GLOBAL PERSPECTIVES on the UNITED STATES

ISSUES AND IDEAS SHAPING INTERNATIONAL RELATIONS

GLOBAL PERSPECTIVES
on the UNITED STATES

ISSUES AND IDEAS SHAPING
INTERNATIONAL RELATIONS

VOLUME III

David Levinson and Karen Christensen, Editors

BERKSHIRE PUBLISHING GROUP
Great Barrington, Massachusetts

Published by:
Berkshire Publishing Group LLC
314 Main Street
Great Barrington, Massachusetts 01230
www.berkshirepublishing.com

Printed in the United States of America

Library of Congress Cataloging-in-Publication Data
Global perspectives on the United States : issues and ideas shaping
international relations / David Levinson and Karen Christensen, editors.
   p. cm.
   Includes bibliographical references and index.
   ISBN 978-1-933782-07-2 (alk. paper)
   1. United States—Foreign relations—2001–   2. United States—Foreign
public opinion.   3. International relations.   I. Levinson, David, 1947–
II. Christensen, Karen, 1957–
   E895.G564 2007
   973.93—dc22   2007020025

EDITORIAL AND PRODUCTION STAFF

Project Directors
David Levinson and
Karen Christensen

Project Coordinators
Jennifer Frederick and Karen Advokaat

Editorial Staff
Erin Connor, Scott Eldridge,
and Marcy Ross

Photo Coordinator
Scott Eldridge

Copyeditors
Francesca Forrest and Mike Nichols

Production Coordinator
Jennifer Frederick

Designer
Joseph DiStefano

Composition Artist
Brad Walrod/High Text Graphics, Inc.

Proofreader
Mary Bagg

**Information Management
and Programming**
Trevor Young

Indexer
Peggy Holloway

Printers
Thomson-Shore, Inc.

EDITORIAL BOARD

CONTENTS

LIST OF ENTRIES

READER'S GUIDE

INTRODUCTION

David Levinson and Karen Christensen, General Editors

This, the third volume of *Global Perspectives on the United States,* provides the general thematic discussion that ties together the detailed coverage in the first two volumes, which provide a nation-by-nation survey of perspectives on the United States. The current volume offers students, journalists, and political observers a chance to explore wider issues in U.S. foreign relations, a subject that is of growing interest and concern to U.S. citizens. Only 20 percent of U.S. citizens have passports, a very low percentage compared with Europeans, and, with the exception of recent immigrants, few U.S. citizens are truly proficient in a second language. But these facts, used to criticize the United States, need context. The United States is a large, diverse nation separated from Europe and Asia, the other major world regions, by oceans. The United States is also the only nation that throughout its history has seen its ethnic and religious diversity as a source of strength.

Americans do care about their place in the world and are proud when they see their nation admired and imitated. And there have been a variety of organized efforts throughout U.S. history to build goodwill and also to educate U.S. citizens about global perspectives. The Peace Corps is probably the single best program the United States has ever created to build positive world opinion, while U.S. study abroad programs reflect the belief that America's educated elite should experience life in other parts of the world.

In the appendix to this volume, we list a number of projects that reflect the desire of our editorial team and authors to help Americans understand their world and to help people elsewhere in the world to understand the United States and its influence. One of these is the Glimpse Foundation, which publishes a magazine and hosts an extensive website to share information from young people living and working abroad, activities it undertakes because "it is in the interests of our country and our world to ensure that everyone, young and old alike, can learn through the experiences of their peers and children who are living abroad. After all, what better way is there to improve international relations and encourage world peace than to foster new generations of global citizens who are constantly seeking to better understand the world they live in?" Efforts like this are essential adjuncts to the expert academic insights provided in this volume.

It is also crucial to point out that while many of the articles published here illuminate negative perceptions of the United States today, they also provide essential historical and cultural context. It is not our intention to be anti-American, and we are not suggesting that the problems of image and relationship that the United States has today are solely the responsibility of the current administration. The United States, like other powerful countries, naturally faces international scrutiny, experiences criticism, and is tested by events in ways that smaller and less powerful nations are not. We see our effort to inform and elucidate as representative of one

of the fundamental principles of the United States—that the free exchange of ideas is an essential right, and that all individuals have a right to their own opinions.

Changing World Opinion

After Americans declared themselves free of English rule in 1776 and prevailed in the subsequent war for independence, the newly established democratic republic became a beacon of freedom, democracy, and liberty for people around the world. Later events enriched this image. U.S. involvement in World War I and, more significantly, in World War II added the roles of liberator and rebuilder to its global image. Many people around the world yearned after the American way of life. True, there was also a dark side to the U.S. image: its history of slavery, continuing racism, and support for despots during the Cold War. But most people in most nations thought highly of the United States. In 2003, this changed. When the U.S. invaded Iraq in March, without the support of the world community, people everywhere began to question American values, motives, and even competence. And as the war has gone badly, perspectives on the United States have continued to decline most everywhere (except in parts of Africa and Eastern Europe). The United States is viewed more as an occupier, destroyer, and go-it-alone empire than as a global beacon of freedom and hope.

Understanding Others' Perspectives

For several years running, public opinion research has told us that many people around the world no longer trust the United States, that they oppose the Iraq War, and that they object to U.S. foreign policy. The U.S. government has tried to improve the nation's image through such initiatives as the establishment of the position of Undersecretary of State for Public Diplomacy and Public Affairs at the Department of State, a position held by longtime senior Bush aide Karen Hughes. But the undersecretary seems to be operating under the assumption that to improve its image, all the United States needs is to do a minimal number of isolated and highly publicized good deeds. The articles in this volume make it clear, from past as well as modern examples, that such an approach does little to build long-term positive perceptions, especially in today's world, where negative views of the United States are both so broad and so deep.

Meanwhile, far too little serious thought has been given to how and why people form their opinions about the United States

and what causes them to change those opinions and perspectives. For example, how does the notion of modernity (which is closely associated with the United States) fit into the Islamic worldview? The answer is that it doesn't; many Muslims believe that modern values cannot coexist with Islamic laws and customs. Or, to take another example, how did the Cold War influence the perceptions of nonaligned nations? The answer is that it made them very nervous because every decision and every action was made in the ominous shadow of the possibility of nuclear war.

And how about the role of mass media? The political theorist Daniel Bell, speaking to this point in the spring 2006 issue of *Dissent* magazine, remarked, "In 2004, [Chinese] state television, for the first time in history, broadcast the U.S. presidential elections live, without any obvious political slant. (I suspect that the turmoil surrounding the 2000 U.S. presidential elections, along with the 2003 U.S.-led invasion of Iraq, discredited U.S.-style democracy among many Chinese, and the government has less to fear from the model.)" Clearly mass media has an enormous influence on world opinion. Unless we discover how factors such as these influence people's thinking and perceptions, we can never expect to have a full understanding of perspectives on the United States, and we certainly cannot hope to significantly influence those perspectives.

The push for this volume of essays came from several contributors to our companion work, *Global Perspectives on the United States: A Nation by Nation Survey,* which provides articles on perspectives on the United States from 140 nations and regions. Contributors to that work told us that beyond documenting perspectives on the United States, it is equally important to identify and discuss how and why nations and peoples form those perspectives, especially when common threads can be identified. This work, *Global Perspectives on the United States: Issues and Ideas Shaping U.S. International Relations,* is a companion to the earlier work, which came out in February 2007. Together, the three volumes enrich our understanding of the role and place of the United States in the world at this critical time in history.

The book is written by and for a wide array of people and organizations—libraries (public, academic, school), government agencies, corporations, international agencies, and nongovernmental organizations, in short, any organization whose members and community want the latest thinking about perspectives on the United States around the world. Our editorial board and contributors represent a dozen different disciplines and fifteen nations. Our broad, interdisciplinary approach makes this volume an important resource for high school and college courses in disciplines such as political science, history, anthropology, geography, management, regional studies, media studies, and American studies.

While there are many factors that influence perceptions of the United States that are specific to one nation or region, there is also a long and varied list of general factors that cross time and place. Some are very broad concepts, such as nationalism and democracy, that in the modern world account for far more than just perspectives on the United States. Others are far more specific; they include USAID and the Peace Corps, programs designed to change life in other nations and therefore by intent also to influence perceptions of the United States. Still other factors, such as U.S. music and television, have widespread influence on cultures around the world and affect how people form opinions of the United States. In addition, historical factors such as slavery continue to inform perspectives on the United States. Finally, major world events such as World War II or the terrorist attacks of September 11, 2001, both change the world order and alter perspectives on the United States. In short, we have amassed a complex list of some 100 factors—events, trends, ideas, programs, processes, and relationships—that tell us much about how and why the United States is perceived the way it is around the world.

Content

This volume provides ninety-five articles and one appendix. The articles are supplemented by illustrations and sidebar text, much of which is primary historical political text that provides real-life examples of issues discussed in the articles. All articles are accompanied by a bibliography that directs the reader to more focused sources on the topic. Each article opens with a brief abstract that summarizes a salient conclusion of the article. An extensive index, blind entries, cross-references, and a reader's guide help readers navigate the volume.

Many of the articles focus primarily on politics, foreign relations, and law, but others focus on business and commerce, media, and popular culture. These other topics, which are important in developing an understanding of perspectives on the United States, are reexplored and debated at Berkshire's related website, LoveUSHateUS.com, and will be the subject of further Berkshire print and online publications. The articles fall into nine general subject-based categories:

❏ Organizations whose activities influence perceptions of the United States, including the Peace Corps and the United States Information Agency (USIA).
❏ Historical events, developments, or eras that altered perceptions of the United States. Topics include the U.S. Civil War and Reconstruction, the Cold War, and Immigration to the United States.
❏ Core American values and beliefs, which often form the basis of how Americans and other define the United States and thereby shape perceptions over time. Topics in this category include the American Dream, Equality, Modernity, and Religious Pluralism.
❏ Policies and actions of the U.S. government, which often directly affect other nations and influence perceptions. Topics in this category include U.S. Foreign Policy after September 11, 2001, and the United States and the Middle East Peace Process.
❏ Cultural contact and communication between and among nations, which in the modern world have an enormous influence on perceptions. Topics in this category include Anti-Americanism, Mass Media, and Pop Culture.
❏ Relations between the United States and other nations and regions. Such relations have special significance in the contemporary world. Topics in this category include Relations with Africa, Special Relationship (U.S.-Russia), and U.S. Role in NATO.
❏ U.S. policy and action regarding global trends and issues. Topics in this category include AIDS, the Drug Trade and the War on Drugs, and Environmental Issues.
❏ U.S. global business and involvement in the global economy. Topics in this category include Economic Globalization, Trade Agreements, and Transnational Corporations.
❏ Elements of the perception-forming process. Topics in this category include Elite vs. Mass Perspectives on the United States and Islamic Worldview.

THE COVER DESIGN

The Statue of Liberty, a nineteenth-century gift from the people of France, is a beloved landmark in the harbor of New York City. It is a symbol of escape from oppression and of the United States' welcome to immigrants from around the world. The big automobile can be seen either as a symbol of American opportunity, mobility, and innovation or as a symbol of its excessive consumption and impact on the environment. The McDonald's arches are well-known around the world, and represent both positive and negative aspects of U.S. culture and influence. Finally, the hooded figure comes from the infamous images of the Abu Ghraib prison in Iraq, where prisoners were tortured and humiliated by U.S. soldiers. By using this range of visual elements, we've aimed to show the varied icons and ideas that have influenced what the world thinks of the United States.

Acknowledgements

This work represents a bit of an about-face for Berkshire Publishing, which is known for publishing about the world and not about the United States only. But it fits perfectly with our global publishing program because of its emphasis on viewing issues and topics from all points of view. Many contributors to past projects have joined in this one, and in fact to launch it, we sent a general e-mail to our wide-ranging community of past contributors. We were flooded with suggestions and encouragement—some three hundred e-mails within the first twenty-four hours! Our thanks go to all these people, many of whom did not write for the project directly but put us in touch with far-flung colleagues.

We want to acknowledge the many contributions of our staff, especially our project coordinators. Karen Advokaat worked on the volume's early stages, and Jenn Frederick took the many disparate pieces of the project and brought them all to a smooth finish. Our Berkshire editorial team—Marcy Ross, Liz Steffey, Erin Connor, and Scott Eldridge—worked hard on the articles, sidebars, and photos. Our senior copy editors Francesca Forrest and Mike Nichols copyedited these articles to a high shine while preserving the unique vocabulary and style of our international contributors. Mary Bagg helped us to catch our mistakes, and Peggy Holloway compiled the comprehensive and valuable index. Designer Joe DiStefano created the page and cover designs, and Brad Walrod, the composition artist, transformed our content into a finished book.

CONTRIBUTORS

Akram, Ejaz
American University in Cairo
Islamic Worldview

Alexandre, Laurien
Antioch University
Feminist Movement and Women's Rights
Mass Media—Debates and Divides

Andressen, Curtis A.
Flinders University
Businesses Overseas, U.S.
Cold War, Post Era
IMF, World Bank, and IDB, U.S. Role in

Antwi-Boasiako, Kwame Badu
Stephen F. Austin State University
Relations with the United Nations, U.S.

Basu, Lopa
Ohio State University
Nobel Peace Prize

Bendik-Keymer, Jeremy
The American University of Sharjah
Human Rights

Bhawuk, Dharm P.S.
University of Hawaii, Manoa
Cultural Diversity, U.S.

Bromark, Stian
Oslo, Norway
Western Europe, Cultural Relations with

Buddan, Robert
University of West Indies
Perspectives on the United States, Theory of

Buzzanco, Robert
University of Houston
Iraq Wars

Calkins, Laura M.
Texas Tech University
Gay and Lesbian Rights Movement
Vietnam War

Capelos, Tereza
Leiden University
Elite vs. Mass Perspectives on the United States

Carter, James
Independent Scholar
Alternative U.S. History

Chiddick, John
La Trobe University
Middle East Peace Process
NATO, U.S. Role in

Crowley, Louise J.
University of Birmingham
Pop Culture—U.S. Films

Dao, Loan
University of California, Berkely
Pop Culture—U.S. Music (Hip-hop)

Drucker, Susan J.
Hofstra University
Government-controlled Media, U.S.

Eccleston, Richard
University of Tasmania
Corruption, Political and Business

Eldridge II, Scott
Berkshire Publishing Group
U.S. Civil War and Reconstruction

Everts, Philip
Leiden University
Use of Force Internationally, Views on U.S.

Fowler, Janice E.
Capella University
U.S. Civil Rights

Friedman, Saul S.
Youngstown State University
Anti-Semitism

Fry, Gerald W.
University of Minnesota
Peace Corps
Tourism

Glass, William R.
Warsaw University
Religious Fundamentalism, U.S.

Goldberg, David M.
College of DuPage
Relations with Latin America, U.S.

González, Francisco E.
The Johns Hopkins University—School of Advanced International Studies
Special Relationship (U.S.-Mexico)

Grace, Miriam
The Boeing Company
Leadership Models

Gronn, Peter
University of Glasgow
Diffusion of Knowledge, Global

Gumpert, Gary
Communication Landscapers
Government-controlled Media, U.S.
Mass Media—Concepts and Technologies

Gupta, Vipin
Simmons College
Multinational Corporations

Hataley, T.S. (Todd)
Queens University
Drug Trade and the War on Drugs

Herbjørnsrud, Dag
Oslo, Norway
Western Europe, Cultural Relations with

Horgan, John C.
Concordia University, Wisconsin
Environmental Issues

Houghton, David Patrick
University of Central Florida
Political System as a Model, U.S.

Husbands, Christopher T.
London School of Economics and
   Political Science
Perspectives on the United States, Visitors'
Radicalism and Populism, U.S.

Imai, Lynn
University of Maryland
Equality

Jeszenszky, Géza
Budapest, Hungary
Soviet Empire, Collapse of

Joyner, Christopher C.
Georgetown University
Trade Agreements

Kenley, David L.
Elizabethtown College
Nationalism

Kislenko, Arne
Ryerson University
Foreign Policy after September 11, 2001,
   U.S.
World War II

Knight, Andrew P.
University of Pennsylvania
Equality
McDonaldization

Kolla, Edward James
Johns Hopkins University
International Law

Kollmeyer, Christopher J.
University of Aberdeen
Globalization, Economic

Kouveliotis, Kyriakos
Centre for Strategic Studies
Intelligence Agencies

Lebiecki, Tomasz M.
Opole University
Colonial Period and Early Nationhood

Leitich, Keith A.
North Seattle Community College
September 11, 2001

Lloyd, Robert B.
Pepperdine University
Empire, U.S.

Locke, Edwin A.
University of Maryland (Emeritus)
American Dream
Founding Principles of the United States

Madison, Julian
Southern Connecticut State University
Slavery and Abolitionism

McKay, George
University of Central Lancashire
Americanization

Mestenhauser, Josef A.
University of Minnesota
Exchanges, Cultural and Scientific

Nantambu, Kwame
Kent State University (Emeritus)
AIDS

Nasong'o, Shadrack Wanjala
Rhodes College
Colonialism and Neocolonialism

Neumann, Caryn E.
Ohio State University
Overseas Americans (Expatriates)
United States Information Agency

Nirenberg, John
School for International Training
Culture Overseas, U.S.

Ockerman, Herbert W.
Ohio State University
Nobel Peace Prize
Appendix: U.S. Agencies & Organizations

O'Connor, Brendon
Griffith University
Anti-Americanism
Homogenization of World Culture
Sports

Okumu, Wafula
Conflict Management Centre
Relations with Africa, U.S.

Pacella, Daniel
Ryerson University
Cold War
Imperialism, U.S.

Pennington, Christopher John
University of Toronto
Exceptionalism, U.S.
Special Relationship (U.S.-Canada)
World War I

Regets, Mark C.
National Science Foundation
Brain Drain

Robert, Dana L.
Boston University
Missionaries

Rowland, Leon F. "Skip"
Banner Cross Consulting Group
Leadership Models

Roy, Joaquín
University of Miami
Relations with the European Union, U.S.

Salamone, Frank A.
Iona College
Popular Culture—U.S. Music (Jazz, Rock)

Shafer, Ingrid H.
University of Science and Arts of
   Oklahoma
Christian Nation, United States as
Religious Pluralism, United States and

Singh, Robert
Birkbeck College, University of London
Special Relationship (U.S.-U.K.)

Smith, Kristen
Temple University
International Agreements and Summits

Stearns, Peter N.
George Mason University
Consumerism
History of United States in World Opinion

Stewart, Marine N.
JIJUMA Global Services &
    International Language Center
Linguistic Imperialism and English

Suganuma, Unryu
Obirin University
Relations with APEC, U.S.

Sundberg, Norman D.
University of Oregon
Tourism

Takacs, Stacy
Oklahoma State University
Media Corporations
Pop Culture—U.S. Television

Trepanier, Lee
Saginaw Valley State University
Special Relationship (U.S.-Russia)

Tucker, Richard P.
University of Michigan
Ecological Footprint, U.S.

van Willigen, Niels
Leiden University
Conflicts, Civilizational and Cultural

von Heyking, John
University of Lethbridge
Democracy
Modernity, United States and

Yagasaki, Noritaka
Tokyo Gakugei University
Immigration to the United States

Zukas, Alexander M.
National University
Green Revolution

Zukas, Lorna Lueker
National University
*U.S. Agency for International
    Development*

WORLD MAP

Greenland

Canada

United States

Mexico

Bahamas

Cuba

Dom.
Jamaica
Haiti Rep.
Puerto
Rico

St Kitts & Nevis
Antigua & Barbuda
St Lucia
Barbados

Belize
Guatemala
Honduras
El Salvador
Nicaragua
Costa
Rica
Panama

St Vincent & the Grenadines

Grenada

Trinidad & Tobago

Dominica

Venezuela

Guyana

French
Guiana

Colombia

Suriname

Ecuador

B r a z i l

Peru

Bolivia

Chile

Paraguay

Uruguay

Argentina

Falkland Islands

South Georgia

Papua
New Guinea

Solomon Islands

Somoa

Vanuatu

Fiji

Tonga

New Zealand

GLOBAL PERSPECTIVES
on the UNITED STATES

ISSUES AND IDEAS SHAPING
INTERNATIONAL RELATIONS

AIDS

The United States' leadership in combating AIDS is lauded by many nations, but some still question the Bush administration's emphasis on abstinence.

AIDS (acquired immunodeficiency syndrome) is caused by the human immunodeficiency virus (HIV). HIV/AIDS is transmitted mainly by unprotected sexual contact with an infected person, needle sharing with an infected person, and transmission from an infected mother to her child during pregnancy or childbirth or shortly after childbirth while breastfeeding.

As a result of the alarming global transmission of AIDS, in 1988 the United Nations launched its World AIDS Day as "an annual global observance of the HIV/AIDS epidemic, which serves to raise awareness, educate the public and fight prejudice" (National HIV/AIDS Action Alert 2004, 28). Every year World AIDS Day focuses on one aspect of HIV/AIDS. For example, the theme for World AIDS Day in 2006 was "Accountability."

Global Impact

At the end of 2005, according to data in *UNAIDS 2006 Report on the Global AIDS Epidemic,* 38.6 million people worldwide were living with HIV, 4.1 million people were newly infected with HIV, and an estimated 2.8 million people died because of AIDS.

Globally, the HIV/AIDS epidemic breaks down in several ways. In Asia, according to 2005 data, 8.3 million people were living with HIV, with two-thirds of that number coming from India. Of these 8.3 million, just shy of one million were newly infected, and approximately 600,000 deaths were due to AIDS.

Sub-Saharan Africa is one of the areas most heavily affected by AIDS. Three-quarters of all women in the world who live with HIV live in sub-Saharan Africa, and 24.6 million people, or 64 percent, of all people with HIV live there. In 2005, it was estimated by UNAIDS that 2.7 million people in sub-Saharan Africa were newly infected with HIV, and two million adults and children died of AIDS.

In Latin America, approximately 140,000 people were newly infected with HIV in 2005, bring the total number of infected people in Latin America to 1.6 million. Among children under the age of fifteen, roughly 32,000 were living with HIV, and in 2005, AIDS claimed 59,000 lives. Nearly 300,000 people were on antiretroviral treatments—a treatment for HIV/AIDS—by the end of 2005. In the Caribbean, 330,000 people were living with HIV

by the end of 2005, with 2,000 of them being children under the age of fifteen, and 37,000 newly infected people.

In Central Asia and Eastern Europe, AIDS is a growing problem, with 220,000 people newly infected in 2005, and 1.5 million people overall living with HIV/AIDS. Between 2003 and 2005, the number of people living with HIV has increased by more than one third. Deaths due to HIV/AIDS have nearly doubled since 2003 as well, with approximately 53,000 dying due to the disease in 2005.

In 2005 new infections in North America and western and central Europe numbered 65,000, which brought the total of those living with HIV/AIDS to two million. However, due to the wide use, availability and distribution of antiretroviral drugs, the number of deaths due to HIV/AIDS was about 30,000, a relatively low number. In the United States, approximately 1.2 million people were living with HIV in 2005.

Against such a cataclysmic backdrop it is important to have a deeper understanding of U.S. policy on the AIDS pandemic.

U.S. Policy

During his administration (1993–2001), President Bill Clinton framed the spread of HIV/AIDS in terms of global catastrophe and national security. Specifically, in April 2000, Clinton said the spread of AIDS had the potential to "topple foreign governments, touch off ethnic wars, and undo decades of work in building free-market democracies abroad" (Gellman 2000, 16A).

During its time, the Clinton administration requested $100 million in congressional funding for programs designed to fight the spread of AIDS in Africa and Asia, upwards of $1 billion in loans annually to sub-Saharan African countries to purchase AIDS, malaria, and polio drugs, and integrate AIDS/HIV education into military training. Clinton was also the first president to create a so-called "AIDS czar" in the president's cabinet.

The AIDS policy of the administration of President George W. Bush falls under the rubric of the "President's Emergency Plan for AIDS Relief" (PEPFAR), which included the "A-B-C approach" ("Abstain, be faithful and use a condom").

In a speech in Philadelphia, Pennsylvania, on 23 June 2004,

President George W. Bush spelled out the U.S. policy as follows: "I think it's really important for us to focus on prevention. We can learn from the experiences of other countries when it comes to a program to prevent the spread of AIDS, like the nation of Uganda. They've started what they call the A-B-C approach to prevent this deadly disease. That stands for Abstain, Be faithful in marriage and when appropriate use Condoms. I like to call it a practical, balanced and moral message" (President Bush 2004).

This policy was elaborated in a speech delivered by Dr. E. Anne Peterson, assistant administrator for global health at the United States Agency for International Development (USAID), at the twenty-fifth international AIDS conference in Bangkok, Thailand, on 15 July 2004. In her presentation, Peterson said "U.S. programs in the future will work more to link those (faith-based) caregivers to nongovernmental organizations and governments that are U.S. partners in working to cope with the epidemic. Faith-based caregivers are an untapped resource in helping to expand the cadres of people devoted to caring for people living with HIV/AIDS."

As part of PEPFAR, the Bush administration pledged $200 million in 2001 for a fund to underwrite programs to prevent and treat AIDS, tuberculosis, and malaria worldwide. The administration also wanted the fund "to respect the patents of drug manufacturers as an incentive to develop new drugs and treatments" (Abejo 2001, A3).

In addition, President Bush's $15 billion emergency plan aimed at fighting AIDS was mostly directed toward 14 African countries. Haiti and Guyana were the only two Caribbean countries receiving U.S. funds. However, U.S. funds come with a series of requirements, including one that stipulates that a portion of the money is earmarked for abstinence-first programs. The president's emergency plan also focuses on preventing new infections, and providing care for children and orphans affected by the disease.

Linking U.S. policy with the 2004 World AIDS Day's theme, Dr. Roy Austin, U.S. ambassador to Trinidad and Tobago, said, "[Our] focus is preventing mother-to-child transmission of HIV. The U.S. quickly trained 14,700 health workers and built capacity at over 900 different health care sites to prevent this tragedy" (Austin 2004, A27). He said the United States "also supports behavior change strategies, including education for girls that build self-esteem, allows for informed choices and fosters the communication skills to say 'no' to sex" (Austin 2004, A27).

Perspectives on U.S. AIDS Policy

Although the international community on the whole has lauded the U.S. policy on AIDS, critics have questioned the administration's perspectives on abstinence.

The cost of antiretroviral drugs and other AIDS treatments, are

A poor woman in Lesotho, a nation in which one in three adults is infected with HIV. Source: istock/Bart Coenders.

part of the challenge of fighting AIDS globally. The World Health Organization (WHO) has already "put its seal of approval on four new generic Indian products...but they are not enough to reach everybody" (Abejo 2001, A3). Developing countries especially are urging U.S. and European drug companies to make generic drugs available, and in some cases to allow their patents on antiretroviral treatments to be lifted so companies that make generic versions can make the cheaper antiretroviral drugs sooner.

The British minister of international development stated that "the UK [does] not support the U.S. over its reluctance to endorse the use of cheaper, generic drugs to fight the disease" (Boseley 2004, A21). The British government has also publicly rejected "the Bush doctrine that sexual abstinence is the best way to stop the spread of the (HIV/AIDS) pandemic" (Boseley 2004, A21). On the contrary, the British plan focuses "on the reproductive rights of women and their need to protect themselves, recognizing abstinence is frequently not an option in some of the worst-hit parts of the world and that husbands are unfaithful" (Boseley 2004, A21).

Many in the international community contend that abstinence is not the most effective method to prevent the spread of AIDS. "Abstinence makes no sense without concomitant adult societal sexual behavior change. In most cases, adults influence the behavior of youths" (*Trinidan Guardian* 2004, 29). For its part, the Vatican blames the spread of AIDS on an "immunodeficiency" of moral values, among other factors. The Vatican suggests that "for greater efficiency in the fight against HIV/AIDS, all forms of discrimination in the treatment of those with the illness must be eliminated" (Reuters 2004, 28).

CRITICISMS OF THE BUSH AIDS POLICY

The following excerpts from major newspaper articles point out some of the perceived shortcomings of the Bush administration's AIDS programs overseas.

GAO Report on Bush Aids Plan

An 87-page GAO report criticized the President's Emergency Plan for AIDS Relief (PEPFAR) because a large part of the funding going "to promote abstinence and fidelity is causing confusion in many countries and in a few is eroding other prevention efforts, including ones to reduce mother-to-child transmission of the virus." The abstinence policy "is basically unworkable," said Paul Zeitz, director of the Global AIDS Alliance. "This shows the problem very clearly and starkly." (*Washington Post,* 4 April 2006)

Bush Policy on Condoms

The U.N. and a number of advocacy groups for AIDS patients have charged that the Bush administration policy had led to a shortage of condoms in Uganda, increasing the risk of infection for many people, particularly married women and adolescents. Jodi Jacobson, executive director of the Center for Health and Gender Equity in Washington, D.C., said that "there has been a dangerous and profound shift in U.S. donor policy from comprehensive prevention, education and provision of condoms to focus on abstinence only." (*New York Times,* 30 August 2005)

Source: Bush's AIDS Policy Is "Basically Unworkable." (2007, January 23). Retrieved March 14, 2007, from http://thinkprogress.org/2007/01/23/sotu-bushs-aids-policy-is-basically-unworkable

The Future

The loudest message coming out of 2004 World AIDS Day was a plea for an end to the "genderization of HIV/AIDS." Gender inequality is the major driving force behind the AIDS pandemic. Women often have difficulty negotiating safer sex with their partners because of women's lower social status, economic dependency on men, and fear of violence. Men traditionally don't like to use condoms because of the way men have been socialized. Women are socialized to believe that men are dominant in a relationship. Younger women, in particular, who are often the target of older men in search of safe sexual partners, find it more difficult to assert themselves. In addition poor women are more susceptible to becoming infected because of the economic correlation of the pandemic.

However, as the epidemic of AIDS continues to spread across the globe, there is a responsibility and a need for greater steps. To take then-U.N. Secretary General Kofi Annan's words from the 2005 World AIDS Day: "It requires every president and prime minister, every parliamentarian and politician (and indeed, every member of society) to decide and declare that 'AIDS stops with me'" (National HIV/AIDS Action Alert 2007, 11–14).

Kwame Nantambu

Further Reading

A word to the wise: Abstinence. (2004, December 11) *Trinidad Guardian,* p. 29.

Abejo, J. (2001, May 12). Bush pledges $200 million to fight disease worldwide. *Akron Beacon Journal,* p. A3.

AIDS talks start off with grim news. (2004, November 24). *Guardian,* p. 17.

Austin, R.L. (2004, December 1). U.S. working hard in battle against HIV/AIDS. *Trinidad Guardian,* p. 27.

Bosley, S. (2004, July 16) U.K. policy on AIDS leaves U.S. isolated. *Guardian*, p. A21.

Bush pledges $200 million to fight disease worldwide. (2001, May 12). *Akron Beacon Journal*, p. A3.

Farley, M. (2001, June 26). U.N. chief to world: Face facts on AIDS. *The Plain Dealer*. p. A1.

Gellman, B. (30 April, 2000). AIDS is declared threat to national security, *The Washington Post*, p. A16.

Hawkins, B. D. (2003, January 30). A predator paradise. *Black Issues in Higher Education*, *19*(5) 21–27.

Kelly, M. J., & Bain, B. (2003). *Education and HIV/AIDS in the Caribbean*. Miami, FL: Ian Randle Publishers.

Long, S. (2004, November 24). U.N. report: AIDS Caribbean's number one killer: We must reach T&T schools. *Guardian*, p. 12.

McDermott, J. (1991, June 23). Asia—Epicenter of the AIDS epidemic. *Washington Post*, p. A21.

McGeary, J. (2001, February 12). Death stalks a continent. *Time*, 36–45.

Mokool, M. (2004, December 13). Women and AIDS. *Trinidad Guardian*, p. 23.

National AIDS Coordinating Committee. (2004). *Some facts about AIDS and HIV*. Port-of-Spain, Trinidad: Caribbean Epidemiology Centre.

National HIV/AIDS action alert. (2004, December 22). World AIDS: Keep the promise. *Sunday Express*, pp. 11–14.

Nessman, R. (2001, June 6). AIDS expert for U.N. warns epidemic is likely to worsen. *The Plain Dealer*, p. 12A.

President Bush discusses HIV/AIDS initiatives in Philadelphia. (23 June, 2004). Retrieved 12 April, 2007 from http://www.whitehouse.gov/news/releases/2004/06/20040623-4.html

Relly, J. (2000, February 26). HIV infection in the Caribbean. *Plain Dealer*, p. 2.

Reuters. (2004, December 11) Vatican blames poor values for AIDS spread. *Trinidad Guardian*.

Rosenberg, P. S. (1995, November 24). Scope of the AIDS epidemic in the United States. *Science*, *270*, 1372–1375.

Shaw, A. (1999, September 16). U.N. agency says AIDS scourge is making Africa a "killing field." *Plain Dealer*, p. 7A.

The fight against AIDS. (1995, December). *Background Brief, BB 1.PSP7, BB28/95*, 1–5.

U.N. urges better help for women, girls. (2004, December 1). *Trinidad Sunday Guardian*, p. 27.

U.S.: Fewer teens having sex. (2004, December 14). *Saturday Express*, p. 45.

U.S. working hard in battle against HIV/AIDS. (2004, December 1). *Guardian*, p. 27.

WHO: World has failed to get AIDS drugs to victims. (2004, July 11). *Trinidad Guardian*, p.19.

Alternative U.S. History

This alternative view of American history emphasizes class divisions, internal conflict and offers a sober counter to the more triumphant perspective of the American past.

An alternative historical view of U.S. history directly challenges and even undermines some of the fundamental assumptions of the mainstream view. Alexis de Tocqueville, the French statesman and author who toured the United States in the nineteenth century, wrote in his 1835 work *Democracy in America* that the great advantage of the Americans was that they had been born equal instead of becoming so. They began their national history as a democracy and never had to suffer a democratic revolution. The new U.S. republic thus differed from the nation-states of Europe by avoiding the feudal stage in its national development. Consequently, its own path to independence and nationhood required the maintenance of the status quo rather than its destruction. This historical reality narrowed the alternatives in the country's political evolution and, thus, has lent historical weight to a consensus view of the U.S. past.

Consensus History

Tocqueville's observation has proven durable over the many years since. Other commentators have echoed the sentiment suggesting that Americans are in general agreement about the larger themes and phenomena of their nation's past. That past, from the colonial period to the present, is often portrayed in ways that minimize conflict and class division. Characterized by an abiding faith in the U.S. national experiment and a belief in the righteousness of the U.S. cause, the mainstream historical narrative continues to determine the parameters of public discourse.

This narrative reached its zenith during the 1950s. Historians and others writing within the milieu of the global Cold War and the domestic "red scare" began arguing that a broad consensus always had existed among Americans. On the most important issues, such as the early colonial experience, the American Revolution, nineteenth-century reform, populism and progressivism, and the New Deal, Americans generally cast their differences aside and came together in the interest of solving problems and moving the nation forward. They united around a set of core ideals and values that included a federal government of limited power, the supremacy of property rights, and the inalienable rights of the individual. U.S. society was relatively homogeneous and stable,

with everyone sharing in, and benefiting from, these core values. This consensus view of history deemphasized or erased altogether evidence of substantive conflict in the nation's past.

The United States was different, or exceptional, according to this view. The national development of the United States differed from that of other nations in the Western world. It was born imbued with a liberal ideology impervious or indifferent to alternatives. Despite episodic difficulties such as the political rebellions of the eighteenth century, the class struggles of the nineteenth century, or the racial violence of the twentieth century, the nation maintained its faith in that set of core values and always triumphed over these internal obstacles in ways that benefited everyone. This general frame of reference regarding the U.S. national historical experience continues to be highly influential. Consequently, Americans possess an exceptionalist understanding of the country's past and are resistant to and even hostile to an alternative view.

Alternative History

Nevertheless, an alternative historical view winds its way through this cultural consensus. Finding its own roots in the writings of the progressive historians around the turn of the twentieth century, this alternative view of U.S. history emphasizes class divisions and internal conflict and offers a counter to the more triumphant view of the U.S. past.

By the 1960s the growing criticism of the Vietnam War, coupled with an often-violent government reaction toward the civil rights movement in the South and the sluggish pace of liberal reform generally, provided the impetus for this alternative view. Historians and other writers began to place more emphasis on the history of conflict in the nation's past. Various exponents of what was termed the "new left" began to articulate a critique of U.S. society that was structural and systemic. The U.S. past, these historians argued, had not been the placid, trouble-free place suggested by earlier historians. Rather, it had always been a place wrought with conflict and great passionate debates over the very course of the nation at nearly every stage. Contradicting the suggestion that most Americans were in agreement on most

A PEOPLE'S HISTORY

Howard Zinn's A People's History of the United States *is considered one of the core documents of alternative U.S. history. In this extract from the book, Zinn recounts part of the story of the growth of American industry in the late 1800s.*

While some multimillionaires started in poverty, most did not. A study of the origins of 303 textile, railroad, and steel executives of the 1870s showed that 90 percent came from middle- or upper-class families. The Horatio Alger stories of "rags to riches" were true for a few men, but mostly a myth, and a useful myth for control.

Most of the fortune building was done legally, with the collaboration of the government and the courts. Sometimes the collaboration had to be paid for. Thomas Edison promised New Jersey politicians $1,000 each in return for favorable legislation. Daniel Drew and Jay Gould spent $1 million to bribe the New York legislature to legalize their issue of $8 million in "watered stock" (stock not representing real value) on the Erie Railroad.

The first transcontinental railroad was built with blood, sweat, politics and thievery, out of the meeting of the Union Pacific and Central Pacific railroads. The Central Pacific started on the West Coast going east; it spent $200,000 in Washington on bribes to get 9 million acres of free land and $24 million in bonds, and paid $79 million, an overpayment of $36 million, to a construction company which really was its own. The construction was done by three thousand Irish and ten thousand Chinese, over a period of four years, working for one or two dollars a day.

The Union Pacific started in Nebraska going west. It had been given 12 million acres of free land and $27 million in government bonds. It created the Credit Mobilier company and gave them $94 million for construction when the actual cost was $44 million. Shares were sold cheaply to Congressmen to prevent investigation. This was at the suggestion of Massachusetts Congressman Oakes Ames, a shovel manufacturer and director of Credit Mobilier, who said: "There is no difficulty in getting men to look after their own property." The Union Pacific used twenty thousand workers—war veterans and Irish immigrants, who laid 5 miles of track a day and died by the hundreds in the heat, the cold, and the battles with Indians opposing the invasion of their territory.

Source: Zinn., H. (1995). A people's history of the United States: 1492–present (pp. 248–49). New York: Haper Perennial.

---

issues, this new generation of historians argued that differences abounded. Although elites had always set the agenda, ruled the nation, determined policy, and possessed most of the nation's resources, they did so amidst rancorous debate and violent conflict and were at times forced to accommodate their critics.

Domestically, the United States had always been a society divided between the haves and have-nots. Class divisions had, in fact, been written into the early republic's founding documents. The Constitution itself had been crafted by elites wary of excessive democratic forces. Those forces had come to the fore during the course of the war for independence and its aftermath to voice their own grievances over taxation, tariffs, political participation, and self-rule. When an army of one thousand indebted farmers led by Daniel Shays marched on the colonial government in Massachusetts to demand economic justice and an end to punishing taxation, the elites were frightened into action to prevent the spread of like sentiments and what they judged to be mob rule. In the Constitution, drafted months later, the founding fathers produced not a revolutionary document but rather a conservative one that ensured continued elite rule and kept democracy at bay. Any consensus was limited to the small group of propertied white men who drafted the document. Certainly poor farmers, women, blacks, and indentured servants had little input or positive impact on the proceedings.

Revisionist scholars thus came to view the United States explicitly in terms of its class divisions. Deeply rooted and codified at the nation's very founding, these divisions proved determinant factors in the national evolution that followed. Viewed in this way, the industrialization process of the nineteenth century perpetuated those class distinctions through the advent of wage labor and the imposition of and repetition of the rhythms of industrial factory work. The agrarian reform movement that grew into populism is better understood as a class-based struggle between the nation's farmers and eastern elites of the banking, financial, and commercial sectors. Similarly, the progressive reform movement of the early twentieth century is in part the reaction of corporate liberals to growing popular antipathy and hostility toward corporate power. Thus, a series of reforms designed to protect corporate interests and to stave off radical alternatives was ushered through the legislative branch.

The New Deal (the legislative and administrative program of President Franklin D. Roosevelt) of the 1930s also constituted a conservative experiment to ameliorate the severest suffering of out-of-work Americans and ride out the Great Depression until economic recovery. Contradicting many critics who labeled the New Deal measures as radical, revisionist scholars point out that the president did little more than attempt to save the U.S. liberal capitalist system through a series of conservative reforms that did not threaten the sanctity of private property or the rights of the individual. The administration made no attempt to redistribute the

nation's resources and even proved reluctant to spend adequately on social welfare programs.

Analyses of the nation's foreign relations also found that in most cases the pursuit or protection of material interests characterized U.S. forays into the world from at least the period after the Civil War. During the nineteenth century the U.S. government intervened repeatedly in the affairs of Latin American nations. The rationale for such intervention had always centered on the perpetuation of liberty and the spread of political democracy. During the 1960s and into the 1970s research pointed toward a different set of conclusions. The United States acted not as a benefactor to the people of Latin America and the world but rather as counterrevolutionary and protector of the status quo. After a series of interventions to overthrow democratically elected governments in the years after World War II, the U.S. government then provided military aid to right-wing and repressive regimes that ensured continued private investment and an appropriately stable political environment. A militarist policy in the world provided for a high level of production and spending, the expansion of jobs, the maintenance of wages, and the broadening of the middle class at home. This "guns and butter" strategy buttressed U.S. economic and military might during much of the Cold War.

Consensus History vs. Global View

These features of U.S. history and of the U.S. role in the world remain poorly understood and little known among a broad cross-section of Americans. Many Americans continue to accept those earlier notions of both the U.S. past and of U.S. foreign policy. Despite a large and growing body of research to the contrary, many Americans' view of the nation's past more closely resembles the triumphalist view. Consequently, analyses and viewpoints that emphasize class divisions or material interests as formative elements of the U.S. national experience are viewed as radical departures from the more mainstream narrative. That liberal ideology, present since the nation's founding and always impervious to alternatives, is partly responsible for this phenomenon.

Those people beyond the borders of the United States, however, particularly those with direct experience with U.S. foreign policy, have a fundamentally different view of the United States. Whether in Latin America, the Middle East, Asia, or even in Europe, the growth and prevalence of U.S. power after World War II have produced a sharp split between the perception and the reality of the U.S. government's use of its power. People around the world have for decades recognized the United States as a superpower. They have also recognized that the United States is willing to use its power in the world to shape events. Yet, they increasingly question U.S. aims and view with great suspicion its leaders' assurances of the protection and perpetuation of liberty and democracy as its motive forces. Consequently, the world's view of the United States is often markedly at odds with the view of Americans themselves.

The twentieth century brought the rise of a virulent and often violent anti-Americanism around the world. The decade after the mid-1950s, for example, included more than 170 demonstrations, riots, and terrorist attacks aimed specifically at the United States. Anti-American attacks and demonstrations have continued over the years. International political theorists and foreign relations specialists have begun to analyze this anti-Americanism as a distinct phenomenon from, for example, anti-British or anti-Russian sentiment. The prevalence of anti-Americanism has only grown in the years ending the twentieth century and beginning the twenty-first. The process of globalization, dramatically hastened during the 1990s, bore all the hallmarks of U.S. economic expansion as the country's corporate exponents—such as McDonald's, Nike, and Starbucks—became ubiquitous. As the United States became even more visible in the world, it became a greater target for hostility and resentment of the use of its power. One historian has concluded that anti-Americanism serves many masters. Economic grievances, envy, powerlessness, political/economic competition, cultural snobbery, and many more issues are all manifest in anti-Americanism.

The opening of the twenty-first century brought the most horrific manifestation of anti-Americanism in the nation's history: the terrorist attacks of September, 11, 2001. Understandably, Americans reacted with shock and horror. They also reacted with near total disbelief that anyone would want to perpetrate such a heinous act upon the United States. That disbelief is in part the result of the sharp disconnect between Americans' view of the nation and the view from outside the United States. For much of their national history Americans have been insulated from the world. Protected by two large oceans and surrounded by relatively weaker neighbors, the United States has not had to seriously consider the threat of invasion. Its development was unburdened by outside threats, just as it was also unburdened by internal alternatives. For all of these reasons, an alternative historical perspective has not taken root in the United States in a way that would broaden public discourse and deepen historical understanding.

James Carter

See also Corruption, Political and Business; Exceptionalism, U.S.; Human Rights; Radicalism and Populism, U.S.; Relations with Indigenous Peoples, U.S.; U.S. Civil Rights; U.S. Civil War; Vietnam War

Further Reading

Bernstein, B. J. (1968). *Towards a new past: Dissenting essays in American history.* New York: Pantheon Books.

Hartz, L. (1955). *The liberal tradition in America.* New York: Harcourt, Brace and World.

Hofstadter, R. (1989). *The American political tradition and the men who made it.* New York: Vintage.

Hofstadter, R. (1996). *The paranoid style of American politics and other essays.* Cambridge, MA: Harvard University Press.

Kolko, G. (1977). *The triumph of conservatism: An interpretation of American history, 1900–1916.* New York: Free Press.

McPherson, A. (2006). *Yankee no! Anti-Americanism in U.S.-Latin American relations.* Cambridge, MA: Harvard University Press.

Stiglitz, J. E. (2003). *Globalization and its discontents.* New York: W. W. Norton.

Young, A. F. (Ed.). (1984). *The American revolution: Explorations in the history of American radicalism.* DeKalb: Northern Illinois University Press.

Zinn, H. (1995). *A people's history of the United States.* New York: Harper.

American Dream

Since the founding of the republic, people have immigrated to the United States with the dream of building a life that promised freedom from tyranny along with the chance for economic prosperity.

When Christopher Columbus discovered the Americas in 1492, North America was, relatively speaking, sparsely inhabited by natives who lived as hunter gatherers or (with few exceptions) primitive planters (Bowden 2003). Columbus's discovery was followed by a long stream of immigrants, initially from Europe but eventually from all over the world. Over time, the stream turned into a deluge, and between 1821 and 2002, over 68 million people immigrated to the United States. They came from the United Kingdom, Germany, France, Italy, Ireland, the Netherlands, Austria, Hungary, Russia, Mexico, the Philippines, Cuba, China, Korea, Vietnam, India, Canada and many other countries. Most immigrants, especially in the eighteenth and early nineteenth centuries, were poor and came at great risk by means of long and dangerous sea voyages. Many twentieth century immigrants, specifically those from Communist countries, had to risk their lives to escape from totalitarian dictatorships.

The Land of the Free

Why were immigrants attracted to the United States? In "The New Colossus," the famous poem inscribed over the main entrance of the Statue of Liberty, Emma Lazarus wrote: "Give me your tired, your poor, Your huddled masses yearning to breathe free." This quote is often used to sum up one of the bold, founding principles written into the U.S. Constitution; that all U.S. citizens would be free from political, religious, and economic tyranny. Early immigrants were often political and religious refugees, many were ruled by feudal aristocracies or monarchies. Those born into poverty struggled to survive and, in most cases, had little or no social and economic mobility, and were often denied freedom of religion and of speech in their homelands. Eighteenth century commentator Hector St. John de Crevecoeur (Letter III) contrasted Europe with America, writing, "Here [in America] are no aristocratic families, no courts, no kings, no bishops, no ecclesiastical dominion . . . no princes for whom we toil, starve and bleed . . . [man's] labor is founded on the basis of . . . self-interest" (St. John de Crevecoeur, 1995).

Once the United States became an independent nation and ratified its constitution in 1788, it became the first example of a country in which laws protected men's freedom to express their own views, practice their own philosophies (political and religious), buy their own land, start their own businesses, and work to create wealth and prosperity for themselves and their families. All men were equal before the law, albeit at that time excluding women and African-Americans. Citizens elected their own political leaders and representatives. Colonial rule was replaced by self-rule, and the United States became a constitutional republic.

Founding Principles

The American Dream was made possible by the founding principles of the United States. The first was confidence in reason, which was the essence of the eighteenth century Enlightenment; it represented the triumph of reason over centuries of ignorance, superstition, and religious dogma. It was the view that the universe followed natural laws which could be discovered by science. The second principle was egoism: the view that man could properly pursue his own happiness. The third principle was a consequence of the first two: that all men were equal in possessing individual rights, that man did not exist to serve governments but that governments existed to "serve" men—that is, to protect its citizens against coercion and lawlessness. The concept of individual rights was an expression of individualism, the concept that man is an end in himself not a means to the ends of others and that each individual is responsible for earning his own living. These revolutionary principles were what prompted Thomas Paine to exclaim, "We [Americans] have it in our power to begin the world over again" (Peikoff 1982, 111).

Laissez-faire Capitalism

Laissez-faire capitalism opposes regulation or interference by the government in economic affairs beyond the minimum necessary. During the eighteenth century, the United States came closer to practicing the system of laissez-faire capitalism than had any country or at any time in world history. This largely unfettered capitalism resulted in a century of unprecedented opportunity and

wealth . By the early twentieth century, the United States had become the wealthiest and most powerful nation on earth.

A corollary of a free economy is what sociologists call "social mobility," meaning people can rise and fall from the social strata into which they were born. Among the American business elite of 1870, 43 percent started from poverty (Mills 1945). Thirty-eight percent of American millionaires in the nineteenth century came from poor families (Sorokin 1925). One example of this is Andrew Carnegie, who emigrated, virtually penniless, with his family from Scotland to Pittsburgh in 1848. Carnegie, starting at age thirteen, began to look for opportunity. He worked in a textile mill, learned bookkeeping at night, became a messenger boy, studied French, took lessons on elocution and manners, went to work for a railroad (where he received several promotions), ran a telegraph office, made several unsuccessful investments, and took charge of a bridge manufacturing company. He ended up in the steel business where, through brilliant management, he built the largest steel company in the world, and eventually sold it for close to half a billion dollars. He was a self-made millionaire and made many of his partners millionaires as well.

Such rags to riches stories still happen today. For example, Jack Welch, the former CEO of General Electric, was the son of a railroad conductor (Locke 2004). During his tenure as CEO, the company created over $300 billion in stockholder wealth, and Welch became a multimillionaire in the process.

The American Dream

The American Dream means controlling your own destiny. For many of the early immigrants to the United States, it was a dream that, in large part, had been unthinkable in their mother countries.

Calvin Colton, a prominent journalist, wrote in 1844, "Ours is a country where men start from a humble origin, and from small beginnings rise gradually in the world, as the reward of merit and industry, and where they can attain the most elevated positions, or acquire a large amount of wealth, according to the pursuits they elect for themselves. No exclusive privilege of birth . . . stand[s] in their path; but one has a good chance as another, according to his talents, prudence and personal exertions. This is a country of self-made men."

The America Dream was always an aspiration; most Americans, including immigrants, were—and are—optimistic. They were confident that they could succeed in improving their lives. The Dream, of course, was not a guarantee of success. Early immigrants had to face many hardships. There were many potential threats: wars with the British rulers, civil strife, attacks by Native Americans, the vicissitudes of nature, illness, injury, exhaustion from hard labor, starvation, and more. And probably only a small percentage possessed the industry and ability to truly succeed in fulfilling the American Dream.

A large, single-family home in northern Ohio. To many, owning one's home is part of the American Dream. Source: istock/Denise Kappa.

"THE NEW COLOSSUS" BY EMMA LAZARUS

Emma Lazarus wrote "The New Colossus" to help raise money for the pedestal of the Statue of Liberty, and it was eventually carved into that pedestal. This poem captures what the statue symbolized to the millions who migrated to the United States around the turn of the twentieth century.

Not like the brazen giant of Greek fame,
With conquering limbs astride from land to land;
Here at our sea-washed, sunset gates shall stand
A mighty woman with a torch, whose flame
Is the imprisoned lightning, and her name
Mother of Exiles. From her beacon-hand
Glows world-wide welcome; her mild eyes command
The air-bridged harbor that twin cities frame.
"Keep ancient lands, your storied pomp!" cries she
With silent lips. "Give me your tired, your poor,
Your huddled masses yearning to breathe free,
The wretched refuse of your teeming shore.
Send these, the homeless, tempest-tost to me,
I lift my lamp beside the golden door!"

Source: Statue of Liberty National Monument. Retrieved March 14, 2007, from http://www.libertystatepark.com/emma.htm

In the twenty-first century, despite legal limits on immigration and the physical dangers of crossing U.S. borders illegally, the American Dream still continues to attract people from all over the world. People from Cuba and other Caribbean nations travel by flimsy rafts and risk drowning trying to make it to U.S. shores. People trek daily through the deserts surrounding the U.S.-Mexico border, often risking death by heat stroke or dehydration.

The fact that the United States is considered a "free country" does not mean that all Americans have been treated justly. It took a bloody civil war to abolish slavery, and African-Americans were politically disenfranchised for over a century after the civil war. Asian-Americans have often been viewed as second-class citizens. Japanese-Americans were even placed in internment camps during World War II. Italians have been called demeaning names. Jews have been discriminated against in many professions. Catholics were looked down on by Protestants. Latinos continue to face discrimination as the newer wave of immigrants to the United States. Nonetheless, the prejudices against different immigrant groups have—almost as a rule—gradually broken down as assimilation into U.S. culture takes place over generations. And overall, no other "melting pot" society in history has ever succeeded as well the United States.

Edwin A. Locke

See also Brain Drain; Cultural Diversity, U.S;
Founding Principles of the United States;
Slavery and Abolitionism; U.S. Civil Rights

Further Reading

Bowden, T. (2003). *The enemies of Christopher Columbus.* Cresskill, NJ: Paper Tiger.

Colton, A. (1844). *Junius Tracts*, No. 7: 15.

Locke, E. A. (2004). Jack Welch. In G. Goethals, G. Sorenson, & J. Burns (Eds.), *Encyclopedia of leadership*, Volume 4 (pp. 1632–1635). Thousand Oaks, CA: Sage.

Mills, C. W. (1945). The American business elite: A collective portrait. *Journal of Economic History*, Volume V, Supplement, 20–44.

Peikoff, L. (1982) *The ominous parallels: The end of freedom in America.* New York: Stein and Day.

Sorokin, P. (1925). American millionaires and multi-millionaires. *Journal of Social Forces*, Vol. III, 627–640.

St. John Crevecoeur, J. H. (1995) Letters from an American farmer: Letter III, retrieved 13 April, 2007, from http://xroads.virginia.edu/~Hyper/CREV/letter03.html

Americanization

The influence of American values and practices is often affected by overt acts of U.S. foreign policy. The U.S. response to 9/11 resulted in an increase in anti-Americanization sentiments around the world.

Americanization is the process by which the influence of the United States pervades and is experienced, desired, and resisted in other parts of the world. Americanization is often a result of overt acts of U.S. foreign policy, previously demonstrated by the Monroe Doctrine of 1823, by U.S. presidents of the 1840s, and by the Marshall Plan aid distributed for the reconstruction of Europe after World War II. More common, though, is the use of the term *Americanization* through the twentieth century, referring to the ways in which the icons and cultural practices of the United States are embraced by or imposed on other peoples. During periods of international tension or crisis such as the Cold War, the political, economic and cultural symbols of Americanization have worked together. Specifically, government-funded international propaganda exercises have included jazz trumpeter Louis Armstrong touring the USSR, European exhibitions of the paintings of radical artist Jackson Pollock, and the establishment of U.S. studies programs in a number of European universities.

Americanization is often understood in relation to modernization for good reasons. In part because of the key U.S. role in the development of mass media and related popular cultural forms (Hollywood movies, pop music, pulp fiction, the Internet), much of the global impact of the country has been felt in such arenas, whether as dramas of desire or anxiety. Of course, the term *Americanization* is also used in the context of the period of mass immigration to the United States in the late nineteenth and early twentieth centuries and refers to the formal and informal processes, such as language, education, acculturation, consumerism, and rituals of nation building, by which European and other migrant groups to the United States became—were "translated" into—Americans.

Modernization and Globalization

In statements that seem to confirm the validity of the process of Americanization, Gertrude Stein and Henry Luce each declared the twentieth century "the American century." The complexity of the term derives from the questions it raises about global power, the switch of the imperial center from Europe to the United States

in the twentieth century, the legacy of the Cold War, possible overlapping of the processes of modernization more fundamentally and Americanization as a specific instance, the extent to which culture itself is understood as a controlling or standardizing phenomenon, and the degree to which the reception of exported culture is characterized by passivity or active appropriation. For Peter Taylor Americanization is the "process of emulation and adaptation under the condition of consumer *modernity*" (Slater and Taylor 1999). Taylor also argues that the period of "capacious" Americanization came to an end in the 1970s, to be followed by the contemporary state of "resonant" Americanization in which, although U.S. culture is ubiquitous, its condition is hybrid: "American influences are clear but . . . national cultures remain intact" (Slater and Taylor 1999, 6).

Recently the term has become problematic, even outdated, for some cultural theorists who debate globalization and postnationalism. As we move into global cultural economies, with related synergies (combined actions or operations) of media, information technology, and transnational capital, the borders of the nation-state become less significant than transactional networks, so that the flow and system of exchange bear less relation to the fixed boundaries of single countries. For John Tomlinson the contemporary challenge is to "consider alternative ways of thinking about globalized culture that do not keep us continually in the shadow cast by national cultures" (Tomlinson 1999, 105). Whereas on the one hand, Stuart Hall has defined postmodernity as "the way the world has dreamed itself American" (Brooker 1992, 24), on the other hand, theories and practices of globalization, as a postnational phenomenon, question the usefulness of *Americanization* as a term today. Thus, for some critics the development of the notion of a *global popular*, as seen, for instance, in corporate syncretism (the combination of different forms of belief or practice) in the entertainment and media industry—whereby multinational companies may combine U.S. and Japanese business interests while outsourcing the manufacture of merchandise to developing countries in order to saturate European markets—blurs any previously discrete national boundaries. Such critics would argue that this situation makes a term such as *Americanization* of more historical than contemporary relevance. In Tomlinson's view we are instead within a "global capitalist monoculture" (Tomlinson 1999, 81).

Contact Zones of Americanization

Mary Louise Pratt's idea of the "contact zone" is useful when considering the dynamics and politics of cultural exchange. Contact zones are the space or times in which "disparate cultures meet, clash and grapple with each other often in highly asymmetrical relations of domination and subordination—like colonialism, slavery, or their aftermaths," leading to an intersection or merging of "subjects previously separated by geographic and historical disjunctures" (Pratt 1995, 4, 6–7). Americanization has been viewed as a benign or positive contact zone process in which the world's most energetic economy and cultural innovator produces images, models, and ideals that appeal to notions of liberty, democracy, opportunity, and pleasure. It has also been viewed malignly as a contact zone process by which indigenous cultures and desires around the world are threatened, even erased, under a homogenizing smother of exported U.S. pop culture.

Looking at the export rhetoric of Americanization positively, it constitutes a discourse of democracy, even liberation. In fact, some people even argue that the utopian dream of the land of "America" was imagined by Europeans before its discovery. The European fiction that is "America," then, both predated and has seemingly survived the invention of the "real" United States. For Europeans it was (perhaps still is) one of those "epic worlds that derive their attraction from the fact that 'America' is non-Europe, that it provides a counterpoint to our culture, a utopian realm for our dreams of escape" (Kroes 1993, 313). What Rob Kroes has identified as a key aspect of U.S. cultural experimentation, the capacity to juxtapose "King Lear and King Kong, Rimbaud and Rambo, Plato and Puzo," has a democratizing impulse (Kroes 1993, 307–308). One can read it as a self-conscious effort to offer an alternative to the Old World high cultural consensus of Europe, a challenge to its elite forms, a celebration of (in Walt Whitman's phrase) "the word democratic, the word en masse" (Whitman, 1900). In *Anti-Oedipus*, even Gilles Deleuze and Félix Guattari celebrate the capacity of "flight" of U.S. artists, who know how to "scramble the codes, to cause flows to circulate.... They overcome a limit, they shatter a wall, the capitalist barrier. And of course they fail to complete the process, they never cease failing to do so" (Deleuze and Guattari 1996, 132–133). Further, the experience of exported U.S. culture has indeed frequently been based on liberation—the counterculture of the 1960s, which became a massive international youth movement, with radical politics of rights and liberation, style, pop music, and experimental ways of living and gathering, is a key instance of a cultural moment largely (although not exclusively) originating in the United States and embraced with enthusiasm by youth around much of the world. That black youth in western Europe have often looked to African-American struggles and styles for templates and forms of expression can be explored as another example of Americanization offering liberation. Americanization is frequently bound up with discourses of youth, newness, and modernity.

The most negative position with regard to the influence and experience of U.S. culture overseas is that under the term *cultural imperialism*. Here, phenomena such as the legacy of hemispheric opposition to the Vietnam War or international support campaigns for indigenous peoples resisting U.S. interventions in Latin America have contributed to the pervasive and persistent critical rhetoric of "Yankee, go home!" More culturally, the United States, and in particular its popular culture, is feared for its role in the leveling down (even dumbing down) of other societies. For George Ritzer (1996), one sociocultural form in particular evidences the process most starkly, and it is one that has struck a chord within and outside academia: Ritzer coined the term *McDonaldization* for "the process by which the principles of the fast-food restaurant are coming to dominate more and more sectors of American society as well as of the rest of the world" (Ritzer 1996). Other terms used, theoretically or pejoratively, include *Coca-colonization* and *Disneyfication*. These forms of U.S. consumption (or the consumption of the United States) have inscribed within them variously power, pleasure, and fear. A reverse reading argues that debates about cultural imperialism are not so much concerned with any U.S. imperial authority but are instead symptoms of the attenuation of European cultural and political authority. There is also a certain elite defensiveness in this position.

Anti-Americanisms?

In some ways the terrorist attacks of September 11, 2001, made it difficult to explore versions of what is often termed *anti-Americanism*. The enormous impact of those events obstructed and even made apparently insignificant earlier or other manifestations of anti-Americanism. At the same time they had the effect of making all voices critical of the United States appear heinous and treacherous: The political rhetoric of "those who are not with us are against us" allowed little room for criticism of or active opposition to U.S. foreign policy or even of criticism of U.S. export culture. In fact, September 11 is one of those moments (others may be the strategic anti-Americanism of the nineteenth-century abolitionist movement in Britain or the sustained protest around the world against the neo-imperial military project of the U.S. war in Vietnam through the 1960s) that makes understanding versions of anti-Americanism more timely, and essential.

For some people anti-Americanism is primarily emotive, generated by envy, snobbery, or fear of the United States as the global

PROJECT FOR THE NEW AMERICAN CENTURY

The following passage is the Statement of Principles for the Project for the New American Century, a non-profit organization founded in 1997 with the goal of promoting American global leadership.

American foreign and defense policy is adrift. Conservatives have criticized the incoherent policies of the Clinton Administration. They have also resisted isolationist impulses from within their own ranks. But conservatives have not confidently advanced a strategic vision of America's role in the world. They have not set forth guiding principles for American foreign policy. They have allowed differences over tactics to obscure potential agreement on strategic objectives. And they have not fought for a defense budget that would maintain American security and advance American interests in the new century.

We aim to change this. We aim to make the case and rally support for American global leadership.

As the 20th century draws to a close, the United States stands as the world's preeminent power. Having led the West to victory in the Cold War, America faces an opportunity and a challenge: Does the United States have the vision to build upon the achievements of past decades? Does the United States have the resolve to shape a new century favorable to American principles and interests?

We are in danger of squandering the opportunity and failing the challenge. We are living off the capital—both the military investments and the foreign policy achievements—built up by past administrations. Cuts in foreign affairs and defense spending, inattention to the tools of statecraft, and inconstant leadership are making it increasingly difficult to sustain American influence around the world. And the promise of short-term commercial benefits threatens to override strategic considerations. As a consequence, we are jeopardizing the nation's ability to meet present threats and to deal with potentially greater challenges that lie ahead.

We seem to have forgotten the essential elements of the Reagan Administration's success: a military that is strong and ready to meet both present and future challenges; a foreign policy that boldly and purposefully promotes American principles abroad; and national leadership that accepts the United States' global responsibilities.

Of course, the United States must be prudent in how it exercises its power. But we cannot safely avoid the responsibilities of global leadership or the costs that are associated with its exercise. America has a vital role in maintaining peace and security in Europe, Asia, and the Middle East. If we shirk our responsibilities, we invite challenges to our fundamental interests. The history of the 20th century should have taught us that it is important to shape circumstances before crises emerge, and to meet threats before they become dire. The history of this century should have taught us to embrace the cause of American leadership.

Our aim is to remind Americans of these lessons and to draw their consequences for today. Here are four consequences:

❑ we need to increase defense spending significantly if we are to carry out our global responsibilities today and modernize our armed forces for the future;

❑ we need to strengthen our ties to democratic allies and to challenge regimes hostile to our interests and values;

❑ we need to promote the cause of political and economic freedom abroad;

❑ we need to accept responsibility for America's unique role in preserving and extending an international order friendly to our security, our prosperity, and our principles.

Such a Reaganite policy of military strength and moral clarity may not be fashionable today. But it is necessary if the United States is to build on the successes of this past century and to ensure our security and our greatness in the next.

Source: Project for the New American Century. (1997, June 3). Retrieved March 15, 2007, from, http://www.newamericancentury.org/statementofprinciples.htm

superpower, for others it is even a form of contemporary racism (made more worrying by virtue of its apparent acceptability). The idea of the "United States-as-threat"—whether in the straightforward sense of militarily or through accusations of cultural imperialism—can elicit negative responses from other cultures around the world. Is this understandable? Is it even valid? It's useful here to consider critics of U.S. export power from *within* the United States. As one example, the political writer and linguist Noam Chomsky has explored aspects of the "rogue state" U.S. foreign policy and capital. Another example is writer and critic Edward Said, whose works have reminded us that a lack of consensus exists within the United States about the war against terrorism and that the internal "forest of dissent" against the Iraq War (2003) may be contemporary evidence of the "obstinate dissenting traditions of the US—the unofficial counter-memory of an immigrant society" (Said 2003, 167, 169).

Commentators such as these supply critical material about U.S. activities from within its boundaries and establishments, illustrating that criticism is not the preserve of non-Americans, that a lengthy tradition of critiquing global power exists, even when exerted by U.S. interests, and that distinctions need to be articulated between different kinds and usages of anti-Americanism. An awkward form of internal or domestic anti-Americanism, from the other end of the political spectrum, is the far-right patriot or militia movement, which frequently argues that it is against the U.S. government but, perversely, is for the United States in

its claims to defend the "original" ideals and constitution of the country.

Different contexts exist for external expressions of anti-Americanism, depending on the political or historical relationship between the United States and, for example, the Caribbean, Central or South America, the Cold War eastern bloc, western Europe, or al-Qaeda. The anti-Americanism expressed by many people in Chile during the early 1970s, at a time when their democratically elected (Marxist) government was destabilized and a military dictatorship put in its place with the aid of the covert action of the U.S. Central Intelligence Agency, may be evident and explicable. Anti-American propaganda in Communist regimes during the Cold War was one politico-cultural activity in the struggle for the protection and extension of spheres of influence. At the same time, an oversimplified view of anti-Americanism should be avoided: Many Cubans have forcefully criticized the U.S. economic blockade of their country while at the same time they use Cuba's unofficial second currency of the U.S. dollar; while Russian leaders during the Cold War criticized the decadence of U.S. culture, and capital, young Russian intellectuals and artists formed a subculture known as the "Shtatniki" (after the Russian word *Shtaty,* "the States"), wearing U.S. suits and listening to jazz music. The contradictions and compromises within anti-Americanism require careful attention and illustrate that anti-Americanism is not a monolithic entity.

Old versus New Empires

People have made significant expressions of cultural resistance to or resentment of the development of mass media and the dominant export cultures of the United States. The twentieth century, for instance, was punctuated by regular moral panics around the latest craze emanating from the United States, which would generally also involve youth pleasure and autonomy and a generational disruption. European elders railed against the symptoms of what they perceived as a nervous, vacuous, immature export culture, whether in the form of hot jazz, gangster films and gun culture, comic books, juvenile delinquency, rock and roll, LSD, fast food, video nasties, gangsta rap and gun culture, and both jogging and obesity. Although each alone may appear a relatively minor novelty, and some are demonstrably more dangerous than others, reactions to them contributed to a current of distrust of the United States and its pop cultural pleasures from significant sectors of European society. A concomitant sense existed of European traditions being threatened, cheapened, "dumbed down" by such Americana, and the strength and longevity of the antagonistic experience of the United States by such sectors should not be underestimated.

Even in 2004, when Britain and the United States were military allies in the Iraq War, a European survey showed that 51 percent of Britons continued to feel that their ways of life were threatened by exported U.S. culture.

These kinds of articulations signify varying degrees of crisis or uncertainty in the (cultural, national, political, or religious) identity of their proponents. From this perspective what might be termed *anti-Americanism* is less reflective of the United States and its political, economic, or cultural force and is instead a symptom of an identity in transition, not emergent but residual, even terminal. For example, strands of British anti-Americanism through the twentieth century explain the consequences of Britain's loss of status as the major world power. Between the 1930s and the 1950s, an ideologically loaded range of cultural organizations and leaders united in the articulation of "United States-as-threat." The purpose of this charge from a whole range of British cultural critics, was to preserve Anglo-European cultural authority. The frequently proclaimed "special relationship" with the United States is often more fraught and ambivalent than political leaders would care to utter. French manifestations of anti-Americanism have been identified as symptoms of cultural anxiety in France, as its key signifiers of national identity are perceived to be under threat from U.S. cultural imperialism: The production and consumption of French cuisine and wine are seen by traditionalists to be threatened by U.S. fast food and drinks or by genetically modified agriculture originating in the United States, and the French film industry seems to fight a constant battle with Hollywood. Even the French language is subject to protectionist action—public radio in France must limit the amount of English-language pop music broadcast, for instance. Examples such as these from Britain and France indicate that anti-Americanism says as much about its proponents and their construction of identity as it does about U.S. hegemony.

How far did the events of September 11, 2001, complicate or confirm the survival of anti-Americanism as a sociopolitical (as well as cultural) phenomenon? On the one hand, even in a globalized world, postnationalism has its limits because the single nation-state of the United States was targeted. On the other hand, al-Qaeda itself appears to be or have been a significantly postnational organization, with members from a number of countries, West and East. Others have identified in the attack on the United States an outdated, residual analysis on the part of al-Qaeda, evidence of a retrogressive understanding based on national boundaries (which has been interpreted as also then a retrogressive ideology). Retrogressive or otherwise, the world's only superpower experienced a powerful contemporary manifestation of the extent to which it can be criticized, opposed, even hated. A spate of publications with titles such as *Why Do People Hate America?* and *The Eagle's Shadow: Why America Fascinates and Infuriates the World* shows the

resurgence of critical interest here. Globalization apparently has not entirely removed the need for an identifiable national friend or enemy (nor has globalization quite fully yet become the new friend or enemy), and the United States is so grand in its achievements, energy, and ambition that each person can still find in it some version of the friend or enemy he or she wants.

George McKay

See also Western Europe, Cultural Relations with; Homogenization of World Culture

Further Reading

Barber, B. (1996). *McWorld vs. jihad: How globalism and tribalism are reshaping the world.* New York: Ballantine.

Brooker, P. (Ed.). (1992). *Modernism/postmodernism.* Harlow, UK: Longman.

Bryman, A. (2004). *The Disneyization of society.* London: Sage.

Campbell, N., Davies, J., & McKay, G. (Eds.). (2004). *Issues in Americanization and culture.* Edinburgh, UK: Edinburgh University Press.

Chomsky, N. (2000). *Rogue states: The rule of force in world affairs.* London: Pluto Press.

Deleuze, G., & Guattari, F. (1996). *Anti-Oedipus: Capitalism and schizophrenia.* London: Athlone Press.

Gilroy, P. (1993). *The black Atlantic: Modernity and double consciousness.* London: Verso.

Hebdige, D. (1988). *Hiding in the light: On images and things.* London: Routledge.

Hertsgaard, M. (2002). *The eagle's shadow: Why America fascinates and infuriates the world.* London: Bloomsbury.

Kroes, R., Rydell, R. W., & Bosscher, D. F. J. (Eds.). (1993). *Cultural transmissions and receptions: American mass culture in Europe.* Amsterdam: Free University Press.

Kroes, R., & van Rossem, M. (Eds.). (1986). *Anti-Americanism in Europe.* Amsterdam: Free University Press.

Pratt, M. L. (1995). *Imperial eyes: Travel writing and transculturation.* London: Routledge.

Ritzer, G. (1996). *The McDonaldization of society: An investigation into the changing character of contemporary social life* (Rev. ed.). Thousand Oaks, CA.: Pine Forge Press.

Said, E. (2003). Global crisis over Iraq. In L. Rinder (Ed.), *The American effect: Global perspectives on the United States, 1990–2003* . New York: Whitney Museum of American Art.

Sardar, Z., & Wyn Davies, M. (2002). *Why do people hate America?* London: Icon.

Slater, D., & Taylor, P. J. (Eds.). (1999). *The American century: Consensus and coercion in the projection of American power.* Oxford, UK: Blackwell.

Tomlinson, J. (1999). *Globalization and culture.* Cambridge, UK: Polity.

Whitman, Walt (1900) *Leaves of Grass.* Retrieved April 12, 2007, from http://www.bartleby.com/142/1.html

Anti-Americanism

Feelings of bigotry, anger, and even hatred toward the United States and its people, exhibited by many nations and people of the world, have often coexisted with attitudes that embrace American culture.

Anti-Americanism is not a comprehensive or coherent belief system or ideology, but rather a series of beliefs and prejudices regarding the United States that have haphazardly been labeled anti-Americanism. The term was first associated with eighteenth- and nineteenth-century European cultural laments about U.S. manners and uncouthness and then, as the United States becomes a global power, more politically and economically based criticism came to the fore. Most recently, in the last decades of the twentieth century, what has been labeled anti-American terrorism has reared its head. What is important to stress is that these phases of anti-Americanism are not mutually exclusive; early forms of criticism continue in later periods and the criticisms of one era often reinforce those of another. A combination of these strands can be seen when President George W. Bush is derided as the "toxic Texan." Both his policies on environmental matters and his uncouth (to some foreign eyes) Texan image are combined in this common caricature.

Defining Anti-Americanism

Arguably the best book written on anti-Americanism during the twentieth century is *The Rise and Fall of Anti-Americanism* (1990), an edited collection of French scholarship on the topic. In this volume the political scientist Marie-France Toinet suggests that the use of the term anti-Americanism "is only fully justified if it implies systematic opposition—a sort of allergic reaction—to America as a whole" (Lacorne, Rupnik, and Toinet 1990, 219). A broader definition is offered by Alvin Rubinstein and Donald Smith, who see anti-Americanism "as any hostile action or expression that becomes part and parcel of an undifferentiated attack on the foreign policy, society, culture and values of the United States" (1988, 35). Bringing us much closer to the common use of the term is Robert Singh's suggestion that—as Justice Potter Stewart observed with regard to pornography—we instinctively "know it when we see it."

Because there is no agreed-upon definition, what differentiates anti-Americanism from reasonable criticism of the United States is often confused or even deliberately distorted. Since September 11, 2001, defenders of the United States have been particularly prone to label criticisms of the U.S. anti-American, often with the intent of silencing debate. At the same time, increasing numbers of people are expressing their frustrations and anger with the U.S. in a manner that is fairly labeled anti-American. Another conceptual problem is the fact that an aversion to the United States often coexists, within a nation or an individual, with an embracing of the United States. One method for understanding anti-Americanism is to consider it in four phases.

The Problem of Manners

The earliest form of anti-American comment tended to be cultural criticism of the lack of taste, grace, and civility in U.S. habits and everyday life. European writers such as Charles Dickens and Frances Trollope built up a picture of Americans as rude and indifferent to manners or polite conversation. The French statesman Talleyrand (1754–1838) denigrated the United States when he observed that it had "thirty-two religions and just one dish" (quoted in Judt 2003, 24). And summing up nineteenth-century European intellectuals' criticisms of the United States, the Norwegian writer Knut Hamsum commented that "America is a very backward country culturally" (1889, 15). However, what infuriated Europeans the most was that this backwardness and uncouthness was combined with what they regarded as a cocksure arrogance. Reflecting on this, the historian Simon Schama writes, "By the end of the nineteenth century, the stereotype of the ugly American—voracious, preachy, mercenary, and bombastically chauvinist—was firmly in place in Europe" (2003). This cultural critique has remained a constant of transatlantic relations, with Europe depicted as the aesthetic bulwark against rampant U.S. consumerism, corporatism, and industrialism.

Cold War Anti-Americanism

After World War II, as the United States became fully engaged in international politics and involved in a global Cold War with the Soviet Union, political anti-Americanism became more significant. At the simplest level, to be pro-Soviet was to be anti-American

(or in, U.S. domestic parlance, un-American). Although this is a very reductionist approach, it is one largely adopted by the sociologist Paul Hollander in his *Anti-Americanism* (1995). Although recruitment to the pro-Soviet cause was undoubtedly hindered by the behavior of the Soviet regime, Communist parties in Europe, particularly in France, had some success arguing that the United States was intent on global military and economic domination and needed to be opposed. Possibly the most noted early Cold War anti-American rallies were large protests organized by the French Communists against the Korean War. These included a sizable antiwar gathering when the U.S. military commander General Matthew Ridgway visited Paris in 1952. The French Communists lambasted Ridgway, dubbing him the "bacterial general" based on their claims that the United States was engaged in germ warfare in Korea. By the time of the Vietnam War a much broader range of leftist parties in Europe and elsewhere were heavily involved in organizing antiwar activities, which were frequently criticized as being anti-American.

Not all post–World War II criticism of the United States was leftist, however. An interesting case in point is French political opposition to U.S. foreign policy in the early Cold War. French commentary and politics from the 1930s through the early Cold War era have created the broadly held view that anti-Americanism is significantly a French tradition, buoyed in France in particular by a resentment of U.S. power and the United States' emergence from the two world wars of the twentieth century stronger rather than weaker. The right-wing Gaullist Party and its leader Charles de Gaulle (the French president from 1958 to 1969) challenged U.S. policy in a number of areas during the 1960s.

Many consider political anti-Americanism in Britain and West Germany to have come to a head during the 1980s, with the growth of public antipathy toward U.S. bases and to the deployment of further tactical nuclear weapons on their soil. This backlash against U.S. bases was also felt in the Philippines, Japan, and South Korea. Japan scholar Chalmers Johnson has written ominously about the potential the latter two countries hold for anti-Americanism in his book *Blowback*. For Johnson anti-Americanism is the ubiquitous form of blowback occasioned by U.S. policies. He and others have suggested, for example, that the CIA's support of the Afghan mujahideen and Osama bin Laden resulted in perhaps the most stunning incident of anti-American blowback—the terrorist attacks of September 11, 2001. As this example suggests, criticisms of the United States' use of its military and political power have continued beyond the end of the Cold War and remain a major source of what is often labeled anti-Americanism. The key difference in these current foreign policy debates and conflicts is that the Soviet Union no longer exists as an alternative pole or source of support.

SINCLAIR LEWIS ON ANTI-AMERICANISM

U.S. author Sinclair Lewis often portrayed a less-than-flattering picture of Americans in the first half of the twentieth century. His 1929 novel Dodsworth *chronicles the European travels of Sam Dodsworth, a self-made industrialist, and his social-climbing wife. In the extract below, a German professor presents Dodsworth and his wife with some strong opinions about the United States and its citizens.*

America wants to turn us into Good Fellows, all provided with the very best automobiles—and no private place to which we can go in them. When I think of America I always remember a man who made me go out to a golf club and undress in a locker room, where quite uninvited men came up and made little funny jokes about Germany and about my being a professor!

. . . [A]nd most Americans who think they have "seen Europe" go home without any idea at all of its existence and what it stands for, and they perceive of Europe just loud-tongued guides, and passengers in trains looking unfriendly and reading *Uhu* or *Le Rire*. They have missed only everything that makes Europe!

Source: Lewis, S. (1962). Dodsworth (pp. 276–277). New York: Dell. (Original work published 1929)

Post–Cold War Anti-Americanism

It was widely predicted that the end of the Cold War would usher in a new era of harmony on political and ideological matters. Hollander, for example, predicted that there would be a reduction in anticapitalist sentiment, which for him is one of the key strands of anti-Americanism. However, rather like predictions of the end of ideology a generation earlier, these pronouncements turned out to be premature. New issues have led to unparalleled disagreements between former NATO allies, with the 2003 Iraq conflict the most obvious example.

At a general level, the end of the Cold War led the world into what has been widely dubbed the age of globalization. The anti-Americanism of this period is frequently associated with the anti-globalization movement and its fears of a world dominated by U.S. capitalist interests and U.S. culture. These anti-globalization concerns often extend beyond anxiety over U.S. dominance, but nonetheless the rhetoric and protests of these movements more often than not single out U.S. multinationals, U.S. influence on the International Monetary Fund and the World Bank, and the United States' failure to sign the Kyoto protocol when seeking a

FRANCES TROLLOPE ON AMERICANS

The Domestic Manners of the Americans (1832), *written by British author Frances Trollope, remains a classic view of the United States by a visitor from abroad. In this extract from her book, Trollope takes aim at a debate between the social reformer Robert Owen who "challenged the whole religious public of the United States to discuss with him publicly the truth or falsehood of all the religions that had ever been propagated on the face of the earth" and the Reverend Alexander Campbell. Her observations are remarkably similar to those made about contemporary debaters in the United States—particularly in the political arena.*

Neither appeared to me to answer the other; but to confine themselves to the utterance of what they had uppermost in their own minds when the discussion began. I lamented this on the side of Mr. Campbell, as I am persuaded he would have been much more powerful had he trusted more to himself and less to his books. Mr. Owen is an extraordinary man, and certainly possessed of talent, but he appears to me so utterly benighted in the mists of his own theories, that he has quite lost the power of looking through them, so as to get a peep at the world as it really exists around him. . . .

It was said, that at the end of the fifteen meetings the numerical amount of the Christians and the Infidels of Cincinnati remained exactly what it was when they began.

This was a result that might have been perhaps anticipated; but what was much less to have been expected, neither of the disputants ever appeared to lose their temper. I was told they were much in each other's company, constantly dining together, and on all occasions expressed most cordially their mutual esteem.

All this I think could only have happened in America. I am not quite sure that it was very desirable it should have happened any where.

Source: Trollope, F. (1949). Domestic manners of the Americans (pp. 152–153). New York: Vintage Books.

---

place to lay the blame for globalization's ills. Similarly, it is often the United States that is held most at fault for world poverty, environmental degradation, and global conflict. Some of these criticisms are fair and justified; others are indiscriminate and are rightly called anti-American. Amongst many in the anti-globalization movement, America has become a code word for all the various ills of the world, reminiscent of its use in the mid-nineteenth century, when "America was already a synonym in certain French circles for whatever was disturbing or unfamiliar about the present" (Judt 1992, 188).

With a backdrop of widespread skepticism about the United States in the post–Cold War period, the attacks of September 11 elicited a mixed response from the rest of the world, something which took many Americans by surprise. Reflecting the noted insularity of their society, Americans seemed largely unaware of how they and their country were viewed around the globe. U.S. society found itself asking, "Why do they hate us?" in reference to terrorists and their supporters.

Anti-American Terrorism

The violent anti-Americanism made concrete by the September 11 attacks has undoubtedly had a sobering effect on discussions of anti-Americanism. However while September 11 marked a new phase of anti-Americanism, the concerns of the previous phases have continued largely unabated. Nor does September 11 mark a hard and fast start date for violent anti-Americanism, which in fact can be traced to earlier events, such as politically motivated attacks on Americans in Beirut, Lebanon, from the 1970s onwards, the Iranian hostage crisis of 1979–1980, the 1993 detonation of a van bomb in the underground parking lot in the World Trade Center, the 1998 car bomb attacks on the U.S. embassies in Nairobi, Kenya, and Dar es Salaam, Tanzania, and the 2000 suicide bombing of the USS *Cole* in Aden Harbor, Yemen. All of those attacks had anti-American motivations, but before September 11 they were thought of more as random events.

In many respects the terrorist attacks of September 11 were quintessential anti-American acts, which satisfy all of the competing definitions of anti-Americanism. In targeting the Pentagon and the World Trade Center, the terrorists deliberately chose two famous symbols of U.S. power while indiscriminately killing civilians who were predominately Americans. When asked by interviewers to justify the attacks, bin Laden claimed that the evils committed by the United States justified a suspension of Islamic laws regarding murder. Furthermore, he stated that U.S. civilians were a legitimate target because they vote in their leaders and their taxes fund their military (and help fund Israel's military, which is used, in bin Ladin's words, to massacre Palestinians). The philosopher and historian Theodore Zeldin has described anti-Americanism as pathological, arguing that "to hate a whole nation, to love a whole nation, is a clear symptom of hysteria" (Lacorne, Rupnik, and Toinet 1990, 35). Although al-Qaeda's terrorist anti-Americanism fits this pathology, its outlook even in all its irrationality is arguably more strategically oriented toward pushing the United States out of the Middle East and the broader Islamic world than Western leaders have generally acknowledged.

Moving Beyond Anti-Americanism

From laments about U.S. uncouthness to al-Qaeda's denouncements of the United States supposed occupation of sacred Muslim sites in the Middle East, criticism of the United States has a varied and broad history. Cultural criticisms have remained a constant in anti-American discourse, particularly as the specter of Americanization is increasingly resisted. Once the United States became recognized as a great power by the rest of the world, political and economic concerns also became a central plank of anti-American rhetoric. Finally and most recently, we have seen the emergence of anti-American terrorism. This division of anti-Americanism into different periods is similar to Moises Naim's identification of "five 'pure' types: politico-economic, historical, religious, cultural, and psychological" (2002, 104). As these broad categories suggest, hating certain things about the United States is easy, but to hate the nation and its people as a whole is difficult given the variety and contradictions the United States encapsulates. This hatred generally relies on stereotypes or caricatures that tell one more about the individual or group passing judgment than they do about the United States. None of this is to suggest that the United States is above reproach. However, prejudiced rhetoric weakens otherwise justifiable critiques of the United States' many faults and at the same time hinders the ability to appreciate the promise that the United States still holds for itself and the world.

Brendon O'Connor

See also History of United States in World Opinion; Perspectives on the United States, Visitors'; Use of Force Internationally, Views on U.S.; Western Europe, Cultural Relations with

Further Reading

BBC News. (2003, June 16). Poll suggests world hostile to U.S. Retrieved December 22, 2004, from http://news.bbc.co.uk/2/hi/americas/2994924.stm

Hamsum, K. (1969). *The cultural life of modern America.* Cambridge, MA: Harvard University Press. (Original work published 1889)

Hollander, P. (1995). *Anti-Americanism.* New Brunswick, NJ: Transaction Publishers.

Johnson, C. (2002). *Blowback: The costs and consequences of American empire.* London: Time Warner.

Judt, T. (1992). *Past imperfect: French intellectuals, 1944–1956.* Berkley: University of California Press.

Judt, T. (2003, May 1). Anti-Americans abroad. *The New York Review of Books, 50*(7), 24–27.

Lacorne, D., Rupnik, J., & Toinet, Marie-France (Eds.). (1990). *The rise and fall of anti-Americanism: A century of French perception* (G. Turner, Trans.). London: Macmillan.

Naim, M. (2002, January-February). Anti-Americanisms: A guide to hating Uncle Sam. *Foreign Policy, 81*(1), pp. 103-104.

O'Connor, B. (2004, Spring). Bush-bashing: The hated and the haters. *Griffith Review, 5,* pp. 211-221.

Pew Research Center for the People and the Press. (2003). America's image further erodes, Europeans want weaker ties. Retrieved December 22, 2004, from http://people-press.org/reports/display.php3?ReportID=175

Rubin, B., & Rubin, J. C. (Eds.). (2002). *Anti-American terrorism and the Middle East.* Oxford, UK: Oxford University Press.

Rubinstein, A., & Smith, D. (1988, May). Anti-Americanism in the Third World. *Annals (AAPSS), 497,* 35–45.

Schama, S. (2003, March 3). The unloved American. *The New Yorker.* Retrieved December 22, 2004, from http://www.newyorker.com/fact/content/?030310fa_fact

Singh, R. (in press). Are we all Americans now? In B. O'Connor and M. Griffiths (Eds.), *The rise of anti-Americanism.* London: Routledge.

Anti-Semitism

This look at the origins of anti-Semitism examines why and how this religious hatred has been allowed to persist to this day in the United States.

The term *anti-Semitism* (hatred of Jews) was coined by a German, Wilhelm Friedrich Marr, in 1873. The term was, Marr felt, a legitimate definition of the cultural conflict being waged between "Germanism" and "Judaism" in the heart of Europe. For Marr, Jews, only recently emancipated from ghettos, represented the vanguard of destructive nonwhite masses poised to overthrow Christianity and Western civilization. One of Marr's adversaries, Leon Pinsker, a Jewish physician, put it more simply. Reflecting on pogroms (massacres) in Russia that killed fifty thousand of his kinsmen in 1881–1882, Pinsker labeled judeophobia a "psychic aberration," an incurable, hereditary disease that had been transmitted for two thousand years (Pinsker 1882).

In fact, animosity toward Jews predates the charge of deicide (the act of killing a divine being or a symbolic substitute of such a being) to which Pinsker referred. Two thousand years before Jesus was crucified, Canaanites, Amalekites, Edomites, and Moabites opposed territorial aspirations of Abraham, the first Hebrew. When Israel claimed to have a special relationship with a god that was immanent (indwelling) in the universe, Greeks and Romans thrashed the Jews in a series of wars (the Gezerot of Antiochus Epiphanes, 175–160 BCE; the Great Jewish War, 66–70 CE; and the Bar Kochba Revolt, 132–135 CE) that left the Jews scattered and homeless throughout the world.

Shunted from country to country, Jews were not permitted to own land, enter guilds, or marry Christians or Muslims. Refuge secured through payment of a special *leibzoll* (head tax) was temporary. Even in lands where Jews prospered for a century or two (Mesopotamia, Spain, England, Poland) their hosts inevitably turned against them, inventing heinous tales. Church fathers from Eusebius to Martin Luther employed homilies attacking Jews. Anti-Semitism at this time was characterized by an array of horrendous stereotypes. Jews were said to cheat non-Jewish customers, to have a peculiar stench *(foetor judaicus)* from bathing in sewer water, to have cursed Christ and Christians in their prayer services, and to be followers of Satan who engaged in host desecration, well poisoning, and ritual murder.

The civilized world experienced a surge of anti-Semitism in the medieval/early modern period. Anti-Jewish discrimination was institutionalized in the Byzantine codes of Theodosius and Justinian and the Islamic rule of Umar. What started as name-calling in defense of religious credos grew into intimidation, boycott, and assault. Unchecked by ruling establishments, bands of anti-Semites orchestrated massacres in the Rhineland during the Crusader epoch (1095–1270 CE), in North Africa (1200–1400), in Iberia during the Inquisition (1480–1820), and in Russia under Ivan the Terrible.

Jews and Capitalism, Communism

Challenged by John Locke, Isaac Newton, and Baruch Spinoza to embrace reason, non-Jews had to admit that Jews bore little resemblance to the "fright-wigged monsters" that inhabited their nightmares. Nevertheless, during the commercial revolution a few anti-Semitic stereotypes were especially perpetuated in bank houses around the world. As the economist Werner Sombart wrote regarding this stereotype, Jews were perceived as "atoms of money which flow[ed] and [were] scattered but which at the least inclination reunite[d] into one principal stream" (Sombart 1951, 175). There was paranoia that Jews unfairly manipulated stock markets, yet at the same time were also supposedly leading the proletarian revolution. It mattered little that not one of the great socialist revolutionaries was raised as or identified as a Jew.

Eugenics

In the nineteenth century Charles Darwin and Gregor Mendel opened the door to a discussion of evolution and differentiation between and within species. Eugenicists (proponents of the science that deals with the improvement, as by control of human mating, of hereditary qualities of a race or breed) such as Francis Galton, Arthur deGobineau, Houston Stewart Chamberlain, Madison Grant, Lothrop Stoddard, and Richard Wagner warned of the threat posed by the Jewish "race"—considered to be slack-jawed cretins bred in the caves of Italy or the ghettos of Galicia—to the rest of humanity. To these eugenicists, Jews were as different from Anglo-Saxons as bacteria were from human beings. But by mid-century millions of immigrants, many of them Jews, were

Furnaces at the Auschwitz concentration camp in Poland. Source: istock.

demanding equality in Germany, England, and the United States. Unfortunately, their demands were met with formidable resistance during this era when Paul de LaGarde advised, with bacteria one does not negotiate, but instead exterminates it.

Proclaiming Gresham's law of racial purity (bad blood drives out good), some Europeans and their U.S. counterparts instructed that nature has an aversion to miscegenation (the crossing of bloodlines). Jews especially understood the power of blood. Although seemingly weak and few in numbers, they had managed to survive, with little change to their character or person, by condemning intermarriage while eroding barriers with gentiles. This sexual phobia was the basis that informed German Nazi leader Adolf Hitler's *Mein Kampf* twenty-five years later and inspired the Nuremberg Laws, *Kristallnacht,*—"night of broken glass," when Jewish shop windows were smashed, and looted, across Germany—and the use of Zyklon B poison gas a decade after as a means to kill Jewish prisoners in concentration camps.

The Holocaust

Hitler and the Nazis believed their anti-Jewish actions to be legitimate ("self-defense") because the Jews not only intended to bastardize good, white racial stock, but also to seize political power throughout the world. Evidence of this Jewish plot came from novels such as *Biarritz* (purporting to tell of a secret meeting of rabbis in Switzerland) and conferences such as the World Zionist Congress, summoned by Theodor Herzl in Basel in 1897, or printed fabrications such as the *Protocols of the Elders of Zion*, which has been used to justify everything from the Easter 1903 pogrom in Kishinev in Moldova to the shipment of Jews to their deaths in Treblinka and Auschwitz in Poland in 1943.

The men and women who participated in that last endeavor (dubbed "14f13" in Nazi newspeak) never admitted that they were motivated by hatred. Rather, they were engaged in a holy mission—the furthering of a "biocracy" in which mistakes of nature would be erased through *gnadentod* (mercy killing). It was not a simple process. Eugenics teachings were celebrated in the United States long before the Nazis mandated sterilization.

On the eve of World War II European states shut their borders to refugees (most of whom were Jews). Refugees were persecuted in many lands, unwelcome in any. When the Western democracies finally confronted the threat of fascism in the spring of 1940, their military planners were outwitted and humiliated. A spirit of collaboration dominated Europe. Emulating their Nazi overlords, European states introduced anti-Jewish codes. States defined Jews by race, called for an Aryan attestation in employment, introduced quotas in professions and schools, confiscated Jewish property,

seized residences, burned synagogues and destroyed cemeteries, beat people on the streets and sent them to nonexistent relocation camps hundreds of miles from their homes. Some European states surpassed even the Nazis in their brutality. Germany may have been the center of this genocidal plan, but an insensitive world rationalized inaction as the Holocaust played out.

In some views, Europe has not done a good job of confronting the legacy of the Holocaust. Until the dissolution of the Soviet Union, many nations denied any responsibility for the massacres. Some countries (Austria, Lithuania), claiming to be victims of persecution themselves, continue to deflect reparations applications. Others (France and the low countries), influenced by large numbers of immigrants from the Middle East, have embraced an "even-handed" approach to Jewish issues, meaning that even the most blatant of anti-Semitic incidents (assassination of an artist in Holland, desecration of synagogues and cemeteries in France) are played down. All of which bemuses Germans and Poles, both of whom have been flogged repeatedly in the past half-century.

A Different World: The United States

The United States seemed immune to criticism on the issue of anti-Semitism until the release of classified documents in the late-1960s. Since then a veritable industry focusing on the U.S. role in the Holocaust has developed. Scholars differ about the nature of policies pursued by the administration of President Franklin D. Roosevelt, but they do not question the existence of widespread anti-Jewish prejudice in that period. Unlike Europe, the United States managed to restrain its own bigots (Father Charles Coughlin and the Christian Front, Fritz Kuhn and the German-American Bund, William Pelley's Silver Shirts, as well as the naïve millions who supported Charles Lindbergh and America First). Perhaps this situation occurred because no single ethnic group could lay claim to being "pure Americans." Pilgrims and Puritans came to the New World seeking religious freedom and instituted one of the most reactionary systems in Massachusetts. Baptists, Quakers, and Jews were warned out of that society. However, they found other places along the ever-expanding frontier—Rhode Island, Pennsylvania, Ohio, Kentucky, Iowa, and Oregon, where a man's religion counted less than his reliability. In that regard the United States, with its legacy of Roger Williams, Thomas Jefferson, Abraham Lincoln, Emma Lazarus, Louis Brandeis, and Martin Luther King Jr., seemed different from Europe.

Public opinion polls conducted during the last sixty years reveal a less appealing side of the United States. During the

Holocaust a substantial number of Americans (between 30 and 50 percent) responded in the negative when asked if they would work with, live next door to, date, or marry a Jew. As late as the winter of 1944–1945 most people surveyed doubted stories of extermination camps. Throughout the war years Americans listed Jews as the least likable minority in the country. Twenty-five years later a majority told Anti-Defamation League pollsters they could support an anti-Semitic candidate for president in times of economic distress.

Anti-Zionism and Israel

Anti-Zionism—opposition to a Jewish State, Israel specifically—is also a persistent problem, akin to anti-Semitism. In the wake of the terrorist attacks of September 11, 2001, many Americans were asking what they had done to warrant such hostility. From a cave in Afghanistan al-Qaeda leader Osama bin Laden emerged to offer an indictment: Americans are arrogant. They ignore the aspirations of Muslims around the world, supporting corrupt, oppressive monarchies, exploiting oil resources, and desecrating the Holy Land by their physical presence in Saudi Arabia.

Years before, in 1968, President Lyndon B. Johnson endured a similar tirade from Soviet Premier Aleksei Kosygin. Why, Kosygin wanted to know, did the United States support Israel? Didn't Johnson realize he was alienating hundreds of millions of Muslims and compromising U.S. strategic interests around the world? To which Johnson is reported to have replied, "because it is right." American Jews, as well as Jews around the world, have been grateful for such support of Israel—though in the wake of a post-9/11 world, these ties to Israel may have awakened a new brand of anti-Semitism.

Saul S. Friedman

Further Reading

Fackenheim, E. (1978). *The Jewish return into history.* New York: Schocken.

Flannery, E. (1985). *The anguish of the Jews: Twenty-three centuries of anti-Semitism.* New York: Paulist Press.

Friedman, S. (1993). *Holocaust literature.* Westport, CT: Greenwood Press.

Hay, M. (1950). *The foot of pride.* Boston: Beacon Press.

Levin, N. (1968). *The Holocaust.* New York: Crowell.

Lewis, B. (2004). *Crisis of Islam: Holy war and unholy terror.* New York: Modern Library.

Mosse, G. (1978). *Toward the final solution.* New York: Howard Fertig.

Perry, M., & Schweitzer, F. (2002). *Anti-Semitism: Myth and hate from antiquity to the present.* New York: Palgrave.

Pinsker, L. (1882). *Autoemancipation.* Berlin: Author.

Poliakov, L. (1974). *The Aryan myth: A history of racist and nationalist ideas in Europe*. New York: New American Library.

Sachar, H. (1958). *The course of modern Jewish history*. Cleveland, OH: World Publishing.

Samuel, M. (1940). *The great hatred*. New York: Knopf.

Sombart, W. (1951). *Jews and modern capitalism* (M. Epstein, Trans.). Glencoe, IL: Free Press.

Trachtenberg, J. (1943). *The devil and the Jews*. New Haven, CT: Yale University Press.

Viereck, P. (1941). *Metapolitics: The roots of the Nazi mind*. New York: Capricorn Books.

Waite, R. (1977). *The psychopathic god: Adolf Hitler*. New York: Basic Books.

Brain Drain

The international migration of highly skilled workers is an important part of economic policy for most nations and a key part of the globalization of economic, scientific, and cultural activities.

Brain drain, *brain gain*, and *brain circulation* are metaphors for the effects of large movements of highly skilled people across international borders. Each term was first commonly used in discussions of the migration of science and technology workers to the United States but now is used to describe a geographically broader phenomenon.

The first term, *brain drain*, is the oldest and best known, originating from discussions in the United Kingdom of the negative effects for Britain of the migration of scientists, engineers, and other highly skilled workers to the United States during the 1950s. Although *brain drain* is still used to describe movements between Europe and the United States, it is now more commonly used to describe movement of educated workers from less-developed countries to developed countries.

The terms *brain gain* and *brain circulation* came into use in the late 1990s by researchers who wished to stress that the effects of highly skilled migration on both sending and receiving countries are too complex to be described in terms of national losers and winners. Rather than emphasizing highly skilled migration as a problem, a focus on the circulation of brains looks at the gains that result both for the global economy and specifically for both sending and receiving countries.

Size and Importance of Brain Circulation

Highly skilled migration has become increasingly important to all countries as economic, scientific, and cultural activities become more globalized. According to the National Science Board, in the United States as of 2004, nearly 30 percent of doctorate holders in science and engineering occupations were foreign born. Numerous countries during the 1990s and early 2000s adopted policies to make their countries more attractive to highly skilled foreign labor. Policies to provide incentives for highly skilled workers to migrate have included easy access to temporary work visas, easing the path to citizenship; active recruitment and immigration preferences for foreign students; personal income tax reductions; and the promotion of English as a work language.

Highly skilled migrants are particularly important for national

economic strategies as the importance of science and technology grows in what has been labeled the "new economy." Employment in science and engineering occupations in the United States has grown from 2.6 percent of the labor force in 1983 to 3.9 percent in 2001 (from 2.9 to 5.6 million workers). Many economists believe that the technological innovation created and maintained by this segment of the labor force has been the key source of productivity and economic growth in industrial countries. For the United States in particular a large portion of this growth in science and engineering employment has been made possible by the relative attractiveness of the United States to foreign scientists and engineers.

At the same time, many countries focused on the numbers of people leaving. Frederic Docquier and Abdeslem Marfouk estimated that many counties had a significant proportion of their tertiary-educated population (having roughly the equivalent of a U.S. associate degree or higher) living in thirty industrialized countries, reaching 40.9 percent of tertiary-educated workers in Caribbean countries. Although smaller and poorer countries certainly tended to have a larger proportion of their educated workers abroad, significant highly skilled emigration was also found for larger countries (China and India were estimated to have 4.2 percent of their tertiary-educated workforce abroad) and for many more developed countries (Canada, 4.9 percent; Germany. 8.8 percent; United Kingdom, 16.7 percent).

Knowledge Flows and Social Networks

Economic and technological advantages accrue to countries that are sending, as well as those receiving, the flow of knowledge through the social networks created by migration.

In some cases this flow is in the form of scientific knowledge transfer—migrants bring knowledge from their previous employers or universities to their new jobs in a different country or to their country of origin after they return. Migrant scientists and engineers are also more likely to collaborate with colleagues from their old institution and with former graduate students with professors and students at institutions where they studied.

In other cases knowledge transfer is of a more mundane, but

still important, type. Migrant social networks, both with co-nationals and with persons in host countries, can lead to sales contacts, to a cross-national understanding of business practices and procedures, and just generally to increased business opportunities. This is particularly true when the migrants are highly skilled and work in either in science and technology or management.

Effects on Human Capital Creation

International labor markets for highly skilled workers create incentives for persons to invest in their own skills *(human capital)*. Although movement across borders may decrease the incentives for governments to invest in higher education, it is nevertheless true that people pay most of the total costs of their education, if only in terms of the lost wages while they are in school. Thus, the ability to market skills internationally, increasing wages and job choices, is likely to increase the global stock of human capital and the global ability both to produce goods and services and to produce new knowledge.

Highly skilled migration may result in a greater stock of human capital even in the sending countries. Although they lose the talents of highly skilled natives, this loss is sometimes temporary. Many highly skilled migrants return to their country of origin after a period abroad, bringing with them human capital gained in the host country both through formal education and through job experience. Even without a return migration, source countries may gain human capital through the incentives created through additional economic returns on the skills of their natives. For in-

stance, some persons may be willing to invest in training knowing that their skills would be valued internationally but in the end stay at home. In addition, the interaction of domestic highly skilled workers with the highly skilled workers in a country's diaspora (the migration of a people away from a homeland) may create job opportunities.

Receiving countries are clear gainers in human capital, benefiting from the labor of highly skilled workers and graduate students (who help to produce new knowledge as teaching and research assistants). However, some concerns have been raised about the effect of highly skilled migration on the incentives for natives in receiving countries to seek high levels of skills. Studies of heavy highly skilled migration to Israel after the collapse of the Soviet Union have suggested a reduction of about one native entering a highly skilled field for every eight immigrants with the same training. Despite this displacement of natives, this fact suggests that a large proportion of the migration of highly skilled people represents a net gain in human capital for receiving countries.

Remittances

Direct transfer of money from migrants to their country of origin has become an important benefit to sending countries. In 2002, remittances by migrants totaled $130 billion. Highly skilled migrants have much higher incomes from which to make contributions but may also be less likely to leave immediate family members behind in their country of origin. Thus, some controversy continues over what proportion of total remittances comes from the highly skilled.

MEDICAL BRAIN DRAIN ON SOUTH KOREA

The following passage describes the costs and consequences of Korean medical professionals emigrating to foreign countries in the 1960s and '70s.

It costs more than $20,000 [in South Korea] to produce a physician through the process of a 6-year medical education and a 5-year training in internship and residency. A substantial portion of the doctors, produced at such an expensive cost, have emigrated to foreign countries, resulting in a serious loss in national manpower resources. This brain drain of medical professionals has caused a setback to our national health program. According to recent statistics compiled by the Ministry of Health and Social Affairs, a total of 3,800 doctors including dentists and "Oriental medicine" doctors have migrated to foreign countries. The figure constitutes 22 percent of the total 16,800 registered doctors in 1975. An annual average of 300 doctors flowed

to foreign countries during the period from 1969 to 1975. The number represents about a fourth of the total annual graduates from fourteen [Korean] medical schools. Consequently, the physician-population ratio, which decreased through the 1960s to 1,851 in 1973, has increased to 2,064 in 1976. This reversal is also applicable to nurses, dentists, and "Oriental medicine" doctors. This massive outflow of medical professionals has created a dislocation in the present government's attempt to formulate a comprehensive national medical insurance program. Government is now trying to solve the so-called problem of "the rural villages without doctors." Fortunately, the manpower shortage in medical fields is likely to be improved because the United States, which has accepted the majority of Korean medical professionals, is planning to restrict the entry of foreign medical workers.

Source: Hankook Ilbo. (1976, November 1).

Two science technicians examine the results of their experiments. Source: istock/Laurence Gough.

Do the Poorest Countries Benefit?

An important criticism of the viewpoint that sending countries also gain through highly skilled migration is that this gain may not be true of the poorest countries. Very poor countries are less likely to have products and services to sell via their diaspora, are less likely to be able to attract back their migrants, and are less likely to be able to benefit from research collaborations with foreign universities and companies. For all of these reasons, highly skilled migration may indeed represent a brain drain for the poorest countries.

Questions also are raised about social versus economic value. These questions seem sharpest when movement is between very poor and developed countries. If highly skilled migrants move to a country where their skills are more highly compensated, this move will usually mean in a market economy a movement to where their skills will contribute the most to the production of new goods, services, or economically valued knowledge. However, this argument becomes uncomfortable when the movement of doctors and nurses is from underserved countries to the more developed world.

However, how poor does a country have to be in order for brain circulation to be largely a brain drain? India was estimated to have a per capita GDP of only $2,900 in 2004, despite an average growth rate of 6 percent since 1990. However, India in the 1990s was a prominent example of a country benefiting from the complex ties of its businesses and universities with the Indian diaspora abroad.

Outlook for Poor Countries

Highly skilled international migration has become an important part of national economic policy for most nations and a key part of the globalization of economic, scientific, and cultural activities. International social networks, the more efficient transmission and creation of knowledge, and the stimulation of human capital growth may all lead to positive effects of highly skilled migration on both sending and receiving countries. However, it may be more difficult for the poorest countries to benefit from the migration of its educated citizens, and these countries may experience what truly may be called a "brain drain."

Mark C. Regets

See also Exchanges, Cultural and Scientific; Immigration to the United States; Nobel Peace Prize

Further Reading

Bhagwati, J. N., & Hamada, K. (1974). The brain drain, international integration of markets for professionals and unemployment: A theoretical analysis. *Journal of Development Economics, 1*(1), 19–42.

Carrington, W. J., & Detragiache, E. (1999, June). How extensive is the brain drain? *Finance and Development*, 46–49.

Docquier, F., & Marfouk, A. (2004). Measuring the international mobility of skilled workers. Retrieved January 7, 2005, from http://papers.ssrn.com/sol3/papers.cfm?abstract_id=625258

Grubel, H. G., & Scott, A. (1966). The international flow of human capital. *American Economic Review, 56*, 268–274.

Institute for International Education. (2004). *Open doors 2004: Report on international educational exchange.* New York: Institute for International Education.

Johnson, J., & Regets, M. (1998). *International mobility of scientists and engineers to the United States: Brain drain or brain circulation?* Arlington, VA: National Science Foundation.

Lowell, L. B. (2002). *Some developmental effects of the international migration of highly skilled persons.* Geneva, Switzerland: International Labour Office.

National Science Board. (2004). *Science and engineering indicators 2004.* Arlington, VA: National Science Board.

Regets, M. (2001). Foreign science & technology personnel in the United States: An overview of available data and basic characteristics. In *OECD innovative people: Mobility of skilled personnel in national innovation systems.* Paris: Organisation for Economic Co-Operation and Development.

United Nations Department of Economic and Social Affairs. (2004). *World economic and social survey 2004: Vol. 2. International migration.* New York: Author.

Businesses Overseas, U.S.

The relocation of business overseas is increasingly common in the expanding global marketplace. Often based on the availability of raw materials and unregulated labor, this trend results in the maximization of profits.

Profit in business is based on competitive advantage. This fact means that if a business can increase its revenues by moving to a location where production costs are less, then that business will do so. The evidence of this fact is all around us. Software is developed in India, and washing machines are made in China, both products based primarily on low-cost labor. Japanese corporations locate their production facilities in Europe, partly to avoid protectionist legislation and partly to access design and production expertise. Korean companies manufacture in Vietnam and Indonesia (not to mention China) to access potentially huge markets. U.S. businesses make similar decisions based on similar market analyses.

Snapshot of U.S. Businesses Overseas

The United States has the world's largest economy, and it is politically the most powerful country in the world. Hence, its economic impact is felt directly and indirectly across the globe. The value of U.S. assets overseas is approximately $9 trillion (as opposed to the nearly $12 trillion worth of foreign ownership in the United States). This is a broad category, of course, including all types of investment and ownership offshore.

More narrowly, if one considers direct U.S. investment in foreign countries (what the U.S. Department of Commerce calls "U.S. direct investment abroad" [USDIA], by the end of 2005 the total was just over $2 trillion. USDIA is defined as "the ownership or control, either directly or indirectly, by one US resident of at least 10 percent of the voting securities of an incorporated foreign business enterprise or the equivalent interest in an unincorporated foreign business enterprise" (Koncz and Yorgason 2006, 27). Hence, U.S. investment includes shares bought in foreign companies or foreign subsidiaries of U.S. companies. U.S. businesses also increasingly are using holding companies, in which "US parents own foreign affiliates that own other foreign affiliates" (Koncz and Yorgason 2006, 24). This indirect form of ownership, which is based on the advantage of different operating environments, now accounts for approximately 30 percent of all U.S. foreign investment and makes U.S. investment overseas much harder to view in precise terms.

Multinational corporations (MNCs) are powerful economic entities. The largest five hundred corporations in the world, in terms of income, have a total annual revenue of more than $11 trillion, with profits in excess of $400 billion. They hold more than $33 trillion in assets and employ approximately 36 million people worldwide. Of these 500 corporations the United States has 162, followed by Japan with 126. The largest U.S. MNCs are, in order, Ford, General Electric, Exxon, and General Motors. In terms of profitability the United States has seven of the top ten and thirty-one of the top fifty most profitable firms.

Geographically the United Kingdom is ranked first as a recipient of U.S. investment, at nearly 16 percent of the total, with Canada second at just over 11 percent. The Netherlands is next at nearly 9 percent, followed by Australia at about 6 percent. Bermuda is the fifth-largest recipient of U.S. investment, but this ranking reflects Bermuda's position as a base for MNCs, which in turn operate globally. Hence, the investment is not in Bermuda itself.

If we look at the categories of U.S. overseas investment, clear patterns emerge. Manufacturing is the largest category overall, including the following subcategories in diminishing size: chemicals, computers, transportation equipment, and food. The second-largest category, almost as large as manufacturing, is finance and insurance (excluding depository banks), followed by wholesale trade and mining.

In terms of economic categories by geographical region, clear patterns also emerge. In terms of Europe, manufacturing is most important, and this ranking is particularly the case in terms of chemicals, computers, transportation equipment, and food, in descending order. Finance and insurance is the second-largest category, followed by wholesale trade.

The Netherlands and the United Kingdom are the major recipients of investment in food, and their positions are reversed in terms of investment in chemicals. The United Kingdom is the main recipient of investment in machinery, followed by Ireland. With respect to computers, Ireland is number one, followed by the United Kingdom. In terms of transportation equipment, the United Kingdom is first; Germany is second.

In terms of finance and insurance the United Kingdom is by far the largest recipient of U.S. investment, followed by the

Netherlands; in wholesale trade Germany is first, followed by the United Kingdom and the Netherlands.

In Latin America, finance and insurance is the category of greatest U.S. investment, and manufacturing is second. Bermuda is by far the biggest recipient of investment in this region, but, as noted earlier, this ranking is meaningless in terms of the final destination of the investment. Mexico is the second-largest recipient of U.S. investment in this category.

Manufacturing is the second-largest category for Latin America. Within this category chemicals is number one, followed by primary and fabricated metals and transportation equipment. Brazil and Mexico consistently receive the most investment in these categories.

In the Middle East mining is understandably the most important, given the region's oil resources, followed by computers and electronic products. The United Arab Emirates figures most prominently in the former category and Israel in the latter.

Reasons for Relocating Overseas

Businesses have many reasons to either relocate overseas or to establish a foreign subsidiary, invest in a foreign company, or establish a joint venture. The decision depends on a host of variables, including costs, legal constraints, the length of time a business expects to be in a foreign market, and the nature of the country's business climate and long-term prospects.

Not surprisingly, Canada is a major receiver of U.S. business. The signing of the North American Free Trade Agreement (NAFTA) in 1992 gave the U.S.-Canada relationship a sharp boost, recognizing the trade complementarities of the two countries. Canada is the major provider of raw materials to the United States, and U.S. businesses are naturally interested in owning the industries that supply these materials (both as a means of profit and as a means of protecting the supply source). Hence, the oil industry in Canada is dominated by U.S. companies, and associated work, such as building pipelines, shows up in the investment statistics. This pattern has been enhanced in recent years as the price of oil on the world market has skyrocketed.

Statistics on the locations of U.S. direct investment also highlight the cultural affinity of the countries involved. This affinity has been studied under the heading of "psychic distance," meaning that companies tend to develop foreign affiliates or to invest in countries that are perceived as being similar to their own.

In some respects this phenomenon is simply common sense: Most U.S. businesses can work more easily in the English (or, in some cases, Spanish) language. However, in culturally similar countries a perception also exists that business mores and customs are also similar and therefore more understandable. In short, people find doing business in such countries easier. In part this perception accounts for the dominance of Europe and the Americas in

A U.S. businessman putting together a globe jigsaw puzzle suggests the complexity of conducting business in the global marketplace. Source: istock/Rob Friedman.

U.S. investment. At the same time, of course, profit has to be the underlying principle.

In the past decade exceptions to this perception have occurred. As Mataloni and Yorgason state, "MNCs [are] centered in other high income countries, particularly Canada and Europe. However, since 1999, value added has grown most rapidly in several low-to-middle-income countries (including China, Poland and India)" (Mataloni and Yorgason 2006, 39). Two examples—that of General Motors and Motorola—highlight the move to China, given the burgeoning market in automobiles and cell phones in that country. Indeed, U.S. foreign affiliates grew faster than the parent corporations during 1999–2004.

Complicated Business

The picture is, however, complex. For example, a substantial proportion of MNC trade is intrafirm trade, in which one part of a company exports components to another part of the same company. This trade is one reason why country-based trade statistics are not accurate. A U.S. company in China exporting to the U.S. market shows up in China's trade surplus, but this portrayal of trade is not accurate. Intrafirm trade is also substantial, accounting for 62 percent of all U.S. exports and 39 percent of all imports of goods, and the figures highlight the power of MNCs.

Many issues are connected with the role of U.S. businesses overseas. One issue is technology transfer and the complexities pertaining to whether this transfer gives a foreign country a long-term advantage over the United States in economic or security terms. Another issue is the extent to which U.S. businesses and U.S. politicians work together to maximize the influence of the United States in areas deemed to be strategically important. Examples are Kuwait and Iraq with their supplies of oil.

Another issue is that of exporting jobs, namely the job losses that occur in the United States when a U.S. MNC moves its manufacturing or service industry offshore to take advantage of a lower-cost environment. This issue is clearly as much political as economic.

A moral dimension of U.S. businesses overseas also reflects the role of MNCs more generally. Given the power of economic globalization and the speed and depth of internationalization of corporations, some critics say MNCs are exploitative of labor (i.e., by relocating to countries where labor is least expensive and least regulated) and outside of the boundaries of government control (particularly if the MNCs are incorporated in a country that does not have substantial legal constraints). Moreover, the broad movement to deregulation, signaled by the World Trade Organization (WTO), means that corporations are growing in power. This issue

lies beneath anti-WTO demonstrations, first put significantly on public view in Seattle, Washington, in 1999.

The counterargument, from the corporate point of view, is that a company will produce the best goods at the lowest price by focusing on the maximization of profits and that such a process will benefit society in general, both consumers and employees. A net economic gain accrues worldwide, although naturally this gain may benefit some countries more than others.

In conclusion, many issues must be considered when looking at U.S. businesses overseas. A straightforward economic dimension exists in which companies seek to maximize their profits through competitive advantage. This dimension has been the major driving force of corporations, accelerated in recent years through the power of economic globalization.

However, investment is more than economics; it occurs within a geopolitical context in which the interests of countries must also be taken into account. The decision to extend NAFTA to include Mexico and perhaps South America is clearly more than an economic decision. Consider U.S. trade with both China and Taiwan, where economic decisions have substantial political impact. Hence, a dynamic tension exists between governments and corporations, and this tension is particularly clear in the United States, the world's biggest economy and its only remaining superpower.

Curtis A. Andressen

See also McDonaldization; Multinational Corporations

Further Reading

Bakan, J. (2004). *The corporation: The pathological pursuit of profit and power.* London: Constable.

Chandler, A. Jr., Amatori, F., & Hikino, T. (1997). *Big business and the wealth of nations.* Cambridge, UK: Cambridge University Press.

Dethloff, H. (1997). *The United States and the global economy since 1945.* Fort Worth, TX: Harcourt Brace.

International Labour Organisation. (1997). Multinational corporations. Retrieved March 28, 2007, from http://www.itcilo.org/english/actrav/telearn/global/ilo/multinat/multinat.htm

Kelly, D., & Grant, W. (2005). *The politics of international trade in the twenty-first century.* New York: Palgrave Macmillan.

Koncz, J. L., & Yorgason, D. R. (2006). *Direct investment positions for 2005: Country and industry detail.* Retrieved March 28, 2007, from http://www.bea.gov/international/ai1.htm#BOPIIP

Mataloni, R. Jr., & Yorgason, D. R. (2006). *Operations of U.S. multinational companies.* Retrieved March 28, 2007, from http://www.bea.gov/international/ai1.htm#BOPIIP

Porter, M. (1990). *The competitive advantage of nations.* New York: Free Press.

Yoffie, D., & Gomes-Casseres, B. (1994). *International trade and competition* (2nd ed.). New York: McGraw-Hill.

Christian Nation, United States as a

Many Americans identify, formally or informally, with Christianity, and U.S. society has been shaped by Christian traditions and beliefs, but is Christianity the established, official religion of the nation?

"Christian" as a term refers to a person or group of people who identify, formally or informally, with one of thousands of denominations based on the teachings of Jesus Christ. "Christian" can also largely be understood as living by what one considers to be the principles taught by Yeshua/Jesus almost two thousand years ago. In the United States that can vary as widely as Bruce Barton's *The Man Nobody Knows* (1925), which portrays Jesus as a model for a successful advertising executive; James H. Cone's *A Black Theology of Liberation* (1970), which looks at Jesus through the lens of suffering and anger of the oppressed African-American community; and the Ku Klux Klan organizer Wesley A. Swift's Church of Jesus Christ Christian, a white supremacy Aryan Nations splinter group. Pat Robertson, Robert Schuller, Mother Angelica, and Jesse Jackson all are highly visible representatives of some form of late twentieth-century Christianity.

The history of Christianity accounts for this diversity. By the fourth century CE numerous versions of Christianity already existed, and although a series of councils tried to establish uniformity, doctrinal and liturgical differences remained. Then, in 1054 CE the Catholic (Western) and Orthodox (Eastern) branches of Christianity formally separated, and in the early sixteenth century the Reformation began the process that would lead to the eventual splintering of the Western church into thousands of major and minor denominations whose "divisions are so extreme... that sincerely and devoutly held beliefs by the most conservative Christians may well be considered blasphemy by the most liberal, and vice-versa" (Religious Tolerance Org. n.d.).

Denominational Diversity

According to a 2001 American Religious Identification Survey (ARIS) study cited at Adherents.com, 159,030,000 people or 76.5 percent of the U.S. population identify with one of the Christian denominations, including Catholic, Baptist, Protestant, Methodist, Lutheran, Presbyterian, Pentecostal (Charismatic), Episcopalian (Anglican), Mormon (Latter-day Saints), Churches of Christ, Jehovah's Witness, Seventh-Day Adventist, Assemblies of God, Holiness, Congregational (United Church of Christ), Church of the Nazarene, Church of God, Eastern Orthodox, Evangelical, Mennonite, Christian Science, Church of the Brethren, Born Again, Nondenominational Christians, Disciples of Christ, Reformed (Dutch Reformed), Apostolic, Quaker, Full Gospel, Christian Reform, Foursquare Gospel, Fundamentalist, Salvation Army, Independent Christian Church, Covenant Church, and Jewish Christians. More than 240,000 adults do not fall into the preceding categories.

In terms of overall patterns, Andrew Greeley—a persistent critic of Robert Bellah's "civil religion" secularization model of society—argues convincingly, based on analysis of social indicators, for what he calls a "stability model" of late-twentieth-century U.S. religions in general and Christianity in particular, with "no discernible change in belief in God, the divinity of Jesus, life after death, the existence of heaven, and divine influence on the Bible" (Greeley 1989, 116). This steady-state model appears to have held for centuries. Almost two hundred years ago the French aristocrat and lawyer Alexis de Tocqueville wrote, "There is no country in the whole world, in which the Christian religion retains a greater influence over the souls of men than in America: and there can be no greater proof of its utility, and of its conformity to human nature, than that its influence is most powerfully felt over the most enlightened and free nation of the earth" (Tocqueville n.d., 294).

Hence, the statement, "The United States is a Christian nation," is true if we think of "Christian nation" as a nation most of whose citizens freely identify themselves as Christians living in a society that has been largely shaped by institutionalized Christian traditions and beliefs—in the same sense that Western civilization itself reflects multifaceted, emergent Christianity. Evidence for this conclusion can be easily obtained by anyone with access to the Internet and a search engine that shows the proportionately large number of churches and institutions associated with Christianity throughout the United States. Several online databases make it easy to check the frequency of names of businesses, organizations,

and institutions in specific geographic areas. The category "church" elicits thousands of hits. Even a simple telephone book suffices to demonstrate the pervasive presence of institutional Christianity throughout the United States.

United States Is Not a Christian Nation

However, the statement "The United States is a Christian nation" is false if it is understood to mean that Christianity is the established official religion of the United States or even that Christianity and so-called Christian values are or should be legally privileged in the United States. More importantly, the intuitively convincing truth that the United States is a Christian nation in the sense discussed in the first section of this article often leads to the equivocation of arguing that the United States is also a Christian nation in the second sense.

The extent of this tension is exemplified by the fact that the words of Supreme Court Justice David J. Brewer have been used to argue both that the United States is a Christian nation and that it is *not* a Christian nation. His 1892 opinion in *Holy Trinity Church v. United States*, an immigration case, is often cited as proof that the United States is a "Christian nation" in the second sense because Brewer, the son of missionaries and a devout Christian, had used the phrase to indicate that a statute prohibiting bringing foreigners to this country under contract to perform labor in the United States ought not to be applied to a church hiring a minister because "this is a Christian nation" and the ministry is not unskilled labor. However, the appropriateness of using this opinion as precedent should have been settled by Justice Brewer himself, who wrote in a subsequent book:

> But in what sense can it be called a Christian nation? Not in the sense that Christianity is the established religion or that people are in any matter compelled to support it. On the contrary, the Constitution specifically provides that "Congress shall make no law respecting an establishment of religion, or prohibiting the free exercise thereof." Neither is it Christian in the sense that all of its citizens are either in fact or name Christian. On the contrary, all religions have free scope within our borders. Numbers of our people profess other religions, and many reject all. Nor is it Christian in the sense that a profession of Christianity is a condition of holding office or otherwise engaging in public service, or essential to recognition either politically or socially. In fact, the government as a legal organization is independent of all religions. (Brewer 1905, 13)

Founding Fathers and Christianity

However, not defining the United States as a Christian nation in the second sense does not mean that the Founding Fathers cannot or should not be considered Christians. Those who assume that deists are non-Christians tend to hold a narrow understanding of Christianity. They fail to recognize that many of the main ideas of the European Enlightenment (a philosophic movement of the eighteenth century marked by a rejection of traditional social, religious, and political ideas and an emphasis on rationalism), such as faith in progress, rationality, and human perfectibility, were among ideals associated with the Christian humanists of the Italian Renaissance. The Jefferson Bible (a summary of what Jefferson considered to be the noble and moral teachings of Jesus, taken from the gospels, and stripped of supernatural elements), with its emphasis on Jesus as moral teacher, is a powerful example of the Enlightenment spirit at work in the New World, a world Jefferson hoped would be governed by God-given human reason and would avoid the Old World pitfalls of inner-Christian persecutions caused by superstition and bigotry.

The pronounced critique of institutional religion of many Enlightenment thinkers should not be interpreted as rejection of Christianity, an ungodly and arrogant substitution of the secular for the sacred, but rather as a further development (and possibly a flowering) of essential Christian principles that flow both from incarnational theology and the example and teachings of Jesus. These principles include—despite nineteenth-century anathemas by popes and other Christian leaders condemning many of them—respect for persons, call for individual accountability, social justice,

---

THE FIRST AMENDMENT

One of the most talked about aspects of U.S. law is the first amendment, and the freedoms of speech, religion, and press it describes. However, the interpretations on that amendment are many. Below is the full text of the first amendment.

Amendment I to the United States Constitution
Congress shall make no law respecting an establishment of religion, or prohibiting the free exercise thereof; or abridging the freedom of speech, or of the press; or the right of the people peaceably to assemble, and to petition the government for a redress of grievances.

Source: United States Constitution: Bill of rights (2006) Retrieved March 19, 2007 from http://www.law.cornell.edu/constitution/consti tution.billofrights.html

A U.S. flag and a church steeple, perhaps symbolizing closeness yet separation of church and state. Source: istock/David Meaders.

democracy, equality, human rights, and liberty of thought. When the devout Lutheran Immanuel Kant defined the Enlightenment as humanity's leaving behind immature childhood and coming of age, and Harvey Cox, citing Saint Paul and pointing to parables attributed to Jesus, views secularization as "unlocking the gates of the playpen" (Cox 1965, 131), the "secular city" becomes part of the process of actualizing what has traditionally been called the "Kingdom of God."

Treaty of Tripoli

Opponents of the position that the United States is a Christian nation tend to refer to the late eighteenth-century Treaty of Tripoli, negotiated with the *dey* (regent) of Tripoli to protect U.S. ships from Algerian pirates near the Barbary Coast of north Africa:

> The position that the United States is a "Christian Nation" is dealt a serious blow by the fact that, as early as 1797, the government specifically said that it is not a Christian Nation. The occasion was a peace and trade agreement between the United States and Muslim leaders in North Africa. The negotiations were conducted under the authority of George Washington, and the final document, known as the Treaty of Tripoli, was approved of by the Senate under the leadership of John Adams, the second president. This treaty states, without equivocation, that the "...government of the United States is not, in any sense, founded on the Christian religion." (Cline, n.d.)

Quite apart from the assumption that the occasion would encourage drafters of the document to make Americans appear as distinct from potentially crusading Christians as possible, the translation of the document is inaccurate, and strong evidence indicates that Article 11, which contains the crucial phrase, was not part of the original treaty at all but rather was inserted by the *dey* of Algiers to "mollify certain concerns of the Pasha of Tripoli about entering into a Treaty with an 'infidel' (non-Islamic) nation" (Eidsmoe 1987, 415).

Benjamin Franklin

Another frequently cited passage by those who wish to argue that the United States is not a Christian nation is Benjamin Franklin's assessment of Jesus:

> As to Jesus of Nazareth, my Opinion of whom you particularly desire, I think the System of Morals and his Religion, as he

left them to us, the best the world ever saw or is likely to see; but I apprehend it has received various corrupt changes, and I have, with most of the present Dissenters in England, some Doubts as to his divinity. (Van Doren 1938, 777)

Thus, evidently Franklin was not a Christian.

That conclusion, however, is not at all evident. Being a Christian does not demand uncritical acceptance of doctrines developed over almost two millennia by Christian thinkers and endorsed by patriarchs, popes, and other officials of institutional Christianity. The arguments for the position that the United States was not founded according to Christian principles rests on the premise that (1) Christians automatically cease being Christians if they engage in critique of certain supposedly essential doctrines held by major official Christian groups, such as Orthodox, Catholics, or Baptists and/or (2) that Christians cannot support the separation of church and state and/or (3) that Christians would never choose religious freedom over religious truth.

Doctrinal pluralism has, however, been part of the multiple Christian paths from shortly after the Crucifixion. Like its parent, Judaism, Christianity has never been a monolith. Throughout the history of Christianity men and women of faith have debated points of doctrine, discipline, and morals, and although the divinity of the Christ is largely accepted, interpretations vary widely as to exactly what it means. Some would argue that all who respect and accept the moral code of Jesus can legitimately be considered Christians—and that includes Benjamin Franklin and Thomas Jefferson, whom John Eidsmoe would exclude.

World Reaction to U.S. Christianity

World reaction to the bewildering variety of U.S. forms of Christianity tends to be a function of the cultural context of the observer, who is often incapable of grasping the nonmonolithic nature of U.S. Christianity and may view the opinions of the representative of a particular Christian perspective as someone who speaks for "*the Christian church in the United States.*" In 2004 one of the most widely publicized exports of conservative U.S. Christianity was Mel Gibson's *The Passion of the Christ.* According to the online edition of the Lebanese newspaper *The Daily Star,* the film "has been embraced by Arab Muslims and Christians alike, with some dismissing allegations *The Passion of the Christ* is anti-Semitic and others making clear such charges are part of its appeal" (*Daily Star* staff 2004).

Another *Daily Star* article focused on former presidential candidate George McGovern's remarks that "the US role in the

(Middle East) has often been obstructive and, at times, destructive," adding that the United States "grossly overstepped its bounds in Iraq" (Hishmeh 2004). McGovern is quoted as calling the progressive faith-based alliance Churches for Middle East Peace (CMEP) a "significant player" in Washington and insisting that the group would ensure that "every member of Congress and every leader in Washington understands the responsibility we have to foster peace in our world" (Hishmeh 2004).

Neither Mel Gibson nor George McGovern is alone as "spokesperson" for U.S. Christianity. In addition to ubiquitous television evangelists, Americans who live or write abroad help form world understanding of the U.S. religious scene. The German daily *Die Welt* published a post-election column by the conservative U.S. head of Berlin's Aspen Institute, Jeffrey Gedmin, who ridiculed the notion, expressed in other German media, such as *Der Spiegel,* that President George W. Bush's reelection constituted a victory of an intolerant, crusading bigot, beloved by the Christian Right. According to Gedmin, European anti-Americanism and opposition to the Iraq War (2003) are driven largely by anti-Semitism and Bush is an ordinary centrist Methodist. However, *Die Welt* also published a translation of an analysis by Harvard professor Niall Ferguson, who called President Bush "a messianic American Calvinist" whose sensibilities and moral oversimplifications "resonate irresistibly with a critical mass of Americans right across the country" and for whom "Faith has secured…a second term" (Ferguson 2004). Ferguson's opinion echoes a 2002 *Le Monde* article: "The more the US mobilises for war, the more ordinary Americans must be persuaded to reduce their view of the world to good versus evil, Western liberalism versus Islamic terrorism or, most primitively, us versus them. Nuance, balance and any sense of reciprocity must cease. Learning to see the world from varying points of view must be eliminated so that only one view will predominate. Anyone who questions it must be denounced for siding with the terrorists and cast out of the community of faith" (Lazare 2002).

On the other hand, Jim Lobe, in a 2003 article in *Asia Times Online,* viewed Christianity as a potential antiwar force in the United States, writing that "a recent *Wall Street Journal*–NBC News poll showed that Catholic support for war has fallen sharply in the past few months" and that "the National Council of Churches of Christ, which includes the mainstream Protestant denominations, has spoken out against the drive to war for months" and that, "except for the South[ern] Baptists, by far the most conservative US denomination—which, like radical Islamists, has long been hostile to equal rights for women—Bush's war plans appear to enjoy only scattered support among Christian and Jewish congregations" (Lobe 2003).

Defining Moments

Frank Lambert, in his *The Founding Fathers and the Place of Religion in America,* writes what can provide a summary of this topic:

These two defining moments in American history, 1639 and 1787, frame the central question of this book: How did the Puritan Fathers erecting their "City upon a Hill" transform into the Founding Fathers drawing a distinct line between church and state? The answer lies in the changing meaning of freedom in the concept of freedom of religion. To the Puritans who fled persecution, Massachusetts Bay represented the freedom to practice without interference the one true faith, which they based solely on the Bible, correctly interpreted. Thus religious freedom in the "City upon a Hill" meant freedom from error, with church and state, though separate, working together to support and protect the one true faith. Those who believed differently were free to go elsewhere and sometimes compelled to do so. The Founding Fathers had a radically different conception of religious freedom. Influenced by the Enlightenment, they had great confidence in the individual's ability to understand the world and its most fundamental laws through the exercise of his or her reason. To them, true religion was not something handed down by a church or contained in the Bible but rather was to be found through free rational inquiry. Drawing on radical Whig ideology, a body of thought whose principal concern was expanded liberties, the framers sought to secure their idea of religious freedom by barring any alliance between church and state. (Lambert 2003, 3)

Hence, the United States can be considered a nation founded on Christian principles as long as the term *Christian* is defined broadly and the Enlightenment is understood as a legitimate expression of Christian values. The U.S. Constitution did not specifically endorse faith in God or a particular denomination or religion precisely because the Founding Fathers realized that state governments should be free to decide religious issues without federal compulsion. On the other hand, although the deists of the infant nation can be considered Christians in the above inclusive sense, it is inappropriate to identify them (or the United States of today) with the conservative political and social agenda of the contemporary Religious Right.

Ingrid H. Shafer

See also Religious Fundamentalism, U.S.; Religious Pluralism, United States and

Further Reading

Adherents.com. (n.d.). Largest religious groups in the United States of America. Retrieved January 16, 2007, from http://www.adherents.com/rel_USA.html

Armstrong, K. (1991). *The battle for God: A history of fundamentalism.* New York: Ballantine.

Brewer, D. J. (1905). *The United States: A Christian nation.* Philadelphia: John C. Winston Company.

Church, F. (1991, 1996). *God and other famous liberals: Recapturing Bible, flag, and family from the Far Right.* New York: Walker.

Church, F. (2002). *The American creed: A spiritual and patriotic primer.* New York: St. Martin's Press.

Cline, A. (n.d.) *Is this a Christian nation?* Retrieved April 23, 2007, from http://atheism.about.com/library/FAQs/cs/blcsm_gov_xiannation.htm

Cox, H. (1965). *The secular city.* New York: Macmillan Paperback.

Daily Star staff. (2004, April 5). *The Passion of the Christ* generates strong reactions in Middle East. *The Daily Star.* Retrieved December 28, 2004, from http://www.dailystar.com.lb/article.asp?edition_id=10&categ_id=4&article_id=1581

Dreisbach, D. L. (1996). The Constitution's forgotten religion clause: Reflections on the Article VI religious test ban. *Journal of Church and State, 38,* 261–295.

Dreisbach, D. L. (2002). *Thomas Jefferson and the wall of separation between church and state.* New York: New York University Press.

Eck, D. (2001). *A new religious America.* San Francisco: Harper.

Eidsmoe, J. (1987). *Christianity and the Constitution.* Grand Rapids, MI: Baker Books.

Ferguson, N. (2004, November). Bush oder: Die Entschlossenheit [Bush or: Determination]. *Die Welt,* p, 5. Retrieved October 29, 2004, from http://www.welt.de/data/2004/11/05/355664.html?s=1

Gedmin, J. (2004, November). Das fromme Amerika [Pious America]. *Die Welt,* p. 9. Retrieved October 29, 2004, from http://www.welt.de/data/2004/11/09/357769.html?s=1

Greeley, A. M. (1989). *Religious change in America.* Cambridge, MA: Harvard University Press.

Hishmeh, G. (2004, March 1). US Christian groups push for Mideast peace. *The Daily Star.* Retrieved December 28, 2004, from http://www.dailystar.com.lb/article.asp?edition_ID=10&article_ID=265&categ_id=2

Hutchinson, W. R. (2003). *Religious pluralism in America.* New Haven, CT: Yale University Press.

Jefferson, T. (1989). *The Jefferson Bible: The life and morals of Jesus of Nazareth.* Costa Mesa, CA: Noontide Press.

Kramnick, I., & Moore, L. (1996). *The godless Constitution: The case against religious correctness.* New York: W. W. Norton.

Lambert, F. (2003). *The Founding Fathers and the place of religion in America.* Princeton, NJ: Princeton University Press.

Lazare, D. (2002, August). A new conformity, deference and authoritarianism: America's patriot games. *Le Monde diplomatique.* Retrieved December 28, 2004, from http://mondediplo.com/2002/08/11america

Lobe, J. (2003, February 19). In the West a moral case is made. *Asia Times Online*. Retrieved December 28, 2004, from http://www.atimes.com/atimes/Middle_East/EB19Ak02.html

Massa, M. S. (1999). *Catholics and American culture*. New York: Herder and Herder.

Religious Tolerance.Org. (n.d.). Divisions within Protestantism. Retrieved October 12, 2004, from http://www.religioustolerance.org/chr_divi2.htm

Tocqueville, A. (n.d.). *Democracy in America: Vol. 1*. New Rochelle, NY: Arlington House.

Van Doren, C. (1938) *Benjamin Franklin*, p. 777. New York: The Viking Press.

Wills, G. (1990). *Under God: Religion and American politics*. New York: Simon & Schuster.

Civil Rights

See U.S. Civil Rights

Civil War and Reconstruction

See U.S. Civil War and Reconstruction

Climate Change

See Ecological Footprint, U.S.; Environmental Issues

Cold War

The Cold War was caused by the ideological conflict between the United States and the Soviet Union, but as these two nations jockeyed for influence and allies to support their own interests around the globe many nations suffered the effects.

The U.S. journalist Walter Lippmann coined the term Cold War in 1947 to describe the intense military, economic, and political rivalry between the United States and the Soviet Union following World War II. Although scholars generally identify 1945–1950 as the official start of the Cold War, its origins lie in the Russian Revolution of 1917, and it did not end until the collapse of the Soviet Union in 1991.

The Revolution of 1917 and World War II

The Russian Revolution of March 1917 toppled Czar Nicholas II and shocked the other Allied Powers (France, Britain, Italy, and the United States). By October of the same year, the Russian provisional government led by Alexander Kerensky had fallen to Vladimir Ilyich Lenin and the Bolsheviks. The U.S. president Woodrow Wilson considered Bolshevism a threat to Western interests, and in August 1918, Wilson sent troops into Russia to help British and French forces push back the Bolsheviks. Although publicly stating a desire to avoid intervention in Russian affairs, Wilson also authorized a U.S. expedition into Siberia to aid Czech forces fighting the Bolsheviks. Those efforts ultimately failed, and U.S. troops left Russia early in 1920. The Union of the Soviet Socialist Republics was formed in 1922 from the territory of the former Russian empire.

The 1939 German-Soviet Nonaggression Pact kept the Soviet Union from entering World War II until June 1941, when Hitler invaded, prompting the Soviet Union to enter on the side of the Allies. From the 1943 Battle of Stalingrad onward, the Soviet Union was able to push German forces west and establish a Soviet presence in Eastern Europe. With the collapse of the Third Reich on 8 May 1945, Allied occupation of Germany began. British, U.S., and Soviet leaders met near Berlin for the Potsdam Conference (17 July 1945–2 August 1945) to discuss the reconstruction of Germany and negotiations with Japan. U.S. officials considered Germany vital to the economic reconstruction of Western Europe, while the Russian leader Joseph Stalin was determined to secure Russia's eastern border against future German threats. At the conference, U.S. officials announced that the United States possessed a new weapon of extraordinary destructive power and issued the Potsdam Declaration demanding Japan's unconditional surrender. Japanese leaders in Tokyo rejected unconditional surrender, and U.S. officials balked at compromise. On 6 August 1945 U.S. president Harry S. Truman authorized the use of the atomic bomb on Hiroshima. Three days later, the United States dropped another atomic bomb on Nagasaki. Japanese leaders issued their unconditional surrender to the United States on 14 August 1945.

The diplomatic advantage the atomic bomb gave the United States was undeniable, and the Truman administration believed Russia could be encouraged to offer concessions in Eastern Europe after witnessing the attack on Japan. By using the bomb to bring about the war in the Pacific before the Russians could enter the region, the United States sought to curtail Soviet influence in the region. However, while Washington moved quickly to enter nations newly liberated from the defeated Axis and retreating colonial powers (French, Dutch, and British), Stalin similarly sought expansion of the Soviet Union.

The Truman Doctrine

The Soviet Union and the United Stated had respective ideological and economic interests in mind as they sought to rebuild parts of Europe and the Pacific. Stalin insisted on securing Russia's eastern borders, and as a result, Poland, Finland, Romania, and Bulgaria came under Soviet influence at the conclusion of postwar boundary settlements.

From Moscow, the U.S. diplomat George F. Kennan cabled the "long telegram," depicting the Soviet Union as an aggressive power guided by rigid Communist ideology, and urging U.S. officials to be firm with the Soviets. Two weeks later, on 5 March 1946, the former British prime minister Winston Churchill spoke in Fulton, Missouri, of the "iron curtain" that had descended in Europe, referring to the Communist presence.

On 12 March 1947, Truman outlined the Truman Doctrine, a policy of containment with reference to the Soviet Union, and of-

fering support to anyone attempting to resist subjugation. In July, Kennan, the director of the State Department's Policy Planning Staff, publicly called for a strong counterforce to the expansionist ideology of the Soviet Union.

The implementation of the Truman Doctrine encouraged U.S. intervention abroad. In 1953, a CIA-sponsored coup overthrew a nationalist Iranian premier, Muhammad Mosaddeq, who was perceived as dangerously left leaning. The following year, the CIA orchestrated the overthrow of Guatemalan president Jacobo Arbenz after he initiated land reform measures. The most sustained intervention came when U.S. military advisers entered Vietnam in the mid-1950s. The U.S. military presence in the region increased to 543,000 troops by 1969, and the United States remained embroiled in war until a cease-fire was agreed upon in 1973.

THE TRUMAN DOCTRINE

The following passage is an extract from President Harry S. Truman's address before a joint session of congress on 12 March 1947. This address, known as the Truman Doctrine, was a statement of U.S. foreign policy aimed to contain communism and is often used to mark the starting point of the Cold War.

The gravity of the situation which confronts the world today necessitates my appearance before a joint session of the Congress. The foreign policy and the national security of this country are involved. . . .

One of the primary objectives of the foreign policy of the United States is the creation of conditions in which we and other nations will be able to work out a way of life free from coercion. This was a fundamental issue in the war with Germany and Japan. Our victory was won over countries which sought to impose their will, and their way of life, upon other nations.

To ensure the peaceful development of nations, free from coercion, the United States has taken a leading part in establishing the United Nations. The United Nations is designed to make possible lasting freedom and independence for all its members. We shall not realize our objectives, however, unless we are willing to help free peoples to maintain their free institutions and their national integrity against aggressive movements that seek to impose upon them totalitarian regimes. This is no more than a frank recognition that totalitarian regimes imposed on free peoples, by direct or indirect aggression, undermine the foundations of international peace and hence the security of the United States.

The peoples of a number of countries of the world have recently had totalitarian regimes forced upon them against their will. The Government of the United States has made frequent protests against coercion and intimidation, in violation of the Yalta agreement, in Poland, Rumania, and Bulgaria. I must also state that in a number of other countries there have been similar developments.

At the present moment in world history nearly every nation must choose between alternative ways of life. The choice is too often not a free one.

One way of life is based upon the will of the majority, and is distinguished by free institutions, representative government, free elections, guarantees of individual liberty, freedom of speech and religion, and freedom from political oppression.

The second way of life is based upon the will of a minority forcibly imposed upon the majority. It relies upon terror and oppression, a controlled press and radio; fixed elections, and the suppression of personal freedoms.

I believe that it must be the policy of the United States to support free peoples who are resisting attempted subjugation by armed minorities or by outside pressures.

I believe that we must assist free peoples to work out their own destinies in their own way.

I believe that our help should be primarily through economic and financial aid which is essential to economic stability and orderly political processes. . . .

It would be an unspeakable tragedy if these countries, which have struggled so long against overwhelming odds, should lose that victory for which they sacrificed so much. Collapse of free institutions and loss of independence would be disastrous not only for them but for the world. Discouragement and possibly failure would quickly be the lot of neighboring peoples striving to maintain their freedom and independence.

Should we fail to aid Greece and Turkey in this fateful hour, the effect will be far reaching to the West as well as to the East.

We must take immediate and resolute action. . . .

The seeds of totalitarian regimes are nurtured by misery and want. They spread and grow in the evil soil of poverty and strife. They reach their full growth when the hope of a people for a better life has died. We must keep that hope alive.

The free peoples of the world look to us for support in maintaining their freedoms.

If we falter in our leadership, we may endanger the peace of the world—and we shall surely endanger the welfare of our own nation.

Great responsibilities have been placed upon us by the swift movement of events.

I am confident that the Congress will face these responsibilities squarely.

Source: The Avalon Project at Yale Law School. (1997). Retrieved March 15, 2007, from http://www.yale.edu/lawweb/avalon/trudoc.htm

Institutionalizing the Cold War, 1945–1948

Although Soviet-American cooperation had led to the creation of the United Nations in 1945, postwar differences remained pronounced. The creation of the U.S.-dominated World Bank, the International Monetary Fund, and the United Nations Relief and Rehabilitation Administration were intended to provide Western Europe with the stability needed to effectively resist the Soviet Union.

On 5 June 1947, George C. Marshall, the U.S. secretary of state, called for the creation of the Marshall Plan (the European Recovery Program) to jump-start the European economy. The Soviet foreign minister, V. M. Molotov, announced that the Soviet Union would not participate in the Marshall Plan, which he termed economic imperialism.

A further manifestation of deepening hostility between Western Europe and the United States on the one hand and the Soviet Union on the other was the Soviet Union's Berlin blockade in 1948. Berlin, which was located in the Soviet-controlled section of Germany, was controlled in part by the Western Allies and in part by the Soviet Union. In an effort to get the Western powers to give up control of their portion of Berlin and to prevent them from consolidating economic gains in the portion of Germany under their control, the Soviet Union initiated the blockade. The United States and Britain countered with an airlift and an embargo on exports from Soviet-controlled Eastern Europe, and in 1949 the Soviets ended the blockade. The British, French, and U.S.-controlled portions of Germany united as the Federal Republic of Germany (West Germany), and the Soviet-controlled portion became the German Democratic Republic, or East Germany.

Militarily, containment of the Soviet Union took the form of the North Atlantic Treaty Organization (NATO), a North Atlantic defense pact. The treaty, signed in Washington on 4 April 1949, assured collective security for its signatories. The Soviet Union responded to NATO with the Warsaw Pact in 1955.

The Arms Race

By 1955, a nuclear arms race was under way. The Soviets exploded an atomic bomb in August 1949, and in 1952 the United States tested its first hydrogen bomb. The Soviets followed with a hydrogen bomb test in 1953. The proliferation of arms can be attributed largely to a U.S. review of military and foreign policy that occurred in 1950 and that inspired the National Security Council Paper Number 68 (NSC-68). That paper predicted prolonged international tension and Soviet military expansion. As a result,

Washington officials deemed it necessary to maintain the United States' dominant global position and to persuade the U.S. public to support larger defense budgets and higher taxes. During the presidency of Dwight Eisenhower, the U.S. nuclear stockpile rose to 22,229, defense budgets averaged $40 billion per year, and one million U.S. troops were stationed overseas. In the Soviet Union, Stalin's successor, Nikita S. Khrushchev, kept pace militarily and outstripped the United States in the space race. In 1957 the Soviets launched the first artificial satellite and successfully fired the first intercontinental ballistic missile.

The Cuban missile crisis of 1962 showed the world the dangers of the Cold War arms race. In 1958–1959, a Communist revolution replaced the dictator Fulgencio Batista with Fidel Castro, who looked for support—including military support—from the Soviet Union. In 1962, when the United States discovered that the Soviet Union had placed nuclear missiles on the island, President John F. Kennedy imposed a naval blockade around Cuba to stop further arms shipments. A tense U.S.-Soviet standoff lasted for fourteen days, but at last the Soviet Union agreed to remove its missiles (the U.S. made a secret pledge to remove its missile from Turkey in return, and promised not to invade Cuba) and nuclear war was narrowly avoided.

The crisis fueled the arms race as the Soviets, exposed as being militarily inferior, became determined to catch up to the United States. Meanwhile, U.S. policy makers fine-tuned the concept of massive retaliation against the Soviets, formulating the notion of "mutually assured destruction" (MAD), based on the ability to absorb a nuclear first strike and to deliver a more potent second strike.

The Cold War in Asia

In Asia, the United States received a blow in 1949 when Mao Zedong and the Communists triumphed over Chiang Kai-shek and the Nationalists in China's civil war. Mao established the People's Republic of China, but the United States refused to recognize it, continuing to treat Chiang Kai-shek's government, which had fled to the island of Taiwan, as the legitimate government of all China. Although Mao's approach to Communism was at variance with Moscow's, the 1950s saw the formation of a Sino-Soviet alliance.

Korea, which had been annexed by Japan in 1910, had been freed from Japanese domination at the end of World War II, but had been divided into two zones of occupation (a U.S. zone and a Soviet zone), with the thirty-eighth parallel as the dividing line. On 25 June 1950, Communist North Korea made a bid to reunite the two halves by force, launching an attack on South Korea. In the absence of the Soviet delegate, the U.N. Security Council

A view from the roof of the Checkpoint Charlie station hut in West Berlin. Source: istock/John Sigler.

passed a resolution that called on U.N. member nations to come to South Korea's aid, and Truman soon ordered U.S. aircraft and warships into action below the thirty-eighth parallel.

The two sides battled up and down the entire length of the Korean peninsula, with the North first driving U.S.-led forces to the bottom of the peninsula and the U.S.-led forces then pushing the North Korean forces back almost to the border with China. China then lent its support to North Korea, and the U.S.-led forces were pushed back behind the thirty-eighth parallel. General Douglas MacArthur, the commander of U.S. troops in Korea, favored attacking China at this point and was relieved of his command when he refused to accept Truman's decision to the contrary. The Korean War having become a stalemate, on 27 July 1953 an armistice was signed. Korea remained divided along the thirty-eighth parallel. The war further eroded Sino-American relations, but strengthened U.S.-Japanese ties as $3 billion in U.S. military orders revitalized Japanese industry. Significantly, the war brought NSC-68 recommendations into effect, with the budget of the Department of Defense increasing from $17.7 billion to $52.6 billion in the 1953 fiscal year.

The Vietnam conflict, mentioned earlier, was a significant example of the Cold War playing out in Asia. After World War II, Vietnam resisted French attempts to return the nation to its colonial status. Like Korea, Vietnam was divided into a Communist-controlled northern portion (North Vietnam) and a non-Communist southern portion (South Vietnam). Fearing that Communist victory in Vietnam would lead to other nations in Southeast Asia becoming Communist, the United States opposed North Vietnam. In the end, however, it withdrew its forces, and two years later, in 1975, Vietnam was reunified as the Socialist Republic of Vietnam.

Détente

In spite of U.S. involvement in Vietnam, the early 1970s saw Cold War tension diminishing. Sensing a Sino-Soviet split, U.S. president Richard Nixon and his chief of national security, Henry Kissinger, sought limited cooperation with the People's Republic of China. A lagging U.S. economy, the lure of a massive Chinese market, and desire to withdraw U.S. troops from Vietnam made détente the buzzword for Nixon and Kissinger's diplomacy.

Détente led to arms reduction talks between U.S. and Soviet leaders. However, both rounds of the Strategic Arms Limitation Talks (SALT) failed to produce lasting disarmament legislation. SALT-II negotiations ended in 1977 when the Soviets deployed 500,000 troops into Afghanistan in an effort to control an increasingly independent-minded client Communist government there.

The End of the Cold War

During his election campaign in 1980, the Republican presidential candidate Ronald Reagan condemned the Soviet expansionist strategy. Upon his election, Reagan produced unprecedented military budgets and furthered the use of covert operations. In 1985 the Department of Defense's budget was a record high of $390 billion and CIA initiatives to overthrow anti-U.S. governments were continuing with verve.

When Mikhail S. Gorbachev became general secretary of the Soviet Communist party in 1985, he called for a restructuring of the hobbled Soviet economy (perestroika) and the liberalization of authoritarian political systems (glasnost). In 1986, Gorbachev stopped Soviet deployment of intermediate-range missiles and froze nuclear weapons tests. He withdrew Soviet forces from Afghanistan in 1988 and reduced support for socialist rebels in Nicaragua and Cuban troops in Angola. Despite the Reagan arms buildup, Gorbachev cut military spending in the interest of economic rebuilding.

In 1989, Gorbachev informed East European officials that Soviet forces would not intervene in any uprisings. Within a year, popular uprisings in Hungary, Poland, Czechoslovakia, Romania, Bulgaria, and finally, East Germany, ousted Communist leaders from power in those former satellite nations. The Berlin Wall, erected in 1961 to prevent the flight of East Germans to West Germany, came down in November 1989, with free elections promised for 1990. In 1990, Lithuania, Estonia, Latvia, and the Ukraine declared their independence, and in the same year Gorbachev was awarded the Nobel Peace Prize. On Christmas Day 1991, the Soviet Union ceased to exist and Boris Yeltsin became the president of the Russia Federation.

Assessment

While the Cold War was centered around the ideological conflict between the United States and the Soviet Union, its effects were experienced worldwide. Remaining nonaligned was difficult, as nations that sought to remain neutral were considered susceptible to Communist influence and therefore a threat to U.S. national security. Meanwhile, every decision and every action was made in the ominous shadow of the possibility of nuclear war, which grew along with U.S. and Soviet military budgets. The disintegration of the Soviet Union meant victory for the United States, but the worldwide presence of nuclear weapons continues to be a significant threat to humanity.

Daniel Pacella

See also Intelligence Agencies; International Agreements and Summits; Soviet Empire, Collapse of; Western Europe, Cultural Relations with

Further Reading

Chomsky, N. (2003). *Hegemony or survival: America's quest for global dominance.* New York: Metropolitan Books.

Crockatt, R. (1995). *The fifty years war: The United States and the Soviet Union in world politics, 1941–1991.* London: Routledge.

DePorte, A.W. (1986). *Europe between the superpowers: The enduring balance* (2nd. ed.). New Haven, CT: Yale University Press.

Dockrill, M. (1988). *The Cold War, 1945–1963.* London: MacMillan.

Dunbabin, J. P. (1994). *International relations since 1945: A history in two volumes: Vol. 1. The Cold War: The great powers and their allies.* London: Longman.

Dunbabin, J. P. (1994). *International relations since 1945: A history in two volumes: Vol. 2. The post-imperial age: The great powers and the wider world.* London: Longman.

Gaddis, J. L. (1987). *The long peace: Inquiries into the history of the Cold War.* New York: Oxford University Press.

Gaddis, J. L. (1997). *We now know: Rethinking Cold War history.* New York: Oxford University Press.

Grosser, A. (1980). *The western alliance: European–American relations since 1945.* New York: Vintage.

Halliday, F. (1986). *The making of the second Cold War.* London: Verso.

Hyland, W. G. (1988). *Mortal rivals: Understanding the hidden pattern of Soviet–American relations.* New York: Simon & Schuster.

Hyland, W. G. (1991). *The Cold War: Fifty years of conflict.* New York: Times Books.

Iriye, A. (1974). *The Cold War in Asia: A historical introduction.* Englewood Cliffs, NJ: Prentice-Hall.

Kakar, M. H. (1995). *Afghanistan: The Soviet invasion and the Afghan response, 1979–1982.* Berkeley and Los Angeles: University of California Press.

Parkinson, F. (1974). *Latin America, the Cold War, and the world powers, 1945–73.* Beverley Hills, CA: Sage.

Rees, D. (1967). *The age of containment: The Cold War, 1945–1965.* New York: St. Martin's Press.

Rodman, P. (1994). *More precious than peace: The Cold War and the struggle for the Third World.* New York: Charles Scribner's Sons.

Walker, M. (1995). *The Cold War.* New York: Owl Books.

Zinn, H. (2003). *A people's history of the United States: 1492–present.* New York: HarperCollins Publishers.

Cold War, Post Era

The end of the Cold War was marked by an event—the fall of the Berlin Wall and the flow of people, and culture, across the divide of Germany—that foreshadowed the emergence of the United States as a solitary world power.

The Cold War was the political and military standoff between the USSR and the United States that endured from about the end of World War II until the late 1980s, its end signaled by the fall of the wall dividing East and West Germany in 1989 and the collapse of the Soviet Union in 1991. The end of the Cold War was momentous in terms of the global role of the United States. Since then the United States has been the sole remaining superpower, and although this condition has meant unprecedented political influence by the United States in world affairs in the post–Cold War period, constraints on U.S. power remain.

Cold War

World War II was a watershed in modern international relations. The United States emerged as one of the major victors, along with Britain, France, and the USSR—the former enemies of Nazi Germany in particular. Even before the end of the war, however, clear divisions existed between the USSR and the Allies. These divisions were based on the two sides' differing views of the postwar world order: in an economic sense, communism versus capitalism, and politically, authoritarianism versus democracy.

The Cold War itself, as the name implies, was a war without direct and major confrontation between the rival parties—essentially the USSR and the United States. Confrontation was inhibited by the new concept of mutually assured destruction (MAD). If the USSR and the United States had used their weapons of mass destruction on each other, especially nuclear weapons, the result would have been massive devastation in both countries. This unthinkable outcome was a huge incentive to maintain the peace, although the world did come to the edge of nuclear war during the Cuban Missile Crisis of 1962.

A number of key events set the Cold War firmly in place. At the end of World War II the countries liberated from the Germans by the USSR came under the latter's control, an event that led England's Winston Churchill in 1946 to declare that an "iron curtain" had descended across the continent. In Asia, North Korea came under Soviet influence, and cooperation, if uneasy, took place between China and the USSR. Recognizing the divisions between the United States and the USSR and the aggressive for-

eign policy of the latter, U.S. President Harry Truman in 1947 announced the Truman Doctrine, a policy of confronting and containing Communism around the world. By 1948 the Soviet attempt to blockade West Berlin, which was located within East Germany, led to the Berlin Airlift signaling again U.S. opposition to Soviet domination. (The Berlin Airlift was the American response to the USSR blockading the ground transportation route between West Germany and Berlin—located within the territory of East Germany. Between June 1948 and May 1949, all supplies to Berlin were flown in by the U.S. Air Force—an early example of Cold War confrontation.)

Succeeding events cemented the Cold War in place. In 1949 the USSR exploded its first atomic bomb. In the same year Chinese Communist leader Mao Zedong proclaimed the victory of Communism in China. In 1950 the Cold War became temporarily hot when North Korea attacked the southern half of the peninsula, and the U.N., led by the United States, responded militarily. In short, in the space of five years the world's international relations had hardened into a bipolar world, and this condition was to last for four more decades.

End of the Cold War

The end of the Cold War in some respects came about slowly. The fundamental flaw in the communist system was an inefficient economy. In a system where people were paid the same regardless of the type or amount of work they did, incentive failed, and economic development slowed. Moreover, a centrally planned economy proved not as efficient as a capitalist one. These facts were soon evident in the USSR, but its totalitarian system did not allow such difficulties to develop into public political problems. Huge amounts of money were funneled into military and defense systems to remain on a par with the United States and to pay for a lingering war in Afghanistan. However, the result of diverting so much money toward defense spending was a relatively poor consumer products base. With capitalism succeeding in the United States and with the capacity for its additional military development thereby increased (and with President Reagan spending massively on new defense programs such as the Strategic Defense Initiative

and advanced submarine technology), the USSR could not sustain its defense systems, and the economy of the Soviet Union effectively collapsed. (The collapse has been viewed by many as a clear demonstration of the superiority of capitalism over communism. The USSR was able to compete militarily with the United States for many years as it diverted most of the resources of the state into the military sector rather than the production of consumer goods. Ultimately, however, capitalism's ability to stimulate individual motivation—leading to both greater production and consumption—won out over communism.)

Concurrently, Mikhail Gorbachev gained the leadership position in the USSR in 1985 and proceeded to end the Cold War with the United States via the democratization of the Soviet Union (glasnost) as well as reinvigoration of the economy (perestroika). The former movement, in particular, unleashed nationalistic forces in the component parts of the USSR, and by 1991 it had begun to break up into separate countries. Some countries, such as the Ukraine and the Baltic states, left the union, whereas others, such as Chechnya, have active independent movements. The replacement of the USSR—the Commonwealth of Independent States—is a shadow of its predecessor.

United States as the World's Policeman

Is the world a safer place now than it was during the Cold War? On the one hand, the danger of MAD has receded, although China remains a nuclear power, and the threat of nuclear weapons being stolen or sold on the black market exists. Generally speaking, however, the threat of massive global destruction has been reduced.

The United States has emerged as by far the greatest military power in the world. Consider the following passage from Paul Dibb in Australia:

> [The U.S.] is a power without parallel in world history. And it is unlikely to face a peer competitor, or even a combination of hostile powers, in the foreseeable future. The U.S. accounts for 32 percent of world GDP and more than 43 percent of world military expenditures. It spends more than $US 1 billion a day on defense. It dominates more than half of global military production and almost 60 percent of world military R&D spending. (Dibb 2003, 2)

If one supports the U.S. worldview and role in contemporary international relations, then the foregoing figures provide some comfort. If one questions the U.S. worldview, the figures indicate something to be feared—a country without an external control in international affairs.

Cost of Maintaining the Peace

However, is this scenario truly the case? What limits U.S. power in a post–Cold War era? One of the most significant factors in this question must be the cost of acting as the policeman to the world. In the case of Iraq, for example, the U.S. government was willing to invade the country without the support of key European allies such as France and Germany. It had the military power to complete the invasion and to remove Saddam Hussein. However, even before major hostilities ceased the U.S. administration began pressing other countries to support the cost of the war and the continued policing of the country. Therefore, although the military power of the United States is overwhelming, its capacity to fund major military campaigns and then pay for subsequent operations is questionable—given that the cost of the war was estimated to be $456 billion by September 2007, with total expenditures estimated to be in excess of $1 trillion. Moreover, given the substantial U.S. budget deficit, it is dependent on foreign countries to service its debt.

Rise of Terrorism

The rise of terrorism is also, to an extent, a response to the dominance of the United States in world affairs. Because currently no country can match the United States in military power, the only way to attack Americans and their allies is through terrorism. In this respect the world continues to face danger, but it is the danger of random acts of violence, not the danger of massive nuclear destruction. This fact is the underlying reality of the terrorist attacks of September 11, 2001.

Contemporary terrorism such as that promulgated by al-Qaeda is also attempting to promote the concept of a battle of religions, along the lines of Samuel Huntington's "A Clash of Civilizations." (Huntington's basic premise is that future wars would occur along cultural lines, with the Islamic and Christian worlds two of those in conflict.) In this respect the volatility of the Middle East in particular does not bode well for long-term peace, and because other nations depend on the region's oil, this volatility is a significant problem for the future.

Role of the United Nations

Liberal thinkers saw the immediate post–Cold War period as a time when multilateral approaches to global problems were predominant. The Clinton administration generally pursued a policy of inclusion, of discussion over conflict. Where conflict did oc-

cur, as in the states of the former Yugoslavia and Somalia, it was conducted under U.N. auspices.

The Bush administration, however, has clearly indicated that U.S. interests come first and that it is willing to make decisions without the support of the U.N. The clearest example of this policy is the decision to invade Iraq in 2003. This policy is an outcome of the United States being the only remaining superpower. It may be useful for the United States to have allies, but if necessary the United States has sufficient power to make independent decisions. In the long term, however, the United States must have allies to effect permanent change in troubled regions.

Global Trade and Globalization

The United States has the world's largest economy, and Japan and China, with the second- and third-largest economies (using gross national product as the measure), respectively, depend significantly on U.S. consumers for their export success. Although this consumerism may be substantially funded by U.S. debt, worldwide a strong belief remains in the strength of the U.S. economy. Hence, the United States remains an integral part of the global economy in the post–Cold War period.

Accompanying the significant role of the United States in global trade is the continuing spread of U.S. culture. With the increase in the ease and speed of communications, U.S. values and customs are finding rapid transmission in the English language and American films, music, and fashion. Although this trend produces a degree of backlash in some countries, the influence of the United States in cultural terms no doubt is greater than ever before. This is not to say, however, that all countries accept U.S. ideals, and one does not have to look any further than the anti-U.S. demonstrations associated with the invasion of Iraq for evidence.

Old Friends, New Friends

The post–Cold War era in an analytical sense has become much more complicated. In a bipolar world, with the USSR on one side and the United States on the other and various parts of the world cooperating either closely or loosely with one superpower or the other, a person could relatively easily understand the motivations and decisions of different countries. Today this situation is no longer the case. The self-interest of each country might involve decisions that fifteen years ago would have seemed unthinkable, and this situation is further complicated by the practice of often putting economic considerations at the forefront of international relations.

Photo of a traffic sign at the Berlin Wall in 1988, at the border between East and West Berlin. "The end" painted on the sign refers to the collapse of the Soviet Union the following year. Source: istock.

Looking Ahead

The United States in some respects has power that is unprecedented in the world. The questions are what the United States will do with this power, and what do other countries expect it to do. The United States is not required to play a major role, either in economic or political terms, but an overall benefit accrues if it does so. One example is the U.S. role in the World Bank and International Monetary Fund—which act as guarantors of the world financial system—a role that the United States has played since the mid-1940s. All countries benefit from this stabilizing force, and this arrangement in turn benefits the United States.

In many current issues, whether they have to do with environment, security, or trade, cooperation between countries is an imperative. One of the more recent questions is the extent to which the United States will play a multilateral as opposed to a unilateral role. Pressures exist for it to move in both directions.

The post–Cold War period is an uncertain one. Flashpoints include North Korea and the Taiwan-China relationship in Asia and Israel and Iraq in the Middle East. What part should the United States play in these flashpoints? How should the United States respond to an emergent China as a substantial economic as well as military power or to Japan as it begins to move to a more preeminent role in international affairs? In short, although the post–Cold War period may not be as overtly dangerous as the Cold War period, significant challenges lie ahead for the only remaining superpower.

Curtis A. Andressen

See also Environmental Issues; Exchanges, Cultural and Scientific; Human Rights; Iraq Wars; Special Relationship (U.S.-Russia)

Further Reading

Dibb, P. (2003, January–June). A world divided. *Strategic and Defence Studies Centre Newsletter,* 2–3.

Huntington, S. (1993, Summer). The clash of civilizations. *Foreign Affairs, 72*(3), 22–49.

Ignatieff, M. (2003). An American empire? *Australian Universities Review, 46*(1), 3–8.

Joffe, J. (1999). *The future of the great powers.* New York: Orion.

Johnson, C. (2000). *Blowback: The costs and consequences of American empire.* Boston: Little, Brown.

Nye, J. (2002). *The paradox of American power: Why the world's only superpower can't go it alone.* New York: Oxford University Press.

Ruggie, J. (1997). *Winning the peace: American and world order in the new era.* New York: Columbia University Press.

Wallerstein, I. (2002, July/August). The Eagle has crash landed. *Foreign Policy, 131,* 60–68.

Winston S. Churchill: "Iron Curtain Speech." (1946, March 5). Retrieved April 24, 2007, from http://www.fordham.edu/halsall/mod/churchill-iron.html

Yahuda, M. (1996). *The international politics of the Asia-Pacific, 1945–1995.* London: Routledge.

Colonial Period and Early Nationhood

The rift between Europe and the United States has widened as a result of U.S. policies following September 11, 2001, but the origins of this divide can be traced back to eighteenth century colonial America.

Despite the outpouring of worldwide solidarity with the United States after the terrorist attacks of September 11, 2001, the early twenty-first century also brought a widening of the geopolitical rift between governments in the Old World and the New World. The political causes of that rift can be traced back to colonial America and the first cracks in the colonies' loyalty to their mother country of Great Britain that would result in the birth of a new nation.

On the surface the geopolitical rift may not, as yet, seem dangerously wide. Despite the bitterness of the transatlantic disagreement over the extent to which the United States—the self-designated global policeman—should resort to such invasive methods of peacekeeping as preemption, interventionism, and nation-building, and the legitimacy of those approaches, Europe and the United States are otherwise stalwart allies against the global threat of terrorism that has scarred nations on both sides of the Atlantic. From this perspective the new enemy is unmistakably perceived as a clear and present danger to the fundamental values and ideals cherished in Western civilization, regardless of any political disagreements.

The rift between the Old World and New World goes much deeper, however, than the differences of opinions concerning appropriateness or legitimacy of particular measures taken to forestall the destruction of their common heritage. Instead, the rift at its core is a fundamental dispute that revolves around an issue of critical importance—the legitimacy of foreign interventionism in the affairs of sovereign nations. On either side of the Atlantic, there are different answers to the crucial question of whether circumstances exist in which violation of a people's right to self-determination could be legally justifiable. Unlike the United States, which appears predisposed to act quickly, decisively, and unilaterally whenever a new threat has been identified, Europe displays a traditional disinclination toward interventionism in domestic affairs of other countries, even when implemented on behalf of human rights and democracy.

The Old World's self-constraint comes largely from the continental tradition of jurisprudence and parliamentary supremacy: A particular government may be tyrannical or autocratic, but as long

as it remains legitimate—that is, established in accordance with the will of the sovereign—it deserves recognition, even reluctantly, by other governments. The U.S. tradition of jurisprudence is deeply embedded in a belief in the existence of higher (natural) law that must be not only protected where its rule is already established, but also disseminated where it is still absent—a philosophy of the supremacy of law that began to take a distinct shape during late colonial America and the early United States.

Notions of Sovereignty and Supremacy of Law

The eighteenth-century debates between Whigs and Tories concerning the essence of the English constitution, the nature of the colonies' relationship with Parliament, and ultimately the question of sovereignty ignited a firestorm that was soon to produce a unique and endemic branch of political philosophy—U.S. constitutionalism. Once a legitimate child of seventeenth- and eighteenth-century European philosophical currents, it would soon reject the forthcoming development of insular constitutional thought and claim the title of the only defender of the true spirit of the British constitution—this matchless conglomerate of tradition, custom, and Anglo-Saxon jurisprudence that the colonists would perceive as the one and only guarantee of their natural rights and for which they would be thus ready to go to war, even with Great Britain itself.

The idea of sovereignty, to which eighteenth-century American colonists were already strongly attached, was barely one hundred years old by the mid-eighteenth century. Having emerged during the English Civil War in the seventeenth century, it had become a canon of Whig political philosophy during the Glorious Revolution of 1688. Its philosophical foundation rested on two concepts. One concept was that of ultimate, undivided power supreme to all other laws and thus subject to no law, and considered law unto itself. This idea that came to England through the writings of Jean Bodin (1530–1596), a sixteenth-century French jurist and natural law philosopher whose efforts were directed toward justification

A governmental building in Colonial Williamsburg, Virginia. Source: istock/Chris Coleman.

of monarchical supremacy. By "sovereign," however, Bodin meant supreme, not arbitrary power, as it should be constrained with limitations deriving from legal, religious, and pre-national origins. The actions of the sovereign still had to embody "the law of nature and of God." By the end of the seventeenth century—through the writings of the German natural law philosopher Samuel von Pufendorf (1632–1694) and the English philosophers Thomas Hobbes (1588–1679) and John Locke (1632–1704)—the idea of natural rights had become deeply ingrained in English philosophical thought and, consequently perceived as providing for a political system in which the arbitrary power of the sovereign was effectively limited by natural rights of the people.

It was the understanding of the colonists that while leaving their mother country and taking possession of the eastern coast of North America in the name of their king, the colonists were not, at the same time, leaving behind the rights and privileges they were entitled to as British subjects. Stephen Hopkins (1707–1785), a governor of Rhode Island and a signer of the Declaration of Independence, wrote in his *Grievances of the Colonies Candidly Examined* (1765):

> The terms of their freedom, and the relation they should stand in to the mother country, in their emigrant state were fully settled; they were to remain subject to the king, and dependant on the kingdom of Great Britain. In return they were to receive protection, and enjoy all the rights and privileges of freeborn Englishmen. (Hopkins 1974, 8)

King George III would be told a few years later by the Company of Rhode Island in the Roxbury Declaration of 14 December 1772, that the colonists' ancestors were relocated to the colonies, removed from Britain, under the promise that they would share in the equal rights and privileges of those subjects of the crown who remained in Britain. In other words, the rights to life, liberty, and property that Hobbes and Locke had described were inalienable and the possession of those rights, the colonists solemnly believed, were guaranteed in the English constitution.

Living thus under the "free and happy Constitution" of England, the colonists had every reason to perceive themselves as faithful subjects of the Crown who were as much culturally and nationally British as politically British, even at the very dawn of the war with their mother country. Except for some radical Whigs, who amounted to about a quarter of the population, colonists would not seek independence until they concluded that the defense of their natural rights demanded such sacrifice. "We are truly sensible how much our safety and happiness depend on a constitutional connection with Great Britain," Georgia's Provincial Congress resolved in 1775, and "nothing but the being deprived of the privileges and natural rights of Britons could ever make the thought of a separation otherwise than intolerable" (Coleman 1982).

Consequently, the colonists would not hesitate to cross the Rubicon when the necessity of the crossing was eventually made obvious to them by the English-born pamphleteer Thomas Paine (1737–1809) and his popular *Common Sense* (1776). The rationale was incontestable. In accordance with natural law, as Paine would argue, the British constitution not only was the ultimate guardian of civil freedoms of those fortunate enough to find themselves under its jurisdiction but also imposed duties on them. In addition to the enjoyment of the constitutional guarantee of their inalienable rights and privileges, the colonists were under obligation to transmit, preserve, and defend those rights and privileges when they were threatened. Paine's words caught like fire because his reasoning reflected only what the colonists had been increasingly feeling toward the end of the eighteenth century. As an example, in 1774, while the North Carolina constitutional delegates still used the term "British Americans," they were not willing to give up their rights, as that would be disgraceful to their ancestors who fought to preserve them.

U.S. Constitutionalism and Parliamentary Sovereignty

At the heart of the conflict between the colonies and their mother country lay the discrepancy between the eighteenth-century political reality of England and the largely idealistic picture that the colonists had harbored since their ancestors' departure for the New World. For a century the insular political system had slowly but persistently evolved toward parliamentary supremacy, in which virtual, not actual, representation would constitute a basis for its legitimacy, a new political system in which Parliament would be treated as an entity representative of the entire British population and thus entitled to legislate for all parts of the vast empire, regardless of its actual representative nature. The idea of parliamentary sovereignty was at the same time irreconcilable with the traditional construction of the British constitution, which might have been already fading in Great Britain but was still vibrant in the colonies, where the evolution of the insular system would pass largely unnoticed.

It was still a common understanding in the colonies that the security of the colonists' rights could be guaranteed only by the existence and recognition of fundamental laws as the only check on arbitrary power. And fundamental laws as a valid political concept would inevitably cease to exist under the rule of parliamentary supremacy, which the British system of government was practically to transform into by the nineteenth century.

By refusing to accept the inevitable, the colonists were thus defending the original meaning and interpretation of the English constitution, which—they believed—was indispensable, were they to remain the free people they had always believed themselves to be under its rule. In their "address to the Inhabitants of the Colonies," aiming at refuting the accusation of conspiracy to sedition, John Dickinson (1732–1808), a member of Delaware Constitutional Convention of 1792, and James Wilson (1742–1798), a member of the

THE FIRST THANKSGIVING PROCLAMATION

On 20 June 1676, the governing council of Charlestown, Massachusetts, held a meeting to determine how best to express thanks for the fortune that had seen the safe establishment of this colonial town.

The Holy God having by a long and Continual Series of his Afflictive dispensations in and by the present Warr with the Heathen Natives of this land, written and brought to pass bitter things against his own Covenant people in this wilderness, yet so that we evidently discern that in the midst of his judgements he hath remembered mercy, having remembered his Footstool in the day of his sore displeasure against us for our sins, with many singular Intimations of his Fatherly Compassion, and regard; reserving many of our Towns from Desolation Threatened, and attempted by the Enemy, and giving us especially of late with many of our Confederates many signal Advantages against them, without such Disadvantage to ourselves as formerly we have been sensible of, if it be the Lord's mercy that we are not consumed, It certainly bespeaks our positive Thankfulness, when our Enemies are in any measure disappointed or destroyed; and fearing the Lord should take notice under so many Intimations of his returning mercy, we should be found an Insensible people, as not standing before Him with Thanksgiving, as well as lading him with our Complaints in the time of pressing Afflictions:

The Council has thought meet to appoint and set apart the 29th day of this instant June, as a day of Solemn Thanksgiving and praise to God for such his Goodness and Favour, many Particulars of which mercy might be Instanced, but we doubt not those who are sensible of God's Afflictions, have been as diligent to espy him returning to us; and that the Lord may behold us as a People offering Praise and thereby glorifying Him; the Council doth commend it to the Respective Ministers, Elders and people of this Jurisdiction; Solemnly and seriously to keep the same Beseeching that being perswaded by the mercies of God we may all, even this whole people offer up our bodies and soulds as a living and acceptable Service unto God by Jesus Christ.

Source: Info USA: Basic documents and writings. (n.d.). Retrieved March 15, 2007, from http://usinfo.state.gov/usa/infousa/facts/funddocs.htm

Constitutional Convention of 1784 and associate justice of the U.S. Supreme Court (1789–1798), would thus explain: "let neither our enemies nor our friends make improper inferences from the solicitude which we have discovered to remove the imputation of aiming to establish an independent empire. Though an independent empire is not our *wish,* it may—let your oppressors attend—it may be the fate of our countrymen and ourselves" (Dickinson 1970, 469).

Modern U.S. and European Jurisprudence

Toward the end of the eighteenth century U.S. and English constitutional thoughts were at a crossroads and about to take two separate paths that were never again to converge. Priority given to natural rights as well as the tradition of common law led to the creation of the U.S. Constitution (1787), a document that has ever since served as an articulation of the belief in the supremacy of higher law over statutory law as the only effective guarantee of freedom and democracy.

European jurisprudence—based on the concept of Roman law and influenced by the political philosophy of such thinkers as the French philosopher and author Jean-Jacques Rousseau (1712–1778), for whom a democratic legislature, as the sovereign, was to perform the role of the guardian of civil liberties—would grow around the idea of supremacy of positive law and thus lead Europe toward parliamentary supremacy. In revolutionary France, for example, the articulation of civil rights, included largely in the *Declaration of the Rights of Man and Citizen,* would become tantamount to the legislation of normative acts that served to constrain the executive and the judicial branch. By the end of the nineteenth century European jurisprudence, largely under the influence of the precursors of the positive school of law, such as John Austin (1790–1859) or Karl Magnus Bergbohm (1840–1927), would eventually reject in its entirety the concept of natural law as the source of legislation and establish positive law—which Austin would then base solely on the sovereign's will and sanctions—as the only subject of jurisprudence.

Accordingly, in European jurisprudence the sovereign—people through their representatives in the legislative branch—is now freed from the constraints of legality of its actions, which results in legality of every act properly legislated as law. Even tyranny—

illegitimate as it might otherwise be for jurisprudence based on the idea of supreme natural law—remains legal in the absence of a higher law that could claim to the contrary. Therefore, it is natural that justification of armed interventions in sovereign countries for the sake of establishing there democratic forms of government cannot be reconciled with the European legalistic tradition as easily as it might be reconciled with the tradition in the United States. The U.S. nation was founded on the philosophical and moral imperatives of natural—not positive—law, which have since given priority to the substance of democracy rather than to its form or procedures.

Tomasz M. Lebiecki

See also Founding Principles of the United States; Special Relationship (U.S.-U.K.)

Further Reading

Bailyn, B. (1992). *The ideological origins of the American Revolution.* Cambridge, UK: Belknap Press.

Coleman, K. (Ed.). (1982). *Colonial records of the state of Georgia.* Athens: University of Georgia Press.

Dickinson, J. (1970). *Writings.* Cambridge, UK: Da Capo Press.

Hopkins, S. (1974). *The rights of colonies examined.* Providence, RI: Bicentennial Foundation.

Lutz, D. S. (Ed.). (1998). *Colonial origins of American Constitution.* Indianapolis, IN: Liberty Fund.

Middlekauff, R. (1985). *The glorious cause: The American Revolution, 1763–89.* Oxford, UK: Oxford University Press.

Middleton, R. (2002). *Colonial America: A history (1565–1776).* Oxford, UK: Blackwell.

Paine, T. (2003). *Common sense, rights of man, and other essential writings.* New York: Penguin Books.

Rakove, J. N. (1997). *Original meanings: Politics and ideas in the making of the Constitution.* New York: Vintage Books.

Reid, J. P. (1986). *Constitutional history of the American Revolution.* Madison: University of Wisconsin Press.

Saunders, W. (Ed.). (1999). *The colonial records of North Carolina.* Temecula, CA: Reprint Services Corp.

Schechter, S. L. (Ed.). (1990). *Roots of the republic: American founding documents interpreted.* Madison, WI: Madison House.

Tocqueville, A. (2000). *Democracy in America.* New York: Perennial Classics.

Urofsky, M. I. (Ed.). (1994). *Basic readings in U.S. democracy.* Washington, DC: United States Information Agency.

Colonialism and Neocolonialism

In the decades and centuries since countries stopped expanding their empires through colonies, a new form of colonialism has emerged based on economic and financial dominance and supported by international trade policies.

Colonialism is the imposition of a country's sovereignty over other nations or territories beyond its own borders. The purpose of such imposition is usually to facilitate economic domination of the resources, labor, and markets of the colonized people for the benefit of the colonizing country. Neocolonialism, on the other hand, is a process of the international system in the postcolonial era. The essence of neocolonialism is that although former colonies have obtained their political independence and have all the constitutional trappings of international sovereignty, in reality their economic systems are dominated by external forces, and their political policies are also directed by external forces. Such forces do not necessarily come from the original colonial powers; the United States, for instance, is often accused of neocolonialism in Africa and Asia even though it is not a former colonial power in these areas.

Roots of Colonialism

Colonialism has its roots in the demographic and social problems generated by the mechanization of agriculture and the displacement of peasants from land through land consolidation; the process of urbanization; and an emerging atmosphere of religious intolerance in Europe, especially in England. These factors contributed to the migration that led to the colonization of the Americas, New Zealand, and Australia, among other areas.

Colonialism also was advanced by the economic dynamics spawned by the Industrial Revolution in Europe in the nineteenth century, which led to high productivity of industrial goods that could not be profitably consumed locally. The high productivity in turn resulted in the near-exhaustion of raw materials for industries. Consequently, European nations began to acquire colonies in Asia, Africa, and the Pacific to secure sources of raw materials and markets for their goods. These colonial ventures reached a crisis in the early 1880s after stiff competition among rival colonial powers over competing claims in Africa led to the Berlin Conference of 1885, which partitioned Africa between seven colonial powers: England, Belgium, France, Germany, Italy, Portugal, and Spain.

There were two types of colonialism: settler and non-settler. Settler colonialism involved migration of significant populations from the colonial power to the colony for permanent settlement as was the case in Australia, Latin America, New Zealand, North America, and South Africa. In non-settler colonies, comprising most of Africa and Asia, little migration took place from the colonial metropolis to the colony for purposes of permanent settlement. This dichotomy explains why the settler colonies were developed while the non-settler ones were underdeveloped. Resources in the settler colonies were exploited and invested in the colony while non-settler colonies were designed as reservoirs of cheap labor and sources of raw materials whose resources were extracted and transshipped to the colonial powers.

Settler colonialism, with the exception of South Africa, was characterized by two types of relationships between colonizers and colonized. The first involved what Ronald Horvath (1972) refers to as extermination of the colonized peoples and the creation of new nation-states in the image of the ones the colonial settlers had migrated from. Examples here include the European occupation of Tasmania, and the extermination of the natives of large areas of Australia, Canada, New Zealand, and the United States. The second type of relationship between settlers and natives was one of assimilation of the latter. Herein, the culture and social values of the colonizer were presumed to be superior to those of the colonized and thus assimilation was a one-way traffic from the colonizer to the colonized. The Hispanicization of Latin America and the Philippines, the Arabization and Islamization of the Middle East, and the Sinization of East and Southeast Asia are examples of this form of colonial relationship.

Non-settler colonies in Africa and Asia were characterized by relations between colonizers and colonized that Horvath describes as relative equilibrium. Herein, there was neither extermination nor assimilation of the native populations. The two groups lived apart or in some cases side by side and although some cultural changes occurred among natives, there was no deliberate policy of their wholesale acculturation or eradication. This was the case even in colonies with some significant presence of colonial settlement including South Africa, Kenya, Indonesia, and Zimbabwe.

United States and Colonialism

The conventional view in the United States is that colonialism was a European enterprise and thus that the United States has nothing to do with colonialism and neocolonialism. Instead, the country's

valiant revolution against England and the resultant democratic institutions are used to showcase the United States as an exemplar of democratic governance and a champion of political freedoms and individual liberties. The United States was founded not by natives of the continent but rather by settlers from England, who came not as emigrants who would adapt to the ways of a new continent but rather as pilgrims who would create a New England in the image of the one they had left behind.

The doctrine of "manifest destiny," by which the United States justified expansion from the Atlantic to the Pacific, the displacement and killing of Native Americans, and the forceful annexation of large tracts of land from Mexico, was not any different from the "civilizing" justifications of European colonialism in Africa and Asia. Additionally, U.S. incursions into the Caribbean and Latin America, albeit brief, were colonial in nature and established lasting political influence. For instance, the Spanish-American War of 1898 won Cuba's independence from colonialism. After defeating Spain the United States retained the Spanish colonies of the Philippines and Puerto Rico as colonies. Just like the colonial powers of his time, U.S. president William McKinley viewed these islands as unfit to govern themselves, and hence the United States had the duty to govern them. The United States never owned up to being a colonial power even as it engaged in a three-year war against Filipinos who had envisaged ridding themselves of Spanish colonialism.

Nevertheless, the United States was a source of inspiration for forces fighting against European colonialism in Africa and Asia. Colonial rivalries over territories in Africa and the Ottoman province of Bosnia in Europe led to intensification of an arms race among the colonial powers and the solidification of the alliance system that contributed to the outbreak of World War I. Yet, the colonial powers were unwilling to state their war aims because the aims included secret territorial claims. It took U.S. president Woodrow Wilson's Fourteen Points policy to lay the groundwork for a negotiated settlement to end the war. The Fourteen Points comprised basic principles, including free trade, freedom of the seas, open agreements, as well as a variety of geographic arrangements emphasizing the principle of self-determination and democracy.

The fifth of Wilson's Fourteen Points was particularly pertinent to colonized peoples as it called for a free, open-minded, and absolutely impartial adjustment of all colonial claims based on a strict observance of the principle that in determining all such questions of sovereignty the interests of the populations concerned must have equal weight with the equitable claims of the government whose title is to be determined. Furthermore, Wilson's idealistic exposition facilitated the formation of the League of Nations to moderate international issues in such a way as to avoid war. Former German

colonies in Africa were placed in trusteeship under the League of Nations' mandates system as future self-governing territories, giving colonized peoples hope of future independence.

U.S. anticolonialism was again manifested in Southeast Asia, where Japan was the only Asian country to become a colonial power when it colonized Korea and Taiwan after its decisive military victories over China in 1895 and Russia in 1905. To extend its imperial reach, Japan invaded and annexed Manchuria Province from China in 1931. The League of Nations's efforts to mediate the issue proved fruitless while England was unsure of which side to support because of concern over its colonies in the Far East, especially Hong Kong and Singapore. The United States reacted by slapping sanctions onto Japan in the interests of keeping China united for "free trade." Japan responded by bombing Pearl Harbor in 1941, thereby drawing the United States into World War II. In July 1941 President Franklin Roosevelt and English prime minister Winston Churchill issued the Atlantic Charter on the aims of the war against fascism.

The third principle of the charter was of critical significance to colonized peoples around the globe fighting for liberation. It stressed respect for the right of all peoples to choose the form of government under which they will live and reiterated the signatories' wish to see sovereign rights and self-government restored to those who had been forcibly deprived of them.

Interestingly, although the Soviet Union—which had been attacked by Germany barely a month prior to the issuance of the charter—was to sign the charter, Soviet leader Joseph Stalin was put off by the charter's principle of "one world," wherein states abandoned their traditional beliefs in a reliance on military alliances and spheres of influence. Even Churchill was not particularly enthusiastic about the principle but went along mainly because in the spring of 1941 the U.S. Congress had approved the Lend-Lease Program, by which the aid promised by Roosevelt to war-weary England began to flow. Hence only Roosevelt was a genuine believer in the possibility of a world governed by democratic processes, with an international organization playing the role of arbiter of disputes and protector of international peace and security.

United States and Neocolonialism

After the independence of most colonized countries by the 1960s, neocolonialism manifested itself in the domination of the economies of the newly independent countries by their former colonial powers. The United States entered the ranks of neocolonial powers under the guise of fighting communism within the context of the Cold War. On the basis of this guise, the United States

propped up dictators around the world simply because they were anticommunist even when they perpetrated gross violations of human rights against their own citizens. Similarly, the United States was not averse to sabotaging—and sponsoring or abetting coups against—leaders viewed as being procommunist and thus opposed to U.S. interests.

The U.S. invasions of Grenada in 1983, Panama in 1989, and Iraq in 2003, are also seen as neocolonialism by many people around the world. With regard to Iraq the United States would like to be seen as liberator rather than invader and occupier. Indeed, in his 2004 State of the Union address, President George W. Bush sought to counter perceptions that his military action against Iraq was imperialistic by denying any U.S. desire to dominate the world or to have an empire. Whatever the motivation for conquering Iraq, the fact is that the eventual Iraqi government will be more pliant to U.S. strategic interests than was the Saddam Hussein regime. Such pliancy is a key attribute of neocolonial relations.

Overall, the end of the Cold War was heralded as a triumph of Western values of liberal democracy and free markets over the Soviet Union's state capitalism and totalitarianism. Pressure began to be applied to less-developed countries to democratize and liberalize their economies. Critics of the process, however, view it as Western imperialism under the cloak of globalization. Whereas the democratic trajectory has yielded positive results for hitherto oppressed peoples, the economic trajectory, spearheaded by the "Washington consensus" between the U.S. government, the World Bank (led by an American), and the International Monetary Fund (led by a European), has facilitated penetration of the markets of less-developed countries by multinational corporations from the developed world. Terms such as *McWorld* and *Cocacolonization* have been coined to describe the ubiquitous presence of U.S. corporations around the globe and the pervasiveness of U.S. culture.

Future Trends

Neocolonial discourses of global power have shifted from the "civilizing mission" of nineteenth-century colonialism through U.S.-sponsored discourses of anticommunism and modernization of the Cold War to a new universalistic language of democracy and free markets. Trade policy is the new instrument of global domination. Accordingly, developing countries will increasingly demand their right to protect their own weak economies from unfair competition, as symbolized by their position that led to the collapse of the Cancun World Trade Organization talks in 2003. Nevertheless, given the sheer size of the U.S. economy and the technologically competitive edge of its business corporations, it will remain economically dominant for a long time to come. Accusations of neocolonialism against the United States will thus remain part of the global economic discourse, especially as long as the perception remains that the country is quick to use its military might to pursue its interests. To obviate this perception, the United States might have to heed Theodore Roosevelt's caution: to walk softly even as it carries the biggest stick in the world.

Shadrack Wanjala Nasong'o

See also Globalization, Economic

Further Reading

Blanchard, W. H. (1996). *Neocolonialism American style, 1960–2000.* Westport, CT: Greenwood Press.

Boahen, A. A. (1989). *African perspectives on colonialism.* Baltimore: Johns Hopkins University Press.

Cooper, F. (2005). *Colonialism in question: Theory, knowledge, history.* Berkeley: University of California Press.

Hochschild, A. (1998). *King Leopold's ghost: A story of greed, terror, and heroism in colonial Africa.* New York: Mariner.

Horvath, R. J. (1972). A definition of colonialism. *Current Anthropology, 13*(1), 45–57.

Loomba, A. (2005). *Colonialism/postcolonialism.* New York: Routledge.

Mamdani, M. (1996). *Citizen and subject: Contemporary Africa and the legacy of late colonialism.* London: James Currey.

Nkrumah, K. (1965). *Neo-colonialism: The last stage of imperialism.* London: Panaf Books.

Ostler, J. (2004). *The Plains Sioux and U.S. colonialism from Lewis and Clark to Wounded Knee.* Cambridge, UK: Cambridge University Press.

Presbey, G. M. (2004). Mahmood Mamdani's analysis of colonialism applied to the U.S.-led war on Iraq. Retrieved March 16, 2007, from http://them.polylog.org/5/apg-en.htm

Sartre, J. P. (2006). *Colonialism and neocolonialism.* New York: Routledge.

Zinn, H. (1980). *A people's history of the United States.* New York: Harper and Row.

Conflicts, Civilizational and Cultural

In World War II the United States was seen as a liberator and restorer of European civilization, but in the war on terror it is seen as an occupier whose goal is to upend and change Islamic civilization.

If *culture* is defined broadly as "a group's attitudes, beliefs, symbols, and values" and if *conflict* is defined as "an incompatibility between two or more goals," a conflict between cultures would be an incompatibility between the attitudes, beliefs, symbols, and values of one group and those of another group. World War II (1939–1945) could be classified as a cultural conflict when one understands the war to have been a conflict between the culture of liberal democracy on the one hand and the culture of fascism on the other hand. The current U.S. war on terrorism is a cultural conflict when one follows the logic of the administration of President George W. Bush and perceives the war as a war between the culture of liberal democracy on the one hand and the culture of violence (terrorism) on the other hand.

The role of the United States in these two conflicts has led to two different perspectives in global society. At the end of World War II the United States was perceived as a liberator. At least among the Allies, people had a common understanding that under U.S. leadership fascism had been defeated and democracy saved. This perception was strengthened during the postwar years when Japan and a part of West Germany were administered by U.S. military forces. These military administrations laid the basis for the Japanese and West German transformation from totally defeated enemies into successful democratic allies of the United States.

On the other hand, the U.S. war on terrorism has caused many U.S. enemies and allies to perceive the United States as an occupier rather than a liberator. The second Iraq War (2003), which is being fought in the name of the war on terrorism, has resulted, many people feel, in an occupation of Iraq. Instead of decreasing cultural conflict between the United States and the Iraqi people, the U.S. military presence has seemed to foster it.

Starting with the assumption that global perspectives of the United States are at least partly shaped by its involvement in cultural conflicts, this essay examines the different global perspectives of the United States that were created as a result of the military administrations of Germany (1945–1949) and Japan (1945–1952) on the one hand and the military administration of Iraq on the other hand. Why does global society perceive the United States as a liberator of Germany and Japan but as an occupier of Iraq?

Defining Occupation and Liberation

The terms *occupation* and *liberation* can be understood as two qualifications of the neutral term *military administration. Military administration* is defined as "the military control of a country by another country." A military administration turns into a (political) liberation when the objective is to set the population of the foreign country free from an oppressive political system. A military administration becomes an occupation when it is installed in order to control the foreign population mainly or even exclusively for the gain of the military administration itself. The choice of qualification depends on the eye of the beholder; does global society perceive a U.S. military administration as being for the benefit of the administered population or for the benefit of the United States?

We can identify two necessary conditions for an administration to be perceived as a liberator. First, the military administration should be considered *legitimate*. If global society regards a particular U.S. military administration as illegitimate, global society is unlikely to perceive it as a liberator. The war preceding a military administration is a source of legitimacy or illegitimacy. In that respect global society should consider the preceding war to be just.

Second, the objective of liberation—the establishment of a new and better political system—should be achieved. A military administration is perceived as a liberator only when it is *effective* in setting the administered people free from a restrictive political system. That liberation includes not only the liberation as such (in the case of Iraq the toppling of Saddam Hussein's regime), but also the successful establishment of a new political order. The U.S. military administrations in Germany and Japan complied with both conditions.

United States as a Liberator: West Germany

At the end of World War II global society perceived the United States as a liberator when it led the Allied invasion of Europe in

order to defeat fascism. Fascist control over Europe was politically suppressive (to say the least), and liberating Europe from it was the main objective of the Allied war effort.

The war ended with an unconditional surrender of Germany, and the country had to accept a military administration by the Allied powers. Germany was divided into four zones, each administered by British, Russian, French, or U.S. military forces. Under the political pressures of the unfolding Cold War (1945–1990), Germany was divided into a western part (under U.S., British, and French influence) and an eastern part (under Russian influence).

The United States established a robust military presence in its zone. A key document of the U.S. administration stated that there should be established a "stern, all powerful military administration of a conquered country, based on unconditional surrender, impressing the Germans with their military defeat and the futility of any further aggression" (Dobbins 2003, 7).

Global society regarded this stern military administration as legitimate because it was the result of a just war. The Allied invasion of Germany had clearly been a reaction to German aggression. In 1939 and 1940 most of western Europe had been invaded and occupied by German military forces. The United States became involved in the war after Japan attacked the U.S. naval fleet at Pearl Harbor on 7 December 1941 and after the Nazi regime of Germany officially declared war on the U.S. government a few days later. Given this aggression, the U.S. postwar determination to prevent Germany from becoming a threat ever again was considered to be legitimate.

In order to reach that objective, U.S. authorities decided to rebuild Germany and to turn the enemy into an ally. This transformation proved to be successful. A crucial factor in the success was the German acceptance of total defeat, which resulted in a cooperative attitude. No significant violent resistance against U.S. or other Allied forces developed, allowing a rapid demobilization. The number of U.S. troops declined from 1.6 million troops in 1945 to 370,000 one year later.

As a result of the cooperative attitude of the West German population, partial sovereignty was returned during the first year of military administration. By January 1946 political life was being reborn on a local level when elections were organized in the U.S. zone. Between 1947 and 1948 significant political authority was returned to the West Germans in all three zones. In 1949 countrywide elections were held, resulting in establishment of the Federal Republic of Germany.

Economic reconstruction was strongly stimulated. Stimulation included not only direct financial aid, but also the subordination of war reparation payments to economic recovery. According to the so-called first charge principle, economic revenues were first used for reconstruction purposes; reparation payments to countries that had suffered under the German occupation were a secondary priority. West German economic output recovered rapidly in 1946. A few years passed before the country was on its prewar production level, but during the military administration the foundation was laid for the German "economic miracle" of the 1960s.

The political and economic reconstruction went hand-in-hand with the destruction of what remained of the Nazi regime. Important Nazi leaders were tried during the Nuremberg War Crimes Tribunal, and the entire state apparatus was dissolved and rebuilt from the bottom. For the Americans and their allies, the enemy had been not the German population as such, but rather the Nazi regime. The German public shared that point of view, and without denying its role in supporting the regime, the public came to regard the successful military administration as a liberation from the dictatorship of the Nazi Party. The oppressive and destructive political system had been replaced with freedom, security, and economic prosperity.

United States as a Liberator: Japan

The same process occurred in Japan. Like Germany, Japan was defeated at the end of World War II. In August 1945 two nuclear bombs dropped on the cities of Hiroshima and Nagasaki ended the war in the Far East. Japan's surrender was as unconditional as Germany's. The difference was that the subsequent military administration was entirely in U.S. hands. The Allied powers were represented in two international councils, but in practice a U.S. general, Supreme Allied Commander Douglas MacArthur (1880–1964), was in charge. Under the leadership of MacArthur a military administration comparable with the one in Germany was established.

The military administration in Japan was considered legitimate by global society because the preceding war was regarded as a just war. With Germany, Japan was held responsible for starting World War II. Since the 1930s the Japanese empire had systematically expanded, and on 7 December 1941, the imperial regime had attacked the U.S. fleet at Pearl Harbor. Because of this direct attack on the United States, the U.S. effort to prevent future aggression by Japan was considered to be clearly legitimate.

U.S. authorities decided to adopt the same strategy as in Germany: A military administration would start by rebuilding the country in order to transform it from an enemy into an ally. Again, this strategy proved to be successful because of a cooperative attitude by the Japanese. The Americans had expected a violent

confrontation when they entered Japan with ground troops, but instead they were received by "women who called 'yoo hoo' to the first troops landing on the beaches in full battle gear, and men who asked what it was the conquerors wished" (Dower 1999, 24). Acceptance of defeat turned into cooperation with the U.S. authority.

Economic reconstruction was fostered by financial aid and economic reform programs. Large industrial conglomerates were disbanded, and a program of land reform was launched in order to undermine the power of rural elites who were held responsible for Japan's aggression. Although the effects of these reforms are ambiguous, the basis of Japan's economic power in the 1960s and 1970s was clearly laid during the military administration.

As for the political reconstruction and disbandment of the wartime imperial regime, less thorough results were achieved in Japan than in Germany. In Japan the War Crimes Tribunal was created, but many officials escaped prosecution, at least partly because the military administration relied on a system of indirect rule in which existing Japanese governance structures were allowed to carry out administrative tasks under U.S. supervision.

The most important example of U.S. use of an indigenous institution was the Japanese emperor. Although Emperor Hirohito is considered to have been at least partly responsible for Japan's aggression, the United States decided to retain him in order to support the rebuilding program. However, his large role in politics was downsized to a symbolic function by a program of democratization. A modern constitution was written that not only curbed the power of traditional elites, but also denounced war as a method of solving disputes.

The military administration of Japan proved to be successful. With the end of the military administration in 1952, the oppressive imperial system, which in the end had also brought war and destruction to the Japanese population, had been replaced with a system that was able to produce freedom, security, and prosperity.

United States as an Occupier: Iraq

The Iraq War (2003) and the subsequent military administration of Iraq were carried out in the name of the war on terrorism. The war on terrorism had begun immediately after the terrorist attacks on the World Trade Center in New York and the Pentagon in Washington, D.C., on September 11, 2001, for which the terrorist network al-Qaeda, led by Osama bin Laden, was held responsible. The U.S. military response focused initially on Afghanistan and its Taliban regime because that country proved to be the main base of al-Qaeda.

However, the war on terrorism was not limited to Afghanistan. Immediately after September 11 President George W. Bush called for a preemptive and proactive strategy, aimed at the pursuit of terrorists all over the world. Not only individual terrorists but also any state harboring suspected terrorists were targeted by what became known as the "Bush Doctrine."

The Bush strategy was broadened when he delivered his State of the Union speech in January 2002. The list of potential targets was expanded with the so-called axis of evil: Iraq, North Korea, and Iran were named as potential targets of a preemptive strike because they had repressive regimes and were suspected of having weapons of mass destruction (WMDs). The Bush administration feared that these regimes would sell WMDs to terrorists or would use them in a direct attack on the United States.

The Bush administration especially regarded the regime of Iraqi president Saddam Hussein as a vital threat to the security of the United States, and the administration decided to launch a military campaign with the goal of regime change. Hussein's regime was destroyed in one of the swiftest and most successful military campaigns ever. With the United Kingdom, the United States formed the Coalition Provisional Authority (CPA), which began to administer Iraq in April 2003 and handed over formal authority to an Iraqi interim government on 28 June 2004.

In several respects the military administration of Iraq was not that different from the military administrations of Germany and Japan. First, it was preceded by a total defeat of the regime. Second, it was aimed at eliminating a (perceived) threat to U.S. vital interests. Finally, the military administration was focused on political and economic reconstruction. The aim was to establish a viable democratic state that posed a threat to neither the United States and its allies nor to the region. As with Japan and Germany, the aim of the military administration was to transform an enemy into an ally.

Despite these similarities, global society perceived the military administration of Iraq not as liberation but rather as occupation. Whereas legitimacy and effectiveness explain why the military administrations in Germany and Japan were perceived as liberations, illegitimacy and ineffectiveness explain why the military administration of Iraq was perceived as an occupation.

The perception of global society that the Iraq War and the military administration lack legitimacy is remarkable, given the broad international support for the war on terrorism immediately after September 11, 2001. In October 2001, when the military operations against the Taliban regime and al-Qaeda bases in Afghanistan started, the United States was supported by a broad coalition. This coalition was not only a representation of U.S. Western allies, but also included Arabic and other Muslim countries. However, by the time the Iraq War had begun, important members of the

coalition, such as France, Germany, and Turkey, had left. What had happened?

The first cracks in the coalition appeared when Bush delivered his State of the Union speech in January 2002. When the United States began to broaden the agenda of the war on terrorism, the coalition started to fall apart. However, the definitive blast to the broad coalition came when the Bush administration could not convince global society that its arguments for starting a military campaign against Hussein were valid. Three main arguments were made. First, the Iraqi regime was accused of having links with al-Qaeda and thus of being indirectly co-responsible for September 11. Second, Iraq was suspected of having WMDs and of being willing to use them against the United States or its allies or to sell them to terrorists. In possessing WMDs, the Bush administration argued, Iraq had violated several resolutions of the United Nations Security Council. Third, Hussein's regime brutally oppressed the Iraqi population, and regime change would therefore improve the lives of many people.

The first two arguments implied that the United States was reacting to Iraqi aggression. Following these arguments, Hussein's regime was punished for its complicity in the September 11 attacks and was preempted from using WMDs against the United States. However, whereas it had been obvious to global society that both Germany and Japan were the aggressors during World War II, that was not the case with Iraq in the war on terrorism. A direct link between the Iraqi regime and al-Qaeda was not proven, and WMDs were not found in Iraq. Those two deficits made both the arguments of punishment and preemption invalid to global society.

The remaining argument, that the Iraqi regime repressed its own population, was certainly valid. With Hussein in power, the Iraqis lived under an oppressive political system that restricted them in many ways. In that sense, the war and the military administration were a liberation.

However, this argument could not convince global society for two reasons. First, the objectives of punishment and preemption seemed more important to the Bush administration; the administration often repeated these objectives. The United States could not convince global society that liberation was the main objective of the war. Second, the military administration did not prove to be effective. The U.S. presence could not prevent the development of an insurgency, fed by different Iraqi groups with equally different political objectives but united in their resistance to the military administration as well as to Iraqi political institutions established under U.S. supervision. The regime of Hussein had been convincingly defeated, but its staunchest supporters and insurgents from other political or religious factions had not been.

The CPA proved to be incapable of establishing law and order

and pacifying the territory. Even the arrest of Hussein in December 2003 did not lead to the expected decrease of violence. Between 1 May 2003, when Bush declared the end of major combat operations, and 28 June 2004, the day sovereignty was formally transferred to an Iraqi interim government, about eighty large pacification operations were carried out by U.S. troops. Instead of early troop reductions, as had been the case in Germany, the number of troops used in the Iraq War (about 150,000) was maintained and at times even slightly increased.

Whereas it proved to be relatively easy to deal with the remainder of the Nazi regime in Germany and the imperial government in Japan, the elusiveness of the insurgency in Iraq proved to be impossible to overcome in only one year of military administration. Therefore, authorities decided that despite the transfer of formal authority from the CPA to the Iraqi interim government, the U.S. military would stay in order to assist with stabilization. However, in the following years the insurgency has prevented the Americans from repeating the early successes that had been achieved in Germany and Japan; economic and political reconstruction has been seriously hampered by the insurgency. Moreover, violence between the different communities within Iraqi society has increased to such an extent that many observers have feared a full-scale civil war. In such an unstable environment, it has proved to be impossible to build sustainable domestic institutions to the same extent as had been done in Germany and Japan. Creating a new political order has proved impossible thus far.

Future Perspectives

One can argue that if the civilizational conflict between the United States and Iraq does not improve, then the U.S. government will become increasingly isolated within global society, coming to be viewed more and more as an occupier. As explained earlier, the U.S. military administrations in Germany and Japan were regarded as liberations because they were legitimate *and* effective. In both countries the oppressive regime was replaced with a system that brought freedom, security, and prosperity in a relatively short period of time. The Germans and Japanese experienced a "new beginning" in the sense of a new political order (Arendt 1990, 35). The lack of effectiveness—and thus a "new beginning"—and the illegitimate basis of the Iraq War created the perspective that the United States is an occupier rather than a liberator of Iraq.

Given the Bush administration's argument for the Iraq War, one might wonder how the U.S. invasion of Iraq can ever become perceived as legitimate by global society, but effectiveness can theoretically still be achieved. For that to happen, the current situation, in which the only success that can be claimed is regime

change, must evolve into a "new beginning." If the stabilization mission proves to be effective in the long term, producing freedom, security, and prosperity for the Iraqi people, the war and the CPA will probably be perceived with hindsight as liberation.

The civilizational conflicts in Germany and Japan were resolved, and the regions stabilized, with the help of two main factors that were not used as effectively in the case of Iraq. Large troop numbers coupled with the winning-over of the hearts and minds of the population were the two key elements in the successful liberation of both Germany and Japan. From the outset the United States had relatively fewer troops in Iraq than it had in Germany and Japan. If the troop-population ratio of Germany had been used in Iraq, the United States would have had no fewer than 2.5 million troops in Iraq in 2003. But troop numbers are easy to measure and control compared to the second element for building a stable political system. Winning the hearts and minds of a population is crucial, yet all the more difficult to control and plan. In order to win the hearts and minds of Iraqis, some argue, the United States would have to become a genuine partner of the Iraqi political institutions. That would involve negotiating with the insurgents, just as the United States did in 2004 in order to end the insurgency of the Shia cleric Muqtada al-Sadr and his followers. It certainly involves the avoidance of scandals such as the Abu Ghraib scandal in 2004, which revealed that U.S. troops had tortured Iraqi prisoners. It has also been argued that an increase in U.S. troops in order to assist the weak Iraqi security forces in providing security for the Iraqi population will help win them over. This would seem a strange necessity after three years of military presence, would face opposition from the increasing pressure from the U.S. public "to bring the boys and girls home," and would be a logistical challenge with the limited availability of additional military forces. However, in West Germany the number of U.S. troops increased again in 1955, but this time the increased troops were there not to administer the defeated Germans but rather to defend West Germany, as a NATO ally, against the Warsaw Pact.

The current situation in Iraq is different in many respects, but in order to resolve this complex cultural conflict, it needs at least as much U.S. commitment as Germany did.

Niels van Willigen

See also Iraq Wars; Islamic Worldview; Middle East Peace Process; World War II

Further Reading

Arendt, H. (1990). *On revolution.* London: Penguin Books.

Baker III, J., Hamilton, L., et al. (2006). *The Iraq study group report.* New York: Vintage Books.

Bremer, P. (2006). *My year in Iraq: The struggle to build a future of hope.* New York: Simon & Schuster.

Calleo, D. P. (2004). The broken West. *Survival, 46*(3), 29–38.

Dobbins, J. F. (2003). *America's role in nation-building.* Pittsburgh, PA: RAND.

Dodge, T. (2004). A sovereign Iraq? *Survival, 46*(3), 39–58.

Dodge, T. (2005). *Iraq's future: the aftermath of regime change.* Abingdon, UK: Routledge.

Dower, J. (1999). *Embracing defeat: Japan in the wake of World War II.* New York: New Press.

Edelstein, D. M. (2004). Occupational hazards: Why military occupations succeed or fail. *International Security, 29*(1), 49–91.

Fawn, R., & Hinnebusch, R. (Eds.). (2006). *The Iraq War: Causes and consequences.* Boulder, CO: Lynne Rienner Publishers.

Feldman, N. (2006). *What we owe Iraq: War and the ethics of nation building.* Princeton, NJ: Princeton University Press.

Fukuyama, F. (2006) *Nation building: Beyond Afghanistan and Iraq.* Baltimore, MD: Johns Hopkins University Press.

Killick, J. (1997). *The United States and European reconstruction: 1945–1960.* Edinburgh, UK: Keele University Press.

Peterson, E. (1977). *The American occupation of Germany: Retreat to victory.* Detroit, MI: Wayne State University Press.

Schonberger, H. B. (1989). *Aftermath of war: Americans and the remaking of Japan, 1945–1952.* Kent, OH: Kent State University Press.

Ziemke, E. F. (1975). *The U.S. Army in the occupation of Germany, 1944–1946.* Washington, DC: Center of Military History.

Consumerism

While consumerism as a practice dates back to the seventeenth century in Western Europe, it has grown tremendously in modern times, with the United States earning a reputation as the leading consumer nation.

Consumerism is devotion to the acquisition of material goods that are not necessary for subsistence. Consumerist societies feature a variety of institutions designed to purvey desirable but unnecessary goods and to encourage desire itself. They also feature a value structure in which people measure their own lives and the condition of their society in significant part by opportunities for acquisition. Consumerist societies, finally, emphasize variety and change in goods; stability is downplayed in favor of fads and novelties; even nostalgia for things past can become part of a faddish procession of styles.

The United States was not the original home of modern consumerism, though by the late eighteenth century significant interest began to build on knowledge of consumer patterns in England. Over the long run, the United States has taken the lead in global consumerism, establishing itself as a trend-setter with its national fashions shaping global trends. Consumerism and Americanism have become widely associated.

Some elements of consumerism go far back in the human experience, including, for example, delights in human adornment not necessary for warmth and decency. Upper classes in many agricultural civilizations marked themselves off in part through consumerism. A common progression, as in the classical Mediterranean or in later Arab societies, involved upper-class groups initially establishing their societal status through military and political leadership but then gradually transitioning to a more expressive, materialist style of life. Their elevated status was demonstrated in their standard of living.

However, even in the most prosperous agricultural civilizations consumerism was constrained by several factors. Foremost was the fact that the majority of the population—peasants and artisans—had a narrow margin of subsistence and therefore did not have the means to adopt consumerist trends. There were also groups who had the disposable resources and income, but whose religion dictated an attention to otherworldly rather than material goals. Available surplus was in this way channeled into collective religious display—the adornments of churches or mosques—rather than into consumerism. Many societies also emphasized the importance of unchanging—or, more commonly, slowly evolving—fashion. Ancient Roman senators, for example, might delight in togas made from newly imported Chinese silks, but the togas themselves were of a standard style, not an opportunity for extensive individual display. European guilds had expressive costumes, denoting the jewelers' or the butchers' craft, and these costumes required resources not, strictly speaking, needed for subsistence. However, the emphasis was on commonality, not individual expression, as well as on durability. This activity was not consumerism, although it did involve materialist expression. Finally, many societies had social strictures and regulations that forbid or discouraged certain classes or groups, regardless of their means, from imitating the fashions of their superiors.

Consumerism recurrently showed up in agricultural societies, but it never became a dominant theme. Bursts of interest were often followed by government or religious campaigns to enforce greater austerity and conformity. During the Tang dynasty (618–907 CE) in China, for example, royal consorts such as Yang Kuei-fei indulged in exotic costumes, influencing the tastes of many others in the elite. However, Yang was put to death by disapproving court officials. In Europe sumptuary laws often regulated display according to standards of social hierarchy, religious priority, and conformity.

Origins

The origins of modern consumerism date to the seventeenth and eighteenth centuries in Western Europe. During the seventeenth century, for example, a tulip craze swept the increasingly commercially prosperous Netherlands. Investments in new strains of tulips, even purchases of paintings of tulips, marked the craze, one of the first "have to have" movements, beyond elite levels, in world history. More systematically, several developments by the eighteenth century marked the permanent arrival of consumerism. Shopkeepers (whose numbers rapidly expanded in Britain and elsewhere in Western Europe) devised more attractive window displays for goods. They advertised in the new urban newspapers, sometimes using testimonials from aristocrats for products as banal as a new kind of razor. Loss leaders were introduced—goods with marked-down prices that would lure buyers into a store, where buyers would often purchase other goods. Manufacturers such as Josiah Wedgwood began to do market surveys of product styles

(in his case, china and porcelain) to determine what to manufacture. In other words, the apparatus of modern consumerism was rapidly developing.

New motivations for and expressions of consumerism were also developing. People began bequeathing consumer items to family members in their wills, a clear sign that these items were acquiring new emotional meaning. Thefts of consumer goods rose rapidly. Second-hand sales did as well; with clothing taking the lead, indicating the spread of consumerism to lower levels of society. Consumer goods gained a new place in family rituals. Tea and coffee sets and more elaborate place settings marked novel kinds of family dining, in which women set the tone for family togetherness around more stylish consumer items. Levels of comfort were redefined, and the idea of being comfortable became increasingly acceptable: During the eighteenth century, for example, the British began to imitate the new French habit of using umbrellas, amid some debate as to whether this new desire to keep dry in the island's incessant rain signaled a softening of British character. Consumerism also began to affect leisure: By the late eighteenth century villages began to import urban music groups for their festivals rather than rely on traditional participatory entertainment; other new spectator interests, for example, in traveling circuses, began to spread in Europe as well. By the 1830s, when department stores first developed (initially in Paris, as an agglomeration of smaller clothing shops), going shopping itself became a popular pastime.

Was increased consumerism a response to the real needs of an evolving world or was it largely a matter of manipulation by manufacturers and advertisers? Several causes contributed to this fundamental redefinition of human purpose. Europe's growing role in world trade contributed to the prosperity of many groups, but with an ever-present gap between the rich and the poor. It also brought new goods. Sugar was the first popular consumer item in Europe that depended on imports. Cotton cloth, from India, greatly encouraged consumerism in clothing because cotton cloth could be dyed in colorful hues, and its low costs increased availability of fashionable styles. Changes in culture contributed as well. Many Europeans became more secular, which facilitated materialistic interests. At the same time, new ideas about romance heightened an interest in consumer items that might increase personal appeal. The spread of manufacturing not only generated new goods, but also put new groups into contact with money and urban styles. Many domestic manufacturing workers, for example, in the Swiss countryside, although not very affluent, used some of their wages to buy city-style clothing rather than accept village conventions. Population growth and growing commercialism blurred social lines. Many children could no longer expect to inherit land because of population pressure; denied this conventional

badge of success, those who could turned to consumerism as an alternative, and more individualistic, way to express themselves and their accomplishments.

Precisely because it was novel, consumerism generated backlash. Upper-class moralists condemned lower-class families who defied conventional barriers with their purchasing power. A common accusation, doubtless true in some cases, was that consumerism was inducing people to live beyond their means, harming family well-being in the long run. Although both genders participated in modern consumerism, women often indulged in it more heavily because it gave them an outlet for expression that they were often denied in society. Women were consequently criticized for the consumerist inclinations. Of course, the tensions between consumerism and proper religious devotion were often noted. At many points critics have worried that consumerism was undermining proper values and self-discipline, at best making life more superficial, at worst undercutting essential civic virtue. Discomfort with consumerism is an important part of its modern history.

After consumerism was established in Western Europe, a couple of major changes propelled modern consumerism forward in the nineteenth and twentieth centuries. Other societies began to imitate European interests. The United States, which had lagged a bit in consumerism in the eighteenth century, began to display new interest in French clothing styles from the 1840s onward. Department stores spread from Western Europe, hitting Russia by the 1850s and the United States at about the same time. Japan's move toward new global contacts soon involved consumerism. Department stores began to spread in Tokyo from the 1890s onward, particularly in districts where foreign interests were particularly marked. Department stores in Shanghai and other Chinese cities, from 1900 onward, similarly were linked to international quarters. For urban Africa, Chinua Achebe's novel, *No Longer at Ease,* set in the 1920s in Lagos, Nigeria, describes a consumerist lifestyle so desirable that many individuals began to violate traditional family obligations in order to stay in the city for consumerist enjoyments.

By 1900, as a key part of this general dissemination of consumerism, the United States was emerging as a consumer leader. The nation had a key advantage: its huge national market, especially compared to individual European nations. This meant that U.S. marketing systems designed for its own national audience could be exported easily into other smaller countries. By 1920, for example, Hollywood emerged as the film capital of the world as key companies began to use the same marketing techniques that had worked across the United States to set up affiliates abroad. The same momentum would later apply to the international spread of McDonald's and Disney. The nation also lacked a strong aristocratic or artisanal tradition, which elsewhere slowed consumerist

People shopping at a shopping mall.
Source: istock/Volker Kreinacke.

trends. Objections to consumerism existed in the United States, but they were not as deeply rooted as they were in Europe or Asia. By 1900, both working- and middle-class families in the United States began to depend increasingly on consumerism to compensate for stresses in the workplace including (for the middle class) the decline of entrepreneurial opportunities in favor of corporate management hierarchies. By the twentieth century, there were signs that American dependence on consumerism as a means of gauging life satisfaction was exceeding other consumerist societies elsewhere, leading among other things to a willingness to work longer hours in favor of greater income for consumer spending.

Resisting the Urge to Splurge

Of course, this international spread of consumerism was not universal. Many people stayed away from the new outlets, arguing that new goods or styles were unnecessary, that local, traditional styles would suffice. Many people also criticized modern consumerism for all the standard reasons plus its foreign qualities. Consumerism could also be channeled into protest movements. In India and elsewhere by the 1920s boycotts of certain goods (in the case of Indian nationalists, British goods) showed an ability to restrain consumerism in the interests of political goals.

The intensification of consumerism initially took place in the West, led by the United States, with Japan following closely behind.

Department stores were already more elaborate than eighteenth-century shops, and more capable of manipulating popular desires. By the 1860s a new disease, kleptomania, marked the advance of consumerism: People, particularly middle-class women, stole items they did not need, simply because they had internalized the compulsion to acquire. Advertising, using new technologies and illustrations, became more sensual and ubiquitous. Formal advertising agencies arose in the United States in the 1870s. Middle-class people began to find consumerism increasingly acceptable, shifting interests away from hard work for its own sake. Many factory workers, dissatisfied with routine jobs, began to turn greater interest into money wages that could buy more goods and recreations—their lives, in other words, increasingly revolved around consumerism. Leisure began to turn to consumerism, with spectator sports and popular theater and soon the movies: Consumers as spectators began to purchase a great deal of leisure from commercial professionals. Consumerism also spread increasingly into childhood, with babies surrounded by consumer items such as teddy bears (named for U.S. president Teddy Roosevelt around 1900). Parents were advised to guide their children's consumerism, as well as use it as a motivation for good behavior. Advertisements began to target children directly, particularly as more children began receive allowances of money from their parents (a U.S. innovation of the 1890s).

By 1900 the influence of the American consumer culture began to influence consumerism elsewhere. The U.S. market grew larger

than European national markets, stimulated new consumer forms and interests, for example, mail order catalogues and the emergence of professional advertising agencies. Both blue and white collar workers became more interested in consumer satisfactions, though they were often portrayed as contributions to increased work capacity of family life. While American critics of consumerism were present, they had less tradition than those in Europe because of the less traditional social structure and culture of the U.S. Consumerism was now anchored firmly as a part of American life. It also contributed to products and models that were quickly adopted into consumer societies elsewhere, such as the "dime" store, movie houses, and consumer-oriented toys for children.

Intensifying consumerism hit global levels by the later twentieth century, and indeed the further expansion of consumerism became a key part of globalization. Japan and the West, including the United States, became centers for the export of popular styles; by 2003 the sale of "cool" products, such as music, animation, and electronic gadgets popular with youth, became the largest export category for Japan. Popular restaurant chains such as McDonald's, British and U.S. rock music, fashions such as blue jeans, and amusement resort chains such as Disneyland and Club Med showed the international currency of consumerism. Holidays began to be transformed: The Mexican middle class began to shift Halloween into a need to buy costumes and candy for the kids; Christmas buying spread to Islamic Istanbul; the purchase of gifts and greeting cards began to be part of Ramadan, the traditional Islamic celebration of abstinence.

That consumerism has its superficial side is obvious. It also, however, allows individuals and groups a new chance for expression, often outside the traditional power structure. This expression is part of its appeal to women and also, increasingly, to youth. A young man, interviewed in a Hong Kong McDonald's, perhaps best expressed the complexities involved in interpreting modern consumerism. He noted that he did not particularly like the fast food—he preferred traditional fare—but he loved to go to McDonald's just to see and be seen, to feel part of a larger international community. And he also didn't mind annoying his parents, who would have preferred that he eat with them at home.

Again, to be sure, resistance existed and continues to exist. Religious groups within Islam and elsewhere protested this foreign invasion of materialism. The evolution of consumerism continues to spark important cultural debates within many societies.

Consumerism has become a global phenomenon, but objections to consumerism remain and are stronger in some places than in others. For example, the United States and the Middle East, both societies with strong religious commitments, nevertheless express different levels of concern about consumer habits. Though religious leaders in both regions are concerned about undue materialism, the debate in Islam is more vigorous. American leadership in consumer tastes is not absolute; the Japanese for instance also play an important role in trend-setting. But the association of consumerism and Americanization is very strong, so that objections to consumerism, in many societies, easily generate objections to the United States in general, and vice versa. At the same time, admiration for the U.S. standard of living often vies with strong objections to, for example, U.S. governmental policy. The United States has played a large role in defining and disseminating the consumer society and because of this it is the subject of intense scrutiny.

Peter N. Stearns

See also Ecological Footprint, U.S.; Environmental Issues; McDonaldization; Media Corporations

Further Reading

Brewer, J., & Porter, R. (Eds.). (1993). *Consumption and the world of goods.* New York: Routledge.

Campbell, C. (1989). *The romantic ethic and the spirit of modern consumerism.* Oxford, UK: Basil Blackwell.

Skelton, T., & Valentine, G. (Eds.). (1997). *Cool places: Geographies of global youth culture.* London: Routledge.

Stearns, P. N. (2001). *Consumerism in world history: The global transformation of desire.* London: Routledge.

Tobin, J. (1992). *Re-made in Japan: Everyday life and consumer taste in a changing society.* New Haven, CT: Yale University Press.

Williams, R. (1982). *Dream worlds: Mass consumption in late nineteenth century France.* Berkeley: University of California Press.

Corruption, Political and Business

The close relationships between U.S. government and the U.S. businesses that influence the free market have created a global backlash, including the image of an overly-influenced, and occasionally corrupted, political system.

The United States is regarded as the home of free enterprise, a country in which market liberalism is cherished and the corporate sector thrives. Although the U.S. brand of free-market capitalism is widely celebrated, many beyond America's shores criticize the political influence of American business, arguing that corporate actors are able to subvert the public interest and, in some instances, corrupt the political process. Perhaps the most pervasive and influential example of such sentiments are found in populist accounts of the influence of American corporate interests in the formation of U.S. foreign policy including the Iraq War. For example, the works of Noam Chomsky (a U.S. citizen) have become a rallying point for international critics of American foreign policy with his book, *9–11* (2001), being translated into over twenty-five languages. Concerns about the influence of business and the extent of "money politics" in the United States also extend well beyond foreign policy. Indeed the proponents of campaign finance reform in mature liberal democracies such as Canada, Australia, and the United Kingdom are motivated by a desire to avoid American-style money politics and corporate lobbying. Despite such perceptions, it is important to note that all political systems are vulnerable to corruption and while it can be argued that the fragmented nature of political decision making in the United States combined with a liberal political culture provide significant opportunities for the promotion of private interests and corruption, this institutional vulnerability is also a strength because such practices are ultimately open to scrutiny from partisan opponents, rival government agencies and a host of effective public interest groups. The ability of such countervailing groups to limit corruption is one of the enduring strengths of U.S. democracy.

Defining Political Corruption

Political corruption has many dimensions and is itself a contested concept. At a general level political corruption can be regarded as conduct that promotes sectional interests and private gain at the expense of the general interest and the public good. However, identifying political conduct that promotes private interests over the public good is nearly impossible. For example, is it corrupt for a politician to promote the interests of a firm from which he or she has received a campaign donation? Or is that politician simply providing legitimate constituent services? A narrower view of corruption might focus on the legality of the conduct of state officials or of those trying to influence public decision making.

Yet, this type of legalistic definition of corruption overlooks a great deal of legal political activity that many people regard as being both unethical and contrary to the public interest. Narrower still is the view that political corruption occurs only when public officials gain an unlawful material advantage—a view expressed by President Richard Nixon in a private conversation with White House lawyer Charles Colson on the Watergate tapes. The president stated "they say it's the greatest corruption in history—that's baloney. Nobody stole anything. The whole point is nobody made any money" (Horsley 1974). Many shades of gray appear to exist. Ultimately what constitutes corrupt conduct will depend on historical patterns of political practice and prevailing norms regarding appropriate political conduct in a particular society at a given time. In this context we need to acknowledge that business is an extremely important and powerful political actor, in capitalist democracies generally, and in the United States in particular. Although we should expect business to exert significant influence, if this influence is excessive and is exercised by means that are either unlawful or fail to meet widely held standards of ethical behavior, then such influence constitutes political corruption.

Business and Politics: Corruption or Influence?

Because definitions of corruption are context dependent, we must understand key elements of the business-government relationship in the United States. The single most important feature of the U.S. state and of government-business relations is the significance of liberal political institutions and values. At an institutional level the U.S. state is built on the ideal of republican government, a system of government with clear constitutional divisions of power designed to protect the public interest from sectional domination. Although we could reasonably expect this constitutional design, with its emphasis on limiting state power, to provide a degree of protection from political corruption, ironically this fragmentation

The Enron building in downtown Houston, Texas, headquarters of the company at the center of one of the largest business corruption scandals in U.S. history. Source: istock/Nitin Sanil.

of power also tends to favor sectional interests generally and business in particular relative to collective concerns.

The U.S. political system is unique among those of advanced democracies in its relative lack of collectivist political institutions and forums. The bureaucracy is divided between federal and state jurisdictions and across a myriad of operationally specific agencies. This fragmentation of state agencies tends to limit political

independence of government, leaving it more vulnerable to the particular demands of powerful interest groups and firms. Business itself is not organized into coherent representative structures as is the case in many other advanced industrial economies. This fact tends to limit the potential for a more negotiated and deliberative approach to policymaking and often results in parochial lobbying from major stakeholders who compete with one another in a given policy arena. Often the best-resourced and best-connected interests prevail.

Perhaps most significantly, in many respects political parties in the United States are relatively weak. This weakness is especially true in terms of the discipline the parties hold over their parliamentary members. The fact that U.S. politicians regularly vote against their party leadership on controversial bills limits the ability of U.S. political parties to aggregate the competing interests of the many constituents they seek to represent. This situation makes it more difficult to implement a more balanced policy platform that is consistent with majority opinion.

In summary the U.S. state is highly fragmented, and the government-business relationship is pluralistic. Although this arrangement provides important insulation from systematic corruption of the political system, it provides opportunities for business to achieve political influence. Perhaps more than any other, the U.S. version of liberal democracy provides for a close relationship between politicians and their immediate constituents. This relationship in turn has created a culture in which politicians unashamedly promote the interests of local constituents, even at the expense of national policy objectives. Given this context, providing such "constituent services" should not be regarded as being corrupt. However, a close constituent-representative relationship can easily lead to politicians becoming overly dependent on powerful business interests to support and finance their political careers.

Taxation

Taxation is among the most invasive of all government activities, with tax policy decisions having the potential to make a massive impact on a company's bottom line. Under these circumstances it is hardly surprising that corporations invest significant political resources trying to gain commercial advantage under the tax code. Nowhere is this fact more apparent than in the United States. Taxation experts describe the U.S. taxation system as being one of the most "schedular" in the world, in that the tax code is riddled with industry-, regional-, and even firm-specific exemptions that have been inserted into the law by lawmakers representing various constituencies. One estimate put the total value of tax exemptions during the period from 2000 to 2004 at almost $400

billion. Although some exemptions may have a legitimate public policy purpose, many do not. Part of the problem with corporate tax exemptions is the lack of transparency around them because they are not subject to the same budget-reporting standards as expenditure items. Despite the enormous sums involved, it is all too often almost impossible to establish precisely who benefits from corporate tax expenditures.

Government Procurement

Another area in which people have expressed concerns about political corruption in the United States is government procurement. Beyond collecting taxes and regulating almost every aspect of commercial activity, modern governments are significant commercial actors in their own right. Although the United States does not have a history of state-owned enterprises, the government is a massive and increasing consumer of goods and services. Given the potential financial rewards associated with winning government contracts, some people have long been concerned that tendering firms will support particular candidates or political parties in the hope of influencing government contracting.

Perhaps the best-known analysis of the linkages between U.S. government and big business was C. Wright Mills's theory of the military-industrial complex, which in the 1950s argued that U.S. government had been captured by a small "power elite" dominated by the chiefs of large defense corporations. Mills claimed that politicians had become dependent on the defense industries for campaign support and patronage, effectively corrupting U.S. government and compromising foreign policy. Although Mills was writing almost a half-century ago, similar concerns have been expressed about the relationship between the administration of President George W. Bush and contractors involved in the reconstruction of Iraq.

Halliburton

A recent example of where U.S. defense procurement has attracted international attention are the claims that a subsidiary of the Halliburton corporation (which had been run by Vice President Dick Cheney until 2000) had been awarded contracts that could be worth an estimated $18 billion for logistical support and oil field reconstruction in Iraq on a "no-bid" basis. Although such claims of improper dealings between the Republican administration and the Halliburton corporation are, in part, the product of the partisan politics and Democrat-authored Congressional reports, a combination of the size of the contracts and the lack of transparency

associated with the tendering process left the Bush administration open to charges of political corruption.

Campaign Finance

Many business interests are extremely powerful. Large corporations in particular can channel investment into particular jurisdictions and provide high-profile endorsements of specific candidates or policy positions. However, the most direct means by which business can support a particular candidate or party is through the direct provision of financial contributions. From the perspective of politicians, securing financial support is becoming even more critical as the cost of running election campaigns escalates—some estimates for total U.S. campaign spending during the 2004 election year were as high as $4 billion. The concern here is that the more dependent candidates and political parties become on massive political donations, the more beholden they become to the

The Watergate building in Washington, DC, associated with the Nixon political scandal on the 1970s. Source: istock/ Daniella Zalcman.

donor's interests. This concern clearly has implications for the public interest in government.

The debate about campaign finance has a long history across the democratic world, and nowhere is this fact truer than in the United States as reformers have tried to reduce the scope and improve the disclosure of campaign finance for more than a century. Despite these initiatives to control campaign finance, political parties and their donors have continued to find means to legally fund political campaigns. Although the most recent attempt to rein in political donations closed "soft money" donations, this closure simply prompted both major political parties to devise new ways of subverting the system. For example, in the 2004 presidential election an estimated $386 million was raised and spent through groups that promoted strongly partisan views but that were not formally related to political parties or candidates and hence were exempt from the laws. Although the illegal funding of U.S. political campaigns is not widespread, the fact that U.S. campaign expenditure continues to grow perpetuates concerns that business donors will continue to exert excessive influence over U.S. government. Certainly Jeffrey Birnbaum's quip that the United States is the world's great "donocracy" continues to hold true.

The Future

The United States prides itself on being one of the world's great liberal democracies. Although, as in any political system, political corruption exists in the United States, a real virtue of the U.S. state, with its constitutional division of political power, is that corruption is unlikely to become systemic given that a number of public agencies can counter an abuse of power from within. The Watergate crisis during Nixon's administration was dealt with by a combination of a Senate committee and the Supreme Court, and the Halliburton case has been investigated by a number of agencies.

Ironically, however, this fragmentation of power and the absence of collectivist institutions leaves the U.S. political system open to the influence of sectional interests and, in extreme cases, corruption. Because U.S. politicians tend to act as independent representatives and because success in the U.S. political system requires significant financial resources, as the examples provided here demonstrate, incentives and opportunities will always exist for business in particular to subvert the political process.

Richard Eccleston

Further Reading

Bernstein, C., & Woodward, B. (1974). *All the president's men.* New York: Simon & Schuster.

Birnbaum, J. (2000). *The money men.* New York: Crown Publishers.

Center for Responsible Politics. (2004). '04 elections expected to cost nearly $4 billion. Retrieved February 9, 2007, from www.opensecrets.org/pressreleases/2004/04spending.asp

Chomsky, N. (2001). *9–11.* New York: Seven Stories Press.

Grossman, M. (2003). *Political corruption in America.* Santa Barbara, CA: ABC Clio.

Hacker, J., & Pierson, P. (2002). Business power and social policy: Employers and the formation of the American welfare state. *Politics and Society, 30*(2), pp. 277–325.

The heat is on Halliburton. (2004, June 26). *The Economist.*

Horsley, K. (1974). *The highlights of the Watergate tapes.* New York: Hawkes Publishers.

Johnston, M. (1982). *Political corruption and public policy in America.* Monterey, CA: Brooks & Cole.

Lowi, T. (1969). *The end of liberalism.* New York: Norton.

Martin, C. (1991). *Shifting the burden: The struggle over growth and corporate taxation.* Chicago: University of Chicago Press.

Mayer, K. (1991). *The political economy of defence contracting.* New Haven, CT: Yale University Press.

McSweeny, D. (2000). Parties, corruption and campaign finance in the United States. In R. Williams (Ed.), *Party finance and political corruption.* London: Macmillan.

Mills, C. (1956). *The power elite.* New York: Oxford University Press.

Nader, R. (2000). *Cutting corporate welfare.* New York: Seven Stories Press.

Olson, M. (1965). *The logic of collective action: Public goods and the theory of groups.* Cambridge, MA: Harvard University Press.

Peters, G. (1991). *The politics of taxation: A comparative perspective.* Cambridge, MA: Blackwell.

Steinmo, S. (1993). *Taxation and democracy: Swedish, British and American approaches to financing the modern state.* New Haven, CT: Yale University Press.

Two new reports criticize Halliburton's contracts in Iraq. (2004, July 21). *House of Representatives Press Release.*

Vogel, D. (1989). *Fluctuating fortunes: The political power of business in America.* New York: Basic Books.

Williams, R. (Ed.). (2000). *Party finance and political corruption.* London: Macmillan.

Wilson, G. (2003). *Business and politics: A comparative introduction* (3rd ed.). New York: Palgrave.

Cultural Diversity, U.S.

The U.S. population is an amalgamation of a diverse group of people. However, some believe that the United States has shifted away from the "melting pot" mentality, as more people embrace their "old country" cultures.

Cultural diversity in most societies has arisen from the migration of people from one part of the world to another over a long period of time. However, the United States has seen an unprecedented flux of people in less than two hundred years. This influx has led the United States to become one of the most culturally diverse nations in the world today. The racial/ethnic composition of the United States, out of a total population of 288,378,137 in the year 2000, is shown in Table 1.

The group that people refer to as "white" or "Caucasian" in the United States is a mixture of many European people, such as the English, Irish, German, French, and Spanish, which can be seen in the breakdown of the fifteen largest ancestries in the United States presented in Figure 1. Similarly, the Pacific Islanders comprise a wide variety of cultural groups, including Native Hawaiians, Chamorro, Samoans, Tongans, and Micronesians. Asians include Chinese, Filipinos, Japanese, Koreans, Vietnamese, and South Asian Indians. Hispanics or Latinos include Mexicans,

Puerto Ricans, Cubans, and others from South America. Diversity within the United States and how issues related to that diversity are addressed have important implications for both national and international relations.

Melting Pot

Societies deal with cultural diversity differently. For a long time the United States has been an example of the melting pot model in which different peoples of European descent adopted English as their language. Because the American colonies were British, English, the language of the empire, was readily adopted by non-English-speaking immigrants to the United States. The melting pot model evolved in the United States in this worldview, which assumed that it is ideal for a country to have a homogeneous culture. In this worldview people of different cultures are encouraged

Table 1. Racial/Ethnic Composition of the United States by Population and Percent

RACE/ETHNICITY	POPULATION	PERCENT	RACE/ETHNICITY	POPULATION	PERCENT
White	215,333,394	74.7	Native Hawaiian and other Pacific Islander	397,030	0.1
Black or African-American	34,962,569	12.1	Native Hawaiian	51,878	
American Indian and Alaska Native	2,357,544	0.8	Guamanian or Chamorro	76,062	
Cherokee tribal grouping	309,459		Samoan	56,736	
Chippewa tribal grouping	114,492		Other Pacific Islander	112,354	
Navajo tribal grouping	293,802		Some other race	17,298,601	6.0
Sioux tribal grouping	120,066		Two or more races	5,557,184	1.9
Asian	12,471,815	4.3	Hispanic or Latino (of any race)	41,870,703	14.5
Chinese	2,882,257		Mexican	26,781,547	
Filipino	2,282,872		Puerto Rican	3,781,317	
Japanese	833,761		Cuban	1,461,574	
Korean	1,246,240		Other Hispanic or Latino	9,846,265	
Vietnamese	1,418,334				
Other Asian	1,489,129				

Source: U.S. Census Bureau (2000).

Figure 1. Fifteen Largest Ancestries in the United States, 2000

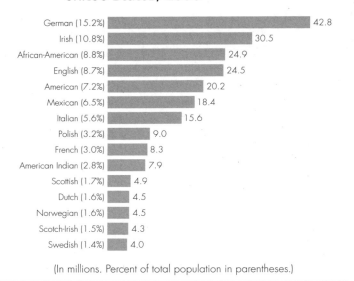

Ancestry	Millions
German (15.2%)	42.8
Irish (10.8%)	30.5
African-American (8.8%)	24.9
English (8.7%)	24.5
American (7.2%)	20.2
Mexican (6.5%)	18.4
Italian (5.6%)	15.6
Polish (3.2%)	9.0
French (3.0%)	8.3
American Indian (2.8%)	7.9
Scottish (1.7%)	4.9
Dutch (1.6%)	4.5
Norwegian (1.6%)	4.5
Scotch-Irish (1.5%)	4.3
Swedish (1.4%)	4.0

(In millions. Percent of total population in parentheses.)

Source: U.S. Census Bureau (2000).

to surrender their differences in favor of a "mainstream" language, norms, work ethic, and so forth, that is, one culture, and in effect immigrants to the country are expected to assimilate into the host culture. For example, many people in Germany expect migrants from Turkey and other countries to assimilate by accepting the German language and culture and thus subscribe to this model. Other countries maintain homogeneity by shutting out people who are different from their own. For example, Japan has refused to receive migrants on the grounds that they will reduce the quality of life in that society.

Psychologists posit that humans strive for optimal distinctiveness, which amounts to maintaining a delicate balance between the forces toward assimilation and merging with groups and the forces toward differentiation from groups. From this theoretical perspective people are unlikely to totally assimilate, as was assumed in the melting pot model. What would be optimal for a person depends both on idiosyncratic factors and on cultural factors that shape that person. For example, people living in a multicultural society are likely to have a higher tolerance for differences than are people living in homogeneous cultures, and thus they may be comfortable having multiple identities simultaneously assimilating in different groups depending on the context.

The United States is undergoing a social shift away from the melting pot model to the multicultural model or what can be termed the "salad bowl" metaphor, in which every ingredient in a salad bowl retains its distinctive quality, and the distinctive

qualities add to each other. The model of multiculturalism assumes that each cultural group can preserve much of its original culture without interfering with the smooth functioning of the society. The spirit of multiculturalism requires, ideally, that each person develop a good deal of understanding of the point of view of members of the other cultures and learn to make attributions concerning the causes of behavior of members of the other cultures that are more or less like the attributions that these members make in explaining their own behavior. Many cities in the world are becoming increasingly multicultural, and according to the 2000 U.S. Census, Hawaii is the state in which the largest number of people claimed to belong to more than one ethnic ancestry. Thus, Hawaii may be in the vanguard of a demographic shift that may transform the world into a salad bowl in which each ingredient has its own unique characteristic but is part of something larger that values diversity.

History of Conflict between Majority and Minority Groups

The history of conflict between two ethnic groups is an important antecedent of perceived dissimilarity, and a policy of multiculturalism helps address this dissimilarity through dialogues. Having such dialogues between various ethnic groups in the United States is a characteristic of U.S. democratic and liberal society. However, a strong undercurrent causes conflicts between various ethnic groups from time to time. And these conflicts shape not only the mindsets of immigrants to the United States but also the national policies of the countries they come from. For example, the lingering conflict between whites and African-Americans can be traced back to slavery, which started right after the Western settlers arrived in North America. Despite the legal freedom of blacks since 1865, it took one hundred years and a civil rights movement to provide equal rights to African-Americans. Often subtle, but sometimes open, discrimination against African-Americans still is prevalent. The history of conflict and the recurrence of discrimination in the workplace and in other domains of social life cause tension between whites and African-Americans as well as immigrants from Africa.

The very foundation of the United States is mired in ethnic conflicts because European settlers decimated the Native Americans and drove them away from their lands to reservations. When European settlers arrived in North America, it was populated by more than ten million Native Americans; only one-fifth of that number remains today. Most of the Native Americans were victims of disease that white settlers brought, and many others were killed in the wars that settlers created to capture resources.

The U.S. government formally adopted a policy of Indian removal in 1825, motivated by the desire to capture Native American lands that contained gold and other minerals. This policy led to the forced removal of the Cherokee, Chickasaws, Choctaws, Creeks, and Seminoles in 1833. The entire Cherokee tribe was forced to move from Georgia by the U.S. government under the leadership of Presidents Andrew Jackson and Martin Van Buren despite the Supreme Court ruling against moving Native Americans from their homeland. Of the sixteen thousand Cherokees who were forced to move from Georgia to the settlements in Oklahoma, about four thousand died along the 1,600-kilometer trek. The Cherokees walked for a year to move to Oklahoma, and the trail they followed is referred to as the "Trail of Tears" because of their hardship and loss of life. Later, at the Sand Creek Massacre in Colorado on 29 November 1864, more than two hundred Southern Cheyennes and Arapahos were killed despite the fact that their leader, Black Kettle, raised the flag of peace as well as the flag of the United States. Such events have led people to call the killing of Native Americans the "American Genocide"; this history continues to be an obstacle to peace between Native Americans and the white majority.

Despite the culture of openness guaranteed by the democratic system and the free press in the United States, a history of conflict between ethnic groups leads to misunderstanding between people coming from different parts of the world to make a home here. Culture is transmitted through generations orally, and significant historical milestones often shape the worldview of people and their perspectives on other ethnic groups. For example, the Chinese Exclusion Act of 1882 prevented Chinese immigrants from entering the United States for ten years, but extensions of the act prevented Chinese immigrants from entering the United States and from becoming naturalized citizens for more than sixty years until passage of the Chinese Exclusion Repeal Act in 1943. More than one hundred years have passed since the exclusion act was promulgated, but it remains a source of misunderstanding between Caucasians and Chinese immigrants.

Racial prejudices can be amplified during difficult times, and this fact was reflected in the war hysteria and failure of leadership during World War II, which led to internment of Japanese-Americans in the United States. The internment of Japanese-Americans, authorized by Executive Order 9066 issued by President Franklin D. Roosevelt, affected more than one hundred thousand Japanese-Americans. Worse, the Supreme Court upheld the constitutionality of this presidential decision in 1944. A formal apology from the U.S. government came during the administration of President Ronald Reagan in 1988. The Japanese-American community still lives with this nightmare.

The Hispanic community also has had a history of conflict with the white majority. The Mexican-American War (1846–1848) is an important historical marker between Mexico and the United States. That war was fought over Texas and led to Mexico losing a large area of its territory, which included what is today California, New Mexico, Colorado, Arizona, Wyoming, Nevada, and Utah, to the United States under the Treaty of Guadalupe Hidalgo. Many of the battles fought in Texas have different symbolic meaning for Mexican-Americans and Caucasians. Similarly, other Latinos have their own history of conflict with the United States. Because of this history Latinos can have difficulty trusting Caucasians.

Native Hawaiians were the original inhabitants of Hawaii, but over the years they have become a minority group, and today they are a marginalized cultural group in what once was their own country. The Native Hawaiian culture went through five

A diverse U.S. business team sits at an office conference table. Source: istock/Jeffrey Smith.

phases of cultural erosion—loss of population, loss of religion, loss of land, loss of language, and loss of political power. When Captain Cook arrived in Hawaii in 1778, 300,000 to 800,000 Native Hawaiians lived on the islands. The Native Hawaiian population was decimated by the diseases that white people brought. In 1819 the traditional Kapu system of laws and regulations was abolished; in 1848 land reform allowed white settlers to purchase land from the natives; in 1896 the Hawaiian language was banned in school; and in 1898 the Hawaiian monarchy was overthrown, despite a treaty between the monarch and the U.S. government. Hawaii was annexed by the United States in 1950. However, a strong sovereignty movement exists in Hawaii. Texas and California may be integrated into the United States, but Hawaii is still struggling for freedom after the illegal annexation by the United States.

The Future

In view of the history of conflict between the majority and various minority groups in the United States, we can understand that strong undercurrents of mistrust exist among minority communities. The occasional events of discrimination in the workplace, racial slurs, and hate crimes that members of minority communities experience further crystallize and bolster their minority identity and the associated prejudice against the majority community. It is perhaps surprising that minority groups and their cultural practices flourish in the United States despite such strong histories of conflict. The democratic system, freedom of speech and press, and the symbolization of the many economic success stories of people from all ethnic communities in the United States are evidence that the social system is quite fair and that the system does allow everybody to pursue his or her dream. Cultural diversity in the United States is clearly progressing toward positive multiculturalism against all odds.

Dharm P. S. Bhawuk

See also American Dream

Further Reading

Brewer, M. B. (1991). The social self: On being the same and different at the same time. *Personality and Social Psychology Bulletin, 17,* 475–482.

Legters, L. (1988). The American genocide. *Policy Studies Journal, 16*(4), 768–777.

Robinson, G. (2001). *By order of the president: FDR and the internment of Japanese Americans.* Cambridge, MA: Harvard University Press.

Seiden, A. (2004). *The Hawai'ian monarchy.* Honolulu, HI: Mutual.

Silva, N. (2004). *Aloha betrayed: Native Hawai'ian resistance to American colonialism.* Durham, NC: Duke University Press.

Triandis, H. C., Kurowski, L. L., & Gelfand, M. J. (1994). Workplace diversity. In H. C. Triandis, M. D. Dunnette, & L. M. Hough (Eds.), *Handbook of industrial and organizational psychology: Vol. 4* (2nd ed., pp. 767–827). Palo Alto, CA: Consulting Psychologists Press.

U.S. Census Bureau. (2000). Census 2000: Demographic profile highlights. Retrieved April 12, 2007, from http://factfinder.census.gov

Zangwill, I. (1914). *The melting pot: Drama in four acts.* New York: Macmillan.

Culture Overseas, U.S.

American popular culture—including music, fashion, and sport—is ubiquitous overseas. This widespread familiarity has brought both love, and contempt, for the American way of life.

When the Berlin Wall was demolished in 1989, a precursor to the dissolution of the Soviet Union in 1991, some Americans took it as a confirmation that capitalism and the U.S. way of life were the optimal economic system and style of living. American conventional wisdom had strong ideas about what made a successful state: privatization of government services, free trade, an unregulated business environment, shareholder value as the primary measure of corporate executive performance, and the marketplace as the determinant of the value and lasting worth of virtually any good or service. The demise of Communist and socialist systems at the end of the Cold War left the United States as the sole remaining superpower and neocapitalism the dominant economic system. As such, U.S. culture has been embraced and reviled for all that it has come to symbolize as well as for its impact in the world.

Impact of U.S. Culture Abroad

There are many definitions of culture. Geert Hofstede, a Dutch psychologist, defined it as "the collective programming of the mind which distinguishes the members of one human group from another" (Hofstede 1984, 21). U.S. culture as experienced in the United States by Americans is, however, very different from U.S. culture as experienced abroad by non-Americans, either through its representation in the media or through interaction with Americans living abroad. A culture is viewed and experienced most fully in its home environment. When others try to make sense of U.S. culture through symbols and products from the United States, the behavior of Americans they see, or news reports about the acts of the government of the United States around the world, inevitably a distorted picture emerges. What is vitally important, however, is not the veracity of the perspectives, but the perspectives themselves and the possible reasons for their existence.

The ubiquity of U.S. culture, U.S. political influence, and the dominance of U.S. economic interests in a variety of forms inevitably lead those in the rest of the world to develop a love-hate relationship with things American. Like it or not, deliberate or otherwise, the United States is now engaged in the world as an empire. Its economic standing drives the world's economy, its national interests, its preferred form of world trade and develop-

ment, and its inhabitants' urge to satisfy their wanderlust, propel U.S. corporations, soldiers, and tourists into every hamlet on the planet. Whether it is the U.S. presence in Saudi Arabia that angers fundamentalist Muslims, U.S. energy companies in Myanmar (Burma), Nigeria, and elsewhere that inflame the tempers of human rights and environmental activists, or American tourists in Mexico that offend local sensibilities with indecorous behavior during a college spring break, the presence of Americans alters the psychological, economic, and cultural landscape in the communities in which they alight.

The scholars Margaret and Melvin DeFleur surveyed over 1,200 middle-class high school students in twelve countries and found that those young people were "convinced, for example, that [Americans] are violent, materialistic and want to dominate other people. On the whole they believe that [Americans] do not respect people unlike [themselves], are not generous, are not concerned about the poor, that [Americans] lack strong family values and are not peaceful. They also believe many [Americans] engage in criminal activities and many American women are sexually immoral" (DeFleur and DeFleur 2002). The source of these beliefs, according to the DeFleurs, is the mass communications media, which thrive everywhere on the sensational and the unusual. The sale of U.S. entertainment in the forms of music CDs, movie DVDs, programming via satellite, cable, the Internet; and, increasingly, copycat styles of nightclubs, video game parlors, and lifestyle magazines all over the world magnify the perception of the U.S. presence. Violence, public sexual symbols and behavior, profanity, and rebelliousness simultaneously become the fashion and are perceived as what is wrong with the United States. There is a type of cultural schizophrenia at work. While the youth gravitate to the latest pop cultural icons from the United States, the elites decry the results of the influence such imports have. But it is also the elites who profit from their importation, both financially and by expanding their own identity as global citizens who increasingly share the language of modernity with the United States.

The U.S. Role in World Politics

In the first decade of the twenty-first century, U.S. culture and the U.S. role in the world is rated more unfavorably by the rest of the

world than it has been since World War II and possibly since its founding. Ironically, the devastatingly negative perception of the United States follows on the world's outpouring of sympathy and its expressed positive feeling in the aftermath of the September 11, 2001, attacks on the World Trade Center in New York City and the Pentagon in Washington, D.C. The results of a survey reported in the *Guardian* (U.K.) show "that in Australia, Britain, Canada, France, Japan, Spain and South Korea a majority of voters share a rejection of the Iraq invasion, contempt for the Bush administration, a growing hostility to the US . . . But they all make a clear distinction between this kind of anti-Americanism and expressing a dislike of American people. On average 68% of those polled say they have a favorable opinion of Americans. The 10-country poll suggests that rarely has an American administration faced such isolation and lack of public support amongst its closest allies" (Travis 2004, 4).

We should remember, however, that although today the United States is the avatar of modernity and the target for both the respect and resentment that comes with sole superpower status, the United States is just the most recent in a long succession of Western "Great Powers." One hundred years ago the British empire, upon which "the sun never set," dominated the globe.

U.S. Business and Trade Practices

For many years, U.S. business practice overseas was typified by images of sweat shops where indigenous women and children were paid insignificant wages to produce cheap goods for the West that were nevertheless beyond the reach of the local workers. Free trade, championed by the United States, has often been seen as a one-way street, with the United States criticizing developing countries' attempts to protect their infant industries but quick to protect its own. Anti-globalization campaigns have attempted to convert free trade into fair trade; campaigners have enjoined multinational corporations to pay local people a living wage and to offer them the same rights and privileges afforded labor in the developed world.

U.S. companies' increasing practice of outsourcing professional services, so unpopular in the United States itself, has created a favorable perception of U.S. culture in the receiving countries. In the high-tech back offices of U.S. companies in India, for example, many Indians find opportunities where previously there were none. In Chennai (Madras), India, for example, because U.S. companies hire on the basis of talent and not caste, they have brought relief to young Indian professionals by reversing a millennia-old practice of discrimination that excluded otherwise qualified individuals.

According to Katherine Boo, a senior fellow at the New America Foundation, "The Americanization of Chennai has been so swift and . . . so quiet that many of its citizens do not yet grasp the change in their cultural and literal landscape. An animation company makes cartoons seen by American children on Saturday mornings. Radiologists read American MRIs, clerks adjudicate patients' insurance claims, and programmers automate Medicaid eligibility for an entire Midwestern state. Chartered accountants complete U.S. tax returns while underwriters certify U.S. mortgages" (Boo 2004, 57).

To employees of Office Tiger (the U.S. outsourcing firm Boo studied) and the many Indian employees and their families and communities that are benefiting from U.S. outsourcing, their glimpse of U.S. culture is unique and thought provoking, since they see in great detail the contours of a significant slice of typical U.S. life as it is experienced at home.

U.S. Products

U.S. tourists discover that even if they travel to such remote locations as the "golden triangle," where Thailand, Myanmar, and Laos meet, they are likely to stumble across an advertisement for Coca-Cola tacked to a tree or to find that their guide is smoking a Marlboro cigarette, wearing Levi's jeans, and a New York Yankees baseball cap. U.S. logos and consumer products are everywhere, and recent anti-globalization protests may indicate that some people have reached a psychological saturation point even if the market has room for more. McDonald's seems to be the corporation most critics love to hate: It represents so much about the U.S. cultural juggernaut that critics find offensive, whether because of the visibility of their golden arches in 120 countries, their less-than-healthy menu choices, or their product and behavioral standardization. Jose Bove, a onetime French farmer and longtime anti-globalization activist, ransacked a half-completed McDonald's in a protest against bad food and U.S. trade policy that hurt French farmers. He gained further recognition in North America as a critic of genetically modified foods and led demonstrations in Brazil against Monsanto, a U.S. multinational chemical company that has pioneered genetically modified foods.

Despite those protests, however, people outside the United States show a great fondness for U.S. products, both tangible and intangible. They choose to eat at McDonald's, compete to study at a U.S. school abroad, watch MTV to find out the latest music hits and teen fashions, tune in to CNN for international news updates, enjoy a trip to a Disney theme park in Paris, Hong Kong, or Tokyo, and turn out in huge numbers to watch an exhibition

game of professional U.S. basketball teams in China because they enjoy the experience.

Perceptions of Americans

U.S. tourists also affect how others view U.S. culture. When Americans travel, their body language, verbal expression, manner of relating to local people, behavior toward one another, and appearance all send messages that observers receive and use to form impressions of U.S. culture. Americans abroad are street-level ambassadors, whether they like it or not. They are instant symbols of whatever the perceiver imagines the United States to be, but they also influence that mental construct, and if they are open and communicative, respectful, and sensitive to local manners, they may make local people's impressions of the United States more favorable.

There is much about Americans that people in the rest of the world generally admire: Americans' sense of humor, openness, ease at communicating with others, willingness to experience the world and alter traditions, innovate and create new things, and voluntarily organize to solve mutual problems and share mutual interests are sources of admiration. Creating the world's first modern republic, being the first to successfully rebel against a colonial power, establishing a system of checks and balances in the governance structure, and disestablishing the church from the state are considered enlightened accomplishments. Though there are those who take issue with those qualities and actions, for people who value choice, self-determination, and freedom, the United States has been the standard.

People also admire Americans' innovation: moon landings, polio vaccines, personal computers—Americans have been at the leading edge of pure and applied scientific research. In fact, the very idea of being an American is largely understood to mean anyone living in the United States regardless of ethnic origin or family roots who can either be a documented resident, or a native or naturalized citizen. The willingness of the U.S. to recognize and welcome talent from all places on Earth has caused a "brain drain" from places less hospitable to divergent, creative and independent thinking. America has much to be grateful for when considering the vast contributions of its immigrant population Further, the world scientific community has appreciated the U.S. tradition of sharing information and its contributions to the world's storehouse of knowledge. Americans working abroad have exemplified this. While in some ways violating local norms of secrecy, privilege, and hierarchy, the can-do, let's-focus-on-results-first approach has also been admired, and thousands of students from all parts of the globe have flocked to graduate schools in the United States.

The other side of the coin, however, is that expatriate Americans are often perceived as loud, impatient, demanding, and dangerously ethnocentric. Their comparative advantage in the world has led many Americans to believe that therefore they are right, best, valid, while the other is less than developed, inferior, backward. The flash and loudness, the swagger and sense of entitlement, the offensiveness of disregarding, discounting, and failing to respect local customs and practices is too frequently observable. Non-Americans also dislike Americans' reliance on agreements and contracts and their legalistic approach to business relationships at the expense of the personal relationships that in most societies form the ultimate basis for business trust and keeping commitments.

Looking Forward

Perceptions change over time. While apparently at their nadir at the moment, perceptions of U.S. culture abroad seem to change readily according to U.S. behavior on the world stage. With a prolonged positive reversal of recent U.S. behavior, it is possible that the perceptions of U.S. culture held by the rest of the world may change for the better.

John Nirenberg

See also Imperialism, U.S.; McDonaldization; Missionaries; Modernity, United States and; Overseas Americans (Expatriates); Peace Corps; Pop Culture—U.S. Advertising; Pop Culture—U.S. Film; Pop Culture—U.S. Music (Hip Hop); Pop Culture—U.S. Music (Jazz); Pop Culture—U.S. Television; Sports; Tourism

Further Reading

Abramsky, S. (2004, July 23). Waking up from the American dream. *The Chronicle of Higher Education, 50*(46), B9–B10. Retrieved January 12, 2005, from http://chronicle.com/free/v50/i46/46b00901.htm

Boas, F. (1920). Methods of ethnology. *American Anthropologist, 22,* 311–322.

Boo, K. (2004, July 5). The best job in town. *The New Yorker,* 54–69.

DeFleur, M., & DeFleur, M. L. (2002, October 17). Why they hate us. *Global Beat Syndicate.* Retrieved January 12, 2005, from http://www.lengel.net/gbs/image/hateus.html

Hofstede, G. (1984). *Cultures consequences: International differences in work-related values.* Beverley Hills, CA: Sage.

Huntington, S. (1996). *The clash of civilizations.* New York: Simon & Schuster.

Klein, N. (2000). *No logo.* New York: Picador.

Lederer, W., & Burdick, E. (1958). *The ugly American.* New York: Norton.

Stewart, E., & Bennett, M. J. (1991). *American cultural patterns: A cross-cultural perspective.* Yarmouth, ME: Intercultural Press.

Travis, A. (2004, October 15). We like Americans, we don't like Bush. *The Guardian,* 4. Retrieved January 12, 2005, from http://www.guardian. co.uk/uselections2004/viewsofamerica/story/0,15221,1327568,00. html

Wagnleitner, R., & Tyler, M. (Eds.). (2000). *Here there and everywhere: The foreign politics of American culture.* Hanover, NH: University Press of New England.

Democracy

Democracy is often described as an ideal system where freedom is seen in the highest regard. But as the United States "spreads" democracy around the globe it has become a rallying point for those opposed to U.S. culture and politics.

The United States has the oldest democratic constitution in the world. For much of the history of that constitution it has inspired democratic movements throughout the world, and emergent democracies often imitate its key provisions while adapting them to local conditions. Even when U.S. foreign and domestic policies prove less popular, the U.S. democratic constitution is often admired.

Yet, democracy consists of more than a constitution and laws. It also consists of the values of a political culture that help to create and sustain those laws. The French writer Alexis de Tocqueville (1805–1859), in his influential *Democracy in America*, wrote that U.S. democracy is the product both of laws and of mores (political culture) as well as the geographic circumstances of the United States. People's perceptions of U.S. democracy depend on which of the three dimensions they focus on. Whereas the Constitution is popular, people are more likely to criticize the United States' political culture and its particular approach to human rights, equality, economics, and political values. For example, the Iranian reformer Abdolkarim Soroush (b. 1945) praises the institutional devices of democracy that promote freedom, including separation of powers, elections, checks and balances, as well as the freedom of the press and intellectual freedom. However, he argues that the Western world lacks sufficient moral character, or what he calls "internal freedom," to ensure that those institutional devices produce a just society: "In the Western world we see injustice, colonialism, and arrogance toward other countries alongside the pursuit of liberty. There is external freedom, but no one is interested in internal freedom" (Soroush 2000, 104). Soroush reflects a common view outside the United States that the institutional and legal devices of the United States are exemplary, but its political culture cannot necessarily be followed. Outside the English-speaking world, perceptions of U.S. democracy have been shaped by cultural considerations. Conversely, observers from the English-speaking world have shown a greater likelihood to consider democracy in its constitutional sense.

Meaning of Democracy

Democracy is a form of government that dates back to ancient Athens. Historically the term *democracy* signified a corrupt form of government in which the rule of the people was unrestrained by law or by other groups. According to Aristotle (384–322 BCE), democracy, understood as unrestrained rule by the many, is as bad if not worse than tyranny, which is unrestrained rule by a single ruler. The founders of the United States preferred the term *republic* instead, and today people usually use the term *liberal democracy* to signify the mixture of democratic sovereignty of the people with the liberal and antimajoritarian principle of securing rights and freedoms.

People today give democracy a wide variety of meanings and labels, including "liberal democracy," "people's democracy," "representative democracy," "republic," "compound republic," "commercial republic," "procedural democracy," "deliberative democracy," "participatory democracy," and "cosmopolitan democracy." These labels emphasize central characteristics of democratic rule, including the degree to which it represents and is responsive to popular will, the degree to which popular will is informed by deliberation and counsel, and how much power "the people" hold and how much is checked by nonpopular institutions, including a monarch or judiciary. Central to all of these labels is the insight that democracy is a form of government that requires maximal expression of people's values that must be combined with institutional restraints and devices that ensure respect for rights and freedoms.

The founders of the United States considered numerous historical examples of democracy when they framed the Constitution. Ancient Athens was the primary example of a political society based on equality and liberty, but the founders considered also the Roman republic, the Netherlands, Poland, and, of course, Great Britain. They weighed the strengths and weaknesses of each democracy, considering the degree to which each secured popular sovereignty, how well each balanced deliberative and administrative powers, and how well each balanced stability and freedom.

Central to the founders' concerns, however, was framing a constitution that is democratic but that does not sow the seeds of its own destruction. To further this end, they distinguished between a democracy and a republic. Writing in *Federalist No. 10*, James Madison (1751–1836) distinguished a democracy from a republic in two crucial ways. First, a republic delegates representatives to "refine and enlarge the public views" (Hamilton, Jay, and Madison 2001, 46–49). The founders understood democracy as majoritarian,

populist, and dangerous to liberties. Conversely, a republic constrains popular will with laws and representative institutions that check and balance one another as much as they check and balance popular will. Representative institutions allow for enhanced opportunities for measured and informed deliberation. Second, democracies have historically been small, and the United States was from its origin a large and commercial society. The ancient ideal of universal political participation of the citizenry is impractical in a large commercial society. Even so, an expanded republic has the additional benefit of diversity, which decreases the probability that a single majority can tyrannize minorities. An expanded republic would be composed of a plurality of minorities, none of whom could dominate the others: "The smaller the society, the fewer probably will be the distinct parties and interests composing it; the fewer the distinct parties and interests, the more frequently will a majority be found of the same party. . . . Extend the sphere, and you take in a greater variety of parties and interests; you make it less probable that a majority of the whole will have a common motive to invade the rights of other citizens" (Hamilton, Jay, and Madison 2001, 47–48). The founders recognized that a republic intertwines representative institutions with a large society exhibiting a diverse range of interests and values in its political culture. Keeping the distinction between institution and political culture in mind, we turn now to international perspectives on U.S. democracy, which have traditionally focused on culture.

Democratic Circumstances, Laws, and Mores

Perhaps the best-known and most influential account of democracy in the United States, by either an American or a non-American, is Tocqueville's *Democracy in America*, which he published in two volumes in the first half of the nineteenth century. In that account he argues that democracy in the United States is maintained by three principal causes: (1) its particular geographical and historical situation, (2) its laws and institutions, and (3) its habits and mores (or culture). "Providence," he felt, had blessed the United States with geographic distance from Europe as well as a sparsely populated continent to settle, making the establishment and maintenance of democracy easier than in Europe, where hostile neighbors and nondemocratic traditions made creating a new form of government extremely difficult. Even so, the particular genius of U.S. democracy resides in its laws and in the "habits and mores," or political culture of its people.

Tocqueville singles out three aspects of U.S. laws as particularly

The Statue of Liberty in New York harbor. Source: istock/Natalie Helbert.

effective in maintaining democracy. First, the federal division of powers between the national and state governments is critical to maintain the power of an extended republic while maintaining the security of a small one. For Tocqueville the size of the state creates a potential danger in which the system's checks and balances on factions will render them too powerless and make individuals dependent on a central state. The federal system allows people to participate in and exercise effective political power in smaller political units like the states, which (1) provide a counterbalance to the national government and (2) give a wider range of people experience in political participation than the national government alone can provide. Second, Tocqueville felt that self-government finds its purest expression in townships, where the fruits of self-government can be seen most directly because people there govern the place that encapsulates their day-to-day existence. Finally, the judiciary restrains the popular will by asserting the power of the Constitution.

Tocqueville extensively analyzed the intellectual and moral dispositions, or mores, of Americans. Religion, he felt, is foremost among the mores sustaining democracy. Unlike fellow Europeans who associated religion, especially the Roman Catholic church, with monarchy, Tocqueville argues that U.S. forms of individualistic religiosity contribute to democratic culture. Religion restrains and elevates their materialistic passions and encourages Americans to think of the common good and to be beneficent toward others. The separation of church and state strengthens religion because it is no longer associated with a particular political position and thus can express itself in purer forms. Common sense and pragmatic intellectual habits and attitudes also maintain democracy because anyone can determine whether something "works," which contributes to the ability of everyone to participate in self-government. This situation differs from that in Europe, whose traditions and public intellectual and ecclesiastical authorities are not open to being challenged, much less understood.

Tocqueville also analyzed mores that undermine democracy. The principal one that corrodes democracy is individualism, for which he provides a relatively precise definition: "Individualism is a reflective and peaceable sentiment that disposes each citizen to isolate himself from the mass of those like him and to withdraw to one side with his family and his friends, so that after having thus created a little society for his own use, he willingly abandons society at large to itself" (Tocqueville 2000, 482). Individualism is related but not reduced to self-interested commercial activity because it is influenced as well by intellectual habits and the individual's perception of his or her equality vis-à-vis others. Individualism involves the constriction of public space around the individual who finds his or her freedom in mass society difficult to bear. Tocqueville anticipates the twentieth-century sentiment of the "lonely

crowd" in which individuals become lost and anonymous in mass society because of the difficulties of maintaining community and of sensing the significance of one's individual life.

PREAMBLE TO THE CONSTITUTION OF THE UNITED STATES OF AMERICA

The preamble to the U.S. Constitution written in 1787 outlined the basic purpose of establishing a democracy and has since served as inspiration for the development of democratic systems around the world.

We the people of the United States, in order to form a more perfect union, establish justice, insure domestic tranquility, provide for the common defense, promote the general welfare, and secure the blessings of liberty to ourselves and our posterity, do ordain and establish this Constitution for the United States of America.

Source: The National Archives experience. (n.d.). Retrieved March 19, 2007, from http://www.archives.gov/national-archives-experience/charters/constitution_transcript.html

Focus on Culture

Of the three causes sustaining democracy—circumstances, laws, and mores—Tocqueville identifies mores, or culture, as the most important, while also noting the crucial influence of the other two, especially laws. He is unusual in this respect because most foreign critics of the United States have focused on its culture, whereas its earliest critics in the eighteenth century focused on its geography. Tocqueville regarded mores as having an important influence on laws, while the majority of interpreters regarded mores as determinative of laws because they were influenced by modern scientific and monocausal theories of human behavior that state that politics is determined by nonpolitical variables: "American discourse has been instrumental to efforts to remove political science from a central position and to replace it with a rival discipline: first 'natural history' (biology), then a deductive or abstract modern social science, then history, then aesthetics, and finally, today, postmetaphysical philosophy and literary and cultural criticism" (Ceaser 1997, 13). Whereas Tocqueville balances the political and cultural components of democracy in his analysis, for most other international observers since the founding of the United States, democracy has been restricted to its cultural dimension.

If Tocqueville considers circumstances and geography as merely

TOCQUEVILLE AND U.S. DEMOCRACY

Alexis de Tocqueville (1805–1859) is most famous for his work *Democracy in America*. This two volume book stemmed from a visit to America in 1831, which was set up for Tocqueville by the French government. The trip was originally intended to retrieve information about U.S. prisons; however, during visits to cities such as Boston, New York, Philadelphia, and New Orleans, he began to make critical observations about the United States.

After a nine-month stay in the United States, Tocqueville published the first volume of *Democracy in America* which portrayed his fascination with American politics, and focused on the success of the American form of government. Tocqueville believed that the United States was of

such great interest "because, there, the future could be studied in the present . . . to understand America in 1830 . . . would be to understand, also, the future in Europe" (Higonnet, 1976). Tocqueville maintained a relatively positive view not necessarily of America's culture, but of its political system. It was Tocqueville's belief that the French government could be improved by following the American example.

Source: Higonnet, P. (1976) Alexis de Tocqueville, 1805–1859. In Marc Pachter, (Ed.), Abroad in America: Visiators to the new nation, 1776–1914 (pp. 53–61). Reading, MA: Addison-Wesley.

among the variables promoting democracy in the United States, eighteenth-century natural historians George Louis Leclerc (commonly known as the "Count de Buffon") (1707–1788) and Cornelius de Pauw (1739–1799) developed racial and environmental theories to explain the "degeneracy" of the United States. De Pauw, for instance, argues that the climate in the United States produces sluggishness that in the end undermines self-government. He advocates deforestation and draining of marshes to increase political and economic vitality (Ceaser 1997, 38).

According to James Ceaser,

[T]he connection between politics and culture in America discourse was forged in the political and philosophical debates over the French Revolution. On the Left, defenders of the French Revolution sought to distinguish it from the American Revolution, which they argued was grounded on the principle of interest and on a defective understanding of modern thought. . . . On the Right, the conservatives opposing the French Revolution chose to view the American and French Revolutions as twin embodiments of modern rationalist thought. . . . [I]f America was not anarchic, it was at any rate banal. It had no art, no taste, no depth. Nothing built on the shaky ground of reason and rights could ever support an impressive cultural edifice. (Ceaser 1997, 11)

Defenders of the French Revolution argued that it was driven by what Condorcet (1743–1794) calls the "new philosophy," according to which rational thought "derived its conclusions more from abstract speculation than from an acquaintance with the facts of a particular time and place" (Ceaser 1997, 71). As a result, these defenders rejected the pragmatism and religiosity of the American Revolution as superstitious, backward, and base because they thought democracy and freedom need a scientific foundation more elevated than self-interest. Condorcet argues in his *Sketch for an Historical*

Picture of the Progress of the Human Mind that the human race moves through ten stages in its history toward a realm of freedom. The French Revolution surpassed the American Revolution as a purer expression of democratic rule. He gives the principle of separation of powers as an example of the deficient democracy of the United States. For Condorcet and other figures of the French Enlightenment (a philosophic movement of the eighteenth century marked by a rejection of traditional social, religious, and political ideas and an emphasis on rationalism), only the Pennsylvania constitution, with its unicameral legislature, appealed to their rationalist views that required democracy to be a pure sovereignty. They did not share the U.S. founders' skepticism of pure democracy and their desire to place institutional checks and balances on government because Condorcet and other figures of the French Enlightenment prized pure theory over experience. Pure sovereignty appealed to their sense of rationalism more than the U.S. separation of powers system, which was predicated on human attributes in addition to rationality, including self-interest, passion, and ambition.

Defenders of the French Revolution rejected the American Revolution as too pragmatic, whereas conservative critics of the American Revolution, such as Joseph de Maistre (1753–1821), rejected it because it ignored tradition and based itself on abstract principles like those of the French Revolution. Some conservatives, most notably Edmund Burke (1729–1797) of England, defended the American Revolution. A member of Parliament who criticized the French Revolution, Burke was one of the few British defenders of the colonists against the monarchy. However, he overlooked the philosophy of natural rights upon which the Constitution was based and instead characterized the American Revolution as a matter of Englishmen defending their rights as Englishmen. His defense of the American Revolution was based on culture, not on political considerations.

The connection between democracy and culture during the

French Revolution was severed throughout the nineteenth and twentieth centuries, with various theories of human and social behavior grounding commentaries of U.S. democracy. The latter part of the nineteenth and twentieth centuries brought influential economic interpretations of U.S. democracy, including *The American Democracy* by British socialist Harold Laski. The early twentieth century brought numerous German commentaries on the United States, almost all of them focusing critically on U.S. political culture as too lowbrow, which reflected the dominance of cultural analysis in German intellectual circles. An exception was political philosopher Eric Voegelin (1901–1985), whose *On the Form of the American Mind* and related articles on U.S. political and legal institutions questioned the cultural approach. French analysts in the nineteenth century focused on racial and ethnic dimensions. For example, Arthur Gobineau (1816–1882) argued that the mingling of races allowed by the democratic commitment to freedom and equality would undermine political society. In the latter part of the twentieth century critics from the left drew upon French literary and cultural theories to argue that U.S. democratic principles, including liberty and equality, are Eurocentric and white and have failed to speak to non-Europeans. Democracy must expand and be made more representative in order to include non-Europeans in the U.S. melting pot. Ironically, this criticism, like that of Burke on the right, roots the principles of democracy in culture and overlooks the principled political arguments for democracy that do not depend exclusively on culture.

One generally needs to look to the Anglo-American orbit of commentators to find sustained examinations and criticisms of the constitutional and political—as opposed to economic or cultural—dimensions of U.S. democracy. Among such commentators were the founders of Canada in the mid-nineteenth century. They inherited British constitutional traditions and ideas, including responsible government, and they shared the principles of consent and liberty as well as federalism with the Americans. Even so, the U.S. Civil War and the emergency powers exercised by Abraham Lincoln made the Canadian founders skeptical of the U.S. design of separation of powers and popular sovereignty. John A. MacDonald (1815–1891), Canada's first prime minister, felt that the British Crown was a bettor guarantor of liberties and that the U.S. doctrine of residual powers, which bestowed all powers not explicitly listed in the Constitution to the states, was too decentralist and left the national government too weak to defend the nation. In the words of the Canadian statesman Georges Etiennes Cartier (1814–1873), "in our federation the monarchical principle would form the leading feature, while on the other side of the lines, judging by the past history and present condition of the country, the ruling power was the will of the mob, the rule of the populace. Every person who had conversed with the most intelligent American statesmen and writers must have learned that they all admitted that the governmental powers had become too extended, owing to the introduction of universal suffrage, and mob rule had consequently supplanted legitimate authority" (as cited in Ajzenstat, Romney, Gentles and Gairdner 1999, 185). The necessity of founding a new regime beside the United States induced Canada's founders to focus on the political and legal dimensions of U.S. democracy: They had to craft their own institutions and looked to the United States as one of two primary examples of a functioning democracy, just as James Madison and the other U.S. founders had considered various historical examples of democracy.

A Broader Agreement

Democracy in the United States is both praised and criticized as well as misunderstood by non-Americans. The U.S. Constitution has been a source of inspiration since its creation. However, since Tocqueville's examination of the circumstances, laws, and mores of U.S. democracy, most of the emphasis on U.S. democracy has been on its mores, including its political culture, economy, and intellectual culture. Academics and constitutional lawyers have focused on the constitutional and legal dimensions of U.S. democracy, whereas more popular discourse and media have focused on its political culture.

One reason for the emphasis on culture is the lack of appreciation for the distinctive political science that framed the Constitution, a science that treats politics as an activity in its own right and does not reduce politics to cultural, economic, metaphysical, climatic, ethnic, or racial categories. Tocqueville provides another reason when he observes the appeal of democratic ideas and institutions to people worldwide. Liberty, equality, and consent seem universally applicable, and the U.S. Constitution serves as a role model for later constitutions at the same time that its very appeal makes it seem familiar to non-Americans. The familiarity of the Constitution ironically induces commentary and criticism on the cultural dimensions of U.S. democracy because the political and legal dimensions get taken for granted. Both international criticism and praise of U.S. democratic culture take place within a broader agreement over the design of its democratic Constitution.

John von Heyking

See also Equality; Founding Principles of the United States; Perspectives on the United States, Visitors'; Political System as a Model, U.S.

Further Reading

Ajzenstat, J., Romney, P., Gentles, I., & Gairdner, W. D. (Eds.). (1999). *Canada's founding debates.* Toronto, Canada: Stoddart.

Beck, E. R. (1968). *Germany rediscovers America*. Tallahassee: University Press of Florida.

Ceaser, J. (1997). *Reconstructing America: The symbol of America in modern thought*. New Haven, CT: Yale University Press.

Hamilton, A., Jay, J., & Madison, J. (2001). *The federalist*. Indianapolis, IN: Liberty Fund. (Original work published 1788)

Laski, H. (1948). *The American democracy: Commentary and interpretation*. New York: Viking Press.

Lipset, S. M. (1990). *Continental divide: The values and institutions of the United States and Canada*. New York: Routledge.

Soroush, A. (2000). *Reason, freedom, and democracy in Islam: Essential writings of Abdolkarim Soroush* (M. Sadri & A. Sadri, Trans.). Oxford, UK: Oxford University Press.

Tocqueville, A. (2000). *Democracy in America* (H. C. Mansfield & D. Winthrop, Trans.). Chicago: University of Chicago Press. (Original work published 1835, 1840)

Voegelin, E. (1995). *On the form of the American mind* (R. Hein, Trans.; J. Gebhardt & B. Cooper, Eds.). Columbia: University of Missouri Press. (Original work published 1928)

Voegelin, E. (2003). *Published essays, 1922–1928: The collected works of Eric Voegelin: Vol. 7* (M. J. Hanak, Trans.; T. W. Heilke & J. von Heyking, Eds.). Columbia: University of Missouri Press.

Voegelin, E. (2003). *Published essays, 1929–1933: The collected works of Eric Voegelin: Vol. 8*. (M. J. Hanak, Trans.; T. W. Heilke & J. von Heyking, Eds.). Columbia: University of Missouri Press.

Diffusion of Knowledge, Global

Knowledge has traveled around the world for centuries. Over time, different institutions and systems have played parts in this increasingly complex trafficking of knowledge, even while experts have struggled to explain just how.

Knowledge travels, and global traffic in forms of knowledge has existed throughout world history. The general phenomenon of global flows and movements, which includes knowledge, has been a longstanding focus of interest among scholars, particularly in the social sciences and the humanities. The late Edward Said, for example, articulated the idea of "interculturalism" (Viswanathan 2004, 114–115), or the global migration, intermingling, and interpenetration of cultural realms and formations. Yet, scholars do not have a universally agreed-upon concept with which to express this idea of global circulation. The term that perhaps best captures the generic dimensions of global movement is *diffusion*. This term has been defined by Strang and Meyer as "the socially mediated spread of some practice within a population" (Strang and Meyer 1993, 114–115).

In the diffusion of numerous forms and systems of knowledge, the United States has played a significant historical role. By World War I, according to most economic, industrial and military indicators available to historians, the United States had become a great power. Just as European imperial states once were, American institutions became major sources of diffusion. The ensuing traffic in cultural icons, technical know-how, commodities and tastes (e.g., techniques of mass industrial production, genres of music and entertainment, and theories of management) permeated numerous realms of human endeavor, and was comprehensive in its adoption and impact. Notwithstanding this pivotal innovative and influential global role, the United States has also been a recipient of knowledge. In relation to the public role of intellectuals and their knowledge in society, for example, it remains captive of old world influence, as an "aura of Europe-envy" pervades discussion among Americans (Collini 2006, 243).

Knowledge

Knowledge can be interpreted broadly to include the entire range of available ideas, information, skills, capabilities, and data to which humans, both individually and collectively, have access. This knowledge ranges in complexity from simply understood, idiosyncratic, and isolated factual material to theoretical knowledge conceptualized in erudite propositional logic. Knowledge also takes a variety of formats, including inscription as alphabetized discourse (e.g., texts), imagery (e.g., film), symbolism (e.g., product branding), and technology (e.g., computer language programs).

Boisot's fourfold typology (classification based on types or categories) provides a helpful starting point for understanding the movement of knowledge. He distinguishes public knowledge (that which "passes" for knowledge in a society), commonsense knowledge (tacit although shared, practical, experience-derived know-how), proprietary knowledge (knowledge that is formalized, structured, and commodifiable), and personal knowledge (knowledge that is uniquely individual and subjective). These distinctions show that the potential for diffusion is greater with some types of knowledge than others. This potential is affected by two important dimensions of knowledge: codification and abstraction. Although each of these four types of knowledge may be codified (i.e., arranged in varying layers, categories, or levels of complexity of meaning), the simpler and more universal the coding scheme (e.g., traffic light colors), the stronger the likelihood of both knowledge diffusion and uptake. Restrictive or particularistic coding (e.g., a localized language dialect), on the other hand, limits access and impedes diffusion. With knowledge abstraction (e.g., symbolic logic), the purpose is to better manage data or even reduce its proliferation and to simplify information processing. Here, the denser the coding (e.g., mathematical formulae), the greater the possible ease of diffusion, but the more limited the general access to diffused messages. For these reasons, although the available space for human knowledge may be open-ended or even infinite, at any one point in time diffusible knowledge is likely to occupy only part of that space.

Diffusion

In the social sciences (especially anthropology, sociology, economics, and political science), few, if any, fully elaborated theories of diffusion exist. Instead, diffusion is mostly accorded the status of a process. Its use is generally associated with the idea of innovation, so that a practice that diffuses is likely to be perceived as new, different, or better than a prevailing set of arrangements. Some authors have an occasional and misplaced tendency to equate

diffusion with "exchange." This tendency has the unfortunate consequence of reducing the movement of knowledge to a form of market relations. A more productive understanding, however, which is the basis of this discussion, is to reposition diffusion in two closely aligned contexts: first, learning, and second, social and cultural change.

Taking the first of these suggestions, the difference between exchange and diffusion becomes clear. A market is a system of preference allocation among competing units whose relations are regulated by commodity pricing and/or legal contracts, the object of which is to facilitate the voluntary exchange of utilities. If, for the sake of argument, knowledge serves as an example of a utility, then it may be commodified (i.e., accorded a market value) to be bought and sold like any other good or service. Thus, proprietary knowledge in Boisot's sense may be transacted for a price in the guise, say, of commercially hired expertise or patented intellectual property. Now, although a marketplace certainly exists for at least some knowledge, clearly not all knowledge has an exchange value. Diffused knowledge, by contrast, is of indeterminate value because the potential adopters (i.e., Strang and Meyer's "population") put a price on knowledge by deciding what they might want to procure and the worth of that to them. In these circumstances, adopters acquire diffusing knowledge in their capacity as learners, with the intention, as March (1999) has suggested, of learning from the experience of others. As part of a process of learning from others, then, diffusion may be said to have occurred "when members of the collective are no longer dependent upon the original holders of the knowledge or skill" (Tompkins 1995, 69–70). Moreover, although market exchange relations are by definition reciprocal (i.e., they require buyers and sellers), diffusion relations may be reciprocal, but equally they may be unidirectional. To illustrate reciprocal diffusion, Bayly cites the nineteenth-century example of the professional civil service, developed in British India and the colonies and subsequently "imported back into Britain" (Bayly 2004, 256). This example contrasts with other nineteenth-century examples of one-way transmission, in which "the Western state form was exported lock, stock, and barrel" (Bayly 2004, 258).

In regard to the second suggestion of social and cultural change, as Bayly's examples attest, diffusion is inherently challenging, possibly even revolutionary, in its contextual effects on the status quo and established sets of interests because people's awareness of the new and different possibilities provided by diffusing knowledge establishes a basis for them to compare, critique, and strive for betterment. This possibility is augmented by the relative absence of rules and conventions to regulate diffusion. In terms of geographical boundaries, for example, the operation of diffusion processes is unrestricted. In this sense diffusion may occur within cultural and social units (e.g., families and neighborhoods) or between

them (e.g., across entire societal and cultural divides). Whatever the units concerned, knowledge may diffuse in a number of modalities. These modalities include imitation, assimilation, translation, copying, cloning, adaptation, borrowing, and contagion. As it diffuses, the flow of knowledge is also patterned according to different trajectories. These trajectories are determined by combinations of velocity, scope, and intensity of movement. Moreover, the cultural penetration of diffusing knowledge is likely to vary in depth, breadth, duration, and scale, depending on the degree of permeability of the barriers to cultural learning and the absorptive capacity and readiness of host populations to adopt.

The agencies of diffusion are many and varied. Historically, they have included the forces of imperialism, trade, travel, tourism, migration, and diasporic relations (relating to the scattering of a people away from a homeland), along with networks of strategically positioned sets of agents (i.e., influential individuals). Finally, the diffusing and adopting units encompass a range of formations, including (in addition to the cultural and societal wholes or parts already mentioned) dynasties, empires, states, and nations. With each of these examples of agents of diffusion, allowance has to be made for varying strengths and degrees of structural integration because, as Ballantyne notes of powerful historical empires, these amounted to an "assemblage of networks, complex threads of correspondence and exchange that linked distant components together and ensured a steady, but largely overlooked, cultural traffic" (Ballantyne 2002, 133).

Globalization, Diffusion, and Knowledge

Current awareness of knowledge diffusion and its significance has quickened as a result of the attention being accorded such phenomena as the "knowledge economy," the competitive advantage among nations, and especially globalization, described by Hopkins as the "catch-word of the day" and arguably "the most important single debate in the social sciences" (Hopkins 2002, 1).

Globalization is not new. Indeed, Hopkins has distinguished four sequential and overlapping forms of globalization, of which the final one is the most recent. These forms are archaic globalization (the period of preindustrialization and the emergence of the nation-state), proto-globalization ("military fiscalism" for the period 1600–1800), modern globalization (incorporating the rise of nation-states and the process of industrialization), and postcolonial globalization (from the 1950s). Nor is globalization, in any of these four forms, synonymous with diffusion. Nevertheless, scholars are concerned with various globalizing forces, which include the pattern of their diffusion, their origins, and the intended

and unintended outcomes that they yield. An increasing number of historians, in particular, are seeking a global, comparative understanding of historical change, which contrasts with a previously dominant concern in the profession with "national history." In their efforts to account for longitudinal rates and trajectories of social and cultural changes, for the relative absence or presence of influential ideas, ideologies, philosophies, knowledge, and developmental trends during different eras and in disparate parts of the globe, scholars have focused on the comparative similarities, differences, and rates of progress across the range of formations previously mentioned. In this regard an abiding academic interest during Hopkins's postcolonial period has been the relationship between culture, economic growth and prosperity, and democracy. This interest has given rise to theories of "modernization."

Modernization

The focus of modernization theory is comparative social development, in particular why some societies managed to industrialize before others and the ways in which they negotiated the transition from premodern to modern status. This body of theory rose to prominence in the 1950s and 1960s, after which it fell into abeyance until its revival in the final two decades of the second millennium. Its emergence coincided with the Cold War, during which "free world" and "command economy" models of industrialization contended with one another. This concurrence complicated modernization theorists' goal of explicating transformational social change as a diffusible theory and knowledge base because different or parallel pathways to "modernity" seemed to exist. Thus, to what body of knowledge or models might developing, post–World War II new nations turn in order to ascertain the causes of their seemingly arrested or lagging development and to inform states' policies? Likewise, what kinds of assumptions about development would underwrite the development initiatives of aid agencies and donor nations? Furthermore, problems existed with the binary terminology generated by modernization theory because "traditional" versus "modern" and even "undeveloped" versus "developed" and later still "periphery" versus "center" and "South" versus "North" seemed to imply the superior status of the latter, as opposed to conveying a bald assertion of differences in status.

Because so many of them were the earliest to modernize, superiority became the privilege of Western rather than non-Western nations, a status that appeared to be confirmed for modernization theorists with the collapse of the Soviet empire in 1989. By the time modernization got its second wind, then, only one, broadly Western route to modernity seemed to exist. This development gave

a new twist to scholars' accounts of the comparative measurement of nations' economic performance because it fueled discussion of the idea of the "West versus the rest" and heralded the possibility of an inexorable convergence around Western cultural values and models of democracy.

Convergence, Divergence, and Hybridization

Although Hobsbawm is by no means an apologist for modernization, and although he disavows the condescension implicit in such attributions of cultural superiority, Hobsbawm is nonetheless emphatic about the recent historical hegemony (influence) of the West. "The twentieth-century history of the non-Western or more exactly non-north-Western world," he writes, is "determined by its relations with the countries which had established themselves in the nineteenth century as the lords of human kind" (Hobsbawm 1995, 200). Few more unequivocal statements can be made about the significance of geographically biased diffusion than this one.

Although an appealing seductiveness may exist about the idea of the uptake of diffusing global knowledge converging around one or a small number of models, difficulties exist in substantiating the claim. For a start, who exactly are the members of the West? The G8 (a group of eight major nations—Canada, France, Germany, Italy, Japan, United Kingdom, United States, and Russia—that meets to discuss economic issues)? The Organisation for Economic Co-Operation and Development (OECD)? Next, how can there be a West when the states that might be assumed to comprise it have a demonstrable absence of institutional uniformity and practice, let alone homogeneity of values, ethnicity, and linguistic composition? Then, of course, within such supposedly convergent conglomerates as the West one or a few member nations often make counterassertions of paramount influence over the remainder. Thus, for the nineteenth century the "exceptional" accolade of historians has been bestowed on Europe. However, should it have been England, as the first "new," industrial nation? In the twentieth century the claim to exceptionalism was wrested by the United States. What, then, of divergence, the counterclaim that nations or groups of nations have forged historically different pathways to nationhood and statehood?

Divergence challenges such phenomena as "Eurocentrism," along with simplistic notions of "success story" diffusion, by articulating powerful counterclaims about the combined influence of "endogenous" factors (i.e., home-grown endowments and resources), timing, and opportunity in stimulating or delaying economic take-off in otherwise comparably positioned societies. This kind of reasoning conduces, in turn, to the possibility of hybridization, the argument that "what is required is a blending of both [diffusionist and endogenous explanations of change]" (Bayly 2004, 295). Thus, when cultural knowledge and practices diffuse, the reality of an encounter between diffusers and adopters is more likely to be one of accommodation, give-and-take, and even fusion of knowledge from its respective sources than one of crude assimilation. Historically, hybridization has meant that host society traditions have been simultaneously ruptured by an infusion of Western ideas, with a corresponding parodying and subversion of those same ideas by non-Westerners.

In Perspective

Global movements of knowledge, both in respect to the content of the particular knowledge that moves and the accruing body of theory that seeks to account for that moving knowledge, are exceedingly complex. In their explanations of such movements, scholars have mostly resorted, explicitly or implicitly, to a version of diffusionist discourse with which to construct their arguments. The increasing popularity of global historiography (the writing of history), however, suggests that a reappraisal of diffusion may be timely. Unless used sparingly and unless accompanied by detailed explorations of the dynamic factors involved, claims to the effect that a political ideology or scientific knowledge "diffused" to a particular destination can be problematic at best or even downright misleading. Such claims are equivalent to those that invoke evolutionary explanations of change, with such typical locutions as "a new situation evolved."

Each explanatory framework—diffusion and evolution—runs the risk of invoking a kind of closet "naturalness" or implicit inevitability as the key to understanding change, thereby eliding the significance of agency, the structural and cultural patterning of agency, and the forces of power and influence that are always manifest as agents seek to realize their individual and collective interests. With these caveats in mind, as a discursive vehicle for elucidating macro-scale phenomena, such as global movements of knowledge, diffusion continues to have much to recommend it.

Peter Gronn

See also Brain Drain; Exchanges, Cultural and Scientific; Linguistic Imperialism and English

Further Reading

Ballantyne, T. (2002). Empire, knowledge and culture: From proto-globalization to modern globalization. In A. G. Hopkins (Ed.), *Globalization in world history* (pp. 115–140). London: Pimlico.

Bayly, C. A. (2004). *The birth of the modern world, 1780–1914.* Oxford, UK: Blackwell.

Biggart, N. W., & Delbridge, R. (2004). Systems of exchange. *Academy of Management Review, 29*(1), 18–49.

Boisot, M. H. (1995). *Information space: A framework for learning in organizations, institutions and culture.* London: Routledge.

Collini, S. (2006) *Absent minds: Intellectuals in Britain.* Oxford, UK: Oxford University Press.

Hobsbawm, E. (1995). *Age of extremes: The short twentieth century, 1914–1991.* London: Abacus.

Hopkins, A. G. (2002). Introduction: Globalization—An agenda for historians. In A. G. Hopkins (Ed.), *Globalization in world history* (pp. 1–10). London: Pimlico.

Knöbl, W. (2003). Theories that won't pass away: The never-ending story of modernization theory. In G. Delanty & E. F. Isin (Eds.), *Handbook of historical sociology* (pp. 96–107). London: Sage.

Lipset, S. M. (1996). *American exceptionalism: A double-edged sword.* New York: W. W. Norton.

March, J. G. (1999). *The pursuit of organizational intelligence.* Oxford, UK: Blackwell.

Pomeranz, K. (2000). *The great divergence: China, Europe, and the making of the modern world economy.* Princeton, NJ: Princeton University Press.

Strang, D., & Meyer, J. W. (1993). Institutional conditions for diffusion. *Theory & Society, 22,* 487–511.

Tompkins, T. C. (1995). Role of diffusion in collective learning. *International Journal of Organizational Analysis, 3*(1), 69–85.

Viswanathan, G. (Ed.). (2004). *Power, politics and culture: Interviews with Edward W. Said.* London: Bloomsbury.

Drug Trade and the War on Drugs

The U.S. war on drugs emphasizes disrupting production and distribution of drugs, and has been pooled into the larger war on terrorism so that efforts to curtail the drug trade—and "narcoterrorism"—have risen to a new level of intensity.

The U.S. war on drugs was initiated during the early administration of President Ronald Reagan and has continued to the present, however overshadowed or incorporated it might be within the war on terrorism. The war on drugs was defined by a substantial increase in resources dedicated to drug interdiction and drug enforcement, as well as a strategy of attempting to enforce U.S. narcotics laws beyond U.S. borders.

Background

In the United States the war on drugs has focused primarily on the disruption of the supply side. This focus has resulted in the development of a three-part strategy: first, to disrupt drug production at its source; second, to interrupt the shipment of drugs en route to the United States; and third, to provide increased street-level enforcement, along with more severe punishment. Between 1981 and 2000 the amount of federal money spent annually on drug control in the United States increased from $2 billion to almost $15 billion.

Drugs and drug-related problems were not new to U.S. society in the 1980s, nor was the Reagan administration the first government to try to deal with the problems associated with illegal narcotics. The history of illegal narcotics in the United States is well documented. President Reagan was, however, the first president to declare the drug trade a threat to national security. In a speech delivered in September 1981, President Reagan proposed a "narcotics enforcement strategy" that included "a foreign policy that vigorously seeks to interdict and eradicate illicit drugs, wherever cultivated, processed or transported" (Carpenter 2003, 11). At the same time he announced formation of the Special Council on Narcotics Control to coordinate efforts to stop drugs flowing into the United States. By April 1986 the war on drugs was formally raised to the highest security priority when President Reagan signed National Security Decision Directive (NSDD) 221, declaring that drug trafficking is a threat to U.S. security.

Support for the Reagan war on drugs was echoed by subsequent administrations. For example, in the cover letter of the National Drug Control Strategy (NDCS) for 1989, President George H. W. Bush stated that "America's fight against epidemic illegal drug use cannot be won on a single front alone; it must be waged everywhere" (Holden-Rhodes 1997, 41). In 1989 President Bush demonstrated his commitment to the war on drugs, in particular his willingness to take the war beyond the geographic confines of the United States and to substantially increase the material and human resources committed to the war. In December 1989 U.S. military forces invaded Panama, motivated in part by President Manuel Noriega's alleged ties to drug traffickers.

It was also in 1989 that the U.S. military started taking a formal role in the war on drugs. As part of the Bush administration's National Drug Control Strategy, Joint Task Force Six (JTF-6) was created to lend support to civilian law enforcement agencies in the war on drugs. The mission of JTF-6 was to "serve as a planning and coordinating headquarters to provide support from the Defense Department to federal, state and local law enforcement agencies" through support activities such as "aerial reconnaissance and surveillance training, transportation assistance, ground radar monitoring, training and general engineering support" (Dunn 1996, 134). Finally, under the Anti-Drug Abuse Act of 1988 a concept known as "high intensity drug trafficking areas" (HIDTA) was created. Areas within in the geographic United States that exhibited characteristics of serious drug-trafficking problems, to the degree that they impacted other areas of the country, were designated as HIDTAs and subsequently qualified for additional resources to fight the war on drugs.

In the early 1990s President Bill Clinton also demonstrated a commitment to continue combating the trade and use of illegal narcotics. In an effort to raise the profile of the antidrug campaign Clinton made the director of the Office of National Drug Control Policy a part of the Executive Office of the President (EOP) and appointed that director as a member of the National Security Council. Clinton was also instrumental in increasing military assistance and support to Latin American and Andean region nations to aid in the fight against drug production and transportation.

A marijuana plant growing in a field of opium poppies in southern Afghanistan. Note scarring on the poppy heads where the farmer has cut the heads to make them produce opium gum, which is harvested and turned into opium, the base element of heroin. Source: istock.

War on Drugs and George W. Bush

Under the administration of President George W. Bush the basic strategy for the war on drugs has continued, and to some degree the resources used in fighting the war on drugs have been enhanced. The Bush administration continues what it refers to as a balanced approach to the war on drugs, which includes three strategies: proactive action in preventing drug usage; intervention and treatment; and disruption of the market for drugs. The nature of the war on drugs, however, has been challenged by two significant factors: the rise in the production and use of synthetic drugs and the war on terrorism.

Under the George W. Bush administration funding for the war on drugs rose slightly between 2002 and the projected budget for fiscal year 2008. In 2002 almost $11.5 billion was spent on drug control; by 2008 that amount will have risen to almost $12.9 billion. In terms of distribution, for fiscal year 2008 $8.3 billion of a projected $12.9 billion drug control budget, or just over 63 percent, is dedicated to funding programs aimed at disrupting the supply side of the drug equation. The budget for fiscal year 2008 also includes $1.6 billion, or 12.4 percent, for education- and community-based

outreach programs, and $3 billion, or 23.3 percent, for drug abuse intervention and treatment centers.

Central to the international initiatives in the war on drugs is the Andean Counterdrug Initiative. This program was conceived during the Clinton administration as Plan Colombia but repackaged and expanded upon during the George W. Bush administration. The Andean Counterdrug Initiative provides counternarcotics support to the Andean region countries of Bolivia, Colombia, Peru, Ecuador, Brazil, Venezuela, and Panama. Funding to this region supports programs such as crop eradication, alternative crop programs, interdiction of narcotics and chemicals necessary for the production of narcotics, support for local law enforcement and judicial systems, anticorruption efforts, infrastructure support (such as the Critical Flight Safety Program in Colombia), and drug awareness programs.

The five strategies noted above incorporate a variety of methodologies to reduce drug production and trafficking. In support of the first strategy, the United States assists in crop eradication, by supplying source countries with chemical herbicides, technical assistance, and specialized equipment and spray aircraft. In addition, the U.S. Agency for International Development (USAID) provides funding to encourage alternative sources of income for people in-

volved in the production of illegal drugs. In an effort to enhance interdiction and law enforcement capabilities in source countries, the second strategy, the United States funds antidrug enforcement training programs in more than seventy countries. In addition, specialized equipment and expertise in the form of Drug Enforcement Administration (DEA) personnel are used to assist foreign police agencies in their antinarcotics role. The third strategy of the U.S. international narcotics control strategy is building cooperation with and between source countries. Although the United States advocates bilateral and multilateral agreements as a mechanism for helping to control drug production and trafficking, it admits that this approach has not been overly effective in stemming the flow of illegal narcotics. From the U.S. perspective, agreements that lack strong enforcement mechanisms, consistent interpretation of anti-drug goals, and the political will to stem the flow of illegal narcotics have a limited effectiveness. The fourth strategy, sanctions and/or economic assistance, uses reward and punishment to encourage countries to support U.S. antinarcotic goals. Under the current certification process, countries deemed to be uncooperative toward U.S. antinarcotics policy are threatened with a combination of aid and economic sanctions. The fifth strategy, institutional development, focuses on developing and strengthening law enforcement and judicial institutions in drug-producing and transit countries in order to support the larger U.S. goals in the war on drugs.

Undoubtedly, the United States is the global leader in the war on drugs, and as such U.S. drug policy has impacted individual states in a variety of ways. And while each state will have its own perspective on U.S. drug policy, ranging from cooperation, to a benign indifference, to some degree of outrage at the intrusive nature of the war on drugs, weighing out a variety of considerations will ultimately determine each state's reaction to U.S. drug policy. The case of Canada is instructive in this regard. Even though Canada has been repeatedly identified in the annual U.S. *National Drug Control Strategy* as a source country for certain narcotics, strong economic ties and similar law enforcement and legal values have resulted in substantial bilateral efforts to combat drug trade and production within and between the two countries. In many Latin American and Asian countries, by contrast, U.S. drug policy is considered by many to be a policy of cooperation by coercion (Ayling 2005, 377). Indeed, Carpenter (2003) argues that U.S. drug policy in Latin American has had a net effect of decreasing local support for anti-drug efforts. Moreover, a lack of viable economic alternatives narcotic production in Latin America (Sharpe 2006, 485) and Afghanistan (Medler 2005, 290) means U.S. drug policy in these countries will be met with at a minimum indifference, or worse, violent opposition.

The Future

Under the Bush administration the war on drugs has been forced to take a back seat to larger foreign policy priorities, notably the war on terrorism, which has necessarily dominated public resources. At some level, however, the war on terrorism and the war on drugs have crossed paths to the degree that the two wars are, in some cases, fighting the same battles. New terminology—such as *narcoterrorism*—has entered the lexicon to describe the nexus between terrorism and drug trafficking. So intertwined are the terrorist and drug worlds that eighteen of the forty-two organizations on the U.S. List of Foreign Terrorist Organizations are linked to drug trafficking. Nowhere is this issue more problematic for the United States than in Afghanistan, where opiate production and trafficking are intricately entwined with the Taliban former regime, the al-Qaeda terrorist network, and provincial warlords with multiple and questionable loyalties. Furthermore, as Afghan narcotics are trafficked from Afghanistan to destinations around the globe, revenues are siphoned off by various groups along the route, including terrorist organizations. Moreover, research suggest

WAR ON DRUGS AFFECTS PRISON POPULATION

In August [2000], the U.S. Department of Justice revealed that the number of men and women behind bars in the United States at the end of 1999 exceeded two million and the rate of incarceration had reached 690 inmates per 100,000 residents—a rate Human Rights Watch believed to be the highest in the world (with the exception of Rwanda)... . The unrelenting war on drugs continued to pull hundreds of thousands of drug offenders into the criminal justice system: 1,559,100 people were arrested on drug charges in 1998; approximately 450,000 drug offenders were confined in jails and prisons.

According to the Department of Justice, 107,000 people were sent to state prison on drug charges in 1998, representing 30.8 percent of all new state admissions. Drug offenders constituted 57.8 percent of all federal inmates.

Source: Human Rights Watch World Report 2001: United States. (2001). Retrieved March 19, 2007, from http://www.hrw.org/wr2k1/usa/index.html

that areas of armed conflict, where drug production existed before the start of conflict, are more likely to experience an increase in drug production as rebel groups use drug production and trafficking as a means to fund their conflict.

The crossover between the war on terrorism and the war on drugs will, in all likelihood, continue. As the war on terrorism progresses and terrorist organizations look for alternative means to fund their respective causes, policymakers will increasingly address this issue with a greater convergence of strategies and assets.

T. S. (Todd) Hataley

See also Relations with Latin America, U.S.

Further Reading

Ayling, J. (2005). Conscription in the war on drugs: Recent reforms to the U.S. drug certification process. *International Journal of Drug Policy, 16,* 376–383.

Carpenter, T. G. (2003). *Bad neighbor policy: Washington's futile war on drugs in Latin America.* New York: Palgrave Macmillan.

Cornell, S. E. (2005). The interaction of narcotics and conflict. *Journal of Peace Research, 42*(6), 751–760.

Duke, S. B., & Gross, A. C. (1993). *America's longest war: Rethinking our tragic crusade against drugs.* New York: Putnam and Sons.

Dunn, T. (1996). *The militarization of the U.S.-Mexico border: Low intensity conflict doctrine come home.* Austin: University of Texas Press.

Holden-Rhodes, J. F. (1997). *Sharing the secrets: Open source intelligence and the war on drugs.* London: Praeger.

Inciardi, J. A. (2002). *The war on drugs III.* Boston: Allyn and Bacon.

Lock, E. D., Timberlake, J. M., & Rasinski, K. A. (2002). Battle fatigue: Is public support waning for "war"-centered drug control strategies? *Crime and Delinquency, 48,* 380–398.

McCoy, A. W., & Block, A. A. (Eds.). (1992). *The war on drugs: Studies in the failure of U.S. narcotics policy.* Boulder, CO: Westview Press.

Medler, J. D. (2005). Afghan heroin: Terrain, tradition and turmoil. *Orbis, 49*(2), 275–291.

Miller, J. (2004). *Bad trip: How the war against drugs is destroying America.* Nashville, TN: WND Books.

Perl, R. F. (2006, July 21). International drug trade and U.S. foreign policy. *Congressional Research Service Report for Congress.* Retrieved February 26, 2007, from http://fpc.state.gov/documents/organization/76892.pdf

Powell, B. (2007). Inside the Afghan drug war. *Time, 169*(8), 11–17.

Sharpe, K. (2006). Realpolitik or imperial hubris: The Latin American drug war and U.S. foreign policy in Iraq. *Orbis, 50*(3), 481–499.

Tracey, S. W., & Acker, C. J. (2004). *Altering American consciousness: The history of alcohol and drug use in the United States, 1800–2000.* Boston: University of Massachusetts Press.

White House. (2007). *National drug control strategy.* Retrieved February 26, 2007, from http://www.whitehousedrugpolicy.gov/publications/policy/ndcs07/ndcs07.pdf

White House. (2007). *National drug control strategy FY2008 budget summary.* Retrieved February 26, 2007, from http://www.whitehousedrugpolicy.gov/publications/policy/08budget/08budget.pdf

Wright, J. (2006, March 1). Afghanistan's opiate economy and terrorist financing. *Jane's Intelligence Review, 18*(3) 36–42.

Ecological Footprint, U.S.

Admiration of U.S. affluence has given way to anger at Americans' wasteful consumption of the world's limited resources, and to an image that the United States does not care about global warming, or see it as a threat to the world.

As the world's greatest economic and strategic power, the United States has drawn on resources of the entire planet, causing ecological decline and pollution. U.S. strategic power spread globally after the Spanish-American War of 1898, but it began with commercial expansion beyond the borders of the original Thirteen Colonies. The U.S. ecological empire has not been very different from that of other industrial powers, but during the twentieth century it became by far the most widespread in history. After 1900 Americans were in the forefront of the global economy, with large-scale investment capital, innovative corporate organization, and ever-expanding consumer markets at home. The environmental impacts accelerated accordingly. However, Americans have also made important contributions toward more sustainable management of the world's natural resources.

Tropical Crops

The earliest environmental impact beyond the nation's borders emerged in late colonial times, when Yankee traders began buying cane sugar grown on Caribbean islands and selling it to consumers along the eastern seaboard. Since the first European colonial settlements in the tropical Americas in the 1500s, African slaves in European colonies had cleared virgin forests in the tropical lowlands to grow sugar cane. By the early 1800s the U.S. market surpassed that of Europe, and Cuba became the largest cane sugar producer in the Americas, its central region almost entirely cleared of forest.

Coffee became the greatest forest-clearing crop in Latin America after 1800, and the U.S. market quickly dominated, especially for coffee from southern Brazil and Colombia, which have been by far the world's greatest coffee producers for almost two hundred years. Endless rows of coffee trees grew where forest had formerly stood; the plantations produced heavy soil erosion, degrading wide hillside regions.

Around 1900 bananas joined the ranks of tropical forest clearers when two giant agro-import corporations, United Fruit and Standard Fruit, imported bananas from Costa Rica, Honduras, and other Central American countries. The two companies created vast plantations, purchasing wide stretches of tropical lowland forest

from governments eager to "conquer" tropical nature and increase their revenue. What had been natural species-rich ecosystems became one-crop plantations, but monocrops inevitably invite invasion from specialized pests and diseases. From 1910 onward crop diseases devastated the banana plantations. The first agrochemical pesticides were only partially effective, so the companies' plant-breeding stations slowly hybridized disease-resistant varieties of bananas. Meanwhile the companies began moving to new areas every twenty years, cutting down additional native forests where the diseases had not yet reached. On depleted soils chemical fertilizers have artificially maintained soil productivity since the 1960s, but at the cost of soil and water pollution. In the struggle against declining soil fertility and crop pests, U.S. chemical corporations led by Monsanto and Dow developed international markets for chemical fertilizers and pesticides. Until the 1960s few people realized that DDT and other farm chemicals were poisoning soil and water as well as farm workers in countries like the Central American republics.

Another corporate strategy was to diversify crops. By the 1960s other tropical fruits, especially citrus and pineapples, replaced older banana plantations. Each crop contributed to tropical forest clearance as U.S., European, and Japanese consumers supplied their dining tables.

Some forests were simply cut down and burned. However, potential profits from sales of tropical hardwoods were being lost. By the 1920s the fruit companies organized logging subsidiaries to ship mahogany to U.S. furniture makers and builders, and tropical timber began benefiting U.S. companies and consumers. However, replanting multispecies tropical forests is almost impossible, so timber companies have usually created tree farms, single-species softwood plantations hardly different from any other one-crop production.

Political Dimension: Strategic Resources

Many other natural resources of the world came under pressure from the expanding U.S. industrial economy from the late 1800s onward. During World War I the U.S. government realized that a

ECOLOGICAL FOOTPRINT

An Ecological Footprint is "a measure of how much biologically productive land and water an individual, population or activity requires to produce all the resources it consumes and to absorb the waste it generates using prevailing technology and resource management practices" (Global Footprint Network). It is measured in "global hectares" because trade is global network and an individual or country's Footprint now includes resources from around the world. The Footprint ratings below indicate how many global hectares the average person in each nation consumes.

Top Ten Nations in the Total Ecological Footprint Rating (2003)

United Arab Emirates	11.9
United States	9.6
Canada	7.6
Finland	7.6
Kuwait	7.3
Australia	6.6
Estonia	6.5
Sweden	6.1
New Zealand	5.9
Norway	5.8

Source: Global Footprint Network. (2007). Retrieved March 22, 2007, from http://www.footprintnetwork.org/

series of natural resources from far-flung locations was strategically important for U.S. military purposes, and the government's interests merged closely with corporate operations. Only one strategic commodity was a plantation crop: natural rubber, which was essential to the automotive industry. After 1905 Goodyear and other U.S. tire corporations cleared forests for large rubber plantations in Southeast Asia. Then in 1926 Firestone began the world's largest plantation in Liberia in west Africa, in close cooperation with the State and Commerce Departments. In each rubber-growing country endless rows of rubber trees replaced wide tracts of tropical forest or subsistence farms. U.S. industry, especially automobiles, provided an insatiably expanding market for natural rubber until synthetic (petroleum-based) rubber appeared as an alternative in World War II. From then onward the expansion of tropical rubber plantations slowed appreciably as production of the two types of rubber became roughly equal. However, this situation meant large increments in U.S. consumption of petroleum, over half of which now comes from sources outside the United States.

Petroleum is equally essential to an industrial economy as well as its military machine, although its production has different environmental costs. By the early 1900s U.S. oil corporations penetrated the world's largest oil reserves in the Middle East, creating profound mutual dependency and strategic entanglements between the United States, Saudi Arabia, Iraq, Iran, and other countries. Then Mexico, Venezuela, Nigeria, and other suppliers joined the ranks of U.S. suppliers. The direct environmental impacts of oil production have centered on intense pollution near production facilities and shipping ports.

Military Role

In addition to massive consumption of fossil fuels, the U.S. military has constructed hundreds of military bases around the world, especially from World War II onward into the Cold War. Each base has had environmental costs: roads, airstrips, power plants, pollution of nearby areas, downstream, and coastal zones. Weapons testing has also had ecological costs. One of the most dramatic resulted from nuclear bomb testing in the Pacific, especially in the 1950s, which destroyed or contaminated not only islands but also surrounding waters for many years after the tests. Finally, during the Vietnam War the U.S. military destroyed many thousands of acres of forest by spraying Agent Orange and other defoliants.

Managing Natural Resources

In reaction to these destructive trends, some Americans saw the need for more efficient resource use to maintain both long-term corporate profits and the broader public and ecological health. In the 1930s planners began coordinating region-wide water use. The Tennessee Valley Authority, the world's first integrated river basin planning authority, became the model for systems of water management and hydropower development around the world after World War II. Scores of countries hired consultants from the U.S. Army Corps of Engineers and the U.S. Bureau of Reclamation to design high dams and power generators, and the U.S. engineering companies that had built Hoover Dam and other early U.S. large dams competed successfully for contracts to build dams around the world. These projects brought many benefits but also fundamentally disrupted living river systems, and the new reservoirs drowned species-diverse forests, rich soils, and rural communities. Only after the 1960s did these projects incorporate any environmental impact planning.

Broader understandings of the need to manage entire natural resource systems outside the United States more carefully emerged

after World War II and accelerated around 1970, the turning point for global environmental awareness. In the 1950s the organization Resources for the Future began issuing reports assessing natural resource use outside the United States. Then Lester Brown launched the Worldwatch Institute, analyzing and publicizing a wide spectrum of global environmental urgencies and the policy challenges to the United States. And in 1981, after Ronald Reagan became president, environmental officials from his predecessor Jimmy Carter's administration helped found the World Resources Institute to study long-range U.S. interests in an ecologically healthy biosphere (the part of the world in which life can exist).

Parallel to nongovernmental planning groups, governmental and international aid agencies began recognizing the vital environmental dimension of economic development around 1970. The U.S. Agency for International Development, in communication with its Canadian and European counterparts, added environmental assessments to its agenda in areas such as crop development, tropical forestry, and water resources. The Peace Corps hired dozens of tropical foresters, many of them committed to the new trend in tropical forestry: the difficult challenge of sustaining tropical ecosystems while selectively harvesting valuable timbers.

None of this was enough to reduce the rate of global ecological deterioration; other conservationists increasingly demanded that natural ecosystems and biodiversity be preserved intact from

development. Wildlife protection movements in the United States had begun to look beyond national borders around 1900 and to cooperate with friends in other countries. The National Audubon Society was the first because many bird species loved by U.S. birdwatchers spent winters in the Caribbean and Latin America. By the 1920s the American Committee for International Wildlife Protection began organizing surveys of endangered animals and wildlife protection laws in many countries. In 1948 its leading voice, Harold Coolidge, helped found the International Union for the Protection of Nature, under United Nations auspices.

Other U.S. environmental organizations gradually joined the movement, notably the Sierra Club, which had defended wilderness since 1892. In the 1960s, under David Brower's leadership, the Sierra Club began addressing international issues such as national parks and tropical deforestation. In 1969 Brower founded Earth Island Institute explicitly as an international network of environmentalists to confront more global controversies, including nontraditional conservation issues such as nuclear weapons and overpopulation. The need for Americans to cooperate with friends around the world was now obvious. Conservation International, an offshoot of the World Wildlife Fund, built into all its tropical programs experts and grassroots leaders from the local countries. This tactic was the only way to avoid the trap of U.S. conservationists imposing their priorities on developing countries facing the needs and pressures of local populations.

Traffic jam on an interstate highway.
Source: istock/ Jim Pruitt.

Population Control

Along with affluent economies' high levels of resource consumption and pollution generation, overpopulation is perhaps the most fundamental and controversial issue relating to global ecological health. By the 1960s the population boom became a critical international challenge, and both private and governmental aid programs have slowly increased family planning programs. Since then U.S. governments have shifted between Democratic administrations' active support of international family planning (through both the United Nations and private organizations) and Republican administrations' opposition to funding most population aid. Among nongovernmental organizations, the Audubon Society has led an environmental coalition since 1980 to support U.S. contributions to global family planning programs. Other organizations have argued that concern for high birth rates in developing countries must be matched by a challenge to overconsumption in affluent countries. Neither public officials nor most environmental organizations in the United States have been willing to confront this issue in a sustained way.

Global Warming

All of the accumulating ecological stresses around the world contribute to the greatest threat of all: global warming. The leading engine of global warming is U.S. industrial and automotive pollution, which has begun to have severe impacts on polar regions, island countries, coastal zones, forests, food production, and water resources. Scientists and environmentalists are largely agreed on this, but corporations and the federal government are responding only slowly. What governments should do has become a highly political issue. Democratic administrations starting with that of President Carter have cooperated closely with international research and legislation to slow the trend toward atmospheric pollution. Republican administrations from President Reagan onward, in contrast, are determined not to limit U.S. political sovereignty by international treaties or to restrict the private sector's freedom of initiative.

Implications

The United States has never been the only metropolitan country involved in the global race to control natural resources. It has al-

ways been in competition with others; thus, sorting out the specific U.S. influence on particular environmental problems can be difficult. However, for the past century the U.S. footprint has been by far the largest on the biosphere. This footprint has produced many-sided and accelerating ecological pressures, partly offset by improved environmental management. The huge U.S. footprint has had a major impact on other societies' views of U.S. power and place in the world. Global admiration of U.S. dynamism and affluence has been increasingly offset by anger (among both governments and populations) at Americans' wasteful consumption of the world's limited resources.

Richard P. Tucker

See also Environmental Issues

Further Reading

Brown, L. R. (2003). *Plan B: Rescuing a planet under stress and a civilization in trouble.* New York: W. W. Norton.

Ehrlich, P., & Ehrlich, A. (2004). *One with Nineveh: Politics, consumption and the human future.* Washington, DC: Island Press.

French, H. (2000). *Vanishing borders: Protecting the planet in the age of globalization.* New York: W. W. Norton.

Kennedy, D., & Riggs, J. A. (Eds.). (2000). *U.S. policy and the global environment.* Washington, DC: Aspen Institute.

Maguire, A., & Brown, J. W. (Eds.). (1986). *Bordering on trouble: Resources and politics in Latin America.* Bethesda, MD: Adler and Adler.

McNeill, J. R. (2000). *Something new under the sun: An environmental history of the twentieth-century world.* New York: W. W. Norton.

Princen, T., Maniates, M., & Conca, K. (Eds.). (2002). *Confronting consumption.* Cambridge, MA: MIT Press.

Richards, J. F. (2003). *The unending frontier: An environmental history of the early modern world.* Berkeley: University of California Press.

Russell, E. (2001). *War and nature: Fighting humans and insects with chemicals from World War I to Silent Spring.* Cambridge, MA: Cambridge University Press.

Schmidheiny, S. (1992). *Changing course: A global business perspective on development and the environment.* Cambridge, MA: MIT Press.

Schneider, S., Rosencranz, A., & Niles, J. (Eds.). (2002). *Climate change policy.* Washington, DC: Island Press.

Speth, J. G. (2004). *Red sky at morning: America and the crisis of the global environment.* New Haven, CT: Yale University Press.

Tucker, R. P. (2000). *Insatiable appetite: The United States and the ecological degradation of the tropical world.* Berkeley: University of California Press.

Vandermeer, J., & Perfecto, I. (1995). *Breakfast of biodiversity: The truth about rain forest destruction.* Oakland, CA: Food First Books.

Elite vs. Mass Perspectives on the United States

Across the globe, the opinions of the United States held by political elites differ widely compared to those held by the middle and lower classes—the masses—due in large part to the influences on those groups of people.

The cultural, political, or economic elites and the masses (average people) in many nations have significant differences in their perspectives on the United States. Political scientists study the gap in the opinions of elites and masses by focusing on the mechanisms of how they think. Being able to determine the influences on such opinions has significant implications for appreciating, in its complexity, the universe of psychological and political mechanisms that shapes global perspectives on the United States.

The Puzzle of Elite vs. Mass Opinion

To understand the inconsistency between elite opinion and mass opinion, we first need to clarify the two concepts. Elite opinion is based on the preferences of academics, media officials and journalists, corporate executives, leaders of think tanks or special interest groups, and policy experts, all of whom shape the foreign and domestic policies in their countries. Mass opinion is a reflection of what the average citizen thinks and feels about politics. As Gregory Markus describes, mass opinion does not reflect the issues and concerns on which active publics deliberate. Rather, it is the "product of a purely formal arithmetic operation by which typically poorly informed, casually maintained, critically unexamined, and privately held considerations about politics are aggregated into an ersatz vox populi" (Markus 1994, 635).

The divergence between mass opinion and elite opinion of the United States is evident in polling data. On the one hand, Vladimir Shlapentokh, Joshua Woods, and Eric Shiraev report highly critical elite opinions of the United States after examining the reports of more than four thousand articles from leading newspapers across the world. On the other hand, the Pew Global Attitudes Project, a worldwide opinion poll administered by the Pew Research Center across forty-four countries, shows that mass public ratings of the United States are low but that the country manages to maintain its power of seduction.

This discrepancy between elites and masses is not limited to

perceptions of the United States. Similar discrepancies are evident in the policy preferences of elites and ordinary citizens in many western European democracies such as France or Sweden or post-Soviet countries such as Russia and Ukraine. In the United States it is rather the rule than the exception that elites and average citizens hold strikingly different opinions on issues such as globalization, the role of the United Nations (U.N.), and immigration. Particularly in the case of immigration, differences create a gap of 46 percent. As the Worldviews 2002 Survey indicates, whereas 60 percent of the public considers immigration a critical threat to the country's interests, only 14 percent of the elites are in line with this position.

Belief Systems in Elites and Masses

In order to account for this gap between the elites and the masses, we will examine how they think about politics and focus on their considerations when they form political judgments. Political science research provides evidence that not everyone thinks in the same way. For example, elites are more informed than the masses regarding political issues and more sophisticated in their political orientations. However, differences in the amount of political information cannot alone explain differences in opinions.

The process of opinion formation is complex, and to shed light on this process, we borrow insights from studies on public opinion. Converse in 1964 argued that the political ideas of elites and masses operate within "belief systems." A belief system is an ideology, a configuration of ideas and attitudes in which the idea elements are tied together by some form of functional interdependence. This interdependence, defined as "constraint," is an essential element of any ideology because it assures consistency among the multiple elements.

How people think about the political world depends on the complexity of their political belief systems. This organization of associations of cognitions has infinite variations, with some cognitions being more central and meaningful than others, involving

more information and being used more often. In other words, the political belief systems of people vary according to three dimensions: their size, their range, and their constraint of interconnected cognitions. These three dimensions taken together define the level of political sophistication of each person.

In a classic article published in 1987 Luskin put the elementary elements of sophistication on the table and offered measurements of the concept, attempting to "measure mind's height by the shade it casts" (Luskin 1987, 864). Luskin's aim was to pinpoint the type of political thinking that can distinguish sophisticates from nonsophisticates and to evaluate different types of measures used. He concluded that knowledge measures outperform other more complex indicators, and since then many scholars have used his recommendation for the creation of instruments in public opinion surveys. Sophistication, sometimes referred to by terms such as *expertise, knowledge,* and *cognitive complexity,* is central to the way we understand mass politics. High sophisticates differ from low sophisticates in the way they process information, in the way they reach their preferences, and in the level of their political involvement.

Formation of Political Judgments

To understand how sophisticates and nonsophisticates, or elites and masses, reach their preferences, we now focus on the individual-level dynamics of opinion formation and change and examine the considerations that induce people to think one way or another. In his classic political science book entitled *The Nature and Origins of Mass Opinion,* published in 1992, John Zaller took the basic idea of Converse and constructed a theory regarding the reaction of masses and elites to political information. His main argument is that the average person reaches political decisions on the basis of "considerations" that are mentally accessible at the time. For example, the probability of favoring a particular policy depends on the number of accessible favorable considerations in one's head. These considerations, which determine the public's reactions to political events, leaders, and policies, are influenced by a host of factors, some individual and some related to the political environment.

An opinion, then, is the outcome of a complex process that involves the reception of information, its acceptance or rejection, its storage in memory, and finally its retrieval and salience over other considerations. One factor that is crucial in the cycle of opinion formation is a person's level of political awareness. Political awareness precedes political sophistication, which comes later as the ability to integrate acquired information.

Political awareness is naturally related to reception of information because it is correlated highly with exposure and attention to mass media. Consequently, on the one hand, as awareness increases, the likelihood of receiving political messages also increases. On the other hand, in high levels of political awareness the likelihood of accepting a message decreases, and as a result the probability of attitude change declines. To understand this situation, we turn to the role of intraindividual political predispositions, such as partisan or ideological preferences. Politically aware individuals have more crystallized and tightly organized attitudes. Consequently, as awareness increases, the number of consistent considerations increases, and inconsistent considerations decrease. This situation suggests the existence of partisan or ideological resistance to inconsistent messages. When highly aware people see that a message is inconsistent with their values, because they have a higher number of consistent existing considerations, they are able to counteract a dominant message.

This discussion has interesting applications in understanding the nature of the opinion gap between elites and masses. Elites are exposed to more information but accept less. Average citizens are more difficult to reach but more penetrable because they lack firm beliefs and considerations that anchor them to particular positions. The aware elites make better counter arguments because they have more contextual information and stronger convictions.

Message-level factors also play a significant role in how opinions are formed. As Zaller notes, attitude formation and change are directly related to the capacity of a message to "penetrate the consciousness of the members of the public" (Zaller 1992, 152). When a message is of low intensity, it can bring change only among highly aware people. Average people are not alert enough to receive low-intensity messages, whereas elites have the high levels of awareness necessary for the reception of such messages. Message familiarity is a second determinant of how opinions are formed. The higher the familiarity, the less the overall change of attitudes among the highly aware. For the least aware, however, the impact of high-familiarity messages is stronger.

In Zaller's model the considerations that the average citizen uses in forming an opinion are affected by the way the topic has been framed in elite discourse. The understanding of public opinion becomes more complicated when no single point of view exists among political elites and instead political issues have two sides. Dominant and countervalent messages affect sophisticates and nonsophisticates differently. In an environment of competing political messages and divided elites, conflicting messages reach to a different degree the high- and low-informed segments of the public. Awareness heightens the impact of values, and members of the public follow the elites, sharing their general ideological

positions. Using opinion formation during the Vietnam War as an example, Zaller accounts for the impact of predispositions and awareness on the opinion formation of people in favor of the war ("hawks") and those against the war ("doves"). The "hawkishness" and "dovishness" of people, interacting with their levels of political awareness, produced interesting patterns in political decision making. The more politically aware doves could best sort out the prowar messages from the antiwar messages. The more aware doves were, as a result, more able than less-aware doves to accept the antiwar messages and reject the prowar ones. Highly aware hawks, on the other hand, were best equipped to resist the antiwar messages that existed in the information environment.

The main lesson from that situation is that opinion formation is not a single-factor procedure. Intraindividual factors, such as the level of awareness and predispositions, interact with the political environment and shape the direction of political decisions. The elites, being politically aware, are better able to discern which messages are consistent with their predispositions when they receive information from other elites. The average citizen is less capable of identifying messages correctly and is thus more easily influenced by the communication of opposing elites. This social phenomenon has important implications for the ability of political elites to communicate their policies to the general public and to mobilize support for political issues. At the extremes, as with the issue of immigration mentioned earlier, large differences between elite opinion and mass opinion can lead to policy stalemate.

Perspectives on the United States

Perspectives on the United States range from total hostility, condescension, and resentment to total advocacy, as the country is hated and loved by different elites and masses around the world. International affairs is a complex environment, with multiple and opposing considerations, and, as we saw earlier, the opinions of elites and masses reflect differences in these considerations. As Andrew Kohut, Bruce Stokes, and Josef Joffe recently show in their books on world opinion, leaders, and U.S. perceptions, extreme favorable and unfavorable opinions are represented by political elites, whereas masses generally hold middle-range and benign opinions toward the United States.

Several factors can explain this phenomenon. In the complex world of international politics, the masses might have difficulty following all that takes place. Issue salience influences their opinions. For issues that have immediate effect on their daily lives—for

example, the economy or a terrorist attack on one's hometown—we expect attitude consistency. In the event of two-sided communications, we would expect polarization of the masses, following the political elites. On the other hand, for issues that are more remote, the masses rely on the mix of considerations that is available in the information environment. Of these considerations, some refer to U.S. foreign policy and military strategies and could be unfavorable, but others bring to mind considerations of U.S. culture—for example, art and films or science and technology developments—which are for the most part favorable. This situation results in a reserved mix of opinions that is also detected in public opinion surveys, such as the one by the Pew Research Center discussed earlier.

For elites, on the other hand, symbolic issues related to power are the most salient in their belief systems. These symbolic issues appear, time and again, in interviews with political elites as the main considerations on the basis of which elites evaluate the United States. Perspectives on the United States as an economic and military superpower, an authority figure, a bully, or a charitable giant are related to issues of national interest and security. On the basis of these favorable or unfavorable considerations, elite opinions polarize and crystallize, diverging from the opinions of the masses.

The challenge that lies ahead for the United States is to cultivate favorable relationships abroad with both elites and masses. The Pew Global Attitudes Project shows that the most positive assessments of the United States come from India and Poland, where favorability ratings are at 71 percent and 62 percent, respectively. The most negative assessments come from Muslim nations, with Jordan scoring a low at 21 percent. European nations provide modest scores between 40 percent and 60 percent. A careful consideration of the determinants of opinions of the elites and the masses in these countries, the intensity and stability of their belief systems, and an understanding of the systemic factors that support their development can shed light to the origins of these ratings beyond regional trends. Mass opinion and elite opinion might seem "worlds apart," but a solid understanding of their determinants can bridge the gap. In their study in post-Soviet states Miller, Hesli, and Reisinger show that where stability and accountability are lacking, where fully developed networks of interest groups and free flow of political information are lacking, even the opinions of elites lack constraint and consistency. On the other hand, as Niemi and Weisberg point out, when the masses are politically involved, discuss their preferences, or mobilize, their attitudes become more crystallized, reaching levels of constraint similar to those of political elites. These findings point to the same direction: Building bridges between the United States and the world's elites and masses is not just wishful thinking. It is a challenging task that calls for improving our understanding of the complexities of public opinion and the cognitive mechanisms of judgment formation.

Tereza Capelos

See also Mass Media—Concepts and Technologies; Mass Media—Debates and Divides; Perspectives on the United States, Visitors'; Pop Culture—U.S. Advertising; Pop Culture—U.S. Film; Pop Culture—U.S. Music (Hip Hop); Pop Culture—U.S. Music (Jazz); Pop Culture—U.S. Television; Tourism

Further Reading

Converse, P. E. (1964). The nature of belief systems. In D. E. Apter (Ed.), *Ideology and discontent* (pp. 206–261). New York: Free Press.

Converse, P. E., & Pierce, R. (1986). *Political representation in France.* Cambridge, MA: Belknap Press of Harvard University Press.

Granberg, D., & Holmberg, S. (1988). *The political system matters.* Cambridge, MA: Cambridge University Press.

Jennings, M. K. (1992). Ideological thinking among mass publics and political elites. *Public Opinion Quarterly, 56,* 419–441.

Joffe, J. (2006). *Uberpower: The imperial temptation of America.* New York: W. W. Norton.

Kinder, D. (1998). Opinion and action in the realm of politics. In D. Gilbert, S. Fiske, & G. Lindzey (Eds.), *The handbook of social psychology* (4th ed., Vol. 1, pp. 778–867). Boston: McGraw-Hill.

Kohut, A., & Stokes, B. (2006). *America against the world: How we are different and why we are disliked.* New York: Times Books.

Luskin, R. C. (1987). Measuring political sophistication. *American Journal of Political Science, 31*(4), 856–899.

Markus, G. B. (1994). Reviewed work(s): The nature and origins of mass opinion by John R. Zaller. *The Public Opinion Quarterly, 58*(4), 633–636.

Niemi, R., & Weisberg, H. (1984). *Controversies in voting behavior.* Washington, DC: Congressional Quarterly Press.

Pew Global Attitudes Project. (n.d.). Retrieved March 18, 2007, from http://pewglobal.org/

Reisinger, W., Miller, A., & Hesli, V. (1995). Public behavior and political change in post-Soviet states. *Journal of Politics, 57*(4), 941–970.

Shlapentokh, V., Woods, J., & Shiraev, E. (2005). *America: Sovereign defender or cowboy nation?* Aldershot, UK: Ashgate Publishing.

Worldviews 2002 Survey. (n.d.). Retrieved March 18, 2007, from http://www.worldviews.org/

Zaller, J. (1992). *The nature and origins of mass opinion.* Cambridge, MA: Cambridge University Press.

Empire, U.S.

While the age of empires came to an end after World War II, many view the United States as the twenty-first century's de facto empire due to its economic might, military strength, political stability, and cultural appeal.

One of the ironies of history is that a republic committed to liberty, equality, inalienable rights, and self-determination should be called an "empire." Indeed the United States—whose ideas, examples, and actions did much to undermine the imperialist empires of the world—now finds itself referred to variously as "empire," "hegemon" (a political state having influence), "imperialist," "hyperpower," or "superpower." This irony requires a close examination of the nature of such a U.S. empire. Of particular importance is how leaders around the world perceive U.S. influence. These perceptions, in turn, define, constrain, and augment the U.S. "empire."

Understanding Empires

What then is an empire? An empire is a political conglomeration of culturally, linguistically, and ethnically diverse nationalities, covering an extensive territory, and ruled directly or indirectly by one nation for its own benefit. The classic example of empire, the Roman Empire, was created by Rome's conquest of the peoples and territory around the Mediterranean Sea. Within this empire those who enjoyed Roman citizenship were accorded special privileges. In the nineteenth century Britain established the first truly global empire with colonies in Africa, Asia, and the Americas. These two empires were alike in that empire was gained through military conquest.

The British and Roman empires are but two examples of what has been the norm for human political organization. Historically, empires arose as a group gained and then consolidated control over a certain region of the world. Such empires expanded, competed with neighboring empires, and eventually collapsed from foes within or outside the empire. Thus, empire replaced empire until the twentieth century. However, as Western ideas of self-determination and nationalism percolated among peoples throughout the international system, and as the shock of major wars weakened a Europe that had exercised preeminent control over the world for half a millennium, empires fell into disrepute. World War I brought the demise of the German, Austro-Hungarian, and Turkish (Ottoman) empires. World War II led to the collapse of the French, British, and Portuguese empires.

The end of the Cold War led to the disintegration of the Soviet (Russian) Empire, the last of the world's great empires. However, instead of the rise of replacement empires, what arose was an international system of nearly two hundred independent sovereign states.

The collapse of the Soviet Empire had three effects that are important in understanding views of a U.S. empire. First, Russia, the successor state, lacked the power to make it a true rival of the United States, effectively ending a unique bipolar era of the international system. Second, ideologically, Marxism had presented an alternative to Western liberal democracies as a way of organizing human political, social, and economic life. Thus, and importantly, the Soviet Union's disintegration not only ended an empire but also discredited the major ideological challenge to Western capitalism and democracy. Third, in the resultant unipolar era of U.S. dominance, newly independent states were left with few real alternative allies to the United States.

U.S. Preeminence

Thus, the twenty-first century began with the United States facing no rival able to match it in economic might, military prowess, technological sophistication, political stability, or cultural charisma. A few statistics underscore the power of the United States with relation to other countries. The United States ranks third in the world in population and fourth in territorial size. The United States has the third largest population, behind India and China. The U.S. population is 300 million out of an estimated world population of 6.5 billion, but the U.S. economy dwarfs the economies of every other country in the world. Even if one allows for cost-of-living adjustments related to local prices (purchase power parity), the U.S. economy is nearly the size of the next three ranked countries (Japan, China, and India) combined. The U.S. dollar is the world's reserve currency, which gives it an enormous financial advantage over that of any other country.

In defense the United States spends one-third more than the next ten countries combined. The United States alone is able to project its power through a fleet of aircraft carriers, intercontinental ballistic missiles, long-range bombers largely undetectable to radar,

A U.S. military Apache helicopter gunship over the Middle East. U.S. military might is seen by some as one element of the "U.S. Empire." Source: istock/Pete Masson.

and troop and equipment transport aircraft. Satellites circling the Earth foster both intelligence and communication. U.S. nuclear weapons could completely obliterate any country in the world.

U.S. science and technology have powered both military and economic progress. In the past century Americans routinely dominate the ranks of Nobel Prize winners. Americans have created or fostered the development of nuclear weapons, spacecraft, computers, software, the Internet, medicines, and high-yield agriculture. In fact, it is difficult to see how the world's rapid population growth could have been sustained without U.S. medical and agricultural technology.

Politically, the United States is a long-standing democracy that has proved adept at adjusting to the enormous demographic, territorial, economic, and cultural changes it has experienced in the two centuries of its existence, as well as to grave domestic upheavals and foreign challenges. U.S. cultural products of literature, films, television, food, and software exert a profound influence on people around the world. U.S. brands such as McDonald's, Coca-Cola, and Microsoft are known everywhere. The English language is now the world's lingua franca in international diplomacy and business.

These factors clearly point to the United States as the world's preeminent state but do not necessarily prove the case for empire. It is one thing to say the United States exercises the influence typi-

cal of an empire; it is quite another thing to say that the country therefore is an empire. To use an analogy, a company town is one in which a single company owns, controls, and integrates all aspects of the life of the townsfolk. This type of town, traditionally associated with the mining or textile industries, is really quite different from a town with a dominant employer whose influence permeates the life of the people, but whose interests are not completely identical with those of the townspeople.

U.S. Empire

Thus, although one can readily argue that the United States is the world's preeminent state, is it also an empire? If the United States is an empire it is indeed a peculiar one. In terms of land, labor, capital, and ideas, the United States acts in some ways that are not typical of past empires. The United States shows little appetite for acquiring and retaining foreign lands outside the North American continent. After the Spanish-American War in 1898, for example, the United States obtained Cuba and the Philippine Islands from Spain. In 1903 the Panama Canal Zone was acquired in perpetuity. Japan was occupied by U.S. forces in 1945. Yet, in all cases, after a relatively short period of occupation, the United States withdrew from these lands.

Perspectives on U.S. Empire

In Asia two former leaders of neighboring countries—former Singapore prime minister Lee Kuan Yew and former Malaysian prime minister Mahathir bin Mohammad—have written extensively on the U.S. Empire. The two see U.S. influence quite differently. In a 1994 interview, for example, Lee expressed a favorable disposition toward the United States and its influence in Asia. He pointed out features of U.S. life that he particularly liked. These features included an open and easy relationship among ethnically, racially, and socially different people, an openness to argument over what is best for society, and the accountability of public officials. He also believed U.S. military influence helped preserve regional stability in Asia.

Lee was, however, critical of what he saw as an overall breakdown of civil society. The indicators of this breakdown included the widespread availability of guns and drugs, violence, vagrancy, and crime. He argued that the United States had leaned too far in the direction of personal freedom at the expense of an orderly society.

In contrast, in a 2001 interview on a U.S. television network program, Mohammad was highly critical of the United States and its international influence on a whole range of issues. He argued that U.S. subsidization of its agriculture benefited a rich country at the expense of poor ones who are locked out of its markets. Foreign-owned banks and businesses set up shop in a country and then compete with and defeat nationally owned firms.

In Africa the statesmen of two major countries, President Hosni Mubarak of Egypt and former President Nelson Mandela of South Africa, also differ in their views on U.S. influence around the world. In a number of speeches Mubarak has emphasized Egypt's special relationship with the United States, Egypt's support for political and economic liberalization in Africa and the Middle East, and its solidarity in opposition to terrorism. He praised U.S. efforts to resolve the Arab-Israeli conflict. Mandela, in contrast, employed unusually harsh rhetoric in the lead-up to the Iraq War (2003), strongly condemning the United States for unilateral military action in a January 2003 speech to the International Women's Forum in Johannesburg.

Republican Empire in a Globalized World

The influence of such world leaders matters in understanding past, present, and future perspectives of the United States. All leaders agree that the United States occupies a position of great influence in the world. Most see this influence as fostering global security, although the Iraq War clearly has caused some reassessment of that view. U.S. political and economic ideals are likewise praised and considered worthy of emulation. Many world leaders are concerned, however, that the moral foundation of the United States is crumbling. Of particular concern to these leaders is the fact that U.S. cultural exports are undermining local traditions and values. There is also concern that economic liberalization around the world—globalization—has harmed many people. Rightly or wrongly, these impacts are laid at the feet of the United States. Such varied figures as Mandela and Mohammad argue that globalization is leading to global inequality.

Thus, in looking at the question of a U.S. empire, one is left with the conclusion that whether or not the United States meets a technical definition of *empire*, people around the world perceive the United States as having influence most commonly associated with an empire. The United States may be a de facto empire in an age of globalization. Clearly, all the processes and influences of such profound developments as modernization, Westernization, and globalization are not really under the control of the United States. Foreign leaders appreciate the positive contributions of a U.S. empire but have an expectation of U.S. leadership in addressing the more negative aspects of U.S. influence on the world.

Robert B. Lloyd

See also Foreign Policy after September 11, 2001, U.S.; Imperialism, U.S.; Linguistic Imperialism and English; Modernity, United States and

Further Reading

Bacevich, A. J. (2002). *American empire: The realities and consequences of U.S. diplomacy.* Cambridge, MA: Harvard University Press.

Boot, M. (2001, October 15). The case for American empire. *Weekly Standard, 7*(5).

Cohen, E. A. (2004). History and the hyperpower. *Foreign Affairs, 83*(4), 49–63.

Fergusson, N. (2004). *Colossus: The price of America's empire.* New York: Penguin Press.

Fukuyama, F. (2004). *State-building: Governance and world order in the 21st century.* Ithaca, NY: Cornell University Press.

Gaddis, J. L. (2004). *Surprise, security, and the American experience.* Boston: Harvard University Press.

Jervis, R. (2003, July/August). The compulsive empire. *Foreign Policy, 137,* 82–87.

Kagan, R. (1998, Summer). The benevolent empire. *Foreign Policy, 111,* 24–36.

Kagan, R. (2003). *Of paradise and power: America and Europe in the new world order.* New York: Alfred A. Knopf.

Kennedy, P. (1987). *The rise and fall of the great powers: Economic change and military conflict from 1500 to 2000.* New York: Random House.

Kupchan, C. (2002). *The end of the American era: U.S. foreign policy and the geopolitics of the twenty-first century.* New York: Alfred A. Knopf.

Nye, J. S. (2002). *The paradox of American power: Why the world's only superpower can't go it alone.* Oxford, UK: Oxford University Press.

Nye, J. S. (2004). *Soft power: The means to success in world politics.* New York: Public Affairs.

O'Brien, K., & Clesse, A. (Eds.). (2002). *Two hegemonies: Britain 1846–1914 and the United States 1941–2001.* Aldershot, UK: Ashgate.

Pei, M. (2003, May/June). The paradoxes of American nationalism. *Foreign Policy, 136,* 30–37.

Rothkopf, D. (1997, Summer). In praise of cultural imperialism? *Foreign Policy, 107,* 38–53.

Stiglitz, J. E. (2003). *Globalization and its discontents.* New York: W. W. Norton.

Zakaria, F. (1994). Culture is destiny: A conversation with Lee Kuan Yew. *Foreign Affairs, 73*(2), 109–126.

Environmental Issues

U.S. environmental activists helped found the modern environmental movement in the twentieth century, but the United States has since fallen behind other countries in protecting the environment and fighting global climate change.

The environmental policies of individual nations affect not only their domestic ecological systems, but also global ecological systems. Whether in absolute or per capita terms the United States ranks high in most surveys among the world's largest consumers of natural resources, especially oil, natural gas, coffee, copper, lead, and zinc. The Unites States also ranks as one of the world's largest polluters. For instance, whereas the United States accounts for around only 4 percent of the world's population, it produces 25 percent of all carbon dioxide emissions.

However, the United States has also been at the forefront of some global environmental initiatives. Although U.S. environmental philosophy appears compatible with that of the rest of the globe, as evidenced in numerous laws and international agreements, the implementation of this philosophy has differed from administration to administration. Those differences have caused sharp criticism in the current global debate.

In general, any government's environmental policy is the set of initiatives it intends to pursue to address a wide range of environmental concerns. Cathryn McCue, Kevin Wolf and Jeffrey Muhr have identified five key questions which governmental actions respond to when formulating environmental policy.

1. Should government intervene in the regulation of the environment or leave resolution of environmental problems to the legal system or market?
2. If government intervention is desirable, at what level should that intervention take place? In the United States, for example, how should responsibility for resolution of environmental problems be divided between and among federal, state and local governments and who should have primary responsibility?
3. If government intervenes at some level, how much protection should it give? How safe should the people be and what are the economic trade-offs necessary to ensure that level of safety?
4. Once environmental standards have seen been set, what are the methods to attain them? How does the system control the sources of environmental obstruction so that the environmental goals are met?
5. Finally, how does the system monitor the environment for compliance to standards and how does it punish those who violate them?

Answering these questions about any one environmental issue produces the near impossibility of formulating one single environmental policy for the United States. Environmental policy is instead a complex set of interlocking, and sometimes conflicting, rules, laws, and regulations that are subject to a whole host of influences, "including the policy beliefs of elected officials, the health of the economy, anticipated costs and benefits of laws and regulations, federal-state relations, public opinion, media coverage of environmental issues and efforts by corporations, environmental groups, and scientists to influence public policy" (Kraft 2006).

Background and Perspectives on U.S. Policy

It was in the early part of the twentieth century that the U.S. federal government initiated the modern conservation movement. President Theodore Roosevelt and Gifford Pinchot, head of the U.S. Forest Service, recognized that the natural resources of the country, although bountiful, were not limitless. Their expansion of the national forests and parks along with establishing national wildlife refuges linked environmental preservations with human health. Roosevelt was also close friends with John Muir, a naturalist who went on to found the Sierra Club. Muir differed philosophically with Roosevelt and Pinchot as to the objectives of environmental conservation. Muir believed that species protection and wilderness preservation were ends in themselves while Roosevelt and Pinchot maintained the link between natural resources and human needs. These two basic perspectives have come to typify much of the environmental debate in the United States over time. However, it is Pinchot and Roosevelt's perspective that has become one of the basic philosophical underpinnings of U.S. environmental policy: protecting nature for its own sake while accounting for human needs. It is a philosophy that is still apparent in the administration of the current president, George W. Bush.

International Perspectives
Overall, the rest of the globe does not view U.S. environmental policy favorably. Whether people are polled on the environment in general or on more specific issues—for example, global warming,

EXTRACT FROM THE KYOTO PROTOCOL

The United Nations Framework Convention on Climate Change, commonly known as the Kyoto Protocol, is an international agreement that calls for a 5.2 percent reduction of greenhouse gas emissions of industrialized nations by the year 2012. The United States refused to ratify the treaty during both the Clinton and the Bush administrations for a variety of reasons, one of which was the cost it would take to implement the reforms. The United States remains the only leading industrialized nation that has not ratified the treaty, which has perpetuated the image of the United States as a "rogue" nation in its disregard for the international community. Listed below are some of the treaty's requirements.

Article 2

1. Each Party included in Annex I, in achieving its quantified emission limitation and reduction commitments under Article 3, in order to promote sustainable development, shall:

  (a) Implement and/or further elaborate policies and measures in accordance with its national circumstances, such as:

   (i) Enhancement of energy efficiency in relevant sectors of the national economy;

   (ii) Protection and enhancement of sinks and reservoirs of greenhouse gases not controlled by the Montreal Protocol, taking into account its commitments under relevant international environmental agreements; promotion of sustainable forest management practices, afforestation and reforestation;

   (iii) Promotion of sustainable forms of agriculture in light of climate change considerations;

   (iv) Research on, and promotion, development and increased use of, new and renewable forms of energy, of carbon dioxide sequestration technologies and of advanced and innovative environmentally sound technologies;

   (v) Progressive reduction or phasing out of market imperfections, fiscal incentives, tax and duty exemptions and subsidies in all greenhouse gas emitting sectors that run counter to the objective of the Convention and application of market instruments;

   (vi) Encouragement of appropriate reforms in relevant sectors aimed at promoting policies and measures which limit or reduce emissions of greenhouse gases not controlled by the Montreal Protocol;

   (vii) Measures to limit and/or reduce emissions of greenhouse gases not controlled by the Montreal Protocol in the transport sector;

   (viii) Limitation and/or reduction of methane emissions through recovery and use in waste management, as well as in the production, transport and distribution of energy;

  (b) Cooperate with other such Parties to enhance the individual and combined effectiveness of their policies and measures adopted under this Article, pursuant to Article 4, paragraph 2(e)(i), of the Convention. To this end, these Parties shall take steps to share their experience and exchange information on such policies and measures, including developing ways of improving their comparability, transparency and effectiveness. The Conference of the Parties serving as the meeting of the Parties to this Protocol shall, at its first session or as soon as practicable thereafter, consider ways to facilitate such cooperation, taking into account all relevant information.

Source: Kyoto Protocol to the United Nations Framework Convention on Climate Change. (n.d.). Retrieved May 1, 2007, from http://unfccc.int/resource/docs/convkp/kpeng.html

carbon emissions, or energy—the world's view of U.S. policy is unfavorable. This view may in part be explained by a general sense of anti-Americanism felt by the international community. The 2005 Pew Global Attitudes Survey concluded that U.S. favorability ratings were at their lowest of any point in modern times, ranging from single-digit approval (Jordan) to the mid-fiftieth percentile (Great Britain). Suspicion of U.S. power, the U.S. penchant for unilateralism, its failure to address global problems, and general skepticism about the nation's motives and honesty are contributing factors to the globe's unfavorable view of the United States. However, the survey also noted some positive aspects of the U.S. relationship with the rest of the globe. Views of the democratic values of the United States, with its way of life and its role as the world's lone superpower, are favorable. Nevertheless, the survey reported that 70 percent of foreigners believe that the United

States pays little or no attention to the interests of other nations. This opinion is reflected in international surveys about U.S. environmental policies.

International policy data for 2006 show the United States at or near the bottom of polls on the question of which country is most trusted to address environmental concerns. In a 2006 Angus Reid/MacLean's world poll, the United States placed last among the twenty countries surveyed on the question, which addressed the need to reduce damage to the environment even if doing so means slower economic growth. Only 70 percent of Americans agreed with that sentiment, whereas the world average was 87 percent (Mexico led the survey, with 95 percent favoring reducing environmental damage). In another 2006 poll, released by the Climate Action Network-Europe, the United States ranked fifty-third out of fifty-six countries that contribute at least 1 percent of

greenhouse gas emissions in the world. The United States, currently the world's largest emitter of greenhouse gases, was ranked ahead of only China, Malaysia, and Saudi Arabia (the world's largest exporter of oil).

In 2006 the United States ranked last in a Pew Global Attitudes Survey on the issue of global warming. Only 19 percent of Americans expressed any worry over global warming (the Chinese ranked just above Americans at 20 percent), whereas 66 percent of Japanese and 65 percent of Indians expressed worry, a 40 percent gap between the United States and other parts of the world. In another 2006 Pew survey on the image of the United States abroad, the results again confirmed a lack of trust by the rest of the globe of the United States concerning the environment. India (23 percent), Canada (16 percent), Poland (14 percent), and Jordan (10 percent) were the only countries whose respondents tallied double-digit favorable opinions of the United States on the question, "Whom do you trust to protect the global environment?" Every other respondent country tallied in single digits, indicating that the rest of the world looks to any other country but the United States for leadership in environmental concerns. The poll indicated no consensus on an alternative to the United States.

In light of such low opinions, observers were surprised by President George W. Bush's remarks on the environment in his 2007 State of the Union address. The president proposed to reduce U.S. dependence on gasoline while promoting alternative fuels and higher fuel standards. Although environmental activists noted little progress from similar proposals made by the president during the preceding year, foreign leaders in Germany and Great Britain remained optimistic about the president's environmental plans while recognizing the need for U.S. leadership on global environmental concerns.

The national energy policy proposed by the Bush administration in early 2001, and enacted 28 July 2005 in the Energy Policy Act of 2005, relies on expanding oil production (particularly in ecologically sensitive areas); constructing new oil, coal, and nuclear power plants; expanding all refineries; and giving additional tax-funded subsidies to the oil and nuclear energy industries. The policy makes no attempt to curb emissions that lead to global warming. The international environmental organization Greenpeace termed the policy "a scam" and nothing more than "a speedy payback to the oil, gas, utilities and mining interests" (Greenpeace 2001). This sentiment was echoed in a BBC report in which the policy was described as a payback for large campaign contributors, especially Texas-based energy businesses, which contributed $50 million to the 2000 Bush-Cheney election campaign.

Loss of Leadership

Whereas U.S. policy favors paying subsidies to promote coal-burning, the Earth Policy Institute reports that most other industrial countries are decreasing their use of coal. The United

A paper plant processing pine trees produces a large amount of smoke. Source: istock.

Kingdom has been replacing coal with natural gas, and Germany has been increasing its use of wind energy to replace coal. The Earth Policy Institute indicated that the United States has surrendered its leadership position in both wind and solar energy development to Europe (wind) and Japan (solar).

U.S. policy also has been criticized along a broader range of environmental issues. As of August 2006, the United States refused to adopt provisions of the Stockholm Convention on Persistent Organic Pollutants and the Rotterdam Convention on the Prior Informed Consent Procedure for Certain Hazardous Chemicals and Pesticides in International Trade. These conventions—adopted by twenty-seven and 160 countries, respectively—seek to eliminate persistent chemicals and to control the trade in toxic chemicals.

On a more positive note, U.S. policy has been applauded for its stand against the killing of whales by Japan and Norway. A number of international groups, led by the International Fund for Animal Welfare and the World Wildlife Fund, thanked President Bush for his position on the issue, a position he shares with previous administrations. The president also received praise in 2006 for designating the country's first National Marine Monument along the northwestern Hawaiian Islands. The monument is home to more than seven thousand marine species. The designation prohibits commercial fishing for five years and prohibits all recreational and commercial activity of any kind. Additionally, the *International Conservation Budget,* published by Conservation International, the Nature Conservancy, Wildlife Conservation Society, and the World Wildlife Fund, recognized U.S. contributions to global conservation, especially the work of the U.S. Agency for International Development (USAID). USAID, along with nongovernmental organizations and other partners, is working to support forestry reform in Liberia, protect coral reefs in Indonesia, and expand protected areas in the Congo River basin forest. However, the report also highlighted concerns that the AID budget would be cut, which could have a negative impact on conservation efforts; in the end the budget actually increased $500,000 from the 2005 fiscal year.

Perhaps no other issue has stirred the international community's reaction in the past decade than global warming, especially the Bush administration's decision not to implement the terms of the Kyoto Protocol. The protocol, an amendment to the 1992 United Nations Framework Convention on Climate Change, called upon signatory nations to adhere to limitations to reduce greenhouse gases produced by emissions. Agreed to by the Clinton administration in 1997, the protocol was never ratified by the U.S. Senate because it was viewed as being potentially harmful to the U.S. economy and because it excluded some developing countries, especially China and India, from compliance. Despite the fact that Bush campaigned for the presidency in 2000 with promises to

reduce carbon dioxide as a pollutant, one of his first actions as the newly elected president in March 2001 was to announce U.S. withdrawal from the protocol. The administration justified withdrawal on the basis of the same arguments advanced by senators, but also questioned the science behind claims of global warming. Negative reaction was swift from other governments and environmental groups.

Climate Disaster

International environmental groups have claimed that U.S. behavior contributes to potential climate disaster. The Natural Resources Defense Council (NRDC) criticized the Bush administration for making misleading statements about the Kyoto Protocol. The NRDC pointed out that the U.S. Senate had never voted against ratifying the protocol, that developing countries are not exempt from the protocol because they were signatories to the earlier 1992 convention, that the Bush administration offered no proof of the potential harms to the U.S. economy, and that the administration offered no alternative. The NRDC argued that the administration was pandering to the energy industry. Germany's largest environmental group, Naturschutzbund Deutschland, termed the U.S. withdrawal a "catastrophe" and with other environmental groups began searching for ways to boycott U.S. businesses responsible for emissions.

Since 2001, in poll after poll, the United States has continued to rank low in terms of its perception of the seriousness of global warming in comparison with the perception of the rest of the world. A World Public Opinion poll in 2006 showed that even though the percentage of Americans who believe global warming and climate change are very serious has increased from 31 percent in 2003 to 49 percent in 2006, those percentages were below the world average of 65 percent. Only China, Indonesia, Kenya, Nigeria, the Philippines, and South Africa ranked lower in the thirty-nation poll. An earlier GlobeScan Incorporated poll found U.S. concern about global warming at 76 percent (combining those who responded that the issue is either very serious, 49 percent, or somewhat serious, 27 percent), but that figure still left the United States in the lowest rankings. That poll also showed that Americans ranked highest in the percentage of people who believe climate change not to be a serious problem (21 percent), whereas the world average was 8 percent.

On a brighter note, a 2006 Pew Global Attitudes Survey showed that 91 percent of Americans were aware of the issue of global warming; although that number was slightly below the number in other industrialized nations, it was significantly higher when compared with public awareness in developing countries.

Nevertheless, the survey also revealed that barely half (51 percent) of Americans personally worry a great amount or a fair amount about the issue, ranking the United States last in this six-nation poll behind Japan (93 percent), France (87 percent), Spain (85 percent), Great Britain (67 percent), and Germany (64 percent). A 2006 Chicago Council on Global Affairs poll concluded that nearly half (46 percent) of Americans see global warming as a threat and feel that the United States should take immediate action even if that action involves significant costs. Again, however, Americans' concern ranked them last in the poll of six nations as they ranked global warming sixth of all the threats facing the country, below the world average ranking of third.

The Bush administration and the United States continue to receive failing marks from the rest of the world in policies on global warming. In a 2007 poll conducted by the Program on International Policy Attitudes and the British Broadcasting Corporation (BBC), adults in twenty-five countries expressed 56 percent dissatisfaction with the U.S. government's handling of global warming, whereas 27 percent expressed approval. An Intergovernmental Panel on Climate Change report entitled *Climate Change 2007: The Physical Science Basis, A Summary for Policymakers* concluded "that global warming is accelerating, that human activity is responsible for this warming, and that it is likely irreversible for centuries, even if greenhouse gas emissions are stabilized." This report was endorsed by the Bush administration's energy secretary, Samuel Bodman. However, the administration continues to rely on developing new technologies to reduce emissions rather than on limiting emissions, as preferred by other industrialized nations within the framework of the Kyoto Protocol.

John C. Horgan

See also Ecological Footprint, U.S.; Green Revolution;
U.S. Agency for International Development

Further Reading

British Broadcasting Corporation. (n.d.). Science & nature: TV and radio follow-up. Retrieved February 19, 2001, from www.bbc.co.uk/nature/environment/conservationnow/global/

Globe Scan. (n.d.). Retrieved March 23, 2007, from www.globescan.com

Greenpeace. (2001). Bush-Cheney national energy policy delivers another blow to the Earth. Retrieved March 23, 2001, from www.greenpeace.org

Intergovernmental Panel on Climate Change. (2007). Climate Change 2007: The Physical Science Basis. Summary for Policymakers. Retrieved March 10, 2007 from www.ipcc.ch/SPM2feb07.pdf

Kohut, A. (2006). *America against the world.* New York: Henry Holt.

Kraft, M.E. (2006). Public policy decision making. Retrieved April 5, 2007, from http://www.pollutionissues.com/Pl-Re/Public-Policy-Decision-Making.html

McCue, C., Wolf, K., & Muhr, J. (2003). Environmental policy. In M. Boatman, et al. (Eds.), *Environmental Encyclopedia,* 3rd *edition.* Detroit, MI: Gale.

Pew Global Attitudes Project. (n.d.). Retrieved March 23, 2007, from www.pewglobal.org

Speth, J. G. (2005). *Red sky at morning: America and the crisis of the global environment.* New Haven, CT: Yale Nota Bene.

United Nations Environment Programme. (n.d.). Retrieved March 23, 2007, from www.unep.org

Watching America. (n.d.). Retrieved March 23, 2007, from www.watchingamerica.com

World Directory of Environmental Organizations. (n.d.). Retrieved March 23, 2007, from www.interenvironment.org/wd/

World Public Opinion. (n.d.). Retrieved March 23, 2007, from www.worldpublicopinion.org

Worldpress.org. (n.d.). Retrieved March 23, 2007, from worldpress.org

Equality

American society has always fought for, protected, and promoted the opportunity for everyone to be treated equally, emphasizing individual opportunity in contrast to some other societies that place more value on collectivism.

Equality has been a core value of the United States since the first European settlers arrived. Many of the colonists who migrated from Europe during the 1600s and 1700s came to escape inequitable treatment because of race, religion, or creed. The people who provided the basis for U.S. culture were, in a sense, seeking equality. Indeed, the U.S. value of equality is clearly stated in the Declaration of Independence of the thirteen colonies, a document that played a pivotal role in their separation from England. The declaration, drafted by Thomas Jefferson (1743–1826) in 1776, boldly proclaims, "We hold these truths to be self-evident, that all men are created equal..."

The way in which U.S. citizens value equality is specific—it is an equality of individual opportunity. Rather than ascribing equal status to people throughout life, the essence of U.S. equality is that all people begin life with the same opportunities and the same potential. What each person does with these opportunities is a matter of his or her ambition and work ethic. Thus, ironically, differences between individuals in the United States are valued. Individual differences are important because of the belief that they are not the result of inequitable original opportunities given by society but rather of individual attributes. The Constitution, which provides the foundation for U.S. government, clearly emphasizes many of these ideas. Serving as a guide for legislation in the United States, the Constitution has consistently protected and promoted the equal opportunity of individuals.

Concern with equal opportunities for all people is strongly linked to the U.S. belief in each person's inalienable right to self-direction and development. In this way the U.S. value of equality is bound inseparably with U.S. individualism. Inequality is presumed to result not from different opportunities, which are contextual or situational characteristics. Rather, inequality is presumed to result from ambition and work ethic, which are individual characteristics. Therefore, to understand how and why Americans value equality of individual opportunity, it is imperative to understand U.S. individualism, a core dimension of U.S. culture.

For the sake of simplicity, we discuss equality and individualism in the ideal and general sense, acknowledging that there are within-culture variations and historical events inconsistent with idealized values. Different groups of people have been excluded from this idea of equality through the U.S.'s history, such

as African-Americans and women. However, we discuss the ideals of equal opportunity and individualism in the sense that they have served to guide and drive tendencies toward rectification of unequal treatment. The civil rights movement of the 1960s and 1970s in the United States is one such example.

Individualism and Collectivism

Since the 1960s cross-cultural research in psychology, sociology, and anthropology has burgeoned on the potent cultural dimension of individualism and its counterpart, collectivism. Simply put, *individualism-collectivism* refers to the degree to which a society builds social experience around individuals versus groups. In highly individualistic societies, individuals are relatively independent of groups; a person's decisions and behavior are relatively separate from any groups with which he or she may be affiliated, such as family or school. In highly collectivistic societies, on the other hand, a person's decisions and behavior are interdependent with and closely guided by any groups with which he or she may be affiliated. The relationship between individuals and collectives in collectivistic societies is much stronger than in individualistic societies.

Cross-cultural research in psychology and anthropology, in particular, has provided a broad overview of how various cultures rank in terms of individualism-collectivism. Consistently, across multiple, distinct research programs, the United States scores as the most individualistic country in the world. Other Western nations, such as Australia, Great Britain, and Canada, also score high on measures of individualism. At the other end of the continuum, Eastern nations, such as China and Singapore, and some Latin American nations, such as Panama and Guatemala, score as the least individualistic (or most collectivistic) nations in the world. Clearly such striking differences, with respect to how societies view the relationship between individuals and collectives, have important implications for a multitude of societal norms and values, as well as for individual cognitions and behaviors. For example, theory and research suggest that people in individualistic societies have different views of the self than do people in collectivistic societies. People in individualistic societies

view the self as unique, autonomous, and independent, whereas those in collectivistic societies view the self as bound to others, determined by others, and interdependent. These differing views of the self serve to drive different patterns of behavior. People in individualistic societies tend to strive to become independent from others and express their unique attributes; individual dispositions and personalities give meaning to the self. People in collectivistic societies, however, tend to strive to maintain the fundamental connectedness of individuals to each other; social relationships give meaning to the self.

More overt manifestations of individualism and collectivism exist in societies. One example is familial structure, or the manner in which a society defines the family. In individualistic societies the tendency is to define the family by nuclear boundaries. Thus, the family consists of a core unit of parents and their children, who are expected to define themselves separately from their family. A child in an individualistic society is encouraged to express his or her uniqueness and differences from parents. In collectivistic societies, on the other hand, the family unit tends to be a much broader social network, including extended family members such as grandparents, aunts, uncles, and cousins. Children in collectivistic societies tend to define themselves by and identify with their extended family. Parents emphasize to their children the importance of representing, protecting, and caring for other family members.

Horizontal and Vertical Individualism, Collectivism

To explain how U.S. individualism and the U.S. ideal of equal opportunity are interrelated, a finer distinction of individualism-collectivism must be made. Cross-cultural theorists and researchers have suggested that the cultural dimension of individualism-collectivism is really a multidimensional facet of culture. Specifically, scholars have indicated that individualism-collectivism can be broken into horizontal and vertical types, with *horizontal* referring to an emphasis on equality and *vertical* referring to hierarchical differentiation. Crossing individualism-collectivism with horizontal-vertical yields four basic categories.

In societies characterized by *horizontal individualism*, individuals desire autonomy and independence from groups (characteristic of individualistic societies) but do not necessarily seek high distinction and status (characteristic of horizontal societies). Swedish culture is a good example of horizontal individualism. Individuals are respected as autonomous beings, separate from groups, and generally want to "do their own thing." Individuals do not tend to seek distinction and high status.

Horizontal individualism can be contrasted to *vertical individualism*, which emphasizes competition and striving to be the best (characteristic of vertical societies). In societies characterized by vertical individualism, people distinguish themselves from groups through individual competitions with others. U.S. culture is a good example of vertical individualism. Americans value and promote autonomy through competition.

In societies characterized by *horizontal collectivism*, interdependence is tremendously important. People see great similarity between themselves and others. Horizontal collectivists emphasize common goals and sociability, and they do not submit easily to authority. Rather, equal status and the common good are paramount. A good example of horizontal collectivism is the Israeli kibbutz, in which people value a common interdependence and similar level of status.

Vertical collectivism, on the other hand, emphasizes the importance of hierarchy and power differences in collectivistic societies. People are interdependent and value group identification to the extent that they sacrifice personal goals and desires for the good of the group, as desired by group authorities. Thus, group authorities have respected power over those lower in the group hierarchy, who are expected to submit to the will of authority. The group authority, people believe, represents the overall interests of the group. Japanese culture is a good example of vertical collectivism. Group and collective identification is important, but hierarchical structures are prevalent.

Vertical Individualism and U.S. Equality

As stated earlier, empirical research has generally found the United States to be a vertical, individualistic society. Many of the aspects

AMENDMENT XV TO THE U.S. CONSTITUTION

The Fifteenth Amendment (1870) was one of the Reconstruction Amendments passed after the Civil War. Its purpose was to enfranchise former slaves. However, it was not until the Voting Rights Act in 1965, that the fifteenth amendment was actually enforced in all states.

Section 1. The right of citizens of the United States to vote shall not be denied or abridged by the United States or by any state on account of race, color, or previous condition of servitude.

Section 2. The Congress shall have power to enforce this article by appropriate legislation.

Source: Emory Law School: Historical Documents. (2006). Retrieved March 19, 2007, from http://www.law.emory.edu/cms/site/index. php?id=3110#7738

A "Welcome" sign to the upscale community of Beverly Hills, California, as symbol of both equality and inequality, depending on one's perspective. Source: istock/Ivan Cholakov.

not valued or expected in the United States (after all, Americans generally desire just one champion), competitions are ideally among those who have been afforded the same opportunities and chances to grow or improve. For example, in many U.S. professional sports leagues, rules restrict the total amount of money each team can pay its players, with the goal of ensuring an environment of fairness.

Thus, the idea that all are created equal is a manifestation of vertical individualism—all are created equal but are expected to work to become different. Americans value equality of opportunity because it ideally ensures that competitions will reveal the individual attributes (not the situational characteristics) that lead to individual differences. In working to improve from the same starting point, individuals distinguish themselves through their abilities, rather than through inequitable beginnings.

Implications

The U.S. value of equality is an equality of opportunity for individuals. The link between U.S. equality and vertical individualism is important because it reveals the core cultural roots of a fundamental U.S. value. When compared directly with horizontal collectivistic cultures such as the Israeli kibbutz, the United States appears quite different. However, differences between cultures are not valence distinctions. Rather, they are simply differences. Each cultural pattern has its own positives and its own negatives. Furthermore, any judgment of what is positive or negative depends on one's cultural perspective. In the case of the United States, vertical individualism stimulates creativity, ambition, and high levels of individual effort. However, extreme competition can also result in high levels of stress and possible unethical practices driven by a pressure to "be the best."

Above all, understanding the depths and roots of U.S. equality facilitates greater understanding of U.S. culture—politics and economics, for example. The U.S. form of government, the democratic republic, clearly is infused with the values of equal opportunity and individualism. Ideally, officials are elected to hold positions of power based on their attributes and abilities. Virtually anyone in the United States has the opportunity to run for office and rise to power. Thus, the election process embraces the value of equal opportunity. Elections are competitions among individuals for positions of power, a clear manifestation of vertical individualism. Similarly, U.S. economic policies are driven by the value of equal opportunity. The market economy, as practiced in the United States, encourages open competition in the marketplace—may the best company or product prevail. Government regulations are put in place to ideally ensure the equal opportunity of all individuals and organizations to introduce products to the market.

of vertical individualism are well represented in U.S. society, such as competing and distinguishing oneself from groups or collectives. Vertical individualism is also manifested powerfully in the U.S. ideal of equal opportunity. Although equal outcomes for all are

An understanding of the cultural roots of U.S. equality more fully informs a global perspective on the United States. U.S. international policies, economic standards, and foreign relations are greatly influenced by this powerful cultural ideal. From its inception, U.S. society has protected and promoted the equality of individual opportunity. This behavior can be contrasted to that of other societies that ascribe more strongly to traditions of collectivism and value interdependence. By seeing how U.S. culture differs from other cultures with respect to individualism and equality, we see the global perspective more completely.

Andrew P. Knight and Lynn Imai

See also Human Rights; Slavery and
Abolitionism; U.S. Civil Rights

Further Reading

Coons, J. E., & Brennan, P. M. (1999). *By nature equal: The anatomy of a Western insight.* Princeton, NJ: Princeton University Press.

Ekirch, A. A. (1977). Individuality in American history. In F. Morely (Ed.), *Essays on individuality* (pp. 291–316). Indianapolis, IN: Liberty Press.

Gannon, M. J. (2004). *Understanding global cultures: Metaphorical journeys through 28 nations, clusters of nations, and continents* (3rd ed.). Thousand Oaks, CA: Sage Publications.

Hofstede, G. (1984). *Culture's consequences: International differences in work-related values.* London: Sage Publications.

Hofstede, G. (1991). *Cultures and organizations: Software of the mind.* London: McGraw-Hill.

Hoover, H. (1922). *American individualism.* Garden City, NY: Doubleday, Page & Co.

House, R. J., Hanges, P. J., Javidan, M., Dorfman, P. W., & Gupta, V. (2004). *Culture, leadership, and organizations: The GLOBE study of 62 societies.* Thousand Oaks, CA: Sage Publications.

Markus, H. R., & Kitayama, S. (1991). Culture and the self: Implications for cognition, emotion, and motivation. *Psychological Review, 98*(2), 224–253.

Murrin, J. M., Johnson, P. E., McPherson, J. M., Gerstle, G., & Rosenberg, E. S. (2004). *Liberty, equality, power: A history of the American people* (2nd ed.). Fort Worth, TX: Harcourt Brace College Publishers.

Nisbett, R. E., Peng, K., Choi, I., & Norenzayan, A. (2001). Culture and systems of thought: Holistic versus analytic cognition. *Psychological Review, 108*(2), 291–310.

Pole, J. R. (1992). The individualist foundations of American constitutionalism. In H. Belz, R. Hoffman, & P. J. Albert (Eds.), *To form a more perfect union: The critical ideas of the Constitution* (pp. 73–106). Charlottesville: University Press of Virginia.

Schoeck, H. (1977). Individuality vs. equality. In F. Morley (Ed.), *Essays on individuality* (pp. 145–176). Indianapolis, IN: Liberty Press.

Triandis, H. C. (1994). *Culture and social behavior.* New York: McGraw-Hill.

Triandis, H. C. (1995). *Individualism and collectivism.* Boulder, CO: Westview Press.

Triandis, H. C., & Gelfand, M. J. (1998). Converging measurement of horizontal and vertical individualism and collectivism. *Journal of Personality and Social Psychology, 74*(1), 118–128.

Exceptionalism, U.S.

U.S. exceptionalism refers to a perception of the United States as a superior nation because of its unique history. In the twenty-first century this notion is embodied in the U.S. mission to spread democracy around the world.

Americans have always believed that they are a special people with a special destiny. This is the essence of American exceptionalism, the idea that the United States is set apart from other nations by its unique national character and a global mission to spread the values of freedom and democracy. Americans have embraced this national myth for more than two centuries. It holds that the Americans possess trademark qualities of rugged individualism and entrepreneurial spirit, a willingness to fight for democratic principles, and a strong sense of morality and idealism. These qualities are coupled with the belief that the United States is endowed with a special responsibility to serve as a global champion of liberal and democratic values.

Understandably, the rest of the world has had mixed feelings about U.S. exceptionalism. The global community has often accepted and encouraged the moral and political leadership of the United States. Americans have always been willing to fight for their freedoms, and particularly since the late 1800s, they have been willing to lend their support to the struggles of others peoples for such freedoms. This was the case in both world wars and the Cold War, which left only the United States standing after an epic standoff with the authoritarian Communism of the Soviet Union.

On the other hand, Americans' belief in their own exceptionalism has fostered considerable resentment and frustration around the world. Many peoples do not accept the smug premise that the United States is superior to other nations. U.S. leaders tend to present their foreign policies as driven purely by selfless and virtuous motives, but in reality, those policies are often as self-serving and unscrupulous as those of any other global power. The United States has justified its intrusions into the business of other nations in part on the grounds that it is exceptional—but the intrusions have often been unwelcome nevertheless. The affected populations have found it galling that U.S. leaders champion freedom and democracy in their rhetoric but ignore those ideals when doing so serves U.S. strategic interests. U.S. exceptionalism has therefore been a mixed blessing for the rest of the world.

The Roots of U.S. Exceptionalism

There is no precise definition of exceptionalism and no particular historical moment at which the idea was first conceived. The no-

tion that Americans are a special—and specially blessed—people was prevalent long before the actual foundation of the United States. The Puritans who founded the Massachusetts Bay Colony believed that they were blessed by God with the chance to begin life anew in a promised land. Such religious convictions were common among early New England settlers, and the notion that God literally blessed America—a notion that is likely familiar to anyone who has ever listened to a U.S. political speech—has been an important component of exceptionalist thought.

Religious conviction instilled the idea that Americans occupied a blessed land, but geography helped to make that conviction a believable one. North America is endowed with remarkable geographic advantages. It occupies an enormous physical space. It has ample arable land and natural resources of immense economic value. For early European settlers, it seemed a gift from God for virtually unlimited Christian settlement. The Atlantic and Pacific oceans also provided a defensive buffer between it and the imperialist powers of Europe and Asia. Thus geography allowed the United States, once established, to survive its early years and develop into a great power.

Racial ideology also played a role in exceptionalist thinking. White settlers used the notion of racial superiority to justify their expansion into Native American lands. They presumed that the "savages" were on the losing end of history, destined to surrender their lands to the Anglo-Saxon race. Racial ideology helped U.S. leaders to rationalize egregious policies toward Native Americans, as well as the longstanding practice of African-American slavery. When the United States pursued expansionist foreign policies in the late nineteenth century, racial assumptions were also used to justify "civilizing" foreign lands such as the Philippines and exercising predominant influence over the affairs of Latin American nations.

The last formative influence on the development of exceptionalism as an intellectual concept was political philosophy. When it was founded, the United States was conceived as a nation that would cherish individual freedom, political and economic liberalism, and republican democracy. These ideals turned an isolated colonial struggle against Britain into what political philosophers such as Thomas Paine (1737–1809) saw as a watershed moment in recorded history. Americans were not just struggling for their own independence, but for the universal principles of freedom and de-

mocracy. This assessment of the significance of the Revolution is one of the critical assumptions behind U.S. exceptionalism.

Affects of U.S. Exceptionalism, 1783–1898

It goes without saying that the notion of U.S. exceptionalism has affected not only the course of U.S. history, but also that of its global neighbors. This was not so great a concern at first, since the United States' first leaders believed that the country ought to steer clear of the murky waters of international diplomacy. George Washington (1732–1799) warned that foreign entanglements with the corrupt powers of Europe and Asia would only corrode the exceptional moral fiber of the U.S. citizenry. It was better to remain a beacon of democracy, shining for all the world to see, than to pursue an aggressive or expansive foreign policy beyond U.S. shores. This perception of the appropriate global role for the United States, dubbed isolationism, dominated U.S. foreign policy until the late nineteenth century, and its lingering influence can still be detected.

A reluctance to venture abroad did not prevent the United States from pursuing rampant expansionist policies across North America. The presumption that the United States had a right to trample its continental neighbors owed much to the concept of exceptionalism. In the 1840s, the U.S. journalist John O'Sullivan coined the phrase *manifest destiny* to describe the divine mission of the United States to take over the continent. The process itself had begun long before and was punctuated by territorial gains such as the 1803 Louisiana Purchase, war with Canada from 1812 to 1814, and war with Mexico from 1846 to 1848. The most terri-

tory was gained from the brutal campaigns waged against Native Americans over the course of the nineteenth century.

In the same century the United States announced that, as an exceptional nation, it had a claim to the entire Western Hemisphere. In 1823 the Monroe Doctrine warned European powers to avoid any further colonization of Latin America. Since that time the United States has rarely tolerated much opposition to U.S. political and economic objectives in the region, and various Latin American nations have been subjected to intervention and even occupation. In 1895 the United States Secretary of State Richard Olney declared that it was "practically sovereign on this continent," and threatened Great Britain with war over a minor dispute over the border of Venezuela (Paterson 1999, 2–3).

Expansion, and Intervention, 1898–1945

By the beginning of the twentieth century, the traditionally isolationist course of U.S. foreign policy had undergone a substantial change. In the late 1890s the idea of exceptionalism helped to justify a new foreign policy: expansion of U.S. political and economic power to the far corners of the globe. The trigger was the Spanish-American War of 1898, in which the United States annihilated feeble Spain and captured its colonies of Cuba, Puerto Rico, Guam, and the Philippines. President William McKinley (1843–1901; served 1897–1901) was motivated to declare war both out of sympathy for the Cubans, who were suffering under cruel Spanish tyranny, and by the perception that U.S. political and economic interests, such as expansion into the fabled "China market," could be furthered by the war. His serene faith in U.S.

United States Capitol Building in Washington, DC, known around the world as a major symbol of the U.S. government. Source: istock.

THE ORIGINAL "CITY UPON A HILL"

This excerpt is from the famous 1630 sermon "A Modell of Christian Charity" delivered by the first governor of the Massachusetts Bay Colony, John Winthrop. U.S. president Reagan quoted this sermon in his own farewell address over three hundred years later to emphasize the greatness of the United States.

Now the onely way to avoyde this shipwracke and to provide for our posterity is to followe the Counsell of Micah, to doe Justly, to love mercy, to walke humbly with our God, for this end, wee must be knitt together in this worke as one man, wee must entertaine each other in brotherly Affeccion, wee must be willing to abridge our selves of our superfluities, for the supply of others necessities, wee must uphold a familiar Commerce together in all meekenes, gentlenes, patience and liberallity, wee must delight in eache other, make others Condicions our owne rejoyce together, mourne together, labour, and suffer together, allwayes haveing before our eyes our Commission and Community in the worke, our Community as members of the same body, soe shall wee keepe the unitie of the spirit in the bond of peace, the Lord will be our God and delight to dwell among us, as his owne people and

will commaund a blessing upon us in all our wayes, soe that wee shall see much more of his wisdome power goodnes and truthe then formerly wee have beene acquainted with, wee shall finde that the God of Israell is among us, when tenn of us shall be able to resist a thousand of our enemies, when hee shall make us a prayse and glory, that men shall say of succeeding plantacions: the lord make it like that of New England: for wee must Consider that wee shall be as a Citty upon a Hill, the eies of all people are uppon us; soe that if wee shall deale falsely with our god in this worke wee have undertaken and soe cause him to withdrawe his present help from us, wee shall be made a story and a byword through the world, wee shall open the mouthes of enemies to speake evill of the wayes of god and all professours for Gods sake; wee shall shame the faces of many of gods worthy servants, and cause theire prayers to be turned into Cursses upon us till wee be consumed out of the good land whether wee are going.

Source: Hanover Historical Texts Project. (2001). Retrieved March 14, 2007, from http://history.hanover.edu/texts/winthmod.html

superiority also justified keeping the Philippines and retaining de facto control of the other newly acquired territories. Who could better civilize these backward peoples, McKinley publicly mused, than the benevolent and anti-imperial United States?

The idea that Americans were ideally suited to this mission was reinforced by the same amalgam of religion and racial ideology that had helped to create the notion of U.S. exceptionalism in the first place. Other global powers noted the hypocrisy of this premise as they watched the United States brutally suppress a revolution in the Philippines from 1899 to 1902 and use its growing military and economic muscle to turn Latin America into a virtual U.S. dependency. President Theodore Roosevelt (1858–1919; served 1901–1909) was fond of "speaking softly and carrying a big stick," and proclaimed the right of the United States to exercise an international police power over the Western Hemisphere. His assumption of U.S. superiority, in the fullest political, economic, and racial sense, was shared by successive twentieth-century presidents.

Woodrow Wilson (1856–1924; served 1913–1921) led the United States through World War I. He was a devout Christian and an equally devout believer in U.S. exceptionalism. To Wilson, the United States was a supremely moral nation, the only nation that could act as an impartial mediator for the warring European states. The United States did not enter the war until 1917, and then it was with the stated intention of "making the world safe for democracy." Wilson envisioned "peace without victory" and laid out his Fourteen Points for the settlement of the conflict. He hoped to build a peaceful and prosperous world order drawing on U.S. values of

political and economic liberalism. At the Paris Peace Conference of 1919, Wilson made a valiant effort but had limited success in his attempt to reshape the world according to this prescription. It said much about his belief in exceptionalism and his grand vision of a more internationalist role for the United States in international affairs that he even tried.

In the 1920s the United States retreated somewhat to isolationism, but from 1933 to 1945, President Franklin Roosevelt (1882–1945) gradually moved toward the sort of internationalist foreign policy that Wilson had championed. World War II helped to enshrine permanently in Americans' consciousness the idea that the United States had to step up and fulfill its destiny as leader of the "free world." Americans were rather late in entering the war against totalitarian Germany, Italy, and Japan, but their influence on the outcome of the war was immense. Roosevelt eased his fellow Americans toward a more internationalist conception of their global mission and relied on the traditional ideas of exceptionalism to explain this policy shift.

U.S. Leadership of the "Free World"

The United States emerged from World War II as the most powerful nation in the world. In 1945 it accounted for half of the world's manufacturing output, and U.S. power, so amply demonstrated during the war, was reinforced by the United States' sole possession

of the atomic bomb. There was a global consensus that the Allies had fought the good fight against the evils of fascism. Now the authoritarian Soviet Union emerged as a threat to global freedom and democracy. From the U.S. point of view, more frightening than the Soviet Union's desire to control Eastern Europe was the alleged grand conspiracy of the Soviet dictator Joseph Stalin (1879–1953) to spread Communism to all parts of the world. This was an exaggeration of the real scope of the Soviet threat, but President Harry Truman (1884–1972; served 1945–1953) nevertheless concluded that the United States had to lead world opposition to the Soviet Union in the emerging Cold War.

Between 1945 and 1950, Truman moved the United States toward the sort of global leadership role that Wilson had envisioned after World War I. This time the shift away from isolationism was permanent, and it was justified by familiar ideas relating to the exceptional character and special mission of the United States. The Truman Doctrine of 1947 declared that the United States would support free peoples everywhere against the expansion of Communism.

In the early postwar era the United States received widespread global support for their new superpower role. The fear of Britain and France in the late 1940s was not that the United States would intervene too much in global affairs, but that it might not intervene enough. For its part, in the early postwar period the United States lived up to its lofty rhetoric about promoting free peoples abroad. Instead of punishing its defeated foes, the United States moved quickly to rebuild the economies of West Germany and Japan and to establish democratic governments in both nations. The United States' European Economic Recovery Plan (or Marshall Plan, named for the U.S. secretary of state George C. Marshall), which operated between 1948 and 1953, brought roughly $13 billion of aid to exhausted, economically depleted Western Europe and helped ensure stability and democracy there.

The deeply instilled idea of U.S. exceptionalism, with its emphasis on the United States' special mission as a defender of freedom and democracy, helped to prepare Americans psychologically for the Cold War. It also, however, created blind spots in the U.S. outlook on the world. Americans' good-versus-evil mind-set led U.S. leaders to make alarmist assumptions about the motivations of the Soviets, whose supposed desire to initiate another world war was debatable at best. It also helped to propagate a distorted world view in which any left-wing nationalist movement abroad was seen as part of a global conspiracy, directed from the Kremlin and designed to undermine a U.S.-led democratic world order. This mind-set led to needless interventions in the affairs of other nations around the world, often in support of undemocratic leaders so long as they were opposed to Communism.

As it had in the past, the idea of U.S. exceptionalism also helped to justify broad intervention around the globe over the course of the Cold War. The Central Intelligence Agency (CIA) used covert tactics to help get rid of uncooperative governments in Iran, Guatemala, and Chile, among other nations. Direct military intervention was also employed in Korea from 1950 to 1953 and in Vietnam from 1961 to 1973. The latter conflict escalated into a tragic and bloody war that ended in a North Vietnamese victory over the U.S.-backed South, tarnished the image of the United States, and called into question the whole idea of exceptionalism. Massive bombing campaigns and widely reported atrocities committed by U.S. soldiers against Vietnamese civilians shocked people both inside and outside the United States, which for the first time ever had been humbled and defeated.

Americans experienced a crisis of confidence in the wake of the Vietnam War. Some pundits wondered if the defeat in Vietnam marked the end of U.S. exceptionalism, as the United States seemed weakened and beleaguered both military and economically. This period of self-doubt did not last long. The 1980s saw the revival of a simple, inspiring brand of exceptionalism, the credit for which can largely be placed with President Ronald Reagan (1911–2004; served 1981–1989), who denounced the Soviet Union as an evil empire and (quoting the first governor of the Massachusetts Bay Colony) hailed the United States as a "shining city on a hill." Reagan could not imagine that other nations would wish to embrace anything but the U.S. model of democracy and free trade. When they did choose otherwise, as was the case in leftist Nicaragua, El Salvador, and Grenada, he did not hesitate to intervene with CIA or military operations. Reagan was supported by the religious right in the United States, which was fitting, as religion had influenced the idea of U.S. exceptionalism from the outset, and this helped to reinforce the uncritical view that the United States was naturally good and its enemies naturally bad.

In the 1990s Americans felt they had even more reason to believe that their nation was blessed. The United States outlasted the Soviet Union, which crumbled economically during the 1980s and was dissolved in 1991. This left the United States as the only remaining superpower and the unquestioned leading nation in the world. In 1991, after an Iraqi invasion of Kuwait, President George H. W. Bush (b. 1924; served 1989–1993) assembled an international coalition that drove Iraq out. This stirring success vindicated the idea, nurtured since the Wilson years, that the United States would assume the leadership of a prosperous and democratic world order.

The Future of U.S. Exceptionalism

If anything, Americans have been more convinced than ever of their own exceptional character and position in world affairs in the early twenty-first century. In the wake of the terrorist attacks of September 11, 2001, in which Islamic extremists crashed planes into

New York City's World Trade Center and the Pentagon, President George W. Bush (b. 1946; served 2001–present) adopted a unilateral new conception of U.S. exceptionalism. His Bush Doctrine asserted that the United States possessed the right to preemptively attack any nation, at any time, in the defense of its national security. This policy was implemented despite global protest in March 2003, when the United States invaded Iraq and deposed its leader, Saddam Hussein (1937–2006). Bush justified the war on grounds that Hussein possessed weapons of mass destruction, a claim that was questionable at the time and that was later revealed to be false. U.S. credibility has suffered abroad as a result of this aggressive and openly militaristic shift in U.S. foreign policy.

This new and virulent strain of U.S. exceptionalism has done much to alter global perspectives on the United States. The idea that Americans are a special people, blessed by God and endowed with a mission to promote freedom and democracy in the world, is not new by any means, but its newly aggressive articulation and the United States' concomitant willingness to use military force to solve global problems are new. These changes have overshadowed the historic U.S. devotion to the values of freedom and democracy, which have previously earned the United States much respect and goodwill abroad, and raised troubling questions about the wisdom and legitimacy of U.S. leadership on future international issues.

Christopher John Pennington

See also American Dream; Democracy; Founding Principles of the United States; Religious Pluralism, United States and; Sports

Further Reading

Berman, L. (1982). *Planning a tragedy: The Americanization of the war in Vietnam.* New York: W. W. Norton.

Chomsky, N. (2004). *Hegemony or survival: America's quest for global dominance.* New York: Henry Holt.

Collin, R. H. (1985). *Theodore Roosevelt, culture, diplomacy, and expansion: A new view of American imperialism.* Baton Rouge: Louisiana State University Press.

Costigliola, F. (1984). *Awkward dominion: American political, economic, and cultural relations with Europe, 1919–1933.* Ithaca, NY: Cornell University Press.

Dorrien, G. (2004). *Imperial designs: Neoconservatism and the new Pax Americana.* New York: Routledge.

Fahrang, M. (1981). *U.S. imperialism: From the Spanish-American War to the Iranian revolution.* Boston: South End Press.

Gaddis, J. L. (1997). *We now know: Rethinking Cold War history.* Oxford, UK: Clarendon Press.

Glaser, E., & Wellenreuther, H. (Eds.). (2002). *Bridging the Atlantic: The question of American exceptionalism in perspective.* Washington, DC: German Historical Institute.

Herring, G. C. (2002). *America's longest war: The United States and Vietnam, 1950–1975* (4th ed.). Boston: McGraw-Hill.

Horsman, R. (1981). *Race and manifest destiny: The origins of American racial Anglo-Saxonism.* Cambridge, MA: Harvard University Press.

Hunt, M. H. (1987). *Ideology and U.S. foreign policy.* New Haven, CT: Yale University Press.

Joy, M. S. (2003). *American expansionism, 1783–1860: A manifest destiny?* New York: Longman.

LaFeber, W. (2002). The Bush doctrine. *Diplomatic History, 26*(4), 543–558.

Leffler, M. (2003). 9–11 and the past and future of American foreign policy. *International Affairs* [Great Britain], *79*(5), 1045–1063.

Link, A. S. (1971). *The higher realism of Woodrow Wilson and other essays.* Nashville, TN: Vanderbilt University Press.

Lipset, S. M. (1996). *American exceptionalism: A double-edged sword.* New York: W. W. Norton.

Lockhart, C. (2003). *The roots of American exceptionalism: History, institutions and culture.* New York: Palgrave Macmillan.

McCrisken, T. B. (2004). *American exceptionalism and the legacy of Vietnam: U.S. foreign policy since 1974.* New York: Palgrave Macmillan.

McEvoy-Levy, S. (2001). *American exceptionalism and U.S. foreign policy: Public diplomacy at the end of the Cold War.* New York: Palgrave.

Noble, D. W. (2002). *Death of a nation: American culture and the end of exceptionalism.* Minneapolis: University of Minnesota Press.

Paterson, T. G. (Ed.). (1999). *American foreign relations since 1895.* (Vol. 2). Boston: Houghton Mifflin.

Stephanson, A. (1996). *Manifest destiny: American expansionism and the empire of right.* New York: Hill and Wang.

Weston, R. F. (1972). *Racism in U.S. imperialism: The influence of racial assumptions on American foreign policy, 1893–1946.* Columbia: University of South Carolina Press.

Williams, W. A. (1988). *The tragedy of American diplomacy* (New ed.). New York: W. W. Norton.

Exchanges, Cultural and Scientific

Nearly two million people each year are involved in international exchanges, creating a global knowledge network in which the United States plays a large role and which can serve as a venue for improved intercultural relations.

On first blush, the idea of exchanging people for educational purposes appears to be very simple. On reflection, however, it is a multidimensional, multidisciplinary, massive idea of global scope. The purpose of this article is to describe briefly these complex dimensions of the field that is part not only of U.S. national policy, but also of nearly every country in the world. It is no wonder that this complex system touches the lives of thousands of participants, as well as their families, their employers, their home countries, and the many people they encounter in host countries while pursuing their educational goals.

However, study abroad programs are not always well understood. There are many reasons for this, one being that people are socialized and acculturated to their own countries and have sometimes have difficulties conceptualizing things of global nature. Another reason is that people tend to think in terms of a single frame of reference, whatever it may be.

The decision to study abroad is not a simple one. It involves certain knowledge of the host country; preparation for the trip; finding resources to make it possible; searching for additional resources (often involving the government-sponsored information services); selecting suitable institutions; and assessing consequences of such decision for future employment upon return. While studying in the U.S., for example, an international student often encounters Americans from all over the country, as well as other international students and scholars. Some researchers suggest that the "incidental" or "implicit" learning about a different culture that goes along with studying abroad is often more important than formal academic learning. Students continually reflect on these experiences, collect pictures and mementos that they share with their families at home, and establish friendships with individuals and families in the host countries. Upon return home, they utilize and apply their new knowledge. They often form professional and academic partnerships with scholars of the host country.

There are at least four dimensions (frames of reference) of this field and its complexity: first, it is costly; second, it involves knowledge and its production, utilization, and transfer; third, it involves intensive and dynamic learning about the host as well as home cultures; and finally it is cultural diplomacy at its best that hopes to accomplish positive experiences based on first-hand knowledge of both societies.

Characteristics of the "Field"

A cultural or scientific exchange can be considered a system even though that system's projects are spread across many countries; its expected outcomes are based on unexamined assumptions about educational and value-added benefits and epistemologies (purposes and practices of higher education, access to it and primary educational philosophies); its origins may be in diverse intellectual traditions embedded in academic disciplines and research; and its management is performed by hundreds of unrelated organizations such as ministries, academies, universities, professional associations, foundations, and brain trusts. A system is a system even without one overarching formula, if it has the connected themes that exchanges have: similarity of goals; future orientation; production, transfer, and utilization of knowledge and skills; and development and maintenance of global partnerships and linkages. The "field" has its own tradition, subspecializations, and record of accomplishment. It also has its own culture, social psychology, politics, and economics. It serves millions of "clients" who believe in its goals and makes a significant contribution to international relations and understanding. It is relevant to the job market and is congruent with global trends. Although it is fragmented and undervalued, it is emerging as a global system that has coalitions to support it. Systems have subsystems and in turn are part of larger systems, such as governments, universities, corporations, foundations, and voluntary associations. Consistent with most theories of learning and functioning of the brain, such complexity and diversity often cause people to see only things that are organized by a single domain; complex systems require explanation through multiple perspectives. The expanding literature of the field suggests at least four major perspectives expressed as metaphors: exchanges (1) as business, (2) as knowledge factories, (3) as cultural diplomacy, and (4) as laboratory of complex global

relations. Before considering these it may be useful to provide a brief description of the scope of the "field."

Scope of the Field

Statistics demonstrate the field's scope and importance. The American Council of Education (ACE) reported that in 2004 nearly two and a half million students studied in countries other than their own, an increase of 56 percent from 1999 when 1.68 million students studied in other countries (ACE, Issue Brief, October 2006). This number does not include performing artists, youth, high school students, athletes, military personnel, missionaries, religious workers, trainees, and teachers. Virtually all countries send and receive people in these exchange categories and regulate their flow through laws, regulations, treaties, and executive agreements. To qualify as an exchange program does not require reciprocity of one for one; exchanges mean that countries agree to provide frameworks and programs that facilitate the implementation of mutual exchange policies. The IIE statistics also indicate that during 2003 572,509 foreign students were in the United States, whereas U.S. students studying abroad numbered 174,629 (from a total enrollment in postsecondary institutions of 13,383,553). Cumulative figures show that foreign student enrollment increased dramatically from 34,232 in 1964–1965. However, because of a variety of complex reasons, that number declined in the United States over two years (2002–2003) by 1.1 percent and 6.4 percent respectively; the number of applicants declined even more dramatically. However, other countries experienced substantial increases of foreign students, notably Great Britain, which had 222,571 students (an increase of 15 percent), Germany, which had 185,179 students (an increase of 10 percent), and France, which had 134,785 students (an increase of 81 percent). In addition to regularly enrolled students (by definition of their immigration visa status), the United States hosted 43,003 "special" students enrolled only in English language courses and 82,905 foreign scholars and researchers, 18 percent of whom were from China. The most encouraging aspect of these statistics is the substantial increase of U.S. students studying abroad. Their number has increased by 8.5 percent since 2002.

Exchanges as Business

Recently the U.S. Department of Commerce started reporting a new category of trade—money transfers from foreign students. In 2005 the amount was $13 billion. The British, by comparison, claim that foreign students spent 13 billion pounds off campus. The Organisation for Economic Co-Operation and Development

(OECD) predicts that the future potential income is even greater, when high schools will graduate 16 million potential candidates for universities in 2025 (an increase from 11 million in 2000). The International Development Program of Australian Universities (IDP) estimated that by the year 2025, 7 million "mobile" students will be available for study globally. Many countries are discovering the profitability of education as export; the General Agreement on Trade in Services (GATS) placed this item on its 2006 agenda. Foreign students are predicted to form 25–50 percent of all student enrollments in countries with capacity to absorb them—and many countries are already building such capacity.

This increase in foreign students, and the potential income they represent, has created a drive for higher education reform in countries that want to compete for the unattached students. The higher education establishment in the United States appears complacent because of the presumed superiority of its university system that it ignores the global trend and may be unprepared to face such global competition.

Exchanges as Knowledge Factory

Exchanges as knowledge factory are driven by the globalization paradigm that focuses on global changes from industrial production to "knowledge and innovation" societies associated with learning, teaching, knowledge production, utilization and dissemination, and relevant cognitive skills. It stresses the need to deal with dramatic changes and to acquire a level of competency not often emphasized in undergraduate education, such as communicating skills and thinking competencies, including critical, creative, comparative, metathinking, and self-regulating competencies. All exchanges are transfer programs of subject-matter knowledge, skills, and application to the job market. Participants also acquire "incidental" cultural knowledge of both the home and host country because both filter what, how, and why knowledge is learned. Different pieces of knowledge are gained differently; some are gained through formal learning; others implicitly, informally, or experientially.

The knowledge perspective is neglected in research and practice for two major reasons: first, because theories of cognition are confusing about expected outcomes from cross-cultural learning. The key questions not answered are (1) how participants process new information for which prior education has not created mental categories, (2) whether participants view the host culture through the eyes of their own (the so-called etic perspective), (3) whether they can switch their "codes" from etic (from the outside of a culture, looking in) to emic (from the inside of a culture, looking out)

THE KOREAN SCIENTISTS' AND ENGINEERS' ASSOCIATION

The following excerpt describes a program of scientific exchange that was established between South Korea and the United States.

The Korean Scientists' and Engineers' Association was created in 1971 by scientists and technical engineers, most of whom entered the United States as students and established successful professional careers in American science and technology. The association has two main goals: (1) to exchange new ideas and news of the accomplishments of its members; (2) to contribute to the technological and scientific development of South Korea. The South Korean government was indirectly involved in the formation of the association partly because South Korea needs Korean-American "brains" in its process of rapid industrialization.

The association has its headquarters in Washington D.C. and twenty-two branches throughout the United States. In 1978 some 1,500 Korean scientists and engineers were organized in the association. Its major activities include: (1) annual seminars in Seoul, with the participation of South Korean scientists; (2) sending newly produced tools, machine equipment, and new books to South Korea. In 1977 the association made a "Mutual Assistance Treaty" with the Korean Institute of Science and Technology (KIST), which is called the "Korean brain tank." An ex-president of the association was cited by the South Korean government for his devotion to the establishment of the association.

Source: Kim, I. (1981). New urban immigrants: The Korean community in New York. Princeton, New Jersey: Princeton University Press.

---

without judging which culture is better, (4) how they integrate new learning with prior learning, (5) whether they are aware of and in control of their thinking when comparing, (6) whether they sustain new learning and keep producing new knowledge continuously, and (7) whether they understand global trends. Funds for research of these and related questions have not been available for several decades, thus dissertations are the only sources of knowledge about these processes. Many of these dissertations have been produced recently, but unfortunately they tend to be dominated not by what and how people learn, but rather how people adjust, how well they do academically, and how satisfied they are with the achievement of personal growth and development. Although these concerns are important, especially for liberal arts students, they provide only anecdotal evidence about exchange experiences.

The second reason for the lack of data is the complexity of the field; it has too many variables to study. The field needs to know not only what individuals learn, but also their institutions. Research about the effects of institutional functioning in this field indicates that academic institutions do not keep adequate records and depend on "seat time" spent in class and grades obtained. They tend to look at study abroad as a shortcut to all international education without raising questions about its effectiveness and sustainability. Many institutions convey an ambiguous message about the importance of exchanges, with the result that only 9.1 percent of graduates have even minimal education in understanding the global dimension of living and working.

Exchanges as Public Diplomacy

The exchange field created an infrastructure of organizations that provides a friendly, accepting, and educational environment in which cultural diplomacy can function. Virtually every community with a college that enrolls foreign students has a volunteer organization that provides home stay, specialized services, speakers' programs, tours, field trips, and other creative programs that allow people to become unofficial ambassadors and vice-versa, to participate in this aspect of foreign policy. First-hand knowledge of other countries is admittedly the best educational bargain. It can accomplish simultaneously education in the subject matter, better understanding of other cultures, and insight into one's own. In Europe the exchanges of persons programs have become the main instruments of European integration. Although the academic field of international relations has been slow to acknowledge this area as its legitimate subfield, a significant public feels a need to promote its country and its values. The public diplomacy perspective on which the field was based since the end of World War I will be helped by recently passed legislation on U.S. intelligence in which the "soft" approach to conveying the core values of the U.S. experience will receive priority and funding to counter negative images of the United States abroad, especially in the Islamic world and in Europe.

Exchanges as Laboratory of Global Relations

Focusing on the people who are "exchanged" is only a part of the story. To make exchange programs work most countries have provided a highly organized, professionally oriented, and leadership-driven infrastructure to provide services for such expanding populations. This infrastructure includes professional associations concerned with selection, recruitment, reception, language training, orientation, financing, assessment of experiences,

reentry to home countries, establishment of standards, accreditation of foreign credentials, and counseling services. Many of these services helped establish academic subfields that have enriched internationalization efforts of our universities, such as intercultural communication, comparative education, or cross-cultural counseling. To provide a common framework for exchanges, several coordinating organizations monitor the field. Counterpart organizations outside the United States began establishing multinational and global coalitions that help provide unity of the exchange field. Most importantly, the presence of foreign students and returned home country nationals has created a giant "true" global laboratory of international and intercultural relations in which one finds virtually every variable of human and social relations, ranging from adjustment processes to complex and theoretical issues of global interdependence. The growing literature in the field reflects those concerns and issues.

Issues and Problems

Every field that requires funding must justify itself. Explaining a complex field outside of the national mainstream is especially difficult. Our culture conditions us to seek quantified data based on causal relationships to outcomes. Social science methodologies are not sufficiently developed to study multidimensional causation and multidisciplinary variables. Moreover, some of the disciplines that have provided intellectual foundation for international education, such as cultural anthropology, are seeking deep understanding rather than cause-and-effect relationships. On the other hand, qualitative research methods tend to be anecdotal, imprecise, and limited in scope; for example, what can we conclude from students' statements that "this was a life-changing experience" or "I learned a lot about the host country" or "the most important thing I learned is that people are people everywhere" or "I keep in touch with the host culture by occasionally eating its native dishes"? The first issue is then for the field to explain itself as an educational bargain with multiple benefits involving high risks worth taking. This may require different explanations to members of Congress, to the media, to Presidents of Universities, and to faculty and students of colleges and universities. The field also needs to compensate for the current trend of going abroad for short periods of time by providing sophisticated orientation programs for which high-quality methods do exist.

The second issue is tension between two contemporary global trends in higher education: massification and globalization. These trends are not sufficiently well understood. Massification is related

The Bolshoi Theater in Moscow, home of the Bolshoi Ballet, a frequent participant in cultural exchanges. Source: istock.

to internationalization and is focused on expanding educational programs to facilitate access of underrepresented populations. Internationalization implies relationships among states in which exchanges are within the authority of national governments, whereas globalization is an ambiguous external force that bypasses and occasionally undermines governments. The field needs to find links between these forces; democratization is such a link.

The third issue is sustainability. Research indicates that returned exchange students lose their skills over time because these skills are not self-renewing and self-regulating. Some longitudinal studies suggest that former participants recall their past experiences fondly but as an arrested frame dated to the time of their sojourn. Hanvey proposed that personal knowledge of people from other countries helps develop these metalearning skills.

A related issue is the role of international students, who are the most underutilized and underappreciated educational tool. Many studies and dissertations document their isolation from the mainstream cultures and their tendency to enclose themselves in their own cultural communities without associations with people of the mainstream host country culture. Many social psychological, linguistic, and cultural reasons exist for this problem, which U.S. students abroad experience also. The solution depends on whether foreign students are regarded as "insiders" or "outsiders"—and that depends on the frame of reference and ethnocentrism of the hosts as well as the guests; the beginning of the solution may be in the campus "ethos" on the living circumstances and on the culture of the classroom. A solution is needed because foreign students are the key to the development of three important skills: metalearning, creative thinking, and sustainability. Hanvey suggested that sustainability of international knowledge and interests depends on two factors: understanding of trends and personal knowledge of people from other countries. Complementing this concept, Csikszentmihalyi addressed creativity and suggested that it is especially difficult to teach because it is unusual. Instead of attempting to teach it in the classroom, he recommended another method he called "heterogeneation"—mixing together many people who are as different as possible (Mestenhauser 2002b, 165–213).

A more subtle benefit could accrue from personal experiences of foreign students; they have to figure out how and why our system of education works in order to function in it successfully. This helps them develop the metalearning skill that gives them an advantage not only in studying, but also in sustaining their continued learning after graduation. Many native students, including minority students, would benefit from such a skill—and from resulting networking possibilities.

Finally, a disturbing trend was reported in the *New York Times* (21 December 2004) by an OECD analyst who called attention to changes in the thinking about exchanges. In addition to purely fiscal motives, he suggested that a trend that emerged in the 1990s is beginning to replace the objective of cultural diplomacy with a "brain gain" program that is using foreign students as recruits to fill important posts in science and technology. This trend is based on the competitiveness paradigm and, if not reversed, will harm any programs designed to educate foreign students to return to their countries to participate in their development.

It bears repeating that educational exchanges of persons are the only aspect of national policy in which thousands of people can participate actively and which allows positive cooperation between the government, educational institutions; business and commerce; and foundations and many non-profit educational societies. The field makes a cumulative contribution to individual development, institution building, and national and international relations. The impact can be seen best if viewed through the multiple frames of reference suggested in this article and understood as a "soft aspect" of international cultural relations as distinguished from propaganda and impression management (Arendt 2005). Furthermore, the impressions that participants in educational exchanges acquire depend not only on the kinds of experiences they have while abroad, but also on what the citizens of the host country actually know about their country of origin. There are thousands of people working in government agencies, in the universities, and as volunteers in civic societies who, in contact with exchange students, practice this soft approach in combination with some of the best academic, social, and cultural traditions that the United States has to offer. They have many hopeful stories to tell about the multiple and life-long benefits of this field that keep giving and that allow people around the world to respect the ideals of the United States even in the face of disagreements with our official policies.

Josef A. Mestenhauser

See also Brain Drain

Further Reading

Abroad View Magazine. (2004). Retrieved January 17, 2007, from http://www.abroadviewmagazine.com/archives/spring_04/

Altbach, P. G. (Ed.). (1994). *The international academic profession: Portraits in fourteen countries.* New York: Carnegie Foundation.

American Council on Education. (2006). *Issues Brief, October 2006: Students on the move: The future of international students in the United States* (pp. 1–16). www.acenet.edu/programs/international

Arendt, R. T. (2005). *The first resort of kings: American cultural diplomacy in the twentieth century.* Washington, D.C.: Potomac Books, Inc.

Barrows, T. S. (1981). *College students' knowledge and beliefs: A survey of global understanding.* New Rochelle, NY: Change Magazine Press.

Bond, S., & Lemasson, J.-P. (Eds.). (1999). *A new world of knowledge.* Ottawa, Canada: International Development Research Centre.

Carnegie Corporation. (2000). *Education for international understanding and global competence.* New York: Author.

Chandler, A. (2000). *Paying the bill for international education: Programs, partners and possibilities in the millennium.* Washington, DC: NAFSA: Association of International Educators.

Czikszentmihalyi, M. (1996). *Creativity: Flow and the psychology of discovery and invention.* New York: HarperCollins.

Dillon, S. (2004, December 21). U.S. slips in attracting the world's best students. *New York Times.* Retrieved January 16, 2007, from http://www.nytimes.com/2004/12/21/national/21global.html

Frankel, C. E. (1965). *The neglected aspects of foreign affairs: American educational and cultural policy abroad.* Washington, DC: Brookings Institute.

Goodwin, C. D., & Nacht, M. (1983). *Absence of decision: Foreign students in American colleges and universities.* New York: Institute of International Education.

Goodwin, C. D., & Nacht, M. (1988). *Abroad and beyond: Patterns in American overseas education.* Cambridge, MA: Cambridge University Press.

Hanvey, R. (1979). *An attainable global perspective.* New York: Global Perspective in Education.

Harari, M. (1992). Internationalizing the curriculum. In C. B. Klasek (Ed.), *Bridges to the future: Strategies for internationalizing higher education* (pp. 52–80). Carbondale, IL: Association of International Education Administrators.

Hayward, F. M. (2000). *Internationalization of U.S. higher education.* Washington, DC: American Council on Education.

Headland, T. N., Pike, K. L., & Harris, M. (Eds.) (1990). Emics and etics: The insider/outsider debate. In *Frontiers of anthropology, Vol. 7.* Newbury Park, CA: Sage.

Huisman, J., & van der Wende, M. (Eds.). *On cooperation and competition: National and European policies for the internationalization of higher education.* Bonn, Germany: Lemmens.

Institute of International Education. (2004). Open doors. Retrieved January 16, 2007, from http://opendoors.iie.network.org

Lambert, R. D. (1989). *International studies and the undergraduate.* Washington, DC: American Council on Education.

Mestenhauser, J. A. (2002a). Critical, creative and comparative thinking in internationalization of universities. In *Internationalization of universities* (pp. 55–77). Winnipeg, Canada: University of Manitoba Press.

Mestenhauser, J. A. (2002b). In search of a comprehensive approach to international education: A systems perspective. In W. Gruenzweig & N. Rinehart (Eds.), *Rockin' in Red Square: Critical approaches to international education in the age of cyberculture* (pp. 165–213). Muenster, Germany: Lit Verlag.

Mestenhauser, J. A., & Ellingboe, B. J. (Eds.). 1998. *Reforming the higher education curriculum: Internationalizing the campus.* Phoenix, AZ: Oryx Press; Washington, DC: American Council on Education.

Riegel, N. D. (1951). *Cultural Contacts Project: An evaluation of the long-time effects of international exchange in Belgium.* Princeton, NJ: Woodrow Wilson School of Public and International Affairs.

Scott, P. (Ed.). 2000. *The globalization of higher education.* Buckingham, UK: Open University Press.

Williams, G., & Kelly, C. (2004). United Kingdom. In J. Huisman & M. van der Wende (Eds.), *On cooperation and competition: National and European policies for the internationalization of higher education.* Bonn, Germany: Lemmens.

Feminist Movement and Women's Rights

While U.S. feminism has contributed to the international women's rights movement, the two have not always been perfect partners. The achievement of women's rights worldwide hinges upon understanding differences in class and culture.

Many people in the United States assume that U.S. values have been in the forefront of the struggle for women's equality internationally and that U.S. women have been leaders in that struggle. Although those assumptions contain some truth, it is equally true that U.S. values and U.S. women have been both an inspiration to and a constraint on the international women's movement.

International Women's Movement: First Wave

The earliest efforts of women to organize internationally for their rights were inspired by the French Revolution and by the principles found in the earliest feminist writings, the first being the treatise *A Vindication of the Rights of Women* (1792) by the British activist Mary Wollstonecraft. Later inspiration came from the writings of the British philosopher John Stuart Mill, who in *The Subjection of Women* (1869) made an impassioned argument for the recognition of women's personal, legal, and political rights, including the right to work outside the home, the right to higher education, and the right to equal rights in the institution of marriage.

Researchers say the U.S. women's rights movement was actually sparked by the refusal to seat U.S. women delegates at the World Anti-Slavery Convention held in London in 1840. Eight years later the U.S. suffragists Elizabeth Cady Stanton and Lucretia Mott organized the first women's rights conference in the United States, with three hundred men and women meeting in Seneca Falls, New York. The conference sought to apply principles of the Declaration of Independence to women. The conference's *A Declaration of the Rights of Women* reads, "We hold these truths to be self-evident: that all men and women are created equal" (Anderson 2000, 168). The National Women's Rights Convention (October 1850), representing women from nine states, endorsed "equality before the law without distinction of sex or color" and made news in Europe (Anderson 2000, 8). Black women leaders such as Sojourner Truth and Harriet Tubman made significant contributions

to antislavery efforts and to women's equality, although tensions existed between the U.S. abolitionist movement and the women's movement. The British wife of John Stuart Mill, Harriet Taylor, was so inspired by these events in the United States that she wrote the *Enfranchisement of Women*, which she sent back to the United States. The National Women's Suffrage Association (now the U.S. League of Women Voters) pushed for suffrage, a move that resulted decades later in the Nineteenth Amendment to the U.S. Constitution. This fight for the right to vote was the focus of U.S. women's efforts for many decades.

All of this is to say that, from the French Revolution to Seneca Falls, from Britain to Germany to the United States, women united to fight for the cause of fullest equality. At the height of the Victorian period, these women insisted on political equality, called for a new kind of marriage, claimed the right to divorce, and argued than an unjust economic system forced women into poorly paid jobs. The first *international* women's congress was held in Paris (1878) in connection with the World Exposition. Neither the people in attendance nor the movement itself was monolithic or unified. Issues included abolition, nationalist and revolutionary strategies, liberal to radical social reform, and often conflicting national agendas.

The striking aspect of the first wave of the international women's movement was that it was based on a web of international feminist connections. The web was inspired by socialist struggles in Europe and abolitionist efforts in the United States as well as by temperance and moral reform movements in many countries. The web was supported by innovations in travel (such as trains and faster steamships) and in communication (such as the telegraph). Letters and news moved back and forth primarily between women in the United States, England, Germany, and France.

Although the role of U.S. women leaders in these first-wave international organizations was significant, U.S. interests tended to be more narrowly focused on suffrage rather than on the wider range of issues held by the European constituents. The impact of U.S. women on the international women's movement during these years was to narrow the wide range of issues to one: voting rights.

The leadership of U.S. women as well as of their European colleagues must also be seen in a larger context of the race, ethnicity, nationality, and class bias of all three of the international women's organizations, which originated and grew primarily in Europe and the United States. The real and perceived obstacles to equal participation of all women created a movement of predominately elite, Christian, older women of Euro-American descent. In addition to the limitations of participation in terms of financial resources and the dominance of certain languages, unacknowledged cultural assumptions about the natural leadership of Euro-American societies were a pervasive factor. Despite the constitutions of all three organizations, which welcomed women of all countries and races, Euro-American women were considered more emancipated and more modern, and thus naturally more deserving of leadership roles. These biases and obstacles were present through much of the twentieth century, finally being challenged in second-wave international women's organizations.

Second Wave

In the United States, after securing the vote in 1920 many middle-class women moved into medical, educational, government, and legal professions. By 1945, after being motivated by events such as the Great Depression and World War II, women's activism took on issues such as peace and disarmament. In the 1960s the civil rights movement inspired a renewed struggle for women's rights as well. Students on college campuses criticized the materialism of U.S. culture and the hypocrisy of U.S. foreign policy. A new and vocal women's movement arose in the United States. Groups such as Women's Strike for Peace and the League of Women Voters found new voice. Publication of Betty Friedan's *The Feminine Mystique* (1963) and founding of the National Organization for Women (NOW, 1966) addressed middle-class women's frustrations and their struggle for equal political and economic rights.

In many ways NOW represented a modernized version of the Seneca Falls *Declaration of the Rights of Women*, reclaiming for women the ideals of equal participation and individual rights. However, just as in the century past, this reclamation did not speak for a large number of women. NOW presumed a model of political activity that was essentially individualist, recalling the early suffragists' focus on the relationship between the individual citizen's rights and the state. However, many women could not identify with the dilemmas of the middle-class professional woman. Challenges arose both internationally and domestically, with more radical women's organizations taking on issues that fundamentally challenged the nation's economic and political status quo.

The period after 1975 brought growth in women's movements worldwide. The United Nations International Women's Year (1975) and the subsequent United Nations Decade of Women (1975–1985) were major factors in stimulating local activities in countries in both the North and South hemispheres, as well as spawning international connections, shared resources, active networks, and global conferences. The three major international women's conferences held during the decade measure women's shifting understandings of each other and demonstrate the changing nature and presence of the United States and U.S. women leaders in the movement.

What made this second-wave international women's movement so much more diverse and complex than the first was the multiplicity of women's issues. First, women's movements in Africa and Asia had worked alongside anticolonialist struggles and had

WOMEN OF THE WORLD UNITE IN BEIJING

In 1995, representatives from 184 governments and women from nearly 2,500 nongovernmental organizations gathered in Beijing for the Fourth World Conference on Women and produced an agreement recognizing that investing in women's health and rights is the key to solving global challenges. In February and March 2005 the International Women's Health Coalition asked women gathered in New York City to commemorate the tenth anniversary of the Beijing conference to write brief statements on what the Beijing conference meant to them. The following is the statement of Maria José Rosado of Católicas pelo Direito de Decidir (Catholics for the Right to Decide) in Brazil.

For me, Beijing was deeply moving. I experienced that meeting as a singular historic moment. Thousands of women from all over the world, gathered in a distant Asian country—distant at least relative to Brazil, where I come from. The variety of colors, faces, languages, ways of dressing and behaving—Should we hug? Should we kiss? Should we put our hands together as if in prayer and bow our heads? Countless ways of greeting one another. We were different. Even in our ways of thinking and expressing our ideas and dreams about feminism.

But at the same time, we were one, sole woman. That universal, abstract, and nonexistent woman was there—palpable, recognizable, identifiable—when, in the name of all women in the world—black, white, poor, famished, wealthy, educated, illiterate, believers, atheists, agnostics—in the name of all of them we shouted to the world, "Here we are. And our lives deserve respect. We want dignity, equality and justice for all of the women of the world!" That's what Beijing was. An unrepeatable experience of the possibility of universal solidarity.

Source: International Women's Health Coalition. (2005). Retrieved May 25, 2007, from http://www.iwhc.org/resources/index.cfm

nurtured a strong female presence. New countries in Asia, Latin America, and Africa had declared themselves unaligned to the Cold War's bifurcation of the "free" West and the "communist" East. Second, the growth of large international bodies, such as the World Bank, the United Nations, and nongovernmental organizations (NGOs), had created structures and forums for international women's voices to be heard. Third, more accessibility to travel and financial resources enabled women from many more countries to participate and to share their experiences as women. Women in these countries brought different experiences of being women.

The second-wave international women's movement reflected a multiplicity of global experiences and perspectives. The leadership roles of U.S. and European women and of Western values, as witnessed in the first wave, were questioned. Whereas U.S. women tended to focus on electoral politics and individual human rights, many Third World women focused on poverty, health, disease, and other issues that affected women, children, and men. Women more concerned with women's equality were often viewed as agents of Westernization and "modernization," privilege, and individualism. Many women from the South criticized Western gender perspectives that ignored interlocking systems of race, class, and gender because their experiences led them to believe that their relegation to second-class citizenship stemmed from racism and poverty as much as from male-dominated institutions. The narrower focus of single-issue and single-gender organizing common in the United States was not acceptable to the experienced and well-organized voices of women from around the world. Western ideals of modernity and progress were often dismissed, and "feminism" was stigmatized and resented as the unpopular outgrowth of Western cultural imperialism. These were often difficult times for U.S. women involved in international women's organizations.

A sign outside a Greek Orthodox monastery in Greece stating the tradition of not allowing women to enter. Source: istock/Vinko Murko.

Bill of Rights for Women

One of the major foci of the international women's movement since the Decade of Women has been passage of the Convention on the Elimination of All Forms of Discrimination against Women (CEDAW), adopted in 1979 by the U.N. General Assembly. It is often described as an international bill of rights for women. It defines what constitutes discrimination against women and sets up an agenda for action to end such discrimination. As of 18 March 2005, 180 countries—more than 90 percent of the members of the United Nations—are party to the convention. The fact that the United States is not one of the ratifying countries speaks to the involvement of U.S. leadership in the cause of women's rights at the international level.

To the same degree that the world witnesses globalization and its discontents, the rise of fundamentalism and its opponents, and simultaneously growing poverty and prosperity, the international women's movement faces conflicts and contradictions. It is not a single, homogeneous women's movement, not a single issue or single entity. It continues to be enriched with common experiences based on gender and, at the same time, fraught with differences also based on gender.

The United States—through its Constitution and its strong women leaders—has played a role in creating and supporting the international women's movement. At the same time, Western cultural assumptions and political values have often limited the scope of that movement's efforts and have presumed a universality of women's issues that does not exist. Current international women's organizations are trying to decentralize power, equalize access to resources, and question assumptions of universality in order to create a movement that will suit the needs of women worldwide.

Laurien Alexandre

Further Reading

Anderson, B. (2000). *Joyous greeting: The first international women's movement, 1830–1860*. New York: Oxford University Press.

Bulbeck, C. (1998). *Re-orienting Western feminisms: Women's diversity in a postcolonial world*. Cambridge, UK: Cambridge University Press.

Dean, J. (1996). *Solidarity of strangers: Feminism after identity politics*. Berkeley and Los Angeles: University of California Press.

Evans, S. (2000). Decade of discovery: The personal is political. In B. Smith (Ed.), *Global feminisms since 1945* (pp. 141–163). New York: Routledge.

Miles, A. (1996). *Integrative feminisms: Building global visions 1960s–1990s*. New York: Routledge.

Mohanty, C. (2003). *Feminism without border: Decolonizing theory, practicing solidarity*. Durham, NC: Duke University Press.

Rupp, L. (1997). *Worlds of women: The making of the international women's movement*. Princeton, NJ: Princeton University Press.

Smith, B. (Ed.). (2000). *Global feminisms since 1945*. New York: Routledge.

Foreign Policy after September 11, 2001, U.S.

Prior to 2001, U.S. foreign policy was strong globally, but not intrusive, and oftentimes cautious. September 11, 2001, changed that, as U.S. policy became more polarizing, and singularly focused on terrorism.

As the Cold War ended in the early 1990s the United States emerged uncontested as the most powerful nation in the world. Some observers anticipated that a new era in international relations would ensue, predicated on the domination of the United States as the preeminent military and economic power. Indeed, with the collapse of the Soviet Union and its empire one can understand why many people believed the United States had "won" the Cold War. Clearly the liberal international economic order championed by the United States had in effect become the global norm. Even the People's Republic of China, the last major communist power, was fully engaged in a capitalist transformation. Similarly, as the United States led an international coalition against Iraq in 1991, a new era in collective security seemed to have begun. Some people even imagined that the United States would become the champion of the United Nations and spearhead democracy and economic development around the world.

Such optimism was, however, fleeting. Senior officials in the administration of President George H. W. Bush (1989–1993) recommended maintaining a military force so powerful that none could challenge it, thus ensuring that U.S.—not necessarily global—interests would be protected. Although nothing came of it then, the corresponding notion of "preemptive" foreign policy aimed at maintaining U.S. power did not go away. It was shelved during the administration of William Clinton (1993–2001) who, critics complained, was too passive in the face of major international crises. Clinton's detractors argued that the United States was slow to respond to the 1994 genocide in Rwanda, did little to push for fundamental change in the world's autocracies, and offered only rhetoric in combating major global issues such as poverty, AIDS, and environmental deterioration.

In fact, both Bush and Clinton were cautious foreign policy presidents. They preferred to act only when the international system was confronted with a major crisis and rejected the notion that U.S. power should be aggressively projected even in advancing what were widely seen as just causes. Both feared that an overextension of U.S. power would lead to endless demands and be antithetical to the "new world order" based on collective security and the rule of international law.

Thus, by the turn of the millennium it was apparent the United States was a somewhat reluctant global police officer. As some observers pointed out, a difficult paradox had emerged for U.S. power. On the one hand, the United States was expected by many in the international community to solve a multitude of problems. On the other hand, many criticized the United States when it did intervene, accusing it of imperialism. The question of a U.S. "empire" dominated international affairs, particularly in the absence of a singular, clearly identifiable foe. Potential adversaries such as China and Russia lacked the means, and possibly even the intent, to fundamentally challenge the United States. The European Union offered a strong economic balance to the United States but had neither the political organization nor the inclination to oppose U.S. leadership in international affairs. Whether by design or by accident it was evident that in its military might, economic strength, and cultural prominence, the United States led a unipolar international order without much challenge.

In this context George W. Bush came to the presidency in January 2001 after one of the closest and most controversial elections in U.S. history. Foreign policy was clearly not his priority. Interviewed by Boston's WHDH TV in November 1999 while running for his party's nomination, Bush was asked to name leaders in four major hotspots around the world: Chechnya, Taiwan, Pakistan, and India. Flustered by the question, Bush managed to get only one leader right, curtly naming "Lee" as Taiwan's president. The episode confirmed Bush's disinterest in foreign policy, but for some harsher critics, especially those abroad, it confirmed something far worse: that Bush also lacked the intellectual skills to lead the country, let alone champion the "new world order."

"We Are All Americans"

Then came the terrorist attacks of September 11, 2001. In the immediate aftermath of September 11 much of the world supported the United States with genuine sympathy. The French newspaper, *Le Monde*, declared "Nous sommes tous Américains" ("We are all Americans"). The British *Mirror* likened the attacks to "War on

U.S. NATIONAL SECURITY STRATEGY, SEPTEMBER 2002

In September of 2002, the U.S. National Security Strategy was set forth. Section three of the strategy—"Strengthen Alliances to Defeat Global Terrorism and Work to Prevent Attacks Against Us and Our Friends"—begins with a quote from a speech delivered by President George W. Bush on 14 September 2001. President Bush stated: "Just three days removed from these events, Americans do not yet have the distance of history. But our responsibility to history is already clear: to answer these attacks and rid the world of evil. War has been waged against us by stealth and deceit and murder. This nation is peaceful, but fierce when stirred to anger. The conflict was begun on the timing and terms of others. It will end in a way, and at an hour, of our choosing." Following are extracts from that section of the National Security Strategy.

The United States of America is fighting a war against terrorists of global reach. The enemy is not a single political regime or person or religion or ideology. The enemy is terrorism—premeditated, politically motivated violence perpetrated against innocents.

In many regions, legitimate grievances prevent the emergence of a lasting peace. Such grievances deserve to be, and must be, addressed within a political process. But no cause justifies terror. The United States will make no concessions to terrorist demands and strike no deals with them. We make no distinction between terrorists and those who knowingly harbor or provide aid to them.

The struggle against global terrorism is different from any other war in our history. It will be fought on many fronts against a particularly elusive enemy over an extended period of time. Progress will come through the persistent accumulation of successes—some seen, some unseen.

Today our enemies have seen the results of what civilized nations can, and will, do against regimes that harbor, support, and use terrorism to achieve their political goals. Afghanistan has been liberated; coalition forces continue to hunt down the Taliban and al-Qaida. But it is not only this battlefield on which we will engage terrorists. Thousands of trained terrorists remain at large with cells in North America, South America, Europe, Africa, the Middle East, and across Asia.

Our priority will be first to disrupt and destroy terrorist organizations of global reach and attack their leadership; command, control, and communications; material support; and finances. This will have a disabling effect upon the terrorists' ability to plan and operate.

We will continue to encourage our regional partners to take up a coordinated effort that isolates the terrorists. Once the regional campaign localizes the threat to a particular state, we will help ensure the state has the military, law enforcement, political, and financial tools necessary to finish the task.

The United States will continue to work with our allies to disrupt the financing of terrorism. We will identify and block the sources of funding for terrorism, freeze the assets of terrorists and those who support them, deny terrorists access to the international financial system, protect legitimate charities from being abused by terrorists, and prevent the movement of terrorists' assets through alternative financial networks.

Source: The White House. (2002). Retrieved March 22, 2007, from http://www.whitehouse.gov/nsc/nss/2002/nss3.html

---

the World." Spain's *El Correo* ran a single-word headline: "Muerte" ("Murder"). Leaders from many nations condemned the attacks and applauded Bush as he vowed to bring those responsible for the violence to justice. Even more moving were the responses from ordinary people. Thousands left flowers, cards, and mementoes at U.S. consulates and embassies around the world. Spontaneous vigils were held in many faiths and in many countries. Both government and religious leaders throughout the Islamic world condemned the attacks as cowardly and "un-Muslim." Remarkably, longtime foes of the United States joined the chorus. Libyan leader Muammar Gadhafi—a sponsor of terrorist groups himself—called the events "horrifying" and urged Muslims to respect the U.S. people. Iranian President Mohammed Khatami expressed his "deep regret" and extended sympathies to the victims' families. Even the government of North Korea, an international pariah, called the attacks a "tragedy" and sent its regards for the U.S. people.

The sympathy continued when later that month the North Atlantic Treaty Organization (NATO) invoked Article 5 of its charter, stipulating that an attack on one member of the alliance

is an attack on them all. In doing so, members endorsed the U.S.-led invasion of Afghanistan in October 2001, aimed at destroying al-Qaeda camps, capturing its elusive leader Osama bin Laden, and toppling the extremist Taliban regime that gave him safe haven. Britain, Canada, France, and other NATO members immediately contributed soldiers to the fight. Several non-NATO countries, such as Pakistan, Uzbekistan, and Georgia, also aided in Bush's war on terrorism by hosting NATO bases and providing valuable intelligence. Even countries ostensibly worried about U.S.-led military action, such as China and Russia, sanctioned the invasion. Indeed, international public opinion, including that in the Islamic world, supported the invasion, which most people saw as a specific and justifiable reprisal for the terrorist attacks.

International sympathies for the United States were, however, ultimately limited. Many people around the world worried about the stark simplicity—some would say "stupidity"—of Bush's proclamation a few days after September 11 that "you're either with us, or with the terrorists." Many also questioned motivations behind his now-infamous reference to an international "Axis of Evil" in

January 2002. In three simple words Bush fundamentally under-mined nearly twenty years of behind-the-scenes diplomacy with Iran designed to promote a more moderate leadership there. Some even blame Bush for the retrenchment of religious conservatives in Iran. His harshest critics point out that in his conservatism and religiosity, Bush is little different than the fundamentalists he seeks to destroy.

Yet, nothing has been more controversial or divisive with re-spect to U.S. foreign policy since September 11 than the decision to invade Iraq. During the 2000 presidential election the Bush camp called for full implementation of the 1998 Iraq Liberation Act, a congressional statement advocating the overthrow of Sad-dam Hussein for his repeated violations of international laws. After Bush became president, he continued to call for action. Prominent members of the Bush cabinet, including Vice President Dick Cheney and Secretary of Defense Donald Rumsfeld, had long advocated invading Iraq. Deputy Secretary of Defense Paul Wolfowitz and Chairman of the Defense Policy Advisory Com-mittee Richard Perle had helped to create and nurture the idea of preemptive foreign policy during their service in the administration of Ronald Reagan (1981–1989). In fact, two senior Bush adminis-tration officials, Paul O'Neill and Richard Clarke, acknowledged that the invasion of Iraq had been planned long before September 11. It was a top foreign relations priority for Bush even before the war on terrorism commenced.

Bush first made public the case against Iraq on 12 September 2002, when he addressed the U.N. Security Council, focusing on weapons of mass destruction (WMDs) that Hussein was known to have had in 1991 and was suspected of still having. After consider-able debate the council adopted a compromise resolution (1441) that ordered continued weapons inspections and the threat of "serious consequences" should Iraq obstruct inspections. However, the U.N. stopped short of authorizing any military action. Security Council members China, Russia, and France made it clear that Resolu-tion 1441 did not endorse either multilateral or unilateral force. Undaunted, in October 2002 the Bush administration pushed the U.S. Congress to authorize action against Iraq, notwithstand-ing that a majority of Americans favored further diplomacy to war. Then, in February 2003 Secretary of State Colin Powell ad-dressed the U.N. General Assembly, arguing that Hussein had not only WMDs but also tangible connections to al-Qaeda. Experts doubted such connections given that al-Qaeda violently opposed secular Muslim leaders such as Hussein and repeatedly called for their deaths. However implausible the connections, September 11 was linked to Saddam Hussein in the Bush administration's justification to invade Iraq. The United States, with the support of the United Kingdom and Spain, put forth a new U.N. resolu-tion authorizing force but faced considerable opposition from other Western allies, including Canada, France, and Germany. Facing almost certain French and Russian vetoes at the Security

Fist of an angry protestor at the New York City antiwar protest March 2004. Source: istock/Ben Thomas.

Council, the United States withdrew the resolution but prepared for invasion nonetheless.

Into the Breach

Despite international protests, including one on February 15 that drew almost ten million people in more than eight hundred cities worldwide, President Bush authorized military action against Iraq on 20 March 2003. The United States and a coalition of allies went to war against the wishes of the United Nations and world opinion.

Immediately there were questions about the legality and consequences of the invasion, but there was little question about its initial success. Within just three weeks Iraqi forces were defeated, and Hussein's regime fell. On 1 May 2003, Bush optimistically proclaimed that the mission was accomplished: Combat operations were over, and the coalition had won. However, the occupation and reconstruction of Iraq proved infinitely more difficult than anyone in the Bush administration had predicted. In fact, the lack of an extrication plan and the inability or unwillingness of U.S. officials to anticipate the insurgency that has unfolded have shocked most observers. Nonetheless, in November 2004 Bush won the presidential election decisively, this time without controversy. Many people around the world who opposed Bush now questioned the U.S. electorate who returned him to office.

Since then the insurgency in Iraq has devolved into civil war, and both domestic support and international support for Bush have declined. As of 1 May 2007, nearly 3,400 Americans and 70,000 Iraqis had been killed in the fighting, the vast majority of them since Bush had announced "victory" four years earlier. Even more troubling is the possibility that because of the war in Iraq, previously unlikely connections between Islamic terrorist groups have, in fact, been built, in effect strengthening the United States' enemy in the war on terrorism. Public opinion in generally pro-Western Muslim countries, such as Turkey, Egypt, and Malaysia, has turned against the United States. Extremist movements there have gained support. Public approval in the West among the United States' historical allies has been similarly lowered. Whereas the majority fully supported the United States after September 11, most now openly criticize it for its continuing occupation of Iraq and seeming indifference to international opinion.

The Bush administration has also been widely criticized for a number of other foreign policy matters since September 11. Preoccupied with Iraq and terrorism, Bush has been accused of ignoring the reemergence of an autocratic Russia and the growing power of China. U.S. policy with respect to global climate change, human rights law, and a host of other international issues has also lagged. In sum many analysts argue that the United States has in effect forfeited its leadership of the international order. In some parts of the world the United States is seen as parochial, arrogant, aggressive, and even ignorant about the rest of the world. It remains to be seen whether the United States can restore its image and recapture the support it once enjoyed in the world, or whether we are witnessing the definitive decline of the U.S. empire.

Arne Kislenko

See also Imperialism, U.S.; Iraq Wars

Further Reading

Clarke, R. A. (2004). *Against all enemies: Inside America's war on terror.* New York: Free Press.

Daadler, I. H., & Lindsay, J. M. (2005). *America unbound: The Bush revolution in foreign policy* (Rev. ed.). Hoboken, NJ: John Wiley and Sons.

Gaddis, J. L. (2005, January/February). Grand strategy in the second term. *Foreign Affairs, 84*(1), 2–15.

Jervis, R. (2006, Summer). The remaking of a unipolar world. *Washington Quarterly, 29*(3), 7–19.

Lieber, R. J. (2005). *The American era: Power and strategy for the 21st century.* Cambridge, MA: Cambridge University Press.

Mead, W. R. (2004). *Power, terror, peace, and war: America's grand strategy in a world at risk.* New York: Random House.

Packer, G. (2005). *The assassin's gate: America in Iraq.* New York: Farrar, Straus, and Giroux.

Founding Principles of the United States

The expression of individualism lies at the core of the U.S. founding principles set forth in the 1700s. There are concerns that the United States is heading away from individualism and becoming a more collectivist society.

The founding of the United States of America was not a historical accident but the product of philosophical ideas, most fundamentally the ideas of two philosophers: Aristotle (384–322 BCE) and John Locke (1632–1704). The United States was founded at the peak of the intellectual period known as the Enlightenment, a period during which reason prevailed over religious dogma—a triumph that had its roots in ancient Greece but that took some two thousand years to reach fruition. Describing the Enlightenment, the philosopher Leonard Peikoff observes, "For the first time in modern history, an authentic respect for reason became the mark of an entire culture" (1982, 102).

Influence of Aristotle and Locke

Aristotle, the foremost philosophical champion of reason in ancient Greece, held that one gains knowledge about the real world by using reason and logic to identify what one observes by means of one's senses. Aristotle was also an advocate of egoism; he held that one's proper goal in life is the achievement of one's own happiness. Reason and egoism form the base of the concept of individual rights, although the latter concept was not formulated until much later.

John Locke's *Second Treatise of Civil Government*, published near the end of the seventeenth century, was the first consistent, systematic presentation of the concept of individual rights. Locke argued that individuals possessed "natural" rights, including the rights to life, liberty, and property. (By the right to property, Locke meant the right to earn it and to keep what was earned.) These rights, Locke held, stemmed from man's nature and were prior to and superior to governments and their laws. Thus individuals did not exist to serve governments but rather governments were formed and existed in order to serve the individual by protecting his rights. Locke argued that people should be free from coercion and interference by others, including the state. This was the most revolutionary political idea in human history—a complete reversal of the traditional conception of the relationship between the individual and the state.

The United States' founding principles were an expression of individualism. Individualism holds that the individual is real and

not merely a subunit of a larger organism. Individuals are the units of value and ends in themselves, not a means to the ends of others. Individualism contrasts with the doctrine of collectivism, which holds that the group (tribe, state, race, class, and so on), not the individual, is the real entity and the unit of value. Collectivism advocates the sacrifice of the individual to the group. The founding fathers of the United States held that reason demonstrated that "all men are created equal"—equal not in their abilities or achievements but in their rights to "life, liberty, and the pursuit of happiness." Contrary to common belief, the United States was not founded as, nor was it ever intended to be, a democracy in strict terms, that is—a form of government studied and sometimes practiced by the ancient Greeks meaning unlimited majority rule. The founding fathers were students of history and knew that the tyranny of the many is no better than tyranny of the one or of the few. The United States was and is a constitutional republic. Thus no one's rights can be voted away or infringed upon by others.

The application of the principle of individual rights to politics meant limited government. The powers of and limits on government enumerated by the U. S. Constitution were to be exercised for the purpose of protecting citizens' freedom of action rather than destroying it. For example, the first amendment to the Constitution states that "Congress shall make no law respecting an establishment of religion, or prohibiting the free exercise thereof." By enacting that amendment, the founding fathers replaced domination by religion, so common throughout history, with intellectual freedom.

The application of the principles of egoism and individual rights, including property rights, led in economics to laissez-faire capitalism and the idea that individuals had the right to trade freely with others (assuming no fraud or coercion) and to keep the rewards of their efforts.

The Spread of Individual Liberty

When a principle as radical as that of individual rights is formally adopted by a country, the traditions and premises of past centuries are not suddenly overthrown. There will inevitably be opposition and thus delay in applying the new principles consistently. Two

The visages of the four presidents carved into Mount Rushmore in South Dakota symbolize the founding principles of the United States, such as liberty, independence, and equality. Source: istock/Bonnie Jacobs.

traditions that the United States acquired from the past were slavery and gender inequality.

The United States did not invent slavery; it inherited it. Slavery had existed since ancient times and had been allowed and encouraged by the British government in its colonies, including its North American colonies. There was also an element of political compromise involved in the nascent United States' acceptance of slavery. Thomas Jefferson's original draft of the Declaration of Independence included a strongly worded repudiation of the institution of slavery, but this section was taken out for fear that the southern states would not join the fight for independence against the British if that repudiation were retained.

But after the United States became independent, the nation was faced with a dilemma. Slavery was obviously incompatible with the concept of individual rights. There were rationalizations to the effect that slaves were not fully human, but these rationalizations could last only so long. Either the country's core principles had to be repudiated or slavery had to be abolished. It took almost ninety years to do it, but slavery was finally eradicated after a bitter and bloody civil war. It took many more decades before blacks were treated as equal before the law.

Full equality for women before the law (including the right to vote and the same rights with respect to property that men had) had never existed in human history at the time the United States became independent. It took Americans almost 150 years to establish women's equality before the law.

Challenges to the Founding Principles

It might be assumed from the foregoing that the twentieth century would mark the final triumph of the Enlightenment and thus of the United States' core principles. At first, this seemed to be true. The United States became the freest, wealthiest, and most powerful nation on earth. It became a beacon that drew millions of foreign immigrants "yearning," as the words on the base of the Statue of Liberty put it, "to breathe free." The United States became a melting pot, a blend of people of different nationalities, races, religions, and social backgrounds, united by the common principles of reason, individualism, and freedom. Though prejudices existed, there were no ostensible royal or class privileges, and in theory all people had the chance to better themselves.

Nevertheless, from the time the nation's core values were first articulated, the seeds of opposition to them were already being sown. First, the founding fathers were not themselves philosophers, and they were not fully consistent in their advocacy of reason. They were to some degree religious. Many were deists who believed that God created the universe, which was then governed by the laws of nature, discovered by science. They also believed that religion was the only source of morality, and since Christianity was the religion that influenced them most heavily, they were not fully consistent in their advocacy of egoism, either, as Christianity holds self-sacrifice to be the highest moral virtue.

Second, Immanuel Kant's *Critique of Pure Reason* (1781) appeared only five years after the Declaration of Independence. Kant was the first philosopher to present an elaborate, comprehensive system of thought challenging the ascendancy of reason, premised on a claim that reason was incapable of knowing reality. From the perspective of Enlightenment thinking, this was the beginning of a long, downward slide in philosophy, with Kant's followers building on his critique until everything collapsed into postmodern skepticism, the doctrine that objective, certain knowledge is totally impossible. Postmodernism also holds that the individual's ideas are determined by society, a position that denies that the individual is a real, sovereign entity.

As reason gradually became dethroned philosophically, there was no means to rationally defend the morality of egoism, the doctrine that the individual should act in his or her own self-interest and one of the founding principles of the United States. Kant regarded self-sacrifice, a contrasting founding principle, as the essence of virtue, a position he justified, ultimately, by an appeal to faith. But without recourse to reason and egoism, the concepts set forth in the U.S. constitution of individual rights and political and economic freedom came under threat.

Champions of individual liberty have noted that the United States' core principles are currently under sustained attack. They argue that reason is being gradually replaced by feelings, group opinion, fundamentalist religion, and, as noted, skepticism, and that egoism is progressively being replaced by altruism, the doctrine of self-sacrifice. The meaning of the concept of individual rights is being altered in the public consciousness from freedom of action to entitlements—benefits that some people are forced by the government to provide to other people. They also argue that individualism is being replaced by collectivism, as group (racial, religious, sexual) membership is coming to be seen as more important than self-made character.

The Future

As the founding principles of United States have evolved over the centuries, differing interpretations and practical applications of these principles have caused many more contradictions to also evolve so that now, in early decades of the twenty-first century, some consider the United States to be at a crossroads with a few contrasting possibilities for the future.

One possibility is that skepticism and loss of confidence in the mind will lead eventually to social collapse, because a society that is skeptical of all values and all principles cannot function. The inevitable result of such social and political chaos is dictatorship; for when enough people declare that they have no answers, stand

for no values, and do not know what to do, then someone or some group that claims to know, by some ineffable means, what to do can fill that vacuum and force the masses to accept its rule.

Another possibility is that the United States will be dominated by fundamentalist religion, which has risen in popularity and acceptance in the last decades of the twentieth century and first years of the twenty-first. Currently, however, although fundamentalists are passionate, numerous, and well organized, they do not yet have a large enough following for such dominance.

Alternately, the United States could return to the nation's core principles, but this time with a stronger, more consistent philosophical base. Ayn Rand's philosophy of Objectivism presents a defense of the validity of reason, of the morality of egoism with its associated virtues, and of the concept of individual rights. Some argue that if the United States were to choose this path, it might rise to new heights of freedom and prosperity; but if not, it is likely to begin a gradual demise, and be remembered for its lost ideals.

Edwin A. Locke

See also American Dream; Christian Nation, United States as; Colonial Period and Early Nationhood

EXCERPT FROM JOHN LOCKE'S SECOND TREATISE OF CIVIL GOVERNMENT (1620)

In "Of Political or Civil Society," Chapter 7 of his Second Treatise of Civil Government, *John Locke makes the case for a person's right to life, liberty, and estate (what we now think of as possessions and property).*

Man being born, as has been proved, with a title to perfect freedom, and an uncontrouled [*sic*] enjoyment of all the rights and privileges of the law of nature, equally with any other man, or number of men in the world, hath by nature a power, not only to preserve his property, that is, his life, liberty and estate, against the injuries and attempts of other men; but to judge of, and punish the breaches of that law in others, as he is persuaded the offence deserves, even with death itself, in crimes where the heinousness of the fact, in his opinion, requires it. But because no political society can be, nor subsist, without having in itself the power to preserve the property, and in order thereunto, punish the offences of all those of that society; there, and there only is political society, where every one of the members hath quitted this natural power, resigned it up into the hands of the community in all cases that exclude him not from appealing for protection to the law established by it.

Further Reading

Becker, C. (1922). *The declaration of independence: A study of the history of political ideas.* New York: Random House.

Kant, I. (1965). *The critique of pure reason.* (N. K. Smith, Trans.). New York: St. Martin's Press. (Original work published 1781)

Locke, E. A. (2003). *Post modernism in management: Pros, cons and the alternative.* Amsterdam: JAI (Elsevier).

Locke, J. (1986). *The second treatise on civil government.* Buffalo, NY: Prometheus Books. (Original work published 1690)

Peikoff, L. (1982). *The ominous parallels: The end of freedom in America.* New York: Stein & Day.

Peikoff, L. (1991). *Objectivism: The philosophy of Ayn Rand.* New York: Dutton.

Rand. A. (1992). *Atlas shrugged.* New York: Signet. (Original work published 1957)

Rubenstein, R. E. (2003). *Aristotle's children.* Orlando, FL: Harcourt.

Gay and Lesbian Rights Movement

During the 1900s the United States became a leader in the global movement for gay and lesbian rights. But growing U.S. social conservatism in the early 2000s has resulted in other countries taking the lead in the movement.

The United States was not the first Western country in which an organized movement to secure legal, political, and economic rights for gays and lesbians developed. However, its large population, its influential civil rights movement, and its tradition of democratic self-expression combined to make the United States a leader in human rights developments, including rights for gays and lesbians, until a major conservative upsurge in the late twentieth and early twenty-first centuries undermined the U.S. gay and lesbian rights movement, leaving it well behind similar movements in other Western countries.

By the early twentieth century in larger U.S. cities, notably in New England, California, and the upper Midwest, secretive gay and lesbian networks were giving rise to more developed gay and lesbian communities. White gay male culture centered on social clubs, bathhouses, roadhouses, cafes, and bookstores. White lesbians occasionally frequented some of the same venues, particularly bars and bookstores. African-American gays in the South found few safe gathering places, but in the North they slowly developed underground club and cafe societies, including venues on the Chitlin Circuit, which was a circuit of black-owned clubs where black entertainers—some of whom were gay or lesbian—could perform. By the 1920s gays and lesbians were the targets of prohibition enforcement, blue laws, antigay violence, and police raids at a time when a shift in U.S. medical opinion ascribed homosexual desire and activity to pathology and mental disease.

By midcentury U.S. gay activism had begun to focus on legal issues, in part because of the experience of World War II. During the war the U.S. armed services maintained racial segregation in housing and unit assignments, tolerated race-based and antigay violence within the ranks, and imposed sanctions on gay and lesbian service personnel. Many gays received administrative discharges, also known as "blue tickets" or "blue discharges." Those personnel found to be, or rumored to be, homosexual could be arrested and removed from military service altogether, without receiving veterans' benefits.

Mattachine Society

In 1948 the widely publicized *Kinsey Report* on adult sexual behavior in the United States revealed the wide experience of homoerotic and homosexual activity. Thus, even at the height of McCarthyism, the U.S. gay rights movement continued to grow. In 1951 San Francisco nightclub owners prevailed in litigation establishing the right of businesses to cater to a gay and lesbian clientele, and in Los Angeles a new organization, the Mattachine Society, advocated for personal rights and liberties of gays, educated potential political allies, and defended its right to use the U.S. Postal Service for delivery of its newsletter. By 1953 Mattachine had some one hundred chapters in southern California, and a lesbian counterpart organization, the Daughters of Bilitis (DoB), was formed in San Francisco in 1955. Both Mattachine and DoB adopted cautious tactics, emphasizing small community contacts and relying chiefly on education for eventual improvement in the status of homosexuals.

For U.S. gays and lesbians, the 1950s were a period of deep distrust of law enforcement, medical professionals, and society at large. In 1952, for example, the American Psychiatric Association issued a policy proclamation that homosexuality is a mental disorder. As a consequence, gays and lesbians were both socially stigmatized and economically threatened: To retain their jobs in the educational, medical, government, and social work fields gays and lesbians had to avoid disclosure of their personal lives to co-workers, superiors, clergy, and family members. This need to protect employment—and accompanying benefits, including access to housing and medical care—by remaining "in the closet" persisted in U.S. conservative southern and western states until well into the early 2000s.

In the early 1960s the U.S. gay rights movement accelerated, largely because of the accomplishments of the African-American-led civil rights movement and the growth of the anti-Vietnam War movement. Between 1965 and 1967 gay and lesbian activists became more radicalized and adopted new tactics that quickly spread to Europe. Gays began holding public meetings, demonstrations, and marches demanding civil rights for homosexuals.

Bar raids and arrests, first in Hollywood and Los Angeles in 1967 and then in the Greenwich Village quarter of Manhattan outside the Stonewall Bar in June 1969, provoked resistance by gays and lesbians and opened a new phase in U.S. gay rights activism. Gays, lesbians, and supporters rallied publicly to confront conservatives and antigay law enforcement officers. In 1969 a radical organization, the Gay Liberation Front (GLF), was formed in New

York City, and affiliated groups formed quickly in California and the Midwest. GLF chapters concentrated on local issues such as discriminatory hiring practices and police entrapment. In 1969 and 1970 meetings of the new North American Conference of Homophile Organizations (NACHO) became involved in broader social issues by endorsing the emerging women's rights movement and calling for U.S. withdrawal from Vietnam. Splits soon developed between cautious and radical leaders. The Gay Activists Alliance (GAA), which broke from the GLF in late 1969, was dedicated to gay rights issues only, eschewing broader progressive initiatives. GAA successfully pushed for several concrete legal changes, including decriminalization of sodomy in three states in 1971; in the same year a federal court ruling banned the firing of homosexual civil service employees. In 1973 GAA also pushed the American Psychological Association to repeal its "mental disease" definition of homosexuality. Less-politicized gay and lesbian groups also emerged, while in major cities and on university campuses

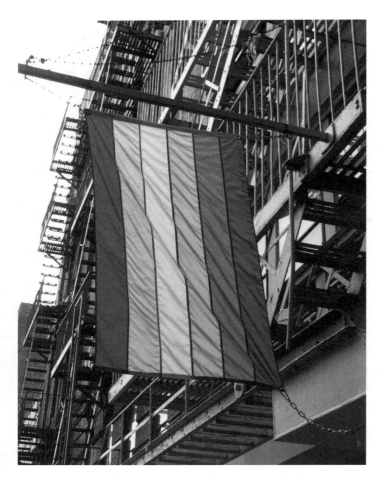

The Gay Rights Rainbow Flag hanging from a pole off of fire escape in New York City's West Village. Source: istock/Harry Lines.

new publications were founded and public "gay pride" celebrations were organized.

European Developments

Gay and lesbian groups overseas, particularly in Europe, followed U.S. developments closely. GLF-style activist organizations were quickly formed in the late 1960s in most western European countries. In Britain, for example, the North Western Committee of the Homosexual Law Reform Society, formed in the early 1960s, reorganized in 1969 as the Committee (later "Campaign") for Homosexual Equality (CHE), which sought legal equality for gays and lesbians in Britain. By 1972 CHE had some sixty local chapters and affiliates. In London a GLF organization founded on the U.S. model was formed in 1970; it hosted workshops, conducted education campaigns, and developed a speakers' bureau. GLF chapters were organized in Birmingham, Manchester, Edinburgh, and other large cities.

The U.S. Stonewall-era gay rights movement also stimulated the gay rights movement in West Germany. Students at German universities and polytechnics gathered to see the German documentary film *Not the Homosexual Perverse, But the Society in Which He Lives,* which portrayed the political activism of the U.S. gay and lesbian movement in the late 1960s. Public demonstrations created pressures for reform, and in 1969 the ruling Social Democratic Party decriminalized homosexual acts. Decriminalization laws were adopted at the same time in Austria and Finland, whereas in the Netherlands conservative leaders dominated the gay rights movement. They did, however, endorse equal access for gays and lesbians to public housing, education, and careers in military and public service.

The U.S. gay rights movement in the 1970s also sparked increased activism beyond Europe. GLF-style groups formed in Mexico City in 1971 and in Argentina in 1973. In Australia and New Zealand the gay rights movement gathered strength from domestic anti-Vietnam War movements. In Sydney and Melbourne, Australia, gay rights advocacy groups emerged in 1969. Sydney's Campaign against Moral Persecution (CAMP) formed chapters nationwide and by 1971 was publishing a journal, organizing protest marches, and contesting local elections. Under these pressures, Australia's federal government decriminalized homosexual acts in those zones governed directly by the national government.

Beginning in the late 1970s a popular movement based in U.S. conservative churches and social organizations began to react against the successes of the women's and gay rights movements. Local ordinances assuring equal rights were rescinded, notably in Miami, Florida, where entertainer Anita Bryant developed

a national coalition called "Save Our Children" and linked her fight against Miami's equal rights law to the criminal activities of male pedophiles. This theme energized the growing U.S. conservative movement, and in 1978 equal rights clauses that had been adopted in the early 1970s were repealed in Minnesota, Kansas, and Oregon. Oklahoma's state legislature voted to permanently dismiss teachers who were gay or lesbian or who "advocated" gay rights or homosexuality. In November 1978 in San Francisco an opponent of a citywide Gay Freedom Day event shot and killed the city's mayor and a city council member, Harvey Milk, then the most widely known openly gay elected official in the United States. Police raids and antigay violence increased. Backed by well-funded evangelical organizations, empowered by the failure of the Equal Rights Amendment to the U.S. Constitution, and reinforced by the candidacy and election in 1980 of conservative Ronald Reagan as president, a resurgent "new right" claimed to defend traditional social conventions and launched a vigorous antigay rights campaign. Since the Reagan era the United States has lagged behind western Europe in extending civil and political rights to gays and lesbians.

New Rights, Few Rights

Three principal areas demonstrate where the U.S. has lagged in extending rights to gays and lesbians: funding for HIV-related prevention and education initiatives; the inclusion of gays in national military service; and legal recognition of monogamous, long-term gay and lesbian relationships. In the United States HIV and AIDS were popularly called "the gay plague" during the 1980s, and the emergence of the disease provided new opportunities for both misinformation about homosexuals, particularly men, and antigay discrimination and violence. The Reagan administration was slow to respond, and federal support for clinical research remained limited until the early 1990s, when President Bill Clinton increased funding for HIV/AIDS public education and research. After some 400,000 deaths in the United States, clinical trials finally identified a multidrug "cocktail" that allowed much longer survival for those infected with HIV. Clinton did not, however, fulfill his promise to overturn the ban on homosexuals serving in the U.S. armed forces. Instead, in 1993–1994 a "don't ask, don't tell" policy was introduced under which homosexuals may serve, provided they do not explicitly reveal their sexual orientation. In this regard the United States has fallen behind such allies as

Britain, where an all-volunteer military permits homosexuals to serve openly, and Israel, where gays and lesbians serve as part of mandatory military service.

Further, in the late 1990s and early 2000s U.S. gay rights activists began calling for legal recognition of same-sex "domestic partnerships" that would provide gay and lesbian couples with the same legal, civil, and economic privileges and responsibilities enjoyed by heterosexual married couples, including access to medical insurance coverage, income tax breaks, legal standing as next of kin, and Social Security benefits. Rulings in U.S. state courts that found restrictive marriage laws unconstitutional added momentum to the campaign, but a nationwide backlash against gay unions quickly developed: Its goal was to stop all legal recognition of "same-sex marriages," also known as "civil unions." By 2007 forty-five states had enacted laws or adopted amendments to state constitutions limiting marriage and all its rights, benefits, and responsibilities to heterosexual couples. Meanwhile, in many countries, including Canada, Britain, Germany, Portugal, Belgium, France, and the Netherlands, same-sex unions have been legalized. Not surprisingly, the U.S. gay and lesbian rights movement has lost much of its international influence.

Laura M. Calkins

Further Reading

Adam, B. D. (1987). *The rise of a gay and lesbian movement (social movements past and present).* Boston: Twayne Publishers.

Duberman, M., Vicinus, M., & Chauncey, G. Jr. (Eds.). (1989). *Hidden from history: Reclaiming the gay and lesbian past.* New York: Meridian Books.

Faderman, L., & Eriksson, B. (Eds.). (1990). *Lesbians in Germany: 1890's–1920's.* New York: Naiad Press.

Lesbian History Group. (Ed.). (1993). *Not a passing phase: Reclaiming lesbians in history 1840–1985.* London: Women's Press.

Marcus, E. (1992). *Making history: The struggle for gay and lesbian equal rights 1945–1990: An oral history.* New York: Harper Perennial.

Miller, N. (1995). *Out of the past: Gay and lesbian history from 1869 to the present.* New York: Vintage Books.

Globalization

See Americanization; Globalization, Economic; Homogenization of World Culture; McDonaldization

Globalization, Economic

The global economy is no longer just a network of intertwined national economies. It has grown into a single entity responsible for a variety of new forms of international cooperation, but also a new form of global imperialism.

Globalization can be defined as a far-reaching societal transformation that increasingly causes the world to function as a single integrated society rather than a mosaic of independent countries separated from one another by national borders. As a result of globalization, many forms of human interaction now extend well beyond the borders of individual countries or regional groupings of countries. Like many previous societal transformations, globalization both enhances and threatens our collective well-being. On one hand, it increasingly binds disparate social groups together, making them interdependent in numerous and complex ways, although this interdependency is not always obvious at the local level. This aspect of globalization clearly creates new opportunities for international cooperation and mutually beneficial interactions among diverse people. But, on the other hand, globalization can threaten our collective well-being as well. Since globalization extends the scope of human interactions beyond the regulatory control of individual countries, many social and economic processes now transpire without much government oversight. This aspect of globalization will likely produce serious problems for years to come, as countries around the world grapple with the inability to solve collective problems originating at the transnational level—problems such as global warming, environmental degradation, terrorism, economic crises, the spread of disease, and so forth. Because globalization is a complex and geographically dispersed process, it is not surprising that social scientists disagree on many of the issues surrounding it.

The Causes of Economic Globalization

Arguably, the confluence of four historical events, each occurring between the late 1960s and the early 1990s, produced the requisite conditions for our present-day movement toward the integration of national economies into a single world market, a process that social scientists typically call economic globalization. The first of these events, starting in the late 1960s and continuing well into the 1970s, was the occurrence of an usually harsh and prolonged economic downturn in many advanced industrial countries. Unlike other recessions, this one was exacerbated by soaring rates

of inflation, triggered in part by a series of oil embargoes and the growing capacity of organized labor to negotiate wage increases. The resulting bout of stagflation—a period of slow economic growth coupled with high rates of inflation—considerably eroded the profitability of many corporations. Reacting to this situation, many corporations operating in the United States and other advanced industrial countries sought to reduce their labor costs by relocating their routine production jobs to low-wage regions of the world economy.

The second event, occurring along with this severe recession, was the advent of the information revolution, which began most notably with the invention of the microchip in 1972. The information revolution ushered in a new round of what the British geographer David Harvey calls "time-space compression"—the ability of technological advancements to reduce the amount of time required to transport people, physical goods, and information across geographical distances. For the average person, this made the world seem smaller, creating the much-lauded global village effect. For major corporations, the information revolution fulfilled a crucial requirement for economic globalization by enabling them to conduct business with overseas subsidiaries, subcontractors, and suppliers more easily.

Third, beginning in the early 1980s and continuing today, political leaders in many advanced industrial countries began implementing policies that facilitate economic globalization. Known as the Washington Consensus in the United States and neoliberalism elsewhere, this set of policies initially sought to overcome the slow economic growth of the 1970s by rolling back government social programs, reducing business regulations, privatizing government-controlled sectors of the economy, and lowering barriers to international trade and capital flows. The United States, arguably the country where these ideas enjoy the widest political support, significantly contributed to the spread of neoliberalism by encouraging other countries to embrace these policies and by influencing the standard practices of prominent international economic organizations. In the latter case, for example, U.S. policy makers and their academic advisers persuaded the International Monetary Fund and the World Bank to modify their lending policies. Since the 1980s, these two international financial institutions have typically required borrowing countries to implement neoliberal reforms

as a condition for loan eligibility. However, this practice has been controversial in many developing countries, primarily because it often increases poverty and income inequality over the short term. Overall, since neoliberalism creates a regulatory climate that facilitates cross-national flows of raw materials, capital, and finished goods, its growing prevalence has been an integral component of economic globalization.

Finally, with the end of the Cold War in 1991, capitalist markets began expanding into formerly socialist regions of the world economy. Before that time, nearly one-third of the world was essentially off limits to capitalist development. But this changed rapidly during the early 1990s, as policy makers in formerly socialist countries sought to improve their sagging economies by welcoming investments from foreign capitalists. It was at this time that the term *globalization* came into common usage, as it expressed the emergent reality that capitalism has become a truly global economic system. Clyde Prestowitz, a former Reagan administration trade official, points out that this process essentially created three billion new capitalists, many of whom are successfully competing for jobs formerly held by Americans.

Historical and Contemporary Economic Globalization

Despite widespread discussions about how economic globalization affects our daily lives, social scientists studying the topic disagree over whether it constitutes a historically unprecedented phenomenon. In a broad context, this debate yields two competing arguments. One argument maintains that, over the last two hundred years, the world economy has experienced several waves of economic globalization, and that the most recent wave, which is often called contemporary economic globalization, has not extensively reordered the centuries-old configuration of the world economy. The other argument, conversely, maintains that the current wave of economic globalization has indeed produced a qualitatively new and historically unprecedented economic system, one that for the first time in history closely approximates a truly global economy.

A small but growing number of social scientists, with the British social and political theorists Paul Hirst and Grahame Thompson being the most notable, see contemporary economic globalization as merely a high point in the ongoing ebb and flow of capitalist development. They assert that contemporary economic globalization simply represents an expansion and intensification of the production and exchange networks that have for centuries characterized the world economy. Their argument rests on two empirical facts. First, analyses of recent trade patterns indicate

that, despite a recent upswing in international economic activity, most trade still occurs within and between three regional economic blocs, centered on East Asia, North America, and Western Europe. This finding implies that recent economic changes have not created a truly global economy. Rather it suggests that free-trade zones, such as North American Free Trade Agreement and the European Economic Union, have created vibrant regional economies, which are closely linked through trade flows. Second, analyses of historical trade patterns reveal three waves of economic globalization occurring since 1795, with each wave being followed by a period of contraction. Interestingly, the similarities between past and present waves of economic globalization can be seen by examining certain historical texts. Writing 150 years ago about the consequences of the geographic expansion of capitalism, the German political philosophers Karl Marx and Friedrich Engels sounded much like present-day scholars describing the consequences of globalization. Capitalism's expansion, Marx and Engels wrote, had

drawn from under the feet of industry the national ground on which it stood. All old-established national industries have been destroyed or are daily being destroyed. They are dislodged by new industries, whose introduction become a life-and-death question for all civilized nations, by industries that no longer work up indigenous raw materials, but raw materials drawn from the remotest zones; industries whose products are consumed, not only at home, but in every quarter of the globe. In place of old wants, satisfied by domestic production, we now find new wants, requiring for their satisfaction the products of distant lands and climes. In place of the old local and national seclusion and self-sufficiency, we have intercourse in every direction, universal interdependence of nations. (Marx and Engels 1998, 39)

Overall, the findings mentioned above imply that recent economic changes merely return the world economy to the norms of the late nineteenth and early twentieth centuries, a time when national economies were deeply embedded within international economic flows. Perhaps more importantly, the findings also suggest that future events will likely reverse our current situation, creating a period in which national economies again become more independent of one another.

However, most social scientists believe that a qualitatively different economic system emerged over the last few decades, one that has subsumed many important national-level economic processes into a worldwide borderless economy. This perspective on economic globalization focuses on the qualitative transformations occurring in the international division of labor. Adherents of this view point out that, for much of the modern era, world trade patterns followed a classic international division of labor, in

which developing countries specialized in growing, extracting, and exporting raw materials to advanced industrial countries, and advanced industrial countries specialized in manufacturing these raw materials into finished goods, which were then sold around the world. But, starting sometime in the early 1970s, the emergence of global commodity chains began to alter this long-standing pattern in world trade.

In global commodity chains, the production process involves a worldwide network of major corporations, subsidiaries, and subcontractors, each of which performs a specific task within a much larger chain of business activities. This arrangement endows corporations with unprecedented levels of organizational flexibility, allowing them to change their product offerings and reallocate their factors of production as market conditions change. The end result, of course, is a finished product. But unlike the previous economic systems, in which the whole range of business activities occurred primarily within one country, products made in global commodity chains may have been developed, financed, manufactured, marketed, and sold in countries located all around the world. Eventually, as this business strategy has become the norm in more and more industries, it has created a new international division of labor, in which developing countries specialize in labor-intensive and low-skilled manufacturing jobs, and advanced (post)industrial countries specialize in high-skilled activities, such as executive management and marketing, banking and finance, engineering and product design, and research and development.

In sum, this dominant view on economic globalization emphasizes that, although current levels of international trade may not be much higher than they were a hundred years ago, our present world economy has been qualitatively reconfigured. In particular, it maintains that the factors of production—raw materials, labor, and capital—are now allocated on a worldwide scale, creating a situation in which the world economy functions less like a system of intertwined national economies and more like a single entity, with product design, finance, manufacturing, marketing, and distribution processes operating concurrently across the globe.

Economic Globalization's Effect on Democracy

Most policy makers and many social scientists see economic globalization as having a positive effect on democracy. During the 1990s, as communism ended, many commentators credited economic globalization with successfully promoting democracy in countries formerly governed by authoritarian regimes. The conventional view holds that democratization typically follows a three-step sequence of events. First, hoping to attract new capital

investment, authoritarian regimes open up their economies to foreign investment. Second, in order to attract and keep foreign investment, authoritarian regimes must loosen their control over the economy, because global investors prefer to operate within liberal market economies rather than state-managed economies. Finally, the ensuing introduction of economic reforms weakens the government's grip over society in general, thereby allowing citizens to leverage their new economic freedoms into political freedom as well. Whether one agrees or disagrees with this logic, the proliferation of democratic regimes since the end of the Cold War has been truly impressive. For example, during the 1990s, the number of national elections held worldwide more than doubled the number held in the previous decade, and experts predict that this trend will continue, with the number of national elections held worldwide possibly doubling again by 2010.

Possibly more than any other scholar, the U.S. sociologist and political theorist Francis Fukuyama anticipated and celebrated the global triumph of democratic capitalism. Shortly after the Berlin Wall fell in 1989, he proclaimed in a now-famous essay that the United States' victory in the Cold War represented the "end of history." In making this statement, Fukuyama was claiming that the political and economic structures of the United States would eventually be emulated by every country in the world, and that consequently the great ideological struggles of modernity had basically been resolved. The future, according to Fukuyama, will not contain any credible challenges to the global hegemony of democratic capitalism.

Despite democracy's global triumph over other forms of governance, some scholars nonetheless hold pessimistic views about the future of democracy. The primary concern is that economic globalization, although it has not officially altered the centuries-old doctrine and practice of state sovereignty per se, does weaken and constrain the ability of governments to define and pursue their own interests. In particular, economic globalization creates an ever-widening mismatch between the territorially delimited authority of national governments and the transnational reach of many important economic processes. The result, many scholars believe, is that national governments are now incapable of controlling many of the domestic effects of economic globalization. Even in the world's strongest democracies, it appears that control over domestic economic issues has been slowly shifting away from citizens and their democratically elected representatives and toward anonymous global market forces and unaccountable decision makers in multinational corporations and international agencies. In this way, economic globalization weakens the sovereignty of nation-states and the democratic mechanisms that hold decision makers accountable to the electorate.

Perhaps more than other institutions associated with democ-

The financial district in downtown Manhattan, New York, the heart of the U.S. global economic empire. Source: istock/Jeremy Edwards.

acy in the post–World World II era, the welfare state and labor unions have been adversely affected by the imperatives of a more economically integrated world. It appears that the open economic borders and flexible production systems associated with economic globalization have upset the previous balance of power between workers and corporations that underpins these two institutions. For example, if government officials push for higher taxes or stricter regulations on business practices, corporations can—albeit with varying degrees of difficulty—shift their affected business functions to other countries with more hospitable business climates. Likewise, if labor unions push for higher wages or better benefits, corporations can outsource their jobs to low-wage regions of the world economy. These outcomes reflect a new political reality in which national governments must increasingly compete against one another to create a business climate that attracts global investors.

Is Economic Globalization a U.S. Project?

Whether operating at the domestic or international level, market economies always rely upon a complex social, legal, and physical infrastructure that only national governments can provide. Even so-called free-market economies do not arise organically out the private sector, but rather are the result of sustained and coherent public-policy choices. For this reason, most social scientists

disagree with popular accounts of how economic globalization originated. Most often, such accounts intimate that economic globalization began when corporations in the advanced industrial countries started relocating their routine manufacturing operations to low-wage regions of the world economy, something that was made possible by technological advancements associated with the information revolution. While the actions of the private sector were clearly important in this process, this view underestimates the degree to which U.S. policy makers and their allies in other advanced industrial countries actively encouraged economic globalization through specific public-policy choices.

It has always been the case that the world's dominant country—for example, Great Britain in the nineteenth century—disproportionately develops and enforces the rules for international trade and commerce. The late twentieth century was no different. During this time, the United States played an indispensable role in organizing and rationalizing the emerging global economic system. The U.S. political scientist Edward Cohen, for example, demonstrates that U.S. policy makers actively pursued economic globalization, in part to spur domestic economic growth, but also to help integrate diverse countries into a community of democratic capitalist countries. Japan and certain European countries acted similarly. These facts suggest that since policy makers in powerful countries have pursued economic globalization, it should be seen as a politically induced phenomenon rather than as a technologically induced one.

Based on this logic, critics of economic globalization often blame the U.S. government for globalization's undesirable side effects. In implementing neoliberal economic policies and opening their economies to global economic flows, many developing countries have experienced economic instability, increasing levels of poverty, and acute social dislocations, the latter resulting primarily from imports undercutting domestic agriculture and craft industries. At the same time, neoliberal economic policies usually make domestic and international owners of capital richer. For these reasons, some critics decry economic globalization as a new form of imperialism, one in which impersonal market forces have replaced previous forms of exploitation, such as colonialism, without significantly altering the economic relationship between the dominant and subordinate social actors.

Christopher J. Kollmeyer

See also Businesses Overseas, U.S.; Colonialism and Neocolonialism; Consumerism; McDonaldization; Media Corporations; Multinational Corporations; Tourism; Trade Agreements

Further Reading

Castells, M. (2000). *The rise of the network society* (Rev. ed.). Oxford, UK: Blackwell Publishers.

Chase-Dunn, C., Kawano, Y., & Brewer, B. (2000). Trade globalization since 1795: Waves of integration in the world-system. *American Sociological Review, 65*(1), 77–95.

Cohen, E. S. (2001). *The politics of globalization in the United States.* Washington, DC: Georgetown University Press.

Dicken, P. (2003). *Global shift: Reshaping the global economic map in the 21st century* (4th ed.). New York: Guilford Press.

Fukuyama, F. (1989, Summer). The end of history? *The National Interest, 16,* 3–18.

Guillén, M. (2001). Is globalization civilizing, destructive or feeble? A critique of five key debates in the social science literature. *Annual Review of Sociology, 27,* 235–260.

Harvey, D. (1990). *The condition of postmodernity: An enquiry into the origins of cultural change.* Oxford, UK: Blackwell Publishers.

Harvey, D. (2003). *The new imperialism.* New York: Oxford University Press.

Held, D., McGrew, A., Goldblatt, D., & Perraton, J. (1999). *Global transformations: Politics, economics, and culture.* Stanford, CA: Stanford University Press.

Hirst, P., & Thompson, G. (1999). *Globalization in question* (2nd ed.). Cambridge, UK: Polity Press.

Marx, K., & Engels, F. (1998). *The communist manifesto: Modern edition with introduction by Eric Hobsbawn.* New York: Verso. (Original work published 1848)

Ohmae, K. (1999). *The borderless world* (Rev. ed.). New York: Harper Collins.

O'Riain, S. (2000). States and markets in an era of globalization. *Annual Review of Sociology, 26,* 187–213.

Prestowitz, C. (2005). *Three billion new capitalists: The great shift of wealth and power to the east.* New York: Basic Books.

Reich, R. (1991). *The work of nations: Preparing ourselves for 21st century capitalism.* New York: Vintage Books.

Robinson, W. (2004). *A theory of global capitalism: Production, class, and state in a transnational world.* Baltimore, MD: John Hopkins Press.

Sassen, S. (1995). *Losing control? Sovereignty in an age of globalization.* New York: Columbia University Press.

Schwartzman, K. (1998). Globalization and democracy. *Annual Review of Sociology, 24,* 159–181.

Stiglitz, J. (2002). *Globalization and its discontents.* New York: W. W. Norton.

Swank, D. (2002). *Global capitalism, political institutions, and policy change in developed welfare states.* Cambridge, UK: Cambridge University Press.

Weiss, L. (1998). *The myth of the powerless state.* Ithaca, NY: Cornell University Press.

Government-controlled Media, U.S.

The U.S. government's use of mass media in shaping foreign relations has at times blurred the lines between public diplomacy and propaganda. Ultimately it is the consumer who must judge the reliability of what is presented.

Who speaks for a nation to people of other nations? In a global world the image of a nation is communicated by tourists, telephone conversations, satellite transmissions, media exports, motion pictures, newspapers and magazines, the transmissions of sporting events, the cultural transplanting of consumable and consumer goods. In the case of the United States, global marketing and branding of U.S. goods from McDonald's and Kentucky Fried Chicken to Nike and Adidas are ubiquitous. In addition, there are the official and semiofficial voices of one nation talking to the citizens and governments of other nations outside the accepted notions of diplomacy. The "targeted media landscape" (i.e., media produced for nondomestic audiences by either governmental or private entities) is significant in disseminating information and shaping perceptions of the United States globally.

The many voices that speak to the world for the U.S. government can be traced to the United States Information Agency (USIA), the precursor of the Voice of America. The USIA (in existence from 1953 to 1999) referred to this form of communication as "public diplomacy." Other people associate "public diplomacy" with propaganda, whereas an alternative conceptualization is that of "soft power" or "power based on intangible or indirect influences such as culture, values, and ideology" with people being converted rather than coerced (Nye 1990).

The USIA's mission was to "understand, inform and influence foreign public promotion of the national interest and to broaden the dialogue between Americans and U.S. institutions and their counterparts abroad" (United States Information Agency).

Voice of America

The Voice of America, the public voice of U.S. national government, began operating on 24 February 1942 (shortly after the United States entered World War II). At that time the United States was one of the few world powers without a government-sponsored international broadcasting service. After World War II a committee investigating whether such broadcasting should continue urged extension of the VOA, noting that the U.S. government could not be "indifferent to the ways in which our society is portrayed to other countries" (Voice of America 2007). VOA's inaugural broadcast, using the transmitters of the British Broadcasting Corporation, featured announcer William Harlan Hale, who stated in German that "the news may be good. The news may be bad. We shall tell you the truth" (Voice of America 2007). The VOA has two goals: (1) to report the news and (2) to reflect U.S. policy. Its charter (quoting Public Law 94-350) stipulates that the "VOA will serve as a consistently reliable and authoritative source of news. VOA news will be accurate, objective, and comprehensive … VOA will present the policies of the United States clearly and effectively, and will also present responsible discussions and opinion on these policies." The journalist and one-time director John Chancellor once observed that the organization is "the crossroads of journalism and diplomacy" (Heil, 2003, 174). Its journalistic code emphasizes the need to strive for accuracy and objectivity, operationalized through traditional journalistic practices such as specified procedures for balance, fairness, and sourcing (i.e., a minimum of two independent, non-VOA sources).

Today the VOA offers more than one thousand hours of news, information, educational, and cultural programming every week in fifty-five languages, reaching an estimated 94 million people. Thirty correspondents at twenty-two news bureaus supply programming to diverse audiences in Africa, the Americas, Asia, Europe, and the Middle East.

The VOA must be understood in the context of its place in the government, which is the result of a long process. The USIA was established in August 1953, but in April 1978 its functions were consolidated with those of the Bureau of Educational and Cultural Affairs of the Department of State. During the Carter administration the USIA was called the "International Communications Agency," but the agency's name was restored to "USIA" in August 1982. The agency was known as the "United States Information Service" (USIS) overseas but did not use that abbreviation domestically in order to avoid confusion with the United States Immigration Service. The 1998 Foreign Affairs Reform and Restructuring Act abolished the U.S. Information Agency in 1999.

Today the Voice of America is governed by the Broadcasting Board of Governors (BBG), which is an independent federal agency established by the International Broadcasting Act of 1994. The BBG is responsible for all U.S. nonmilitary international broadcasting and in 2005 had a budget of $577 million.

According to the VOA, the BBG's mission is "to promote and sustain freedom and democracy by broadcasting accurate and objective news and information about the United States and the world to audiences overseas" (Broadcasting Board of Governors 2007). The *Broadcasting Board of Governors 2003 Annual Report* states:

> VOA audiences are also able to access the latest news and information on the Internet at www.VOANews.com. Continuously updated, English and foreign-language text is presented with photos, audio, and video. Subscriptions to Cyberjournals—daily or weekly VOA email publications—are another popular web feature. (Tomlinson 2003, 4)

Therein a curious problem arises because U.S. citizens are able to watch and listen to VOA broadcasts even though to do so is technically illegal because of the 1948 Smith-Mundt Act (22 USC 1461) which was intended to protect U.S. citizens from propaganda produced by its own government, but the technology of the Internet has made such protection impossible, if not obsolete. When asked about this apparent contradiction, Joseph O'Connell, director of external affairs, indicated that Internet transmissions are considered an extension of international broadcasting and therefore do not violate the letter of the law. However, the Voice of America is not the only government-sponsored voice of the United States.

Broadcasting Board of Governors

As a result of the 1998 Foreign Affairs Reform and Restructuring Act (Public Law 105-277), the Broadcasting Board of Governors "became the independent, autonomous entity responsible for all U.S. government and government sponsored, non-military, international broadcasting," effective 1 October 1999 (Broadcasting Board of Governors 2007). Eight members of the Broadcasting Board of Governors are appointed by the president and confirmed by the Senate; the ninth is the secretary of state. The board presides over five other broadcasting entities besides the Voice of America. These entities reach more than 100 million listeners, viewers, and Internet users around the world. The BBG notes that it has "played an important role in explaining the war on terrorism, helped counter misperceptions and untruths about the United States and provided valuable information about health, sci-

ence, education, politics, the rule of law and the status of women" (Tomlinson 2003, 2).

Radio Free Europe/Radio Liberty (RFE/RL) is a private, nonprofit, U.S. government radio service for central, southeastern, and eastern Europe. It broadcasts one hundred hours a week in twenty-nine languages.

Radio Farda ("Radio Tomorrow" in Persian) combines RFE/RL and VOA facilities and emanates from Washington and Prague. The twenty-four-hour station broadcasts on medium wave (AM 1593 and AM 1539) as well as shortwave and digital audio satellite and on the Internet. Many of Radio Farda's broadcasts are beamed into Iran.

The International Broadcasting Bureau (IBB) is the administrative unit under which the VOA and Radio/TV Marti operate. The latter broadcasts into Cuba and functions under the Broadcasting to Cuba Act of 1983 (Public Law 98-111). The IBB is also the primary organization responsible for the network of transmitting stations and satellite and Internet delivery systems. The IBB Office of Policy is responsible for writing U.S. government editorials.

The fourth of the five entities reporting to the BBG is the Middle East Television Network, which includes Alhurra and Radio Sawa. Alhurra is an Arabic-language news and information satellite television station, and Radio Sawa is an Arabic-language station whose programming originates in Washington and is broadcast via shortwave, medium wave, and the Internet.

Radio Free Asia (RFA) broadcasts in Mandarin, Cantonese, Uyghur, three dialects of Tibetan, Burmese, Vietnamese, Korean, Lao, and Khmer. The broadcasts originate in Washington; bureaus are situated throughout the Far East.

Transparency

The issue of transparency is of significance when considering how these diverse broadcasters shape perceptions of the United States around the world. Some broadcasters, such as VOA, are clearly known to be taxpayer-sponsored. Others are less publicly linked but are widely known or suspected to be, whereas the status of still others may be ambiguous to the audience. Anecdotal evidence indicates that Radio Sawa and Alhurra are generally known to be U.S. organizations, and each includes a statement on its website stating that they are funded by the U.S. Congress and the BBG. The U.S. government's relationship with other broadcasters is marked by greater ambiguity. Such is the case of Radio Free Asia and Radio Free Europe and Radio Liberty (chartered as RFE/RL Inc.), a corporation formed under the laws of the state of Delaware in 1949 and funded by the U.S. government, thereby providing

a degree of limited liability for the government. To add to the complexity in attempting to determine the source, the Office of Marketing and Program Placement (OMPP) of the BBG offers content to radio, television, and cable station owners and programmers interested in rebroadcasting VOA programming. Thirteen hundred affiliate broadcasters receive programming via satellite downlinks and mp3 audio files.

Whether such programming is merely suspected to be or is clearly identified as U.S.-supported, people have tried to jam broadcasts, an increasingly difficult endeavor as signals are moving from shortwave to satellite transmissions and Internet streaming. Recent cases of attempted jamming or blocking have occurred in Iran, Iraq, China, and Cuba.

Indirect Audiences: Military Broadcasts and Beyond

Who speaks for the nation remains a difficult question to answer. In addition to the Broadcasting Board of Governors with its link to the State Department, the White House Office of Global Communications was organized in 2002 "to coordinate strategic communications overseas that integrate the President's themes while truthfully depicting America and Administration policies." The aspect of coordination is not clear, particularly in regard to "public diplomacy."

Until now the public diplomacy model has essentially been a mass communication broadcasting one—the use of the mass media to reach large groups of people located in strategic places around the globe. The primary media were those of shortwave, long-wave, and medium-wave broadcasts and later satellite. However, the Internet, in all of its complexity, represents a new model in which access to information is far more important than directed mass messages aimed at specific locations. Thus, the voice of the nation becomes an aggregate of channels linked and combined with a series of connections. This is a difficult concept to articulate but perhaps can best be demonstrated by describing a short journey in cyberspace. It begins with a visit to the White House Office of Global Communications web site. No password or other authorization is needed, nor is the site restricted to U.S. citizens.

The White House Office of Global Communications links to both the U.S. State Department and the U.S. Defense Department. Among the myriad sites available are the Pentagon Channel; *Around the Services,* a daily half-hour military news feature; and *Studio Five,* a program that includes conversations with the members of the military. All are produced by the Pentagon Channel NewsCenter in Alexandria, Virginia.

The Broadcasting Board of Governors is responsible for *non-military* international broadcasting. Other government voices include Armed Forces Radio and Television Services (AFRTS), part of the Department of Defense, with a mission to "communicate Department of Defense policies, priorities, programs, goals and initiatives" (http://www.afrts.osd.mil/). Programming is directed to U.S. service personnel and Department of Defense civilians serving outside the continental United States in more than 177 countries. The American Forces Network Broadcast Center (AFN BC) is the sole programming source for military radio and television outlets overseas, operating under the umbrella of the Defense Media Center (located at March Air Reserve Base near Riverside, California). Although the intended audience is the U.S. military, when shortwave signals were used the signal reached beyond the boundaries of military bases. Satellite transmissions allow for a more targeted audience. Much of the programming can be accessed via the Internet, enlarging the potential audience.

In a world of flowing information and data the voice of a nation is a complex element. The persuasive impressions, images, and messages of a nation are never simple, never one-dimensional, but in the end the test will always be based on reliability, trust, truth, and verifiability.

Gary Gumpert and Susan J. Drucker

See also United States Information Agency

Further Reading

Alhurra TV. Retrieved February 5, 2007, from http://www.alhurra.com/Sub.aspx?ID=266

Broadcasting Board of Governors. (2007). About the BBG. Retrieved February 5, 2007, from http://www.bbg.gov/bbg_aboutus.cfm

Dizard, W. P. Jr. (2004). *Inventing public diplomacy: The story of the U.S. Information Agency.* Boulder, CO: Lynne Rienner.

Heil, A. L. Jr. (2003). *Voice of America: A history.* New York: Columbia University Press.

Nye, J. S. Jr. (1990, March). The misleading metaphor of decline. *The Atlantic,* 86–94.

Nye, J. S. (2004). *Soft power: The means to success in world politics. Public Affairs.*

Public Law 94-350. Retrieved January 30, 2007, from http://thomas.loc.gov

Puddington, A. (2003). *Broadcasting freedom: The Cold War triumph of Radio Free Europe and Radio Liberty.* Lexington: University Press of Kentucky.

Radio Sawa. Retrieved February 5, 2007, from http://www.radiosawa.com/english.aspx

Tomlinson, K. (2003). *Broadcasting Board of Governors 2003 annual report.* Retrieved January 13, 2007, from http://www.bbg.gov/reports/03anrprt.pdf

144

GLOBAL PERSPECTIVES on the UNITED STATES

Tomlinson, K. (2005). *Broadcasting Board of Governors 2005 annual report.* Retrieved January 13, 2007, from http://www.bbg.gov/reports/05anrprt.pdf

United States Information Agency. (n.d.). Retrieved January 13, 2007, from http://dosfan.lib.uic.edu/usia/

Urban, C. R. (1998). *Radio Free Europe and the pursuit of democracy: My war within the Cold War.* New Haven, CT: Yale University Press.

Voice of America. (2007). About VOA. Retrieved May 16, 2007, from http://www.voanews.com/english/about/

White House Office of Global Communications. (n.d.). Retrieved January 13, 2007, from http://www.whitehouse.gov/ogc/

Green Revolution

U.S. Cold War policymakers believed that the communist revolution thrived on people's poverty. The Green Revolution was seen as a way to alleviate poverty through agrarian reform and halt the spread of communism.

The Green Revolution (GR) has transformed global agriculture radically since the 1940s. Foreign assessment of U.S. involvement in starting and promoting the GR is intimately connected to a variety of overseas perspectives. This includes the value neutrality of Western-style experimental science, the value of emulating U.S. agricultural models, and the goals of U.S. development policies. Within various countries no national or unified perspective on the United States and the GR exists; rather, perspectives are based on the class, educational, and geographic backgrounds of the observers.

Rockefeller Foundation and the Mexican Agricultural Project

The GR is sometimes regarded by non-Americans as a neutral scientific project and at other times as a politically and culturally charged project. It began in U.S. agronomical (relating to a branch of agriculture dealing with field-crop production and soil management) practice a hundred years ago and was first "exported" to Mexico in the 1940s as the result of Rockefeller Foundation (RF) initiatives. The RF had become involved in applying a scientific approach to agriculture in 1906 when it had joined a U.S. Department of Agriculture (USDA) project to persuade farmers in the U.S. South to adopt a package of practices common in the later GR: improved seed types, increased cultivation, fertilization, and mechanization. In its philanthropic projects, which included agricultural "improvement," the RF hoped to rationalize the U.S. social order by promoting the creation and dissemination of useful knowledge. This rationalizing impulse would characterize the missionary-like zeal of later advocates of the GR.

In cooperation with the Mexican government, the RF turned its attention in the early 1940s to boosting Mexican agricultural production. The professionals whom the RF chose to plan and execute the project in 1943 came from Washington State University in Pullman and had worked extensively in the U.S. land-grant agricultural college system. Norman Borlaug, often considered the "father" of the GR and a member of these professionals, won the Nobel Peace Prize in 1970 for his early work on hybrid wheat in Mexico. The commercially oriented science of the land-grant

agricultural college system favored large, commercial farmers who could afford to invest in new technology, and the RF team strove to re-create the U.S. system in Mexico. In attempting to strengthen Mexican agriculture in the face of crop losses in the early 1940s, the RF involved the Ministry of Agriculture, agricultural colleges, and commercial farmers, set up experimental stations, and used U.S. experts, hybrid seeds, and irrigation systems.

Reactions in Mexico

Mexicans had mixed reactions to the RF project. State officials welcomed the outside funding and the revival of agronomy and some agrarian living standards; many agronomists had heard of the abundance of U.S. agriculture and wished to enhance their professional image by emulating U.S. agronomy; journalists praised the "modern" and "progressive" agriculture of the RF project, but the majority of smaller corn-producing peasants, the backbone of Mexican agriculture, received few benefits and were skeptical. The U.S. team selectively bred hybrids of corn and wheat, but Mexicans with small farms were not consulted on their needs because their farms (averaging 3 hectares) were not in a position to adopt expensive practices involved with hybrid seed, especially inorganic chemical fertilizers and irrigation.

Mexicans with large wheat farms fared better, but these were commercial ventures with an export orientation not unlike that of U.S. farms. They could afford the annual purchase of hybrid seed (rather than the peasant practice of saving open-pollinated seed from the harvest) and the timely application of inorganic fertilizers and pesticides so hybrids could reach their highest yields. Where Mexico's economy, social structure, and farming population differed greatly from those of the United States, the RF program was unable to remake Mexican agriculture over in the U.S. image, but by 1963 wheat production had soared, and that was enough. The seeds of the GR were planted, and they would sprout vigorously in Mexico and elsewhere in the Third World following the model laid down by the RF.

The Rockefeller Foundation project reoriented Mexico's agronomists away from their traditional concerns with rural hygiene, economic empowerment, peasant political consciousness, and land

reform (breaking up large, inefficient haciendas and creating small, more efficient peasant plots) toward technical and scientific solutions to the problems of Mexican agriculture. By making larger landholders more efficient and productive, the RF's project eased the pressure from peasants to enact land reform and the countervailing pressure by large landowners to reverse land reform altogether.

Foreign Proponents

After World War II the government and business community of the United States and its allies in Europe, the Americas, and Asia saw itself in a life-or-death struggle against communism. In the eyes of policymakers, communist social revolution thrived on people's poverty, and poverty now appeared to be a global problem. Seeing the increased yields from hybrid wheat in Mexico, business and government leaders in the United States and overseas looked to economic development in the form of the GR to eradicate poverty and blunt the appeal of communism. Proponents of the GR in Asia, Africa, and Latin America had similar backgrounds to the Mexicans who welcomed the RF's project and to the Americans who promoted it: large, commercial, market-oriented farmers, government officials in agriculture and economics ministries, university-trained and commercially oriented agronomists, and bankers. These elites hoped to stabilize class relations and prevent the division of large estates into peasant holdings (land reform). They believed U.S. agricultural science was readily transferable

Farmland in India, where the Green Revolution resulted in the transformation of many small farms into larger business operations. Source: istock/ Ron Mertens.

with the proper infrastructure, and the GR with its land- and labor-saving technologies seemed to offer a politically acceptable solution to the twin problems of malnutrition and land-hungry populations.

Foreign research scientists applauded the U.S. model of funding research stations along the line of the RF's project in Mexico: "The 'tree of research' of the North was transplanted to the South and Latin America became part of a transnational system of research" (Escobar 1994, 37). One of the first major research and training centers that emerged as a result of the RF effort in Mexico was CIMMYT (International Maize and Wheat Improvement Center). Founded in 1966, CIMMYT is a member of CGIAR (Consultative Group on International Agricultural Research), an umbrella organization of various agricultural research centers all over the world that are staffed by scientists from every country in the world. Their training and perspectives align with the U.S. research model that the Rockefeller Foundation transplanted to Mexico in the 1940s.

In the 1970s the World Bank, under the leadership of former U.S. Secretary of Defense Robert McNamara, turned its attention to rural development with the idea of increasing peasant food production by exposing the peasants to market forces. Pursuing this neoliberal idea, the World Bank provided loans to governments with the idea of bringing the requirements of the GR (capital, technology, training, and irrigation) to peasants so they could become small-scale entrepreneurs on the U.S. model. The World Bank planners operated within a purely economic frame of reference: Nature was a material resource, poverty was a lack of development, peasants were food producers, hunger was a result of insufficient agricultural productivity, and capital and technology brought progress. The World Bank and the international research centers affiliated with CGIAR with their native and foreign specialists argued, and continue to argue, that agricultural improvements require unprecedented action carefully guided by experts. Agrarian development experts Yojiro Hayomi, Derek Byerlee, Ruben Echeverria, and C. S. Prakash continue to echo this view of a scientifically guided agriculture in the era of genetically modified crops and biotechnology. Prakash in 2000 presented a letter to the U.N. Commission of Sustainable Development from two thousand scientists who, he said, believe that biotechnology is good for agriculture because it can reduce pesticide use, increase productivity, and grow more nutritious crops. Fellow Indian scientists Gurdev Khush, Kameswara Rao, Seetharam Annadana, and Gurumurti Shantharam also promote greater support for research on creating genetically modified crops and foods. M. S. Swaminathan, "the scientist most responsible for bringing Borlaug to Asia," founded a research institute in India to promote GR solutions to agricultural problems (Prakash 2004).

Foreign Critics of the Green Revolution

Foreign critics of the GR approach to poverty and hunger, such as Arturo Escobar, assert that "massive poverty in the modern sense appeared only when the spread of the market economy broke down community ties and deprived millions of people from access to land, water and other resources" (Escobar 1994, 22). Poverty and hunger were not inherent in peasant subsistence economies that developed visions of community, frugality, and sufficiency to deal with periods of shortages. Writers such as Edmundo Fuenzalida, Pedro Morandé, and Escobar argue that the new transnational research system accelerated peasants' loss of self-sufficiency while it devalued traditional modes of knowing and living on the land.

Critics in Latin America observed that in the first decades of the GR (1950s through early 1970s) output of staple food crops (beans, maize, cassava, plantains) cultivated by peasants stagnated, whereas growth rates of commercial crops (cotton, rice, sugar, soybeans, wheat, coffee) cultivated by entrepreneurs using GR technology for urban and export markets surged. Alain de Janvry noted that GR technology treated food as a commodity, privileged capitalist farmers, and made social class a prime determinant in the success of the GR: Commercial farmers could operate easier in a monetized U.S.-style economy, could afford the inputs and hybrid seeds, and received preferential treatment in protectionist measures and privileged access to research, credit, technology, and irrigation.

Critics are concerned that the GR continues to be guided by U.S. assumptions that disallow any development that is not market-based and that the GR operates with a definition of social progress that is shaped by U.S. culture and history. Class is also an issue: Guy Gran notes that "Neoclassical economists in Washington rather than African peasants define both the problem and the solution for African rural development.... The current situation is a dialogue of elites" (Gran 1986, 277–278). Critics argue that the GR has disrupted and restructured rural economies around the world so that they resemble the economy of the rural United States and are safe places for the investment of excess U.S. capital but that the GR has not eliminated hunger or poverty in those economies. Vandana Shiva in India contends that the GR's high-responsive seeds, developed for U.S.-style farming, perform worse than indigenous varieties in the absence of expensive inputs, result in a loss of biodiversity, and have caused increased pesticide use.

The Future

Under the weight of extensive criticism and growing problems of sustainability, proponents are reassessing the technical components

of the GR but not the scientific, land-grant model of agriculture that underlies it. Proponents are turning to biotechnology and scientifically engineered crops that are more pest- and disease-resistant and need less water to thrive. The commercialization of seed germplasm (germ cells and their precursors serving as the bearers of heredity and being fundamentally independent of other cells) is more extensive than ever, sparking a new controversy around "biopiracy." From the point of view of those who bring the charge, biopiracy is the illegitimate patenting of traditionally accessible genetic material and indigenous knowledge in the Third World by corporations and universities of the First World for private commercial gain. U.S. businesses holding the patents believe their actions are sanctioned by the World Trade Organization's Agreement on Trade-Related Aspects of Intellectual Property Rights (TRIPS), and they look to the U.S. government to uphold those legal rights.

The United States is a leader in defending intellectual property rights globally, especially as they are related to new applications of technology and chemistry, and the United States Patent and Trademark Office (USPTO) is a leader in processing TRIPS claims. The USPTO restricted the patents of a Texas company on basmati rice in 2001 after sustained protest by Indian farmers and a lawsuit by the government of India challenging the company's claims, but it has approved hundreds of patents on plant and animal genetic material that did not originate in the United States. Foreign assessment of U.S. involvement in starting and promoting this second GR will still be intimately connected to the class, educational, geographic, and (increasingly) gender position of the viewer.

Alexander M. Zukas

See also IMF, World Bank, and IDB, U.S. Role in;
U.S. Agency for International Development

Further Reading

Byerlee, D., & Echeverria, R. (2002). *Agricultural policy in an era of privatization.* New York: Oxford University Press.

Cueto, M. (1994). *Missionaries of science: The Rockefeller Foundation and Latin America.* Bloomington: Indiana University Press.

Escobar, A. (1994). *Encountering development: The making and unmaking of the Third World.* Ewing, NJ: Princeton University Press.

Franke, R. (1974). Miracle seeds and shattered dreams in Java. *Natural History, 83*(1), 10–18, 84–88.

Gran, G. (1986). Beyond African famines: Whose knowledge matters? *Alternatives, 11*(2), 275–296.

Khor, M. (2000). Debate on feeding the world. Retrieved October 1, 2004, from http://www.twnside.org.sg/title/2041.htm

Leff, E. (1995). *Green production: Toward an environmental rationality.* New York: Guilford.

Prakash, C. S. (2004). Jimmy Carter, George McGovern, and scientists celebrate "father of the Green Revolution." AgBioWorld.org. Retrieved January 30, 2007, from http:www.agbioworld.org/biotech_info/pr/borlaug90.html

Prakash, C. S. (2004). Technology that will save billions from starvation. Retrieved October 1, 2004, from http://www.agbioworld.org/biotech_info/articles/prakash/prakashart/save-billions.html

Shiva, V. (1989). *Staying alive: Women, ecology and development.* London: Zed Books.

Shiva, V. (1991). The Green Revolution in the Punjab. *The Ecologist, 21*(2). Retrieved October 1, 2004, from http://livingheritage.org/green-revolution.htm

Shiva, V. (1992). *The violence of the Green Revolution: Third World agriculture, ecology and politics.* London: Zed Books.

Visvanathan, S. (1986). Bhopal: The imagination of a disaster. *Alternatives, 11*(1), 147–165.

Visvanathan, S. (1991). Mrs. Bruntland's disenchanted cosmos. *Alternatives, 16*(3), 377–384.

History of United States in World Opinion

The United States has received both praise and condemnation for its role in the world, and has never been absent from world opinions. However, since the mid-twentieth century, the view of the United States has been more negative than positive.

The United States has maintained a somewhat complicated relationship to world opinion from the early nineteenth century to the present. On the one hand, Americans often participated eagerly in world opinion seeking to correct various abuses in various parts of the world; in some important instances, such as the struggle against South African apartheid during the 1980s, the United States actually led the current of world opinion. On the other hand, the United States has sometimes been the target of international moral condemnation. Racial issues have provided the most obvious problems. After World War II, U.S. policies arising from its status as a superpower also attracted international criticism; this was particularly evident in global opposition to the U.S. invasion of Iraq. By the same token, Americans and U.S. leaders have also alternated between seeking the good favor of other countries and resisting outside pressure.

What Comprises World Opinion?

World opinion is not easy to define, as it emanates from no central agency but rather is the aggregate of public opinion from diverse nations and regions. World opinion has never been representatively global, but it always cuts across political and cultural boundaries to some extent. Historically, Western Europe has most commonly taken the lead in world opinion. Canada has developed a commitment to help guide world opinion on issues such as human rights, and Australia has been heavily involved on certain issues. Since World War II opinion emanating from Japan and, more recently, South Korea has had increased importance. U.S. opinion has had great weight from the nineteenth century onward.

The central feature of world opinion, aside from its international quality, is a sense of moral responsibility for people living in remote places. These people generally share no direct ethnic or religious link with those formulating world opinion, simply a sense of common humanity. World opinion requires reasonably regular news about distant places, so that the international public can become informed, and like all manifestations of public opinion,

it demands that relevant policymakers pay attention to it. Finally, world opinion would have no sway if indications of international displeasure did not cause embarrassment for policymakers. One of the reasons world opinion has an effect on the United States is that Americans are relatively responsive to outside pressure; Americans desire to be liked and approved of in the wider world.

World Opinion in Early U.S. History

World opinion in its modern form first made itself felt in the late eighteenth century, on the issue of slavery and the slave trade. A combination of impulses from new Protestant sects, notably Methodists and Quakers, and the broader spirit of the Enlightenment generated the kind of humanitarian thinking that recast one of the oldest social institutions into an abomination. Centered in England and France, but with ramifications elsewhere, antislavery sentiment had much the effect at that time that world opinion was to have from that point onward. Moral intensity was the primary component: slavery was evil, an unacceptable affront to human dignity and the right to freedom. A variety of groups developed to spread the word about slavery and to galvanize demonstrations and petitions. Appropriately, many of these organizations developed international connections, particularly across the Atlantic. The creation of the earliest durable international human rights group, the Anti-Slavery Society, which still exists and is based in London, marked the start of the development of a world opinion infrastructure.

Pictures and stories of individual atrocities gave the antislavery movement the drama on which world opinion so often depends; theatrical renditions of Harriet Beecher Stowe's *Uncle Tom's Cabin* (1852) served as one component in this ongoing effort. A variety of tactics were discussed, including boycotts of slave-produced goods such as sugar. But ultimately it was the strength of numbers and moral fervor that constituted the core strategy. Petitions signed by hundreds of thousands of people, from various social classes, combined with urgent assertion of slavery's evil, pressed lawmakers

in Britain and elsewhere, and slave owners themselves, first to end the slave trade and then to end the institution itself.

This first, and ultimately widely successful, outcome of the assertion of world opinion had various effects on the United States. Many Americans participated extensively in the international effort, often imitating and corresponding with English groups. While the U.S. antislavery campaign was largely national, it certainly acknowledged and benefited from the larger international chorus. At the same time, Southern slavery was one of the targets of the world campaign, particularly after the abolition of the international slave trade and the ending of slavery in British and French colonies. One reason for Lincoln's issuance of the Emancipation Proclamation in 1863 was to defuse British and French sympathies for the Southern cause by bringing the federal government in line with the standards of world opinion on the slavery question. In the very first case of world opinion effecting a change in social practice, then, the United States was already in an ambiguous position, as both a partner in the world outcry and the focus of that outcry, and in Lincoln's response we see the first instance of U.S. conciliatory reaction.

Because of the way it is formed, including its dependence on media coverage, world opinion can often seem inconsistent. Despite the outcry over slavery, the world had no particular reaction to U.S. policy toward the American Indians during the nineteenth century. Few stories claimed atrocities, and insofar as the atrocities were known, the U.S. actions may have seemed unremarkable in the age of European imperialism.

In the later nineteenth century, when the treatment of women became an issue that engaged world opinion, the United States again figured both as participant and target. U.S. feminist leaders, headed by Elizabeth Cady Stanton (1815–1902), were at the forefront of organizing international conferences and forming organizations to deal with women's issues, particularly from the 1880s onward. The effort was clearly directed toward establishing international standards for the treatment of women, with attention paid to "unfortunate sisters" in Asia. A particular campaign focused on so-called white slavery. Many people believed that large numbers of innocent young women and children were being seized on the city streets, to be sold in Russia, the Middle East, and particularly Latin America for purposes of prostitution. Outrage surged, with pitiable individual stories of innocence defiled. Most historians believe that the scare outstripped reality, but there was no question that opinion ran high against white slavery and that it had an impact, ultimately inducing international organizations like the League of Nations to pronounce on the subject and individual governments, particularly in Argentina, to take action to deflect hostile global comment.

At almost the same time, however, world opinion began to target the U.S. practice of lynching African-Americans and Mexicans, a practice that continued during the first half of the twentieth century. European and even Japanese papers began to send reporters to some of the most notorious lynching sites, and their stories back home were damning. Condemnations of lynching constituted one of the first Japanese expressions of opinion on a moral matter on the world stage, with Japanese newspapers emphasizing the contradictions between loudly expressed egalitarian principles and actual behavior in the United States. Media coverage of lynchings provoked frequent petition campaigns and letters from famous individuals excoriating U.S. violence and racism. Again, there was some response; partly to placate Mexican opinion, the federal government began intervening in more cases involving Mexican citizens and in some cases even paid out some compensation to aggrieved families.

World Opinion and the United States in the Twentieth Century

This angle of world opinion, bent on condemning some of the more extreme manifestations of racism, continued after World War II. Even though African-American hopes for international backing in their struggle for civil rights faded against the tensions of the Cold War, international commentary on the U.S. racial scene continued, focusing particularly on Southern segregation. During the 1950s Southerners frequently went out of their way to exempt black foreigners from some of the most blatant discrimination—for example, in restaurants—and savvy local African-Americans sometimes successfully put on a French accent to receive similar treatment. Sensitivity to international criticism continued, though it took far more massive, domestic efforts really to affect basic policies.

As for Americans contributing their voice to world opinion, prior to World War II segments of the U.S. population joined with the West Europeans in protesting Italian and Japanese aggression and the Spanish Civil War, but were unable to stop the aggressors through moral suasion. After the war, the sense that there had been inadequate resistance to repression, particularly as more information about the Holocaust was revealed, helped galvanize world opinion on both sides of the Atlantic.

Nuclear Testing

Without question, world opinion became a more visible and consistent force to some extent during the 1950s and more vigorously from the 1960s onward, and as was true in the past, the United States was both the target of international criticism and, in other instances, a potent voice in international outcry. During the Cold War, world opinion was very critical of the nuclear arms race, and

AMNESTY INTERNATIONAL DECLARATION ON THE USE OF DEATH PENALTY AGAINST CHILD OFFENDERS

In the declaration below, Amnesty International calls on lawyers and other legal professionals to oppose the use of the death penalty against young offenders—particularly those in the United States.

Recognizing that the International Covenant on Civil and Political Rights, the Convention on the Rights of the Child and other international treaties preclude the use of the death penalty against child offenders—people who were under 18 years old at the time of the offence;

Recognizing that all countries have ratified one or more of these treaties;

Recognizing that when the United States reserved the right to execute child offenders on ratifying the International Covenant on Civil and Political Rights, the Human Rights Committee established under that Covenant stated that the reservation was incompatible with the object and purpose of the Covenant and urged that it be withdrawn;

Recognizing that the Inter-American Commission on Human Rights has held that the prohibition of executing child offenders is a rule of customary international law and a norm of *jus cogens*;

Concluding that the use of the death penalty against child offenders in any circumstances violates international law;

Deploring that the United States accounted for 19 of the 35 known executions of child offenders worldwide since 1990, and that it currently holds at least 70 child offenders on its death rows;

Welcoming the decision of the US Supreme Court to reconsider the constitutionality of executing child offenders,

We, the undersigned, call on

The legislatures of US states whose laws still allow the execution of child offenders to raise the minimum age to 18;

The US government to ensure that the United States respects its obligation under international law not to execute child offenders.

Source: Amnesty International. (2004). Lawyers declaration against the implementation of the death penalty on child offenders in the USA. Retrieved May 25, 2007, from http://web.amnesty.org/pages/iln-010504-petition-eng

---

the United States was sometimes singled out for criticism not because its policies were unique—the Soviet Union participated actively in the arms race too—but because unlike the Soviet Union, the United States combined its power with a democratic openness that made it more receptive to criticism.

The initial criticisms centered on atomic weaponry and particularly nuclear testing. Concerns were first voiced in the late 1940s, when the United States was the only nuclear power. Japan contributed, newly conscious of its voice in world opinion on matters of peace and armaments given its World War II experience. Several newly independent nations, headed by India and Egypt, also voiced anxieties, as did several Latin American nations. This initial expression was both hesitant and short-lived, cut off by the Cold War (which largely trumped armaments concerns) and by the general ill-repute of pacifism following World War II. However, the accession of the Soviet Union to nuclear ranks, the steady escalation of nuclear potency and Cold War tension, and particularly the growing realization of the environmental and health consequences of nuclear testing began to generate more widespread and vigorous opposition in world opinion. A U.S. testing accident in the Pacific that doused a Japanese fishing boat with nuclear pollutants, killing one person, provided a dramatic and specific case that galvanized world opinion in a way that abstract principles had not been able to. Australian opinion was drawn in because of the frequent use of the Pacific region for testing. Large

antinuclear movements developed in Western Europe, some of them (in Germany, for example) expressing deep disappointment that power considerations seemed to outweigh democratic principles in the contemporary United States. There were numerous demonstrations before U.S. embassies and educational centers, which in response became so well fortified that they often looked like armed camps.

Toward the end of his administration, President Dwight Eisenhower acknowledged the efficacy of world opinion when he said that while modern weaponry was powerful, world opinion had become even more powerful: The United States joined in negotiations that ended the open testing of nuclear weapons. World opinion was now an acknowledged factor in U.S. military and diplomatic policy.

The Vietnam War

The conclusion of a partial test ban treaty in 1963 and the nuclear nonproliferation treaty in 1968 somewhat allayed world anxiety, though within Europe, demonstrations against the installation of additional U.S. rocketry occasionally occurred. The U.S. war in Vietnam became a new target of international criticism, however. There were protests in various parts of the world—including, of course, the United States—against this assertion of U.S. power and against the bombing attacks that so often victimized civilians as well as the natural environment. The international wave of

student protests in 1968 was directed in part against U.S. Vietnam policies, and demonstrations before various U.S. facilities continued for several years.

Other Foci of World Opinion

The end of the Vietnam War and the gradual easing of Cold War tensions reduced international hostility toward U.S. foreign policy. World opinion focused its criticism on new targets, including South Africa (for its repressive apartheid regime) and Indonesia (for its actions in East Timor, which it had annexed in 1975 and refused to part with until 1999). The United States was only indirectly involved, as opinion mobilizers sought to win official U.S. support against human rights violators, such as South Africa. Large segments of the U.S. public added their voices to international criticism of apartheid and in some instances even led the fight against it. African-American organizations began the international charge against apartheid and, by 1984, were joined by a variety of university campus groups. They pressed private

CHARLES DICKENS ON SLAVERY IN THE UNITED STATES

In his 1842 book, American Notes for General Circulation, *Dickens voices his strong disapproval of the institution of slavery in the U.S. South.*

But again: this class, together with that last one I have named, the miserable aristocracy spawned of a false republic, lift up their voices and exclaim 'Public opinion is all-sufficient to prevent such cruelty as you denounce.' Public opinion! Why, public opinion in the slave States IS slavery, is it not? Public opinion, in the slave States, has delivered the slaves over, to the gentle mercies of their masters. Public opinion has made the laws, and denied the slaves legislative protection. Public opinion has knotted the lash, heated the branding-iron, loaded the rifle, and shielded the murderer. Public opinion threatens the abolitionist with death, if he venture to the South; and drags him with a rope about his middle, in broad unblushing noon, through the first city in the East. Public opinion has, within a few years, burned a slave alive at a slow fire in the city of St. Louis; and public opinion has to this day maintained upon the bench that estimable judge who charged the jury, impanelled there to try his murderers, that their most horrid deed was an act of public opinion, and being so, must not be punished by the laws the public sentiment had made. Public opinion hailed this doctrine with a howl of wild applause, and set the prisoners free, to walk the city, men of mark, and influence, and station, as they had been before.

Source: Dickens, C. (1842). Slavery. In American notes for general circulation *(Chap. 17).*

institutions as well as the U.S. government to withdraw investments from South Africa and to take other measures to press the regime to alter its policies. New atrocities by South African police spurred world opinion further and helped drive its claims home. The U.S. government, initially reluctant, was pressed into increasing advocacy of the antiapartheid cause, and finally between 1990 and 1991 apartheid came to an end. This was one of the most successful cases of world opinion influencing a country's domestic policy, and the United States played an influential role. Similar developments helped bring U.S. intervention in Yugoslavia during its civil war in the 1990s; again in that instance world opinion, including U.S.public opinion, convinced a hesitant but not hostile U.S. policy community to take action.

Other developments in the same period were more complex. First, there was a rise in sentiment against both the environmental and worker-related policies of multinational corporations. Campaigns against these corporations often focused on U.S.-based companies and individuals, though the campaigns were not couched in specifically anti-American terms. A major international protest developed over the McDonald's restaurant chain's use of nonbiodegradable wrappers and its importation of Brazilian beef. (The latter was an issue because the Brazilian beef industry cut down portions of the Amazon rain forest to make rangeland for its cattle.) After initial resistance, McDonald's altered its policies. Concern over U.S. clothing and shoe manufacturers' use of sweatshop labor in developing countries focused on dramatic cases of abuse, and again the corporations often made concessions, at least for a time. Several U.S. entertainers, such as Kathy Lee Gifford, had investments in what turned out to be sweatshop operations, and publicity and the pressure of public opinion forced sometimes tearful apologies and vows to reform. These were important developments, and they did not single out U.S.-based companies alone; Japanese, Korean, and European multinationals were also often targeted.

The Role of Nongovernmental Organizations

The rapid rise and proliferation of human-rights-oriented nongovernmental organizations (NGOs) had more direct implications for the United States. The pattern began with the establishment of the British-based Amnesty International in 1961 and continued with the activities of the U.S.-based Human Rights Watch (established in 1978) and a host of other groups, both international and regional. These groups used their ability to rouse and mobilize public opinion to fight the abuse of human rights. They also steadily expanded the definition of abuse, for example to include not only political executions, but also torture and political imprisonments. Many of their campaigns were directed against Communist and other authoritarian countries. These campaigns frequently involved

extensive participation by U.S. citizens and sometimes even U.S. government approval. However, the organizations were also careful to cite Western cases of human rights abuse, such as British abuses in Northern Ireland. These cases often proved problematic for the United States.

An important confrontation occurred during the administration of President Ronald Reagan in the mid-1980s. NGOs and local reformers uncovered extensive information about assassinations, imprisonment, and torture by U.S.-backed authoritarian regimes in Central America. The Catholic Church also publically protested the many abuses. Under this international cloud of dissent, the United States was gradually forced to alter its policies, withdraw support from the regimes, and accept the inclusion of reform elements in Central American nations. This flexibility demonstrated renewed U.S. openness to global criticism, but the initial policies that countenanced repression did not endear the United States, particularly its conservative political elements, to world opinion.

A more durable rift with world opinion, especially with its West European base, began in the 1990s, when world opinion—spurred by human rights organizations, along with official Catholic opinion—turned against the death penalty, at a time when American reliance on the penalty was increasing. A number of scheduled executions drew widespread international comment, with letters and petitions to state governors to grant reprieves. Relatively few of the appeals found favor, but there were some signs of retreat from the death penalty after 2000 that may have been motivated in part by concern for the United States standing in world opinion

The Administration of George W. Bush

The advent of another conservative administration, that of George W. Bush, in 2000 put the United States at odds with world opinion. The administration was eager to avoid any concessions to international pressure that might compromise national sovereignty and rejected a number of international treaties on the environment, bans on the use of land mines, even on child labor. Several of these conventions had been eagerly supported by U.S. reformers as part of the larger global voice, but the administration's go-it-alone stance highlighted a kind of defiance that represented the views of the segment of the population who feared compromising their beliefs under pressure from foreign standards.

Despite an outpouring of world support for the United States following the terrorist attacks of September 11, 2001, during 2002–2003, as the United States appeared to move inexorably toward an attack on Iraq, world opinion turned decidedly hostile. A host of new and established organizations mobilized demonstrations and petitions against a war that much of the world regarded as unjustified. World opinion clearly did not accept the notion that preemptive strikes against presumed weapons of mass destruction were warranted, at least not without far more extensive efforts through international diplomacy beforehand. On 11 February 2003, probably as many as 25 million people demonstrated against the war, with the heaviest concentrations in North America, Western European countries, Japan, Russia, and Mexico. This was almost certainly the largest international demonstration in world history. Opinion polls confirmed what the demonstrations suggested: 60 to 90 percent of most publics were hostile to the looming war, even in countries in which the government response was more favorable, such as Spain and Italy.

In the United States, the public was divided. Polls suggested that about a third of all Americans agreed with world opinion outright and opposed the war. Another third thought that war might be justified, but should be undertaken only with substantial international agreement. A final third favored war regardless of international opinion. This last strand was embraced by the Bush administration, which defied world opinion in going to war. Initial success in the invasion seemed to deflate the global protest, except in the Islamic world. However, polls suggested increasing hostility to the United States and U.S. policy in most parts of the world; many publics polled regarded the United States as the greatest threat to world peace. In 2004, as the U.S. occupation of Iraq encountered growing difficulties and amid reports of U.S. attacks on civilians and abuses of political prisoners, international censure of the United States grew more acute. As the twenty-first century continues to unfold, the current actions of the U.S. government suggest new complications in the relationship between the United States and world opinion, continuing an already complex history.

Peter N. Stearns

Futher Reading

Drescher, S. (1999). *From slavery to freedom: Comparative studies in the rise and fall of Atlantic slavery.* New York: New York University Press.

Klotz, A. (1995). *Norms in international relations: The struggle against apartheid.* Ithaca, NY: Cornell University Press.

Korey, W. (1998). *NGOs and the Universal Declaration of Human Rights: A curious grapevine.* New York: St. Martin's Press.

Nadelmann, E. (1990). Global prohibition regimes: The evolution of norms in international society. *International Organization, 44,* 479–526.

Rupp, L. J. (1998). *Worlds of women: The making of an international women's movement.* Princeton, NJ: Princeton University Press.

Stearns, P. N. (2005). *Outrage without borders: How world opinion developed and how its impact evolved.* London: Worldwide.

Wittner, L. (1997). *Resisting the bomb: A history of the world nuclear disarmament movement, 1954–1970.* Stanford, CA: Stanford University Press.

Homogenization of World Culture

World cultures in the modern era contain fewer areas that remain unaffected by outside cultures. The rise of capitalism, technological innovation, and human curiosity, has blended cultures in a way previous interactions never did.

Trends in religion, language, fashion, entertainment, art, eating, drinking, and relationships—just some of the components of what might be considered overall human culture—are varied almost beyond comprehension. Further, humanity has innumerable subcultures that most of us know little about. However, the breadth of human cultural diversity has not stopped all manner of commentators from declaring that overall, human culture is becoming increasingly homogenized. Frequently this charge is associated with a belief that human culture is becoming overly Americanized.

Although the development of a shared human or world culture should be seen in the context of globalization, interaction between peoples and cultures is nothing new; trade and migration have been mixing cultures since time immemorial. What is distinctive about twentieth- and twenty-first-century globalization is that it leaves fewer (if any) societies untouched: Indigenous and traditional cultures throughout the world are increasingly familiar with television, commercial music, and consumer trends that make their lifestyles less unique than they once were. Moreover, an overarching global culture of a sort has emerged; its cultural icons include McDonald's, the National Basketball Association (NBA), rock music, Coca-Cola, and Hollywood. Global capitalism, technological innovation, and human curiosity are the motors behind the development of this global culture.

Given this cultural globalization it would be fair to say that people's drinking, eating, listening, and consuming habits across the globe are more homogenized than they have ever been. For example, 78 percent of all soft drinks consumed are produced by the three largest firms—although how culturally significant this is debatable. To paraphrase Sigmund Freud, sometimes a Coke is just a sugary drink and sometimes it is a symbol of U.S. imperialism. A more meaningful indicator of loss of cultural distinctiveness might be the loss of numerous languages and dialects over the last century and the increasing spread of the English language, including its role as the principal language of the World Wide Web. Further, it is estimated that 90 percent of spoken languages will become extinct during this century. Whether these global cultural trends are largely negative and whether they imply a deep

Americanization depends in part on what we mean by the term *homogenization*.

What Is Homogenization?

Homogenization is the process of blending diverse elements into a uniform mixture. The first interpretation of homogenization in a sociological context is to see it as implying a blending of different cultures. From this perspective, the best elements of national cultures are spread around the world, just as cream is spread around milk when milk is homogenized. A metaphor for this understanding of homogenization would be a multicultural food bazaar with stalls of cuisine from all parts of the globe. There is one question that arises from this interpretation: who spreads this variety around the world and who experiences it? Any balanced answer to this question would suggest that this first understanding of homogenization is rather idealized. It is less commonly called homogenization, with scholars preferring terms like cosmopolitanism, pluralism, or hybridization.

The second interpretation of homogenization suggests that it entails a domination of the big over the small, with the outcome being an increased sameness and possibly an increased blandness and corporatization. A metaphor for the second understanding would be a strip of roadside restaurants owned by multinational chains such as McDonald's. This second interpretation is what is more commonly meant by homogenization. The term is generally used to imply a negative process, with an emphasis on the ills of standardization, commercialization, Westernization, and Americanization.

The Context: Globalization

Far too often globalization is treated as an almost entirely economic or technological phenomenon, with the cultural dimension largely ignored. More comprehensive understandings of globalization take into account that cultural dimension, with debates about global cultural homogeny a crucial area of interest and concern.

Globalization, put simply and practically, "refers to the shrinkage of distance on a large scale. It can be contrasted with localization, nationalization, or regionalization" (Keohane and Nye 2000, 105). Moreover, as the world has shrunk, capital, ideas, goods, values, and people have increasingly crossed borders, breaking down boundaries to create what UNESCO has called the "global neighborhood," or what the sociologist John Tomlinson has described as "enforced proximity."

The Global Blending of Cultures

Seen positively, cultural globalization has brought greater diversity and understandings of difference to people around the world. It has broken down the tyranny of distance between peoples. Events such as Nelson Mandela being greeted by the Inuit people of northern Canada with a cry of "Viva ANC!" (UNESCO 1996, 105) or my own memories of sitting next to a group of young Muslim girls clad in traditional headscarves cheering enthusiastically for their Australian Rules football team at the Melbourne Cricket Ground remind us of the marvels of global culture. Conversely, the death of a language reminds us of the costs of globalization.

Cultural blending, or what others call cosmopolitanism, is championed as a departure from narrow, nationalist, and monocultural understandings. Indeed cultural globalization has much going for it, as the political economist Tyler Cowen rightly highlights in his recent Creative Destruction. Some obvious benefits are a greater diversity of food, music, and literature in many parts of the world. When criticizing such cosmopolitan ideals, it is important to remember the threats posed by the opposite extreme—cultural chauvinism and fundamentalism, which can lead to the banning of books or even to actions such as the fatwa against the writer Salman Rushdie for the perceived blasphemy of his novel *The Satanic Verses*. Similarly, supporters of cosmopolitanism such as Cowen fail to recognize that problems of affordability mean that not everyone can experience the richness of choice that cosmopolitanism theoretically makes possible and that not all imported culture is presented as a choice; some of it is imposed.

Cultural Imperialism

Forced migration, religious missionaries, wars against indigenous populations and land seizure, and the imposition of foreign languages and customs have had a long cultural legacy. They have homogenized people—made their behavior more similar—via the barrel of the gun. Cultural imperialism continues to this day, although generally in more subtle forms than colonization and slavery. Extreme forms of cultural imperialism continue in ethnic wars, as documented in Heather Rae's recent *State Identities and the Homogenisation of Peoples*. Schiller and others argue that the spread of commerce, particularly U.S. commerce, is also tinged

with cultural imperialism. At their worst, multinational companies have shown a deplorable lack of regard for local culture. When Nestlé infamously marketed baby formula to impoverished African and Asian mothers with contaminated water supplies, it not only endangered the lives of the babies, it undermined local traditions of nursing by suggesting that bottle feeding was superior. Shell has run oil pipes across Nigeria polluting the streams and lands of Nigeria's Ogoni people, and BHP Billiton polluted the Ok Tedi and Fly Rivers with its mining activities in Papua New Guinea. Human lives have been lost as a result of these actions, and, in the latter two cases, local communities have been unable to farm and fish their traditional lands. This side of globalization cannot be ignored, however it is important to note that, although U.S. companies are among the worst offenders, they are not alone, as

Indian businessman with a laptop talking on a cell phone. Source: istock.

the above actions of a Swiss, a Dutch, and an Australian company remind us. Furthermore, the spread of Western capitalist culture comes with costs and benefits. To focus exclusively on either side of this equation usually reveals more about a commentator's politics than anything else.

Americanization

It is fair to say that U.S. culture is the preponderant culture of globalization. In his introduction to *Many Globalizations,* a broad-ranging study of Americanization and cultural diversity, the sociologist Peter Berger writes, "There is indeed an emerging global culture, and it is indeed heavily American in origin and content. It is not the only game in town . . . but it is the biggest game going and it will likely stay that way for the foreseeable future" (Berger 2002, 2–3). The following chapters of the book document the vast spread of U.S. popular culture around the globe. Some are inclined to see this as imperialism, "with local popular or traditional forms driven out or dumbed down to make way for American television, American music, food, clothes and films" (Jameson 2000, 51). Although the dominance of Hollywood films and the omnipresence of Coca-Cola are hard to deny, U.S. culture is not always adopted or experienced passively.

A fascinating example of this adaptation and hybridization is the development of reggae and dance hall music in the Caribbean in the second half of the twentieth century. As the sociologist Orlando Patterson brilliantly points out in an essay on global culture, far from being overwhelmed by the U.S. music industry and culture, the small Caribbean islands have been a hotbed of invention, much of which has been exported around the world. The current phenomenal success of Caribbean-influenced hip-hop music is just one example among many of successful Caribbean exports. This reminds us that the flow of culture is not one-way. In fact UNESCO figures show that from the 1970s to the 1990s cultural exports from the developing world significantly increased as a percentage of global cultural exports.

In addition, claims that Americanization is leading to standardization often ignore the heterogeneous nature of U.S. culture, not only in its breadth, but also its contradictions. For example, the United States is the home of both an active Christian evangelical movement and a thriving pornography industry.

Proceeding with Caution

Although present-day global culture is much more than a bland corporatized McWorld, a few cautionary points need to be made.

Global corporations are often not respectful of local cultures, and as multinational corporations extend their reach into new markets and search out consumers, they often overwhelm local customs and products. Although globalization offers Third World farmers and musicians new markets, the patterns and rules of world trade and commerce are generally biased against the Third World.

The powerful global media can raise our consciousness about tragedies near and far and bring new stories of wonder and beauty to billions of people, supporting the sociologist Roland Robertson's definition of globalization as both "the compression of the world and . . . the intensification of the consciousness of the world as a whole" (Robertson 1992, 8). However the concentration of media ownership and the distribution power of the major Hollywood film studios limit the ideas and stories people around the world see and get to hear about. Without subsidies, the film, television and music industries in countries such as Australia would be run out of town by U.S. imports. Undoubtedly the power of U.S. enterprise needs to be regulated to keep global culture rich and diverse.

Some worry that U.S. culture is like a virus infecting the dreams, speech, and attitudes of people in the rest of the world. Examples of this are not particularly hard to find: At times, it seems that every second individual in Australia thinks that "Whatever!" is a witty way of telling someone you do not want to listen to his or her point of view. This of course exaggerates the problem, but a healthy skepticism of Americanization is undoubtedly needed. As combatants against homogeny have long cried, *Vive la différence.*

Brendon O'Connor

See also Culture Overseas, U.S.; Diffusion of Knowledge, Global; Globalization, Economic; McDonaldization; Multinational Corporations

Further Reading

Anderson, K. (2003, May). Wine's new world. *Foreign Policy, 136,* 47–54.

Barber, B. (1992, March). Jihad vs. McWorld. *The Atlantic Monthly, 269*(3), 53–65.

Berger, P. (2002). The cultural dynamics of globalization. In P. Berger & S. Huntington (Eds.), *Many globalizations* (pp. 1–16). New York: Oxford University Press.

Cowen, T. (2002). *Creative destruction.* Princeton, NJ: Princeton University Press.

Jameson, F. (2000, July-August). Globalization and political strategy. *New Left Review, 4,* 49–68.

Keohane, R. & Nye, J. (2000, Spring). Globalization: What's new? What's not? (And so what?) *Foreign Policy, 118,* 104–119.

Patterson, O. (1994). Ecumenical America: Global culture and the American cosmos. *World Policy Journal, 11*(2), 103–117.

Rae, H. (2002). *State identities and the homogenisation of peoples.* Cambridge, UK: Cambridge University Press.

Ritzer, G. (1998). *The McDonaldization thesis.* London: Sage.

Robertson, R. (1992). *Globalization: Social theory and global culture.* London: Sage.

Schiller, H. (1976). *Communication and cultural domination.* White Plains, NY: International Arts and Sciences Press.

Schiller, H. (1991). Not yet the post-imperialist era. *Critical Studies in Mass Communication, 8*(1), 13–28.

Tomlinson, J. (1999). *Globalization and culture.* Chicago: University of Chicago Press.

UNESCO. (1996). *Our creative diversity.* Paris: UNESCO Publications.

Human Rights

The U.S. human rights record has been described as both heroic and villainous. A record of leadership in spreading human rights now clashes with the perception that the U.S. is undermining international human rights as a whole.

In the U.S. Declaration of Independence Thomas Jefferson declared that all people have rights to life, liberty, and the pursuit of happiness. Thus, the United States was founded on the basis of natural rights—universal, moral rights of citizens to have what is necessary for a good life. These natural rights were modern philosophy's first form of human rights. The U.S. Constitution was designed to protect these rights, especially the right to be free of domination. However, whereas the U.S. Constitution has been admired since its creation, the U.S. government has often failed to guarantee human rights and is increasingly seen in the world as a new form of imperial power. This hypocrisy has generated criticism—increasingly so from the world human rights movement. On the one hand, the United States is one of the world's inaugural contributors to human rights; on the other hand, the United States has supported the severest of human rights violations. Moreover, it undermines the international structure of human rights as a whole. "From hero to villain" describes the United States in the eyes of the human rights movement.

World Human Rights Movement

The human rights movement is found in almost every country. It consists of nongovernmental organizations (NGOs), regional and international courts, the United Nations (U.N.), official statements by most nation-states; and a diffuse culture of Internet sites, hip-hop and rock songs, posters and graffiti, bumper stickers, and thoughts that guide the lives of millions of people. Nongovernmental organizations include Amnesty International, Human Rights Watch, and Federation Internationale des Ligues des Droit de l'Homme (International Federation of Human Rights Leagues). Courts include the European Court of Human Rights—a regional court—and the International Criminal Court (ICC). The United Nations was chartered with the Universal Declaration of Human Rights. Nations today regularly use the rhetoric of human rights to defray criticism, showing that human rights are increasingly basic to the discourse of national politics.

These elements of the human rights movement may seem rather unconnected, but we can speak of a human rights *movement* because people around the world use these elements to refer to each other. NGOs pressure governments to hand over the accused to the ICC. Cyberspace chat rooms refer people to the Internet sites of NGOs. School children visit the U.N. and recite poems or sing folk songs advocating respect for the dignity of people. A bumper sticker featuring a U.S. flag and the words "These colors don't run the world" connects with the thoughts of another driver, who e-mails her congresswoman to pressure the U.S. government to support U.N. multilateralism and the human rights of military prisoners. Even administrations seen as contemptuous of human rights by the movement try to explain their policies in terms of human rights, as the administration of U.S. President George W. Bush did in 2003 when justifying the invasion of Iraq ex post facto once weapons of mass destruction were not found. A circulation of human rights norms exists in the world today.

The overarching goal of these norms is to translate a universal and minimal morality into international law and the many cultures of the world. That morality is "universal" because it is *for* all humans and supposedly justifiable *to* all humans. That morality is "minimal" because it is supposed to concern only basic human rights. Some cultures may arrange marriages, giving some room for the autonomy of the young. However, all humans deserve the ability to maintain their bodily integrity and so have a right against being tortured. The human rights movement wants to build this minimal morality into international law and the governance of all nation-states. However, the United States often obstructs that goal.

U.S. Might

An increasingly common perception is that the United States obstructs or undermines the consistent spread of human rights in the world. In fact, the human rights movement has long known that the United States supports human rights violations, often covering its actions only enough to appear just. The United States supports human rights violations because such rights limit U.S. power internationally. There are two ways by which human rights limit such power.

First, human rights limit *national power*. Since the Cold War the United States has supported dictatorial regimes, including regimes with policies of arbitrary imprisonment, torture, or wide-

spread state assassination. The United States did so during the Cold War in order to oppose the spread of communism, for instance, in Central America. The United States does so today in order to maintain its interests in a region, for instance the Middle East. The United States also commits its own violations. It has an official policy of torture, for instance, in Afghanistan, as well as an unofficial policy, as witnessed in Abu Ghraib prison in Iraq (2003), where psychological humiliation tactics developed at the Guantanamo Bay, Cuba, holding facility were taught to military police. The thread running through these examples is that the United States has supported human rights abuse for the sake of geopolitical control. Having to support human rights might limit U.S. power by making dictators or torturers illegitimate geopolitical players.

Second, human rights limit *capitalism*. Many corporations depend on the United States for protection of their interests, and some people have said that the national ethos (distinguishing character, sentiment, moral nature, or guiding beliefs) of the United States is capitalism. The United States has benefited greatly from a relatively unregulated capitalist economy, especially on the global scale: The United States uses one-quarter of the Earth's resources.

Human rights, however, place limits on capitalism. For instance, they demand that work conditions be humane and that workers and communities be able to hold corporations responsible for harms done against them. A discourse is emerging from the human rights movement about transnational corporations. Disregarding human rights violations favors capitalism and specifically U.S. corporations that profit from cheap labor conditions and resources internationally.

National power and unregulated capitalism are motives to uphold human rights *inconsistently*. The United States upholds human rights principles in some of its policies but not in others. Such inconsistency is not limited to international affairs.

Domestic Violations

The United States is inconsistent in domestic human rights, too. One of the U.S. practices most offensive to the human rights movement is the death penalty. The death penalty violates the right to life (in one interpretation) or the right to freedom (in another interpretation). No other Western country imposes the death penalty.

PREAMBLE TO THE UNITED NATIONS UNIVERSAL DECLARATION OF HUMAN RIGHTS

After World War II there was a general consensus within the world community that the United Nations Charter did not sufficiently define the rights it referenced. On 10 December 1948, the Universal Declaration of Human Rights, containing thirty articles outlining the view of the United Nations on the human rights guaranteed to all people, was adopted by the United Nations General Assembly.

Whereas recognition of the inherent dignity and of the equal and inalienable rights of all members of the human family is the foundation of freedom, justice and peace in the world,

Whereas disregard and contempt for human rights have resulted in barbarous acts which have outraged the conscience of mankind, and the advent of a world in which human beings shall enjoy freedom of speech and belief and freedom from fear and want has been proclaimed as the highest aspiration of the common people,

Whereas it is essential, if man is not to be compelled to have recourse, as a last resort, to rebellion against tyranny and oppression, that human rights should be protected by the rule of law,

Whereas it is essential to promote the development of friendly relations between nations,

Whereas the peoples of the United Nations have in the Charter reaffirmed their faith in fundamental human rights, in the dignity and worth of the human person and in the equal rights of men and women and have determined to promote social progress and better standards of life in larger freedom,

Whereas Member States have pledged themselves to achieve, in co-operation with the United Nations, the promotion of universal respect for and observance of human rights and fundamental freedoms,

Whereas a common understanding of these rights and freedoms is of the greatest importance for the full realization of this pledge,

Now, therefore,

the General Assembly,

Proclaims this Universal Declaration of Human Rights as a common standard of achievement for all peoples and all nations, to the end that every individual and every organ of society, keeping this Declaration constantly in mind, shall strive by teaching and education to promote respect for these rights and freedoms and by progressive measures, national and international, to secure their universal and effective recognition and observance, both among the peoples of Member States themselves and among the peoples of territories under their jurisdiction.

Source: University of Minnesota Human Rights Library. (2007). Retrieved March 19, 2007, from http://www1.umn.edu/humanrts/instree/b1udhr.htm

The anti–death penalty segment of the human rights movement holds the United States in contempt.

The United States commits other human rights violations that might be called "violations of human vulnerability." They include not providing protection against homelessness and inadequate medical care for all. In the United States—one of the wealthiest and most technologically advanced countries in the world—millions of people struggle with homelessness or lack of adequate medical care. Their lives are vulnerable to a high degree. Both the homeless and those without adequate medical care have shorter life expectancies than those with homes and access to medicine. Moreover, these vulnerable people find their actual freedom abridged, dominated by circumstances that could be in society's control.

The United States deserves acclaim for its rule of law—one of the cornerstones of human rights—but its rule of law works inconsistently. People who are minorities in the strict sense—

Homeless man protesting in front of the White house, exercising his right to free speech. The sign refers to treatment of war on terrorism prisoners at Guantanamo Bay in Cuba. Source: istock/Jim Pruitt.

the poor, African-Americans, Native Americans, Latinos, the uneducated—populate death row and jails or lose trials much more commonly than they should, given trial and sentencing results for members of the majority who face similar charges. As with U.S. might internationally, it seems that U.S. might domestically creates uneven treatment inside the United States.

What Is the United States?

Given these inconsistencies, a question that people ask is, "What is the United States?" On the one hand, the United States was one of the world's inaugural advocates for human rights; on the other hand, the United States serves power: national power, corporate power, power of the culturally or economically privileged. This fact is increasingly true today as the Bush administration has acted to deregulate the world, act unilaterally, reverse centuries of international law by engaging in preemptive war, and expand U.S. power in "the new American century." Given that the United States was founded on modern philosophy's earliest form of human rights—natural rights—and defined itself as supporting the dignity of people, the situation isn't trivial. Nothing less than the dignity of millions around the world and U.S. identity are at stake.

If a necessary condition of identity is that one conform to one's moral principles, then the United States must support human rights. However, if morality is not a necessary condition of identity, then the United States is not necessarily being hypocritical when it supports human rights inconsistently. The problem is that people's moral convictions are basic to their identity, and the moral convictions of the United States are the foundation of the nation because the United States is a constitutional democracy based on a commitment to honor the right of people to be free.

The United States must support human rights—and is hypocritical when it does not—because the nation is founded on its Constitution. This Constitution defines the United States through commitment to protect people from domination—to respect people's right to be free. Thus, when people around the world look at U.S. domestic and international policy with disbelief because it violates human rights, they—and not Americans who support that policy—see the true United States.

Constitutionalism

One of the greatest contributions of the United States to the world human rights movement is its Constitution (1788) with its Bill of Rights (1789 but effectively inactive until the Fourteenth Amendment was ratified). By its design, the U.S. Constitution—through balance of power, democracy, and the rule of law—makes sure the

government does not dominate the people. Here are major elements of the human rights movement today: the rights that people have to hold their government accountable to them and to remain free and the right of all people to due process and equal treatment under the law. When we add the principles of the Declaration of Independence to the legal structure of the Constitution and emphasize the liberties and due process of the Bill of Rights, we see that the United States was defined from its origin as a protector of human rights.

Constitutionalism is important to the human rights movement because the very possibility of human rights depends on it in practice. A right is a legal concept. No true human rights order can exist without a constitutional structure to make the rule of law fundamental to the operation of nations. When nations are governed by a constitution, *moral principles*—not any particular person or group—rule. This rule limits the arbitrary power of any specific interest and maintains strict moral equality. In short, constitutions are important for making governments fair and nondominating. This idea is old in the Western tradition under what is called the "civic republican tradition."

The United States has a historical place in the human rights movement in part because the U.S. rule of law has been admired. Although this rule of law can be inconsistent, people in nonconstitutional countries often covet having a right to fair representation and due process under the law. Such a right means that the *rule* in the United States is to have fair process—rather than the caprice of the powerful—decide a great part of people's lives. Instead, the powerful must hide their attempt to deny people fair process. Think of how fair representation can help workers unfairly accused of a misdeed. Think of how due process can save a falsely accused person.

People also admire the Bill of Rights, the first ten amendments to the Constitution. A striking image of this admiration is the lone Tiananmen Square protester in Beijing, China, in 1989. Two hundred years after the Bill of Rights, he stood alone before a Chinese army tank for the sake of his right to voice his political views. Whereas people in many parts of the world are not free to take part in their government—even to voice their views in public—Americans are. Organizations such as the American Civil Liberties Union (ACLU) work to protect such human rights.

Culture of Freedom and Equality

Central to the U.S. Constitution are moral commitments to freedom and equality. Paraphrasing the Declaration of Independence, *all* humans are equal, and they have a right to freedom and the "pursuit of happiness." These moral commitments—ensconced in constitutional law—have had profound effects on U.S. culture and indirectly on the world human rights movement.

The United States has been a showcase for the liberation of oppressed groups, albeit a showcase with as much inconsistency as liberation. African-Americans (slave and nonslave), women, gays, the disabled, the elderly—all these minority groups have sought freedom and equal respect in U.S. culture and law with some success, although much progress remains to be achieved. All of these developments have been relayed to world culture through U.S. popular media. In fact, the role of U.S. popular media in spreading a culture of freedom and equality is surprising, given the materialism and objectification of women in that media. In countries around the world, young people emulate the ambivalently free women and men they see on U.S. TV shows or hear in U.S. songs, even while those songs advocate being materialistic or suggest that women are objects. The U.S. culture of freedom and equality is expressed through the youth-cultural media at the same time some of the uneven tensions in the United States are expressed.

U.S. Idealism

The United States has severe tensions between its moral and legal identity and its actual policies, between its youth culture and its actual practices, and within media representations themselves. These tensions are reflected in criticism of the United States globally. If one wanted to unify this criticism, one might say simply that the global perspective on the United States regarding human rights is that the United States is laudable for its idealism but not for its reality as an international political agent.

U.S. idealism is both cultural and constitutional. Culturally, U.S. media portray the idea that all humans have an equal right to be free and to be treated with respect. This idea is so radically pursued that its results have hardly been schematized. For instance, the U.S. love of psychotherapy can be seen as a result of this idea. Not only do people have a human right to be respected, but also people have a "natural" right to be free from self-hatred. This pursuit of a free life is idealistic at its core: The attempt is to remake life through an idea. Constitutionally, the United States is idealistic in that its very existence as a nation is inextricable from core moral commitments. These commitments—not age-old ethnicity or sediments of ancient rulers—founded and define the country. At origin, strictly speaking, the country is not tradition but rather idea.

The Early Twentieth Century

At no other time was U.S. idealism more important for the human rights movement than during the early twentieth century, when the United States substantially helped people obtain human rights.

The role of the United States in founding the United Nations after the United States helped to end World War II shouldn't be forgotten. The United Nations has always been an international project. However, it was justly placed in New York City because of the leading role that the United States played in its formation. In the early 1900s President Woodrow Wilson envisioned the need for an international governmental body. His vision partially materialized after World War I in the form of the League of Nations. However, the league's authority was not taken seriously, and only World War II's Holocaust and the need to avoid a third world war—between Russia and the United States—convinced people around the world that the United Nations was necessary.

What ideals would the United Nations follow? So many religious and philosophical perspectives existed among the people chartering the United Nations. Here again a U.S. statesperson—Eleanor Roosevelt—brought people into accord. Scholars of the U.N.'s Universal Declaration of Human Rights (1948) describe how she managed to create a consensus about the document across divergent views. She brought people together in an informal way to work out differences. The Universal Declaration of Human Rights, in turn, became the moral charter of the U.N.—part of the U.N.'s constitution.

Before the United States helped create the United Nations, it helped liberate Europe from fascism during World War II. Many people are critical of the United States recently in part because people set high expectations for the United States. They saw it as a heroic country when it liberated Europe from fascism. Moreover, the U.S. liberation of Europe was understood as an expression of U.S. ideals, among them human rights ideals. Fascism dominated people, and it did not respect any of the rights concerning violence against persons. By liberating Europe from fascism and providing a home for the United Nations, the United States reached midpoint in the twentieth century as a leader in the human rights movement.

However, this period is called the "*early* twentieth century" and not the "*mid*-twentieth century" because by 1945–1948, the United States was already embroiled in the Cold War and the manipulation of geopolitics that has earned the United States a bad name around the world today. What came to fruition in 1948 with the United Nations and the Universal Declaration of Human Rights was a U.S. constitutional idealism that had turned global. However, like an insight of conscience in a power-stressed world, that idealism almost immediately fell under the immense economics at stake for the post–World War II United States and its massive corporate interests. Whether the United States ever recaptures that moment of insight—an authentic translation of its core identity to the world stage—will determine how future generations of human rights supporters around the world view the United States.

Jeremy Bendik-Keymer

See also International Law; U.S. Civil Rights

Further Reading

Cheney, R., Abrams, E., Libby, I. L., Kagan, D., et al. (1997). *The project for a new American century—Statement of principles.* Retrieved March 26th, 2007 from http://www.newamericancentury.org/statementofprinciples.htm

Corwin, E. S. (1955). *The "higher law" background of American constitutional law.* Ithaca, NY: Cornell University Press.

Cranston, M. (1989). *The philosophy of human rights.* Belmont, CA: Wadsworth.

Ellison, R. (2002). *Invisible man.* New York: Random House. (Original work published 1952)

Federation Internationale des Ligues des Droits de l'Homme. (2004). Retrieved October 5, 2004, from http://www.fidh.org

Glover, J. (1999). *Humanity, a moral history of the twentieth century.* New Haven, CT: Yale University Press.

Hardt, M., & Negri, A. (2001). *Empire.* Cambridge, MA: Harvard University Press.

McIlwain, C. (1947). *Constitutionalism: Ancient and modern.* Ithaca, NY: Cornell University Press.

Miller, D. (2003). *Political philosophy, a very short introduction.* New York: Oxford University Press.

Miller, J. (1996). *Search and destroy: African-American males in the criminal justice system.* New York: Cambridge University Press.

Morsink, J. (1999). *The universal declaration of human rights: Origin, drafting, intent.* Philadelphia: University of Pennsylvania Press.

Nussbaum, M. (2001). *Women and human development, the capabilities approach.* New York: Cambridge University Press.

Pettit, P. (1997). *Republicanism, a theory of freedom and government.* Oxford, UK: Clarendon Press.

United Nations. (1948). Universal declaration of human rights. Retrieved October 5, 2004, from http://www.un.org/Overview/rights.html

Zeldin, T. (1996). *An intimate history of humanity.* New York: Perennial.

IMF, World Bank, and IDB, U.S. Role in

International institutions created to tackle substantial debt and poverty in the developing world decades ago now find these problems all the more severe. This is not to say these groups haven't helped, but the problem is ever-present.

The U.S. role in the International Monetary Fund (IMF), World Bank, and Inter-American Development Bank (IDB) can be traced back more than a century. In the 1900s the world banking system was underpinned by the United Kingdom. The United Kingdom was the preeminent world power of the time, and it acted as guarantor of global trade, with the value of currencies directly linked to the gold reserves of a particular country.

The world banking system failed after World War I, with the United Kingdom no longer in a position to look after the world's financial system. U.S. Congress began practicing a policy of isolationism, unwilling to closely involve the United States in European affairs.

At the end of World War II the United States emerged as the wealthiest and most powerful nation in the world. It began to act as the regulator of global finance and trade, the role the United Kingdom had played in the previous century. Today the United States continues to play this role and heads the operation of the International Monetary Fund, the World Bank, and the Inter-American Development Bank.

Postwar Context

Even before the end of World War II the global financial system needed the stability lacking in the 1930s. Some perceive this lack of stability as part of the reason for the rise of Nazism in Germany and communism in many other parts of the world. In 1944 this situation led to the International Monetary and Financial Conference of the United and Associated Nations (known as the "Bretton Woods conference" after its meeting place in New Hampshire), a meeting of forty-four countries that ultimately led to the creation of a number of international institutions that continue to help regulate world finance today.

The landmark Bretton Woods Agreement of 1945 had at least four important components. First, it established the U.S. dollar as the basic currency for world trade, with the dollar being directly linked to the price of gold—thirty-five U.S. dollars equaled one ounce of gold. All other currencies within the U.S. sphere of in-

fluence (that is, noncommunist countries) were in turn linked to the U.S. dollar. The dollar was, idiomatically speaking, "as good as gold."

Second, the General Agreement on Tariffs and Trade (GATT) was established to work toward freer and fairer trade. It is the predecessor of today's World Trade Organization.

Third, the GATT established the International Bank for Reconstruction and Development or, more simply, the World Bank. Its purpose was to provide long-term loans, initially to help with the reconstruction of the war-ravaged countries of Europe and subsequently the general development of the Third World.

Fourth, at Bretton Woods the International Monetary Fund was created. The Great Depression had in large part resulted from the lack of a guarantor of the world financial system. When a country became mired in financial difficulty another nation was needed to step in to make loans and help stabilize that country's financial system, to restore international faith in its economy, and thereby halt its economic decline. The Great Depression had come about and had endured for a decade because no stabilizing force had existed at the time. The United States undertook to provide this stability as lender of last resort under the auspices of international financial cooperation in the form of the IMF. The purpose of the IMF was, therefore, to provide relief to countries with balance-of-payments problems and to manage the fixed exchange rate system created by tying the U.S. dollar to gold. Members of the World Bank were required to be members of the International Monetary Fund because their activities were inherently connected.

Although the foregoing institutions date from the end of World War II, the Inter-American Development Bank was created only in 1959. Its mandate is to help its developing member countries improve their economies and the lives of their citizens through targeted loans.

The IDB is owned by its members—forty-seven countries, including the United States and Canada, sixteen European countries, twenty-six countries in Latin America and the Caribbean, as well as Israel, Japan and the Republic of Korea. Funds come from the developed member countries; recipients are limited to the twenty-six countries in Latin America and the Caribbean.

Role of the United States in the Three Institutions

The World Bank and the IMF are suborganizations of the United Nations, but they operate with effective independence. However, because of the connection with the U.N. these organizations can draw on expertise within other U.N. agencies, such as the World Health Organisation (WHO), the United Nations Educational, Scientific and Cultural Organisation (UNESCO), and the United Nations Development Program (UNDP). The bank can therefore bring a substantial level of knowledge to bear in organizing and coordinating aid projects. In this respect these institutions are truly international in nature.

Although the IMF, the World Bank, and the Inter-American Development Bank are, as their names suggest, institutions based on international cooperation, they remain heavily influenced (both formally and informally) by the United States. On the one hand, this arrangement is logical. After all, the United States is the world's largest economy, has the major global currency, and continues to provide leadership in terms of global trade and finance. On the other hand, the United States is often criticized for forcing its will onto other countries and for putting its national interests first.

United States and the World Bank

The World Bank began operating in 1946 with thirty-eight member states and today includes more than 180. It has created several subsidiary organizations, such as the International Finance Corporation and the International Development Association. Its general purpose, working through these and other structures, is to promote economic growth in poorer countries through targeted low-interest or interest-free loans.

The bank receives some funding through its commercial operations, but its major source of income is contributions from member countries. The United States, for example, has given in excess of $50 billion since the bank's creation. Although the bank is operated along the lines of a corporation (board of governors, executive board), funds are allocated on the basis of member financial support. Therefore, the United States has the largest number of votes, sufficient to veto any proposal.

The World Bank is also a coordinating agency that encourages other funding groups to support World Bank projects. Hence, the power of the bank reaches beyond its immediate resource base. In this respect the bank also works with regional development banks, including the Asian Development Bank, the African Development Bank, and the Inter-American Development Bank, which are all structured along the lines of the World Bank.

United States and the IMF

Although the United States is one of 184 member countries of the IMF, it holds 17 percent of the voting power in the organization. Most of the decisions taken by the IMF require 51 percent of the vote, which prevents the United States from having the capacity to force particular decisions.

On the other hand, the more critical decisions about the structure of the IMF or its lending resources can require up to 85 percent of the votes of the IMF, in which case the United States can exercise a veto. This is not a significant feature of the IMF, however, with respect to its lending operations.

One cannot forget, though, that the United States is the largest donor nation in the IMF, and it can exercise considerable informal power on member states, in both the developing and developed worlds, so its influence is arguably in excess of its voting capacity.

United States and the Inter-American Development Bank

Although the United States holds 30 percent of the votes in the IDB, the largest of any single country, it does not have sufficient direct votes to determine decisions on loan applications. Rather, a majority vote is needed to provide a loan, and the twenty-six developing countries from Latin America and the Caribbean hold 50.02 percent of the votes.

On the other hand, the United States certainly can bring to bear informal pressure, not only by combining its vote with selected developing countries, but also by being the largest financial supporter of the IDB. Moreover, all developed country members of the IDB are required to also be members of the IMF, and the United States also holds considerable influence in that institution. Finally, the United States permanently holds one of the executive director positions on the IDB board of directors.

Long Boom

Whatever criticisms are made of U.S. dominance of these international institutions, it is difficult to argue with the economic results of the quarter-century of global growth after World War II.

The period from 1945 until the beginning of the 1970s featured an unprecedented expansion in the economies connected to the United States. In both Europe and Asia rapid economic growth occurred. Japan and Germany, in particular, with U.S. aid went from being war ravaged and nearly destitute to being two of the most economically powerful countries in the world. Other countries developed along similar lines, whether they were countries

in western Europe or the newly industrializing economies (NIEs) of South Korea, Taiwan, Hong Kong, and Singapore.

Erosion of U.S. Dominance

U.S. global financial leadership began to decline in the early 1970s. By that time the United States had been directly involved in the Vietnam War for six years, and indirectly involved there since the end of World War II. The war had not only brought into question the value of the U.S. fight against communism in Asia, but also had created a huge economic burden on the U.S. budget. President Lyndon Johnson's Great Society ideal of raising the living standards of the nation's poor added a further financial burden.

The U.S. government, under these pressures, began increasing the money supply. With a fixed exchange rate the United States could finance both debt and deficit simply by printing more money. The problem is that this remedy could last only so long as other countries retained their faith in the U.S. economy and currency.

At the same time, the United States began to labor under substantial trade deficits. As Japan and western European countries rebuilt their economies after World War II a significant flow of goods began from the United States to those countries. However, as their economies grew and their manufactured products were able to compete (and often out-compete) with those from the United States, the trade balance was reversed. In part this reversal was caused by the global financial system, which pegged currencies to the U.S. dollar. In many cases the fixed exchange rate, which was arguably appropriate in 1945, was out of date by the early 1970s. Japan was a prime example. In 1971 the yen was still pegged to the U.S. dollar at an exchange rate of 360, a rate left over from just after the war. By that time, after a decade of rapid growth, this exchange rate meant that Japanese products were seriously underpriced in the U.S. market and hurting U.S. manufacturers.

By the late 1960s European banks in particular were growing concerned about the problems in the U.S. economy and began to pressure the United States to demonstrate that it had the gold reserves to support the dollar's link to the gold exchange system. Because the United States could not, in fact, support the level of its currency, U.S. president Richard Nixon took the unprecedented step of removing the U.S. dollar from the gold exchange system, moving the world to a system of freely floating currencies, which in turn significantly devalued the U.S. dollar. President Nixon also added a 10 percent surcharge on imports. Both measures were designed to bring the U.S. economy back into a positive balance-of-payments. Unfortunately, the U.S. dol-

lars held by European banks were suddenly worth far less than before, and this resulted in a lack of faith in the U.S. economy and U.S. leadership.

A More Uncertain World

With the transition to freely traded currencies the global financial system became much less stable. Although the level of a currency should ideally reflect a range of economic fundamentals (the success of businesses, balance of trade, budget surpluses, and so on), it also reflects perceptions in the marketplace, which can vary with little reason. Moreover, predatory individuals and companies can speculate on currencies for personal gain, and this speculation can distort the global financial system.

A second problem of the U.S. dollar default—the largest default in banking history—was that European banks began to look to other countries for investment. At the same time, their accounts with Middle Eastern countries began to grow dramatically with the upsurge in oil prices engineered by the Organization of Petroleum Exporting Countries (OPEC) in 1973. Much of this money found its way into investments in Central and South America.

Debt Crises

Increased volatility in exchange rates contributed to two major debt crises—in Latin America in 1982 and in East and Southeast Asia in 1997. In both cases many countries in the regions saw their currencies fall and their economies slow. They found themselves unable to service their foreign debts.

In both cases the IMF was called in to deal with the worst-affected countries. It stepped in with structural adjustment programs (SALs) to help stabilize the economies and currencies and restore investor faith in the countries. Hence, although the IMF was originally designed to deal with (among other things) a fixed exchange rate system, it has evolved to be a lender of last resort—a stabilizing agent in the world financial system.

The Three Banks Today

The World Bank and the IMF were designed to help poorer countries of the world and to regulate the global financial system as a reaction to the chaos of the 1930s, and the United States took the lead in their establishment and their operations. The IDB had a more limited regional role: to help the developing countries of

Central and South America, but in this case the ideal was also to foster economic development.

One can view these institutions and the U.S. role in them from different perspectives. On the one hand, everyone benefits from a stable financial system, including the United States, and U.S. leadership here is laudable. It is not all altruism, however; the United States was aware that economic growth in the postwar period inhibited the spread of communism in the poorer countries of the world, including those closer to U.S. borders.

Some people also complain that U.S. companies benefit from U.S. involvement in developing economies. This charge was leveled during the financial crisis in Asia in the late 1990s, when U.S. corporations alleged to have unfairly made significant inroads into Asian markets. More recently U.S. corporations have been charged with unfairly securing lucrative contracts for the rebuilding of Iraq.

The IMF is also criticized for the stringent structural adjustment programs it implements in countries with economic difficulties. On the one hand, these countries need guidance to pull themselves out of their (often self-inflicted) problems. On the other hand, such measures can cause significant short-term pain, and those likely to suffer are the poorest people in a country. Indeed, the IMF is often viewed as working in the interests of elites rather than the interests of the poor its programs are designed to help, and in any case the IMF is seen as wielding tremendous power over relatively powerless people.

It is important bear in mind that when these institutions were created substantial debt and poverty existed in the developing world. Unfortunately, after a half-century of operation these two problems are more rather than less severe. The situation may be better today than it would have been without these institutions, but some charge that these institutions are also part of the problem.

The World Bank, the IMF, and the IDB will undoubtedly be called on to do more in the future. The world economic system is more volatile than ever, and problems in one country quickly affect other countries, whether the problems are political, economic, or health-related. For example, the IMF stepped in to help after the 2004 tsunami struck a number of countries in South and Southeast Asia.

These three institutions will continue to play an important role in the future, and the United States will be called on to provide further leadership within these institutions. The leadership that the United States demonstrates will, in part, determine the level of support it receives from the international community.

Curtis A. Andressen

See also Trade Agreements; U.S. Agency for International Development

Further Reading

Allen, R. (2000). *Financial crises and recession in the global economy*. Cheltenham, UK: Edward Elgar.

Aryeetey, E., Court, J., Nissanke, M., & Weder, B. (Eds.). (2003). *Asia and Africa in the global economy*. New York: United Nations University Press.

Bird, G. (1995). *IMF lending to developing countries: Issues and evidence*. London: Routledge.

Dunning, J. (1999). *Governments, globalization and international business*. Oxford, UK: Oxford University Press .

Fischer, S. (2004). *IMF essays from a time of crisis: The international financial system, stabilization, and development*. Boston: MIT Press.

Frazer, W. (2000). *Central banking, crises and global economy*. Westport, CT: Praeger.

Griffiths, M., & O'Callaghan, T. (2002). *International relations: The key concepts*. London: Routledge.

Gwin, C. (1994). *U.S. relations with the World Bank, 1945–92*. Washington, DC: Brookings Institution Press.

James, H. (1996). *International monetary cooperation since Bretton Woods*. Oxford, UK: Oxford University Press.

Kadmos, G., & O'Hara, P. (2000). *International Monetary Fund: Functions, financial crises and future relevance*. Perth, Australia: Curtin University of Economics.

Kapur, D., Lewis, J., & Webb, R. (1997). *The World Bank: Its first half century*. Washington, DC: Brookings Institution Press.

Korner, P., Maass, G., Siebold, T., & Tetzlaff, R. (1984). *The IMF and the debt crisis: A guide to the Third World's dilemma*. London: Zed Books.

Nelson, P. (1995). *The World Bank and non-governmental organizations: The limits of apolitical development*. Basingstoke, UK: Macmillan.

Noble, G., & Ravenhill. J. (2000). *The Asian financial crisis and the architecture of global finance*. Cambridge, UK: Cambridge University Press.

O'Brien, R., & Williams, M. (2004). *Global political economy: Evolution and dynamics*. New York: Palgrave Macmillan.

Payer, C. (1982). *The World Bank: A critical analysis*. New York: Monthly Review Press.

Polak, J. (1994). *The World Bank and the IMF: A changing relationship*. Washington, DC: Brookings Institution Press.

Rogoff. K. (2003, January/February). The IMF strikes back. *Foreign Policy, 134*, 39–47.

Smith, J., & Michie, J. (Eds.). (1995). *Managing the global economy*. Oxford, UK: Oxford University Press.

Yahuda, M. (2004). *The international politics of the Asia-Pacific* (2nd ed.). London: Routledge.

Immigration to the United States

The United States has always been a nation of immigrants, which over time has produced greater cultural diversity. In a shift from earlier centuries, Asian and Hispanic immigrants are playing a larger societal and economic role.

Whereas the population of developed countries in Europe and Asia remains stable or is decreasing, the population of the United States is steadily increasing, having passed 300 million in 2006. This increase is in part natural, but it is also the result of a continuous influx of immigrants. From the Columbian period to the twenty-first century many people have been attracted to the United States. Immigrants modified the world of Native Americans, built a new nation, and contributed to the development of a multiracial, multicultural society. Hence, immigration to the United States is key to understanding the dynamics of the United States.

Immigrants to the United States were and are a diverse lot: manual laborers as well as professionals, scholars, athletes, and artists. They contribute to developing the U.S. economy, diversifying U.S. culture, and advancing the arts, sciences, and technology. In addition to those immigrants admitted legally, many undocumented immigrants reside in the United States, often causing social conflicts within U.S. society.

Origins of Immigrants: Past and Present

We must view immigration to the United States in the global framework by applying the push-pull model of international immigration. When the force of pushing people out of place A and the force of pulling people into place B take place simultaneously, people may migrate from place A to place B. Many parts of Europe pushed people out to the United States at different times for different reasons. People sought new opportunities in the New World across the Atlantic Ocean.

The United States has sustained a magnetic force throughout its history, although the source areas of immigrants have changed historically. For example, from the late nineteenth century many Asians entered the United States; Mexico and other Latin American countries are more recent source areas of immigrants. Historically the United States needed a large labor force to exploit natural resources, to build cities, to develop urban industries, to construct railroads, to advance the farming frontier, and to harvest crops. U.S. innovations in mechanization and automation, industrial reor-

ganization, and rationalization of management have helped people cope with a labor shortage. However, another solution has been to fill worker vacancies by attracting workers—both manual laborers and brain workers—from the world over. Such immigrants have been admitted to the United States on the assumption that they eventually will become Americans and contribute to the development of the nation. Of course, at times immigrants have not been admitted without restrictions; the selection process once barred immigrants from southern and eastern Europe and Asia.

Two turning points changed the source areas of immigrants to the United States. One turning point was the period from the late nineteenth century to the early twentieth century, and the other turning point was the late twentieth century.

Since the establishment of colonies on the Atlantic Seaboard through the late nineteenth century, northwestern Europe was the major source area of immigrants to the United States, as exemplified by the number of immigrants in the period 1841–1860. Among the total of 4.3 million, 93.9 percent came from northwestern Europe, including Ireland (39.3 percent), Germany (32.2 percent), and the United Kingdom (16 percent). Immigration patterns began to change in the period 1861–1880. Whereas 84.6 percent of the total of 5.1 million came from Europe, the percentage from northwestern Europe was reduced to 75.2 (Germany 29.4, United Kingdom 22.5, Ireland 17.0, and Norway and Sweden 6.3). Southern and eastern Europe contributed 3.7 percent. During the period 1881–1900 immigrants from southern and eastern Europe contributed 29.4 percent, whereas those from northwestern Europe further declined (Germany 21.9 percent, United Kingdom 12.1 percent, Ireland 11.7 percent, and Norway and Sweden 10 percent). This trend was increased during the period 1901–1920, when northwestern Europe accounted for only 16.8 percent and southern and eastern Europe for 60 percent. Thus, "new immigrants" replaced "old immigrants" in the immigration flow to the United States.

Although a sustained demand for labor and an ample supply of land and natural resources promoted immigration to the United States, the U.S. government began to selectively admit immigrants on the basis of national origin. The Chinese Exclusion Act of 1882 was the first law to exclude immigrants by nationality. The Immigration Act of 1924 introduced the system of national quotas, which admitted immigrants by national origin on the basis of

population composition surveyed in the 1890 census. That law was intended to restrict immigration from southern and eastern Europe and Japan. The door to the United States remained closed to southern and eastern Europeans and Japanese until the 1960s, when the immigration act was revised to abolish the national quotas system. This revision brought about a surge of new immigration from the 1970s.

Europe's portion of total immigration to the United States declined, accounting for 46.8 percent in the period 1951–1970, whereas Latin America accounted for 31.8 percent and Asia for 10.3 percent. The new trend of immigration to the United States is typified by the period 1971–1990, when Europe accounted for only 12.7 percent. Instead, Asia's portion increased to 37.6 percent (Philippines 7.2 percent, Korea 5.2 percent, China 5 percent, Vietnam 4.9 percent, and India 3.7 percent), and Latin America, including Mexico (19.4 percent), accounted for 44.6 percent. Immigrants from Latin America and Asia combined to have an absolute majority in the immigration flow, reaching 82.2 percent. The trend continues to the present. Europe, especially northwestern Europe, which was once the major source of immigrants to the United States, itself now receives immigrants from other parts of the world to cope with a labor shortage and an aging population.

Growing Impact of Asians and Hispanics

Changes in the source areas of immigration have gradually modified the composition of the population and have augmented the ethnic and cultural diversity in the United States. Increasingly Asians and Hispanics/Latinos are becoming an important part of the U.S. culture and economy. Chinese food and Mexican food have already been integrated into U.S. dining habits. Geographically speaking Asian and Hispanic influence is greatest on the Pacific Coast and in the Southwest. Asians create ethnic enclaves in urban areas with a distinct Asian ethnic landscape, and Hispanic barrios are ever expanding with Latino ways of living.

Particularly important is the Hispanic influence. *A Day without a Mexican,* a film directed by Sergio Arau and released in 2004, depicted the confusion brought about by the disappearance of Hispanics in California. No vegetables are picked, no garbage collected, no baseball games played, and no dishes washed. The movie sarcastically showed that ordinary life of Californians could not be maintained without Hispanics. As a matter of fact, Hispanics account for more than 30 percent of California's population. In the United States, the Hispanic population accounts for 12.5 percent of the total, and that share is increasing. More than half of Hispanics in the United States are Mexican.

The impact of Hispanics in U.S. society was demonstrated on May Day of 2006. A "Great American Boycott" was called for "no school, no work, no shopping, no selling." Hispanics went on strike on 1 May; factories, restaurants, and stores were forced to close, paralyzing the U.S. economy. One million people are estimated to have demonstrated in more than fifty cities throughout the United States, protesting the tightening regulations on undocumented immigrants. Many Hispanics are low-wage manual laborers in factories, farms, construction sites, restaurants, and other service sectors, supporting U.S. economic prosperity from a lower social stratum. If all undocumented immigrants were eliminated some believe the U.S. economy would be paralyzed.

SHORT-TERM IMMIGRATION

The following passage uses the example of Yemini immigrants in Detroit to point out that not all immigrants to the United States come to stay.

The economic motivation underlying Yemeni immigration to Detroit is expressed in the immigrants' overall goals—to make as much money as possible in the shortest period of time, after which they plan to return to Yemen permanently to enjoy the fruits of their labor. Immigration to the United States is perceived by the immigrants as a means to a livelihood (*talib al-raziqh*), while social mobility and material gratification are to take place in the home country, not in the United States. This determination on the part of the immigrants to return home permanently is reinforced by several practices which contribute to the maintenance of their familial and material ties to Yemen. First, most Yemenis leave their families behind in the villages when they emigrate to the United States. An estimated 70–80 percent of the immigrants are married, yet only a small fraction bring their families to live with them in Detroit. Although they advance a host of reasons, religious, cultural, or economic, for not bringing their families to the United States, the determining factor seems to be whether a person believes his return to Yemen is imminent or not. Those who tend to believe their return is imminent hesitate to bring their families to the United States, and thereby avoid the necessity of confronting the various "ideological" proscriptions against family emigration.

Source: Abraham, N. (1983). The Yemeni immigrant community of Detroit: Background, emigration, and community life. In S.Y. Abraham & N. Abraham (Eds.), Arabs in the New World: Studies on Arab-American communities (p. 121). Detroit, MI: Wayne State University.

Cars lined up to pass into America from Tijuana, Mexico. Source: istock/James Steidl.

The impact of Asians is observed in large cities such as Los Angeles, where ethnic towns and ethnic economies thrive. Old Chinatown is located close to downtown Los Angeles, whereas suburban Chinatowns are found in the eastern suburbs of Monterey Park and farther east in Rowland Heights and its vicinity. Recently arrived ethnic Chinese from Southeast Asia are dominant in old Chinatown, whereas wealthy Chinese tend to settle in the outer suburbs, purchasing expensive houses in affluent neighborhoods. Little Tokyo, adjacent to Los Angeles's civic center, once the heart of Japanese community and economy, is losing its ethnic flavor because of redevelopment projects, outmigration of Japanese, and decreasing immigration from Japan in recent years. On the other hand, Koreatown near downtown Los Angeles is thriving with continuous immigration from Korea since the 1970s. Thai Town in the Hollywood area is a much smaller but obvious ethnic landscape. In addition the Los Angeles metropolitan area has Little India and Little Saigon. Development of these ethnic towns reflects the increased immigration from Asia since the 1970s as the Immigration and Naturalization Act of 1965 came into force, and refugees were accepted after the end of the Vietnam War.

Ethnic towns are cultural islands where the newly arrived can find a place to sleep and a job while adjusting to the U.S. way of living. In such cultural islands the culture of immigrants' homeland is re-created and sustained. On the other hand, for many Americans ethnic towns are pockets of foreign cultures and often are seen as tourist attractions.

Immigration to the United States in the Global Perspective

The global perspective of immigration to the United States differs from immigration to other advanced industrial nations in that the United States has continuously attracted immigrants from the world over. European countries once pushed immigrants out to the United States and other parts of the New World. However, Europe now receives immigrants from the developing world. Although Japanese immigrated to the United States and other parts of the Americas from the late nineteenth century to the post–World War II period, Japan now needs foreign laborers because of a declining birthrate and an aging population. Reflecting the socioeconomic and demographic conditions, the source areas of immigrants to the United States have shifted. China and other Asian countries and Mexico and other Latin American countries are now major source areas of immigrants.

Undocumented immigration to the United States is also important in the global perspective. Twelve million illegal immigrants are estimated to be living in the United States. Many of these immigrants enter the United States across the U.S.-Mexican border. Immigration from Mexico, which started in the late eighteenth century when Junipero Serra moved north to build a mission in San Diego, California, has continued. Sharp differences in wages, living conditions, and opportunities across the international border are sustaining forces in driving northward immigration.

Also important is the immigration of scholars and professionals who seek a better research environment and prestige at U.S. universities and research institutions. Many foreign-born professors and researchers engage in higher education and research. U.S. universities also attract foreign students, especially at graduate schools. Foreign scholars and graduate students play an important role in advancing science, technology, and culture in the United States.

Foreign immigrants have also been prominent in professional sports and the arts. Major League Baseball in particular has attracted many baseball players from around the world who dream of becoming a major leaguer. Many from Latin America, the Caribbean and Asia have been successful. Hollywood movies, an important part of U.S. popular culture, have augmented immigration to the United States by spreading U.S. values and the U.S. lifestyle. Actors and actresses, such as Audrey Hepburn from Belgium, were attracted to the United States to participate in filmmaking in Hollywood. Arnold Schwarzenegger, born in Hungary, immigrated to the United States as a bodybuilder and became a movie star before becoming governor of California.

All of these examples illustrate why immigration to the United States is a complex and sometimes controversial phenomenon. People come to the United States for many different reasons, but in the end immigration has undoubtedly contributed to strengthening and diversifying the U.S. economy, society, and culture.

Noritaka Yagasaki

See also Brain Drain; Cultural Diversity, U.S.; Relations with Latin America, U.S.; Special Relationship (U.S.-Mexico)

Further Reading

Allen, J. P., & Turner, E. (2002). *Changing faces, changing places: Mapping southern California.* Northridge: Center for Geographic Studies, California State University.

Arreola, D. D. (Ed.). (2004). *Hispanic places, Latino places: Community and cultural diversity in contemporary America.* Austin: University of Texas Press.

Chan, S. (Ed.). (1991). *Entry denied: Exclusion and the Chinese community in America, 1882–1943.* Philadelphia: Temple University Press.

Ciment, J. (2001). *Encyclopedia of American immigration* (4 vols.). Armonk, NY: M. E. Sharpe.

Foner, N. (2000). *From Ellis Island to JFK: New York's two great waves of immigration.* New Haven, CT: Yale University Press.

Lehman, J. (Ed.). (1999). *Gale encyclopedia of multicultural America: Primary documents* (2 vols.). Farmington Hills, MI: Gale Group.

Lopez-Garza, M., & Diaz, D. R. (2001). *Asians and Latino immigrants in a restructuring economy: The metamorphosis of southern California.* Stanford, CA: Stanford University Press.

Imperialism, U.S.

The United States has been on both ends of imperialism—a former colony, and a controller of territories outside its borders—but has given rise to neo-imperialism, where territorial control is not the only mark of supremacy.

In both academic and mainstream circles imperialism—the policy of extending a nation's power, either through direct territorial control or indirectly, through control of economic or political spheres—is generally considered to denote something negative. However, among historians, securing a precise definition for the term as applicable to the United States has proven difficult. Certainly U.S. imperialism has some similarities to imperialism as practiced by traditional European powers, as the U.S. government was the administrator of territory outside the sovereign United States of America. But, the United States itself was a British colony prior to its successful war of independence, and many of the United States' founding fathers were hostile to the idea of an empire, being advocates of a sovereign republic. However, in 1823 the Monroe Doctrine (articulated by U.S. president James Monroe; served 1817–1825) simultaneously stipulated that the United States would not involve itself in political affairs in Europe and warned European powers not to interfere with U.S. activity in South America. This set the United States upon what could be called a neo-imperialist course—a course that it has continued to follow through the twentieth century and into the twenty-first.

The Spanish-American War and Early Expansion

In April 1898 the United States joined Cuban forces in their fight for independence from Spanish colonialism. It was victorious U.S. delegates, however, not Cubans, who signed a peace treaty with Spain in December of that year. The United States came away from the conference having secured the Philippines, Puerto Rico, and Guam while maintaining informal control over Cuba.

Cuba was granted a limited form of independence. The U.S. Platt Amendment (1903) prohibited Cuba from signing international treaties that might violate its independence, and the United States reserved for itself the right to intervene in Cuban affairs. Cuba was required to cede to the United States land necessary for coaling and naval stations. Also in 1903, the United States constructed a naval base at Guantanamo Bay for which the U.S. government paid a small annual fee.

Of the territory gained in the Spanish-American War, the Philippines proved most intriguing. Under the Treaty of Paris, Spain ceded the Philippines to the United States on 20 December 1898, for 20 million dollars. Many U.S. officials, including U.S. president William McKinley (served 1897–1901) thought the Philippines would be a good stepping stone for access to the lucrative Chinese market. However, the Filipino people resisted U.S. control. The Filipino leader Emilio Aguinaldo eventually declared independence for the Philippines and fought the United States for control of the island. The insurrection collapsed in 1902 with some 200,000 Filipinos dead and 4,165 U.S. casualties. A U.S. civil government controlled the Philippines (establishing virtual Philippine dependence upon the U.S. market) until independence was granted on 4 July 1946.

The Panama Canal

The election of Theodore Roosevelt as president (served 1901–1909) ensured that the United States would continue its expansionist policies. The United States provided moral support (and the threat of force, in the form of naval vessels) to a Panamanian insurrection against the Colombian government (Colombia controlled Panama at the time) when Colombia rejected a treaty that would have allowed the United States to build an isthmus canal. On 18 November 1903 the newly established Panamanian government signed the Hay-Bunau-Varilla Treaty, which called for the United States to build, fortify, and operate the Panama Canal. Panama became a U.S. protectorate. In 1904 the Roosevelt Corollary was added to the Monroe Doctrine; the corollary transformed the ban on European interference in the Western Hemisphere into a promise that the United States would police South America.

Woodrow Wilson and World War I

The presidency of Woodrow Wilson (served 1913–1921) continued previous the administration's policies in Latin America. Wilson believed that concessions gained in that region by U.S. financiers had to be protected even at the cost of violating a nation's sovereignty.

The president thus ordered naval intervention in the Dominican Republic in 1916, and the U.S. Navy maintained a strong presence in the country until 1922. In 1914 Mexico's reform-minded president Francisco Madero was overthrown, and a government that was more supportive of landed interests, headed by a general, Victoriano Huerta, came to power. Wilson ordered U.S. troops to invade Mexico and overthrow Huerta when Huerta's forces detained U.S. soldiers who were accused of entering a prohibited zone.

On the broader world stage, Wilson is famous for his Fourteen Points, proposed at the end of World War I. The United States' late entry into the war in 1917 hastened the defeat of the Central Powers, and an armistice was signed on 11 November 1918. Wilson put forward his Fourteen Points in January 1918, before the war actually ended, as an outline for a peace settlement. He sought to create a climate of international cooperation through an organization of states based on the concept of collective security. The first five points deal with Wilson's vision of a more open world after the war: the removal of tariffs, freedom of navigation on the seas, reduction of armaments, and an end to colonialism. Subsequent points invoke the concept of national self-determination for minor-

ities in Europe. Finally, the fourteenth point suggests the creation of an association of nations to protect the political and territorial integrity of all states. After some debate, European leaders agreed to use the Fourteen Points as the basis for a peace treaty.

Although Wilson had called for national self-determination, former German and Turkish colonies were mandated to the countries that conquered them. Japan claimed China's Shandong Province and some of Germany's Pacific islands. France made further gains in Europe through the Allied occupation of the German Rhineland, which was to be demilitarized, and by acquiring a share of the coal-rich Saar Basin. Italy annexed South Tyrol and Trieste from the collapsed Austro-Hungarian Empire. Such actions contradicted the Fourteen Points but Wilson was unable to prevent the land grab.

Wilson's own actions during the Russian Revolution contradicted the spirit of his Fourteen Points. The ascendancy of the Bolsheviks in Russia in 1918 drew a sharp reaction from the Americans. Anticapitalist, anticlerical, and authoritarian, the Bolsheviks, according to Wilson, had to be stopped. Some 10,000 U.S. troops were sent into Russia. It was not until June 1919 that U.S. troops left Russian soil.

In Europe, after months of acrimonious negotiations, the Paris Peace Conference concluded in January 1920 with the founding of the League of Nations and with peace treaties between the victorious Allies and the various Central Powers (the most important being the Treaty of Versailles, with Germany). Wilson returned home hoping for Senate acceptance of both the Treaty of Versailles and subsequent U.S. participation in the League of Nations. Many Republicans denounced the formation of the League as a dangerous constraint on U.S. sovereignty. With his health failing, Wilson was unable to prevent the Senate from rejecting the treaty. Wilson's progressive internationalism was defeated by traditionally nationalist and isolationist politics in the United States.

"THE GOOD NEIGHBOR POLICY"

In this excerpt from his first inaugural address on 4 March 1933, U.S. President Franklin D. Roosevelt presented the United States as a cooperative neighbor to Central and South America rather than a controlling military power.

In the field of world policy I would dedicate this Nation to the policy of the good neighbor—the neighbor who resolutely respects himself and, because he does so, respects the rights of others—the neighbor who respects his obligations and respects the sanctity of his agreements in and with a world of neighbors.

If I read the temper of our people correctly, we now realize as we have never realized before our interdependence on each other; that we can not merely take but we must give as well; that if we are to go forward, we must move as a trained and loyal army willing to sacrifice for the good of a common discipline, because without such discipline no progress is made, no leadership becomes effective. We are, I know, ready and willing to submit our lives and property to such discipline, because it makes possible a leadership which aims at a larger good. This I propose to offer, pledging that the larger purposes will bind upon us all as a sacred obligation with a unity of duty hitherto evoked only in time of armed strife.

With this pledge taken, I assume unhesitatingly the leadership of this great army of our people dedicated to a disciplined attack upon our common problems.

The Good Neighbor in Latin America

During his presidency, Warren G. Harding (served 1921–1923) continued U.S. occupation in the Dominican Republic and Haiti. In 1930, Rafael Trujillo, a U.S.-trained dictator, took over rule of the Dominican Republic from U.S. forces; he remained in power for more than thirty years. President Calvin Coolidge (served 1923–1929) sent U.S. troops back to Nicaragua (where they had been since 1912) in 1926 after a one-year absence, citing a Communist threat there.

In 1933 President Franklin Roosevelt (served 1933–1945) insti-

THE PLATT AMENDMENT, 1901

The Platt Amendment, passed by the U.S. Congress on 2 March 1901, was designed to govern U.S.-Cuban relations after the U.S. occupation of Cuba ended in 1902. Against the wishes of many Cubans, the provisions of the Platt Amendment below were written into the 1902 Cuban Constitution.

I. That the government of Cuba shall never enter into any treaty or other compact with any foreign power or powers which will impair or tend to impair the independence of Cuba, nor in any manner authorize or permit any foreign power or powers to obtain by colonization or for military or naval purposes or otherwise, lodgement in or control over any portion of said island.

II. That said government shall not assume or contract any public debt, to pay the interest upon which, and to make reasonable sinking fund provision for the ultimate discharge of which, the ordinary revenues of the island, after defraying the current expenses of government shall be inadequate."

III. That the government of Cuba consents that the United States may exercise the right to intervene for the preservation of Cuban independence, the maintenance of a government adequate for the protection of life, property, and individual liberty, and for discharging the obligations with respect to Cuba imposed by the treaty of Paris on the United States, now to be assumed and undertaken by the government of Cuba.

IV. That all Acts of the United States in Cuba during its military occu-

pancy thereof are ratified and validated, and all lawful rights acquired thereunder shall be maintained and protected.

V. That the government of Cuba will execute, and as far as necessary extend, the plans already devised or other plans to be mutually agreed upon, for the sanitation of the cities of the island, to the end that a recurrence of epidemic and infectious diseases may be prevented, thereby assuring protection to the people and commerce of Cuba, as well as to the commerce of the southern ports of the United States and the people residing therein.

VI. That the Isle of Pines shall be omitted from the proposed constitutional boundaries of Cuba, the title thereto being left to future adjustment by treaty.

VII. That to enable the United States to maintain the independence of Cuba, and to protect the people thereof, as well as for its own defense, the government of Cuba will sell or lease to the United States lands necessary for coaling or naval stations at certain specified points to be agreed upon with the President of the United States.

VIII. That by way of further assurance the government of Cuba will embody the foregoing provisions in a permanent treaty with the United States.

Source: Bevans, C.I. (Ed.). (1971). The Platt Amendment. In Treaties and other international agreements of the United States of America, 1776–1949 (Vol. 8, pp. 1116–1117). Washington, DC: United States Government Printing Office.

tuted the Good Neighbor policy with regard to Latin America. The Marines were withdrawn from Latin American countries, the Platt Amendment was revoked, and the president asserted that no nation had the right to intervene in the affairs of another. However, as it had in the Dominican Republic, the United States ensured that pliant leaders stayed in power in Cuba and Puerto Rico. In Mexico, a compromise was reached with the United States following Mexican expropriation of foreign oil companies in 1938. Roosevelt conceded that Mexico owned its raw materials while Mexico agreed to compensate the companies for expropriated properties.

After World War II

Although victorious in World War II, the European Allies lost their overseas empires, with the French losing Indochina (Vietnam, Laos, and Cambodia) in 1954, the Dutch losing the Dutch East Indies (which, as Indonesia, became completely independent in 1954), and the British leaving India, Burma (now Myanmar),

and Ceylon (now Sri Lanka) in 1947, 1948, and 1948, respectively. Meanwhile the Soviet Union, despite sustaining heavy casualties, became a major international power.

President Harry S. Truman (served 1945–1953) continued the internationalist trend initiated by Franklin Roosevelt. The concept of collective security was at the very heart of the creation of the United Nations and the North Atlantic Treaty Organization (NATO). Despite being allies during World War II, the United States and the Soviet Union squared off in a battle between competing economic systems, with the former trumpeting a capitalist economic system while the latter embraced a state-controlled command economy under Communism. It was this conflict, known as the Cold War, that initiated a new wave of U.S. interventions abroad.

The United States set about ensuring its security through both overt and covert means. Overt intervention in Korea in 1950 was followed by a protracted war in Vietnam. Behind the scenes, the administration of U.S. president Dwight D. Eisenhower (served 1953–1961) authorized the overthrow of the Iranian prime minister Muhammàd Mosaddeq in 1953 and the Guatemalan president Jacobo Arbenz in 1954.

Post—Cold War Era

Since the collapse of the Soviet Union in 1991, the United States finds itself the unchallenged superpower in the world. Military intervention against Iraq following Iraqi president Saddam Hussein's occupation of Kuwait in 1991 demonstrated the superiority of U.S. military power to the world. In that conflict the U.S. acted in concert with the United Nations, with the international community in agreement that Iraq's occupation of Kuwait was illegal. In 1998, the United States was one of a group of nations (the Contact Group; other members were Britain, Germany, France, Italy, and Russia) that tried to oversee a peaceful resolution of the conflict between Serbians and ethnic Albanians in Kosovo, Yugoslavia, after alarming incidents of ethnic cleansing. When negotiations broke down, a U.S.-led NATO coalition conducted bombing campaigns against the Serbian military.

Resentment against the United States manifested itself spectacularly in the September 11, 2001, terrorist attacks on New York City's World Trade Center and the Pentagon. In response, President George W. Bush (served 2001–present) waged war on Afghanistan (2002) and Iraq (2003). The war in Afghanistan was supported by many Americans and to a certain degree by the international community; the war in Iraq was almost universally unpopular abroad and widely criticized in the United States itself. The United States' motives for going to war have been questioned, as neither of the two ostensible reasons given for the invasion—that Iraq's government had ties with al-Qaeda, the terrorist organization responsible for the September 11 attacks, and that Iraq possessed weapons of mass destruction—have been supported by fact, and as Iraq is rich in oil resources, which the United States would benefit from controlling. There are those who claim that U.S. actions in Iraq represent the worst possible example of imperialism in the twenty-first century, and the question with regard to Iraq today remains, Is the United States helping to build a nation or merely securing its own interests?

The successful establishment of an autonomous democracy in Iraq could go a long way toward proving that the United States is not imperialist minded in its actions. However, as long as casualties continue to mount and Iraqi resistance to the U.S. occupation spreads, the stigma of imperialism will continue to haunt U.S. policymakers, and if the United States continues to circumvent multilateral institutions such as the United Nations, international observers will continue to brand the United States an imperialist power. Conversely, should U.S. leaders work with the international community in implementing solutions to the world's problems, the United States could well come to be seen in a more positive light.

Daniel Pacella

See also Empire, U.S.; Foreign Policy after September 11, 2001, U.S.; Linguistic Imperialism and English; Modernity, United States and

Further Reading

Becker, W. H., & Wells Jr., S. F. (Eds.). (1984). *Economics and world power: An assessment of American diplomacy since 1789.* New York: Columbia University Press.

Brands, H. W. (1998). *What America owes the world: The struggle for the soul of foreign policy.* New York: Cambridge University Press.

Chomsky, N. (2003). *Hegemony or survival: America's quest for global dominance.* New York: Metropolitan Books.

Clarfield, G. H. (1992). *United States diplomatic history: From revolution to empire.* Englewood Cliffs, NJ: Prentice-Hall.

Cohen, B. J. (1973). *The question of imperialism: The political economy of dominance and dependence.* New York: Basic Books.

Gaddis, J. L. (1983). The emerging post-revisionist synthesis on the origins of the Cold War. *Diplomatic History, 7*(3), 171–190.

Hogan, M. J., & Paterson, T. G. (Eds.). (1991). *Explaining the history of American foreign relations.* New York: Cambridge University Press.

Kennedy, T. C. (1975). *Charles A. Beard and American foreign policy.* Gainesville: University Presses of Florida.

Mills, C. W. (1956). *The power elite.* New York: Oxford University Press.

Nearing, S., & Freeman, J. (1925). *Dollar diplomacy: A study in American imperialism.* New York: B. W. Huebsch & Viking Press.

Ninkovich, F. A. (1999). *The Wilsonian century: U.S. foreign policy since 1900.* Chicago: University of Chicago Press.

Ninkovich, F. A. (2001). *The United States and imperialism.* Malden, MA: Blackwell Publishers.

Parrini, C. P. (1986). Theories of imperialism. In L. C. Gardner (Ed.), *Redefining the past: Essays in diplomatic history in honor of William Appleman William* (pp. 65–83). Corvallis: Oregon State University Press.

Smith, T. (1981). *The pattern of imperialism: The United States, Great Britain, and the late-industrializing world since 1815.* Cambridge, UK: Cambridge University Press.

Williams, W. A. (1972). *The tragedy of American diplomacy.* New York: Dell.

Zinn, H. (2003). *A people's history of the United States: 1492–present.* New York: HarperCollins.

Zunz, O. (1998). *Why the American century?* Chicago: University of Chicago Press.

Intelligence Agencies

Some nations oppose, and others endorse and cooperate with U.S. intelligence-gathering activities. Whether a country cooperates often depends on the shared nature of U.S. intelligence activities, and the benefits to a helpful country.

During the American Revolution in 1775 General George Washington employed a spy based in Boston. Ever since then intelligence gathering has been a vital necessity of the U.S. government due to the size of the U.S. federal government, the geographical area of the United States, and the distance of the United States from much of the rest of the world.

World War I—FBI

By 1908 some people in the federal government feared that foreign secret agents were spying on members of Congress. This fear led Attorney General Charles Bonaparte to establish the Justice Department's Bureau of Investigation, the forerunner of the Federal Bureau of Investigation (FBI).

The Bureau of Investigation undertook many roles in the following forty years. As a police agency, it investigated trafficking in illegal aliens, combated prostitution imported from abroad, searched for fugitives, and started a forensics program, scientifically studying such crime clues as tire tracks, guns, watermarks, and typefaces.

Moreover, the bureau conducted espionage, counterintelligence, sabotage, and code breaking, making its functions more like those of today's Central Intelligence Agency (CIA). On top of that, the FBI acted as a regulatory agency, checking for violations of neutrality laws and coordinating other intelligence agencies of the time, such as MI-8 (a former department of the British Directorate of Military Intelligence) and the Black Chamber (America's first peacetime cryptanalytic organization and a forerunner of the top-secret National Security Agency). The rise of socialism worldwide led the FBI to acquire additional duties: It spied on fascist and Communist groups in the United States, as well as the Ku Klux Klan.

World War II—FBI, OSS, SIS

After the Japanese attack on Pearl Harbor in 1941 the need for a centralized and organized intelligence community was increased. Therefore, in 1942 the Office of Strategic Services (OSS) was founded.

With U.S. involvement in World War II the FBI investigated draft evaders and deserters. The war also gave birth to a new intelligence agency, the Special Intelligence Service (SIS). The role of the Special Intelligence Service was to provide information about Axis activities in South America, a role shared with the FBI.

Meanwhile, more intelligence services, such as the Military Intelligence Service (MIS) and the Interim Research and Intelligence Service (IRIS), were established to organize and expand the intelligence community.

CIA

To counter the threat of Communism the Central Intelligence Agency was established in 1947. The CIA assumed many responsibilities over time and soon became the primary intelligence agency in the United States, conducting espionage, counterintelligence, sabotage, and code breaking. U.S. intelligence operations overseas were solely vested in the CIA.

However, the CIA was involved in some missteps over the years, such as the attempt to assassinate Cuban leader Fidel Castro, the Bay of Pigs fiasco (an unsuccessful attempt by United States-backed Cuban exiles to overthrow the government of the Cuban dictator Fidel Castro), Operation Chaos (a domestic espionage project to monitor college students' protests against the U.S. government's foreign policy in Vietnam), the Watergate scandal, and the misinformation provided before the Iraq War (2003). Such missteps led other institutions such as the FBI and the U.S. Senate to investigate the activity of the CIA.

NSA, NRO, DIA

Soon after establishment of the CIA the need rose for a more effective and specialized organization to conduct cryptology (the enciphering and deciphering of messages in secret code or cipher), eavesdropping, wiretapping, and telecommunications espionage, and in 1952 the National Security Agency (NSA) was established.

In 1961 CIA-Air Force efforts to collect and evaluate aerial

photography resulted in establishment of the National Reconnaissance Office (NRO). The NRO proved itself the next year during the Cuban Missile Crisis, in which aerial photography played an important role.

Also in 1962 the Defense Intelligence Agency (DIA) was established to coordinate the intelligence gathering, analysis, and assessment of other military intelligence agencies.

Today's U.S. Intelligence

The U.S. intelligence system today is a complex maze of interconnected agencies. These agencies report to various authorities. Some agencies are directly under the president, others under federal departments, whereas others serve the House of Representatives or the Senate. All intelligence institutions, however—apart from those directly under the president—are controlled and report to a central authority, the Intelligence Community (IC).

The Intelligence Community has also its own offices. The simple scheme that follows shows the basic relationships among agencies of the intelligence system.

    President
        President's Foreign Intelligence Advisory Board
            (PFIAB)
        Intelligence Oversight Board (IOB)
    National Security Council (NSC)
    Intelligence Community (IC)
        IC Organs
            National Intelligence Council (NIC)
            Central Intelligence for Community Management (CI/CM)
            Office of the National Counterintelligence Executive (ONCIX)
            Associate Director of Central Intelligence for Military Support (ADCI/MS)
        Intelligence Agencies
            CIA, NSA, DIA, NRO, FBI, CTC, TTIC, SSCI

The Intelligence Community covers these areas:

1. SIGINT—Signals Intelligence (NSA)
    a. COMINT—Communications Intelligence
    b. ELINT—Electronic Intelligence
    c. FISINT—Foreign Instrumentation Signals Intelligence
2. MASINT—Measurement and Signature Intelligence (mainly DIA)
3. HUMINT—Human Intelligence (mainly CIA and DIA)
4. IMINT—Imagery Intelligence (mainly National Geo-Spatial Intelligence Agency, NGA)
5. OSINT—Open-Source Intelligence (mainly CIA, ISR)

An example might make the scheme simpler. SIGINT operations almost exclusively concern the National Security Agency (NSA). MASINT operations evolve under the authority of the Defense Intelligence Agency. HUMINT operations usually concern the Central Intelligence Agency and the Defense Intelligence Agency. IMINT operations primarily concern the National Geo-Spatial Intelligence Agency (NGA), and finally, OSINT operations mainly relate to the Foreign Broadcast Information Service (FBIS) and the National Air Intelligence Center (NAIC).

Impending Needs

The United States might not have survived either world war if the country had not been able to gather good intelligence. The peak of intelligence activity occurred during the Cold War, which involved not only U.S.-Soviet espionage and counterintelligence but also wars, covert operations, confrontations, and rivalries: the Korean War, the Bay of Pigs invasion, the Vietnam War, the Cuban Missile Crisis, and the Star Wars (more formally known as the Strategic Defensive Iniative). Information was the ultimate weapon during this time, and the United States was caught up in an information-gathering race.

After the Cold War many people said that further innovation in intelligence gathering was not needed or even possible for the United States. They were proven wrong.

First, mounting anti-Americanism overseas and the development of weapons of mass destruction (WMDs) increased the need for intelligence agencies as well as the number of human resources and operatives around the world. Today the United States is not threatened by another Pearl Harbor, but rather by WMDs and countries that possess them, such as North Korea, Pakistan, India, and Russia. Therefore, in addition to the DIA and NRO, more information and security organizations were formed, North American Aerospace Defense (NORAD) being the most striking example.

Second, the United States needed even more extensive intelligence because of the country's massive economic expansion around the world. Global hotspots such as Serbia and Iraq and the power of China, Russia, and Iran demonstrate how the United States continues to need intelligence to preserve and expand its economic development.

Third, the September 11, 2001, terrorist attacks on New York City and Washington, D.C., opened a new chapter in U.S. intelli-

gence. Agencies across the administrative spectrum of government, such as the Department of Homeland Security, were formed to prevent another terrorist attack. The attacks of September 11 also led to the strengthening of many government agencies, including the Department of Homeland Security, as well as three organizations within the Department of Justice: The Neighborhood Watch Program (NWP), the Terrorism Information and Prevention System (TIPS), and the Terrorism Information Awareness (TIA). These programs require ordinary civilians to spy on their neighbors and colleagues at work and provide feedback. However, these three organizations have raised concerns about human rights, civil liberties, and democracy.

Finally, the feeling of insecurity has created extra demands for the United States by their allies to better utilize their expertise on intelligence. For example, in the first Iraq War (1991), the British Petroleum (BP) company pressured the U.K. government to protect its interests in Kuwait. As a result the U.K. government cooperated more closely with the U.S. during the war. Israeli pressure, on the other hand, motivated by a growing fear of countries such as Iraq, Egypt, Saudi Arabia, and Syria, led the United States to establish information-gathering organizations, mainly think tanks such as the Council on Foreign Relations (CFR).

Perceptions of Other Nations

In today's global village the actions of one country affect many other countries. As U.S. intelligence activity spreads across the globe it causes strong reactions. Negative feelings about U.S. foreign intelligence come from two main areas. The first area is comprised of countries such as Russia, China, Cuba, and North Korea that have been rivals of the United States since the Cold War. The other area is comprised of countries such as Iraq, Iran, Saudi Arabia, and Syria that are new rivals of the United States, mainly since terrorism became a challenge for the United States. However, some nations not only cooperate, but also indeed seek out U.S. interference through U.S. intelligence agencies. In the international community there are feelings of both endorsement and enmity for the activity of U.S. intelligence agencies.

Kyriakos Kouveliotis

Further Reading

Andrew, C. (1995). *For the president's eyes only: Secret intelligence and the American presidency from Washington to Bush.* London: HarperCollins.

Andrew, C., & Dilks, D. (Eds.). (1984). *The missing dimension: Governments and intelligence communities in the twentieth century.* London: Macmillan.

Gates, R. (1996). *From the shadows: The ultimate insider story of five presidents and how they won the Cold War.* New York: Simon & Schuster.

Ranelagh, J. (1986). *The agency: The rise and decline of the CIA.* London: Weidenfeld and Nicolson.

Rhodri, J. (1998). *The CIA and American democracy.* New Haven, CT: Yale University Press.

Rhodri, J. (2002). *Cloak and dollar: A history of American secret intelligence.* New Haven, CT: Yale University Press.

Rhodri, J., & Andrew, C. (Eds.). (1997). *Eternal vigilance? 50 years of the CIA.* London: Frank Cass.

Richelson, J. (1995). *A century of spies: Intelligence in the twentieth century.* New York: Oxford University Press.

Rudgers, D. (2000). *Creating the secret state: The origins of the Central Intelligence Agency.* Lawrence: University Press of Kansas.

Theoharis, A. (2002). *Chasing spies: How the FBI failed in counterintelligence but promoted the politics of McCarthyism in the Cold War years.* Chicago: Ivan R. Dee.

Woodward, B. (1987). *Veil: The secret wars of the CIA 1981–1987.* New York: Simon & Schuster.

Zegart, A. (1999). *Flawed by design: The evolution of the CIA, JCS and NSC.* Stanford, CA: Stanford University Press.

International Agreements and Summits

The United States adheres to most international agreements it enters into, but it has also breached treaty obligations for political reasons. This has harmed the U.S. image, adding to fear and distrust of the United States.

With the growth of technology and communications, cross-border trade, and regional integration, nations of today's world grow increasingly interdependent. Since the end of World War II international agreements and summits have played an important role in shaping U.S. foreign relations. The charters establishing the United Nations and the Organization of American States, for example, created a framework for international cooperation. Agreements establishing the World Trade Organization govern U.S. trade relations with many of its trading partners. Political commitments and relationships resulting from the summit process are equally important. Diplomacy at Group of Seven (G7) summits has resulted in international monetary reforms and economic policy coordination.

International Agreements as Instruments of International Law

The ability to enter into a treaty or agreement with foreign powers is an important attribute of state sovereignty. As noted earlier, treaties have proliferated since the end of World War II and today play an important role in the international community, addressing issues ranging from the environment and human rights to economic cooperation. It is in accordance with the principle of *pacta sunt servanda* (pacts must be honored), that the shared sense of commitment to the treaty is observed. States are hesitant to breach treaty obligations, knowing that if they do not honor treaty commitments, neither will other countries.

International law defines treaties as agreements between states (or at times international organizations) that are intended to be binding upon the parties. The Vienna Convention on the Law of Treaties, which entered into force on 27 January 1980, codifies international law governing treaties. Although the United States is not a member of the convention for political reasons (the convention would grant the executive branch power reserved for Congress), the United States observes the convention as a matter of customary international law.

International treaties generally are multilateral, collaborative

mechanism, or bilateral. Multilateral treaties, legislative by nature, establish agreed-upon norms of behavior or rules of law. Depending on the treaty, a multilateral treaty may be open to all members of the international community or to all members of a large regional group. Collaborative mechanism treaties are created to manage or regulate a specific type of activity. Substantively, these treaties set forth principles and purposes and establish institutional organs responsible for making operational decisions, rules, orders and recommendations. In this sense they differ from multilateral treaties. One of the more famous collaborative mechanism treaties is the 1982 U.N. Convention on the Law of the Sea, setting forth principles and mechanisms governing exploitation of seabed mineral resources. The final treaty type—bilateral—is the most common. These treaties are of a contractual nature and set forth terms of rights and obligations. The United States favors this type of treaty to develop stronger investment and trade relationships with foreign nations.

International Treaties and Agreements from the U.S. Perspective

The United States defines treaties more restrictively than does international law. As noted, for international law purposes a treaty (or agreement) is an international agreement concluded between states and intended to have a legal effect. International law makes no distinction between types of international agreements. The United States, by contrast, distinguishes between treaties and executive agreements. A treaty is an international agreement made with the advice and consent of Congress. An executive agreement is an agreement entered into by the president, based on that office's constitutionally delegated powers or on the advice and consent of both houses of Congress.

The United States also distinguishes between self-executing and non-self-executing treaties. Self-executing treaties, intended to bind parties without implementing legislation, are binding after

ratification. Non-self-executing treaties are not considered U.S. law until they have been enacted by legislation.

Under domestic law treaties and federal legislation are on equal footing; the Constitution refers to both as the "supreme law of the land." When a dispute exists between an international treaty (or agreement) and federal legislation courts will first try to construe statutes and treaties so as to give effect to both. However, when applying this rule is not possible, the statute or treaty that was enacted later in time will prevail as domestic law. In practice this rule means that Congress may override an existing treaty or congressional-executive agreement by enacting legislation—a troubling prospect for many foreign countries entering agreements with the United States. However, if application of this rule results "in the suppression of treaty provisions as domestic law, that result does not relieve the United States of its international obligations" (Treaties and Other International Agreements 2001).

U.S. Treaty Making

The first phase of treaty making is negotiation. Representatives of each government agree on the substance, wording, and terms of the treaty. In the case of the United States, the president has significant discretion. In addition to setting negotiation guidelines, the president has the authority to choose negotiators (although sometimes subject to the consent of the Senate). The second phase is adoption of the treaty by the parties. Adoption means simply that the negotiations have ended and that the terms of the treaty are fixed, not that the treaty has entered into force.

After the negotiation and adoption phases are complete, the president transmits the treaty to the Senate for consideration. For a treaty to be binding under U.S. law, the Senate must approve the treaty by at least a two-thirds majority. After receiving congressional approval, the treaty is returned to the president. Once again, the president has significant discretion; it is the president's decision whether to ratify the treaty.

A treaty becomes binding on the United States after it is ratified by the president. In the case of bilateral treaties, the parties generally exchange instruments of ratification. Multilateral treaties generally enter into force when the parties deposit instruments of ratification as specified by the treaty. After the treaty enters into force, it is legally binding on all parties that ratified it. After a treaty has entered into force, the president issues a proclamation containing a published version of the text to notify the public.

Executive agreements are similar to treaties with respect to the process but with one important distinction—consent. Congressional-executive agreements are entered into with consent of a majority of both houses of Congress. Consent is given by both houses of Congress either before or after the agreement is negotiated. Sole executive agreements are entered into by the president, based on power granted under Article II of the Constitution, often the president's authority as commander in chief. Because these agreements are concluded solely on the basis of the president's constitutional authority, they do not need to be submitted to Congress for consent.

The political checks and balances involved in the treaty-making process are often a concern for parties negotiating treaties with the United States. Treaty negotiations are time-consuming endeavors, requiring significant give-and-take from all parties. Other nations may be hesitant to invest time and political goodwill in treaty making, only to have a treaty rejected by Congress. This prospect is particularly troublesome in the negotiation of trade treaties, which can take years and significant resources to negotiate. To address this problem a special procedure, informally referred to as "fast track," was created by the Omnibus Trade and Competitiveness Act of 1988 and the Trade Act of 1974. Fast track streamlines the approval process for trade negotiations. Under fast track the president submits the text of an agreement to each house of Congress. Each house has sixty days to accept or reject the agreement. Amendments are not permitted.

U.S. Willingness to Honor Treaty Obligations

Overall the United States has regarded treaties as legally binding instruments. The tens of thousands of agreements to which the United States is a party attest to the importance the government places on these instruments as tools of international relations. That said, at times the United States has breached treaty obligations for domestic political reasons. Such breaches have had a negative effect on foreign affairs, giving foreign countries already wary of U.S. political might a further reason to distrust the United States. Two examples of U.S. breaches of treaty obligations are U.S refusal to pay outstanding U.N. dues (angering other members of the U.N. and damaging U.S. credibility) and U.S. refusal to advise alien prisoners of their rights, in contravention of the Vienna Convention on Consular Relations. In the case of *Breard vs. Greene,* the United States was accused of failing to advise a Paraguayan citizen sentenced to die of his rights under the Vienna Convention on Consular Rights. Despite a ruling from the International Court of Justice to the contrary, the U.S. Supreme Court refused to stay the execution. Applying the later-in-time rule mentioned earlier, the Court concluded that the Antiterrorism and Effective Death Act of 1996 superceded the United States' obligations under the Vienna Convention.

International Summits

Summit diplomacy also plays an important role in international governance. In an increasingly interdependent world, summitry provides world leaders with a forum for addressing complex political and economic issues. Today the term *summit* is overused, often referring to endless international gatherings and meetings. For purposes of this discussion the term *summits* refers to meetings at which heads of state meet to address issues of common concern. A common characteristic of these meetings is the attempt of heads of states not merely to react to world events, but rather to shape them according to their own views and convictions.

Three summits that are important from an international relations perspective are the Group of Seven (G7, now G8), Asia-Pacific Economic Cooperation (APEC), and the Summit of the Americas.

Group of Seven (now G8)

Group of Seven summits are held by eight of the major industrialized nations (United States, Canada, United Kingdom, France, Germany, Italy, Japan, and Russia) to address political and economic issues. The presidency of the group rotates among member nations each year. The president sets the group's annual agenda and hosts that year's summit.

Asia-Pacific Economic Cooperation

The Asia-Pacific Economic Cooperation is an organization of the major economies of the region and other important economies, such as the United States. Leadership of APEC rotates on a yearly basis among members, although every other year the chair must be held by a member country of the Association of Southeast Asian Nations (ASEAN). Each year the APEC chair hosts the APEC leaders summit to foster economic cooperation and trade as well as meetings between senior trade and foreign affairs officials.

Summit of the Americas

The Summit of the America brings together heads of state of Western Hemisphere countries to discuss economic, political, and social issues.

Summit Practice and the United States

The United States uses summits as an important part of its foreign relations, using them to address issues ranging from peace in the Middle East and terrorism to economic development and growth. However, in spite of the important role that summits

play in state relations, quantifying their direct contributions can be difficult. Unlike agreements that codify accepted norms and principles, summits are typically part of a larger causal change of events. Moreover, the outcomes of summits are strongly influenced by the political personalities of the president or other politicians involved, as well as by domestic and international political pressures.

In the early days of U.S. summitry, summits were informal, often characterized as fire-side chats. These gatherings of leaders (or top government ministers) tended to be small, personal, and discreet. Because they were discreet, participants felt free to express themselves and often developed strong bonds of trust. An example of early summitry is the Library Group of finance ministers, the predecessor of the Group of Seven. This group first met in the White House library in 1973 and later on the margins of international monetary negotiations to address economic and monetary issues. Its meetings, generally held in secret, were not bound by strict agenda; this setting created an atmosphere in which close working relationships could be established. The ministers often enjoyed companionship based on similar challenges faced in their domestic political environments.

U.S. summitry today has grown increasingly more bureaucratic and institutionalized. Often preliminary negotiations are left to a small group of special representatives called "sherpas." Sherpas meet in preparatory sessions to clarify agendas and issues and to explore possible resolution of disagreements. This process can be frustrating to leaders, who feel restricted by tight policy frameworks and agendas. At the G7 Tokyo Summit in 1993 President Clinton was said to be frustrated by the tight framework and processes at the summit. This situation resulted in Clinton being attracted to a proposal made by Britain's then–prime minister John Major to simplify summit procedures and to concentrate on a few broad issues designated by the leaders themselves, rather than merely speaking from prepared scripts.

Legal Status of Joint Communiqués and Informal Agreements

Joint communiqués are often issued at the end of the summit process. Although not legally binding, these agreements are important instruments of foreign policy. Flexible in nature, they tend to signal broad policy guidelines and demonstrate the goodwill of the nations involved. In discussing the importance of these agreements, former secretary of state Henry Kissinger said that although the agreements "are not binding commitments of the United States…

that does not mean, of course, the United States is morally or politically free to act as if they did not exist. On the contrary, they are important statements of diplomatic policy and engage the good faith of the United States so long as the circumstances that gave rise to them continue. But they are not binding commitments on the United States" (Nash 1994, 515).

Summitry Power and Limitations

Proponents view summitry as collective leadership in an increasingly interdependent world. In practice, summitry provides U.S leaders strong frameworks and foundations for collective action.

Group of Seven initiatives, for example, have resulted in international monetary reform and coordinated economic action. Importantly, summits also play a role in domestic policies. Summits often provide the opportunity to overcome both internal and bureaucratic resistance and to launch new initiatives. At the 1978 Group of Seven summit in Bonn, Germany, for example, President Jimmy Carter agreed to implement measures to reduce oil imports. Despite domestic resistance to these measures, Congress passed an energy package that met summit commitments. When discussing the measures, a senior White House advisor noted, "If a President commits himself to something at a summit, and you can cite that in a meeting, that's a...powerful argument" (Bayne and Putnam 1987, 88). Summits are important in building

---

AN EARLY TREATY WITH ARAB NORTH AFRICA/MIDDLE EAST

This excerpt from the Treaty of Peace and Amity, signed at Algiers 5 September 1795 shows that the United States has had international ties in the Middle East since early nationhood. This treaty was ratified by the United States 7 March 1796.

ARTICLE 1st
From the date of the Present Treaty there shall subsist a firm and Sincere Peace and Amity between the President and Citizens of the United States of North America and Hassan Bashaw Dey of Algiers his Divan and Subjects the Vessels and Subjects of both Nations reciprocally treating each other with Civility Honor and Respect.

ARTICLE 2d
All Vessels belonging to the Citizens of the United States of North America Shall be permitted to enter the Different ports of the Regency to trade with our Subjects or any other Persons residing within our Jurisdiction on paying the usual duties at our Custom-House that is paid by all nations at Peace with this Regency observing that all Goods disembarked and not Sold here shall be permitted to be reimbarked without paying any duty whatever either for disembarking or embarking all naval & Military Stores Such as Gun-Powder Lead Iron Plank Sulphur Timber for building far pitch Rosin Turpentine and any other Goods denominated Naval and Military Stores Shall be permitted to be Sold in this Regency without paying any duties whatever at the Custom House of this Regency.

ARTICLE 3d
The Vessels of both Nations shall pass each other without any impediment or Molestation and all Goods monies or Passengers of whatsoever Nation that may be on board of the Vessels belonging to either Party Shall be considered as inviolable and shall be allowed to pass unmolested.

ARTICLE 4th
All Ships of War belonging to this regency on meeting with Merchant Vessels belonging to Citizens of the United States shall be allowed to Visit them with two persons only beside the rowers these two only permitted to go on board said vessel without obtaining express leave from the commander of said Vessel who shall compare the Pass-port and immediately permit said Vessel to proceed on her Voyage unmolested All Ships of War belonging to the United States of North America on meeting with an Algerine Cruiser and Shall have seen her pass port and Certificate from the Consul of the United States of North America resident in this Regency shall be permittd to proceed on her cruise unmolested no Pass-port to be Issued to any Ships but such as are Absolutely the Property of Citizens of the United States and Eighteen Months Shall be the term allowed for furnishing the Ships of the United States with Pass-ports.

ARTICLE 5th
No Commander of any Cruiser belonging to this Regency shall be allowed to take any person of whatever Nation or denomination out of any Vessel belonging to the United States of North America in order to Examine them or under presence of making them confess any thing desired neither shall they inflict any corporal punishment or any way else molest them.

ARTICLE 6th
If any Vessel belonging to the United States of North America shall be Stranded on the Coast of this Regency they shall receive every possible Assistance from the Subjects of this Regency all goods saved from the wreck shall be Permitted to be Reimbarked on board of any other Vessel without Paying any Duties at the Custom House.

Source: Avalon Project at Yale Law School. (2007). Retrieved March 21, 2007, from http://www.yale.edu/lawweb/avalon/diplomacy/barbary/bar1795t.htm

relationships between leaders. Summits are often credited for the close relationships forged between President Clinton and Russian leader Boris Yeltsin and between President George W. Bush and Russian leader Vladimir Putin.

However, limits to the summit process also exist. Diverse opinions and national interests tend to weaken results. These limits have led some scholars to view summits as mere photo opportunities rather than as important tools of foreign relations. Moreover, although leaders may agree on issues, "summits cannot manufacture national political will where none exists" (Bayne & Putnam 1987). State rivalries are another common problem.

International agreements and summits are important instruments in United States foreign policy. Their unique characteristics make them important tools in traversing the changing international landscape, especially during a time when the United States is often viewed as arrogant and its strong political and military might is often both envied and distrusted in the international community.

Kristen Smith

Further Reading

Agreement establishing the World Trade Organization. (1994). Retrieved April 17, 2007, from http://www.wto.org/English/docs_e/legal_e/04-wto.doc

Bayne, N. & Putnam, R. (1987). *Hanging together: Cooperation and conflict in the Seven-Power Summits* (2nd ed.). London: Sage.

Breard v. Greene, 523 US 371 (1998).

Dalton, R. E. (1999) National treaty law and practice: United States. In M. Leigh, M. R. Blakeslee and L. B. Ederington (Eds.), *National treaty law and practice (Austria, Chile, Colombia, Japan, Netherlands, U.S)*. Washington D.C.: American Society of International Law.

Damrosch, L. F. (Ed.). (2001). *International law, cases and materials* (4th ed.). West Group Publishing.

Kirgis, F. L. (1997). International Agreements and U.S. Law. Retrieved April 17, 2007, from http://www.asil.org/insights/insigh10.htm

Nash, M. (1994). U.S. practice: Contemporary practice of the United States relating to international law. *American Journal of International Law, 91,* 515.

Treaties and other international agreements: The role of the United States Senate. (2001, January). Retrieved April 17, 2007, from.http://www.au.af.mil/au/awcgate/congress/treaties_senate_role.pdf

International Law

With no single, sovereign, entity overseeing international law, but rather a system of agreements between sovereign governments, the area of international law is unclear and has been subjected to wide interpretation and discretion.

International law is the system of rules, principles, procedures, and norms applied to relations between states. The term *international law* is attributed to the English jurist and philosopher Jeremy Bentham and is equivalent to the term *law of nations*. The term *international law* in this sense is often qualified as *public international law* to differentiate it from the term *private international law,* which refers principally to conflicts between the municipal laws of discrete sovereign entities. International law must also be distinguished from quasi-international law. Quasi-international law governs relations in ways similar to international law but often addresses issues in which one of the parties involved lacks an international personality, which usually means that it is not a sovereign state. Quasi-international law would apply, for example, in some disputes between sovereign states and multinational corporations.

The principle of state sovereignty makes international law at once unique from and complex in relation to municipal law systems in a single country. In a single sovereign country laws are promulgated by the sovereign government and enforced through the monopoly on coercive force exercised by sovereign governments. In the international arena, in contrast, no single and recognized sovereign entity, but rather a multiplicity of sovereigns that are equal by definition, promulgates laws.

At its inception, the United States was a great proponent and defender of international law. Although the United States had waged a revolutionary struggle to gain independence from the British Empire, the Founding Fathers were eager, once the war with Great Britain was over, to promote international law as a means of emphasizing its status as an independent nation. Furthermore, the United States was a relatively weak power in the early years of its existence, and many believed international law was an important means to protect the fledgling republic from aggressive European powers.

For much of its history the United States has remained a defender of the international rule of law. President Woodrow Wilson sought to give a legal basis to principles such as national self-determination and collective security in the aftermath of World War I, most notably in the form of the League of Nations. After World War II, the United States was an even stronger promoter of international order based on rules and institutions, and it was the chief architect of the United Nations, the International Monetary Fund, the International Bank for Reconstruction and Development (the World Bank), and various other international organizations that continue to have an active role in international politics.

Since the end of the Cold War, however, the United States has increasingly been accused of ignoring or breaking many tenets of international law—often tenets it had previously championed. Defenders of the United States's behavior assert that it, as the world's only remaining superpower, has special responsibilities that make adherence to the international rule of law difficult. Especially since the attacks of September 11, 2001, some have asserted that the traditional rule of international behavior, most notably the rule of war, are obsolete in an era in which states must combat non-state actors, including "terrorists." The majority of the international community seems to oppose these positions; some of the United States's closest allies have been the staunchest opponents of its recent conduct, especially its decision in 2003 to invade Iraq. Many domestic and international critics maintain that the best way for the so-called "war on terror" to be fought and won is through scrupulous adherence to international law, lest the United States debase itself to the level of its enemies.

Sources of International Law

Because no single, recognized, sovereign entity creates international law, the sources of international law are multiple. Article 38 of the Statute of the International Court of Justice lists the three key sources of international law that the court applies in adjudicating disputes submitted to it. These three sources have received near-unanimous consent as being definitive:

1. international conventions, whether general or particular, establishing rules expressly recognized by states
2. international custom, as evidence of a general practice accepted as law
3. the general principles of law recognized by civilized nations

Treaties or conventions are important sources of international law, but the content of all conventions does not necessarily reflect

The International Court of Justice in The Hague, also known as The Peace Palace. Source: istock/Jan Kranendonk.

international law; in many instances treaties merely represent an accord between two international actors that cannot be considered law as generally applicable to all. Bilateral or multilateral treaties can, however, create obligations that are binding and become law, or they can incorporate tenets of law, the repetition and observance of which serve as evidence of their status as law. What is more, in some cases agreement with or acquiescence to a widely subscribed multilateral treaty such as the United Nations Charter (1945) can give aspects of those conventions the force of international law. United Nations General Assembly resolutions are not necessarily law, although they can serve as evidence of opinion on matters of international law because the General Assembly is the widest international forum for such dialogue.

Customs in international affairs that have been in widespread and consistent use over a significant duration of time can also acquire the force of law. When President Harry Truman unilaterally extended U.S. jurisdiction over the nation's continental shelf he was in contravention of the international law of the time; however, because most countries over the following years extended their national jurisdiction in the same way, national jurisdiction of the continental shelf became a customary feature of international law.

General principles of law recognized by nations represent an important source of international law. For example, the legal principle *pacta sunt servanda* (pacts must be honored), the rule that agreements are binding and to be implemented in good faith,

underpins every treaty negotiated in international relations and is key to the functioning of international society.

Sanctions in International Law

Scholars have argued that because international law lacks coercive sanctions it is more akin to a system of morality in behavior than to law. Sanctions exist in international law; however, just like sources, they are markedly different from those in municipal law. The principles of good faith, diplomatic habituation, national self-interest, and global public opinion often act as sanctions in international law, but only according to the dynamics of the international system at the time and not in a uniform manner. Of course, retaliatory action, even military action, by the party injured by a violation of international law is an obvious sanction, although this retaliatory behavior itself is subject to international law. In recent times international organizations and agencies have increased the scope both for sanctions to be applied to transgressors of international law and for nonmilitary sanctions to be applied. It bears repeating that, even with the growth of international organizations, sanctions are subject to the dynamics of the international arena. Although all actors are equal in principle in international law, actors are never equal in power dynamics, and therefore international law is often not universally applied or enforced.

In the second half of the twentieth century much international

law developed in the context of the Cold War rivalry between the United States and the Soviet Union. After the fall of the Soviet Union, the United States has emerged as the only global super-power and has been in a unique position both to uphold and to breach international law. Many promoters of a more rigorous and widespread system of international law hope that through the increased adoption of such a system, power imbalances will be attenuated and international justice will increase.

Rules and Principles of International Law

Rules of international law are numerous and exist in a myriad of fields. They include, but are hardly limited to, the norms of some diplomatic and consular relations between states, the rules for declaring and waging war, some of the ways treaties are negoti-ated and stay in effect, and many aspects of economic and trade dealings between states. Some of the most fundamental rules of international law are known as *jus cogens* (compelling law) and are the peremptory norms of the law. Well-known *jus cogens* laws include the international prohibitions on genocide and slavery.

The reality of the sovereignty of states is an important principle of international law. How to determine where and when a state is sovereign, how it becomes so, as well as the process by which it is recognized by other sovereign states are all in the purview of international law. Other important principles of international law include consent, reciprocity, responsibility, good faith, finality of awards and judgments, and the freedom of the seas. Treaties also are an important feature of international law, and the 1969 Vienna Convention on the Law of Treaties codified much of the law of treaties. The right to wage war is also subject to international law. International law regarding war has been tabulated principally in the Hague Conventions of 1899 and 1907 and the Geneva Protocol of 1925. The United Nations Charter is also important in this re-spect for its prohibition on waging wars of aggression. Actions of self-defense can legally be undertaken against recognizably illegal acts, but the requirement for self-defense must be compelling and immediate. The qualitative nature of these two needs has meant that controversy has often existed around the legality of military actions characterized as defensive.

History of International Law

As long as human societies have been in interaction, intersocietal law has existed. Rules of behavior and conduct existed between the ancient Greek city-states and in Roman times, as did a conception of a society of nations in Confucian China and ancient India. The legacy of Roman laws and the Roman Empire influenced society

---

ON THE LAW OF WAR AND PEACE (1625)

The extract below is from the 1814 translation of Dutchman Hugo Grotius's De Jure Belli ac Pacis (On the Law of War and Peace). Although written almost four-hundred years ago, this work is considered to have laid the foundations for modern international law.

Chapter 8: On Empire over the Conquered

I. If individuals can reduce each other to subjection, it is not surprising that states can do the same, and by this means acquire a civil, abso-lute, or mixed, dominion. So that, in the language of Tertullian, victory has often been the foundation of dominion, and it often happens, as Quintilian remarks, that the boundaries of states and kingdoms, of na-tions and cities, can only be settled by the laws of war.

Quintus Curtius relates of Alexander, that he said, it was for con-querors to dictate laws, which the conquered were bound to receive. This has always been a general opinion and rule, thus Ariovistus, in Caesar, laid it down as an indubitable right of war, for the conqueror to impose whatever terms he pleased upon the conquered, nor did he suppose the Roman people would allow any one to interpose with them in the discretionary use of this right.

By conquest, a prince succeeds to all the rights of the conquered sovereign or state; and if it be a common. wealth, he acquires all the rights and privileges, which the people possessed. He gains the same right, which the state had before, to alienate the possessions, or to transmit them if he chuses to his descendants, by which means they will become a patrimonial territory.

II. The right of conquest may go even beyond this. A state may hereby lose its political existence, so far as to form an appendage to another power, which was the case with the Roman provinces: or if a king engaged in war against a state, at his own expence, has reduced it to complete subjection, his authority over it becomes an absolute, rather than a limited sovereignty. It can no longer be called an independent state, but, by the right of conquest, forms an integral part of the prince's immediate dominions. Xenophon in drawing the character of Agesi-laus, commends him for requiring no other services and obedience of the cities he had conquered, than what is usually paid by subjects to their lawful sovereigns.

Source: Grotius, H. (1625). On the law of war and peace. Retrieved March 19, 2007, from http://www.constitution.org/gro/djbp.htm

and group interactions through the Middle Ages. In feudal society, with its hierarchy with the papacy and emperor at the summit and its imposed norms in diplomatic relations, trade, and warfare, one can see precursors of international law. Indeed, during the medieval period vigorous philosophic and theological debate concerned what constitutes just and unjust war.

However, not until the late fifteenth century, when the concept of territorial sovereignty became widely accepted, was a coherent approach to international law developed. The approach was spurred in particular by the writings of such Renaissance political theorists as Niccolo Machiavelli and Jean Bodin and the increasing discourse around natural law theories. Natural law theorists were heavily influenced by the discovery of North America by Europeans and by the debates over the acquisition of territory there, the rights of its indigenous inhabitants, and the law of the seas. Theorists also concerned themselves with warfare during this period of frequent, often religious, war in Europe. Hugo Grotius, one of many theorists concerned with natural law, is often called "the father of international law." His treatise *On the Law of War and Peace* was published in 1625, during the early part of the Thirty Years War. The Treaty of Westphalia (1648) at the end of the Thirty Years War enshrined the principle of *cuius regio eius religio* (whose rule, his religion), the principle that secular rulers can settle the religious disputes within their own domains. The Treaty of Westphalia also established the European states' system of territorial sovereign entities, a system that has spread around the world and exists into the twenty-first century.

During the eighteenth century the balance of power between the European great powers was seen as the guiding principle in international relations as well as an important principle of law. The French Revolution helped to reorient the idea of sovereignty away from the person of the monarch to the body politic or citizenry of the nation. During the nineteenth century the increasingly interdependent nature of European society inaugurated the modern era of "international legislation," and treaties were negotiated that dealt with issues as diverse as navigation of inland waterways and the abolition of the slave trade. This period also featured the expansion and application of international law, hitherto a feature of the European states system and those parts of the world that had been European settler colonies in large parts of Africa and Asia. Likewise, in this period the United States emerged as a great power outside the traditional European constellation.

After World War I the development of international law was influenced by new approaches to international relations that people hoped would prevent another such war. On the insistence of U.S. president Woodrow Wilson the League of Nations was created, and international organizations became more common, as did the idea of arbitration in the settlement of disputes. These processes continued after World War II with the founding of the United Nations. Since 1945 other important changes in the way societies interact have affected, and changed what falls within the pale of, international law. Scientific changes, such as the emergence of nuclear power and nuclear weapons, mass intercontinental travel, space travel, and computers and the Internet, have confused or rendered nugatory (inconsequential) certain traditional demarcations of national sovereignty. These and other developments have both challenged established conceptions of international law and given birth to new fields such as space law and Internet law. Likewise, the rapid growth of international trade in the second half of the twentieth century along with the emergence of an increasingly interdependent global banking and financial system fueled a boom in international economic and trade law.

Future of International Law

At the beginning of the twenty-first century the sovereign state remains central to any conception of international law. However, the proliferation of international organizations, of regional communities such as trading blocs that blur traditional definitions of what is the sovereign domain of states, of multinational corporations with global interests and resources that can rival those of some states, and of international nongovernmental organizations that lobby for specific concerns all augur changes in international relations and therefore, implicitly, in international law. One recent change has been an increasing awareness of and concern for the rights of individuals in international law. Increased coverage by the global media of poverty, disease, illiteracy, and genocide and the recognition that these blights affect everyone in an increasingly interdependent world have promoted awareness for international humanitarian and human rights law. Whereas traditional conceptions of international law stress sovereign states as the only actors in international law, some commentators are beginning to evaluate individuals as actors in international law and to recognize their rights in relation to sovereign countries, even to their own state.

Others have predicted the end of international law as we know it. The increasing importance of the individual in international law, the eclipsing of the nation-state, and the emergence of the United States as the only global superpower have led commentators on both sides of the political spectrum to surmise that a new international legal order needs to be erected. Some argue that the international "war on terror" requires a reevaluation of existing law. Others believe that the United States's conduct in this war, especially its invasion in 2003 of Iraq, has fatally undermined the current international system of law. The economic and political growth of the European Union and other regional governments

and organizations may signal a shifting of power towards regional blocs in international affairs. However international law will evolve in the coming years, it is certain that the United States will have a central role in that development.

Edward James Kolla

See also Human Rights; International Agreements and Summits; Relations with the United Nations, U.S.

Further Reading

Akehurst, M. B. (1984). *A modern introduction to international law* (5th ed.). London: Allen and Unwin.

Brierly, J. L. (1963). *The law of nations: An introduction to the international law of peace* (6th ed.). Oxford, U.K: Oxford University Press.

Brownlie, I. (2003). *Principles of public international law* (6th ed.). Oxford, U.K.: Oxford University Press.

Byers, M. (Ed.). (2000). *The role of law in international politics: Essays in international relations and international law.* Oxford, U.K.: Oxford University Press.

Falk, R. A., Kratochwil, F. V., & Mendlovitz, S. H. (1985). *International law: A contemporary perspective.* Boulder, CO: Westview Press.

Grewe, W. G. (2000). *The epochs of international law* (M. Byers, Trans.). Berlin, Germany: Walter de Gruyter.

Hyde, C. C. (1945). *International law: Chiefly as interpreted and applied by the United States* (2nd rev. ed.). Boston: Little, Brown and Company.

Kindred, H. M. (Ed.). (2000). *International law: Chiefly as interpreted and applied in Canada* (6th ed.). Toronto, Canada: Emond Montgomery.

McDougal, M. S., & Reisman, W. M. (1981). *International law in contemporary perspective: The public order of the world community.* Mineola, NY: Foundation Press.

Oppenheim, L. F. L., & Lauterpacht, H. (1955). *International law: A treatise* (8th ed.). London: Longmans.

Von Glahn, G. (1996). *Law among nations: An introduction to public international law* (7th ed.). Boston: Allyn and Bacon.

Iraq Wars

The wars in Iraq—first in 1991, then in 2003—have been two of the most defining moments shaping the image of the United States since 1990, and more recently have been detrimental to U.S. foreign policy, and its image abroad.

Meeting with Iraqi president Saddam Hussein and Iraqi foreign minister Tariq Aziz in 1990, the U.S. ambassador to Baghdad, April Glaspie, was sympathetic to her hosts. She decried "cheap and unjust" media portrayals of Iraq, told the Iraqis that President George H. W. Bush wanted "better and deeper relations with Iraq" and "an Iraqi contribution to peace and prosperity in the Middle East." Responding to Saddam's fears that Kuwait and other Persian Gulf nations might set the price of oil too low and damage the Iraqi economy, Glaspie added, "President Bush is an intelligent man. He is not going to declare an economic war against Iraq" (*New York Times,* 1990).

Glaspie's show of support continued. "I have lived here for years. I admire your extraordinary efforts to rebuild your country. I know you need funds [from oil revenues]. We understand that and our opinion is that you should have the opportunity to rebuild your country" (*New York Times,* 1990).

Then Glaspie uttered what would become one of the more parsed-over comments in contemporary international politics: President Bush and his administration, she explained, "have no opinion on the Arab-Arab conflicts, like your border disagreement with Kuwait. I was in the American Embassy in Kuwait during the late 60s. The instruction we had during this period was that we should express no opinion on this issue and that the issue is not associated with America. James Baker has directed our official spokesmen to emphasize this instruction. We hope you can solve this problem using any suitable methods . . . All that we hope is that these issues are solved quickly" (*New York Times,* 1990).

Just a week later, on 2 August 1990, Iraqi troops invaded and occupied Kuwait, setting into motion a series of global crises and wars that is now in its second decade.

However, the roots of these crises can be traced back much earlier than the 1990s. From a 1958 coup in Baghdad that brought nationalist general Karim Kassim to power, through his 1963 overthrow by Baathists (including Saddam and supported by the United States), to significant U.S. economic and military support of Iraq in its war against Iran in the 1980s, U.S. leaders were involved in Iraqi affairs and supportive of the regime there. By 1990 all that had changed.

Looking for new justifications for a ramped-up military budget and for continued reasons for U.S. global presence after the fall of European communist states, U.S. leaders raised alarms about "nuclear outlaws" and "rogue states." Iraq fit the bill. Thus, five days after the invasion of Kuwait, Bush announced that "this will not stand" and began to deploy military forces, impose sanctions, and put together a coalition to oust Iraq from its southern neighbor, which Iraq still claimed as its own.

The initial phase of the invasion, Operation Desert Shield, lasted through the end of 1990 as the United States and other countries, operating out of Saudi Arabia, put together a force of more than 600,000 troops, the vast majority of them from the United States. For the next few months, as the buildup continued, neither side budged, and hostilities seemed unavoidable. Then, on 17 January 1991, the United States and its allies began a massive air campaign against Baghdad. Saddam barely fought back, instead sending his air force to Iran to escape destruction. Although Iraq did launch Scud missile attacks, the allied forces met little resistance during the air campaign, and when they launched a ground invasion on 20 February 1991, they routed Iraqi forces in a matter of days. The war was over, but the seeds of continued hostilities were planted.

President Bush and his advisors ceased offensive operations on 22 February. However, Shiite Muslims opposed to Saddam in southern Iraq, assuming that allied forces would advance inside Iraq and support them, began an uprising against the regime. U.S. troops, however, remained in their positions, and Saddam struck back brutally, killing perhaps 100,000 Shiites.

Later, and presciently, Bush and his national security advisor, Brent Scowcroft, explained their decision to halt the offensive: "Trying to eliminate Saddam . . . would have incurred incalculable human and political costs. Apprehending him was probably impossible . . . We would have been forced to occupy Baghdad and, in effect, rule Iraq . . . there was no viable 'exit strategy' we could see, violating another of our principles. Furthermore, we had been self-consciously trying to set a pattern for handling aggression in the post–Cold War world. Going in and occupying Iraq, thus unilaterally exceeding the United Nations' mandate, would have destroyed the precedent of international response to aggression that we hoped to establish. Had we gone the invasion route, the United States could conceivably still be an occupying power in a bitterly hostile land" (Bush & Scowcroft 1998, 489). Still, the

United States did not disengage from Iraq. In the aftermath of the Gulf War, U.S.-sponsored U.N. sanctions went into effect and had a devastating impact on Iraq during the next decade or so, causing the deaths of perhaps 500,000 Iraqis, according to the United Nations International Children's Emergency Fund (UNICEF), or even one million, according to other human-rights observers. With a shortage of food, a lack of clean water, serious deficiencies of medical equipment, and a ban on other supplies because they might have a "dual use" in potential weapons development, Iraq was reeling. Despite the outcries from various critics, including Denis Halliday, U.N. humanitarian coordinator in Iraq, the sanctions persisted, with U.S. secretary of state Madeleine Albright acknowledging the hundreds of thousands of deaths, especially among children, but maintaining the U.S. stance.

Even as the sanctions led to a massive death toll and destroyed the Iraqi infrastructure, the United States increased the pressure on Saddam, alleging Iraqi violations of "no-fly zones" in northern and southern Iraq and responding with air strikes. The administration of President Bill Clinton began to invoke the no-fly rules, originally established to protect anti-Saddam Kurds and Shiites, to force Iraq to bend to U.S. wishes, with Clinton publicly calling for "regime change" and offering aid to anti-Saddam forces in the Iraq Liberation Act of October 1998. In December 1998 Clinton launched Operation Desert Fox, a four-day air bombardment in which U.S. and British forces flew more than six hundred sorties against Iraq.

Prior to the air strikes U.S. officials withdrew U.N. weapons inspections teams, led by Scott Ritter, from Iraq, but later Clinton and his successor, President George W. Bush, would claim that Saddam forced the U.N. inspectors out. In any event U.S. officials began to charge that Saddam was developing weapons of mass destruction (WMDs) and posed a regional threat. As Clinton left office in early 2001, U.S.-Iraqi relations were at a low point.

And they would get worse. In the immediate aftermath of the terrorist attacks on U.S. soil on September 11, 2001, the Bush administration zeroed in on Iraq. Although no good intelligence had linked Iraq to the attacks in New York and Washington and although Saddam had long had an adversarial relationship with terrorist leader Osama bin Laden and al-Qaeda, the Bush White House began to prepare for military action against Iraq even as the United States was invading Afghanistan in October 2001 because that country had provided refuge to al-Qaeda forces.

Throughout 2002 Bush ratcheted up the pressure against Iraq with a well-coordinated campaign of disinformation about Saddam's WMD program and links to al-Qaeda. Even though U.N. weapons inspector Hans Blix and the head of the International Atomic Energy Agency (IAEA), Mohamed el-Baradei, were reporting that Iraq was cooperating, albeit slowly, the Bush administration and U.S. media offered a relentless publicity campaign to urge war against Iraq. In November 2002 the U.N., in Resolution 1441, gave Iraq a final ultimatum either to comply with disarmament demands or face attack. The resolution, however, did not

An M1 Abrams Main Battle Tank crew prepares for a combat patrol in Ramadi, Iraq. Source: istock/Craig DeBourbon.

have an automatic trigger mechanism, and the U.N. was to meet again to vote on taking military action against Iraq. Thus, in February 2003 Secretary of State Colin Powell spoke before the U.N. Security Council, offering "facts" about Iraq's weapons program and aggressive intentions.

Powell's "facts," since discredited, were not convincing to most of the world even at the time. As the Bush administration was preparing for war, its only major ally was Britain. Fearing that intervention in Iraq would divert attention and resources from the issue of terrorism, worsen the Israeli-Palestinian issue, and potentially inflame the Arab and Muslim world, Germany, Russia, China, and especially France, as well as almost all the Middle East nations, were publicly critical of the rush to hostilities, and it was clear that the U.S. resolution to go to war against Iraq would not pass the Security Council without one or more vetoes.

Facing such opposition, the United States decided to forgo the U.N. vote and, on 20 March 2003, began an air campaign against Iraq to, as Bush put it, disarm Iraq of WMDs, end Saddam's support for terrorism, and liberate the Iraqi people. The invasion progressed rapidly, Baghdad fell, and Saddam went into hiding in early April. A few weeks later, on May 1, wearing a flight suit, President Bush landed aboard the USS *Abraham Lincoln* and, with a banner declaring "Mission Accomplished" behind him, declared a successful end to hostilities in Iraq.

The war, however, continued as Iraqi partisans—Saddam loyalists, Shiite militia, Sunnis fearing Shiite predominance, and possibly outside Islamist forces—began an insurgency against U.S. forces and their Iraqi allies that continues to this day. The rapid progress of the initial incursion was not surprising, given the overwhelming U.S. force employed and the apparent lack of desire to fight among Iraqi troops. However, the occupation would prove to be much more problematic. Prior to the invasion U.S. commanders, most notably Army Chief of Staff General Eric Shinseki, had warned that the U.S. force of about 100,000 troops would fall far short of requirements for an occupation, and he observed that several hundred thousand soldiers would be needed. Bush and Pentagon optimists such as Defense Secretary Donald Rumsfeld and his undersecretary, Paul Wolfowitz, publicly rebuked Shinseki and other military officials who warned about difficult days ahead and sanguinely concluded that the entire Iraq operation would be over in months.

By mid-2003, however, the insurgency was already a presence in most major Iraq cities, particularly Baghdad and Fallujah, and U.S. casualties began to increase. Still, Bush refused to send significant numbers of troops to Iraq, and the public perception of Iraq, optimistic since the invasion in March, began to dissipate. Meanwhile, Bush's rationales for war—WMDs, links between Saddam and bin Laden, charges of an Iraqi role in the terrorist attacks of September 2001—began to unravel as government officials and congressional investigations exposed and undermined the bases of intervention. By mid-2004, amid the presidential campaign, the country was split about evenly on the efficacy and prospects of the U.S. invasion and occupation of Iraq.

Bush was narrowly reelected that November, but events in Iraq began a swifter downward spiral by 2005. By that time administration claims that the insurgents were outside forces or isolated groups of disaffected Iraqis had been undermined, and U.S. troops were facing well-organized and popular militias and other armed groups. Still, Bush persisted in claiming that the war was going successfully and continued to defend the decision to invade, even as the evidence against WMDs, al-Qaeda, and other issues mounted. More Americans began to oppose the war, with a majority as of May 2007 holding the opinion that the war was a mistake and not going well.

By 2006 Iraq was often labeled a disaster by political figures and the media. In the elections of November 2006, the opposition Democratic Party made Iraq its main issue and shocked the political establishment by taking control of both the House of Representatives and Senate. Once in power in early 2007, the Democrats pushed resolutions to force Bush to establish a timeline for withdrawal, including a supplemental Defense spending bill that was vetoed, and a spending bill that linked reconstruction funding to progress on the part of Iraq's government.

More than four years into the war, more than three thousand Americans and perhaps hundreds of thousands of Iraqis, mostly civilians, have been killed. The insurgency rages, and daily attacks on government buildings, markets, and universities fill the news. Public opposition to the war has continued to grow, and U.S. prestige has fallen commensurately. And the war costs have mounted rapidly, with a total bill of one to two trillion dollars likely.

Although the Bush administration continues to seek "victory" in Iraq—for example, with a surge of twenty thousand troops in early 2007—fewer and fewer optimists remain. Sectarian violence, government disarray, rising protest in the United States, and mounting losses of lives and money have turned the Iraq invasion into perhaps the greatest disaster in U.S. foreign policy history. From the first serious U.S. involvement in Iraq after World War II to the most recent wars, the United States has pursued a path of intervention and aggression with little positive to show for it.

Robert Buzzanco

See also Foreign Policy after September 11, 2001, U.S.; Islamic Worldview; Middle East Peace Process

Further Reading

Bacevich, A. (2002). *American empire: The realities and consequences of U.S. diplomacy*. Cambridge, MA: Harvard University Press.

Baker, J.A., & Hamilton, L.H. (2006). *The Iraq study group report: The way forward—a new approach*. London: Vintage.

Bush, G. H. W. and Scowcroft, B. (1998) *A world transformed*, New York: Knopf.

Chatterjee, P. (2004). *Iraq inc: A profitable occupation*. New York: Seven Stories Press.

Johnson, C. (2004). *The sorrows of empire: Militarism, secrecy, and the end of the republic*. New York: Metropolitan Books.

Miller, T. C. (2006). *Blood money: Wasted billions, lost lives, and corporate greed in Iraq*. New York: Little, Brown and Company.

New York Times. (23 September 1990). Excerpts from Iraqi document on meeting with U.S. envoy. Retrieved May 25, 2007, from http://www.chss.montclair.edu/english/furr/glaspie.html

Ricks, T. (2006). *Fiasco: The American military adventure in Iraq*. New York: Penguin Press.

Islamic Worldview

The concept of *ummah* (the spiritual community of believers) is at the heart of Islamic culture. This sense of *ummah*, and how its clashes with Western culture, have influenced the Islamic worldview and opinions of the United States.

A worldview is an overall perspective from which one sees and interprets the world. This overall perspective is a collection of beliefs about life and the universe held by an individual or a group. A translation of the German word *weltanschauung*, the word *worldview* entered the English language in the mid-nineteenth century. Before the advent of modernity in Europe, all societies held a traditional worldview, in which God played a central role in humanity's self-conceptualization. However, in Western Europe the older view of the world was gradually jettisoned in favor of a materialistic conception of nature—that is, a conception of the world as apprehended through science, in which physical matter and its manifestations and processes were the only reality. Having made this transition, European civilization was able to distinguish, compare, and contrast the operative ideals of the two worldviews.

In the modern era, the theories of evolution and relativity came to hold the authority and exercise the influence that the Christian church had held and exercised in the medieval Christian world. This shift from a traditional way of looking at the world

and adoption of a new "story" of the origin and purpose of life led to a radical shift in how Western societies looked at the cosmos and humanity's place in it. Meanwhile, the rest of the world still held a traditional view of the world, in which the sole purpose of creation is to know its creator (God). The sociologist Peter Berger has called the opposition between these two worldviews a collision of consciousness between the modern and traditional.

The Relevance of the Islamic Worldview

The Islamic worldview is hostile to the materialism and anti-spiritualism that it associates with modernism. A foretaste of the modern world reached many parts of the Muslim world through colonialism. The general resentment the Muslim world feels toward the modernist worldview was in part a response to that colonialism. After World War II, most Muslim areas gradually became independent, but a vast majority of Muslims feel that the Muslim world continues to be ruled indirectly by the West. They feel the condescension of nineteenth-century British colonialism has merely given way to the contempt evident in U.S. foreign policy. The creation of Israel and the United States' unquestioned support for the new state, despite the plight of the Palestinians, is the most important factor in the negative image the Muslim world has of the United States. Almost all Muslims see Palestinian actions not as terrorism but as desperate and suicidal responses to Israel's state terrorism. Whereas this issue is seen by Western analysts as territorial, it is seen by many Muslims through a religious prism.

After the demise of the Soviet Union, the Western world began to see the Muslim world as its new enemy. This was in part due to the clash-of-civilizations thesis offered by scholars such as Bernard Lewis and Samuel Huntington. In the twelve years between the two Gulf Wars (1991–2003), the United States emerged as the world's sole superpower. The tremendous political unrest and increasing anti-American sentiment in the Muslim world led to the terrorist attacks of September 11, 2001. The Muslim world perceived the U.S. response to those attacks as a systematic assault on Islam. Many Muslims feel that U.S. supporters of Israel, whether members of the Christian Right or the U.S. Jewish community, have

LOVE U.S. HATE U.S.

The Love U.S. Hate U.S. website (www.loveushateus.com) is a global experiment. It provides an open forum where people from around the world can read, express, and discuss views on the United States. The following entry deals with 2008 U.S. presidential candidate Barack Obama and his experiences living in the Islamic world, and being an African-American. Obama was born to an American mother, and a Kenyan father, and as a child lived in Indonesia, which is nearly 90 percent Muslim.

I still think we can redeem America but it won't be with more of the same. I laugh at the Democrats who worry about Barack Obama not being seasoned enough. John Kerry had plenty of seasoning but it couldn't make up for his stumbling and bumbling in the public arena. And as for our current president and the decades of collective experience his advisors brought . . . well, we see where that's gotten us.

Whether America is willing to accept an inspirational candidate who by birth and upbringing straddles our racial divide and understands the Muslim world firsthand . . . well, that's another question.

A view from the Citadel of Old Cairo, Egypt, including the ancient Al-Azhar University and mosque. Source: istock/Adrian Beesley.

pushed U.S. foreign policy into a crusade against Islam. Gradually, the prediction of a clash of civilizations seems to be coming true. It is crucial that the Muslim world and the United States develop a deeper understanding of each other in order to build trust and avert or defuse that clash.

It is curious to note that economically and militarily the world's Muslim nations are, with certain exceptions, among the world's least powerful. The perceived threat the Muslim world poses to the West and the United States is out of proportion with its actual power. However, it is true that the Muslim world is replete with physical and human resources. There are some fifty-seven countries with majority Muslim populations, with Muslims living as populous minorities in many non-Muslim nations. The Muslim world also has the world's biggest oil reserves, which gives it strategic importance and is another reason for mutual Western-Muslim understanding.

Elements of the Islamic Worldview

Even though the economic and political structures of the world have become modern, in the sense that capitalism is the predominant economic system, the nation-state the predominant political form, and democracy and pluralism valued political goals, most of the Muslim world still remains traditional in its attitudes and outlook. Muslims believe that "there is nothing that has nothing to do with religion because there is nothing that has nothing to do with God," and thus religion is seen as a foundation for everything (Northbourne 2001, 1).

Muslims assert that the Muslims have remained truly Muslim, whereas many Christians have become secularized and are not particularly Christian. Muslims point out that shariah (Islamic law) is in active use in their daily lives in a way that comparative institutions no longer are in other religions. Shariah is derived from Islamic sources such as the Quran, hadith (sayings of the Prophet Muhammad), and the sunnah (the life of Prophet). The Quran is considered the word of God as revealed to the Prophet, and its exhortations play a major role in defining the nature of humanity and humanity's relationship with the universe. Similarly, the five pillars of the Islamic faith constitute religious rituals that Muslims practice on an hourly, daily, weekly, monthly, and annual basis. The five pillars are: first, the declaration of the oneness of God; second, the five daily prayers; third, fasting during the holy month of Ramadan; fourth, the hajj (pilgrimage to Mecca), to be performed at least once in the lifetime of those who have the capability of doing so; and fifth, the giving of alms to the poor. Although there are slight differences in the ways the different sects of Islam and different regions of the Muslim world practice these rituals, the Muslim worldview remains coherent and unified. It is through the practice of Muslim rituals that Muslims in Malaysia identify with Muslims in Scandinavia. Even though culturally and

ORGANIZATION OF THE ISLAMIC CONFERENCE (OIC) STATEMENT ON THE EVENTS OF SEPTEMBER 11, 2001

Following the bloody attacks against major buildings and installations in the United States yesterday, Tuesday, September 11, 2001, Dr. Abdelouahed Belkeziz, secretary-general of the 57-nation Organization of the Islamic Conference (OIC), stated that he was shocked and deeply saddened when he heard of those attacks which led to the death and injury of a very large number of innocent American citizens. Dr. Belkeziz said he was denouncing and condemning those criminal and brutal acts that ran counter to all covenants, humanitarian values and divine religions foremost among which was Islam.

"Our tolerant Islamic religion highly prizes the sanctity of human life and considers the willful killing of a single soul as tantamount to killing humanity at large," stated Dr. Belkeziz.

He added that on this sad occasion, he was asking the American President, Administration and people to accept his heartfelt condolences over the national catastrophe that befell their country. "The hand of severe justice should apprehend the perpetrators as soon as they have been identified with certainty," Dr. Belkeziz added.

The OIC secretary-general said that the Islamic world as a whole was sharing the pain and sorrow of the American people in this terrible and devastating ordeal. The Islamic world, he stressed, denounced and condemned the perpetrators while sympathizing with the innocent victims, their families, their beloved ones and the entire American people.

Dr. Belkeziz went on to say that the OIC had always been adamant in condemning terrorism. He added that everyone, everywhere, ought to stand most forcefully against such practices committed by those who aim at shaking the democratic system which the American people unanimously embraced through the use of innocent victims as a means to impose their views and achieve their aims.

The secretary-general said that, in a message of condolences to US President George W. Bush, he condemned and denounced the incidents.

In his message, Dr. Belkeziz asked President Bush to accept his condolences for the victims of those savage acts.

Source: Organization of the Islamic Conference. (2001, September 12). Events that took place in the United States of America. Retrieved May 25, 2007, from http://www.oic-un.org/pr/2001/96.html

---

geographically many such Muslims are worlds apart, adherence to the rituals of Islam integrates them into a spiritual community of believers known as the Muslim *ummah*.

The concept of *ummah* is at the heart of the collective identity of Muslims. The *ummah* is considered by Muslims an organic whole. If one part of the *ummah* is suffering, Muslims assert, the other parts cannot be happy. After independence from colonial rule, the Muslim world became divided into economic and national units that were too small to effect a positive change in their predicament, bringing about fragmentation in the economy and politics of the Muslim *ummah*.

Diversity in Islamic Worldview

Multiplicity within the Muslim world should be approached with caution. Western analysts often make the mistake of treating that diversity in the light of the West's own experiences of diversity. The Christian Reformation created a deeper schism in the Western worldview than the various divisions in Islam have created, however: The Shiite and Sunni streams of Islam and their substreams and offshoots are still much more unified than are the numerous Protestant, Roman Catholic, and the Eastern Orthodox denominations in Christianity. Similarly, while the

post-Christian worldview of the nineteenth and twentieth centuries stressed the diversity, transitory nature, and dynamism of phenomena, the Islamic worldview emphasizes oneness because of the principle of the oneness of God. Timelessness is still very much a part and parcel of traditional Muslims' way of life, even though they operate in a world that is being radically transformed by the forces of modernism. Moreover, national consciousness within Muslim nations has not replaced the Islamic worldview; it has only strengthened it.

The Islamic World's Relations with the West

While Muslim regions have either sought modernization voluntarily or have had modernization forced upon them during colonialism, contemporary Muslims' drive toward modernization is not for the sake of modernity. On the contrary, it is to safeguard their identity: In order to defend themselves, Muslim nations must develop industrially, which requires modernization. Muslims have resisted modernism in both its Communist-atheistic form and its Western secular form. The fact that nations in the Muslim world have forged alliances with the United States does not mean that there is a consensus on basic values and outlook on life; from the

point of view of the Muslim nations, those alliances are merely to fulfill strategic imperatives.

The U.S. policy of supporting U.S.-friendly dictators in the Muslim world has led to suppression of democracy on the one hand and to anti-American sentiment on the other. Shortly before stepping down from the presidency of Malaysia, Mahathir Mohamad expressed the resentment of the whole Muslim community at the tenth summit of the Organization of the Islamic Conference (OIC), which was held in October 2003 in Kuala Lumpur, Malaysia. Mahathir said, "Today, we, the whole Muslim *ummah,* are treated with contempt and dishonor. Our religion is denigrated. Our holy places are desecrated. Our countries are occupied. Our people starved and killed. Today, if they want to raid our country, kill our people, destroy our villages and towns, there is nothing substantial that we can do" (Irshad 2003, 86). In the quote above, *they* refers to the West and particularly to the United States.

Many voices within the West and the Muslim world have asked for a dialogue. President Mohammad Khatami of Iran convinced the United Nations to declare the first year of the second Christian millennium as the year of dialogue of civilizations. The chances of genuine, substantive dialogue seem tenuous, however, due to the enormous disparity in political power between the Muslim world and the West, especially the United States.

Some Western scholars have suggested that Muslim nations have not modernized because they have failed to conceive of Protestant-style reform in Islam. Muslim scholars who have accepted that position have become the darlings of Western proponents of the view. However, while on the surface Islam seems to accommodate modernity, many Muslims feel that if Islam is to remain Islam—that is, if it is to take the Quran as the source of its law and hold the Prophet Muhammad as its exemplar—then modernism must be rejected. Most Muslims believe that modernism, as championed by the United States, increases distributive injustice within and among nations. The U.S. government, U.S. corporations, and certain agencies are seen as a morally corrupt forces that want to lift all ethical fetters on social, political, and economic life. Muslims see the modern world system as antispiritual and antithetical to the spirit of justice that is considered central in the message of Islam. Perhaps, if the modern world changes the conditions of modernity and embraces justice, it may be possible to avert the clash of worldviews.

Ejaz Akram

See also Iraq Wars; Middle East Peace Process

Further Reading:

Hossein Nasr, S. (2003). *Heart of Islam: Enduring values for humanity.* San Francisco: Harper.

Hossein Nasr, S. (1990). *Traditional Islam in the modern world.* London: KPI.

Irshad, M. (2003). Mahathir's call to awaken the Muslim Ummah. *Defence Journal, 7*(4), 84–88.

Naugle, D. K. (2002). *Worldview: The history of a concept.* Grand Rapids, MI: Eerdsmans.

Northbourne, L. (2001). *Religion in the modern world.* Ghent, NY: Sophia Perennis et Universalis.

Schuon, F. (1963). *Understanding Islam.* London: Allen & Unwin.

Leadership Models

The explosion of multinational firms has encouraged the widespread use of U.S.-based business leadership models. These formulaic approaches to leadership changed how businesses around the world were formed.

There are many different types of leadership, from political to spiritual to communal. This article focuses on models of leadership in business. As U.S. businesses have grown into multinational, global enterprises, their influence on other countries has become increasingly pervasive. Business is a driver of public policy, educational excellence, and social values. Business expansion increasingly creates global cultural convergence, interconnected economics, and interdependent political strategies. American business leadership models such as those discussed in this article, therefore, are a critical determiner of how the U.S. is perceived around the world.

Two of the most important contributions of the United States to leadership technology during the twentieth century were T-groups and total quality management (TQM). T-groups, better known as "sensitivity training groups" or "encounter groups," were an innovation in the technology of education and personal development. TQM, also known as "total quality control" (TQC) and "continuous quality improvement" (CQI), was an innovation in management technology.

Shift in Leadership Focus

From the mid-1800s through the early part of the twentieth century, "people tended to think of the world as being divided into 'leaders and followers'" (Tannenbaum, Weschler, and Massarik 1961, 68). The emergence of the field of human relations and the behavioral sciences shifted the focus from the "behavior of individuals to the behavior of individuals within organizational settings" (Tannenbaum, Margulies, and Massarik 1985, 1). Until the 1930s "very few businessmen in positions of responsibility had received any formal education in management" (Urwick 1961, 417–418). The concept of "getting things done through people" (Urwick 1961, 421) emerged gradually throughout the twentieth century. Sensitivity training and the "quality movement" encouraged the paradigm shift from the "leader to the follower as the important actor" and from "the individual to the group as the action unit" (Bradford, Gibb, and Benne 1964, 17) in organizational settings. T-groups and TQM helped to mature management thought and encouraged dialogue on leadership as an increasingly participatory relationship.

Sensitivity Training in the Twentieth Century

Sensitivity training emerged in the United States in the late 1940s and continued to provide a framework for understanding and improving human behavior in groups during the social movements and business transformations that occurred from the 1960s through the 1990s. The National Training Laboratories (NTL) was the crucible from which sensitivity training emerged. NTL provided a "temporary residential community...dedicated to the stimulation and support of experimental learning and change [that] multiplied across America and abroad" (Bradford, Gibb, and Benne 1964, 3) in the 1960s.

Sensitivity training was a "phenomenon in which individuals participated as learners...[who] studied their own behavior" (Bradford, Gibb, and Benne 1964, 1–2) and became sensitized to multiple forms of feedback from within themselves and from group members. By locating people in a neutral laboratory setting away from their place of work, T-groups established a new process of inquiry. Experienced in small group dynamics, the laboratory trainers focused participants on the "here and now" and on "learning how to learn" (Bradford, Gibb, and Benne 1964, 19) through group participation and interaction. The trainer was vital both for providing the in-laboratory training and for enabling the process of transferring what was learned in the laboratory setting back to the work environment.

Sensitivity-training concepts were pioneered by Kenneth Benne (1948), Leland Bradford (1948), Kurt Lewin (1948), Ron Lippitt (1949) and others and later institutionalized through the scholarship and practice of Chris Argyris (1962), Carl Rogers (1961), Abraham Maslow (1962), Rensis Likert (1961), Edgar Schein, Warren Bennis (1965), and others. The *Journal of Applied Behavioral Science* published much of the early works of these scholar-practitioners.

Continuous Learning Paradigm

As fair employment practices and global competition opened up the modern workplace to a more diverse workforce, sensitivity training was effective in helping people to make the adjustment

from a relatively stable business environment to what became a radically different business model. T-groups integrated "the previously separate functions of action, research, and education in order to support a continuous learning paradigm throughout adult life" (Bradford, Gibb, and Benne 1964, 5). TQM focused on continuous quality improvement through the development of a mental attitude of readiness for continuous learning and change. In the T-group structure each participant "self-reflected on their personal process of learning and involved group members in that process" (Bradford, Gibb, and Benne 1964, 18). Participants formed a "reciprocal relationship" (Bradford, Gibb, and Benne 1964, 19) that fostered mutual learning and growth. TQM emphasized practicing teamwork, learning and working together, and improving communications between management and employees.

Sensitivity Training in the Twenty-first Century

Sensitivity training was the "legitimate and indispensable ancestor to all subsequent experiential techniques" (Vaill 1985, 561). "Process analysis and team building [were] outgrowths of T-Groups" (Lundberg and Bowen 1993, 10), while the "collaborative inquiry" and "environmental consciousness" movements of the 1990s were largely "'re-labeling' of T-Group values" (Lundberg and Bowen 1993, 13). Sensitivity training now often concerns itself with issues of "equity and social justice" (Howard 1999, 31), and many of the names from the early days of sensitivity training are today's leadership scholars.

Trusting the process was sensitivity training's "great insight into human dynamics" (Vaill 1985, 562). The belief "trust the process" (Vaill 1985, 561) was at the core of sensitivity training in the 1960s and was reborn in the continuous process improvement initiatives of TQM in the 1980s and 1990s.

Quality Movement in the Twentieth Century

"Total quality management and other continuous quality improvement programs were among the earliest process-oriented changes shared worldwide" (Parker 1998, 573). The concept and practice of quality control began in the United States in the 1940s but are "usually traced back to the visits of Deming and Juran to Japan in 1950 to assist in the process of industrial reconstruction after World War II" (Ghobadian and Speller 1994, 2). W. Edwards Deming (1900–1994) is associated with statistical process control, but he was also concerned with the human side of the business. Many of the

tenets in his leadership and management principles addressed human interrelationships. Joseph Juran defined quality as "fitness for use," emphasized a customer-led approach in the judging of quality, and believed, like Deming, that "most quality problems are due to management" (Ghobadian and Speller 1994, 3). Principles such as taking the long view, using decisions made by employees in the context of the work, using facts and data, and reducing variation were all part of what came to be called the "quality movement." Metrics "on performance, reliability, price, on-time delivery service and accuracy" (Smith and Fingar 2003, 145) provided the feedback that informed the measurement of quality.

TQM: Bridge between Leadership and Management

TQM is a business mind-set, an organizational philosophy, and a bridge between leadership and management theory and practice. As a business mind-set, TQM "seeks to ensure that every aspect of the organization is controlled, monitored, and directed toward corporate aims" (Webley and Cartwright 1996, 484). TQM is an organizational philosophy of looking for "continuous and ongoing improvement" (Webley and Cartwright 1996, 484). TQM bridges leadership and management by combining the motivation and inspiration of leadership and the statistical controls of management. The TQM movement was implemented through leadership skills, such as open communications, employee inspiration, and goal setting, and management practices, such as "Pareto analysis, histograms, and process flow charting to control processes" (Ghobadian and Speller 1994, 63). "Nine psychological processes [were found] to underlie TQM: identification, equity, equality, consensus, instrumentality, rationality, development, group dynamics, and internalization" (Webley and Cartwright 1996, 1). Many of these psychological processes parallel what would be uncovered in an analysis of sensitivity training processes.

TQM and the United States—A Perspective

Deming was in his fifties when he introduced the Japanese to statistical process control and the principles of quality management, but not until he was in his eighties was TQM widely accepted by U.S. businesses. The value of TQM was recognized in the United States only when it was discovered to be an important "competitive weapon in the free-market system" (Ghobadian and Speller 1994, 53). "The rapid pace of globalization called leaders to find ways to accomplish work faster, cheaper, better" (Parker

1998, 145). As customers demanded more quality in goods and services and lower prices, the market demanded ever-increasing productivity. The dramatic growth of Japanese industry through its employment of continuous improvement techniques drew U.S. business toward TQM.

"Orientation to the group is one of several core beliefs among Japanese businessmen" (Parker 1998, 125). Maasaki Imai (1986) believed that this group orientation was the main differentiator between Japanese and U.S. business practices. He used a simple example like the adoption of the employee suggestion system to illustrate what he saw as a profound difference between Japanese and U.S. approaches to business management.

The employee suggestion system was "an idea that was introduced in Japan by the U.S. Air Force" (Imai 1986, 112) as TQM was beginning to yield profits for Japanese businesses. The suggestion system in Japan was process-focused and emphasized employee participation. Suggestions became a sign for management that "a worker had more skill than a job called for" (Imai 1986, 113), and thus submitting suggestions became a self-motivating activity. Japanese employees submitted millions of suggestions for improvement in order to yield the most business value for their group.

According to Imai, when the suggestion system was adopted back in the United States as a part of the adoption of TQM, it became an activity that emphasized only economic benefits and was results-focused. Imai used this example to highlight what he called the "Western manager's almost exclusive concern with the cost of change and its economic impact" (Imai 1986, 114). Imai believed this to be a major difference between Japanese and U.S. management practices. He argued that the preference for acting independently was reflective of North American individualism. He suggested that the focus on results, not process, was why TQM took so long to be internalized into U.S. business cultures.

Total Quality Management in the Twenty-first Century

Although TQM took more than thirty years to make its way back from Japan to the United States, process improvement has become a mantra in twenty-first-century U.S. businesses. The focus on how work is done (the process) that the quality movement introduced is still creating important shifts in the way business is conducted in the United States. What is being called the "third wave" or "Business Process Management" (Smith and Fingar 2003, 1) is expected to revolutionize global business at a level equivalent to the change that came with the introduction of the relational database to information management practices. Other recent evolutions of TQM are "Six Sigma . . . statistical constructs that measure how far

a process deviates from perfection" (Smith and Fingar 2003, 145) and the concept of a "just-in-time" or "lean" production system, in which processes are optimized to eliminate waste. Lean production processes are triggered by "customer pull" and characterized by the "shortest possible production lead time, which allows the company to respond to the fluctuating orders from the market" (Imai 1986, 27). The "bottom line" of quality control fits well into lean manufacturing principles by which empowered knowledge workers collaborate in self-managed teams and "trust the process" of working together.

Creation of a Participatory Work Environment

Sensitivity training played an important role in creating a work environment in which trust and open communications could foster collaborative work groups. Group learning experiences during the 1960s and 1970s institutionalized the idea of feedback and group process that in some important ways enabled TQM to thrive in the 1980s. T-groups established an innovative process of group inquiry developed by educators and sociologists, and TQM established a revolutionary process of continuous quality improvement through effective team interactions in a business context. T-groups and TQM are leadership models that focused on the role of the individual in the context of the group and together helped to foster more participatory and productive work environments within U.S. organizations.

Parker argued, "Workers, worldwide, are now increasingly viewed as sources of knowledge" (Parker 1998, 314). The trend toward more participatory forms of leadership theory and practice suggests that North American businesses view people working in teams as the productivity engine of the twenty-first century. However, what might we discover if we adopted a more global perspective and asked a more global question: To what extent are North American leadership models accepted and effective in other cultures? And how does that acceptance, or the lack thereof, affect perceptions of the United States? Hofstede and Peterson (2000) questioned the assumption of the universality of Western management theory by raising the question of whether U.S. theories apply abroad. In 1993, partly in response to Hofstede's (1980) seminal work, the Global Leadership and Organizational Behavior Effectiveness (GLOBE) Research Project set out to understand the "extent to which specific leadership attributes and behaviors are universally endorsed . . . and the extent to which the endorsement of leader attributes and behaviors is culturally contingent" (House, Hanges, Javidan, Dorfman, and Gupta 2004, 2). In this ongoing research project, scholars and practitioners from sixty-one cultures across the globe are examining the interplay of leadership and context in an attempt to understand the "impact of cultural variables on leadership and organizational processes" (House et al. 2004, 2). The GLOBE research highlights the complexity of this issue and the increasing importance of cross-cultural and worldwide research to the field of leadership scholarship and practice. Understanding how U.S. leadership theories and practices "play" in other cultural contexts is a step toward understanding how U.S. culture is perceived. Looking at cultures by "clustering" nations based on work-related similarities may provide a way to understand worker attitudes and values in relationship to leadership dimensions. Nations that cluster culturally with the United States (Anglo cluster) may more easily accept U.S.-born leadership models than would countries in the Arab cultures cluster, for example. The explosion of multinational firms since the 1980s adds to this complex dynamic and is an increasing force for global cultural convergence. Any cross-cultural contributions that stem from the twenty-first-century U.S. leadership models that were known as "T-groups" and "TQM" will continue to be assessed within this global world of the twenty-first century.

As the world watches the behaviors in the U.S. business culture, perceptions are formed and, inevitably, are more broadly applied to the culture of the U.S. in general. Ethical, collaborative, and inclusive models of business leadership reflect a society that honors those same values. The behaviors that stem from T-Groups and TQM disciplines are based on a "working together" paradigm that is essential for creating and sustaining positive human relationships in an increasingly interconnected world.

Miriam Grace and Leon F. "Skip" Rowland

See also Businesses Overseas, U.S.;
Multinational Corporations

Further Reading

Argyris, C. (1962). *Interpersonal competence and organizational effectiveness.* Homewood, IL: Dorsey Press.

Ashkanasy, N. M., Wilderom, C.P.M., & Peterson, M. F. (Eds.). (2000). *Handbook of organizational culture and climate* (pp. 401-416). Thousand Oaks, CA: Sage.

Benne, K. D. (1948). Principles of training method. *The Group, 10*(2), 17.

Bradford, L. P. (1948). Human relations training. *The Group, 10*(2), 7–8.

Bradford, L. P., Gibb, J. R., & Benne, K. D. (Eds.). (1964). *T-group theory and laboratory method: Innovation in re-education.* New York: Wiley & Sons.

Delbeco, A. L. (1970, January). Sensitivity training. *Training and Development Journal, 24*(1), 32–35.

Deming, W. E. (1982). *Quality, productivity, and competitive position.* Cambridge, MA: Massachusetts Institute of Technology, Center for Advanced Engineering Study.

Deming, W. E. (1986). *Out of the crisis.* Cambridge, MA: Massachusetts Institute of Technology, Center for Advanced Engineering Study.

Fisher, A. B. (1993, May 31). Japanese workingwomen strike back. *Fortune, 127*(11), 22.

Ghobadian, A., & Speller, S. (1994, May). Gurus of quality: A framework for comparison. *Total Quality Management, 5*(3), 53–70.

Hofstede, G. (1980). *Culture's consequences: International differences in work-related values.* Beverly Hills, CA: Sage.

Hofstede, G., & Peterson, M. F. (2000). Culture: National values and organizational practices. In R. J. House, P. J. Hanges, M. Javidan, P. W. Dorfman, & V. Gupta (Eds.). (2004). *Culture, leadership, and organizations: The GLOBE study of 62 societies.* Thousand Oaks, CA: Sage.

House, R. J., Hanges P. J., Javidan, M., Dorfman, P. W., & Gupta, V. (Eds.). (2004). *Culture, leadership, and organizations: The GLOBE study of 62 societies.* Thousand Oaks, CA: Sage Publications.

Howard, G. R. (1998). *We can't teach what we don't know: White teachers, multiracial schools.* New York: Teachers College Press.

Imai, M. (1986). *Kaizen: The key to Japan's competitive success.* New York: McGraw-Hill.

Juran, J. M. (1989). *Juran on leadership for quality.* New York: Free Press.

Lewin, K., & Lewin, G. W. (1948). *Resolving social conflicts, selected papers on group dynamics (1936–1946).* New York: Harper.

Likert, R. (1961). *New patterns of management.* New York: McGraw-Hill.

Lippitt, R. (1949). *Training in community relations.* New York: Harper & Brothers.

Lippitt, G. L., & This, L. E. (1980, June). Leaders for laboratory training. *Training and Development Journal, 34*(6), 56–65.

Lundberg, C. C., & Bowen, D. D. (1993). Iphigenia; or on the fate of T-Groups. *Journal of Organizational Change Management, 6*(5), 7–14.

Maslow, A. (1962). *Towards a psychology of being.* New York: Van Nostrand.

McFarland, L. J., Senen, S., & Childress, J. R. (1993). *Twenty-first-century leadership.* New York: Leadership Press.

McMurtrie, R., & Gupta, N. (2003, April). Quality: The timeless quest. *Engineering Management, 13*(2), 22–25.

Parker, B. (1998). *Globalization and business practice: Managing across boundaries.* Thousand Oaks, CA: Sage.

Rogers, C. (1961). *On becoming a person.* Boston: Houghton Mifflin.

Ronen, S., & Shenkar, O. (1985). Clustering countries on attitudinal dimensions: A review and synthesis. *Academy of Management Review, 10*(3), 435–454.

Schein, E. H., & Bennis, W. G. (1965). *Personal and organizational change through group methods: The laboratory approach.* New York: Wiley.

Smith, P., & Fingar, P. (2003). *Business process management: The third wave.* Tampa, FL: Meghan-Kiffer Press.

Tannenbaum, R., Margulies, N., & Massarik, F. (Eds.). (1985). *Human systems development: New perspectives on people and organizations.* San Francisco: Jossey-Bass.

Tannenbaum, R., Weschler, I. R., & Massarik, F. (Eds.). (1961). *Leadership and organization: A behavioral science approach.* New York: McGraw-Hill.

Urwick, L. F. (1961). Management and human relations. In R. Tannenbaum, I. R. Weschler, & F. Massarik (Eds.), *Leadership and organization: A behavioral science approach* (pp. 416-428). New York: McGraw-Hill.

Vaill, P. (1985). Integrating the diverse directions of behavioral sciences. In R. Tannenbaum, N. Margulies, & F. Massarik (Eds.), *Human systems development: New perspectives on people and organizations* (pp. 547–577). San Francisco: Jossey-Bass.

Walton, M. (1986). *The Deming management method.* New York: Putnam Publishers.

Webley, P., & Cartwright, J. (1996, December). The implicit psychology of TQM. *Total Quality Management, 7*(5), 483–493.

Linguistic Imperialism and English

Despite the widespread political distaste for the United States and the United Kingdom that has grown over the centuries, English has remained, and will likely continue to dominate, as a global language, at least for the next century.

English is the official language or among the official languages in more than twenty-five countries. This linguistic dominance came about mainly as the result of the British Empire's colonization. The expression, "The sun never sets on the British Empire," indicates that Britain once occupied countries in all hemispheres. However, the United States since its inception has also been responsible for the further diffusion of the English language, especially in the twentieth and twenty-first centuries.

Spread of English by Imperialistic Britain

Not so long ago English was not the global language. During Shakespeare's time only a few million people spoke English, and those speakers lived primarily in England. The language was not even very important to the rest of Europe. In fact, French was the language to know beginning with the Norman Conquest of England in 1066 led by William I, duke of Normandy in France. During this period the English language was superceded by French as the language of culture, and English was much influenced by French.

After the Norman Conquest intercourse with Europe in politics and trade grew and hastened England's rise as a major European power. However, French remained the language of choice and of culture. As a major power Britain developed a fierce rivalry with its former conqueror, France, in conquering, occupying, and influencing vulnerable nations. Their fiercest competition took place on the continent of Africa, which was endowed with natural resources, including diamonds, ivory, gold, oil, and natural gas. Like the French, the British required the colonized indigenous people to learn the language of the colonizer and not the other way around. This policy made things convenient for the British in the long run, but the British would come to frown on the many dialects and accents that developed in English. Even today the British, in broadcasting and other media, work tirelessly to spread British English with completely different pronunciation and spelling from the English of the United States. Through its

sheer economic and military superiority, the United States works even harder to spread its version of English or "American." English, despite its different accents and spellings, binds the United States and the United Kingdom as closely as any loving parent and child despite a role reversal from past years.

Imposition of English by Imperialistic United States

Although the United States was the only British colony to have actually fought and won a war against the British—with the help of the French—the United States embraced the English language. However, as the United States developed, it introduced into the language its own words, which even the British, although initially resistant, have come to use in many cases.

The United States, even in its infancy, produced some of the world's greatest scholars in the English language, including the framers of the Constitution and the Bill of Rights. Americans' love and mastery of the English language were evident in the writing of early American literary geniuses such as Edgar Allan Poe, Henry David Thoreau, Nathaniel Hawthorne, Washington Irving, and Mark Twain (Samuel Langhorne Clemens). In the twentieth century the United States continued producing great writers such as John Steinbeck, Ernest Hemingway, William Faulkner, and Toni Morrison as well as great orators like Dr. Martin Luther King Jr., John F. Kennedy, and Robert F. Kennedy.

U.S. writers and other English-language writers are read worldwide more than writers in any other language. Since translation often loses important meaning, many books and other printed materials are left in their original English. Some of the world's most important international documents, including those of the Geneva Convention and those establishing the United Nations, were originally composed in English as well as French and Russian.

Impact of U.S. Media on the World

The media in English have had an even greater impact on the world than has literature in English. After World War II the number

of nonnative English speakers learning and working in English skyrocketed. The publisher of *Life* magazine reaped the rewards of international subscriptions for years. The *International Herald Tribune*, the *Wall Street Journal*, and *Time* and *Newsweek* magazines can be found on newsstands in most major capitals. British publications such as the *Financial Times*, the *Economist*, and many other English-language publications are available worldwide. Scientists and adventurers around the world read *National Geographic*. Their international medical counterparts read the *Journal of the American Medical Association*.

Although print publications in English, as well as radio news broadcasts in English, which increased during World War II, have been common for years, the advent of international satellite and cable television, led by the Cable News Network (CNN) of the United States, has had a greater influence on diffusing the English language. Studies show that many people speaking limited English improved their English by listening to CNN or the British Broadcasting Corporation (BBC). International journalists rely on U.S. and British national news agencies such as United Press

International and Reuters News for their stories. Most journalists in non-English-speaking countries are required to know English at an advanced level. Many foreign news agencies have formed alliances with English-language news agencies.

U.S. motion pictures have had an even greater impact on diffusing the English language in the global community. Even though some countries such as Italy, Spain, and France often dub over foreign films, including English-language films, a large number of countries use subtitles, and the viewing audiences get to hear the films in their original language. Subtitles are also widely used in foreign language teaching; thus, students hear the language in its original form while reading it to make sure their understanding is correct. In Holland, Denmark, Switzerland, and Norway English-language films are rarely dubbed or subtitled. In these countries children start studying English at an early age, and most speak it fluently by their teenage years.

Much of the revenue of Hollywood's billion-dollar movie industry comes from audiences outside the United States. Many of the movies are seen in their original English-language versions.

FRENCH FURY OVER ENGLISH LANGUAGE

This article from 8 February 2007 explores the loss of identity felt by residents of France who feel that their national language is losing importance as English becomes the language of business and government.

French pressure groups have demanded an end to the dominance of the English language in business in France.

A group of trades unions and language lobbyists say the French language is being reduced to a local dialect.

They have organized a press conference in parliament to demand the right to work solely in French.

One campaigner has dubbed the battle to preserve the supremacy of the French language as a fight against "linguistic hegemony" of English.

"We can no longer tolerate this," said Albert Salon, president of the French-speaking campaigning group, Forum Francophone International.

"We are not against influences of one language by another, or the occasional borrowing of words, but now there is a wholesale substitution of the French language for English."

English E-mails

He said in many companies it had become standard practice for native French speakers to use English even among themselves and French scientists were forced to publish their research, in English, in leading U.S. journals.

"We have nothing against the Brits or the Americans," Mr Salon said.

"But we simply cannot accept that our language is reduced to a local dialect—we are protesting against this linguistic hegemony!."

A recent survey showed that seven percent of French firms used English as their main language and multinational companies often sent e-mails in English to their French employees.

But Pierre Kosciusko-Morizet, CEO and founder of French site Priceminister.com, accepts that having English as a global business language enables him to converse with foreign colleagues in a common tongue.

"Some things are facts and you can't fight against them," Mr Kosciusko-Morizet said.

"We can promote French but I don't see very efficient ways of fighting English. English didn't become the global language of business by fighting other languages," he added.

The BBC's Caroline Wyatt, in Paris, says that President Jacques Chirac is one of the most ardent supporters of those who wish to protect the French language—he once walked out of a meeting in Brussels when a Frenchman began his speech in English.

Source: BBC News. (2007). French fury over English language. Retrieved March 20, 2007, from http://news.bbc.co.uk/2/hi/europe/6341795.stm

A sign in English and Arabic warning of radiation hazards at a captured Iraqi compound. Source: istock/ Craig DeBourbon.

Impact of the Rise of the United States as an Economic Power

Notwithstanding the impact that U.S. literature, U.S. news media, and the U.S. film industry have had on the diffusing of English as the global language, the U.S. economy, led by the military, continues to be the most powerful diffuser of the English language throughout the world. The United States played a major role in World War I, but its success with the Allies in World War II brought the United States to the world stage as a major player. The country was loved by much of the world, especially by the western Europeans who saw the young country as the great liberator. The U.S. military grew by leaps and bounds, and military bases were set up around the world from Japan to Germany to Italy and places in between.

Through the Marshall Plan (European Recovery Program), named for U.S. secretary of state George C. Marshall, the United States poured massive amounts of aid into the rebuilding of western Europe. All documents relating to this aid plan were written in U.S. English. However, where necessary, translations into other languages were made.

Boeing, McDonnell Douglas, and Northrop of the United States were—and to a large extent continue to be—the biggest builders of military and civilian aircraft in the world. All instructions for such aircraft are written in English; the countries buying the aircraft add some translations on commercial flights for their passengers. All flight instructions in all countries are given and received in English. All personnel of commercial airlines should be fluent in English.

The role of the United States in Asia increased with its involvement in the Korean War and the Vietnam War, as well as with the presence of many U.S. military and civilian personnel in Japan. The United States was also involved in writing the constitution of Japan. Thus, as the influence and presence of the United States increased around the world, so did the spread of the English language. Americans perfected a tradition of the French and British during their colonial days: Do not learn the language of the conquered people but instead require the conquered people to learn the language of the conqueror.

English: A Blessing and a Curse

Today English speakers have an advantage when they travel, when they watch a movie, or when they want to read that best-selling Italian or Japanese author. English speakers can enjoy most anything they want because if it wasn't originally written or filmed in English, it will be interpreted or translated into English. We can travel easily because everybody else speaks English, even in Timbuktu and remote areas of China.

This nonchalant attitude of English speakers, particularly Americans and British, is seen as arrogance in many parts of the world, particularly in countries such as France, Germany, Russia, and even Japan, a major U.S. trading partner. Americans' lack of knowledge of foreign languages prompted the late Senator Paul

Simon of Illinois to write *The Tongue-Tied America: Confronting the Foreign Language Crisis* in 1980. Senator Simon gave a tongue-lashing to fellow Americans who speak only English. He believed that our lack of knowledge of other languages causes the United States to lose billions of dollars in business simply because Americans cannot clearly communicate with other sellers and buyers. Simon felt that foreign language study should be a major part of the curriculum in U.S. education from grade school through college.

Through their evolution from old English to middle English and finally to modern English, words and usage have become simplified and flexible. For example, without inflections, the same word can function as many parts of speech. *Swim, drink, walk, kiss, look,* and *smile* can be used as both nouns and verbs. Because of the loss of inflections and its simplicity of form, English is easier to grasp initially than are most other modern languages. The English language freely admits words from other languages. Because it is possible in English writing and speaking to omit prepositions and other parts of speech without changing the meaning, English can be written and spoken in concise sentences. A paragraph conveying the same meaning in Italian is almost twice as long as the same paragraph in English. With the borrowing of words and phrases from other languages and the introduction of technological and business words almost daily, particularly by the United States, the vocabulary in the English language has grown by leaps and bounds in the last century.

TEN MOST AWARDED LANGUAGES FOR NOBEL PRIZE IN LITERATURE (1901–2006)

LANGUAGE	NUMBER OF LAUREATES	PERCENTAGE
English	26	25.00
French	13	12.50
German	12	11.54
Spanish	10	9.62
Italian	6	5.77
Swedish	6	5.77
Russian	5	4.81
Polish	4	3.80
Danish	3	2.88
Norwegian	3	2.88

English Rules

Foreign students of English often complain that English has too many exceptions to rules, and others complain that English *has* no rules. The German political philosopher Karl Marx, who with Friedrich Engels wrote the *Communist Manifesto,* lived in London from 1849 until his death in 1883. When asked how he learned and spoke English so well, Marx, in essence, responded that you just have to learn it by memory and know it. So there you have it. Nothing can explain why this seemingly easy language is actually difficult. There is a saying that German is difficult initially but becomes easier as one continues studying, whereas the reverse is true of English. Many foreigners easily learn basic English, but few progress above the intermediate level unless they apply themselves diligently through continued study, including living in English-speaking countries.

Future of English as the Global Language

Great Britain's dominance as a colonial power and the later rise of the United States as an economic and military power were the major forces that made English the global language. Even as other countries increasingly disapprove of the foreign policies of both the United States and the United Kingdom, English will continue to be the global language for at least the next century. After all, it is the language of business, technology (including the Internet), aviation, sports, the news media and films, or, more simply, the language of money.

Marine N. Stewart

See also Diffusion of Knowledge, Global; Empire, U.S.; Imperialism, U.S.

Further Reading

English—An international language for science? (1967, December 26). *The Information Scientist,* pp. 19–20. Retrieved April 16, 2007, from http://www.garfield.library.upenn.edu/essays/V1p019y1962-73.pdf

JIJUMA International Language Center. (1992–2004). *Collected English language materials.* Rome and Los Angeles: Author.

Schultz, R. (2005). English—The international language. Retrieved April 16, 2007, from http://www.sk.com.br/sk-ingl.html

Simon, P. (1980). *The tongue-tied American: Confronting the foreign language crisis.* New York: Continuum Publishing.

Soars, J., & Soars, L. (1990). *Headway student's book, upper-intermediate.* Oxford, UK: Oxford University Press.

Mass Media— Concepts and Technologies

In the absence of direct or personal contact with other cultures, mass media images and the presence of media form the basis of other cultures' perceptions of the United States, however accurate they may or may not be.

Winston Churchill once said, "A lie gets halfway around the world before the truth has a chance to get its pants on." But when Churchill uttered those words, it took a lie a much longer time to get halfway around the world. Our conception of the world has been radically altered by the acceleration and adoption of communication technology in the intervening years.

Less than two hundred years ago global communication was limited to the speed of the messenger. Today, locomotion (the act of moving from place to place) emphasizes transmission (the conveying of data). The relationship of transmitter to transmission, of person to process, and geography to data has been fundamentally altered. The media theorist Marshall McLuhan said that "with the creation of any new medium or technology a new environment is also created" (McLuhan 1962, introduction). Today's media environment is global in scope. Media content, forms, and economics have all been globalized, with a concomitant effect on perception, interaction, and place attachment.

Classification and Reach of Mass Media

One can divide media into three categories: mass media, micromedia, and convergent media. Mass media are channels of communication targeted at large heterogeneous and geographically disbursed audiences; they include newspapers, books, magazines, radio, television, movies, and the World Wide Web. Generally, acts of communication through mass media lack the opportunity for immediate feedback.

Micromedia are interactive technologies used for point-to-point or interpersonal communication in which the action of the user generates a response from either another human being or a computer program at the other end of the media connection. Examples include telephones, fax machines, and e-mail.

Convergent media are those in which one medium functions as a platform for other media functions, content, or both. For example, the Internet can serve as a platform for telephonic communication and for radio or television transmission, and

mobile phones (cell phones) can function for distribution of text or photos.

Push and Pull

In *Being Digital* Nicholas Negroponte (1995, 170) of the MIT Media Lab argued that "the economic models of media today are based almost exclusively on 'pushing' the information and entertainment out into the public. Tomorrow's will have as much or more to do with 'pulling,' where you and I reach into the network and check out something the way we do in a library or video-rental store today." Television, radio, and newspapers have generally been considered "push" media, sending the same product or information from one source to many recipients. Satellite radio and television, cable television, audio and video recordings (downloadable via the Internet), and webpages, by contrast, allow an individual to "pull" or select sources of information or data on demand.

The Global Media Landscape

How a nation and its people are perceived is contingent upon the source of information and images. The global media landscape is the aggregate of all sources of information. The global media landscape comprises bordered media landscapes, shared media landscapes, targeted media, and imported or syndicated media.

Bordered Media Landscape A bordered media landscape is any nation's domestic media system. It is the sum of communication activity and domestic production. Theoretically, at some point in an earlier stage of media development, the information available and received was containable within and coincided with geographic boundaries. Access to information could be limited by governmental policy, and these limitations were hard to circumvent before the advent of widespread use of the Internet in the late twentieth century and even more so before the advent of radio in the late nineteenth century.

Shared Media Landscape The shared media landscape is that portion of the global media landscape that is accessible more or less to everybody. That media landscape includes both micro- and

mass media. Each geographical entity has available both internal and external media sources. The balance between internal and external, between domestic and foreign media sources, has shifted as telecommunications and information technology have made external contact and content more readily available.

Media barriers, unlike physical barriers, are always porous. Old concepts of transborder data flow have become practically meaningless in the contemporary world. Regulatory power over communication contact and content is undermined when borders become transparent—or even imperceptible—and easily crossed. Jurisdiction, a geographically or territorially based term, is being redefined as well as redistributed by modern media.

Because of technological advances, U.S. media content and forms now reach a global audience. Furthermore, whereas in the past the distribution of sounds and images was mainly unidirectional, it has now become bidirectional. The pager, the personal digital assistant, the laptop, the cell phone, and the television can both receive and transmit audiovisual data and other information. Newspapers and magazines are available online. Radio, television, and movies are downloadable.

Targeted Media Target media are media sources specifically intended to supply information to nondomestic audiences. Both governments and private entities are responsible for targeted media: nationally sponsored targeted media include the United States' Voice of America and Great Britain's BBC World. Privately owned

outlets include CNN International, and international editions of newspapers or magazines such as the *Herald Tribune* or *Time*.

The U.S. government is actively engaged in the international dissemination of its message. The Voice of America is a multimedia international broadcasting service funded by the U.S. government. Operating since 1942, it currently broadcasts a thousand hours of news, information, educational, and cultural programming every week to an estimated worldwide audience of 96 million people. Programs are produced in forty-four languages. VOA broadcasts via shortwave, AM, and FM radio, satellite television, and the Internet (www.VOA.gov), although U.S. law prohibits broadcasting within the United States. The Broadcasting Board of Governors administers all U.S. government broadcasting, which includes, in addition to the Voice of America, Radio Free Europe/Radio Liberty, Radio Free Asia, and Radio and TV Martí (targeted at Cuba). Some of these—Radio Free Europe, for example—combine private administration with government funding.

In 2004 the U.S. government launched al-Hurra ("The Free One") a government-funded Arabic-language satellite TV channel, also operating under the Broadcasting Board of Governors. The channel sees its role as promoting democracy and influencing public opinion in the Arab world, most specifically to counter the perceived anti-American slant of the Qatar-based al-Jazeera and al-Arabiya satellite channels. Al-Hurra is operated by a private corporation called the Middle East Television Network, which is financed by the U.S. Congress.

Satellite dishes on a building in Amsterdam, Netherlands. Satellite reception has made television shows available for viewing around the world. Source: istock.

Imported and Syndicated Programming Imported and syndicated programming—programming originally created in one country but then sold, distributed, or licensed in another—is another component of the global media landscape. U.S. programs are widely available throughout the world in this format. They join U.S. brands, trademarks, or licensed entities and products (for example, McDonald's, Coca-Cola, Starbucks, the New York Yankees, Chicago Bulls and so on) as disseminators of U.S. icons and lifestyles.

Syndication involves the license, distribution, and production of feature films and television programming for television, cable, satellite, and the home video market. Syndication was estimated to earn the United States more than $4 billion as of the start of 2004. Since the 1990s, the U.S.-produced film export market has grown more rapidly than the U.S. domestic film market and film export revenues substantially exceed domestic box-office receipts. Allen Scott, a media scholar, reports that "Hollywood films represent more than half, and sometimes more than two-thirds, of total box-office receipts in major markets" (Scott 2002). As globalization has intensified, the U.S. government has been actively promoting a free-trade agenda generally, in cultural products in particular.

Cultural Imperialism

There has long been recognition that cultures are vulnerable to the impact of foreign media. In media studies, this is called the cultural imperialism thesis (or the media imperialism thesis). The United States has often been accused of cultural imperialism in this regard. In a pull-media context in which access on demand is increasingly available and of high quality, however, imposition is giving way to selection.

Two dominant threads of thought on cultural or media imperialism can be traced to the work of George Gerbner, who studied the effect of heavy exposure mass media and Herbert Schiller, who documented the political economy of media institutions, information flow, and the dominance of the United States in developing countries.

The media critic Douglas Kellner argues that we are witnessing the birth of a "new form of global culture" in which globally produced "images, sounds and spectacles help produce the fabric of everyday life . . . providing the materials out of which people forge their very identities" (Kellner 1995). Critics argue that this global culture "with its hallmarks of homogenization and convergence—is obliterating local cultures, creating in its wake mirrors of American consumer society" (Strelitz 2001).

The cultural consequence most often associated with use of U.S. media has been the adoption of U.S. consumerism. Scholars concerned with the consequences of U.S. cultural influence on indigenous cultures have been criticized, however, for simplistically assuming that the presence of U.S. media automatically results in a cultural influence. The SIM ("Susceptibility to Imported Media") model purports to provide a means to predict what elements people will focus on and retain when they watch imported television. Michael Elasmar, the creator of the SIM model, argues that preexisting beliefs, predispositions, and knowledge about the country of origin of the imported television programming all affect the influence it has on the population that imports it. It is a useful model for understanding the multiple facets of international cultural exchange.

Those concerned about cultural imperialism are also worried about the increasing concentration of media ownership in fewer hands. The global commercial media system, dominated by a small number of U.S.-based transnational media corporations, wields significant power. Deregulation of media ownership and the privatization of television in European and Asian markets have made it possible for media giants to establish powerful distribution and production networks within and among nations. Horizontal integration has resulted in consolidation within the publishing industry, while vertical integration of the global media market has resulted in a few companies gaining ownership of content as well as the means of distribution.

Images and Representations

The meaning attached to media content varies from culture to culture and country to country. In the absence of direct or personal contact with "the other," mediated interactions and mass media images form the basis of perception. Given the high number and high quality of media contacts with the United States, the differences between mediated and direct experiences have become less distinct. The less apparent or obtrusive the medium is, the harder it is to detect the medium's influence.

The premise that media representations structure the perceptions of the audience is fundamental to the work of many media scholars. Despite advances in international travel, many people have no firsthand experience of people from other societies; they depend on notions received from and influenced by media. Media content, whether news or entertainment, is often representative of the conditions, values, and groups within the society that produced it. However, economic, technological, or institutional factors can result in the use of stock characters and a reliance on the shorthand of readily recognizable stereotypical images and themes.

In Plato's "Allegory of the Cave" prisoners sit chained, unable to turn their heads. Behind them a fire burns and reflects the outer world by the casting of shadows on the wall. Unable to see the real objects behind them, the prisoners believe the shadows to be real. Used to the world of illusion, the prisoners resist explanations of reality. Modern media technology encourages individuals to select, view on demand, and obtain high-quality images of the other. However, modern media are also the source of confusion between the real and the mediated illusion. Plato believed that there were invisible truths lying under the surface of things that the enlightened could grasp; by analogy, people in the contemporary world should strive to get below the surface of things when it comes to understanding the truth about the other as presented by the media.

Susan J. Drucker and Gary Gumpert

See also Media Corporations

Further Reading

Artz, L., & Kamaliour, Y. (Eds.). (2003). *The globalization of corporate media hegemony.* Albany: State University of New York Press.

Brennan, S. (2004). NATPE 2004. Retrieved June 1, 2007, from http://www.hollywoodreporter.com/thr/television/feature_display.jsp?vnu_content_id=2068718

Cooper, L. (1938). *Plato: Phaedrus, Ion, Gorgias, and Symposium, with passages from the Republic and Laws.* Ithaca, NY: Cornell University Press.

Desousa, M. (1982). The cultural impact of American television abroad: An overview of criticism and research. *International and Intercultural Communication Annual, 6,* 19–20.

Dorfman, A. (1983). *The emperor's old clothes: What the Lone Ranger, Babar, and other innocent heroes do to our mind.* New York: Pantheon.

Elasmar, M. (2003). *The impact of international television: A paradigm shift.* Mahwah, NJ: Lawrence Erlbaum.

Gerbner, G., Gross, L., Morgan, M., & Signorelli, N. (1980). The "mainstreaming" of America: Violence profile no. 11. *Journal of Communication, 30*(3), 10–29.

Golding, P., & Harris, P. (1996). *Beyond cultural imperialism: Globalization, communication and the new international order.* London: Sage Publications.

Hamelink, C. (1990). *Information imbalance: Core and periphery in questioning the media: A critical introduction.* London: Sage Publications.

International Television Flow Project. (1988). *A report on television stereotypes of three nations: France, U.S. and Japan.* Tokyo: Author.

Kellner, D. (1995). *Media culture: Cultural studies, identity and politics between the modern and the postmodern.* London: Routledge.

Liebes, T., & Katz, E. (1990). *Exporting meaning: Cross-cultural readings of Dallas.* New York: Oxford University Press.

Lull, J. (1999). *Media, communication, culture: A global approach* (2nd ed.). New York: Columbia University Press.

McChesney, R. W. (2000). *Rich media, poor democracy.* New York: New Press.

McLuhan, M. (1962). *The Gutenberg galaxy: The making of typographic man.* Toronto, Canada: University of Toronto Press.

McLuhan, M., & Powers, B. (1993). *The global village: Transformations in world life and media in the 21st century.* New York: Oxford University Press.

Negroponte, N. (1995). *Being digital.* New York: Alfred A. Knopf.

Rogers, E. (1983). *Diffusion of innovations* (3rd ed.). New York: Free Press.

Schiller, H. I. (1976). *Communication and cultural domination.* White Plains, NY: International Arts and Science Press.

Scott, A. J. (2002, November 29). *Hollywood in the era of globalization: Opportunities and predicaments.* Retrieved January 9, 2005, from http://www.yaleglobal.yale.edu/article.print?id=479

Strelitz. (2001, Spring–Summer). *Where the global meets the local: Media studies and the myth of cultural homogenization* (Transnational Broadcasting Studies Archives No. 6). Retrieved January 9, 2005, from http://www.tbsjournal.com/Archives/Spring01/strelitz.html

Thussu, D. K. (2000). *International communication: Continuity and change.* New York: Oxford University Press.

Mass Media—
Debates and Divides

The United States is the most powerful producer of media images in terms of both sheer quantity and pervasiveness in other parts of the world. Despite this prevalence, the impact of U.S. media penetration is unclear.

The flow of media industries, images, and products across borders is as much a hallmark of our globalized world as the flow of money, resources, and people. And as with every variety of these cross-border movements, there are imbalances in the patterns; there are those advantaged and disadvantaged by the movements, and there are debates about fairness, access, impact, and consequences. The most recent incarnation of these long-standing debates over the global flow of information and communications has focused on the digital divide—on the gap between the have and the have-not countries in the field of telecommunications.

It is important to set an international context for transborder information flows and the movement of media products. Media—print, radio, television, film, music, and the like—do not function independently of dominant regional and international politics and trends. In the early twenty-first century, contradictory trends such as globalization and nationalism frame movements of people, ideas, and products across borders. To one degree or another, media production, information access, and communications distribution are also framed by these social, political, and economic trends. Since the first systems of mass media and telecommunications emerged, writes the media scholar Robert McChesney, "their control and structure have been political issues" (1996, 1).

Clearly, the United States wields immense influence in the economic, cultural, and social struggles in this deeply polarized world. Acceptance or resistance to U.S. superpower status is implicit in many fundamentalist challenges to modernity, nationalist challenges to globalization, and regional challenges to economic-cultural hegemony. It is, therefore, not surprising that there is national and regional resistance to the dominance of Western, and particularly U.S., media industries, products, resources, and influence. Yet, at the same time, one can also find evidence of widespread imitation of Western cultural norms spread around the globe in television, advertising, music, movies, radio, and print media. In this complex globalized environment, which is both propelled forward and supported by dynamic media exchanges, how one experiences and interprets the global communications and information system will have much to do with how one frames the U.S. presence and influence in the media debate.

Understanding the Media Debate

There is no question that U.S. cultural presence around the world has reached a zenith—no television production center, publishing enterprise, or news establishment outside the United States can compete on equal terms with the powerful U.S. media giants. The inequality of media presence has widened in the past decades, with media-rich nations becoming richer and media-poor countries falling further behind. As of 1997, for example, over half of the world's people had not yet made a single telephone call. Only 10 percent of the world's population currently uses the Internet, and 85 percent of the world's users are located in the small number of developed countries where 90 percent of Internet hosts are located. As of 2003, there were 862 million illiterate people in the world. Africa produces less than 2 percent of the world's book titles and Latin America just 5 percent; the United States and Europe dominate the industry. Fewer and fewer corporations within Western countries (primarily the United States) control more and more media. Against this backdrop, many individuals, grassroots advocacy alliances, nongovernmental organizations, and UN bodies such as UNESCO argue that the inequity in communication flows and information access must be redressed and rebalanced. These groups see communications as basic to the life of all individuals and communities, and they believe that all people should have fair and equitable access to communication resources and literacy and media skills; all people should be able to protect their cultural identity and participate in decisions regarding media images, media products and resource distribution, and relevant policies.

The Debates in the 1970s and 1980s

While the years after World War II saw tremendous expansion of Western culture (primarily U.S. culture) abroad, many questioned the nature and impact of that global penetration. The economist and media scholar Herbert Schiller did ground-breaking work

examining the role of the U.S. media presence in the world in *Mass Communications and the American Empire* (1969). Schiller offered a comprehensive examination of international mass communications structures and policies and documented the emerging and merged networks of U.S. economics, finances, and communication industries.

By the early 1970s, critical voices were heard around the globe, as the call went up to address the question of control over the flow of global news and mass culture. UNESCO's International Commission for the Study of Communication Problems (1980) noted the increasing importance of mass media and argued for a balanced and nonpartisan approach to meet the challenges. Developing nations argued for a movement from disadvantage and dependence to self-reliance; they advocated for more equal opportunities in the creation and distribution of media. The United States strongly opposed the UNESCO efforts, arguing, among other things, that any efforts to place controls on the media news flow abridged press freedom, and restricting Western ownership of local media outlets abridged the free flow of information. The debates at the United Nations faded in the latter half of the 1980s, though they were not resolved, and disparities between nations were actually growing greater. The reaction from the United States and other Western countries proved to be a significant force in slowing down UNESCO's efforts to redress imbalances. Also, the problems of the great media and communications divide required addressing problems that extended well beyond the sphere of media and UNESCO's purview.

The Struggle Today

As the gap between the information rich and the information poor has continued to grow, the literature on this topic has also grown. Terms such as *cultural imperialism* and references to the digital divide have become commonplace in discussions. Sometimes the rhetoric fails to do justice to the complexities of the challenges. For example, the digital divide should not only refer to the gap between the information-rich Western nations and the information-poor nations of the developing world, but also to the gaps between the rich and poor within Western societies themselves.

UNESCO and many nongovernmental and grassroots alliances continue to focus much of their attention on communications and information issues. A few examples will demonstrate the nature of these contemporary international media advocacy alliances. The People's Communications Charter, for example, recognizes the need to define communication rights and responsibilities such that people are assured of media independence, safeguards for cultural identity, access to cyberspace, and account-

ability. Similarly, the Association for Progressive Communications, an international network of socially oriented organizations that has consultative status at the United Nations, has created an Internet rights charter that stresses that access to information and freedom of expression must be safeguarded if information and communications are to have an empowering role in national, regional, and even individual development. Nor are developing countries the only ones challenging the penetration of U.S. media. France and Canada, for example, have long contested the intrusion of U.S. cultural products and programming and have placed constraints on the flow by, for example, requiring a certain number of nationals to be employed in productions done within the country, in order to support their own national media industries and national culture.

As with all debates, of course, there are multiple positions. With respect to the omnipresence of U.S. media and its influence on the cultural landscape of other nations, there are those who believe that there is in fact more media diversity in the world today than less. The media scholar Benjamin Compaine has suggested that the widely held notion that the world's media is now controlled by a handful of dangerous all-powerful transnational media giants is vastly overstated and argues that a tremendous diversity exists in media outlets, citing newswire services as an example. Compaine believes that national and regional media systems and producers determine their own programming, not the large Western transnational media corporations. Compaine sees today's global media situation as promoting cultural diversity and democracy, rather than undermining it.

One way to approach this debate is to suggest that it is not an either/or situation, but rather that there is both a system of global media flow dominated by U.S. and Western companies and a system of local or national media, which in some cases—Brazil's and India's, for example—is quite robust. Some contemporary media scholars strongly believe that while the dominant trends in communication and information flow are against the fullest balance and diversity, transnational cultural production is shifting toward commercializing local cultural content on a global scale—something that was not the case in the 1970s. "The older systems of one-way cultural distribution—like TV, with people in Tonga or East Asia watching reruns of U.S. Westerns—are in a state of metamorphosis," notes Schiller (Amelan 2003).

This more nuanced dualist approach explains why media consumers around the globe might simultaneously flock to U.S. movies while also enjoying their own indigenous film industries or watch CNN while reading their national newspapers. In fact, one can find instance after instance of local or national media being preferred to U.S. cultural products, even though the U.S. media products dominate the national market. As one Brazilian study concludes,

A U.S. Army soldier surfing the web in Iraq. Source: istock/Amanda Goeke.

"Even though U.S. mass media products contribute to alienation, damage the local culture and serve as imperialist instruments, Brazilian audiences are not passive and vulnerable. The Brazilian public still prefers and values its own national TV programs and music" (Kamalipour 1999, 193).

The Question of Impact on Perceptions

Although no nation holds more power than the United States in terms of the sheer quantity and extent of media penetration into other societies, the impact of U.S. media penetration on perception and public opinion is not predetermined.

It is virtually impossible to assess causality in human behavior, and it is therefore difficult to assert with precision the relationship between media consumption and individual perception. Observers should be careful not to assume that media images broadcast into a region simply enter like serum from a hypodermic needle into the national bloodstream of the people. At the same time, it would be ridiculous not to believe that a repetitive diet of Hollywood movies, violent video games, Madison Avenue advertising, and U.S.-produced news coverage has no impact at all. Again, it is not an either/or situation. Images of nations and peoples are formed through a very complex communication process involving varied information sources within the context of politics, culture, and

values; media consumers' traits (race or ethnicity, class, education level, gender, religion, and the individual personalities) also affect how the information is received.

Cultivation theory, which was developed in the 1970s by the media scholar George Gerbner, explores how people form impressions of the real world based on long-term exposure to television images. Gerbner hypothesized that exposure to recurring patterns of images, themes, and messages through television cultivates a viewer's set of attitudes. Gerbner also stated people's social reality changes with the amount of television they watch. In essence, heavy viewers believe in a reality consistent with the television world they are watching. In terms of national impressions and opinions about other countries, cultivation theory would posit that people's impressions of the United States would reflect and be influenced by their media diet: Their sense of U.S. culture would be affected by how heavy a diet of U.S.-produced television shows and movies they consume. However, there are many cases that seem to contradict this theory, cases in which no clear correlation can be made between a steady diet of U.S. media products and perceptions of the United States and its people.

An individual's opinion about the United States certainly may be cultivated by, informed by, even challenged by media images and information. So too, "the nature and quality of political relations between countries is a critical factor in the images they portray of each other in their mass media" (Kamalipour 1999, 35). Of course, the degree to which media consumers welcome and believe the

images or distrust and disagree with them will also be influenced by the relations of the countries, as well as by the consumers' own characteristics, as mentioned above.

Images of the U.S. around the World (1999), edited by the communications scholar Yahya Kamalipour, brings together eleven different national studies exploring perspectives on the United States in relation to media consumption patterns. When asked their opinions about people in the United States and then about the sources from which they received information, international respondents gave answers that suggest that impressions of Americans in many nations are far from positive in spite of—or perhaps owing to—a heavy diet of U.S. media programming. Alex Fernando Teixeira Primo, who contributed the study from Brazil, notes that "much of the body of relevant knowledge in Brazil holds that American TV programs, movies, music and other cultural products have an alienating power and constitute a form of imperialism, cultural invasion conducted by the U.S. to maintain international hegemony and generate higher profits. At the same time, Brazilian audiences fill movie theaters showing American movies in great numbers, "buy CDs of American music and stay tuned to U.S. TV programs" (Kamalipour 1999, 179). Another study, perhaps closer to home, notes that Canadians hold negative values about the United States and feel that U.S. culture is "swallowing up the whole planet" yet are relatively high consumers of U.S. media (Kamalipour 1999, 166).

The Iraq War and Perceptions of the United States

In the months leading up to and following the U.S. invasion of Iraq, studies documented a rising degree of negative public opinion toward the United States. In 2003, *Business Week* reported that in a majority of twenty countries surveyed, people held America "in much lower esteem than they did a year ago" (*Business Week* 2003, 104). A Pew Global Attitudes survey, published in December 2002, showed that an overwhelming majority of respondents in France and Russia believed that the U.S. policy in Iraq had been driven by the United States' wish to control Iraqi oil. And a survey conducted for the Brookings Institute in six Arab countries in March 2003 found an "unprecedented tide of public opinion running against the U.S" (Telhami 2003, 24).

What has been the role of media in this situation? While recognizing that media do not have a singular casual role in determining a viewer's attitude, nor in confirming or countering a reader's opinion, it is still possible to acknowledge that media organizations may try to cater to audiences and, in commercial enterprises, to

their advertisers. This has definitely been the case when it comes to how the Iraq conflict has been presented by different news services to different audiences around the world.

Many countries had saturation television coverage of the U.S. invasion. However, despite the saturation, major differences existed in the information and images made available to audiences around the globe. Take, for example, the case of CNN, a unit of the distinctly U.S. transnational corporation, Time Warner (then AOL Time Warner). Whereas during the first Gulf War in 1991, CNN's global presentation was uniform, by the time of the 2003 Iraq War, CNN had developed several overseas networks catering to regional audiences. Thus, CNN International (CNNI) presented "more of the gore" (Flint, Goldsmith, and Kahn 2003, B1) than the domestic network did, and viewers of CNN outside of the U.S. were (and are) more exposed to casualties, to interviews about the "dire situation," and to coverage of how Arab nations view the war and broader Middle East issues.

Non-U.S. media are also focusing on information and images not frequently aired in the United States. Arab regional media coverage of the war has focused heavily, for example, on the fact that postwar looting happened in hospitals and museums that were left unprotected by U.S. forces, and not in the oil installations and oil ministries, which were heavily guarded by troops. European media coverage has also differed from U.S. coverage, thus demonstrating the degree to which national coverage does exert autonomy. In Italy, for example, both state and private television stations often broadcast long excerpts from al-Jazeera—not something one is likely to find in the United States—and in Germany, the press has concluded that the U.S. media has "gone through a 'Gleichschaltung,' an ominous word used to describe how the Nazis took over key public institutions" (Flint, Goldsmith, and Kahn 2003, B1).

Faced with negative and hostile global public opinion, governments often try to coordinate public diplomacy efforts to present their side of the story. Along those lines, a panel appointed by the White House argued in October 2003 that the United States must drastically overhaul its public relations efforts to salvage its plummeting image among Muslims and Arabs. "Hostility toward America has reached shocking levels. What is required is not merely tactical adaptation but strategic and radical transformation," recommended the panel (Weisman 2003, 1).

Positive media can only cover up bad reality for so long, however. Even with an overhaul of official public relations and an effort to get ahead of the story and frame the news, it is unlikely that the image of the United States in the eyes of the Muslim world will improve until foreign policy and political relations change course. One cannot blame media for all that is wrong, and one should not

be lulled into the false belief that good public relations are all that is needed to change public opinion.

Laurien Alexandre

See also Media Corporations

Further Reading

Amelan, R. (2003). Communication: From information society to knowledge societies. *The New Courier, 3.* Retrieved June 1, 2007, from http://portal.unesco.org/en/ev.php-URL_ID=14339&URL_DO=DO_TOPIC&URL_SECTION=201.html

America: The view from abroad. (2003, June 16). *Business Week,* p. 104. Retrieved June 1, 2007, from http://www.businessweek.com/magazine/content/03_24/b3837139_mz029.htm

Annan, K. (2001, May 4). In interconnected world all people must have access to Internet, says secretary-general, in World Telecommunications Day message. Retrieved June 1, 2007, from http://www.unis.unvienna.org/unis/pressrels/2001/sgsm7791.html

APC Internet rights charter: Internet for social justice and sustainable development. (2002, November). Retrieved June 1, 2007, from http://www.apc.org/english/rights/charter.shtml

Chesney, R. (1996). The global struggle for democratic communication. *Monthly Review, 48*(3), 1–20.

Compaine, B. (2002, November–December). Global media (think again). *Foreign Policy, 133,* 20–28.

Flint, J., Goldsmith, C., & Kahn, G. (2003, 11 April). A Global Journal Report: CNN gives U.S., world different views. *Wall Street Journal.* B1.

Giffard, C. A. (2000). News agencies, national images and global media events. *Journalism and Mass Communications Quarterly, 77*(1), 8–21.

Jansen, S. C. (2002). *Critical communication theory: Power, media, gender and technology.* Lanham, MD: Rowman & Littlefield Publishers.

Kamalipour, Y. (Ed.). (1999). *Images of the U.S. around the world: A multicultural perspective.* Albany: State University of New York Press.

Tehranian, M. (1999). *Global communication and world politics.* Boulder, CO: Lynne Rienner Publishers.

Telhami, S. (2003, Summer). Arab public opinion on the United States and Iraq: Postwar prospects for changing prewar views. *Brookings Review, 21*(3), 24–27.

Schiller, H. I. (1969). *Mass communications and American empire.* Boston: Beacon Press.

UNESCO. (1980). *Many Voices, One World.* Report by the International Commission for the Study of Communication Problems. UK: UNESCO.

Wresch, W. (1996). *Disconnected: Haves and have-nots in the information age.* New Brunswick, NJ: Rutgers University Press.

Weisman, S. (2003, 1 October). US must counteract image in Muslim world." *New York Times,* Sec. 8, Column 3, Page 1.

McDonaldization

McDonald's is a global model of business success, and its "golden arches" are one of the most recognizable symbols of U.S. culture. Yet in some nations, McDonald's restaurants have been met with protests, petitions, and even riots.

In 1948, brothers Dick (1909–1998) and Maurice (d. 1971) McDonald built the first McDonald's fast-food restaurant in California. The burger joint remained a small-scale operation until 1954, when Ray Kroc (1902–1984) became the first franchisee and began to open McDonald's restaurants at other locations. Following his early success in opening additional McDonald's restaurants, Kroc purchased the rights to the McDonald's concept and brand from the McDonald brothers in 1961 for a price of $2.7 million. Grounded in a focus on quality, service, cleanliness, and value, McDonald's franchises continued to multiply at a feverish pace throughout the second half of the twentieth century, expanding both within the United States and across the globe. The five-hundredth McDonald's opened in 1963, the thousandth in 1968, and the five-thousandth in 1978. In 2003 there were more than thirty thousand McDonald's restaurants operating in 120 countries, serving an estimated 47 million customers each day.

Worldwide, McDonald's "golden arches" and its mascot, the clown Ronald McDonald, are among the most recognizable symbols of U.S. culture; indeed, to many people across the globe, McDonald's is an ambassador of U.S. culture that reflects core values, beliefs, and customs. Fast-food restaurants and perceptions of U.S. culture are powerfully linked, both in the eyes of Americans and non-Americans, and an understanding of the principles of the fast-food restaurant business in general, and of McDonald's in particular, can valuably contribute to an understanding of U.S. culture. Since the early 1990s, a powerful sociological discussion of the characteristics of the fast-food industry and its impact on U.S. culture has developed around the concept of McDonaldization.

the proliferation of large-scale, chain enterprises throughout the United States and the world. Ritzer's thesis is that the principles of fast-food restaurants—efficiency, calculability, predictability, and control—have slowly crept into many other industries, including education, medicine, travel, and entertainment.

Ritzer draws from classic sociological and organizational theories in his discussion of McDonaldization. In particular, he uses the works of the sociologist and political economist Max Weber (1864–1920) and the engineer Frederick Winslow Taylor (1865–1915) to explain the principles of McDonaldization. Both Weber and Taylor wrote of the potential value of rationality in maximizing organizational performance. Weber is well-known for his theory of the bureaucratic organization. In a bureaucracy, roles, tasks, relationships, and responsibilities are rationally developed and assigned. Weber suggested that organizations could maximize efficiency through bureaucratization. Taylor is renowned for his work on scientific management—the process of applying techniques of empirical science to the study and design of jobs. Taylor dedicated himself to discovering and designing the best way to complete work tasks. Managerial applications of Weber's and Taylor's ideas flourished in large-scale industrial factories in the United States in the early 1900s. Although businesses made efficiency gains using these methods, however, many workers protested scientific management and bureaucracy, feeling that their application dehumanized workers and led to increasing monotony in work. McDonaldization is, in a sense, an application of the ideas of Weber and Taylor in the modern workplace. This is evident from the four key characteristics of McDonaldization, examined in more detail below.

Overview of McDonaldization

In *The McDonaldization of Society* (1993), the sociologist George Ritzer introduced the term *McDonaldization* to describe "the process by which the principles of the fast-food restaurant are coming to dominate more and more sectors of American society as well as the rest of the world" (Ritzer 1993, 1). While Ritzer strongly associates his McDonaldization thesis with the fast-food restaurant McDonald's, he does not restrict the concept to the fast-food industry. Rather, he broadly applies the concept to describe

Efficiency

Efficiency refers to an emphasis on finding and using the least costly means to a certain end. In many instances, efficiency entails both low cost and high speed. McDonaldized businesses promise consumers streamlined processes and products; they attempt to deliver the most product for the least effort. The product offered by the quintessential McDonaldized industry—the fast-food industry—is efficient "finger food." Hamburgers, french fries, and single-serving apple pies are designed to be eaten quickly and with

little or no mess. Efficiency also characterizes McDonaldized businesses outside of the fast food industry. For example, in McDonaldized health care clinics, physician-patient interactions are structured to be as cost effective as possible; patients spend minimal time with physicians, whose time is typically very costly. Rather, patients spend time with relatively less costly nurses and physician assistants and complete standardized questionnaires. Reduced physician-patient interactions enhance a clinic's efficient use of resources. From fast food to health care, McDonaldized companies across a range of industries enhance efficiency by offering more simplified, or less idiosyncratic, products and services. In essence, McDonaldized companies offer simplified products.

To achieve maximum efficiency, employees are required to perform their tasks using particular, standardized, and predetermined methods—the most efficient methods possible—in a manner reminiscent of Frederick Taylor's scientific management. For example, cooks at McDonald's must flip the burgers in a particular sequence, after aligning the frozen patties on the grill in six neat rows. McDonald's officials have determined this to be the most efficient means of cooking burgers, with respect to both time and energy costs. In addition to having employees perform tasks in efficient ways, McDonaldized companies enlist the most inexpensive labor: the customer, who works for free. Customers at fast-food restaurants are expected to clean up their own tables, dispose of their own trash, and fill and refill their own drinks. Or, returning to the example of McDonaldized health care, patients are expected to spend copious amounts of time completing standardized forms. By having tasks performed in the most efficient way possible, and by distributing tasks to customers for completion, McDonaldized organizations reduce the overall cost of delivering products and services to and thus are able to maximize profits.

Predictability

McDonaldized enterprises enforce standardization across space and time, and the result is predictability. Many McDonaldized organizations are large-scale chains; they attempt to ensure that customers encounter the same product and the same service regardless of what store they enter or when they enter it. By emphasizing uniform standards across stores, McDonaldized businesses cater to the human desire to avoid risk and seek familiarity. At McDonald's and chains like it, customers have the assurance that they will be purchasing something familiar; they reduce their chances of purchasing a substandard product or experiencing lackluster service.

McDonaldized organizations achieve high levels of predictability through standardized work environments, including standardized inputs and processes. The raw materials and parts that go into

creating a product, such as a hamburger, are of a standard type. At McDonald's, precooked hamburger patties are required to measure precisely 3.875 inches and weigh 1.6 ounces. A hamburger bun must measure 3.5 inches. Similarly, french fries must conform to standard dimensions. In addition to standardized inputs, McDonaldized organizations strive for standardized processes—for instance, in the cooking of hamburgers, mentioned above. Additionally, employee-customer interactions are controlled through scripted dialogues. By specifying precisely how jobs are to be completed, McDonaldized organizations attempt to restrict variety and promote predictability. When standardized inputs are manipulated with standardized processes, the outcome is reliably the same, but the downside is that work becomes mindless, boring, and routine.

Calculability

McDonaldized organizations adhere to the belief that what gets measured is important, and they measure the attributes of their products and processes, including product characteristics, as described above, and service interactions (measuring, for example, speed of delivery). With respect to products, McDonaldized organizations emphasize the quantity of products served or the size of products. For example, the concept of supersizing promoted the quantitative aspect of drinks and french fries. Fast-food product names that stress the quantity rather than the quality of the product include the Big Mac (McDonald's) the Monster Thickburger (Hardee's) and the Bigfoot pizza (Pizza Hut). With respect to processes, McDonaldized companies emphasize speed, which is seen as an indication of efficiency. For example, in the early 1990s, Domino's Pizza marketed its pizza delivery service with the promise that the pizza would arrive in 30 minutes or less, or the pizza would be free.

Quantitative measures facilitate assessment of the efficiency and predictability of products and processes. Quantitative measures also aid McDonaldized companies in marketing the efficiency gains of their products and services. Large-scale tourist agencies market trips based on the number of attractions that travelers will see, for example, and tourist agencies emphasize that travelers will see this large number of attractions in a very limited amount of time. These quantifiable data make it possible to measure the efficiency of the tourist experience. In this manner McDonaldized companies shift customers' attention from quality to quantity.

Control

Control ties the other three characteristics together. Simply put, McDonaldized organizations control inputs and processes so that

they are efficient and predictable, and they use quantifiable measures of success (calculability).

McDonaldized companies control inputs through purchasing contracts that specify precisely the nature of the input to be purchased. In the case of hamburgers, size, fat content, and nature of the meat are all specified. McDondaldized companies control processes through a mixture of nonhuman technology and rigid training and supervision. Human employees are increasingly being designed out of McDonaldized organizations to prevent human variability from disturbing the goals of predictability and efficiency. To prevent human forgetfulness or decision inaccuracy from introducing variation into french fry preparation, McDonald's uses robotic devices that remove the cooked french fries from the cooker at a precise time. To take another example, at airports customers can use self-check-in machines to avoid the necessity of dealing with a customer service representative and the potential variability he or she may introduce. Where McDonaldized organizations still use humans, they are heavily controlled by training and supervision. Supervisors, managers, and workers attend training programs either at or created by corporate "universities." Employees who do not conform to established policies, practices, and procedures have a limited future with a McDonaldized organization.

Customers, too, are subject to control in McDonaldized organizations. For example, at a fast-food establishment, customers must stand in lines, order their food from a limited, predetermined menu, eat their food quickly, and dispose of their own trash.

Implications of McDonaldization

As a cultural phenomenon, McDonaldization has a number of important implications, some positive and some negative. On the positive side, McDonaldization has been hailed for supplying a wide range of goods and services to a large portion of the population. McDonaldization facilitates convenience: customers can obtain goods and services regardless of time or location, and those goods and services are much cheaper, which means that they are within financial reach of a large portion of the population. The uniform nature of McDonaldized organizations promotes the ideas of equality, both with respect to hiring employees and serving customers.

But there are a number of drawbacks. George Ritzer's primary thesis is that in striving for extreme rationality, McDonaldization is, paradoxically, irrational. By dehumanizing workers, it prevents them from using their unique, individual abilities—the abilities that would let them make the most meaningful contribution to the enterprise. A second disadvantage is reduced learning and development within McDonaldized organizations and industries. Because McDonaldized processes and procedures are designed to eliminate variety—the raw material of learning—McDonaldization may reduce the growth and development necessary for sustained, continuous innovation.

The benefits and the drawbacks of a McDonaldized society, such as the United States, are repeatedly debated in academic discourse and in the media, even on a global stage. While McDonald's has been welcomed with great fanfare in numerous countries (for example, in Russia in the 1990s), a movement against McDonaldized organizations grew steadily throughout the 1990s and into the twenty-first century. In some nations, new McDonald's restaurants have been met with protests, petitions, and even riots. This movement against McDonaldization is even manifest in the United States. There are, for example, communities that have passed ordinances prohibiting large-scale retail chains like Wal-Mart from entering their local markets. But while the debate over the benefits and drawbacks of McDonaldization continue, the phenomenon itself remains a powerful feature of U.S. culture, and one that is increasingly experienced by the global society.

Andrew P. Knight

See also Businesses Overseas, U.S.; Globalization, Economic; Homogenization of World Culture; Multinational Corporations

Further Reading

Boas, M., & Chain, S. (1976). *Big Mac: The unauthorized story of McDonald's*. New York: E. P. Dutton.

Bryman, A. (2004). *The Disneyization of society*. London: Sage.

Fishman, C. (2006). *The Wal-Mart effect: How the world's most powerful company really works—and how it's transforming the American economy*. New York, NY: Penguin.

Ford, H. (1922). *My life and work*. Garden City, NY: Doubleday.

Kowinski, W. S. (1985). *The malling of America: An inside look at the great consumer paradise*. New York: William Morrow.

Kroc, R. A. (1977). *Grinding it out: The making of McDonald's*. New York: Berkeley Medallion Books.

Ritzer, G. (1998). *The McDonaldization thesis*. London: Sage.

Ritzer, G. (2004). *The McDonaldization of society* (Rev. ed.). Thousand Oaks, CA: Pine Forge Press.

Schlosser, E. (2001). *Fast food nation*. Boston: Houghton Mifflin.

Taylor, F. W. (1947). *The principles of scientific management*. New York: Harper & Row.

Weber, M. (1978). *Economy and society: An outline of interpretive sociology* (G. Roth & C. Wittich, Eds.; E. Fischoff et al., Trans.). Berkeley and Los Angeles: University of California Press.

Weber, M. (2002). *The Protestant ethic and the spirit of capitalism* (S. Kalberg, Trans.; 3rd ed.). Los Angeles, CA: Roxbury.

Media Corporations

Large media corporations view global expansion as good for their businesses, but questions remain about whether market forces alone can effectively regulate an industry that serves both corporate and public interests.

Globalization has been facilitated by the emergence of new media technologies capable of bypassing geographic boundaries and bringing distant locales into virtual proximity with each other. The images, messages and sensations transmitted over these technologies help shape global perspectives on the United States as well as U.S. perspectives about the world. For that reason, it is important to understand who is responsible for producing and transmitting these messages and to what ends.

Today, in much of the world, media corporations have replaced state governments as the primary owners of media infrastructure and the primary producers of media content. These corporations vary greatly in size, scope, organization, and influence, from small content producers to large hardware manufacturers and multimedia conglomerates, from private enterprises to public service entities, and so on. However, they all tend to treat information and entertainment as commodities to be traded rather than public services designed to promote social understanding. Since many of these corporations are either owned by U.S. citizens, located on U.S. soil, or targeted toward a U.S. audience (at least as a primary market), they are also viewed as promoters of American values and beliefs and sometimes as engines of "Americanization" or "cultural imperialism." Thus, a better understanding of these media corporations—their history, modes of operation, and effects on cross-cultural communications—can help illustrate why global perspectives on the United States assume the forms that they do.

Changes in the Industry since the 1970s

A combination of factors has led the reshaping of the media environment since the 1970s. First, new technologies for the delivery of media messages have emerged to challenge the monopoly ownership and control of media systems previously secured by the natural scarcity of media conduits. The limited spectrum space available for radio and television broadcasting over the airwaves, for example, once encouraged governments to assume a strong role in controlling broadcast systems. Government regulation ensured that signal overlap, or spillover, would be minimal. However, such regulation often resulted in the formation of monopoly enterprises and the restriction of consumer choice. In some societies, this restriction took an extreme form as authoritarian governments commandeered the media for their own propaganda purposes. Most societies, however, established a system of publicly supported but relatively autonomous media networks that would ensure a modicum of pluralism. Britain, for instance, funded its fledgling TV service through a license fee imposed on owners of TV receivers. The money was channeled to the British Broadcasting Corporation (BBC), an autonomous programming agency established to ensure that TV would serve the public interest. In 1955 the British government established a competing commercial service (ITV), but the public service tradition and strong government presence ensured that ITV programming would vary little from the BBC's. These two networks dominated the British TV market until the 1990s, offering a narrow range of programs and formats from which consumers might choose.

Even where mixed systems of public regulation with private commercial ownership evolved (in North and South America and Australia, for example), monopoly ownership of the media and restricted consumer choice were the norm. The United States, for example, was the largest media market in the world but had only three commercial television networks (NBC, CBS, and ABC) until the emergence of the Fox network in 1986. Because of spectrum scarcity, the U.S. government established regulations limiting station ownership, segregating transmission and production functions, restricting the amount of air time available for commercials, and establishing rules to ensure the fair coverage of political topics. Even in the most commercial media market in the world, then, government regulation was relatively robust until the 1970s. A similar story could be told about radio, film, and even print journalism in most locales, although regulation of print media was complicated by free speech traditions in many Western countries.

Since the 1970s, however, new technologies and processes of information packaging have enabled information to be produced and disseminated in much more varied ways and by many more providers. In the television industry, for example, the introduction of cable and satellite technologies, along with devices like the VCR and DVD player, gave consumers all over the world a greater variety of media sources to choose from, thereby undermining

the state's firm control of media policy based on scarcity. Satellite television, in particular, "acted as a kind of 'Trojan Horse' of media liberalization" because it bypassed geographic barriers between nations and undermined the authority of national governments to regulate media content (Sinclair, Jacka, and Cunningham 1996, 2). Governments in Europe and Asia were virtually forced to open their domestic TV markets to commercialization and competition to provide a counterweight to the satellite offerings. For example, the introduction of the British Sky Broadcasting (BSkyB) satellite service in 1989 finally pushed the British government to privatize portions of its TV system and introduce competing channels. Hong Kong-based Star TV accomplished similar effects in India and Taiwan in the early 1990s. In addition to enabling greater consumer choice, technological innovations have made the distinctions between telecommunications, broadcasting, and computer service providers increasingly unimportant. Digitalization—the conversion of information into a uniform binary code that can be decoded by virtually any appliance—makes it possible to carry phone conversations over cable systems, broadcast signals over telephone wires, and computer services over either. This technological convergence means that no logical reason exists to prevent competition between these different providers for similar services.

Regulatory change was also pushed by political forces intent on integrating the global economy. In the 1980s free trade became the political mantra of leaders such as Ronald Reagan in the United States and Margaret Thatcher in Britain, who advocated the elimination of unnecessary government barriers to the flow of all goods, information, ideas, and services. Such reformers embraced the belief that capitalist markets function most effectively when left to correct themselves through the mechanism of competition (a belief known as *laissez faire*). They further argued that market economies are more efficient, flexible, innovative, and responsive to consumer desire than governments because they operate according to the laws of supply and demand. What the people want, the market will provide. Using political and economic leverage, including treaties, promises of foreign direct investment, and international loans, these leaders imposed their political ideas on other nations.

The coherence between promarket politics and the new media environment resulted in a laxer regulatory regime for media corporations. Public media systems were effectively privatized and commercialized to ensure the "free flow" of information across geographic borders. Media corporations were permitted to buy into foreign markets and to diversify their holdings, consolidating both software and hardware under a single corporate umbrella and dabbling in multiple media. Because the terrain of competition was much bigger and more crowded, media corporations felt that they, too, had to get bigger, and a wave of media mergers swept across the industry throughout the 1980s and 1990s.

The result is a "tiered global media market" (Hermann and McChesney 1997, 52) that looks something like a pyramid with a handful of powerful transnational multimedia conglomerates on top, a smaller and less powerful group of regional or niche service providers in the middle, and a huge number of tiny, localized media firms on the bottom who provide specialized goods and services to the other two groups. These tiers are highly articulated through labor and distribution arrangements, joint ventures, co-productions, licensing agreements, and interlocking boards of directors. Because of this high degree of articulation, some critics have argued that cooperation, rather than competition, is the norm among media corporations and that thus the market cannot effectively regulate itself. They also maintain that deregulation threatens the public interest by threatening the diversity of public discourse because corporations control access to and regulate speech within their domains (preferring commercially viable sex and violence to informed political debate, for example). Proponents of media deregulation argue, on the contrary, that it has created more competition and consumer choice and liberated people from government control over expression and the exchange of ideas. If the social effects of media deregulation are open to debate, however, the effects on business practices within media corporations are relatively transparent. A case study of the practices of the Disney Corporation can help illustrate some of the strategies adopted by media corporations to adjust to the new business environment.

Case Study in Contemporary Media Dynamics

The formation of a liberalized global market for media technologies and products, hardware, and software opened media firms to competition not only from start-up operations but also from established media corporations in other locales. This competitive environment heightened the risks associated with the already risky business of cultural production at the same time that it promised exponentially larger returns on investment for successful products, which could now be distributed around the world and in multiple media formats. The rewards were too high to ignore, but the risks too high to tolerate. Savvy media corporations thus attempted to minimize their risks by employing strategies of consolidation, conglomeration, and globalization to grow their businesses.

Consolidation is the vertical integration of corporate holdings such that a single corporation controls all aspects of the production, distribution, exhibition, and sale of its product or service. Conglomeration involves the horizontal diversification of a corporation's holdings into new and sometimes unrelated fields. Globalization is the international dispersal of creative production and

distribution so as to cut costs and increase sales. Even before the deregulatory frenzy of the 1980s and 1990s, Disney was already somewhat horizontally integrated, having established theme parks to exhibit and promote its animated features and copyrighted characters. The parks also provided Disney with an alternate revenue stream through which to finance its film production. However, the corporation was prohibited by U.S. law from owning movie theaters or a television network and thus had to content itself with being a content provider until the early 1990s, when the U.S. Federal Communications Commission (FCC) relaxed its rules on market concentration and cross-media ownership and the U.S. courts ruled that no reason existed to continue segregating cultural production from distribution.

These rulings paved the way for Disney to grow larger by acquiring Capital Cities and its prodigious multimedia holdings, which included newspapers, publishing houses, lucrative cable channels (including ESPN and partial shares of A&E, Lifetime, E! Entertainment, and the History Channel), and the ABC television and radio networks, including ten television stations reaching up to 24 percent of U.S. households and seventy-two radio stations with forty-eight hundred affiliates. With this acquisition Disney provided itself with guaranteed distribution outlets, new sources of finance, and new ways to promote its products in a variety of media and consumer markets. It also gained, through ABC's established connections in Latin America and Asia, an immediate foothold in the global market for cultural programming. Already one of the most recognized brands in the world, Disney could now rush its products to foreign locales directly through its own networks. Owning a variety of media also opened new opportunities for cross-promotion and creative synergy, whereby multiple media holdings enable a corporation to leverage a single concept into many different products. For instance, Walt Disney Productions can create an animated feature film for theatrical release; Disney magazines, the Disney cable channel, and ABC TV and radio affiliates can all promote the film; merchandisers can create products licensed by Disney to bear the likeness of the film's characters, and Disney theme parks and retail outlets can sell these products to consumers. Because Disney owns multiple media outlets, it can also profit from a strategy called "windowing" whereby a product is released slowly through a chain of media outlets so as to maximize profits. For example, Disney might show a feature film first in theatrical release (preferably using its own theaters), then offer the film exclusively to viewers of its Disney cable channel; later it could offer the network premiere of the film on its ABC TV network, and, finally, it could release the film to video and DVD through its own Buena Vista distribution company. As the Disney example illustrates, growing larger through both vertical and horizontal integration enables a media corporation to pool its capital

resources, using profits from one sector to finance production in another and realize profit in new, more flexible ways.

Since 1995 Disney has undertaken a number of ambitious projects to both cut production overhead and leverage its brands globally. ESPN, for example, has been transformed into a multinational, multimedia franchise in its own right with magazines, restaurants, pay-per-view outlets, radio programs, four domestic U.S. cable channels (ESPN, ESPN2, ESPN Classic, and ESPN News), and international cable outlets broadcasting in more than 192 countries. The handling of ESPN International is indicative of a strategy known as "glocalization" whereby corporations seek to globalize their operations by tailoring their products and services to local markets. Thus, ESPN International is broadcast using local languages and local anchors, and coverage includes sporting events of local interest. Another way Disney has attempted to increase its global presence while minimizing its capital risk is through partial ownership of regional media suppliers in foreign locales, such as the Japan Sports Channel, the RTL network in Germany, and the Scandinavian Broadcasting System SA. Disney also aggressively partners with local media production companies around the world, including Tele-München and ZDF in Germany and Hamster Productions in France. Disney has also used joint ventures with other corporations to promote its brands globally, including a ten-year licensing deal with McDonald's to promote its animated features and deals with Sprint and Verizon to present Disney content over mobile phones. By partnering across media and with second- and third-tier media corporations, Disney is able to maintain its competitive edge at a relatively minimal cost. This, too, is indicative of all major media corporations in the global market.

Questions Remain

Consolidation, conglomeration, and globalization enable media corporations to become leaner and meaner so as to compete in the expansive global markets opened through deregulation and free trade. Disney's strategies of integration along with its joint ventures and co-productions are indicative of larger media trends, which now extend into the field of computer and Internet content provision. Giant media corporations of today are looking to partner with or acquire computer firms to add an additional distribution, and potentially retail, outlet to their holdings. If the 1995 merger between Disney and Capital Cities was the largest of its time, Time Warner's merger with online service provider AOL is the largest of today. The goal, however, remains the same: to integrate a variety of media and services under one roof in order to realize benefits that no single division could achieve on its own. Technological innovation and deregulation have made this goal possible.

Although integration and concentration may be good for business, questions remain about whether a pure market model will provide sufficient diversity of expression to insure the public interest. Will market regulation enable media systems to continue educating, informing, and integrating societies? Or will such needs be sacrificed for profit and efficiency? Even in the United States, a global leader in the promotion of free trade, public opinion seems to be shifting away from the market model. When the FCC announced in 2002 that it would eliminate restrictions on cross-media ownership and ownership of multiple television stations in a single market, suggesting that a corporation could own up to 45 percent of a media market without threatening the public interest, a bipartisan coalition of community activists assailed Congress with protest letters, e-mails, and phone calls. As a result, Congress has blocked the FCC recommendations. Although this is a far cry from re-regulating the media in the public interest, it at least signals a modification of pro-market discourse. Media scholar Ben Bagdikian may have put it best when he said, "The threat does not lie in the commercial operation of the mass media. It is the best method there is and, with all its faults, it is not inherently bad. However, *narrow* control, whether by government or corporations, *is* inherently bad" (Bagdikian 2004, 223–224).

Stacy Takacs

See also Mass Media—Concepts and Technologies; Mass Media—Debates and Divides

Further Reading

Bagdikian, B. (2004). *The new media monopoly*. Boston: Beacon Press.
Barker, C. (1997). *Global television: An introduction*. Malden, MA: Blackwell Publishing.
Barnet, R. J., & Cavanaugh, J. (1994). *Global dreams: Imperial corporations and the new world order*. New York: Simon & Schuster.
Byrne, E., & McQuillan, M. (1999). *Deconstructing Disney*. Sterling, VA: Pluto Press.
Compaine, B., & Gomery, D. (2000). *Who owns the media? Concentration and competition in the mass media* (3rd ed.). London: Lea.
Croteau, D., & Hoynes, W. (2001). *The business of media: Corporate media and the public interest*. Thousand Oaks, CA: Pine Forge Press.
Doyle, M. (1992). *The future of television: A global overview of programming, advertising, technology and growth*. Lincolnwood, IL: NTC Publishing.
Garnham, N. (1990). *Capitalism and communication: Global culture and the economics of information*. Thousand Oaks, CA: Sage Publications.
Grover, R. (1997). *The Disney touch: Disney, ABC, and the quest for the world's greatest media empire* (Rev. ed.). Chicago: Irwin Professional Publishing.
Hermann, E., & McChesney, R. (1997). *The global media: The new missionaries of corporate capitalism*. Washington, DC: Cassell.
International Institute of Communications. (1996). *Media ownership and control in the age of convergence*. London: Author.
Murdoch, G. (1990). Re-drawing the map of the communications industries: Concentration and ownership in the era of privatization. In M. Ferguson (Ed.), *Public communication: The new imperatives* (pp. 1–15). Thousand Oaks, CA: Sage Publications.
Nordenstreng, K., & Schiller, H. (Eds.). (1993). *Beyond national sovereignty: International communication in the 1990s*. Norwood, NJ: Ablex Publishing.
Owen, B., & Wildman, S. (1992). *Video economics*. Cambridge, MA: Harvard University Press.
Page, D., & Crawley, W. (2001). *Satellites over South Asia: Broadcasting, culture and the public interest*. Thousand Oaks, CA: Sage Publications.
Sinclair, J., Jacka, E., & Cunningham, S. (Eds.). (1996). *New patterns in global television: Peripheral vision*. New York: Oxford University Press.
Sreberny-Mohammadi, A., Winseck, D., McKenna, J., & Boyd-Barret, O. (1997). *Media in global context: A reader*. New York: Edward Arnold Publishing.
Tumber, H. (2000). *Media power, professionals and policies*. New York: Routledge.
The Walt Disney Company 2005 fact book. (2006). Burbank, CA: Walt Disney Corporation. Retrieved February 1, 2007, from http://corporate.disney.go.com/investors/fact_books.html
Wasko, J. (1982). *Movies and money: Financing the American film industry*. Norwood, NJ: Ablex Publishing.
Wasko, J., Phillips, M., & Meehan, E. (Eds.). (2001). *Dazzled by Disney? The global Disney audiences project*. New York: Leicester University Press.

Middle East Peace Process

Since the 1960s the U.S. has been in a position to promote Middle East peace, but also serve as a champion of Israel. This has led to tensions and questions about whether the U.S. can bring about a settlement for both sides.

The phrase "Middle East peace process" came into common use during the early 1990s, but plans to establish peace in that region are almost as old as the Israeli-Arab conflict itself. The Arab-Israeli war of 1948 ended with a series of truce agreements, and even then proposals were advanced to convert the truce into a more durable peace settlement. The degree of U.S. involvement in such efforts has varied over time. Successive administrations have believed that U.S. interests would be served by a resolution of this conflict because the association of the United States with Israeli policies has put U.S. standing with Arab and Muslim populations in the region at risk. On the other hand, a variety of internal pressures has inhibited the United States from pursuing policies that could be represented as jeopardizing Israel's strategic position. Furthermore, during the Cold War Israel was sometimes regarded as a strategic asset. The efforts of various U.S. leaders to promote a peace settlement have often been tentative and readily sidetracked, although they are not always fruitless. The central problem for United States policy-makers has been how to reconcile the U.S.-Israeli relationship with Washington's broader strategic interests.

Early Peace Overtures (1949–1956)

President Harry Truman (1884–1972) was in office during the establishment of Israel, and his administration gave general support to this process. The United States helped to secure passage of the United Nations General Assembly resolution of November 1947 that called for the partition of Palestine and thereby the creation of the Jewish state. This resolution was opposed by Arab and Muslim states, which considered it unfair to the indigenous population. However, the damage to U.S. standing in the region was for a time mitigated by the fact that the Soviet Union also supported the resolution, despite Moscow's anti-Zionist record, and was therefore in a weak position to benefit from anti-American sentiment thereby generated. Even so, Arab resentment found expression in Egypt's abstention in the United Nations Security Council vote in June 1950, authorizing action against North Korea, and in calls by Syrian politicians for an Arab alignment with the Soviet Union.

Some influential members of Truman's administration feared the strategic and political consequences of an unmodified pro-Zionist stance, and any postwar moves toward a more permanent settlement were likely to be welcome in Washington. Such moves came initially from Syria.

In March 1949 a military coup in Damascus, Syria, brought Colonel Husni Zaim (1897–1949) to power. With a view to securing U.S. aid, Zaim sought a peace settlement with Israel and offered to resettle in Syria 300,000 of the 700,000 Palestinians who had fled or been expelled from their homes in the course of the 1948 war. These overtures were rejected by the Israeli prime minister, David Ben-Gurion (1886–1973), despite U.S. pressure for a more positive response.

Zaim was overthrown and executed in a second coup in August 1949. After a later military leader, Colonel Adib Shishakli (1901–1964), renewed the overtures to Israel, negotiations took place in 1952 and 1953, but without success. In 1954 Shishakli in turn was overthrown, and Syrian politics entered a more radical phase.

Meanwhile, in January 1953 Dwight Eisenhower (1890–1969) entered the White House, having won the November 1952 election as the Republican candidate. The Eisenhower administration sought to adopt a more even-handed approach to Arab-Israeli issues than the preceding Democratic administration. Preoccupied with the Cold War, the Eisenhower administration was anxious to avoid driving the Arab world into the arms of Moscow, an outcome that appeared more probable as the post-Stalin Soviet leadership of Nikita Khrushchev (1894–1971) pursued a policy of wooing Arab states with military and economic aid. During Eisenhower's first term secret indirect contacts were established between the new Israeli prime minister, Moshe Sharett (1894–1965), who held office between December 1953 and November 1955, and President Gamal Abdul Nasser of Egypt (1918–1970). The Sharett-Nasser overtures foundered, however, as a result of a number of incidents, including the death sentences imposed on two Egyptian Jews involved in a sabotage operation in Egypt organized by Israeli military intelligence and the February 1955 Israeli raid on the Egyptian military headquarters in Gaza. After the latter event Nasser terminated contact with Sharett.

A further effort to promote an Israeli-Egyptian accord was then undertaken by Elmore Jackson, a U.S. Quaker acting as a

YITZHAK RABIN ON THE MIDDLE EAST PEACE PROCESS

On 4 November 1995, Yitzhak Rabin—Israel's Prime Minister and Minister of Defense—was assassinated at a peace rally in Tel Aviv's City Hall Plaza by an Israeli who opposed the peace process.

. . . [I]n the more than three years of this Government's existence, the Israeli people has proven that it is possible to make peace, that peace opens the door to a better economy and society; that peace is not just a prayer.

Peace is first of all in our prayers, but it is also the aspiration of the Jewish people, a genuine aspiration for peace.

There are enemies of peace who are trying to hurt us, in order to torpedo the peace process.

I want to say bluntly, that we have found a partner for peace among the Palestinians as well: the PLO, which was an enemy, and has ceased to engage in terrorism. Without partners for peace, there can be no peace.

We will demand that they do their part for peace, just as we will do our part for peace, in order to solve the most complicated, prolonged, and emotionally charged aspect of the Israeli-Arab conflict: the Palestinian- Israeli conflict.

This is a course which is fraught with difficulties and pain. For Israel, there is no path that is without pain.

But the path of peace is preferable to the path of war.

I say this to you as one who was a military man, someone who is today Minister of Defense and sees the pain of the families of the IDF soldiers. For them, for our children, in my case for our grandchildren, I want this Government to exhaust every opening, every possibility, to promote and achieve a comprehensive peace. Even with Syria, it will be possible to make peace.

This rally must send a message to the Israeli people, to the Jewish people around the world, to the many people in the Arab world, and indeed to the entire world, that the Israeli people want peace, support peace.

Source: Yitzhak Rabin's last speech. (1995, November 4). Retrieved May 31, 2007, from http://www.ariga.com/rabin-speech.shtml

Eisenhower persuaded an old friend, Robert Anderson, to undertake a fresh attempt. Anderson pursued his mission until March 1956, but ran up against the same obstacles as had previous efforts. Nasser was unwilling to take the risk of a face-to-face meeting, without which Ben-Gurion (who was then prime minister again) was unwilling to offer concessions. Eisenhower attributed the consequent failure to the intransigence of both parties.

The Drift from Even-handedness (1956–1968)

The abortive Anderson mission was the last U.S. mediatory attempt for more than a decade. From mid-1956 the administration's attention was diverted by the Suez crisis. In October, Israel, Britain, and France launched a military attack on Egypt aimed at overthrowing Nasser. Despite his disapproval of Nasser's policies Eisenhower was opposed to this adventure, and U.S. pressure was decisive both in bringing it to a halt and in securing Israel's withdrawal from the Egyptian territory it had occupied during the conflict. Eisenhower's stand during this crisis was welcomed by moderate Arab opinion, and helped to avert greater damage to Western interests in the Middle East. Thereafter, the Eisenhower administration concentrated on countering the Arab radical forces, which it believed were facilitating the growth of Soviet influence in the region. Arab-Israeli issues were pushed into the background.

John F. Kennedy (1917–1963), who succeeded Eisenhower in 1961, shared his predecessor's concern with containing Soviet power but believed that U.S. interests would be better served by a more sympathetic view of the aspirations of nonaligned powers. Opinions differ about how far this general position was reflected in Kennedy's thinking about Israel and the Arabs. Some regard him as the real architect of the U.S.-Israeli "special relationship," pointing in particular to the September 1962 decision to supply Israel with Hawk missiles, advanced weaponry for the time. Others note his private warnings to Ben-Gurion that the U.S. commitment to Israel would be jeopardized if Israel did not open its Dimona nuclear plant to inspection, suggesting that a major showdown over Israel's nuclear weapons program would have been likely had Kennedy lived longer. We have no way of knowing in which direction he would have moved had he not been assassinated.

No such uncertainty attaches to Kennedy's successor, Lyndon B. Johnson (1908–1973), who showed little inclination to seek a rapprochement with Arab nationalism. Indeed, he substantially increased U.S. military aid to Israel even before the crisis that led to the June War of 1967. This war, sometimes known as the "Six-Day War," began on 5 June when Israel launched what it portrayed as a preemptive strike against Egypt and Syria. It ended with Israel

private citizen, with the knowledge of the Eisenhower administration. During this mediation effort people learned that the Israeli side wanted a face-to-face meeting with Nasser, who was unwilling to agree to such a meeting without greater Israeli concessions than Israel was prepared to offer. Concerned about Nasser's growing alienation from the West, manifested in his arms deal with Czechoslovakia and his opposition to the Western-aligned Baghdad Pact, the administration persevered with mediation efforts after the failure of the Jackson mission. In November 1955

occupying the West Bank and East Jerusalem (taken from Jordan), the Gaza Strip and Sinai Peninsula (taken from Egypt), and the Golan Heights (taken from Syria). The Johnson administration's actions were helpful to Israel both militarily, in the form of arms supplies, and diplomatically, in that the U.S. delegation at the United Nations Security Council opposed demands for the withdrawal of armed forces to prewar lines, thus facilitating Israeli operations. In contrast to the 1956 crisis, the 1967 war produced a marked deterioration in relations between the United States and the bulk of the Arab world, as Egypt, Iraq and others broke off diplomatic relations with Washington. The Soviet Union, though inactive during the war itself, took advantage of the situation and hastened to restore the depleted Egyptian and Syrian arsenals.

One outcome of the war that could be regarded as a contribution to the peace process was United Nations Security Council Resolution 242, adopted unanimously in November 1967. This resolution called for a settlement based on Israeli withdrawal from territories occupied in the recent conflict and on the right of all states in the area to live in peace within secure and recognized boundaries, together with the termination of all belligerency. Known in shorthand as the "land for peace" formula, this resolution has formed the basis for most subsequent peace proposals. It did, however, attract criticism from Palestinians and their supporters because it omitted mention of Palestinian national aspirations.

The aftermath of the June War was otherwise a barren period for peacemaking. The triumphant mood in Israel and the corresponding sense of humiliation in the Arab world all but guaranteed future conflict. Another consequence of the war, or more precisely of the Israeli occupation, was the stimulus given to Palestinian nationalism. The Palestine Liberation Organization (PLO), founded in 1964, became an important actor in regional politics.

Nixon, the Rogers Plan, and the October War

Richard Nixon (1913–1994) assumed office as president in January 1969 and at first seemed inclined to revert to the Middle Eastern stance of the Eisenhower administration, in which he had been vice president. In December 1969 William Rogers, the secretary of state, put forward a peace plan whereby Israel would withdraw from the occupied territories in return for guarantees of its territorial integrity, with only minor adjustments to the territorial status quo obtained before the June War. Rejected by Israel and viewed skeptically by Nixon's influential national security advisor, Dr. Henry Kissinger (b. 1923), the plan was not promoted with any vigor, and the administration's policies became increasingly aligned with Israel's. Nixon later explained that he had not really

expected the Rogers Plan to succeed but thought it important to demonstrate to the Arab world that the United States was not indifferent to Arab concerns about the Israeli occupation.

On 6 October 1973 Egypt and Syria launched attacks on Israeli positions in the Sinai Peninsula and Golan Heights, respectively, with a view to recovering their lost territories. In the ensuing conflict, known to Israelis as the "Yom Kippur War" and to Arabs

YASSER ARAFAT ON THE MIDDLE EAST PEACE PROCESS

In a time of hope, Palestinian leader Yasser Arafat shared the 1994 Nobel Peace Prize with Israeli leaders Simon Peres and Yitzhak Rabin as a result of the Oslo Accords. In the excerpt below from his speech at the Nobel ceremony, Arafat talks of the continuing role of the United States and other leading nations in the peace process.

We started the peace process on the basis of land for peace, and on the basis of U.N. Resolution 242 and 338, as well as other international decisions on achieving the legitimate rights of the Palestinian people. Even though the peace process has not reached its full scope, the new environment of trust as well as the modest steps implemented during the first and second years of the peace agreement are very promising and call for the lifting of reservations, for procedures to be simplified. We must fulfill what remains, especially the transfer of power and taking further steps in Israeli withdrawal from the West Bank and the settlements to achieve full withdrawal. This would provide our society with the opportunity to rebuild its infrastructure and to contribute from its location, with its own heritage, knowledge and know-how in forging our new world.

In this context I call on Russia and the United States of America, the cosponsors of the peace conference, to help the peace process take bigger steps, by contributing to the process and helping to overcome all obstacles. I also call on Norway and Egypt as the first countries to have nurtured the Israeli-Palestinian peace to pursue this worthy initiative that took off from Oslo, to Washington, to Cairo. Oslo shall remain the bright name that accompanies the process of peace, the peace of the brave, as will the name of those countries sponsoring the multilateral talks.

Here I call on all the countries of the world especially the donor countries to speed up their contributions so that the Palestinian people may overcome their economic and social problems and proceed with reconstruction and the rebuilding of infrastructures. Peace cannot thrive, and the peace process cannot be consolidated in the absence of the necessary material conditions.

Source: Yassar Arafat—Nobel Lecture. (1994). Retrieved May 31, 2007, from http://nobelprize.org/peace/laureates/1994/arafat-lecture.html

as the "Ramadan War," the United States flew arms supplies to Israel, while the Soviet Union resupplied Egypt and Syria. In military terms the war ended with another Israeli victory, but its political and psychological results were quite different from those of the 1967 war. Israel's early military setbacks, combined with an Arab oil embargo against the United States, served to dispel the picture of Arab humiliation and impotence. After the war Kissinger, by then secretary of state, promoted agreements for the disengagement of Egyptian and Israeli forces in Sinai and a similar Israeli-Syrian disengagement on the Golan Heights. Furthermore, the psychological preconditions were now in place for more substantial moves toward a settlement, at least between Egypt and Israel. Egypt's foreign policy was being reoriented by President Anwar Sadat (1918–1981), who had succeeded Nasser after the latter's death in 1970. Sadat believed that closer ties with the United States would better serve Egypt's interests than continued

An Arab Muslim and Israeli Jew looking away from each other. Source: istock: Steven Allan.

dependence on Soviet support and, having administered a shock to Israel in 1973, felt able to act on this belief.

Carter, Camp David Treaty, and Its Consequences

The undermining of the Nixon administration by the Watergate scandal, culminating in the president's resignation in August 1974, put the United States in a poor position to undertake major initiatives in the Middle East. The next president to take up the matter was the Democrat Jimmy Carter (b. 1924), who took office in January 1977. Although Carter had expressed pro-Israeli sentiments during the 1976 election campaign, in October 1977 he joined the Soviet leadership in calling for recognition of the legitimate rights of the Palestinians and appeared to favor convening an international peace conference with Soviet participation. Plans for an international conference were, however, undercut by the developing bilateral contacts between Egypt's Sadat and the Israeli prime minister, Menachem Begin (1913–1992).

Begin wished to avoid an international conference, especially one involving Moscow, but was happy to deal with Sadat. In November 1977 Sadat broke with long-standing Arab practice by visiting Israel and addressing its legislature, the Knesset, with a plea for peace. Adjusting to the new situation, Carter invited Sadat and Begin to the presidential retreat at Camp David, Maryland, in July 1978. After months of negotiation the parties agreed on the terms of a peace treaty, which was eventually signed in Washington in March 1979. Its main provisions were that Egypt formally recognized Israel and ended the state of belligerency, and Israel agreed to return the Sinai Peninsula to Egypt.

The Camp David treaty aroused strongly conflicting responses. The United States and the West generally welcomed the treaty as the first formal peace agreement between Israel and an Arab state and possibly a model for others. However, to most of the Arab world it represented betrayal: Sadat had broken the united Arab front, to Israel's strategic benefit, while other Arab territories were still under occupation. Egypt was suspended from the Arab League, and Sadat himself was assassinated by Islamic radicals in October 1981.

The next decade was marked by continuing conflict, notably the Israeli invasion of Lebanon in 1982, which strained the Israeli-Egyptian entente, and the Palestinian uprising known as the *intifada*, which began in 1987. The United States, under President Ronald Reagan (1911–2004), put forward two further peace plans, in 1982 and 1988. Both proposed a degree of Palestinian autonomy, but not independence, and neither made headway. Nonetheless, U.S.-Palestinian relations improved slightly in November 1988,

A ROAD MAP TO PEACE

The following passage is the introduction to the Middle East peace process plan, A Performance-Based Roadmap to a Permanent Two-State Solution to the Israeli-Palestinian Conflict. *This document was a result of a collaboration among several world powers and it was presented in 2003 by the U.S. State Department.*

The following is a performance-based and goal-driven roadmap, with clear phases, timelines, target dates, and benchmarks aiming at progress through reciprocal steps by the two parties in the political, security, economic, humanitarian, and institution-building fields, under the auspices of the Quartet [the United States, European Union, United Nations, and Russia]. The destination is a final and comprehensive settlement of the Israel-Palestinian conflict by 2005, as presented in President Bush's speech of 24 June, and welcomed by the EU, Russia and the UN in the 16 July and 17 September Quartet Ministerial statements.

A two-state solution to the Israeli-Palestinian conflict will only be achieved through an end to violence and terrorism, when the Palestinian people have a leadership acting decisively against terror and willing and able to build a practicing democracy based on tolerance and liberty, and through Israel's readiness to do what is necessary for a democratic Palestinian state to be established, and a clear, un-ambiguous acceptance by both parties of the goal of a negotiated settlement as described below. The Quartet will assist and facilitate implementation of the plan, starting in Phase I, including direct discussions between the parties as required. The plan establishes a realistic

timeline for implementation. However, as a performance-based plan, progress will require and depend upon the good faith efforts of the parties, and their compliance with each of the obligations outlined below. Should the parties perform their obligations rapidly, progress within and through the phases may come sooner than indicated in the plan. Non-compliance with obligations will impede progress.

A settlement, negotiated between the parties, will result in the emergence of an independent, democratic, and viable Palestinian state living side by side in peace and security with Israel and its other neighbors. The settlement will resolve the Israel-Palestinian conflict, and end the occupation that began in 1967, based on the foundations of the Madrid Conference, the principle of land for peace, UNSCRs 242, 338 and 1397, agreements previously reached by the parties, and the initiative of Saudi Crown Prince Abdullah—endorsed by the Beirut Arab League Summit—calling for acceptance of Israel as a neighbor living in peace and security, in the context of a comprehensive settlement. This initiative is a vital element of international efforts to promote a comprehensive peace on all tracks, including the Syrian-Israeli and Lebanese-Israeli tracks.

The Quartet will meet regularly at senior levels to evaluate the parties' performance on implementation of the plan. In each phase, the parties are expected to perform their obligations in parallel, unless otherwise indicated.

Source: U.S. Department of State. (2003, April 30). Retrieved March 20, 2007, from http://www.state.gov/r/pa/prs/ps/2003/20062.htm

---

when Yasser Arafat (1929–2004), chairman of the PLO, persuaded the Palestinian National Council to support a two-state solution to the Palestinian conflict rather than the unitary Palestinian state, which the council had previously advocated. The Reagan administration responded by opening formal dialogue with the PLO, paving the way for further initiatives by Reagan's successor, George H. W. Bush (b. 1924).

Madrid Conference and the Oslo Accords

A confluence of events at the beginning of the 1990s led the George H. W. Bush administration to believe that a comprehensive settlement of the Arab-Israeli conflict was feasible. The collapse of the Soviet bloc between 1989 and 1991 and the defeat of Iraq in the 1991 Iraq War put the United States in a position of unprecedented hegemony. The same developments weakened the radical forces in the Arab world. At the same time, the Bush administration felt the need to demonstrate that the United States was not wholly

insensitive to Palestinian aspirations and put some pressure on Israel to desist from expanding Jewish settlements in the occupied territories.

Under U.S. sponsorship a conference was convened in Madrid in October 1991, attended by Syria and Israel as well as a joint Jordanian-Palestinian delegation, the Palestinians not technically representing the PLO. The conference was followed by bilateral negotiations between Israel and the Arab parties, but by the time Bush left office in January 1993, to be succeeded by the Democrat Bill Clinton (b. 1946), no substantial progress had been made.

An alternative approach was adopted by the opening of secret talks between PLO and Israeli representatives in Oslo, Norway, without U.S. participation. This process was facilitated by the election in June 1992 of a new government in Israel, under the Labor Party leader Yitzhak Rabin (1922–1995), who was readier for compromise than his predecessor had been. The outcome was an agreement on the Declaration of Principles, whereby Israel and the PLO formally recognized each other and laid down an agenda for future negotiation. The agreement, also known as "Oslo I," did not prescribe the form of a final agreement but did provide

for Israeli withdrawal from the Gaza Strip and Jericho. When the Clinton administration discovered what had been happening, Arafat and Rabin were invited to sign their agreement at the White House, which they did on 13 September 1993. This event, and the accompanying handshake between Arafat and Rabin, was greeted euphorically in the West, although with more mixed feelings in the Middle East.

A second agreement, called "Oslo II," was signed in September 1995, providing for the election of a Palestinian council with some legislative powers and further measures of Israeli withdrawal. Meanwhile, a peace treaty between Israel and Jordan was concluded in October 1994. In the context of an apparently improving Israeli-Palestinian relationship, King Hussein of Jordan felt free to give formal expression to the long-standing reality of peace with Israel.

Diplomatic Failure and Renewed Conflict (1995–2000)

From the mid-1990s the optimism generated by the Oslo accords began to fade. Rabin, regarded as a traitor by the far right in Israel, was assassinated by one of their number in November 1995. The following year a Likud-led government came to power under Binyamin Netanyahu (b. 1950), who had never been happy about the accords. Arafat, too, came under attack from Palestinians who believed that he had abandoned the *intifada* in return for insignificant gains.

The election in May 1999 of a new Israeli government under Ehud Barak (b. 1942) led to a fresh round of negotiations with Syria and the Palestinians, this time with U.S. participation. The Israeli-Syrian talks collapsed in March 2000 because Barak, although willing to return the bulk of Syrian territory occupied since the June War, was not prepared to withdraw completely to the prewar lines, a condition insisted on by the Syrian president, Hafez Assad (1930–2000).

Israeli-Palestinian negotiations resumed when Clinton invited Barak and Arafat to a summit meeting at Camp David, which took place in July 2000. This meeting, too, ended in failure, the precise reasons for which are disputed. The official Israeli version, supported by Clinton, is that Arafat turned down a generous offer, which would have granted the Palestinians a state comprising the bulk of the land occupied in 1967. The opposing version is that Barak did not offer the conditions required for a viable independent Palestine but rather a truncated entity in which the Palestinians would have been militarily and economically dominated by Israel. The summit collapse was followed in September by a renewed Palestinian uprising, sometimes called the *al-Aqsa intifada*.

George W. Bush and the Road Map

The first term of President George W. Bush (b. 1946) was dominated by the U.S. response to the September 11 terrorist attacks and the subsequent wars in Afghanistan and Iraq. When, prompted by his allies, he turned his attention to the Palestine question, the result was a document termed the "road map," produced in collaboration with the European Union, the U.N., and Russia but clearly reflecting U.S. thinking. The document, presented in April 2003, called for a series of phased measures, including Palestinian reforms and an end to the uprising, leading to a peace settlement and a Palestinian state by 2005. The plan's supporters noted that Bush was the first U.S. president to call explicitly for a Palestinian state. Critics argued that in most respects the Bush administration was so aligned with the Israeli position, for instance, in its refusal to deal with Arafat, as to undermine U.S. credibility as a mediator. The death of Arafat in November 2004 led Bush to express the hope that the peace process could be revived.

Implications

This discussion has shown that Israeli-Arab peace negotiations have a long history. The degree and form of U.S. involvement in these negotiations have changed over time, but at least since the 1960s the United States has been both the external power most capable of promoting a settlement and the main champion of Israel. This dual role has produced tensions, and a key question for the future is how far it will allow Washington to bring about a settlement that seems just to both sides. A substantial body of evidence now exists, particularly in the form of opinion poll data, suggesting that the standing of the United States in the Arab and Islamic Middle East is closely related to U.S. policy towards the Palestine issue. More than any other single factor, this is mentioned by poll respondents as the primary grievance against the United States, even among people who admire other features of U.S. society and politics. An equitable resolution of the conflict seems clearly to be in the interests of the United States. A settlement that merely reflects the prevailing power balance is unlikely to be durable.

John Chiddick

See also Foreign Policy after September 11, 2001, U.S.; Iraq Wars; Islamic Worldview

Further Reading

Beilin, Y. (2004). *The path to Geneva: The quest for a permanent agreement, 1996–2004.* New York: Akashic Books.

Enderlin, C. (2002). *Shattered dreams: The failure of the peace process in the Middle East, 1995–2002.* New York: Other Press.

Lenczowski, G. (1990). *American presidents and the Middle East.* Durham, NC: Duke University Press.

Lesch, D. W. (2003). *The Middle East and the United States: A historical and political reassessment.* Boulder, CO: Westview Press.

Morris, B. (1999). *Righteous victims: The history of the Zionist-Arab conflict, 1881–1999.* New York: Alfred A. Knopf.

Ross, D. (2004). *The missing peace: The inside story of the fight for Middle East peace.* New York: Farrar, Straus and Giroux.

Rubenberg, C. A. (1986). *Israel and the American national interest: A critical examination.* Urbana and Chicago: University of Illinois Press.

Shlaim, A. (2000). *The iron wall: Israel and the Arab world.* New York: W. W. Norton.

Slater, J. (2001). What went wrong? The collapse of the Israeli-Palestinian peace process. *Political Science Quarterly, 116*(2), 171–199.

Suleiman, M. W. (1995). *U.S. policy on Palestine from Wilson to Clinton.* Normal, IL: Association of Arab-American University Graduates.

Missionaries

U.S. missionaries have at times exercised significant influence on U.S. public opinion and foreign policy because they travel from one culture to another and have firsthand knowledge of international political circumstances.

Missionaries are representatives of churches who cross cultural boundaries to spread the Christian faith. The first task of missionaries is to translate the Bible and other theological documents into vernacular languages of the foreign locale. The task of translation often includes putting the language into written form, compiling a lexicon, and teaching people to read. By the twenty-first century portions of the Bible had been translated into more than twenty-three hundred languages. Missionaries seek to convince people of the correctness of Christian beliefs, to gather them into churches, and to train church leaders. In addition to evangelistic outreach, missionaries engage in humanitarian work, including the founding of schools and hospitals, famine and refugee relief, and the documentation of human rights abuses.

Because missionaries traditionally made long-term commitments to specific groups of people, they were often the first Americans to gain in-depth knowledge of a people's language, history, and customs. One of the most important roles of U.S. missionaries has been to act as representatives on behalf of indigenous peoples vis-à-vis Western governments and media and to communicate knowledge about other cultures to ordinary Americans. Missionaries and their indigenous partners thus act as bridges between U.S. and non-Western cultures.

The first U.S. missionaries worked among Native Americans. The first Bible printed in the Americas was Massachusetts Puritan missionary John Eliot's translation into Algonquian, published in 1661. Both Harvard and Dartmouth colleges were founded in part to train Native American ministers. Although individual missionaries had varied success among Native Americans, widespread support of missionaries did not begin until the 1800s. The first "foreign" mission agency was a cooperative venture among Congregationalists and Presbyterians. Called the "American Board," it raised money by individual subscriptions to send its first missionaries—three married ministers and their wives and two unmarried men—to India in 1812. The British East India Company refused them admittance to British India until an act of Parliament forced them to admit missionaries. Early U.S. missionaries were seen as a nuisance by European colonial powers because such missionaries facilitated social change among subject peoples and because they were imbued with the spirit of "American republicanism" and democracy.

As increasing numbers of Christians in the United States came to support foreign missions, different denominations founded their own voluntary societies to send missionaries. By the 1880s about two thousand Americans had become missionaries, 10 percent of whom worked among Native Americans. As the United States became more involved in foreign affairs before World War I, it overtook the United Kingdom in sending the most missionaries. U.S. Roman Catholic priests and religious sisters also began going abroad in significant numbers after the war. Missions provided opportunities for women to work cross-culturally in education, medicine, and social work, and by the 1910s two-thirds of U.S. Protestant missionaries were female. Female missionaries, both Catholic and Protestant, introduced formal education for girls in Korea, India, China, Japan, and other countries that traditionally opposed the education of women. Missionaries agitated for improved rights for women. They opposed such social customs as female infanticide, forced female seclusion, legalized prostitution, child marriage in India, foot-binding in China, and female genital mutation in north Africa. The first female medical doctors and nurses in China, India, Japan, and Korea were trained by missionaries. The importance of missionaries as interpreters of non-Western cultures was underscored in 1932 when missionary Pearl S. Buck received the Pulitzer Prize for *The Good Earth*, her novel of Chinese peasant life, and the Nobel Prize in literature in 1938.

During World War II Western missionaries were stranded in Southeast Asia and interned by the Japanese as enemy aliens. Roughly half of foreign culture experts during World War II were the offspring of missionaries who had grown up in the affected areas. After the war U.S. missionaries returned to help reconstruct civil, religious, and educational institutions in Japan, the Philippines, and other devastated countries. A new wave of conservative evangelical missionaries moved into small tribal societies in Latin America, Africa, and Southeast Asia to translate the Bible, found churches, and train indigenous pastors. The victory of Communism in China displaced all missionaries there by 1950. During the period of decolonization and national independence movements in the 1950s and 1960s, mainline denominations began questioning the evangelistic motives of mission work, and the number of full-time missionaries from those denominations steadily declined from the late 1960s. However, conservative missionaries, including

Pentecostals, Southern Baptists, and Wycliffe Bible translators, increased in number. The United States continued to send the most missionaries in the early twenty-first century, with more than four hundred agencies sending 45,600 full-time Protestant missionaries in 2002. In addition, hundreds of thousands of part-time mission volunteers regularly participate in building projects, AIDS orphans projects, and other cross-cultural humanitarian ventures.

Missionaries and Foreign Policy

Because of their ability to bridge different worldviews, their willingness to live in obscure and dangerous locations for the sake of their religious commitments, and their relationships with interested supporters, missionaries have at times exercised significant influence on U.S. public opinion and through it on foreign policy. The following are two important examples of such influence.

Near East

Through the founding of secondary schools and colleges during the nineteenth century, missionaries introduced Western learning, including sciences, technology, geography, and civics, into India, east Asia, and the Ottoman Empire. Missionary educators founded such institutions as the American University of Beirut and Robert College of Constantinople (Istanbul), Turkey. Religious minorities often used U.S. missionaries to put them on the path toward modernization. As the Ottoman Empire began to crumble, the Ottomans slaughtered Christian minorities, including Armenians, Nestorians, and Maronites. In the 1890s U.S. missionaries reported on the atrocities they witnessed and provided support for thousands of survivors. In 1915 missionaries began helping survivors of the Armenian genocide. In response to missionary reports the U.S. State Department launched Near East Relief as the first substantial foreign relief operation of the U.S. government. The American Board collected the funds and distributed relief aid through the network of consuls and missionaries in the Ottoman Empire. Near East Relief channeled $117 million from 1915 to 1930 and is credited with keeping the Armenian nation alive.

Concerned for minorities in the Ottoman Empire and elsewhere, President Woodrow Wilson issued his Fourteen Points in 1918. Among the Fourteen Points was the doctrine of the self-determination of minority peoples. W. R. Mead attributes "Wilsonian" foreign policy concerns for human rights to missionary influence as missionaries and their home-based supporters in the nineteenth and early twentieth centuries pressured the U.S. government to promote "a human rights agenda in the developing world" (Mead 2001, 148). The concept of a "global civil society" was partly a result of missionary influence. Missionaries also used church connections as a conduit for the resettlement of oppressed peoples in the United States.

Latin America

After Communists drove out or imprisoned the Western missionaries in China, many Roman Catholic priests and nuns relocated to Latin America during the 1950s to found schools and seminaries. In 1963 Pope John XXIII called for all North American religious communities to send one-tenth of their personnel to Latin America as missionaries. While U.S. Catholic religious workers were moving southward, military dictatorships were overthrowing democratically elected governments throughout the continent. Father Ivan Illich of Mexico charged that the U.S. missionaries were being used as "colonial chaplains" for "Camelot projects." In response to such criticisms, many North American Catholic missionaries adopted a "theology of liberation" and began to stand in solidarity with the oppressed masses suffering under dictatorships. Nuns moved into poor communities, both to witness oppression and to help people organize themselves.

The Banzer Plan, promulgated secretly by Paraguayan dictator Hugo Banzer, authorized death squad attacks on missionaries and church leaders. For standing on the side of the poor, approximately 850 bishops, priests, and nuns were murdered in Central America during the 1970s and 1980s. In 1980 four North American church women were raped and murdered by right-wing militias

MISSIONARY WORK IN THE MIDST OF VIOLENCE

The following is an excerpt from a letter written by Brother James Miller, a Christian missionary and advocate for the poor in Guatemala. It was written shortly before he was killed by a paramilitary death squad on 13 February 1982.

I am personally weary of violence, but I continue to feel a strong commitment to the suffering poor of Central America. "God's ways are not man's ways," says the Bible. God knows why He continued to call me to Guatemala when some friends and relatives encouraged me to pull out for my own comfort and safety, but I have been a Christian Brother for nearly twenty years now, and my commitment to my vocation grows steadily stronger in the context of my work in Central America. I pray to God for the grace and strength to serve Him faithfully by my presence among the poor and oppressed of Guatemala. I place my life in His Providence; I place my trust in Him.

Source: Brett, D.W. & Brett, E.T. (1988). Murdered in Central America: The stories of eleven U.S. missionaries (p. 158). Maryknoll, NY: Orbis Books.

in El Salvador. By documenting abuses against the poor, the missionaries had become a threat to the military junta. As the Reagan administration's Contra war on the Nicaraguan Sandinistas accelerated, U.S. Catholic sisters blanketed churches in the United States with anti-Contra information. Kept informed by Maryknoll missionary sisters, Speaker of the House Tip O'Neill prevented support for the Contras from passing the House of Representatives. North American Catholics meanwhile instituted the Sanctuary Movement to hide undocumented immigrants from Guatemala, El Salvador, and other places fleeing from Latin American dictatorships. Although many conservative Protestants in the United States supported Reagan's Latin American policies, the missionary theology of liberation provided a vital counterweight in public opinion and foreign policy.

Imperialists or Humanitarians?

U.S. foreign missionaries have frequently been suspected of being government agents—a charge that in most cases cannot be substantiated. For example, one of the first U.S. missionaries in 1812, Adoniram Judson, was forced from India by the British but then arrested as pro-British by the Burmese. Critics of the perceived relationship between the U.S. government and missionaries typically fall into two groups: Americans who believe that religious belief should be privatized or that cultural change is inherently bad and leaders of foreign governments or political parties. Governments such as that of Indonesia, for example, routinely deny visas to missionaries because they witness human rights abuses by government forces against tribal peoples. Ambivalence and interpretive shifts accompany African perceptions of missionaries, ranging from the Kenyan politician Jomo Kenyatta's accusation during the 1950s that missionaries brought the Bible but stole the land, to South African politician Nelson Mandela's thanking of missionaries for their educational and human rights work during a meeting of the World Council of Churches in 1998.

Hostilities against missionaries rise and fall with the political context. Often attacks on missionaries are orchestrated to gain publicity by holding them hostage, even though mission organizations refuse to pay ransom. Examples of missionary hostages include Father Lawrence Jenco of Catholic Relief Services and the Presbyterian Reverend Benjamin Weir, held captive by Islamic Jihad in Lebanon in the mid-1980s; Christian and Missionary Alliance leprosy nurse Betty Ann Olsen, held by the Viet Cong for eight months until her death in 1968; and Martin and Gracia Burnham of New Tribes Mission, held by the militant separatist group Abu Sayyaf in the Philippines in 2001–2002. With the United States as the major world power in the late twentieth century, antimissionary rhetoric increased among fundamentalist political parties such as the Hindu nationalist BJP (Bharatiya Janata) in India and the Taliban in Afghanistan. Both within the United States and abroad, antimissionary rhetoric has proven useful as propaganda against Westernization or Judeo-Christian influence.

China

Nowhere else has opinion about missionaries shifted as much as in China, the most common destination of missionaries prior to the Communist era. Because Protestant missionaries entered China under the "unequal treaties" forged after the Opium Wars, the Chinese viewed missionaries as part of the imperial presence. Anti-Christian riots peaked in 1900 during the Boxer Movement, when the Empress Dowager called for a general uprising against all things foreign, including religion and technology. The Boxers killed several hundred foreign missionaries and about thirty thousand Chinese Christians. Paradoxically, the destruction of the Boxers revealed the need of the country to modernize, and thousands poured into missionary schools. When the Nationalist government seized power in 1912, it was pro-Christian and pro-Western. Both Sun Yat-sen and Chiang Kai-shek became Christians and used their status to forge friendships with the West. Missionaries supported the Nationalist regime and represented its interests to Western governments. Medical schools, hospitals, social services, and thirteen mission-founded universities were praised as valuable contributions to China's progress. During the 1920s, however, anticolonial movements swept through student populations, and the government put all mission institutions under Chinese control. The Marxist-inspired Communist movement rejected missionaries and all Christian institutions as imperialistic. Its victory in 1949 meant the end of foreign missions in China and the expulsion of all missionaries. Although official government policy firmly rejects missions, by the late twentieth century a new appreciation for missionary contributions in agriculture, medicine, education, and the arts emerged among intellectual elites searching for the foundation of the West's success. In the 1989 demonstrations at Tiananmen Square in Beijing, some students carried crosses in public processions for the first time in decades. By the early twenty-first century Chinese intellectuals were studying "religion as culture" and reevaluating missionaries as contributors to China's national progress.

The multilayered and changing perceptions of U.S. missionaries demonstrate why they should be analyzed in particular social and political contexts rather than from ideological perspectives.

Dana L. Robert

See also Christian Nation, United States as

Further Reading

Barton, J. (1930). *The story of Near East Relief.* New York: Macmillan.

Bays, D. (Ed.). (1996). *Christianity in China from the eighteenth century to the present.* Stanford, CA: Stanford University Press.

Bays, D., & Wacker, G. (Eds.). (2003). *The foreign missionary enterprise at home: Explorations in North American cultural history.* Tuscaloosa: University of Alabama Press.

Brett, E. (2003). *The U.S. Catholic press on Central America: From Cold War anticommunism to social justice.* Notre Dame, IN: University of Notre Dame Press.

Carpenter, J., & Shenk, W. (Eds.). (1990). *Earthen vessels: American evangelicals and foreign missions, 1880–1980.* Grand Rapids, MI: Eerdmans.

Costello, G. (1979). *Mission to Latin America: The successes and failures of a twentieth century crusade.* Maryknoll, NY: Orbis.

Dries, A. (1998). *The missionary movement in American Catholic history.* Maryknoll, NY: Orbis.

Fey, H. (1966). *Cooperation in compassion: The story of Church World Service.* New York: Friendship Press.

Grabill, J. (1971). *Protestant diplomacy and the Near East: Missionary influence on American policy, 1810–1927.* Minneapolis: University of Minnesota.

Hutchison, W. R. (1987). *Errand to the world: American Protestant thought and foreign missions.* Chicago: University of Chicago Press.

Lernoux, P. (1982). *Cry of the people: The struggle for human rights in Latin America—The Catholic church in conflict with U.S. policy.* New York: Penguin.

Mead, W. R. (2001). *Special providence: American foreign policy and how it changed the world.* New York: Knopf.

Robert, D. L. (1997). *American women in mission: A social history of their thought and practice.* Macon, GA: Mercer University Press.

Robert, D. L. (2002). The first globalization: The internationalization of the Protestant missionary movement between the world wars. *International Bulletin of Missionary Research, 26*(2), 50–66.

Varg, P. (1977). *Missionaries, Chinese, and diplomats: The American Protestant missionary movement in China, 1890–1952.* New York: Octagon.

Modernity, United States and

The United States has been viewed as an agent of modernity—with an emphasis on freedom, science and reason—since its founding, and it has been admired and criticized as modernity takes hold across the globe.

Many people view the United States as the paradigm of the "modern" society because it was founded in the spirit of "modernity" by "reflection and choice," in the words of the authors of the U.S. Constitution (Hamilton, Jay, and Madison 2001, 1). "Modernity" is a broad intellectual category meant to convey a matrix of experiences that originated after the Reformation and Renaissance. It signifies "the fragmentation of the social world, the absence of universally accepted values and norms of behavior, the paramount role of the selfish individual as prototype for the human existence, the public display of private obsessions transmitted in an imagery of chaos and terror, dream, and fantasy, the swift succession of 'fashions' in intellectual and cultural matters, the collective feeling of superiority toward the past and ancient cultures, and the widely spread predilection for disorder, disruptions, disobedience" (Schabert 1979, 123).

Two major components of modernity stand out: (1) the view that the primary attribute of human beings is their freedom and (2) the view that the scientific method is the vehicle for improving humanity's lot in the world, often referred to as the "relief of man's estate." Modernity is a broad category because people have a wide variety of understandings of human freedom, science, and the degree to which freedom and science in fact contribute to human happiness. Some people resist modernity, and others want to extend and perhaps radicalize it and even go beyond it. Even so, modernity has many faces and stages of development. How one evaluates the United States as the symbol and agent of modernity depends not only on one's attitude toward modernity, but also on which modernity one adopts for oneself and which modernity one attributes to the United States. Even so, with worldwide attention paid to the modernity of the United States, it can be said fairly that the United States has been elevated to the status of a symbol or even a concept of philosophy, which no other nation in human history, except perhaps the Roman Empire, has enjoyed or suffered.

Three Waves of Modernity

Modernity is often characterized as having three waves, and men holding views of the first wave founded the United States. The Enlightenment (a philosophic movement of the eighteenth century marked by a rejection of traditional social, religious, and political ideas and an emphasis on rationalism) strongly influenced the founders of the United States. The hallmarks of their political thinking were the liberty of each person to decide how to live his or her own life, equality, limited government, separation of church and state, and representative government. Their political views were drawn from their philosophical views, according to which they viewed human beings as fundamentally rational in the sense that each person can determine his or her own self-interest and act upon it; the universe has a law-like structure that can be understood by the human intellect; the methods of modern science can be used to understand the universe; the methods of modern science can also be used to gain a great deal of technological mastery over the universe.

Ideas such as justice are found in the laws of nature, making reference to the laws of God philosophically unnecessary (although perhaps politically necessary). English and Scottish philosophers of the Enlightenment influenced the founders. For instance, after the Bible, the most quoted author among pamphleteers during the American Revolution was John Locke (1632–1704), one of the key English Enlightenment thinkers whose ideas on tolerance, natural rights, limited government, and freedom continue to inspire classical liberals and "neoconservatives" to this day.

The first wave of modernity contained a tension that would be criticized—but never fully resolved—and even aggravated in later waves. The Enlightenment sees politics as limited because it views self-preservation, not virtue or moral greatness, as its fundamental principle. Human greatness would have to come through the progress of science in understanding and also mastering nature. Dissatisfaction is a common theme and concern among all modern writers because modernity promises the grand project of mastery over nature, but it is conducted by and for a being whose nobility and dignity are difficult to defend under the terms of modernity. The intractable dissatisfaction inherent in modernity is found in the tension between its moral leveling and the technological powers and responsibilities it demands of human beings. The English philosopher Thomas Hobbes (1588–1679), a key first-wave thinker, summarized the combination of low moral stature and great scientific power of modern humanity: "I put for a general inclination of

all mankind, a perpetual and restless desire of power after power that ceaseth only in death" (Hobbes 1994, 58).

Numerous political thinkers criticized the principles of this first wave of modernity. The French philosopher and author Jean-Jacques Rousseau (1712–1778), who inspired Romanticism (a literary, artistic, and philosophical movement originating in the eighteenth century and characterized by a reaction against neoclassicism and an emphasis on the imagination and emotions) as well as the French Revolution, and the German philosopher Immanuel Kant (1724–1804), whose ideas influenced the formation of the European Union, thought that the ideas of first-wave thinkers such as Locke undermine liberty. These second-wave thinkers argued that the natural rights philosophy of the first wave (and of the U.S. Constitution by implication) based itself on a view of nature that associates human nature too closely with the nature of physical objects. Human freedom cannot be adequately defended if humans are seen to be under the same laws of necessity of physical objects. Moreover, freedom and political society have to aspire to something more than simply self-preservation. Not surprisingly, Kant stated that Americans are incapable of civilization because they have "no passion, hardly speak at all, never caress one another, care about nothing, and are lazy" (Rubin and Rubin 2004, 26).

If the first wave of modernity regarded human nature as too static and freedom as too restrictive and insufficiently grand, Rousseau and Kant decided that freedom can be sustained only by regarding human nature and political society in light of an evolving sense of history. Rousseau saw humans evolving in the "state of nature" from a state of innocence to one corrupted by civilization that creates inequality through property and technology. Humans can be made whole again by creating a just society that is of their free making. Unlike first-wave thinkers, this just society would be less concerned about simple physical well being, and it would be more concerned with justice and virtue. Key to Rousseau's idea is the notion that justice, or the general will, is not an abstract principle nor based on the laws of nature or of God. It is a rule of reason produced by the march of history and the development of human rationality. History as progress toward some final state, an "end of history," is the hallmark of second-wave modernity and plays an important role to subsequent thinkers, including the German political philosopher Karl Marx (1818–1883), but also to Americans who view history as progressive in terms of freedom and technological achievement.

Nature, understood as a transcendent ethical standard in the form of natural law or right, no longer has anything to do with politics in second-wave modernity. Nature is restricted to the physical realm, and politics is instead viewed as the realm of history, reason, and will. Second-wave thinkers therefore inspired various Romantic sentiments and ideologies that simultaneously would see human beings as morally good but politics and civilization as corrupt and nature as separate and pure, not to be touched by society. In addition to major segments of French and German society, their ideas helped to inspire a wide variety of ideologies

The famous "Welcome Sign" to Las Vegas, Nevada, a city that symbolizes the decadence targeted by U.S. critics. Source: istock/Jason Walton.

and viewpoints that criticizes the United States. These critics include opponents of capitalism such as Marx; cosmopolitans whose allegiance to transnational organizations such as nongovernment organizations (NGOs) and international law makes them skeptical and critical of U.S. forms of nationalism; legal scholars who regard the constitutional values as progressive (and reject "original intent" as a mode of interpreting the Constitution because first-wave modernity is deemed antiquated); environmentalists who think civilization in the form of industrialization destroys the planet; and nationalists who view the commercial and extended republic of the United States as a threat to small communities characterized by civic virtue and solidarity. These attitudes and ideologies share the second-wave view of history as a progressive unfolding of human potential and civilization. For most of these groups, progress is for the better, although some people, including some environmentalists and romantics, view history not as progress but as regress and corruption. Many of these groups reside on the left wing of the political spectrum, although many nationalists are on the right (even though they selectively borrow from left-wing second-wave ideas). However, most people on the right wing of the political spectrum in the United States, mostly classical liberals and neoconservatives, tend to take their bearings from the U.S. founding and Locke.

If second-wave thinkers turned to history because they regarded first-wave thinkers' views on nature and freedom as too restrictive, third-wave thinkers rejected history as too restrictive and went further by rejecting all transcendent or metaphysical grounds for freedom. German thinkers such as Friedrich Nietzsche (1844–1900) and Martin Heidegger (1889–1976) and the later twentieth-century "postmodern" and "deconstructionist" thinkers whom they inspired postulated that all foundations residing outside the human will are oppressive. They claim that "privileging" one cultural, historical, or metaphysical perspective lies at the root of oppression, including colonialism, sexual and racial discrimination, economic inequality, homophobia, and cultural prejudice. Heidegger, for instance, regarded the United States in apocalyptic terms by regarding its commitment to pragmatism and technology as the quintessentially (first-wave) modern force of technology that destroys human culture. Third-wave modernity (or postmodernism) expresses the sentiment of the "experience of terror and anguish rather than of harmony and peace, and it is a sentiment of historic existence as necessarily tragic" (Strauss 1989, 94). According to this view, all moral and political values are humanly created and not rooted in either nature or history, not to mention premodern categories such as God and revelation. As a result, all values are subject to reevaluation and re-creation, including modern values of freedom and technology themselves: "Modernity could be said to consist of its own self-criticism, held together by the relative stability of the horizon within which the self-criticism takes place" (Cropsey 1986, 174). With third-wave modernity the unease and anxiety of Hobbes's restless search for power after power become most explicit.

Modernity and the United States

From its founding the United States has been seen as the agent of modernity. Eighteenth-century European aristocrats criticized the United States for its commitment to freedom and equality for the same reason that the underclass emigrated there. Karl Marx even wrote to Abraham Lincoln during the Civil War in support of the North against the propertied South. However, Marx and later socialists, as part of second-wave modernity, recognized the ways in which U.S. ideals of freedom and equality, along with representative government and capitalism, are rooted in first-wave modernity.

Perceptions of the United States as an agent of modernity have changed as the rest of the world has modernized. The elites creating the European Union are inspired more by second-wave and in some cases third-wave modernity, and so they regard the United States as too conservative because its modernity, as expressed in terms of classical liberalism, is rooted in the first wave. Similarly, numerous leaders in the developing world since the 1950s have applied the criticisms of capitalism and imperialism in the works of Marx and the Russian Communist leader Vladimir Ilyich Lenin (1870–1924) (both second-wave thinkers) to the United States.

The identification of the United States with globalization is part of this second-wave viewpoint. However, critics of globalization also argue that it undermines community (the criticism also of nationalists) because it replaces the traditions and stories of particular societies with the images of mass media and entertainment. Globalization erodes traditions because it unsettles communities, and mass media, mostly U.S., serve as an ersatz tradition for the dispossessed masses. Globalization is seen as a threat and as a promise, which is rooted in modernity's utopian and dystopian roots.

Many people regard the United States, as the agent of modernity and globalization, with ambivalence. As the Swiss philosopher Jeanne Hersch states: "The Americans make us uneasy because, without wishing us ill, they put things before us for taking... so convenient that we accept them, finding perhaps that they satisfy our fundamental temptations.... Even when we can make a choice between products, we are influenced by a sort of force within ourselves, which we fear because it is indeterminate and indefinable" (Rubin and Rubin 2004, 236). This philosopher's statement reflects the spirit of modernity as it is found in all three waves, whether in Hobbes, Kant, or Heidegger. Unease, dissatisfaction, and criticism are the hallmarks of modernity, and the unease that the United States brings shows it to be perceived as the agent of modernity for many. For Hersch modernity still retains promise for greater freedom. However, unease not just for the United States but for modernity in general also produces hostility, as in many parts of the Islamic world. In that part of the world, many view the United States as Satan understood as not as an "imperialist bully but [as] a smooth operator, a tempter who makes his wares seem so attractive that people want to sell him their souls" (Rubin and Rubin 2004, 167). Part of the reason many parts of the Muslim world oppose the United States is due to the traditional Muslim view that political society serves religion and piety instead of the modern view according to which political society enables science to serve freedom of the individual. However, some people have argued that the "unease" of these parts of the world springs from their acceptance of modernity as well, as manifested in their adaptation of and inspiration from democracy, science, and even modern forms of religiosity. People who adopt premodern, second-wave, and third-wave modern (or postmodern) viewpoints, from European intellectuals to political Islamists, seem to agree that the United States is dangerously attractive, and they draw upon the symbols of their respective modernities to express and justify their unease.

The Future

People have celebrated and criticized the United States as an agent of modernity. Their perception of the United States is colored not only by their attitude toward modernity, but also by the type of modernity they view the United States as representing and what type they themselves have adopted. Today's world exhibits sentiments and ideologies rooted in all three waves (and to some degree premodernity as well). These multiple modernities lead to a diverse range of interpretations of the United States, many of which are self-contradictory.

A Canadian journalist satirized these diverse and contradictory sentiments:

> Fanatical Muslims despise America because it's all lapdancing and gay porn; the secular Europeans despise America because it's all born-again Christians hung up on abortion.... America is also too isolationist, except when it's imperialist. And even its imperialism is too vulgar and arriviste to appeal to real imperialists.... To the mullahs, America is the Great Satan, a wily seducer; to the Gaullists, America is the Great Cretin,

a culture so self-evidently moronic that only stump-toothed inbred Appalachian lardbutts could possibly fall for it.... Too Christian, too Godless, too isolationist, too imperialist, too seductive, too cretinous. (Rubin and Rubin 2004, 225)

This satirical statement reflects the many modern faces of the United States as well as of its critics. Moreover, it reflects the view that the United States is the primary stage in the world on which the diverse views of modernity interact and work themselves out. The United States, insofar as it contains modern and premodern ideals, is an image of Western civilization. Its representative stature continues to set the tone for the rest of the world. The resilience of modernity as well as of the United States shows that the United States will continue to be viewed as its agent for the foreseeable future.

John von Heyking

See also Culture Overseas, U.S.; Mass Media—Concepts and Technologies; Mass Media—Debates and Divides; Pop Culture—U.S. Advertising; Pop Culture—U.S. Film; Pop Culture—U.S. Music (Hip-hop); Pop Culture—U.S. Music (Jazz, Rock); Pop Culture—U.S. Television

Further Reading

Ceaser, J. (1997). *Reconstructing America: The symbol of America in modern thought.* New Haven, CT: Yale University Press.

Cooper, B. (1984). *The end of history: An essay on modern Hegelianism.* Toronto, Canada: University of Toronto Press.

Cropsey, J. (1986). The United States as regime and the sources of the American way of life. In R. H. Horowitz (Ed.), *The moral foundations of the American republic* (pp. 165–180). Charlottesville: University of Virginia Press.

Fukuyama, F. (1992). *The end of history and the last man.* New York: Avon Books.

Hamilton, A., Jay, J., & Madison, J. (2001). *The federalist.* Indianapolis, IN: Liberty Fund. (Original work published 1788)

Hobbes, T. (1994). *Leviathan* (E. Curley, Ed.). Indianapolis, IN: Hackett Publishing. (Original work published 1651)

Manent, P. (1998). *The city of man* (M. A. LePain, Trans.). Princeton, NJ: Princeton University Press.

Marx, K. (1865, January 28). Address of the International Working Men's Association to Abraham Lincoln, president of the United States of America. Retrieved December 14, 2006, from http://www.marxists.org/history/international/iwma/documents/1864/lincoln-letter.htm

Roy, O. (2004). *Globalized Islam: The search for a new ummah.* New York: Columbia University Press.

Rubin, B., & Rubin, J. C. (2004). *Hating America: A history.* Oxford, UK: Oxford University Press.

Sandoz, E. (2001). *A government of laws: Political theory, religion, and the American founding.* Columbia: University of Missouri Press. (Original work published 1990)

Schabert, T. (1979, February). A note on modernity. *Political Theory, 7*(1), 123–137.

Strauss, L. (1989). The three waves of modernity. In H. Gildin (Ed.), *An introduction to political philosophy: Ten essays by Leo Strauss* (pp. 81–98). Detroit, MI: Wayne State University Press.

Voegelin, E. (2000). *The collected works of Eric Voegelin: Modernity without restraint: Vol. 5. The political religions; the new science of politics; and science, politics, and gnosticism* (M. Henningsen, Ed.). Columbia: University of Missouri Press.

Multinational Corporations

Multinational corporate behavior has affected global perceptions of the United States for better or worse. It has caused societies to weigh the cultural, technological, and economic benefits against the price paid by those societies.

U.S. multinational corporations operating overseas and overseas multinational corporations operating in the United States both have shaped global perspectives of the United States. The comparison of social benefits with the social costs of the investment from specific nations' multinational corporations, as opposed to other sources of investment, and the ways in which these social benefits and costs have been strategically and politically constructed all contribute to shaping these perspectives. Although a range of social benefits and costs has been discussed in the media and in literature, the deciding factors include: (1) cultural effects in terms of diversity and multiculturalism (benefits) versus hegemony (costs), (2) technological effects in terms of enhancing the capability of the local nation (benefits) versus hollowing out the technological base to competing nations (costs), and (3) economic effects in terms of the substitution (costs) or complementation (benefits) of employment, income, resource allocation, and growth.

Cultural versus Technological and Economic Effects

In general, technological and economic effects of U.S. multinationals have been perceived more positively by global societies than have their cultural effects. For instance, in the 1950s the generosity of U.S. firms, such as General Electric, in transferring technology under the umbrella of the Marshall Plan were greatly appreciated in western Europe and generated a dramatic economic reconstruction and revival of the local economies. During the 1960s a significant rise in U.S. multinational activity produced considerable social and political discomfort in western Europe. Americans were perceived to be taking over local economies and imposing their culture. National governments, as in France, sought to promote local companies and investments in order to contain the monocultural U.S. influence, which was condemned for its "Coca-Colanization" of Europe.

Maximizing Technological and Economic Gains

Historically, societies globally sought to minimize the cultural costs of U.S. multinationals. Japan executed a policy—which was prevalent in many economically underdeveloped nations—with particular finesse. In addition to restricting U.S. multinational investments in Japan during the 1970s, the Japanese government nurtured a policy of encouraging Japanese companies within the same industry—such as consumer electronics—to seek technological collaborations with leading U.S. corporations. The government sponsored consortia, then facilitated sharing knowledge from U.S. firms among the Japanese firms with a view to developing a robust technological platform that would outsmart technological offerings of U.S. firms competing independently. By the late 1970s Japanese exports to the United States were booming, thereby hurting domestic sales of U.S. multinational firms and worsening the trade deficit of the United States. The U.S. government sought to contain the damage by negotiating voluntary export restraints with the Japanese government, which in turn imposed restraints on the exports of Japanese companies, such as in the auto industry.

To offset the export restraints, during the 1980s Japanese multinationals reluctantly began investing in the United States and in the process even encouraged their domestic vendors to invest in the United States to assure just-in-time deliveries. These multinationals believed the productivity of the investments in the United States to be subpar because of the high cost and inflexibility associated with U.S. labor and lack of adequate appreciation for zero defects and zero wastage in the United States.

As Japanese multinationals criticized the U.S. restrictions as a move away from free trade, they also sensed concern in the United States about the rapid expansion of Japanese multinational investments in the United States and the associated increase in the imports of intermediate inputs and technology, translating into a rising trade deficit.

By the late 1980s and early 1990s Japanese multinationals were beginning to guard their bases by developing linkages with U.S. suppliers. They found the advanced technological base of U.S. suppliers distinctly useful to graduate up, for instance, from an earlier Japanese focus on low-end compact cars to high-end luxury cars. Japanese multinationals announced plans for increased investments in the United States, even as their own domestic operations and domestic market were dropping into doldrums.

Simultaneously, Japanese commentators began talking about the "borderless world" (Ohmae 1990). They questioned the prudence of identifying multinationals with their home nations when

firms such as Honda had realized more investments, sales, and employees in the United States than in their home nation. Indeed, even the Americans were realizing the futility of the traditional "Buy American" campaigns because now a dominant share of the inputs of most U.S. products was manufactured overseas.

Although during the 1970s and 1980s the Japanese government and Japanese multinationals had held distinctly negative perceptions of the U.S. work ethic, productivity, and competitiveness, a sea change was perceptible in the 1990s. The Japanese government now courted U.S. multinationals, such as General Motors, to increase their investments in Japan and to help bail out faltering Japanese firms. Japan's admiration for U.S. technological power strengthened in recent years, with the rapid growth in software, the Internet, and associated technologies in the United States.

Cultural Forces in Technological and Economic Gains

During recent years many nations have promoted more inward investments from U.S. multinationals than from multinationals of other industrially leading nations. Distinctive patterns in the U.S. multinational culture accounted for this shift in global perceptions.

U.S. multinationals are perceived to have stronger organizational systems and greater willingness to transfer their new technologies because of a greater emphasis on the pursuit of global strategies. Global strategies are associated with a geocentric mind-set, in which an attempt is made to minimize the differences in domestic versus international activities. U.S. multinationals appreciate the capabilities of local partners and are willing to provide strategic and global servicing responsibilities to partners and even to offer training and support to help develop world-class delivery capabilities.

Japanese multinationals, in contrast, emphasize international strategies. International strategies are associated with an ethnocentric mind-set, with a greater home-nation orientation, in which advanced technology is retained at home, and only older and peripheral equipment and product designs are transferred to foreign nations. Japanese multinationals tend to appropriate substantial learning from local partners, do not give those partners any credit for their insights, and instead criticize them for not meeting the norms set by operations back home that rely on more expensive and sophisticated technologies and labor.

Finally, European multinationals have traditionally relied on multilocal or multidomestic strategies. Multilocal strategies are associated with a polycentric mind-set, in which strategies are formulated on a country-by-country level. Although like Japanese multinationals, European multinationals, such as Unilever, also retain more sophisticated resources, operations, and products for the European market, significant freedom is often given to the local operations in different nations to develop local vendors and to operate like a local firm. Although the local partners do get opportunities to be engaged, such engagement is more locally or regionally focused, and access to global responsibilities is limited for the partners based outside Europe.

Local Forces in Cultural Effects

The technological and economic gains from the engagement of U.S. multinationals have not been uniformly distributed among all local geographies. If we consider the case of the emerging markets, the benefits have perhaps been greatest for India, followed by China and East Asia and then Latin America.

Until the 1980s European—particularly British and German—multinationals were the prominent foreign players in the Indian market. However, since the 1980s the government of India has promoted investments from, and relationships with, U.S. multinationals to develop India's information technology and associated service industries. Now the United States is the leading trade partner and investor in India, displacing European nations.

China enjoyed substantial Japanese multinational investments around World War II. However, most of these investments were exploitative, focused on taking Chinese raw materials for further processing in Japan and marketing Japanese products in China. During the postwar period Japanese firms expanded these exploitative investments into East Asia. They also began using East Asia as a base to manufacture mature products at lower costs, using older and expensive technology transferred from Japan, and then to export these products to the United States, circumventing the export restraints on Japan. The local East Asian firms also developed capabilities to do the same in their own right and to offer a direct sourcing option to U.S. firms through strategic partnerships.

The benefits enjoyed by China and East Asia from engagement with the United States have been tempered by the substantial social and political concerns in the United States about potential intellectual property rights, environmental, and human rights abuses in China (such as using child labor, poor working conditions, and using pirated technology to achieve below-market costs but with uneven quality) and the strategic vulnerability of relying too much on the volatile economies of East Asia. Incidents of contamination of food materials, such as pet foods, sourced from East Asia have occurred recently.

Moreover, the activities of U.S. multinationals in India and East Asia have been under special scrutiny in the United States

with the increase in offshoring of core processes and services, as the United States was traditionally perceived to have a comparative advantage in the services domain. Nevertheless, firms in India and East Asia, such as Infosys and Lenova, are rapidly upgrading their service and product delivery capabilities and models with support and mentoring from U.S. multinationals. Such mutual collaboration has strengthened the global competitiveness of U.S. multinationals, enabled unprecedented growth in productivity, and allowed the U.S. and global economy to be resilient to such events as the terrorist attacks of September 11, 2001, and the global war on terror. Concurrently, U.S. multinational engagement in Asia is facilitating a rapid growth in China and India and is allowing Asia to become a notable economic, social, cultural, and political power in the international arena.

Unfortunately, involvement of U.S. multinationals in Latin America does not appear to have generated similar levels of developmental gains. In Latin America U.S. firms have tended to transfer their own models, often focused on reducing costs, as in Mexico, or on expanding the market base for their products and services.

Social Benefits versus Social Costs

Overall, despite the evident social benefits of U.S. multinational activity, concerns remain about the potential social costs—especially if U.S. multinationals are allowed to operate unmonitored, without any social and political checks and balances. Within the United States some people are concerned about potential job losses in the United States. Also of concern are strategic vulnerabilities, such as the diffusion of dual-use technologies to China and to nations that the U.S. government associates with terrorism. Outside the United States some people are concerned about U.S. multinationals imposing their economic, technological, and cultural hegemony and creating a dependency syndrome. For instance, in many nations backlash has occurred over the effects of the bottling plants of Coke and Pepsi on groundwater levels, the effects of Wal-Mart and Starbucks outlets on local retailers, the high costs of U.S. technology, and the limits imposed on inclusive and sustainable development.

Maximizing the Social Benefit– Social Cost Ratio

The social benefits given by U.S. multinationals to overseas nations—and by foreign multinationals to the United States—

should be enhanced when a reciprocal technological exchange occurs between multinationals and local firms and other entities. For instance, when U.S. multinationals acknowledge the unique knowledge and contributions of local partners, give them strategic worldwide delivery responsibilities, and offer mentoring and networking to facilitate those responsibilities, the local societies tend to be appreciative. Examples include research and development labs of General Electric and Microsoft in Asia. A major impediment to this technological exchange is a lack of awareness about the capabilities of local firms and local entrepreneurs, which prevents U.S. multinationals from fully recognizing the value of local know-how. Similarly, awareness of the capabilities of local firms in the United States is limited among foreign multinationals, as illustrated by the historical experiences of the Japanese firms mentioned earlier.

Diversity research indicates that people tend to use their own dominant perspectives and to discount the value of the perspectives of minority and underprivileged voices because those voices often remain silent or simply not heard. Indeed, the discourse on multinationals tends to focus on the advantages that multinationals bring to compete in a foreign market. Although the scholars recognize distinct learning advantages of multinationals, the factors that allow distinctive learning unique to a host environment are usually limited to technical know-how. There is an additional need to gain a better appreciation of the cultural factor. Multinationals may gain some benefit in many nations because of common cultural factors or because of the limited importance of cultural conditions in generating that benefit. Other benefits may be unique to specific nations or may be too costly to generate in specific nations because of the huge costs of cultural change.

Future Implications

Growing emphasis on multiculturalism and diversity in the United States puts U.S. multinationals in a unique position to become credible and trusted repositories of authentic local cultural endowments in different geographies. By recognizing, celebrating, and acknowledging the distinctive characteristics of different cultural systems, U.S. multinationals can generate a positive shift in the global perspectives of their initiatives.

Vipin Gupta

See also Businesses Overseas, U.S.; McDonaldization

Further Reading
Abo, T. (Ed.). (1994). *Hybrid factory: The Japanese production system in the United States.* New York: Oxford University Press.

Dunning, J. H. (2002). *Theories and paradigms of international business activity: The selected essays of John H. Dunning* (Vol. 1). Cheltenham, UK: Edward Elgar.

Gupta, V. (1998). *A dynamic model of technological growth: Diffusion of Japanese investment networks overseas.* Doctoral dissertation, Wharton School, University of Pennsylvania, Philadelphia.

House, R. J., Hanges, P. J., Javidan, M., Dorfman, P. W., & Gupta, V. (Eds.). (2004). *Culture, leadership, and organizations: The GLOBE study of 62 societies.* Thousand Oaks, CA: Sage Publications.

Kenney, M., & Florida, R. (1993). *Beyond mass production: The Japanese system and its transfer to the U.S.* New York: Oxford University Press.

Ohmae, K. (1990). *The borderless world.* London: William Collins.

Nationalism

The "nation" is a powerful symbol that elicits tremendous sacrifice from its constituents; nationalism and preserving nationalism have influenced global events for centuries, and will continue to for years to come.

Nationalism, in its various forms, has had a tremendous effect on twentieth-century U.S. history and world history. Nationalism has been a motivating factor in U.S. diplomacy, war, and even economic development. Most Americans have seen automobiles virtually covered with magnetic ribbons proclaiming, "Support our troops" and "God bless America." Undoubtedly, nationalism is a potent force in American society. Conversely, American nationalism has had a tremendous affect on perceptions of the United States around the world.

After the bloody battles of World War I, many people began analyzing the role of nationalism in global events. Why, they frequently asked, would people make such tremendous personal sacrifices in the defense of the nation? What exactly is a nation, and how does it elicit the loyalties of millions of otherwise discrete individuals? In short, what is nationalism, and what role does it play in the lives of a nation's citizens? In his seminal work entitled *Essays on Nationalism,* published in the decade after World War I, C. J. H. Hayes attempts to describe the characteristics of nationalism. Because of nationalism, he explains, "the individual is commonly disposed, in case of conflict, to sacrifice one loyalty after another, loyalty to person, places and ideas, loyalty even to family, to the paramount call of nationality and the nation-state" (Hayes 1926, 94–95). In other words, nationalism is a marker of identity, competing with other markers such as class, gender, and family. However, unlike these competing markers, nationalism, Hayes contends, is more powerful and has a higher claim on a person's loyalty.

Not surprisingly, Hayes does not provide the final definition of nationalism. Since the late 1980s the study of nationalism has exploded among political scientists, historians, sociologists, and scholars of nearly every other academic discipline. Although providing a perfect definition of the word may be impossible, the scholars John Hutchinson and Anthony D. Smith have delineated four dominant schools of thought regarding the concept of nationalism: primordialism, perennialism, modernism, and ethno-symbolism.

Primordialism

Before one can effectively analyze nationalism, one must answer a seemingly simple question: What is a nation? Academics disagree as to what a nation is and when nations come into existence. Some academics, such as sociobiologist van den Berghe, argue that nations have always existed and are merely the political manifestations of prehistoric—or primordial—genetic ties. For instance, according to myth, the Japanese nation emerged from the conjugal love of the deities Izanagi and Izanami. Therefore, the subsequent inhabitants of the islands share physical and biological bonds with each other. It is only natural that these people would create institutions based on their common origins. Although such institutions may change over time, the underlying ties continue to exist, primordialists argue.

This myth, like other such origin myths, has had a powerful influence on the Japanese nation. However, its historical accuracy is obviously suspect. Furthermore, in most cases scientific analyses undermine, rather than support, the claim of common biological and genetic descent. For these and other reasons, the primordial view of the nation has come under sustained attack among intellectuals.

Perennialism

Some scholars, such as John Armstrong, have proposed a more complex definition of nation. Nations, he argues, are not primordial. However, nations have long histories that predate the modern era. Through time nations recurrently thrive and deteriorate. When factors such as religion, government, or culture overlap, the nation emerges as a vital and distinguishable entity. When these same factors diverge, the nation fades and becomes less apparent. Looked at over long periods, these perennial communities are readily apparent. Some of these nations, such as the Jewish nation, have an easily distinguishable past that reaches back to the ancient world. Others, such as the English, Scottish, and Irish nations, have waxed and waned since at least the high Middle Ages. In each case, however, the nation is an old—although not a primordial—entity based on religious, governmental, cultural, or other existing ties.

Modernism

Recent scholarship has tended to move away from both the primordialist and perennialist views of the nation. For example,

researchers such as Ernest Gellner, John Breuilly, and Benedict Anderson contend that the nation is a product of the modern era and that although religious, ethnic, or linguistic communities may have existed prior to the modern era, none of these can be accurately defined as a "nation." Nationalism, they insist, is a modern invention.

These researchers disagree, however, on how and why nations come into existence. Ernest Gellner contends that the nation is a product of modern, industrial society. With the growth of the factory and the concurrent migration of agricultural laborers to the cities, workers found themselves alienated from traditional groupings. In the impersonal world of the city, these people had to communicate and interact with people from beyond their recognized community. Furthermore, their supervisors needed workers who were literate and could function as a unit. Consequently, modern society began emphasizing public education and the standardization of vernacular languages. The result was an emerging sense of belonging, or nationalism. As Gellner explains, "nationalism is not the awakening of nations to self-consciousness: it invents nations where they do not exist" (Gellner 1964, 169).

John Breuilly agrees that nations are a product of modernity; yet, he claims, they are not a function of industrialization but rather are a result of political maneuvering. In their quest to maintain power, Breuilly argues, political elites nurture a sense of nationalism. By defining and controlling national symbols and boundaries, these elites can mobilize and control the masses. Furthermore, they can attempt to discredit or negate competing national narratives. However, because power relations ebb and flow, these narratives are constantly changing. For example, in early twentieth-century China, political leaders idealized women who sacrificed for the

good of the nation. These political leaders, who were universally male, claimed that the "virtuous woman" represented the Chinese nation. Subelite women, however, did not always agree with the portrayal of the virtuous woman. Many women became adept at utilizing the same national rhetoric employed by their male counterparts to alter the symbol of the virtuous woman and thereby expand their political voice in the process. In this case a national symbol, and the nation itself, became a construct fostered and manipulated by those seeking to maintain or enhance their positions in society. In other words, there was no bounded, essential nation.

Other researchers, including Benedict Anderson, have argued that national communities involve more than simply power politics. These researchers have also downplayed the negative implications of political constructivism. Although Anderson agrees that the nation is a modern construct, he says it is not merely a fabrication of the elite. Instead, Anderson argues that the nation is an imagined community that appears as a result of print capitalism. With the emergence of a large, literate public, newspapers and books create a community of linguistically related readers, each imagining himself or herself as part of a larger print culture. After people imagine this community, modern nation-states emerge. The "boundaries" of these nations may change over time, but such changes are not simply the result of political manipulation.

Ethno-symbolism

A fourth group of scholars, which Hutchinson and Smith refer to as "ethno-symbolists," strikes a balance between the perennial-

---

EXTRACT FROM THOMAS PAINE'S RIGHTS OF MAN (1791)

In the wake of the American and French Revolutions, Thomas Paine wrote the influential pamphlet, Rights of Man. Although nationalism was not to become a guiding influence for at least another century, it seems a concept that Paine would have opposed. As he makes clear in the excerpt below, in his view, governments need to earn the loyalty and devotion of its citizens.

When it shall be said in any country in the world, my poor are happy; neither ignorance nor distress is to be found among them; my jails are empty of prisoners, my streets of beggars; the aged are not in want, the taxes are not oppressive; the rational world is my friend, because I am the friend of its happiness: when these things can be said, then may that country boast its constitution and its government.

Within the space of a few years we have seen two revolutions, those of America and France. In the former, the contest was long, and the

conflict severe; in the latter, the nation acted with such a consolidated impulse, that having no foreign enemy to contend with, the revolution was complete in power the moment it appeared. From both those instances it is evident, that the greatest forces that can be brought into the field of revolutions, are reason and common interest. Where these can have the opportunity of acting, opposition dies with fear, or crumbles away by conviction. It is a great standing which they have now universally obtained; and we may hereafter hope to see revolutions, or changes in governments, produced with the same quiet operation by which any measure, determinable by reason and discussion, is accomplished.

Source: Paine, T. (1791). Chapter 5: Principle to practice—ways and means of improving the condition of Europe interspersed with miscellaneous observations. In Rights of Man. Retrieved April 5, 2007, from http://www.ushistory.org/paine/rights/

ists and the modernists. These scholars concede that nationalism is a modern ideology, but they do not agree that the nation is a modern phenomenon. Rejecting the elitism of the modernists, scholars such as Anthony Smith contend that business leaders, political elites, and newspaper publishers could not simply invent national symbols but rather that they had to work with existing, premodern myths, traditions, public memories, and cultural commonalities (including language and religion). In turn, these commonalities facilitate dedication to the nation. Consequently, nations are not simply politically constructed states or ideological institutions. Indeed, nationalism is a powerful force among many stateless peoples (such as the Basques or the Kurds). Smith contends that to understand nationalism, one first must understand those premodern cultural elements uniting a certain group of peoples. Popular, folk, and lower-class elements influence and delineate the form of the nation. By extension, then, modern territorial states are reformations of existing communities. These communities may be called "ethnic groups," "myth-symbol complexes," "ethnies," or "nations," but they certainly existed in the premodern era. Critics of the ethno-symbolists counter by asking this question: If nations emerge from "ethnies," how do "ethnies" originate? Indeed, this debate replaces one ambiguous term ("nation") for another equally ambiguous term ("ethnies").

The Croatian National Theater in Zagreb, Croatia. Such monumental architecture and the institutions they house are important symbols of national pride in many nations around the world. Source: istock/Robert Lerich.

Transnationalism

To add to the contentiousness of nationalism studies, postmodernists such as Khachig Tölölyan and Paul Gilroy have further complicated the issue by discussing the concept of transnationalism. For instance, they point out, a diaspora (a group of peoples separated from a common homeland or nation and living in at least two locales) is an example of a transnational group. Diaspora studies have garnered much attention since the mid-1990s. In many ways diasporas owe their existence to the nation. In other ways diasporas undermine the nation. As Tölölyan suggests, "transnational communities are sometimes the paradigmatic Other of the nation-state and at other times its ally, lobby, or even, as in the case of Israel, its precursor" (Tölölyan 1991, 3). Some diasporic communities exhibit extreme nationalism, whereas others consciously distance themselves from the politics of their homeland.

However, transnational diasporas usually share several additional characteristics. Transnationalists living in a diaspora frequently maintain a memory of their home nation, even if that memory is a product of stories and traditions passed through many generations. Many diasporic people believe that their host nation will never fully accept them, and therefore they are unwilling to surrender their identity with their nation of origin and may even plan an eventual return to their homeland. Corresponding with this desire to return, transnationalists remain committed to the maintenance of their home nation. For all of these reasons, diasporic people develop a sense of community—transcending gender, class, and family differences—that in many ways mirrors the nation itself. Yet, like a nation, diasporas are changing, evolving, imagined communities that lack any primordial, unifying element. Instead, the experience of displacement and marginalization is the glue that holds them together and allows for transnational conversations.

Nationalism and the United States

Nation clearly remains a problematic term for scholars to define. However, regardless of whether the nation is primordial or perennial, whether it is a modern imaginary or a product of ethno-symbolism, the nation is a powerful symbol that elicits tremendous sacrifice from its constituents. Perhaps nowhere has this been more evident than in the United States. Following the attacks of September 11, 2001, President George Bush and millions of Americans rhetorically asked, "Why do they hate us?" Peter Ford, of the *Christian Science Monitor*, attempted an answer. To many around the world, he explained, U.S. military power appears as arrogant swagger. Furthermore, U.S. policies in the Middle East, Latin America, and elsewhere have, at times, appeared hypocritical and overly aggressive. Rather than thoughtfully analyzing the question, many Americans believed "they hate us" because of the superiority of U.S. civilization, culture, and democratic principles. They chose to see any attack from outside not as a violent critique of U.S. foreign policy, but as an assault on the entire "nation" and its constituent members. Therefore, the only acceptable response was a national response. For this reason, thousands of men and women eagerly enlisted in U.S. military forces in the weeks following the September 11 attacks. These individuals were willing to sacrifice their own welfare and security in the defense of an "imagined community." Predictably, this nationalistic response reinforced many U.S. stereotypes for individuals around the globe.

Since 2001, those that have challenged U.S. foreign policy makers have been characterized as un-American. Political elites have channeled feelings of nationalism to further their own policies and goals. At the same time, subelites have also drawn on feelings of nationalism to alter existing policies and political power structures. As seen in the recent U.S. past, nationalism can be either a tool for advancing an individual's personal agenda or a weapon for eliminating competitors. Indeed, nationalism has been a potent force in the past century and promises to influence global events for years to come.

David L. Kenley

See also Americanization; Anti-Americanism; Empire, U.S.; International Law

Further Reading

Anderson, B. (1983). *Imagined communities: Reflections on the origin and spread of nationalism.* London: Verso Editions and NLB.

Armstrong, J. (1982). *Nations before nationalism.* Chapel Hill: University of North Carolina Press.

Berghe, P. van den. (1978). Race and ethnicity: A sociobiological perspective. *Ethnic and Racial Studies, 1*(4), 401–411.

Berghe, P. van den. (1995). Does race matter? *Nations and Nationalism, 1*(3), 357–368.

Bhabha, H. (1994). *The location of culture.* London: Routledge.

Breuilly, J. (1993). *Nationalism and the state* (2nd ed.). Manchester, UK: Manchester University Press.

Clifford, J. (1994). Diasporas. *Cultural Anthropology, 9,* 302–338.

Conner, W. (1978). A nation is a nation, is a state, is an ethnic group, is a . . . *Ethnic and Racial Studies, 1*(4), 377–400.

Ford, P. (2001, September 7). Why do they hate us. *Christian Science Monitor.*

Gellner, E. (1964). *Thought and change.* Chicago: University of Chicago Press.

Gellner, E. (1983). *Nations and nationalism.* Ithaca, NY: Cornell University Press.

Gellner, E. (1994). *Encounters with nationalism.* Oxford, UK: Blackwell.

Gilroy, P. (1993). *The black Atlantic: Modernity and double consciousness.* Cambridge, MA: Harvard University Press.

Hayes, C. J. H. (1926). *Essays on nationalism.* New York: Macmillan.

Hobsbawm, E. (1990). *Nations and nationalism since 1780.* Cambridge, MA: Cambridge University Press.

Hobsbawm, E., & Ranger, T. (1983). *The invention of tradition.* Cambridge, MA: Cambridge University Press.

Hutchinson, J., & Smith, A. D. (2000). General introduction. In J. Hutchinson & A. D. Smith (Eds.), *Nationalism: Critical concepts in political science.* New York: Routledge.

Judge, J. (2001). Talent, virtue, and the nation: Chinese nationalisms and female subjectivities in the early twentieth century. *American Historical Review, 106*(3), 765–803.

Smith, A. (1989). The origins of nations. *Ethnic and Racial Studies, 12*(3), 340–367.

Smith, A. (1991). *National identity.* Reno: University of Nevada Press.

Renan, E. (1990). What is a nation? In H. Bhabha (Ed.), *Nation and narration*. London: Routledge.

Tölölyan, K. (1991, Spring). The nation-state and its others. *Diaspora, 1,* 3–7.

NATO, U.S. Role in

Although the original rationale for NATO was the supposed threat of the Soviet Union to the West, it was only after the Cold War ended that NATO forces were used in armed conflict, against Serbia in the Balkan wars of the 1990s.

The North Atlantic Treaty Organization (NATO) was the main institutional expression of the policy of "containment" adopted by the United States and its allies during the Cold War with the Soviet bloc. The North Atlantic Treaty establishing the alliance was signed on 4 April 1949, with an initial membership of twelve countries. Apart from the United States, these countries were Canada, Iceland, Norway, Denmark, Britain, France, Italy, Portugal, Belgium, Holland, and Luxembourg. Membership was later extended during the Cold War to include Greece and Turkey (1952), West Germany (1955), and Spain (1982). After the collapse of the Soviet bloc at the end of the 1980s, a number of formerly Communist east European nations were admitted to NATO, which by 2004 had twenty-six members.

Although the original rationale for the alliance was the threat said to be posed to the West by the Soviet Union, it has survived the latter's disappearance, thus raising questions about its function and usefulness in the post–Cold War era. Indeed, only after the Cold War was over were NATO forces used in armed conflict—against Serbian forces in the Balkan wars of the 1990s. The key defense clause of the treaty (Article 5) was first invoked in response to the September 11, 2001, attacks by al-Qaeda on New York City and Washington, D.C.

NATO and the Cold War (1949–1989)

The North Atlantic Treaty owed its existence to the belief that member nations needed to ensure a U.S. military commitment to western Europe to counter the conventional armed might of the Soviet Union and to provide a protective barrier behind which the political and economic rehabilitation of the non-Communist part of the continent might proceed after World War II. Supporters of the treaty argued that failure on the part of the Western democracies to demonstrate a collective will and the means to deter aggression would invite a repetition of the events that had led to World War II. Although the terms of the treaty did not nominate a specific enemy, people generally understood that the feared potential aggressor was the Soviet Union. Article 5 of the treaty committed the parties to regard an attack on one or more

of them as an attack on all and to assist those attacked by taking such action as the parties deemed necessary to restore and maintain the security of the North Atlantic area.

From the beginning a clear disparity existed in the relative strengths of the member nations, with consequent influence on their roles in the alliance. The United States was the only possessor of the atomic bomb when the treaty came into being, and although Britain and France were to join the nuclear club in later years, the United States never lost its overwhelmingly dominant strategic position. This disparity was on the whole unproblematic when fear of the Soviet Union was the alliance's cementing force. Resentment of U.S. power, sometimes evident in Europe, was not strong enough to outweigh the presumed advantages of U.S. protection.

Indeed, periods of tension existed within the alliance during the Cold War. One instance was the Suez crisis of 1956, when the United States openly condemned the military attack on Egypt launched by two leading NATO members, Britain and France, and exerted economic pressure to halt the adventure. In the 1960s the French government under President Charles de Gaulle (1890–1970) sought to distance itself from U.S. policy in many respects and in 1966 withdrew from the integrated command structure of NATO, although not from the alliance itself.

Notwithstanding these disputes, the alliance did act cohesively in the final stages of the Cold War, in particular by

NATO MEMBERS IN 2007

Belgium	Hungary	Portugal
Bulgaria	Iceland	Romania
Canada	Italy	Slovakia
Czech Republic	Latvia	Slovenia
Denmark	Lithuania	Spain
Estonia	Luxembourg	Turkey
France	Netherlands	United Kingdom
Germany	Norway	United States
Greece	Poland	

Source: North Atlantic Treaty Organization. (2007). Retrieved March 22, 2007, from http://www.nato.int/

agreeing to the installation of Cruise and Pershing missiles on its members' territory to counter the Soviet Union's SS-20 missiles. This action was taken in the teeth of opposition from Moscow and from west European unilateral nuclear disarmament movements. Subsequent arms reduction agreements between Moscow and Washington were made possible by Soviet acceptance of U.S. terms under the leadership of Mikhail Gorbachev (b. 1931) in the late 1980s.

NATO after the Cold War (1989–2007)

The collapse of the east European Communist regimes in 1989, followed by the dissolution of the Soviet Union itself two years later, raised questions about NATO's purpose in the new world. Given the disappearance of the enemy against whom the alliance had been created, a case could be made for dissolving it, although in practice such calls were only occasionally heard. More disagreement existed over the question of NATO enlargement, and in particular over the extension of the alliance to include former members of the Eastern bloc grouping, the Warsaw Pact. Opponents of such expansion argued that it was unnecessary, risked an overextension of U.S. commitments, and was unduly provoca-

tive to Russia at a time when the latter was trying to construct a viable post-Communist order. Supporters argued that expansion was a means of reinforcing the pro-Western orientation of the post-Communist nations and that Moscow's objections could be overcome by offering a form of NATO-Russian partnership. The latter view prevailed, with the result that by 2004 NATO had admitted nine nations that had formerly been part of the Soviet bloc (Poland, Hungary, the Czech Republic, Estonia, Latvia, Lithuania, Bulgaria, Romania, and Slovakia), as well as Slovenia, a former constituent of the nonaligned Yugoslavia.

NATO and Russia

After the collapse of the Soviet bloc, relations between Moscow and Washington oscillated between periods of amity and periods of renewed tension, and the U.S. interpretation of NATO's function played an important part in this shifting and sensitive relationship. Already unhappy about NATO's eastward expansion, in 1999 Russia strongly opposed the U.S. bombing campaign against Serbia, which was designed to compel a Serb withdrawal from the Albanian-majority province of Kosovo, where an insurgency had developed. On this occasion the Clinton administration, wishing to avoid the appearance of conducting a unilateral U.S. campaign,

NATO soldiers dressed in army camouflage uniform, red berets and boots in a parade during a national holiday in Athens, Greece. Source: istock/Vasiliki Varvaki.

secured NATO's agreement that the operation should be carried out under the aegis of the alliance. NATO thus bypassed the United Nations Security Council, where Russia could wield a veto, bringing relations between Moscow and the Western alliance to their most antagonistic point since the Cold War.

Two years later, however, the September 11, 2001, attacks on the United States by al-Qaeda produced a shift in the opposite direction. Russia, now under the presidency of Vladimir Putin, was trying to suppress a secessionist rising in Chechnya and sought to represent its efforts there as consistent with the "war on terror," which the United States had proclaimed in the aftermath of September 11. The United States wished to use Russian-influenced former Soviet republics in central Asia in its campaign against the Afghan Taliban and al-Qaeda and was therefore ready to play down criticism of Russian conduct in Chechnya. One outcome of this move was the establishment in May 2002 of the NATO-Russian Council, which was designed to promote the common security interests that the parties believed they had.

NATO and Iraq

The decision of the George W. Bush administration to invade Iraq in March 2003 produced a fresh disagreement with Russia, as well as a major rift within NATO itself, perhaps the most serious in its history. France, Germany, Belgium, and Luxembourg joined Russia in opposing the attack on Iraq, and the Turkish parliament refused to allow U.S. forces the use of Turkish territory for a land invasion. There was thus no question of representing the Iraq War as a NATO operation. Instead, the Bush administration gathered together an ad hoc "coalition of the willing," consisting of some members of NATO and some other nations that were prepared to give the United States varying levels of support. The broad strategic consensus obtained during the Cold War years was displaying signs of disrepair. Even some of the NATO nations that had committed forces to Iraq withdrew some or all of them after the invasion in response to domestic pressure. Spain withdrew its troops after the election of a socialist government in March 2004, and Poland announced substantial reductions in its commitment in 2005.

These differences notwithstanding, attempts were made to demonstrate the continued cohesion of the alliance. In August 2003 NATO took over control of the International Security Assistance Force (ISAF), set up to support the new Afghan authorities after the overthrow of the Taliban. The next year, at a summit meeting in Istanbul in June 2004, the alliance agreed to assist the new Iraqi government with a training program to equip it to deal with

local insurgents. NATO's role, however, was explicitly limited to training and technical assistance, not combat.

Prospects for NATO

This discussion has outlined the evolution of NATO from an alliance designed to defend specific territories against a recognized, although formally unnamed, enemy to a body whose purpose is less clear in the aftermath of that enemy's disappearance. One suggested alternative rationale was to confirm the former Warsaw Pact nations in their Western orientation. Another new direction was the development of "out-of-area" operations such as those in Afghanistan and Iraq. The division within the alliance over Iraq, however, illustrated the limitations of this alternative conception of its role. Even as membership of NATO grew, certainty as to its function diminished.

John Chiddick

See also Cold War; Cold War, Post Era; Relations with the European Union, U.S.

Further Reading

Asmus, R. D. (2003). Rebuilding the Atlantic alliance. *Foreign Affairs, 82*(5), 20–31.

Carpenter, T. G. (2001). *NATO enters the 21st century.* Portland, OR: Frank Cass.

David, C.-P., & Levesque, J. (1999). *The future of NATO: Enlargement, Russia and European security.* Montreal, Canada: McGill-Queen's University Press.

Duignan, P. (2000). *NATO: Its past, present and future.* Stanford, CA: Hoover Institution Press.

Gaddis, J. L. (1972). *The United States and the origins of the Cold War, 1941–1947.* New York: Columbia University Press.

Gaddis, J. L. (1982). *Strategies of containment.* Oxford, UK: Oxford University Press.

Kaplan, L. S. (1984). *The United States and NATO: The formative years.* Lexington: University Press of Kentucky.

Kaplan, L. S. (1988). *NATO and the United States: The enduring alliance.* Boston: Twayne Publishers.

Sloan, S. R. (2003). *NATO, the European Union and the Atlantic community.* Lanham, MD: Rowman and Littlefield.

Talbott, S. (2002). From Prague to Baghdad: NATO at risk. *Foreign Affairs, 81*(6), 46–57.

Nobel Peace Prize

Since the Cold War ended, the Nobel Peace Prize has been increasingly awarded to citizens of non-Western nations, indicating that the United States and the West in general may be losing their monopoly of this prestigious prize.

The Nobel Peace Prize is one of five Nobel prizes awarded from a bequest by Alfred Nobel, a Swedish industrialist. The bequest stipulated that the prize be awarded to the person who has done the most or the best work for fraternity between nations, the abolition or reduction of standing armies, and the promotion of peace conferences. The prize is awarded each year at City Hall in Oslo, Norway. The Norwegian Parliament appoints the Norwegian Nobel Committee, made up of five people, which selects laureates for the prize. Nominations are made by a broad spectrum of persons, including former laureates, members of national assemblies, university professors, international judges, and advisors to the committee. The prize can be awarded not only to individuals, but also to organizations that have promoted peace. Recipients often have a long history of promoting humanitarian issues.

From 1901 to 1913 the prize was primarily given to a person involved in a peace movement or to organizations. In 1905 the first female was honored. In 1913 the first socialist received the prize. From 1914 to 1918 World War I and the Red Cross were the primary focus of the committee. Between 1919 and 1939 the League of Nations and the work for peace by individuals were considered important. From 1940 to 1945 World War II was a focus, and another prize was awarded to the Red Cross. From 1946 to 1966 the Cold War and the United Nations had a major influence on the award. In 1949 the first scientist received the award. In 1950 the first black person received the award. Between 1967 and 1989 the Cold War was a major influence on the prize, and the prize became globalized. In 1974 the first Asian person received the award. From 1990 to the present globalization has been a major factor in the award.

No Popularity Contest

The committee's choice for the prize, such as Theodore Roosevelt, Shimon Peres, Yasser Arafat, Le Duc Tho, and Henry Kissinger, is not always popular. Right-leaning groups have been critical of the committee, in some cases accusing the committee of a left-wing bias. When Le Duc Tho and Kissinger were selected, two of the committee members resigned. Other controversies have stemmed from the fact that even though the Norwegian Parliament appoints the committee members, the political makeup of the Parliament often determines the political makeup of the committee. Some recipients, such as Kissinger, Mikhail Gorbachev, and Arafat, have been criticized for their political activity. Some people have criticized the failure of the committee to award the prize to some people who were nominated, such as Mohandas Gandhi, Pope John XXIII, Pope John Paul II, Steve Biko, Herbert Hoover, and Oscar Romero. The also-ran nominee mentioned most often is Gandhi. A few laureates have not always lived up to their reputation after they were awarded the prize, and a few infamous people, such as Adolf Hitler, Joseph Stalin, and Benito Mussolini, have been nominated. However, in spite of controversy, the Nobel Peace Prize is still the most prestigious award of the more than three hundred peace prizes given in the world today.

Western Orientation

A summary of the first one hundred years of the Nobel Prize indicates that most organizations honored have been embedded in Western ideology. Nineteen prizes have gone to people in the United States, both sitting politicians and people more distant from the center of political power. Twelve were given to people in Great Britain, again reflecting both political positions and traditional values, eight to France, four to Germany, five to Sweden, and two to Norway.

In 1936 the first prize was awarded to a person not from Europe or North America, and the next such recipient was in 1960. Beginning in the 1970s the committee began giving the prize to Asians, Africans, and Latin Americans. From the 1970s to the 1980s, as many prizes went to people from Africa, Asia, and Latin America combined as to people from North America and most of Europe combined. In addition, a few prizes are now going to eastern Europe and Israel. The focus has gradually become more global.

How has this system of prize selection affected global perspectives of the United States? Even though the United States does not select the prize winner some critics might reply that Western-oriented friends of the United States do select the winner. The

NOBEL PEACE PRIZE WINNERS SINCE 1989

YEAR	WINNER(S)	COUNTRY	QUALIFICATIONS
2006	Muhammad Yunus, Grameen Bank	Germany	Efforts to create economic and social development from below, banker to the poor
2005	International Atomic Energy Agency, Mohamed ElBaradei	Austria, Egypt	Efforts to prevent nuclear energy from being used for military purposes and ensure the safe use of nuclear energy for peaceful purposes
2004	Wangari Maathai	Kenya	Contribution to sustainable development, democracy, and peace
2003	Shirin Ebadi	Iran	Efforts for democracy and human rights
2002	Jimmy Carter Jr.	United States	Efforts for peaceful solutions to international conflicts and advancing democracy, human rights, and economic and social development
2001	United Nations, Kofi Annan	United States, Ghana	Working for a more peaceful and organized world
2000	Kim Dae Jung	South Korea	Efforts for democracy and human rights in South Korea and east Asia, and for peace and reconciliation with North Korea
1999	Doctors Without Borders	Belgium	Multinational medical and humanitarian efforts
1998	John Hume, David Trimble	Northern Ireland	Efforts to find a peaceful solution to the conflict in Northern Ireland
1997	International Campaign to Ban Landmines, Judy Williams	United States	Work to ban and clear antipersonnel mines
1996	Carlos Felipe Ximenes Belo, Jose Ramos-Horta	Timor	Work toward a just and peaceful solution to the conflict in East Timor
1995	Joseph Rotblat, Pugwash Conferences on Science and World Affairs	United Kingdom, Canada	Efforts to diminish the role of nuclear arms in international politics and to eliminate such arms in the long-term
1994	Yasser Arafat, Shimon Peres, Yitzhak Rabin	Palestine, Israel/ Poland, Israel	Efforts to create peace in the Middle East; signed the Oslo Accords
1993	Nelson Mandela, Fredrik Willem De Klerk	South Africa	Ending apartheid in South Africa
1992	Rigoberta Menchu Tum	Guatemala-Maya Indian	Campaigner for human rights, especially for indigenous peoples
1991	Aung San Suu Kyi	Myanmar (Burma)	Work as a Buddhist, nonviolent, prodemocracy activist and human rights advocate
1990	Mikhail Sergeyevich Gorbachev	USSR	Helped bring an end to the Cold War and the fall of the Iron Curtain
1989	Fourteenth Dalai Lama (Tenzin Gyatso)	Tibet	Religious and political leader of the Tibetan people

Source: All Nobel Peace Prize laureates. (2007). Retrieved May 31, 2007, from http://nobelprize.org/nobel_prizes/peace/laureates/

growing list of recipients from Asia, Africa, and Latin America has certainly blunted this argument and the prize has grown in stature worldwide. No selection system is perfect, but the Nobel Peace Prize selection has weathered criticism on all sides and still has great international appeal.

Herbert W. Ockerman and Lopa Basu

See also International Law

Further Reading

A Nobel Peace Prize for food. (1997). Retrieved June 1, 2007, from www.paulagordon.com/shows/borlaug

All Nobel Peace Prize laureates. (n.d.). Retrieved March 16, 2007, from http://nobelprize.org/nobel_prizes/peace/laureates/

Famous peacemakers. (2007). Retrieved June 1, 2007, from http://peacemakers.szm.com/

International Organisations and the Nobel Peace Prize. (2007). Retrieved June 1, 2007, from http://www.bl.uk/collections/americas/americasnobel.html

Mother Teresa. (n.d.). Retrieved March 16, 2007, from http://almaz.com/nobel/peace/peace.html

Nobel laureates—peace. (n.d.). Retrieved March 16, 2007, from http://womenshistory.about.com/od/nobelpeace/Nobel_Laureates_Peace.htm?terms=Nobel+laureates%97peace

Nobel Peace Prize winners 2006–1901. (2007). Retrieved March 16, 2007, from http://almaz.com/nobel/peace/peace.html

Nobel Prize. (2007) Retrieved June 1, 2007, from http://nobelprize.org/

Rowen, B. (n.d.). Nobel Prize history. Retrieved March 16, 2007, from www.infoplease.com/nobel-prize-history.html

The Nobel Prize & Grand Hotel. (n.d.). Retrieved March 16, 2007, from http://www.grand.no/hist_nobel.asp

United Nations Publications. (2007). Retrieved March 16, 2007, from https://unp.un.org/

Overseas Americans (Expatriates)

Americans living outside the United States fall into two groups: those who accept the cultural and lifestyle differences in their new home, and those who appear to disdain their lives overseas and long to return home.

Enormously affluent and exuberantly free, the United States seems to hold out the promise of unlimited freedom and material gain for anybody who works hard. For centuries it has been a magnet for immigrants seeking a better life. Few Americans have left U.S. shores for other nations. Yet, the ones who have emigrated have both influenced their adopted countries and affected how the United States is perceived by these countries.

The first official U.S. expatriates went abroad because of war. Colonial Tories moved to England before or during the American Revolution. They did not always paint a flattering picture of the new U.S. government and the patriots that had founded it. However, Benjamin Franklin, John and Abigail Adams, Thomas Jefferson, and other notable luminaries and statesmen of the day all spent long periods in Europe and focused on forging diplomatic discourse both before and after the Declaration of Independence was signed. When the war was won and freedom declared, they made new alliances, set up a network of merchant trade, and opened diplomatic relations for a nation in the making. They were prominent in social, as well political, affairs and were under close scrutiny by Europeans for their manners, conversation, and customs. Some Britons were surprised that a colonial could speak so well, as painter Gilbert Stuart discovered.

People in the United States generally believe that whereas people abroad wish to immigrate to the United States, Americans themselves do not wish to emigrate. Persons who move out of the United States do so relatively unnoticed and unrecorded. Statistics on emigration from the United States were last collected during the Eisenhower administration in the 1950s. Despite deficiencies in the data, enough information is available to determine that in the twentieth century the United States lost about 10 million people to emigration. At the start of the twenty-first century, the U.S. was losing about 150,000 people, mostly former immigrants, each year.

Relatively few native-born Americans left the United States in the first decades of the nation's existence. Writer James Fenimore Cooper moved to Italy with his family in 1826. Cooper was vigorously pro-United States and republican. He reverted to his native background in his books, which were viewed by Europeans as novel and informative. During the 1820s and 1830s Cooper helped to illuminate the United States for Europeans who did not wholly understand the American Revolution and its consequences. In time Cooper's writings also contributed to a prevailing feeling in Europe that the United States was overrun with Indians.

In the nineteenth century Americans living abroad were bombarded by questions about the contradiction of a slave population that existed under a government that rested entirely on the doctrine of equal rights. Black Americans often have a different picture of the United States than white Americans.

North to Freedom

A number of African-Americans migrated to Canada to escape slavery. Slavery in Canada formally ended in 1834. At this point, the nation became a place of refuge and resettlement for blacks, particularly after passage of the U.S. Fugitive Slave Act in 1850. These Americans did not present a positive image of the United States. Instead, with their presence and with their stories, they showed the United States to be a place of brutality that lagged behind other powerful nations in its continued toleration of human bondage.

In Africa, Liberia was settled in 1822 by freed U.S. slaves. Liberia's organizers intended to fight the slave trade being conducted along the western coast of Africa as colonists spread the Christian religion and "civilization" among the indigenous population. Under white governors appointed by the American Colonization Society, the colonists had little success in persuading Africans to abandon either domestic slavery or the coastal sale of slaves. Even after gaining independence in 1847, the Americo-Liberians continued dressing in European clothes, speaking English, and modeling their government and society after their mother country. Too many of the former slaves created offense by behaving in the same way colonial rulers had elsewhere. They alienated many west Africans from African-Americans for decades afterward, and, in doing so, harmed the cause of pan-Africanism.

After the Civil War ended slavery in the United States, black Americans continued to leave the United States to escape abusive treatment. Singer and dancer Josephine Baker emigrated to France in 1925 partly to escape segregation and racial discrimination in the United States. Black writer James Baldwin bought a one-way air-

plane ticket to Paris and left the United States in 1948. Sociologist and National Association for the Advancement of Colored People co-founder W. E. B. DuBois moved to Ghana in 1961 after years of persecution by the U.S. government for his communist political views and racial activism. Cartoonist Tom Feelings moved to Ghana because of both a sense of alienation in the United States and a desire for greater economic opportunities. Teacher Priscilla Stevens Kruize emigrated to Ghana to escape U.S. rejection. The presence of these overseas Americans as well as their criticism of U.S. racial policies gave an image of the United States as a land of bigotry.

However, Americans of all races are treated as foreigners by Africans. Ghanaians use the word *abruni* or "not from the family" to refer to Americans. As foreigners, expatriates long received preferential treatment by Ghanaians instead of being treated as just other black persons in a black society. Additionally, Americans in Africa, especially during the Cold War, were sometimes suspected of working for the U.S. government.

The category of U.S. expatriates includes immigrants who lived in the United States before returning to their countries of origin. These people have had, and continue to have, the greatest impact on how the United States is perceived in other countries. This is true particularly in Mexico, at the start of the twenty-first century. Knowledge of the United States has been obtained firsthand by other nationals through letters sent home by emigrants, but also through emigrants who returned home to live after a period of time in the United States. Many immigrants to the United States intend to return home at some point, and the peak period of immigration, between 1880 and 1920, about one in three immigrants in did return home.

Push and Pull

The causes of immigration to the United States are found in the interaction between those forces that drive people out of their countries of origin and those forces that entice them to the United States. Although historians have typically described these forces as "push" and "pull" factors, emigrants did not make much of a distinction between what was pushing them out of Europe, Asia, or Latin America and what was pulling them to the United States. Most of them simply wanted to make a good living for themselves or their families. One of the important influences on foreign perception of the United States was the knowledge of potential economic opportunity. One Pole wrote to the Emigrants Protective Association in Warsaw, Poland, in the first decade of the twentieth century that he had observed Poles returning from the United States with money. He declared that he wanted to go

to the United States to advance, to live decently, and to give his children some education.

Asian immigration to the United States began later than European immigration because of racially motivated immigration restrictions. Substantial numbers of Filipinos choose to immigrate to the United States because of the influence of Americans overseas. They picked the United States because of the democratic ideals that they had learned in U.S.-run schools in the years after the 1898 U.S. colonization of the Philippine Islands. However, this interaction with expatriate Americans left the Filipinos with an unrealistic vision of what their lives in the United States would be like. Carlos Bulosan, a Filipino intellectual who lived in the United States from 1930 until his death in 1956, reported that he felt betrayed because racism blocked his access to beauty, wealth, power, and grandeur.

Most Filipinos, from the first wave of immigration in the early twentieth century to the present, have had their views of the United States shaped by the available economic opportunities. The Hawaiian Sugar Planter's Association sent Americans to the Philippines to recruit contract workers between 1909 and 1934. Upon expiration of the contracts, some of the 119,470 Filipino sugar workers remained, and others returned home. Both groups of workers influenced Filipinos by reporting the number of well-paying jobs available in the United States, in sharp contrast to the jobs offered at below a living wage that attracted thousands of applicants in the Philippines.

The most dramatic growth in the number of overseas Americans occurred after World War II. The United States expanded its political, military, corporate, and humanitarian responsibilities outside of its national borders. The number of overseas diplomatic personnel doubled, spurred by the nation's superpower status as well as by the Foreign Service Reform Act of 1946, which provided for the recruitment of economists and other professionals as well as diplomatic generalists. However, the State Department accounts for only a small percentage of overseas Americans. The armed forces, Central Intelligence Agency, U.S. Information Agency, Peace Corps, and the Departments of Treasury, Commerce, Interior, and Agriculture also send representatives abroad. Since 1946, when it was unusual for Americans to live overseas unless they were missionaries or diplomats, it has become commonplace for Americans to be stationed abroad, if only for a year.

U.S. Children Abroad

With families in tow, government and private-sector personnel began to live and move outside the borders of their U.S. compounds in the postwar years. Sometimes called "third culture kids"

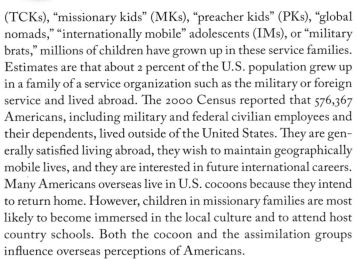

(TCKs), "missionary kids" (MKs), "preacher kids" (PKs), "global nomads," "internationally mobile" adolescents (IMs), or "military brats," millions of children have grown up in these service families. Estimates are that about 2 percent of the U.S. population grew up in a family of a service organization such as the military or foreign service and lived abroad. The 2000 Census reported that 576,367 Americans, including military and federal civilian employees and their dependents, lived outside of the United States. They are generally satisfied living abroad, they wish to maintain geographically mobile lives, and they are interested in future international careers. Many Americans overseas live in U.S. cocoons because they intend to return home. However, children in missionary families are most likely to become immersed in the local culture and to attend host country schools. Both the cocoon and the assimilation groups influence overseas perceptions of Americans.

A distinct dichotomy exists among Americans overseas in their attitudes toward the host country. One group accepts the power outages, the traffic snarls, and the bureaucratic bungling as simply part of the character of the place and appreciates the good things. The other group, infamous as "ugly Americans," goes beyond complaining about local conditions and finds every opportunity to make derogatory comments about the character of the host country nationals. The second group combines with U.S. military excursions overseas to create negative perceptions of the United States.

The U.S. presence in Vietnam damaged international perceptions of Americans. The behavior of U.S. military men in impregnating and abandoning native Vietnamese women did not improve those perceptions, and their children were often ostracized. In December 1987 Congress passed the Amerasian Homecoming Act in response to media depictions of the plight of these children in Vietnam and growing public pressure to intervene on their behalf. The possibility of free immigration to the United States for Amerasians and their relatives had a profound impact on the standing of these children in their communities. They were now golden passports to the United States. There are also many Amerasians in Korea and the Philippines, where the United States had a significant military presence for many years. However, only the Amerasians of Vietnam have attracted widespread support in the United States, partly because of the ongoing U.S. preoccupation with the Vietnam War. The impact of the other Amerasians has, accordingly, been limited.

Caryn E. Neumann

See also Culture Overseas, U.S.; Missionaries

Further Reading

Dashefsky, A., DeAmicis, J., Lazerwitz, B., & Tabory, E. (1992). *Americans abroad: A comparative study of emigrants from the United States.* New York: Plenum Press.

Dunbar, E. (1968). *The black expatriates: A study of American Negroes in exile.* New York: E. P. Dutton.

Ender, M. G. (2002). *Military brats and other global nomads: Growing up in organization families.* Westport, CT: Praeger.

Gershoni, Y. (1985). *Black colonialism: The Americo-Liberian scramble for the hinterland.* Boulder, CO: Westview.

Ross, I. (1970). *The expatriates.* New York: Thomas Y. Crowell.

Shick, T. W. (1977). *Behold the promised land: A history of Afro-American settler society in nineteenth century Liberia.* Baltimore, MD: Johns Hopkins University Press.

Smith, C. D. (1991). *The absentee American: Repatriates' perspectives on America and its place in the contemporary world.* New York: Praeger.

Peace Corps

Probably more than any other group, the Peace Corps has created a positive global image of the U.S., with education and aid programs in dozens of developing countries, and volunteers integrating into the communities they serve.

The Peace Corps was created in response to the Cold War between the United States and the Soviet Union. A novel of social realism entitled *The Ugly American* by William Lederer and Eugene Burdick (1958), with its devastating critique of the poor performance of "tongue-tied" U.S. government personnel serving overseas, inspired the idea of the Peace Corps. Americans fared poorly overseas in contrast to better-trained and more linguistically adept Russians in the "battle for the hearts and minds" of people in the developing world. Senator Hubert Humphrey of Minnesota and Congressman Henry Reuss of Wisconsin proposed the creation of a Peace Corps–like agency in 1960.

After John F. Kennedy defeated Humphrey in the 1960 presidential primaries, Kennedy picked up the idea of the Peace Corps, and it became part of his own campaign. Former President Dwight D. Eisenhower and Vice President Richard Nixon derided the idea and called it the "Kennedy Kiddie Corps" (Textor 1966, 2), but this public derision did not stop Kennedy from implementing what went on to become a very successful program.

Turning Points

Kennedy formally proposed the idea of the Peace Corps on 14 October 1960 as he campaigned on the steps of the Student Union at the University of Michigan before a crowd of ten thousand. After taking office, President Kennedy on 1 March 1961 issued Executive Order 10924 establishing the Peace Corps and asked his brother-in-law, R. Sargent Shriver, to establish and run the agency, which was to become part of the State Department. The agency, however, was only temporary. To make the Peace Corps permanent, Kennedy needed authorization from Congress. Shriver appointed Bill Moyers, a young protégé of Lyndon Johnson, to handle his congressional relations and work for the formal approval of the Peace Corps.

Shriver cleverly began implementing the Peace Corps prior to Congress's acting on the legislation. By the time Congress was ready to act, about two hundred volunteers were already in four countries: Ghana, Colombia, St. Lucia, and Tanganyika. On 22 September 1961, the Peace Corps Act was passed by Congress, and the Peace Corps received an initial appropriation of $30 million. By the autumn of 1965 approximately twelve thousand volunteers were serving in forty-six countries.

Objectives and Basic Operating Principles

In the Peace Corps Act three key objectives were stated:

1. To help developing countries meet their need for trained manpower.
2. To promote a better understanding of the U.S. people on the part of the peoples served.
3. To help promote a better understanding of other peoples on the part of the U.S. people.

The Peace Corps also has three core operating principles:

1. Volunteers would receive intensive training (approximately three months) prior to departure.
2. Volunteers would receive intensive language training related to their assignments.

OUR GLOBAL RESPONSIBILITIES

The excerpt below is from a speech given by President Kennedy just a week before the official establishment of the Peace Corps program.

The benefits of the Peace Corps will not be limited to the countries in which it serves. Our own young men and women will be enriched by the experience of living and working in foreign lands. They will have acquired new skills and experience which will aid the in their future careers and add to our country's supply of trained personnel and teachers. They will return better able to assume the responsibilities of American citizenship and with greater understanding of our global responsibilities.

—*John F. Kennedy, February 21, 1961*

Source: Kennedy, J. F., & Adler, B. (Eds.). (2003). The uncommon wisdom of JFK. New York: Rugged Land.

3. Volunteers would receive roughly the same salaries as their local counterparts. Thus, they are expected to live under modest conditions, earning only a fraction of a typical U.S. salary for the same kind of work.

Basic Facts

To date approximately 170,000 volunteers and trainees have served in 137 countries. Currently approximately 7,500 volunteers are serving in seventy-one countries. Many volunteers now serve in countries that did not exist fifteen years ago, such as Kazakhstan, Georgia, and the Kyrgyz Republic. The current demographic profile of volunteers is 59 percent female, 90 percent single, 15 percent people of color, 6 percent older than fifty, 83 percent with an undergraduate degree, and 15 percent with a graduate degree. The average age of volunteers is twenty-eight, and the oldest volunteer is eighty-one.

The jobs that Peace Corps volunteers perform are negotiated between the host country and the Peace Corps. The most common Peace Corps jobs have been teaching and training. Also many volunteers have been involved in local community development work.

Over time Peace Corps procedures have changed. There were times when couples with children could not serve, for example. Initially training often took place on U.S. college campuses. Later considerable training took place at special sites in Puerto Rico (for Latin American volunteers) and the big island of Hawaii (for Asia-Pacific volunteers). Now all training is done in-country. Initially an emphasis was placed on the recruitment of volunteers with general liberal arts backgrounds who could be provided training in their technical areas. Later more emphasis was placed on recruiting volunteers with existing needed technical skills.

Assessment

Related to the third objective of the Peace Corps, the United States now has an extensive pool of individuals who are knowledgeable in diverse cultures and a multitude of languages. Hundreds have gone on to become scholars and writers, contributing to U.S. knowledge and understanding of developing countries. As would be expected, former volunteers have contributed to the field of anthropology. The Peace Corps has also produced popular writers and people influential in the media, such as the novelist and travel writer Paul Theroux (2000) and Chris Matthews (2001), host of the cable TV news show *Hardball*.

A SYMBOL OF HOPE

The excerpt below is from a speech delivered by Teresa Heinz Kerry, wife of the democratic presidential candidate John Kerry, at the 2004 Democratic National Convention.

To me, one of the best faces America has ever projected is the face of a Peace Corps volunteer. That face symbolizes this country: young, curious, brimming with idealism and hope—and a real honest compassion. Those young people convey an idea of America that is all about heart and creativity, generosity and confidence—a practical, can-do sense and a big, big smile. For many generations of people around the globe, that is what America has represented. A symbol of hope, a beacon brightly lit by the optimism of its people—people coming from all over the world.

Source: PBS Online Newshour. (2004, July 27). Retrieved March 22, 2007, from http://www.pbs.org/newshour/vote2004/demconvention/speeches/heinz-kerry.html

The Peace Corps has also influenced thinking about how to teach other languages effectively, which is relevant to the late Senator Paul Simon's (1980) harsh critique of the failure of U.S. citizens to develop competency in other languages.

The Peace Corps experience has often been transformative for volunteers. The late Harvard social psychologist Gordon Allport (1954) emphasized social contact theory arguing that encounters across diverse cultural and racial groups reduce prejudice and misunderstanding. A number of former volunteers have married members of the indigenous cultures, especially in the Philippines, Chile, and Thailand. In terms of lifestyle former volunteers are likely to be critical of excessive materialism and to belong to the voluntary simplicity movement and a growing group known as "cultural creatives" (Ray and Anderson 2001).

Many people discover teaching through the Peace Corps. Former volunteers are well known for their willingness to take on, for example, challenging inner-city assignments in the United States. Many former volunteers also have a record of civic involvement.

Overall the Peace Corps has clearly helped improve the image of the United States overseas. The cultural and language abilities of many volunteers have helped endear them to their hosts. However, some people have criticized the Peace Corps. Some people in host countries are skeptical of the motives of volunteers and question why they are willing to live so meagerly. Some people accuse volunteers of being "spies for the CIA." President Kennedy was conscious of this potential problem and thus put into place legislation prohibiting intelligence agencies from hiring volunteers in the first five years after their Peace Corps work.

Of the three Peace Corps objectives, most skepticism probably concerns the first—the contribution of volunteers to the development of the host country. The record of achievement of this objective has certainly been mixed, and volunteers have not always had the technical skills needed. Of course, thousands of volunteers have made a difference in the lives of others. Identification and then promotion of local talent are certainly areas of success.

Probably the most severe criticism of the Peace Corps is that it is a large public relations operation designed to enhance the image of the United States in the face of unpopular U.S. foreign actions such as the Vietnam War and the Iraq War (2003).

Spread of the Peace Corps Movement

The Peace Corps has inspired other groups to form Peace Corps–like programs that have no connection to the U.S. government.

Two prominent U.S. examples are Volunteers in Asia, a consortium of Stanford, Pomona, and the University of California at Santa Cruz, and Minnesota Studies in International Development. Many countries now have their own form of the Peace Corps. Table 1 provides data on these organizations.

The Future

Congress has consistently been supportive of the Peace Corps and is considering plans for expansion, with a target of placing ten thousand volunteers overseas. Many people consider the Peace Corps to be the best foreign policy investment the United States has ever made. For thousands of U.S. citizens the Peace Corps has provided intense intercultural and language learning opportunities and transformative experiences.

Gerald W. Fry

Table 1. Government-supported Overseas Volunteer Organizations

Name of organization	Voluntary Service Overseas (VSO)	Canadian University Services Overseas (CUSO)	Peace Corps	French Association of Volunteers of Progress (AFVP)	German Development Service (DED)	Japan Overseas Cooperation Volunteers (JOCV)	Korean Overseas Volunteers (KOV)
Country	United Kingdom	Canada	United States	France	Germany	Japan	South Korea
Year founded	1958	1961	1961	1963	1963	1965	1990
Total # of volunteers to date	30,000+	13,000	170,000	NA	13,000	26,451	1,000+
Total # of current volunteers	1,500	356	7,749	330	1,000	2,537	208
Countries served currently	35+	NA	73	35	40	66	25
Age qualification	20–75	NA	18+	21–30	21+	20–39	20–61
Term of service	2 years	2 years	2 years	2 years	2 years	2 years	2 years
Annual budget	$64.7 million (32.8 million pounds)	$22.6 million (CA$24.3 million)	$308 million	$30.9 million (23 million euros)	$114 million (85 million euros)	$188 million (22.8 billion yen)	NA

Further Reading

Allport, G. W. (1954). *The nature of prejudice.* Cambridge, MA: Addison-Wesley.

Cleveland, H., Mangone, G. J., & Adams, J. C. (1960). *The overseas Americans.* New York: McGraw-Hill.

Elgin, D. (1993). *Voluntary simplicity: Toward a way of life that is outwardly simple, inwardly rich.* New York: Quill.

Illich, I. (1990). To hell with good intentions. In J. C. Kendall (Ed.), *Combining service and learning: A resource book for community and public service* (Vol. 1, pp. 321–323). Raleigh, NC: National Society for Internships and Experiential Education.

Kennedy, J. F., & Adler, B. (Eds.). (2003). *The uncommon wisdom of JFK.* New York: Rugged Land.

Lederer, W. J., & Burdick, E. (1958). *The ugly American.* New York: Norton.

Matthews, C. (2001). *Now, let me tell you what I think.* New York: Free Press.

National Peace Corps Association. (2001). *The directory of returned Peace Corps volunteers & former staff 1961–2001.* Purchase, NY: Richard C. Harris Publishing.

Ray, P. H., & Anderson, S. R. (2001). *The cultural creatives: How 50 million people are changing the world.* New York: Three Rivers Press.

Schwimmer, B. E., & Warren, D. M. (Eds.). (1993). *Anthropology and the Peace Corps.* Ames: Iowa State University Press.

Simon, P. (1980). *The tongue-tied American: Confronting the foreign language crisis.* New York: Continuum.

Textor, R. B. (Ed.). (1966). *Cultural frontiers of the Peace Corps.* Cambridge, MA: MIT Press.

Theroux, P. (2000). *Fresh air fiend: Travel writings, 1985–2000.* Boston: Houghton-Mifflin.

Perspectives on the United States, Theory of

The United States came to achieve world power status—a status that might be under challenge in the twenty-first century—by strategically choosing its relations with other countries based on idealism, as well as political realism.

The United States emerged first as a continental power through its westward expansion, leading to wars with Native American tribes and Mexico and the consolidation of the U.S. frontier by 1890. It then emerged as a regional power, establishing a sphere of influence in the Americas through the Monroe Doctrine (1823), leading to wars with Spain. It ultimately emerged as a world power after World War II, with its primary enemy being the Soviet Union, leading to the Cold War.

The United States has consolidated its status as a world power since the end of the Cold War. However, since then the United States has gone through two phases in attempts to legitimize its status as the world's only superpower and to construct a world order in its image. It first sought to claim that legitimacy through the "new world order" (1992), by which it would fight for democracy and human rights, free trade, and environmentalism. Its main allies were the United Kingdom and Europe, and its main competitor—briefly—was Russian leader Mikhail Gorbachev and his vision of a new world order.

After the terrorist attacks of September 11, 2001, the United States has sought to claim its legitimacy as a superpower in a different way, that is, through the war against terrorism, by which it would fight against terrorist states and organizations to preserve U.S. safety and the cultural values of Western civilization. However, the Iraq War (2003) and the general war against terrorism have been more unilateralist campaigns compared with the multilateralism of the new world order and have isolated the United States from its main allies in Europe and countries around the world, with the United Kingdom remaining its most solid ally. Europe and the rest of the world appear to favor both the multilateral approach and the democratic and free trade agenda of the new world order vision.

During George W. Bush's first term (2001–2005) and the start of his second term, three issues appear to pose the greatest challenge to the world power status of the United States. The first of these is the issue of legitimacy itself. People have questioned the credibility of U.S. leadership because the reasoning behind the war against Iraq (finding and destroying weapons of mass destruction and destroying the al-Qaeda terrorist network) have proven unfounded and/or unsuccessful.

Second, the priority given to the war against terrorism has replaced priorities of democracy and development, issues in which Europe and the rest of the world are more interested. Third, substantial costs to the U.S. economy result, in contrast to the rise in power of the countries of the European Union and China. These costs have caused growing alarm that U.S. economic leadership in the world might be on its way out, considering the weakening U.S. dollar against the EU currency, the growing U.S. trade deficit, and strong economic growth of China.

Strategizing Relations with Other Countries

To understand how the United States came to achieve world power status and why that status might be under challenge at present, one must appreciate how the United States has strategized its relations with other countries over time. Three perspectives are useful.

The perspective of realism sees the world as a Hobbesian (relating to the English philosopher Thomas Hobbes) power struggle in which the strong survive. Countries should therefore rely less on morality and law (because they are generally not respected) and rely more on realpolitik (politics based on practical and material factors rather than on theoretical or ethical objectives) to secure themselves in a balance of powers among states to ensure their survival, if not their dominance. The "Big Stick" policy (1904) of the United States is an example of this perspective.

This perspective arose out of the kind of thinking reflected by the naval strategist Alfred Mahan, who argued that the future security and greatness of the United States depended on building a large naval fleet around the world. Social Darwinists at the time believed that the world was a jungle, that international conflict was inevitable, and that only the strong countries would survive. Religion was sometimes invoked in the cause of realism, for example, that the United States had a duty to take on the "white man's burden" by exporting its supposedly superior culture to backward peoples. This perspective made foreign intervention and imperialism acceptable. The realist emphasis is on national security.

The perspective of idealism sees the world through a Kantian (relating to the German philosopher Immanuel Kant) lens of peace, a product of Enlightenment (a philosophic movement of the eighteenth century marked by a rejection of traditional social, religious, and political ideas and an emphasis on rationalism) philosophy and the Age of Reason. Ideas of liberalism and human progress were founded on the belief that war hinders commerce. Morality and law are important to regulate order among states. Prescriptions of a cosmopolitan world order are offered, such as through the League of Nations and the United Nations. The Good Neighbor Policy and the Alliance for Progress, which favored cooperation with Latin America rather than foreign intervention, were examples of idealism in U.S. foreign policy.

Idealists believe that war is a product of poverty, colonialism, and the security dilemma arising from the anarchical nature of the international system, a system in which no world government exists. President Woodrow Wilson was among those who believed that the League of Nations would provide the regulation needed to avoid wars, allow self-determination for colonized peoples, and promote economic development to meet people's welfare. The idealist emphasis is on international cooperation.

The perspective of structuralism sees the world through a Wallersteinian (relating to world systems analyst Immanuel Wallerstein) lens in which the structures of the world system determine how states behave. Such structures determine the nature of international trade, the dominant positions of multinational corporations, and the military imbalances among states, all of which perpetuate and determine conflict, inequality, dependency, and underdevelopment. The international system is structured so that a hierarchy of inequality exists between states.

International peace movements, ecological movements, and humanitarian nongovernmental organizations (NGOs) have arisen to promote a planetary variant on the world system perspective, saying that all countries would be better off by making trade free and fair, making multinationals more socially responsible, and converting savings from disarmament into peace dividends. These actions would lead to sustainable development of the planet and secure it not just for states in time, but also for people over time, that is, for future generations. The emphasis of structuralists is on global reform.

U.S. Foreign Policy in Perspective

These three perspectives have been present in U.S. foreign policy, but the realist perspective has been most dominant in the last hundred years. Europe, the heartland of the Enlightenment, has been able to build a community of states by discarding the power politics that led to European rivalry in favor of community politics more in line with the idealist and structuralist perspectives. The Soviet Union/Russia had attempted to build the Commonwealth of Independent States in eastern Europe under Gorbachev. However, the United States has not created a community of states in the Americas, which is symptomatic of its problem in legitimizing its moral leadership in the world.

The U.S. presidential election of 2004 was, in part, a choice for U.S. citizens to continue along the realist, religio-ideological, unilateralist path that put national interest first or along a multilateral path with a vision for a community of the Americas espoused by the defeated candidate, John Kerry. U.S. foreign policy makers currently see the world in terms of a struggle between good and evil in which the strong will survive. Phrases such as "evil empire" and "axis of evil" are symptomatic of this perspective. The war against terrorism is the latest example of the dominance of this perspective, supported by a religio-ideological outlook and a military campaign.

Hans Morgenthau, a U.S. scholar and a founding father of U.S. international relations, wrote during the era of the Cold War that, "The protection of the 'free world' from Communism became the main purpose of American foreign policy whether in Europe or Asia and Central America. In its name, or its alias, national security policies were pursued and outrages committed which defied the moral standards by which government theory and practice had traditionally been judged" (Morgenthau and Thompson 1985, 374). That alias is now terrorism.

Realism seems outdated in a globalizing world that is trending evermore toward multilateralism and community politics. This misfit between U.S. foreign policy and global interdependence underlines the difficulty the United States faces in legitimizing its moral status as world leader. The U.S. strategic alliance with Israel, for example, alienates Arab countries. The U.S. strategic engagement with Iraq and then the U.S. military attacks on Iraq are regarded as unprincipled.

U.S. engagement with the former apartheid regime of South Africa was justified purely on realist grounds—to balance the perceived Soviet encroachment through the Horn of Africa—but strongly criticized internationally as insensitive. Its embargo against Cuba, a holdover from the Cold War, is viewed in the Caribbean as outdated and a hindrance to a community of the Americas. Its support for oligarchs in Saudi Arabia, Pakistan, and Haiti against democratic alternatives subverts what Morgenthau calls its "libertarian" and "anti-colonial" tradition.

The United States is a "big brother" to some—democratic or oligarchic, honest or corrupt—but an "ugly American" to others. It continues to have difficulty convincing many countries of the

morality of its leadership. Samuel Huntington remarks that the efforts of the West to promote its values of democracy and liberalism as universal values, to maintain its military predominance, and to advance its economic interests engender countering responses from other civilizations. Decreasingly able to mobilize support and form coalitions on the basis of ideology, governments and groups will increasingly attempt to mobilize support by appealing to common religion and civilization identity.

Huntington follows up this observation by raising questions about the future of the U.S. identity and challenges to preserve its Christian, Anglocentric traditions. Whether the United States will be driven by this ideological and cultural conviction in the future is yet to be seen. The question is which of its historical perspectives will predominate—the realist, idealist, or structuralist.

Robert Buddan

Further Reading

Heine, J., & Manigat, L. (Eds.). (1988). *The Caribbean and world politics: Cross currents and cleavages.* New York and London: Holmes and Meier.

Hettne, B. (1990). *Development theory and the three worlds.* London: Longman Scientific and Technical.

Huntington, S. (1993, Summer). The clash of civilizations. *Foreign Affairs, 2*(2), 22–28.

Macridis, R. (Ed.). (1989). *Foreign policy in world politics: States and regions.* Englewood Cliffs, NJ: Prentice-Hall.

Morgenthau, H., & Thompson, K. (1985). *Politics among nations: The struggle for power and peace.* New York: Alfred A. Knopf.

Perspectives on the United States, Visitors'

From the earliest days of U.S. nationhood, visitors from abroad, particularly Europe, have documented their travels in the United States, intent on informing the rest of the world of their perceptions, both good and bad.

In the context of this article, the word *visitors* has been strictly interpreted. It includes only those who went to the United States with the clear or apparent intention not to settle there permanently, even if the stay of some lasted quite some time. Thus, excluded are writers about the United States such as the radical Thomas Paine (1737–1809) and the German-born psychologist Hugo Münsterberg (1863–1916), both of whom moved to the United States permanently. It also excludes native-born Americans who spent long periods of time abroad, returning intermittently to visit their country of birth; a famous example of such from the twentieth century would be the Chicago-born author and journalist John Gunther (1901–1970). This article also limits itself to the perspectives of historical visitors and does not deal with present-day travelers' impressions of the United States.

Overview

Almost from the foundation of the republic (with the adoption of the U.S. Constitution in 1787), visitors to the United States of America have been keen to publish their views on the nation and describe their experiences there. It has been estimated that between 1815 and 1860, up to two hundred travel accounts were published by various authors, although almost all of them would now be considered worthless even as social commentary on the United States at that time, being ephemeral or obviously unrepresentative in coverage. Still, partiality in content or tone has not stopped several works from achieving lasting reputations. Even many of those that have survived and proved to be of some current interest were, at the time of publication, accused of bias, prejudice, or condescension, especially but not exclusively in the United States.

Some early traveler commentators who went to the United States during the first half of the nineteenth century were principally interested in its viability for economic enterprise and settlement. However, others were curious about its workings as a new style of democracy. After all, the United States was, in the words of the U.S. sociologist Seymour Martin Lipset, "the first new nation." It was the first country of the modern era both to have broken free

from colonial rule and also to have undertaken a republican form of government, a status that necessarily evoked much curiosity about the uniqueness and particularism of its social and political arrangements. Many (though not all) of those writing about it were from Great Britain, the very country from whose institutions and control the United States had deliberately detached itself. Since some authors were self-avowedly either conservative or radical, they approached their task often with a particular axe to grind; the same can be said of some of those who reviewed their published works. Well before the 1850s there was incentive within conservative circles in Britain to denigrate the United States because the British government was worried about the drain of skilled labor emigrating from Britain. However, a more radical political orientation did not necessarily mean a corresponding positive bias of perspective; one of the most famous commentators on the United States of this period, the novelist Charles Dickens (1812–1870), who visited the country in 1842 and later that year published his generally sardonic views about it in his two-volume *American Notes for General Circulation* (1843), had hoped to be favorably impressed but was generally disappointed. Slightly earlier, the British writer Harriet Martineau (1802–1876) published *Society in America* (1837), the product of a sojourn in the United States from September 1834 to August 1836; that work betrayed a similar disappointment. Both Dickens and Martineau considered slavery to be a blight on the United States' democratic credentials—an opinion that in later writers developed into a critique of U.S. race relations, as is evident in one of the most famous outsider accounts of the United States in the twentieth century, *An American Dilemma: The Negro Problem and Modern Democracy* (1944), by the Swedish economist Gunnar Myrdal (1898–1987).

In the period between the Civil War and World War I, the United States attracted commentators—sometimes critical and sometimes awestruck—who were drawn by its incontrovertibly exceptional economic and industrial prowess, which was fueled by a continuous stream of immigrants from Europe. The U.S. historian David M. Potter observed that Americans, living in a country exceptionally endowed with natural resources, were a "people of plenty" whose national character had been shaped by this

economic abundance. The early nineteenth-century concern over whether the United States was a good place in which to invest had been firmly put to rest. Among the themes that recur throughout the two centuries of visitors' commentaries on the United State, it would be appropriate to mention on the positive side egalitarianism (as contrasted with Europe) and an openness and informality in public behavior. On the negative side, however, has been the occurrence of political and financial corruption and the relatively violent character of U.S. society, judged against the standard of most (if not all) European civil societies. The violence mentioned by some earlier writers was often the force used as a means of disciplining slaves. Curiously, more than one earlier writer referred to a purported penchant among Americans for strong alcoholic liquor; examples include the journalist William Cobbett (1763–1835), in his *Journal of a Year's Residence in the United States of America* (1819) and Dickens in his 1843 *American Notes*. Still, by the end of the nineteenth century, those commenting on U.S. workers were more likely to be claiming their relatively greater sobriety in comparison with their European counterparts.

When looking at all this literature, one should be wary of suggesting undifferentiated stereotypes. Some writers would offer a global characterization, before conceding that it was, or might be, specific to particular social statuses, doubtless reflecting the limit of their personal acquaintanceship.

Classifying Visitors' Perceptions of the United States

The following classification scheme is offered as an attempt to organize the large and varied body of literature written by visitors to the United States. First, there are the major magisterial nineteenth-century commentators upon the particularisms of U.S. mores and institutions. Commentators in this category include Henry Bradshaw Fearon (1793–1842), Frances Trollope (1779–1863), who was the mother of the novelist Anthony Trollope (1815–1882), who himself published his own impressions of North America, Harriet Martineau, Alexis de Tocqueville (1805–1859), and James Bryce (1838–1922).

Second, there are social-science writers, essentially economists, who were interested in analyzing the United States as a uniquely successful industrial economy. Works in this genre were especially current from the 1890s to World War I; they were sometimes stimulated by comparisons with the economies of Great Britain, Germany, and France, which were becoming increasingly less dynamic.

Third, there are the sociologists or political scientists, who were particularly attracted to the distinctive character of U.S. industrial

life and of the U.S. worker. They believed that this character explained why a social-democratic political movement on the continental European model had only minimal success in the United States. In a similar vein, while not proper social scientists, several European trade unionists were drawn into writing about aspects of U.S. industrial life and U.S. workers' political movements.

Fourth, there are the novelists who were moved by their experiences in the United States to write nonfiction pieces. From the late nineteenth century, writers such as Rudyard Kipling (1865–1936), H. G. Wells (1866–1946), Arnold Bennett (1867–1931), Hilaire

EXTRACT FROM RUDYARD KIPLING'S AMERICAN NOTES (1891)

In the excerpt below, Kipling delivers quite an opinionated view of the American army.

I should very much like to deliver a dissertation on the American army and the possibilities of its extension. You see, it is such a beautiful little army, and the dear people don't quite understand what to do with it. The theory is that it is an instructional nucleus round which the militia of the country will rally, and from which they will get a stiffening in time of danger. Yet other people consider that the army should be built, like a pair of lazy tongs—on the principle of elasticity and extension—so that in time of need it may fill up its skeleton battalions and empty saddle troops. . . .

Some day, when all the Indians are happily dead or drunk, it ought to make the finest scientific and survey corps that the world has ever seen; it does excellent work now, but there is this defect in its nature: It is officered, as you know, from West Point.

The mischief of it is that West Point seems to be created for the purpose of spreading a general knowledge of military matters among the people. A boy goes up to that institution, gets his pass, and returns to civil life, so they tell me, with a dangerous knowledge that he is a suckling Von Moltke, and may apply his learning when occasion offers. Given trouble, that man will be a nuisance, because he is a hideously versatile American, to begin with, as cock-sure of himself as a man can be, and with all the racial disregard for human life to back him, through any demi-semi-professional generalship.

In a country where, as the records of the daily papers show, men engaged in a conflict with police or jails are all too ready to adopt a military formation and get heavily shot in a sort of cheap, half-constructed warfare, instead of being decently scared by the appearance of the military, this sort of arrangement does not seem wise.

Source: Kipling, R. (1891). American notes (Chap. 6). Retrieved November 2, 2004, from http://eserver.org/books/american_notes.html

Belloc (1870–1953), and G. K. Chesterton (1874–1936) wrote about some of their experiences in the United States, often on the basis of brief visits.

Finally, there are the novelists who let their visits to the United States influence their fiction. The novels of these writers reveal their views about aspects of U.S. society.

The Magisterial Nineteenth-century Commentators

Henry Bradshaw Fearon, who was a wine merchant by profession, wrote *Sketches of America: A Narrative of a Journey of Five Thousand Miles through the Eastern and Western States of America* (1818) as a series of individual reports, recounting a visit between August 1817 and May 1818 made on behalf of English entrepreneurs interested in knowing the suitability of the United States as a place of emigration and economic enterprise.

Frances Trollope's *Domestic Manners of the Americans* (1832) arose initially from jottings made when she was reduced to penury after failed attempts to make a living whilst alone with her children in the United States from 1827. Her observations, including her comments on the universally poor manners of the good citizens of her contemporary Cincinnati, were taken by Americans to be unwelcome products of unjustified pique and personal bitterness. She was certainly unimpressed with what she perceived as Americans' general coarseness of manner, especially toward their supposed social superiors.

Harriet Martineau's *Society in America* received similar criticism in the United States especially because of Martineau's condescension toward Americans' bluntness. Martineau was a radical who had been attracted during her visit by the abolitionists and their work; she was significantly less impressed by the authoritarian structure of the slavery-based South. Indeed, when her views on slavery were published whilst she was still in the United States, she was obliged to alter her itinerary for fear of being lynched in the South as an abolitionist. Alexis de Tocqueville's *Democracy in America* was published in two separate volumes in 1835 and 1840; translations into English appeared in the same respective years. Tocqueville concluded that, despite his ambivalence toward the United States and his suspicion of democracy, this feature was permanent and likely to spread back to Europe. Like James Bryce, who wrote fifty years later, Tocqueville was concerned by the limitations that he saw in bureaucracy and anticipated those twentieth-century elite critics of mass society who deplored the banality and corruption that crept into politics as politicians courted the public. Bryce's two-volume *The American Commonwealth* (1888) was an elaborately detailed description of U.S. life and politics. Bryce

was of the opinion that the United States' political arrangements were not wholly beneficial since total elective democracy produced a peculiar type of political corruption in city politics and also a less-informed electorate than was desirable. In offering detailed descriptions of U.S. political institutions, Bryce also expressed concern over the high levels of political apathy that he observed. This apathy was a factor in his famous explanation of why the "best men" did not go into politics.

Economists on the United States

By the 1890s an interest in the United States as a capitalist country was fully developed, fed by fears in European countries that the United States was outstripping Europe in economic growth and luring away some of Europe's most skilled workers. That was the motivation behind *The American Workman* (1898), a two-volume work by the French economist Émile Levasseur (1828–1911), based on a five-month visit in 1893 at the request of a French learned society. Levasseur's work ranges over many areas, but his calculations that U.S. workers tended to earn more and pay less in real terms for life's necessities than European ones highlighted the superior standard of living in the United States.

Other works, influential in their time, that were inspired by European concern over the United States' successful economic growth and developing competitive advantage were the two-volume *Industrial Efficiency: A Comparative Study of Industrial Life in England, Germany and America* (1906), by Arthur Shadwell (1854–1936) and the report of the so-called Mosely Industrial Commission (*Mosely Industrial Commission to the United States of America, Oct.–Dec. 1902: Reports of the Delegates*, 1903), named after its chief commissioner, the English industrialist Alfred Mosely (1855–1917). Both works are typical of the time in being impressed by the United States' culture of entrepreneurship.

Political Scientists, Sociologists, and Trade Unionists

The works of political scientists, sociologists, and trade unionists are well exemplified by *Why Is There No Socialism in the United States?* (1906), the trenchant work of the German political economist and sociologist Werner Sombart (1863–1941) who visited the United States in 1904. Sombart saw in the higher U.S. standard of living the principal answer to his question, although—contrary to what some have said—that was not his sole answer. Sombart also claimed that the greater degree of social mobility in the

ALEXIS DE TOCQUEVILLE ON AMERICAN ARISTOCRACY

In Chapter 20 of the second volume of his classic work Democracy in America *(1840), Tocqueville discusses how the growth of manufacturing might create an aristocracy in the United States.*

As the conditions of men constituting the nation become more and more equal, the demand for manufactured commodities becomes more general and extensive, and the cheapness that places these objects within the reach of slender fortunes becomes a great element of success. Hence there are every day more men of great opulence and education who devote their wealth and knowledge to manufactures and who seek, by opening large establishments and by a strict division of labor, to meet the fresh demands which are made on all sides. Thus, in proportion as the mass of the nation turns to democracy, that particular class which is engaged in manufactures becomes more aristocratic. Men grow more alike in the one, more different in the other; and inequality increases in the less numerous class in the same ratio in which it decreases in the community. Hence it would appear, on searching to the bottom, that aristocracy should naturally spring out of the bosom of democracy.

But this kind of democracy by no means resembles those kinds which preceded it. It will be observed at once that, as it applies exclusively to manufactures and to some manufacturing callings, it is a monstrous exception in the general aspect of society. The small aristocratic societies that are formed by some manufacturers in the midst of the immense democracy of our age contain, like the great aristocratic societies of former ages, some men who are very opulent and a multitude who are wretchedly poor. The poor have few means of escaping from their condition and becoming rich, but the rich are constantly becoming poor, or they give up business when they have realized a fortune. Thus the elements of which the class of poor is composed are fixed, but the elements of which the class of the rich is composed are not so. To tell the truth, though there are rich men, the class of rich men does not exist; for these rich individuals have no feelings or purposes, no traditions or hopes, in common; there are individuals, therefore, but no definite class. . . .

The territorial aristocracy of former ages was either bound by law, or thought itself bound by usage, to come to the relief of its servingmen and to relieve their distress. But the manufacturing aristocracy of our age first impoverishes and debases the men who serve it and then abandons them to be supported by the charity of the public. This is a natural consequence of what has been said before. Between the workman and the master there are frequent relations, but no real association.

I am of the opinion, on the whole, that the manufacturing aristocracy which is growing up under our eyes is one of the harshest that ever existed in the world; but at the same time it is one of the most confined and least dangerous. Nevertheless, the friends of democracy should keep their eyes anxiously fixed in this direction; for if ever a permanent inequality of conditions and aristocracy again penetrates into the world, it may be predicted that this is the gate by which they will enter.

Source: Tocqueville, A. de. (1840). Democracy in America *(Vol. 2, Chap. 20). Retrieved May 31, 2007, from http://xroads.virginia.edu/~HYPER/DETOC/ch2_20.htm*

United States, the democratic effects of the U.S. political system, and the presence of the frontier (which acted as a social safety valve) helped explain the lack of socialism in the United States. In forming his conclusions, Sombart relied heavily on the works of Levasseur, Shadwell, the Mosely Industrial Commission, and others.

Some well-known European trade unionists contributed to the literature on the U.S. labor movement. For example, Carl Legien (1861–1920), a reformist German trade union leader, wrote *Aus Amerikas Arbeiterbewegung* (From America's Labor Movement) in 1914, based on a short visit in 1912. It described the organizational composition of the U.S. labor movement at the time. Astonishingly, even the senior British trade union leader, Walter McLennan Citrine (1887–1983), made a sea voyage to the United States in November 1940 in order to accept an invitation from the president of the American Federation of Labor to attend its convention; this was written up in *My American Diary* (1941), although that work is essentially a travelogue of impressions rather than a serious analysis of the U.S. labor movement.

Novelists' Nonfiction on the United States

Novelists and journalists of the late nineteenth century were often vitriolic in their denunciation of American urban life. The young Rudyard Kipling, for example, was sarcastic about the brutalities of San Francisco in his controversial *American Notes* (1891), and the crusading English author and journalist William Thomas Stead (1849–1912), who was to die in the *Titanic* disaster, made his views about Chicago clear in the hand-wringing title of his exposé of the city's vice and political corruption: *If Christ Came to Chicago: A Plea for the Union of All Who Love in the Service of All Who Suffer* (1894).

H. G. Wells, in his *The Future in America: A Search after Realities* (1906), was hugely impressed by U.S. dynamism and especially its economic growth, although he was one of the many writers also mentioning varieties of endemic corruption, which he attributed to the excessively individualistic ethos of the United States and a supersensitive concern about money. The title of Hilaire Belloc's

book on the United States, *The Contrast* (1923), encapsulates his general theme, American exceptionalism in physical, social, and political spheres. Belloc thought that the Jewish population in the United States was socially excluded to a greater degree than the Jewish population in Europe.

A taste for literature based upon impressionistic views of the United States and its people persisted until well into the mid-twentieth century; a later example is *My American Friends* (1933) by Lawrence Pearsall Jacks (1860–1955), a British Unitarian minister. Jacks's book, biased as it was in favor of the United States, at least had the merit of being based on better acquaintanceship than is to be derived from a quick visit. Jacks first came to the U.S. in 1886 as a Harvard graduate student, and then made many return visits in later years.

The United States in Europeans' Novels

There is one further way in which many European novelists who visited the United States expressed their reactions to the United States: in actual novels. In tone, these were usually satirical or critical. The sections of Charles Dickens's novel *The Life and Adventures of Martin Chuzzlewit* (published in 1844, shortly after Dickens's disillusioning visit to the United States) describing Martin's sojourn in the United States can be seen only as Dickens's caricature of the ludicrous side of American character. In the maturity of later life Dickens did apologize to U.S. audiences for the humor that he had extracted at the country's expense in some of his youthful writings. He was not alone, however; numerous later European authors included critical themes about the United States in their novels. The first novel of Louis-Ferdinand Celine (1894–1961), *Journey to the End of the Night* (1932), contains a section that made clear the human cost of industrial production in Detroit (he had actually been a staff surgeon at the Ford Motor Company plant there). The novella *The Loved One* (1947) by Evelyn Waugh (1903–1966) is not only a hilarious satire on the Californian funeral business but also contains a number of observations of what Waugh perceived as the general vacuity of the lives of reasonably typical Americans, plus a waspish comment on the oeuvre of U.S.-born anglophile novelist Henry James (1843–1916): "All his stories are about the same thing—American innocence and European experience" (Waugh n.d., 104–5)

There is also an established genre among contemporary European novelists of novels treating some aspect of life in the United States but informed by a deliberately European perspective. Two typical works in this genre are *Stepping Westward* (1965), by Malcolm Stanley Bradbury (1932–2000) and *Changing Places* (1975) by David John Lodge (b. 1935). Both are "campus novels"; the latter features an originally rather retiring English academic who is drawn to a more alternative lifestyle while at a U.S. university that is being swept by late-1960s turmoil. (Despite the use of a pseudonym, the university is known to have been modeled upon the University of California at Berkeley.)

Common Themes

It is legitimate to ask whether there is any common thread in this diverse body of literature. In a sense there is: Whether the writers offer approbation or disapprobation for what they see, there is general agreement that the United States is exceptional. Its political institutions have unique features, its society offers unique incentives, and its national character has features found in like degree in no other country. Lipset has claimed that many outside commentators were attracted by Americans' informality, often attributed to the absence of a feudal past and to a less developed class structure. Perhaps more significant is the country's status—considered in the longer run and despite episodes such as the Great Depression—as the most dynamic and successful example of capitalism on the globe. Its success has contributed to its continuing character as a country based on immigration and has given a national ideology of personal success and advancement some plausibility. Notwithstanding the complexities of historical debate on the topic, the United States' success remains a primary explanation for why the United States did not experience a fully successful social-democratic movement on the European model. As Sombart had said in metaphor, using hyperbole to express an essential truth about the United States, "all Socialist utopias came to nothing on roast beef and apple pie" (Sombart 1976, 106)

Christopher T. Husbands

See also Democracy; History of the United States in World Opinion

Further Reading

Belloc, H. (1924 [1923]). *The contrast*. New York: Robert M. McBride & Company.

Bradbury, M. (1965). *Stepping westward*. London: Secker & Warburg.

Bryce, J. (1888). *The American Commonwealth*. London: Macmillan and Co.

Celine, L. F. (1960 [1932]). *Journey to the end of the night*. New York: New Directions.

Citrine, Sir W. (1941). *My American diary*. London: George Routledge & Sons.

Cobbett, W. (1983 [1819]). *Journal of a year's residence in the United States of America*. Gloucester: Alan Sutton.

Dickens, C. (1874 [1843]). *American notes for general circulation [and Pictures from Italy]*. London: Chapman and Hall.

Dickens, C. (1994 [1844]) *The life and adventures of Martin Chuzzlewit*. London: David Campbell Publishers.

Fearon, H. B. (1819 [1818]). *Sketches of America: A narrative of a journey of five thousand miles through the eastern and western states of America* (2nd ed.). London: Longman, Hurst, Rees, Orme, and Brown.

Ingham, P. (2000). Editor's Introduction to Charles Dickens's *American notes for general circulation* (pp. xi–xxxi). London: Penguin Books.

Ions, E. (1968). *James Bryce and American democracy, 1870–1922*. London: Macmillan.

Jacks, L. P. (1933). *My American friends*. London: Constable & Co.

Kipling, R. (1891). *American notes*. New York: F. F. Lovell Company.

Legien, C. (1914). *Aus Amerikas Arbeiterbewegung* [From America's labor movement]. Berlin: Verlag der Generalkommission der Gewerkschaften Deutschlands.

Levasseur, É. (1900 [1898]). *The American workman*, 2 vols. (T. S. Adams, Trans.; T. Marburg, Ed.). Baltimore, MD: The Johns Hopkins University Press.

Lodge, D. (1975). *Changing places*. London: Secker & Warburg.

Martineau, H. (1981 [1837]). *Society in America*, (S. M. Lipset, Ed., Abbrev., and Intro.). New Brunswick, NJ: Transaction Books.

Mosely Industrial Commission (1903). *Mosely Industrial Commission to the United States of America, Oct.–Dec. 1902: Reports of the delegates*. Manchester: Co-operative Printing Society.

Myrdal G. (1944). *An American dilemma: The Negro problem and modern democracy*. New York: Harper & Brothers.

Nevins, A. (Comp. & Ed.) (1948). *America through British eyes*. New York: Oxford University Press.

Shadwell, A. (1906). *Industrial efficiency: A comparative study of industrial life in England, Germany and America*, 2 vols. London: Longmans, Green, and Co.

Smuts, R. W. (1953). *European impressions of the American worker*. New York: King's Crown Press of Columbia University.

Sombart, W. (1976). *Why is there no socialism in the United States?* (P. M. Hocking & C. T. Husbands, Trans.; C. T. Husbands, Ed.). London: Macmillan.

Stead, W. T. (1894). *If Christ came to Chicago: A plea for the union of all who love in the service of all who suffer*. Chicago: Laird & Lee.

Tocqueville, A. de. (1994 [1835/1840]). *Democracy in America* (A. Ryan, Intro.). London: David Campbell Publishers.

Trollope, F. (1927 [1832]). *Domestic manners of the Americans*, (M. Sadleir, Intro.). London: George Routledge and Sons.

Waugh, E. (n.d. [1947]). *The loved one: An Anglo-American tragedy*. London: Chapman & Hall.

Webb, R. K. (1960). *Harriet Martineau: A radical Victorian*. London: Heinemann.

Wells, H. G. (1906). *The future in America: A search after realities*. London: Chapman & Hall.

Wheatley, V. (1957). *The life and work of Harriet Martineau*. London: Secker & Warburg.

Political System as a Model, U.S.

The U.S. political system mixes a federal authority, divided between executive, legislative, and judicial wings; and governance at state and local levels, a model that has been used to shape new democracies around the world.

Scholars of comparative politics conventionally distinguish between the presidential and parliamentary systems of government. Looking at the world in broad comparative terms, the United States has a presidential system, although specialists in U.S. politics are fond of noting that one should not conclude from this observation that the U.S. president is necessarily the most powerful actor in the system. The key distinction between the two types is that in a parliamentary system there is only one agency or actor that represents the electorate—an assembly or legislature at whose pleasure the executive (often a prime minister) serves; in a presidential system, on the other hand, the legislature and a president are chosen separately, giving the electorate two main agencies of representation. The latter description obviously fits the United States, which elects its president in a process entirely separate from that used to select members of Congress. The other notable features of the U.S. political system are a three-way separation of powers, which divides up authority between the president, Congress and the Supreme Court; a federal system, dividing authority between the federal, state, and local levels of government, with the division between executive, legislature, and judiciary replicated at each of the lower levels; and an electoral college, in which the president is chosen by slates of electors rather than through direct popular vote.

The U.S. system has exerted considerable influence as a model for other states. There are at least four ways in which this influence has operated: (1) the details of specific features of the U.S. system have served as a kind of blueprint for some democratizing states, mostly in Latin America; (2) more generally, the ideas of liberal representative government and national self-determination exemplified in the U.S. system have exerted a more diffuse influence across a broader geographical span; (3) some states, even those with political institutions quite different from those in the United States, have borrowed from the governing style (idealistic rhetoric and attentiveness to media, for example) associated with U.S. politics; and (4) throughout its history, the United States has exerted its military power in an effort to compel other states to take the democratic route and thereby become more like the United States. These four routes of influence are dealt with in more detail below.

The U.S. Model as Blueprint

As Richard Rose, a scholar of public policy, has shown, states often borrow policies and institutions they perceive as successful from other states. That the U.S. system in particular should have influenced the rest of the world is perhaps not surprising, since the United States has long aspired to provide an example ("a shining city upon a hill," to quote President Ronald Reagan, himself quoting John Winthrop, the first governor of the Massachusetts Bay Colony) in the hope that others would seek to emulate it. One of the long-standing motifs of U.S. foreign policy has been its missionary zeal—its a desire to spread U.S. ideas and institutions to other parts of the globe—which has been evident both during its isolationist phases and during its current period of internationalism.

Until World War II, however, U.S. missionary zeal was mostly confined to the Americas. In part as a result, U.S. influence on the actual institutional design of other states has mostly been limited to Central and South America. As a broad generalization, the United States served as the political model for newly democratizing states in the Americas, but elsewhere (particularly in Africa) the Westminster, or parliamentary, model has predominated. Not unnaturally, many of the Commonwealth states (states that were formerly a part of the British empire) copied (or had foisted upon them) a U.K.-style parliamentary system. Except for Asia, where a few presidential systems exist, most democracies have adopted the parliamentary system of governance, and even in Latin America institution builders drew lessons from Europe as well as the United States.

Nevertheless, we can see the influence of the U.S. model in this direct sense right across the Americas, especially in the prevalence of federalism. The three geographically largest states in Latin America—Brazil, Argentina, and Mexico—all not only have federal systems today, but have had them for most of their existence.

Brazil has had a federal system for most of the period since 1891, when it adopted a system so closely modeled on that of the United States that the writers of its constitution went so far as to use the phrase *Estados Unidos do Brasil* (United States of Brazil). In Mexico, most of the constitutions under which Mexicans have lived have included a federal system, obviously inspired by that of its close neighbor. Except during the regime of Juan Perón (1946–1955), Argentina also has had a federal system since 1853.

Also worth noting is the continuing relevance of the U.S. example in the process of European integration. Winston Churchill's notion of a United States of Europe, and the federalist model generally, continues to exert an impact on those who ultimately matter most in the process of European integration: European politicians themselves. Although the Swiss and German models were also influential, the U.S. example provided much of the original impetus for the creation of the new postwar Europe. Even if the federal system in Europe has subsequently developed along lines closer to the German model, the U.S. model had more impact at the outset because it provided an obvious example of the ways in which states with quite different interests and priorities might integrate under a single banner. Some students of European integration, moreover, continue to find the U.S. example instructive; they point out that the United States under the Articles of the Confederation was little more than a loose grouping of national entities—in fact, it was weaker than the current European Union—but subsequently became and remained a strong and viable entity.

Interestingly, some U.S. observers who favor more centralized control of policy making—a tradition that goes back to Alexander Hamilton (c. 1755–1804)—feel that newly democratizing states should not seek to copy the U.S. system of government, since this would merely replicate a political structure they feel hamstrings leadership and encourages deadlock and drift in policy making. "During the 1990s an American scholar traveled to Kazakhstan on a U.S. government-sponsored mission to help the country's new parliament draft its electoral laws," Fareed Zakaria, the editor of *Newsweek International*, notes. "His counterpart, a senior member of the Kazak parliament, brushed aside the many options the American expert was outlining, saying emphatically, 'We want our parliament to be just like your Congress.' The American was horrified, recalling, 'I tried to say something other

than the three words that had come immediately screaming into my mind: 'No you don't!'" (Zakaria 2004, 21–22).

More General U.S. Influence

As already noted, relatively few states worldwide seem to have attempted to copy U.S. political institutions in this way; in the event, even Kazakhstan selected a parliamentary system quite unlike that of the United States. But in order to properly assess the influence of the U.S. political system, we must consider not only the direct, formal adoption of systems that are like the U.S. system—what might be termed institutional blueprinting or copying—but also the influence of the general democratic ideals and institutions long championed by the United States in a more abstract sense. This provides a second avenue of influence.

The United States has probably served as an abstract model or inspiration for others—spreading and advocating the democratic idea in a general sense—to a far greater extent than it has been a

A facsimile of the U. S. Constitution. Source: istock/Royce DeGrie.

model in the sense already discussed. The notion of national self-determination enshrined in the U.S. Declaration of Independence has, not unnaturally, provided a source of inspiration for many nationalist movements. Rhodesia (now Zimbabwe), in its 1965 Unilateral Declaration of Independence from British rule, provides one example. Surprisingly to some, Vietnam provides another striking example. In 1945 the Communist-nationalist leader Ho Chi Minh replicated the opening lines of the U.S. document in his own declaration of independence from the French. Ho and the Americans had been allies during World War II, and Ho fully expected U.S. support for his declaration. In the event, the Cold War intervened, political expediency determined the U.S. response, and successive U.S. administrations sided with the French colonialists and then fought Ho directly in the U.S. war in Vietnam.

The Style of Politics in the United States

A third form of influence has been that exerted by the U.S. style of politics. Glamorous and colorful, often identified with Hollywood images and high-sounding, emotive rhetoric, the U.S. political style is frequently lampooned overseas; its grandiose language and idealistic tone often ring hollow in European ears and sometimes sounds silly and simplistic when contrasted with the more hard-handed, pragmatic language of European politics. Nevertheless, the style of U.S. politics has considerable appeal to many non-U.S. politicians. The Americanization of British politics offers an especially good example. Britain has a parliamentary system that is quite unlike the U.S. system in many respects. Tony Blair, Britain's prime minister, not only invested a great deal of political capital in his relationship with U.S. presidents Bill Clinton and George W. Bush, but has also attempted to appear "presidential" along U.S. lines. In spite of a large parliamentary majority after his landslide victory of 1997, which removed the Conservative Party from power after eighteen years in office, "President" Blair often appeared to govern as if he were living in a system of separated powers, failing to use his large majority in Parliament to make radical changes to policy (something the U.S. system often makes difficult but the British system makes reasonably easy when the governing party has won by a substantial margin).

Tony Blair has also introduced a number of changes to his own system of governing that appear to move him toward presidential government and away from the traditions of parliamentary government. For instance, he has displayed a predilection for announcing policy changes in press conferences (much as a U.S. president or his subordinates would) rather than on the floor of the House of Commons (as has conventionally been done in the

United Kingdom's parliamentary system); he has reduced the number of question times the prime minister holds in the Commons, a move that originally created a storm of protest; and he has often seemed to distance himself from his own party, in a strategy that reminds Americans of Clinton's triangulation strategy, building a personal coalition that appears to place him not inside his own Labour Party but *between* the two main parties. This approach frequently pits him against his own party. Blair has even suggested that the main candidates for office engage in debates prior to general elections, something that has never been done in Britain but that is common in U.S. politics. Whether this represents a real shift in style in British politics or is merely a matter of Blair's personal taste is hard to assess, but the arrival of U.S.-style ad agencies, media consultants, and political advisers in British election politics, and even the importation of U.S. campaign staff to advise candidates in U.K. elections, suggest that something permanent has occurred.

Forced Adoption of the U.S. Political Model

The previous three mechanisms all involve voluntary compliance with the U.S. model; all are the result of some form of admiration for or identification with that model. In assessing the influence of the U.S. political system on others, we should consider not only the voluntary adoption of U.S. institutions and ideas, however, but also the fact that U.S. predominance in the international system at least potentially gives it the power to forcibly *compel* other states to do so. The United States is not merely a passive participant in the spread of liberal democratic norms. A fourth form of influence, then, is the long-established practice in U.S. foreign policy of seeking to force other states to adopt democratic forms of governance. According to the political scientist Mark Peceny, the desire to spread democracy has been the primary motivation behind about one-third of all the military interventions the United States has undertaken around the globe since its founding. This does not mean that the United States has always sought to promote democracy abroad—during the Cold War in particular, U.S. policy makers actively sought to remove from power a number of democratically elected but supposedly anti-U.S. leaders—but the impulse to forcibly export democracy has always been there.

How effective, generally speaking, are such efforts? Two obvious success stories are Germany and Japan, both of which were compelled to adopt democratic institutions after World War II (though interestingly, Japan in particular owes as much to the British parliamentary model as it does to the U.S. one). Most social scientists are not sanguine about the United States' ability to spread

EXTRACT FROM THE ARTICLES OF CONFEDERATION, 1781

The Articles of Confederation were ratified by all thirteen states on 1 March 1781. As the first constitution of the United State, they stipulated a loose confederation of sovereign states and a weak central government. Less than a decade later however, the Articles were replaced by the U.S. Constitution.

Articles of Confederation and perpetual Union between the states of New Hampshire, Massachusetts-bay Rhode Island and Providence Plantations, Connecticut, New York, New Jersey, Pennsylvania, Delaware, Maryland, Virginia, North Carolina, South Carolina and Georgia.

I. The Stile of this Confederacy shall be "The United States of America."

II. Each state retains its sovereignty, freedom, and independence, and every power, jurisdiction, and right, which is not by this Confederation expressly delegated to the United States, in Congress assembled.

III. The said States hereby severally enter into a firm league of friendship with each other, for their common defense, the security of their liberties, and their mutual and general welfare, binding themselves to assist each other, against all force offered to, or attacks made upon them, or any of them, on account of religion, sovereignty, trade, or any other pretense whatever.

IV. The better to secure and perpetuate mutual friendship and intercourse among the people of the different States in this Union, the free inhabitants of each of these States, paupers, vagabonds, and fugitives from justice excepted, shall be entitled to all privileges and immunities of free citizens in the several States; and the people of each State shall free ingress and regress to and from any other State, and shall enjoy therein all the privileges of trade and commerce, subject to the same duties, impositions, and restrictions as the inhabitants thereof respectively, provided that such restrictions shall not extend so far as to prevent the removal of property imported into any State, to any other State, of which the owner is an inhabitant; provided also that no imposition,

duties or restriction shall be laid by any State, on the property of the United States, or either of them.

If any person guilty of, or charged with, treason, felony, or other high misdemeanor in any State, shall flee from justice, and be found in any of the United States, he shall, upon demand of the Governor or executive power of the State from which he fled, be delivered up and removed to the State having jurisdiction of his offense.

Full faith and credit shall be given in each of these States to the records, acts, and judicial proceedings of the courts and magistrates of every other State.

V. For the most convenient management of the general interests of the United States, delegates shall be annually appointed in such manner as the legislatures of each State shall direct, to meet in Congress on the first Monday in November, in every year, with a power reserved to each State to recall its delegates, or any of them, at any time within the year, and to send others in their stead for the remainder of the year.

No State shall be represented in Congress by less than two, nor more than seven members; and no person shall be capable of being a delegate for more than three years in any term of six years; nor shall any person, being a delegate, be capable of holding any office under the United States, for which he, or another for his benefit, receives any salary, fees or emolument of any kind.

Each State shall maintain its own delegates in a meeting of the States, and while they act as members of the committee of the States.

In determining questions in the United States in Congress assembled, each State shall have one vote.

Freedom of speech and debate in Congress shall not be impeached or questioned in any court or place out of Congress, and the members of Congress shall be protected in their persons from arrests or imprisonments, during the time of their going to and from, and attendence on Congress, except for treason, felony, or breach of the peace.

Source: The Avalon Project at Yale Law School. (2007). Retrieved March 22, 2007, from http://www.yale.edu/lawweb/avalon/artconf.htm

democracy through its own actions, however, at least in nations or regions that lack basic liberal representative traditions. Writing in the mid-1980s, the political scientist Samuel Huntington expressed this view when he opined that "the ability of the United States to affect the development of democracy elsewhere is limited. There is little that the United States or any other foreign country can do to alter the basic cultural tradition and social structure of another society or to promote compromise among groups of that society that have been killing each other" (Huntington 1984, 218). On the other hand, the world is currently experiencing a democratic contagion effect that cannot be attributed primarily to domestic factors like those. Whatever the truth of these contending perspectives, the

2003 invasion of Iraq provides a textbook example of the profound difficulties involved in creating democracy from scratch.

We can probably expect transmission or diffusion effects from the United States to the rest of the world to become more extensive with the spread of globalization—which some European and non-Western critics see as little more than the Americanization of culture, economy, and polity—and with the continued preeminence of the United States in the world's economic and political spheres. The United States' prominence will clearly lead others to continue to turn to it as an example of what a democratic system ought to look like. The question remains, however, whether the United States ought to be in the business of forcibly exporting its

ideals and institutions. In the past those who answered affirmatively have won out, but in the present political climate it remains unclear whether the exportation of U.S.-style democracy to the Middle East in particular—assuming that this is possible—is even in the United States' own interests.

David Patrick Houghton

See also Democracy; Equality; Founding Principles of the United States

Further Reading

Huntington, S. P. (1984, Summer). Will more countries become more democratic? *Political Science Quarterly, 99*(2), 193–218.

Peceny, M. (1999). *Democracy at the Point of Bayonets.* University Park: Pennsylvania State University Press.

Rose, R. (1993). *Lesson drawing in public policy: A guide to learning across time and space.* Chatham, NJ: Chatham House.

Zakaria, F. (2004). *The future of freedom: Illiberal democracy at home and abroad.* New York: W. W. Norton.

Pop Culture—U.S. Films

U.S. cinema oftentimes explores political, social, and cultural changes in the U.S. climate, making it one of the best media through which people can experience the United States without being there.

The U.S. film industry, popularly known as "Hollywood," was officially born in 1896. Since that time it has established itself as a global force with its movies shown all over the world, and thus has had an impact on millions of lives. Film is a legitimate social force, arbitrating and negotiating tensions as well as reflecting popular culture and ideology of the era in which films are produced. Consequently, Hollywood film reflects the social, historical, political, economic, and cultural climate within the United States at any given time, attempting to mediate problems endemic to U.S. life as well as to entertain the public. Therefore, film is also a medium that transmits U.S. popular culture to the rest of the world. Film itself generates a perspective of the United States. It influences how people from different cultures perceive and interact with the United States.

Genre

By the 1930s Hollywood studios were familiar with what worked in film and what did not. Audiences identified with certain types of film and responded to them. Consequently, studios established formulas and reproduced them, often to the point of exhaustion. Each formula was identified as a genre—including the Western, gangster film, hard-boiled detective film, screwball comedy, musical, and family melodrama. Although this exploitation of formulas was done expressly to make a profit, it also established U.S. values and, because of Hollywood's global popularity, transmitted them to the rest of the world. The Western is a prime example.

The Western is a genre identified with only the United States, and it effectively mythologizes the nation's unique history. A Western is usually set between 1860 and 1890 (three years before the frontier officially closed) and deals with the westward expansion that occurred during that era. The frontier is not only distinctly involved with U.S. themes and myths, but also metaphorically represents the meeting and merging of impossible choices. The figurative line represents a space where a way of life is disappearing while another one is emerging. It attempts to reconcile numerous dichotomies in order to offer solutions to historical, political, economic, and social problems endemic to U.S. life. For example, law is never the same as justice. Often the institutions of the law

in small-town United States appear as corrupt, and therefore another agency is necessary to ensure that justice prevails. The hero always presents various values and ideals incompatible with those of the town he moves into. For example, his freedom is often at war with the constrictions involved in living in a town. He also introduces an element of the wilderness into the predictable and staid routines of civilization.

The era in which Westerns are located allows these dichotomous attributes of the formative U.S. national character to exist side by side with equal validity and weight. As a result, this genre has been used repeatedly to encourage patriotism. The national mythology generated was valued by Americans in the Western's heyday of the 1950s, a reactionary age in which the Cold War unsettled the nation. President Ronald Reagan also utilized this mythology in the 1980s in order to enhance his credibility and create a national identity of which he was an integral part. Ironically, few Westerns were made during the Depression when the general public had little faith in the United States and its institutions. The Western feeds the image of Americanism and fuels the notion of the United States as elite. Although it conducts a certain image to the global community, it also imposes a particular outlook on the United States itself. It is a genre that has primarily been used to develop national heritage and culture rather than communicate it to the rest of the world. However, in these terms it also enables other cultures to understand the tensions and crises of any given period.

Social Resolutions

Film offers a psychological insight into society, expressing the hopes, fears, tensions, and fantasies of mainstream United States. Marginalized communities, such as hyphenated enclaves, were given a voice with the rise of a stable, better-defined, independent cinema in the 1970s. Perhaps the best-known benefactor of this new cinematic era was filmmaker Spike Lee. His rise to fame was of great symbolic importance because he is an African-American who took advantage of the opportunity to project the African-American voice, to make it heard across the world, and to establish an image apart from the previous stereotypes created by

white United States. Films such as *Gone with the Wind* (1939) had established characters such as Mammy as the normal societal roles for African-Americans. That is to say, their place in society was alongside but subservient to the white, Anglo-Saxon, Protestant (WASP) middle class. This condition persisted into the 1950s and 1960s. However, the 1970s heralded a cinematic change for African-Americans, exposing their own, long-repressed self-image.

In blaxploitation movies, the lone black hero was strong, independent, and hypermasculine. He rejected black bourgeois assimilation values and embodied ghetto culture. Movies such as *Shaft* (1972) effectively allowed film audiences a glimpse of a new culture. Although ghetto culture was established before the 1970s, it was new in terms of cinematic theme because both black and white middle-class audiences had previously suppressed that perspective. However, images of violence and drugs, although accurate and realistic, reinforced the black buck stereotype and perpetuated fear rather than acceptance of this culture as legitimate. Despite this reaction, the blaxploitation era proves that film provides a medium that no longer excludes Americans on account of race, class, or gender. As an audience, we are now privy to most cultures that exist within the United States and to just how complex the structure of society is.

1960s: Door to the Past

History as we know it is relative. Although the images and accounts of certain events we receive through film are unlikely to be absolute in their accuracy, that is not to say that such images and accounts are useless in terms of social and cultural ideology. In *U-571* (2000), for example, the submarine that located and retrieved the German code-breaking machine Enigma is a U.S. sub. In reality it was English, as the director, Jonathan Mostow, was forced to acknowledge in a disclaimer at the end of the movie after an outcry from both those involved in the actual event and the media in the United Kingdom. However, the film transmits a message about the way the United States viewed itself and its global role at the time the film was made. The U.S. government has long considered the nation as world leader, and this view formed the foundation of a number of movies in the late 1990s and into the 2000s, which, in turn, served to impress this role on the rest of the world. This view also gave credibility to the version of history presented by the United States both on and off screen.

The 1960s are perhaps the best era to examine for the relationship between film and history. The decade was one of profound social upheaval, littered with assassinations (President John F. Kennedy in 1963, Malcolm X in 1965, Martin Luther King Jr. and Robert Kennedy in 1968), riots, and protests that disturbed

the status quo and allowed the medium of film to examine those changes in terms of society's transition from Old World values to those of the contemporary, more liberal youth of the United States. As a result, the well-established formulas of 1930s and 1940s Hollywood cinema underwent a period of dispersal and fragmentation. Whereas television and newspapers broadcast the events in terms of what, where, and when, film delved into the psychology of the 1960s and therefore presents the audience with an accurate picture of the culture of that era. Movies such as *The Wild Bunch* (1969) and *Bonnie and Clyde* (1967) were a response to the politics of dispossession that had disillusioned society in a number of ways. These films embodied the antiestablishment ethos (distinguishing character, sentiment, moral nature, or guiding beliefs) that was gathering momentum throughout the era.

The culture of protest centered around two major events—civil rights and the Vietnam War. Both events had caused discontent, a political atmosphere that permeated film. Demands for equality and enfranchisement split the old and the new and caused conflict when society attempted to reconcile the two. The Vietnam War disillusioned all sections of society because the motivation for the war was somewhat ambiguous and the death rate was reaching unprecedented proportions. Not only did this situation enable a countercultural backlash, but also it altered the values of society in general. Society was forced to evolve to accommodate such radical changes. Film mirrored this evolution in order to stay relevant. As a result, both *The Wild Bunch* and *Bonnie and Clyde* heralded a tremendous increase in violence in comparison with the movies released previously, and no morality structure is apparent as the subjective view of the camera paints the apparent villains in a favorable light. This tone cements the films' status as antiestablishment.

The 1960s marked a turning point in the nature and content of film. Hollywood transmits and explains the anxieties of 1960s society, although it does not necessarily offer solutions. Although *Bonnie and Clyde* may not be historically accurate, it is the epitome of ideological exploration and demonstrates that film can also be a powerful tool in the expression of discontent.

Documentary

Although Hollywood feature films rarely appear in documentary form, this medium has recently become popular. The most prominent documentary filmmaker in the United States currently is arguably Michael Moore. Although his commentary on the United States is anything but objective, it provides a specific opinion of U.S. culture. Moore's latest offering, *Fahrenheit 9/11* (2004), transmits the tensions in U.S. society in relation to the Iraq War

(2003). Although the film is specific to the United States, it strikes a resonant chord with Great Britain, where similar discord regarding the motivations of President George W. Bush and Prime Minister Tony Blair to go to war filtered into the media and society in general.

Documentary films of this sort effectively capture the distinct tensions that any given section of society is experiencing during a particular moment. For example, in the film Moore travels to Washington, D.C., with a Mrs. Lipscombe, a woman who lost her son as he fought in Iraq. The film depicts her devastating grief as she cries, arguing with a bystander over who exactly was responsible for her son's death. Her pain was simultaneously experienced by millions of her fellow Americans who had also lost loved ones to the national cause. Moore harvests the seeds of discontent by highlighting how the Bush administration used a national tragedy—the terrorist attacks of September 11, 2001—to push its own agenda. Moore's documentary style purposely examines contentious issues so as to express his perspective alone, allowing no room for a balanced argument. However, his distinct point of view transmits and explains the culture of political discontent that is currently permeating U.S. society.

The Future

Ultimately, while Hollywood films continue to be globally distributed, they will continue to communicate U.S. culture to the rest of the world. Every film released has to be relevant to U.S. society in some way because that is the largest national audience and thus the highest potential gross. If films lose touch with reality, then they will subsequently lose their audience. Cinema will continue to evolve to stay abreast of social and cultural changes and therefore will routinely betray the climate in the United States, whether uncertain or stable, calm or highly charged. Careful analysis of film can enable us to learn about the past and, in certain cases, anticipate the future. Film remains one of the best ways in which one can experience the United States and its multitude of cultures without having to be there. While the Hollywood film industry maintains its global audience, its films will continue to be produced and distributed worldwide.

Louise J. Crowley

Further Reading

Altman, R. (1999). *Film/genre*. London: BFI Publishing.

Belton, J. (1994). *American cinema/American culture*. New York: McGraw-Hill.

Burgoyne, R. (1997). *Film nation: Hollywood looks at US history*. Minneapolis: University of Minnesota.

Carnes, M. (1992). *Past imperfect: History according to the movies*. New York: Henry Holt.

Cook, D. A. (2000). *Lost illusions: American cinema in the shadow of Watergate and Vietnam, 1970–1979*. New York: Scribner's.

Ferro, M. (1988). *Cinema and history*. Detroit, MI: Wayne State University Press.

Finler, J. W. (1988). *The Hollywood story*. London: Octopus.

Fraser, G. M. (1988). *The Hollywood history of the world: From* One Million Years B.C. *to* Apocalypse Now. London: Harvill.

Hill, J., & Church Gibson, P. (2000). *American cinema and Hollywood*. Oxford, UK: Oxford University Press.

Maltby, R. (1995). *Hollywood cinema*. Oxford, UK: Blackwell.

Mast, G. (1996). *A short history of the movies*. Boston: Allyn & Bacon.

May, L. (1983). *Screening out the past: The birth of mass culture and the motion picture industry*. Chicago: University of Chicago Press.

Neale, S. (Ed.) (2002). *Genre and contemporary Hollywood*. London: BFI Publishing.

Neve, B. (1992). *Film and politics in America: A social tradition*. London: Routledge.

Robert, R. (1993). *Hollywood's America: Reflections on the silver screen*. St. James, NY: Brandywine Press.

Rosenstone, R. (1994). *Revisioning history: Film and the construction of a new past*. Princeton, NJ: Princeton University Press.

Schatz, T. (1981). *Hollywood genres*. Boston: McGraw-Hill.

Schindler, C. (1979). *Hollywood goes to war: Film and American society, 1939–1952*. London: Routledge.

Sklar, R. (1975). *Movie-made America: A cultural history of the American movies*. New York: Random House.

Wood, M. (1975). *America in the movies*. New York: Basic Books.

Pop Culture—
U.S. Music (Hip-hop)

Hip-hop music has grown out of the lineage of African music that traveled through the Caribbean to mainland America and emerged into the South Bronx. It has played a huge role in shaping youth perceptions of the United States.

People commonly describe globalization in terms of expansion and movement. A permeation of markets and technologies from the global north into the global south occurs alongside the increased movement of capital, cultures, and people. Proponents of globalization have celebrated internationalized culture as the ultimate development of civilization—signifying the end of cultural clashes and the beginning of "one world, one culture." Critics, on the other hand, argue that cultural globalization is a mass-produced, packaged, and marketed commodity that further exemplifies the capitalist takeover of indigenous cultures for the purposes of expanding markets. A global justice perspective also sees international social justice movements as the key to social change in the time of late capitalist crisis. While globalized markets inundate local economies with useless and overpriced products, local communities produce cultural practices that challenge U.S. or European influence. The multiple worlds that define hip-hop music today demonstrate all three analyses as they are expressed in the overlapping spaces of global and local, commercial, and grassroots hip-hop culture.

Hip-hop's Global Roots

The dominant narrative of globalization tends to map an unidirectional expansionism that begins in the global north, namely the United States, and spreads to other parts of the world. The history of hip-hop is no exception. Dominant narratives of hip-hop locate it as originating in the South Bronx, New York, then filtering into other parts of the country, and finally throughout the world. The term globalization enters the discourse in this last stage. Common narratives view this art form as an African-American phenomenon that became marketed for a world audience.

In fact, hip-hop has been an internationalized musical form since its inception. One could trace hip-hop as a musical evolution in tempo with the migration of Africans into the United States. The musical attributes of hip-hop belong to the lineage of African music that traveled through the Caribbean into the mainland Americas. Hip-hop music falls within a long heritage of resistance music that defines itself in the contexts of forced migration, slavery, and ongoing systemic oppression.

Moreover, the dominant narrative of hip-hop actually situates this syncretic (relating to the combination of different forms) musical history with particular icons. To many people hip-hop began in the impoverished boroughs of the South Bronx with the likes of Jamaican immigrant Kool Herc and the importation of Africa Bambaataa's concept of a "Zulu Nation" from the silver screen to the street party in the mid-1970s. Significantly, hip-hop found "black and brown" roots in the government housing projects that African-Americans as well as Latino and Caribbean immigrants called home. The multicultural immigrant communities in the South Bronx infused hip-hop with international rhythms, beats, and language. From the beginning, this musical genre combined reggae, salsa, and African influences as well as cultural practices indigenous to urban youth in the U.S. In short, hip-hop's origins lie within the scope of immigration of diverse peoples and cultures rather than separate from it.

Yet, the linear historiography of hip-hop contradicts its musical lineage. If we are to conceptualize hip-hop from the musical heritage of Afro-Caribbean beats and verbal arts in the 1800s, blues and jazz in the early twentieth century, and funk, soul, rock, and disco peaking in the 1970s, then it would be more logical to assume that organic versions of rapping and sampling emerged locally throughout the United States. Additionally, if hip-hop represents a "culture of poverty" within urban "ghettoes," then it stands to reason that the elements and cultural production of hip-hop also developed in uneven and circular patterns across the country, regardless of its popularity in the South Bronx. Finally, one could argue that the organic production of hip-hop in poor communities globally reflects the same developmental pattern.

Consuming Blackness in Commercial Hip-hop

The "Special Collector's Edition" of *Vibe* magazine in March 2007 contained a two-page advertisement for the Nissan Japanese car company with the tagline, "The Black Experience is everywhere" (*Vibe* 2007, 5). The ad was photographed in a brightly lit barbershop that mixed traditional Japanese architectural aesthetics with telltale signs of a U.S. barbershop, such as the fluorescent red, white, and blue revolving light in the window. The four Japanese male models and one Japanese female model role-played not only the barber and patrons but also Nissan's interpretation of "the Black Experience." All the men were dressed in baggy pants and oversized T-shirts or jerseys. The woman donned a tight green sweater minidress, gold accessories, brown high-heeled boots, and a 1940s rimmed mafia hat. She had tightly permed short hair, while two men had dreadlocks, and the man with an Afro hairstyle was getting his hair braided. His friend's shaved head was covered with a baseball cap turned backward and he wore a huge diamond earring.

The image conveys the message that a consumer can have access to "blackness" through the consumption of a Nissan, as summed in its new symbol, "SHIFT_respect" (*Vibe* 2007, 5). Nissan is right, though, the "Black Experience" is everywhere. However, the textures of reading this "experience" give us the option to consume African-based culture in exploitative global capitalist hegemony and thereby to wear the "mask" of hypermasculinity and "soulfulness" that has historically been packaged for the white entertainment gaze. Significantly, unlike African-Americans, consumers of commercial black culture can straighten their hair, change their dress and language, and thus remove their identification with "blackness." In short, world markets consume hip-hop culture as African-American culture in three ways: (1) as part of the U.S. image of maverick, violent, hypermasculine, sexually promiscuous, and ostentatious, (2) as black culture that is rich with "soul" and steeped in rebellious resistance, and (3) as the desire for the "American Dream" of material wealth and power, even in poverty.

These African drums represent the traditional rhythms and music patterns that have been incorporated into many contemporary styles of music, including hip-hop. Source: istock.

This photo of graffiti art in Hamburg, Germany, illustrates the globalization of hip-hop. Graffiti art developed as part of hip-hop culture in the United States in the early 1980s, originating in Philadelphia. Source: istock.

The consumption of hip-hop culture as U.S. hegemony also should be contextualized in terms of consumer demographics. For much of the market base internationally, consumers must have access to technology, purchasing power, distribution sites, and, often, knowledge of the English language. Consequently, much of the consumer base abroad is middle-class to upper-class urban youth. The extent to which these youth identify with the "ghetto roots" from which hip-hop claims its voice becomes a site of contention. Domestically, they possess a relatively great amount of privilege compared with their compatriots and may even participate in the oppression of the masses in their own society. Internationally, however, for many youth in the global south, their livelihood even as middle-class people falls far below comparative middle-class standards in the United States. Thus, hip-hop's contradictory position on the world stage functions to perpetuate a U.S. cultural and economic hegemony on the one hand and represents the experiences of oppressed people worldwide on the other.

Hip-hop as a Voice for Global Justice

A global justice perspective of the phrase "the Black Experience is everywhere" associates hip-hop directly with oppression as a human experience beyond borders. The "black body" has histori-

cally been a symbol of racial subjugation in the United States, but perhaps a more complicated interpretation occurs on a global scale. To identify with blackness is to identify with disenfranchisement and resistance against repressive apparatuses. Although a hyper-capitalist lifestyle exists in hip-hop videos, the lyrics represent economically oppressed people's desire, real and imagined, for accumulated wealth and power. The use of performance, including the hyperbolic "spectacles" of music videos, as a safe political expression of the hidden transcript of resistance is seductive (Rose 1994, 100–101). The corporate rank-and-file, suburban youth, and economically marginalized youth across the world can relate to these desires to "break out," at least in the safety of a fictitious narrative. Hip-hop, in essence, represents the resistance of hegemonic power to the extent it legitimizes the expression of one's poverty or one's marginalization while reclaiming one's power through the weapon of music and performance. It is a carte blanche to dream of a better life beyond one's physically confining economic or racial box. Breaking through the parameters of one's scripted life becomes a path to liberation from the prison of social structures imposed on people worldwide.

Aside from the consumption of commercial hip-hop, youth throughout the world in the twenty-first century have severed their experiences of localized alienation and individualized isolation through a music that "saved my life." The ease with which one can now duplicate music through technological innovation

may not have reached many people in the world, but compact disc burners and Internet downloads have allowed independent or underground hip-hop to travel from Oakland, California, to small villages in Cambodia, Ghana, or Palestine through informal social networks of people rather than major record companies and their distributors. This is the site where grassroots, underground hip-hop breeds social movements. However, independent hip-hop recording artist Ise Lyfe asserts that hip-hop is not a social movement but rather the "soundtrack" to movements that fight for economic and social justice. Hip-hop theater performer Aya de Leon complicates Lyfe's analysis with geographical and temporal specificity. She suggests that the "risk" factor of articulating one's oppression can measure the difference between a cultural movement and a social movement. This debatable topic can be further elucidated through specific examples.

Prach Ly is a Cambodian-American emcee who, with his family, came to the United States as a refugee. In 2001 the twenty-two-year old recorded his first compact disc on a karaoke machine in his parents' garage, combining traditional Cambodian instruments and Khmer language with the drum machine and sampling. Prach's music now touches the lives of thousands of Southeast Asian diasporic youth because his lyrics talk of the trauma and genocide in Cambodian history that is not taught in schools or transferred generationally in the community. Similarly, Rico Pabon of Prophets of Rage raps about social issues in the United States and about the liberation of Puerto Rico, from which much of his lyrical and musical influences derive. Salsa music plays an integral role in Pabon's music. His working-class childhood memories in the south Bronx and Oakland and the politics of Puerto Rico inform his lyrics. Although Prophets of Rage has fans in many places, Pabon was shocked to learn that a small village in Ghana had heard his music from a traveler who disseminated copies of it.

Hip-hop documentary filmmaker Eli Jacobs-Fauntauzzi describes "hip-life" in Ghana as a derivative of traditional "highlife" music integrated with hip-hop. Although hip-hop Ghana-style may adopt beats and rapping styles, he points out that some aspects of the culture do not translate across borders. The antiauthority stances of much early or grassroots hip-hop does not translate in Ghana because "your grandparents, your parents, the chief" constitute the governing bodies (Chang 2007, 259–260). In Cuba as well hip-hop becomes a site for a complicated critique of one's poverty without necessarily taking an antigovernment stance. Rather, hip-hop serves as a channel to continue a tradition of resistance and struggle in poor neighborhoods by groups such as Anonimo Consejo, whose members believe that the essence of hip-hop is "inventos" or "making something out of nothing" (Jacobs-Fauntauzzi 2005). South African crew Prophets of da City

(POC) challenges this mantra in its hip-hop pedagogy by arguing that "hip-hop is about seeing something in what we are often told is nothing" (Chang 2007, 262). Cape Town's hip-hop boom was embraced first by "colours," mixed-race communities who are socially positioned as "not Black and not white, but superior to Black and inferior to white" (Chang 2007, 264).

The immigration of multiple cultures into the urban United States, compounded with the exportation of hip-hop as a politically motivated cultural practice, perpetuates the dynamism of this art globally in the twenty-first century. Moreover, many artists such as the ones cited here coalesce their progressive messages and unique musical hybrids with ongoing political organizing in their own communities. This marriage of cultural change with social movement activity bridges the separation of culture from politics and lived experience. Instead, hip-hop continues to be a powerful force in global justice movements as a soundtrack for material struggles, a site for an identity formation that claims the universality of oppression, and a political act of healing through expression.

The Future

The global movement of bodies that has simultaneously multiplied the locations of poverty in the United States and abroad has played a critical role in the phenomenal spread of hip-hop as both a multibillion-dollar commercial industry and a dynamic grassroots, international social movement. Yet, these two planes of analyses are not mutually exclusive. Although commercial hip-hop seeks to expand its consumer base by perpetuating the desire for U.S. material wealth, it also extends the historical image of violent and misogynistic hypermasculinity engrained in U.S. cultural production. Thus, commercial hip-hop arguably entices a world audience to participate in U.S. cultural imperialism at the expense of African-American cultural practices—consumers are encouraged to purchase "blackness" as a product. Further research could shed light on the extent to which youth in other parts of the world actually internalize and adopt the negative images promoted in commercial hip-hop.

Conversely, grassroots, underground hip-hop tends to distribute through informal networks and technologies. Underground hip-hop can contain more positive and politically conscious messages because it is often created in politicized spaces. The journeys of underground hip-hop connect artists, oppressed youth, and social activists alike. Youth who produce hip-hop in noncommercial settings localize their lived experiences of poverty and oppression as well as inculcating the "traditional" musical forms of hip-hop with indigenous instruments, beats, languages, metaphors, and

structures. At these sites of "making something out of nothing," we will find the future of hip-hop as both cultural innovation and social movement.

Loan Dao

See also Pop Culture—U.S. Music (Jazz, Rock)

Further Reading

Chang, J. (2005). *Can't stop won't stop: A history of the hip-hop generation.* New York: St. Martin's Press.

Chang, J. (Ed.). (2007). *Total chaos: The art and aesthetics of hip-hop.* New York: Basic Civitas Books.

Chuck D., & Jah, Y. (Eds.) (1997). *Fight the power: Rap, race and reality.* New York: Dell Publishing.

Dolby, N. E. (2001). *Constructing race: Youth, identity and popular culture in South Africa.* Albany: State University Press of New York.

Hiphoparchives. (2007). Retrieved April 13, 2007, from http://www.hiphoparchives.com/

Jacobs-Fauntauzzi, E. (Director). (2005). *Inventos: Hip-hop Cubano* [Motion picture]. United States: Clenched Fist Productions.

Lipsitz, G. (1994). *Dangerous crossroads: Popular music, postmodernism, and the poetics of place.* New York: Verso.

McBride, J. (2007, April). Hip-hop planet. *National Geographic, 11*(4), 104-119.

Mitchell, T. (Ed.). (2001). *Global noise: Rap and hip-hop outside the USA.* Middletown, CT: Wesleyan University Press.

Rose, T. (1994). *Black noise: Rap music and black culture in contemporary America.* Hanover, NH: Wesleyan University Press.

Pop Culture— U.S. Music (Jazz, Rock)

Many forms of popular U.S. music that have roots in 19th-century African-American culture have often been initially considered rebellious, but can now be heard all around the world and seen as symbols of freedom and democracy.

U.S. music has long influenced European music. Even before the advent of recording technology European composers made trips to the United States to hear African-American music on plantations and in other venues, such as minstrel shows. Indeed, African-Americans had appeared in stage productions even before the Civil War.

Most people are familiar with minstrelsy and its blackface makeup. Even African-American performers used blackface as part of the production. The songs, dance, humor, and instruments were billed as African-American. It is true that some of the music was watered down, a practice that continues into the present. However, at root the music had an African-American basis.

The earliest instance of blacks performing on stage in New York City dates to the 1820s at the African Grove Theater. The first sheet music of a black composer was that of Francis Johnson, published in 1818. Both the African Grove Theater and Johnson's music were in the European tradition. With minstrelsy this situation changed. "Jump Jim Crow," a song that Thomas Rice stole from a black stable boy, was the first truly popular song based on black music. The lyrics, actually, were African-American. The melody was taken from an Irish jig. However, African adaptations to the jig were made. The rhythm was syncopated, and a banjo—a west African instrument—was employed. Thus, a precedent was set and followed by many. The mixture of European and African elements, reimagined in the music, became a staple of U.S. popular music. The formula works to the present.

Tin Pan Alley and Other Early Twentieth-century Forms

Tin Pan Alley was an area of Union Square in New York City that produced a number of major U.S. songs beginning in the 1890s. Advances in technology aided the spread of popular music. The songs tended to be sentimental and to employ many of the mechanisms of African-American music, mixed with European elements.

A natural progression occurred from Tin Pan Alley music to Broadway music. U.S. musical theater emerged as the finest in the world. During this time Thomas Edison's recording technology developed; Broadways songs began to become popular with the wider public. Jerome Kern's "They Didn't Believe Me" was a hit across the country and eventually in much of the rest of the world. George Gershwin became perhaps the major U.S. composer of his period, making fine use of jazz influences. His *Porgy and Bess* was a major hit overseas as well as at home.

"Race music"—aimed at black audiences—also became a major segment of recorded music and reached a larger audience interested in blues and jazz. Paramount and Okeh Records led the field.

Ragtime emerged at about the same time as race music. Ragtime was dance music and essentially piano music. It used many African techniques, included syncopation and accidentals (flats and sharps) to add color to the music. Scott Joplin employed many European elements as well and disliked people improvising on his music. Ragtime is certainly rooted in African-American music, more so than earlier forms of music. It became popular in the United States and overseas. Early recordings and sheet music helped spread the music widely.

Early Appreciation of Jazz in Europe

Among the first Europeans to appreciate jazz were classical composers. Johannes Brahms of Germany, for example, was fascinated with ragtime, a related form. Jazz and related music explored dimensions of music that were fresh and exotic to European composers. The music offered them new avenues of exploration. New recording technologies supplemented the movement of African-Americans to Europe and provided means for musicians to study the new dimensions of the New Orleans masters Jelly Roll Morton and King Oliver. Among the early composers who used jazz was French composer Darius Milhaud, whose ballet *The Creation of the World* in 1923 used polyphonies and jazz instrumentation. Later the U.S. musician Dave Brubeck

studied with Milhaud, using classical devices to extend his own jazz vocabulary.

Over the years, in fact, composers used jazz in classical compositions. In 1902, for example, the U.S. composer Charles Ives began his "Ragtime Dances" for both piano and small orchestra. In the 1920s, with the increase in jazz musicians and the popularity of jazz, syncopations and blues harmonies were openly taken by Paul Hindemith, Maurice Ravel, Igor Stravinsky, and Aaron Copland.

The entrance of the United States into World War I in 1917 helped spread jazz in Europe. A number of jazz musicians lost their jobs because of the closing of Storyville, a New Orleans red-light district. Prohibition put jazz in the illegal and dangerous settings of speakeasies. A number of musicians went to Europe at the close of the war, their way made easier by the work of African-American bandmaster James Reese Europe. The black army bands of James Reese Europe and other black artists not only boosted U.S. morale, but also demonstrated how the new music should be played. A number of musicians stayed in Paris after the war, and others went to Europe to tour after the war ended. Their influence could be heard in the works of Erik Satie, George Auric, and Darius Milhaud, among others.

James Reese Europe

James Reese Europe was a transitional figure in the history of jazz. He employed jazz elements within a symphonic framework. He did so in such a manner that European musicians insisted on inspecting the instruments used by his band members, believing that these had been specially made to produce jazz effects. It was not the last time that this kind of scrutiny occurred. Years later U.S. trumpet players Louis Armstrong and Dizzy Gillespie had their horns examined to see whether the two men had changed their horn designs to hit such high notes. Neither had done so. James Reese Europe also used African harmonies and cross-rhythms in his orchestrations, in many ways anticipating the kind of work that Duke Ellington brought to its acme. Unfortunately, James Reese Europe died young, leaving his fans to wonder in what direction he might have gone after the war.

Nonetheless, he did whet the continent's appetite for jazz. A number of musicians and other performers did their best to satisfy that hunger, a hunger also whetted by Europe's disgust with war and its consequences. The singer and dancer Josephine Baker, for example, took to Europe an act inspired by the spirit of jazz and the Harlem Renaissance. Baker was quite popular in Berlin, an exception to the preference of Berlin audiences for white jazz musicians over black ones. Berlin had the largest concentration of intellectuals in Europe at the time and took readily to the new music. However, the U.S. jazz cornetists Red Nichols and Bix Beiderbecke, for ex-

ample, were favored over King Oliver and Louis Armstrong, at least at first. As the jazz age continued, more African-American musicians included Berlin in their tours, exchanging ideas with German musicians, as they did with French and British musicians.

In addition to European acceptance of jazz, African-Americans had social and cultural reasons for their fondness for Europe. Jazz is about freedom. Many African-Americans regard it as a sacred music. Dizzy Gillespie once said that jazz is sacred because "You make the other fellow sound good." Duke Ellington also regarded his music as sacred. Part of the sacred nature of jazz is found in its relationship to freedom. Thus, not surprisingly many African-Americans viewed Europe as a land of freedom, as more open to racial integration and respect for their work. In Europe a number of African-American musicians and other performers had white females working with them, something that was impossible in the United States between the wars.

Despite some problems, Europeans had a great deal of respect for jazz. Scholarship in Germany, for example, on Louis Armstrong, Duke Ellington, Charlie Parker, Miles Davis, and other jazz originals treated them as great contributors to Western culture in the same manner as Bach, Beethoven, and other giants of the European musical tradition.

Expatriates

In 1932 the most influential jazz musician who ever lived, with the possible exception of Charlie Parker, made his first trip to Europe. Louis Armstrong went to England, where he received his famed nickname "Satchmo" (a shortened version of "Satchelmouth," Armstrong's original nickname). Armstrong was a great success in England. He repeated that success in Denmark, Sweden, Norway, and Holland. Local musicians who had heard Armstrong on his classic records with the Hot Fives and Hot Sevens began to note that he was even greater in person. His tours were expanded during the Cold War after World War II, when he earned the title of "Ambassador Satch."

Shortly after Armstrong's initial tour of Europe, the world's greatest jazz trumpet player found that the world's greatest jazz saxophone player had gone on tour to Europe. The English bandleader Jack Hylton had invited Coleman Hawkins to tour Europe with his band. Because the crowds were so enthusiastic and because Hawkins found a freedom not yet attainable in the United States, he stayed for five years in Europe. During that time he increased his knowledge of modern classical music and harmonies while reveling in the adulation of fans and other musicians. Along with the great alto saxophonist and trumpeter Benny Carter, who stayed in Europe for three years, Hawkins advanced the standard of European jazz.

JAZZ IN SERBIA

The excerpt below reveals that early exposure to American music and culture came about through radio programming and school.

Although at present direct contacts with America are of practically no importance, there are many forms of indirect contact. Every peasant is familiar with Nikola Tesla, who left Yugoslavia as an emigrant boy to become a famous scientist in America. Today the largest Yugoslav radio factory bears his name. Another form of contact is the radio, for "Voice of America" can occasionally be heard over one of the few village radios. One day . . . in the course of a conversation with some village men on the beauties of regional folk music, one of them turned on Radio Belgrade to prove his point, and out blared the American jazz tune, *Rag Mop.* Serbian folk melodies and folk-patterned popular music predominate in the village, but some of the school girls have learned from their teachers the Serbo-Croat versions of such songs as *Jingle Bells, My Darling Clementine,* and *Magic is the Moonlight.*

Source: Halpern, J.M. (1967). A Serbian village. New York: Harper & Row.

Hawkins refused to accompany Hylton to Germany, going to Amsterdam instead. He recorded widely in Europe with European musicians such as the Belgian jazz guitarist Django Reinhardt. As war approached, Hawkins returned to the United States. He allayed all fears that his five years in Europe had weakened his playing with his recording of "Body and Soul," displaying his increased power, warmth, and versatility.

In 1933 the world's greatest jazz band went to Europe, demonstrating that U.S. classical music would be based on the African-American experience and its "folk music" and spirituals. Duke Ellington and his band performed "East St. Louis Toodle-oo," "Mood Indigo," "Creole Love Call," and "Rockin' in Rhythm," among his other compositions. Although these compositions had gained him celebrity, they had not been taken seriously by U.S. classical music critics. As he discovered on his 1933 tour, European critics did take them seriously, both as characteristically U.S. music and as music related to contemporary European music.

Rock and Roll and the Counterculture

In the 1950s a form of music developed from blues, gospel, and other influences, including country music. Rock and roll cap-

tured the youth audience quickly with its antiestablishment feel and direct appeal to the youth culture. In 1954 Bill Haley and the Comets had a major rock and roll hit with "Rock around the Clock," which helped launch the rock revolution. The coming of Elvis Presley, a white man who could sing black, helped solidify rock's hold and spread its sound around the world. Although much black-based music was covered by white performers, by the 1960s many black artists, including Bo Diddley, Chuck Berry, Little Richard, and Fats Domino, were popular with white audiences.

In the 1960s rock and roll became the music of protest. Merged with folk and folk rock, such as the music of Bob Dylan and Joan Baez, it led the musical assault on the Vietnam War and "the establishment." It has continued in its many transformations to be a music of rebellion, and those who opposed the Soviet empire as well as those who opposed Western abuses listened to rock as their music of choice.

International Impact of U.S. Music

It is no overstatement to say that U.S. music is popular around the world in almost all of its forms. It is probably the most cherished of all U.S. cultural contributions. In one way or another U.S. music is the basis or influence for Afrobeat (a combination of West African music, jazz, and funk rhythms), reggae, Australian country music, Russian rock, and bongo flava (a mixture of jazz, hip hop, and Tanzanian music).

Additionally, U.S. music has influenced sexual mores, youth behavior, and attitudes and behavior in general. Strong critics of U.S. music have existed from its earliest days. However, U.S. music has also been heralded as a forerunner of freedom and democracy.

Frank Salamone

See also Pop Culture—U.S. Music (Hip-hop)

Further Reading

Clarke, D. (1995). *The rise and fall of popular music.* New York: St. Martin's Press.

Ewen, D. (1957). *Panorama of American popular music.* Upper Saddle River, NJ: Prentice Hall.

Ferris, J. (1993). *America's musical landscape.* Dubuque, IA: Brown & Benchmark.

Ward, E., Stokes, G., & Tucker, K. (1986). *Rock of ages: The Rolling Stone history of rock and roll.* New York: Rolling Stone Press.

Pop Culture—U.S. Television

The international transmission of television has been characterized as an unequal exchange of goods and services, with U. S. media dominating the global market, using localized productions to enhance and facilitate global appeal.

Although cultural critics in the 1960s touted the technological capacity of television to transcend time and space and to create a global village, the television industry remained highly localized in its content and nationalized in its ownership and regulation until the 1990s. National governments viewed television as an important public servant responsible not only for entertaining but also for informing, developing, and uniting national citizens. For that reason national governments were protective of their television industries, imposing restrictions on foreign ownership of local stations and limiting the flow of foreign programming.

Because people need a lot of money to start a television system and keep it running, however, many developing nations were forced to accept technological assistance and programming from developed nations with a history of international media production. Britain, France, Germany, and the United States, in particular, offered monetary and technological assistance to developing nations (usually former colonies) and traded their programs internationally from the late 1950s on. The international transmission of television has thus been characterized historically by the unequal exchange of goods and services. The national orientation of most television systems gave this unequal exchange a political character, as less-developed countries feared that the imbalance in television flows would enable the more-developed countries to impose their worldviews. They charged that such inequities amounted to "cultural imperialism," the willful imposition of Western (specifically U.S.) culture onto weaker nations.

This debate flourished during the 1970s and 1980s, at which point technological and political developments in the TV industry made the argument for cultural imperialism more difficult to sustain. New technologies, such as the direct broadcast satellite receiver and VCR, enabled television to reach consumers directly, bypassing centralized community antennas and superceding a government's capacity to regulate broadcasting in the national interest. These technological developments accompanied a shift in political and economic perspectives that favored the elimination of national constraints on television development and transmission, a process known as "deregulation." Deregulation eliminated most barriers to the flow of television signals and programs across geographic space. Not only have public television systems been privatized and commercialized (turned over to private corporate

control), but also restrictions limiting foreign ownership of television systems, impeding the ownership of multiple media properties by a single corporation, and restricting program imports in the name of fostering local television production, have all been eliminated or severely qualified. As a result, media corporations have become global in ownership and scope, commanding multiple media systems and markets all over the world and exhibiting loyalty to no single national government. This situation complicates arguments for cultural imperialism, which assume that television flows reflect and transmit national interests. It is difficult to argue, for example, that the U.S.-based production firm Columbia Tristar is imposing U.S. worldviews on others when that firm is actually owned by a Japanese company (Sony).

Television scholars have adopted two basic approaches to understanding the global transmission of television signals and programs. The first is a structural approach that examines the political economy of the global media, asking who owns the infrastructure and controls the regulation of the industry and to what effect. The second approach involves a qualitative analysis of the content of global television flows and how this content is received by local communities. Both approaches complicate the simplistic assumptions on which the cultural imperialism thesis rests, illustrating instead that global television transmission is a complex, multilayered, multidirectional process subject to local feedback.

One-way Street or Multidirectional System?

The structural analysis of global television flows can be traced to the mid-1970s debates over a so-called new world information and communication order (NWICO) within the United Nations Educational, Scientific and Cultural Organization (UNESCO). These debates pitted developing nations, who argued that national control of television systems was necessary to prevent their economic and political subordination to the West, against the Western powers, who advocated the "free flow of information" across geographic borders. To clarify the terms of the debate, UNESCO commissioned a study to determine the extent and direction of television traffic around the world. Released in 1974, the study concluded

that international television flows constituted a "one-way street" flowing from the large exporting countries in the West to the rest of the world, with little reciprocal program exchange. For example, whereas developing nations filled an average of 30 percent of their program schedules with imported fare, mostly from the United States, the United States imported only 1 percent of its programming from abroad. A follow-up study in 1983 noted marginal decreases in international imports but concluded that "the trends discovered in the 1973 study seem to persist in 1983: one-way traffic from the big exporting countries to the rest of the world" (Varis 1993, 10). Although these data clearly illustrated the existence of a structural imbalance in television flows, they did not prove that negative cultural effects resulted from this imbalance, although this was the conclusion of the original authors.

Researchers seeking a more nuanced analysis of television traffic have noted important trends and absences in the original UNESCO report. For example, the original UNESCO report ignored the presence of significant regional export flows in order to emphasize the dominance of U.S. programming. These regional flows have assumed only greater importance in the age of satellite TV and recorded media transfers, which cut across national and international broadcast flows. This situation has led some researchers to argue that television transmission is better conceptualized by "a dynamic, regionalist view of the world" that takes note of "the intricate and multidirectional flows of television across the globe" (Sinclair, Jacka, and Cunningham 1996, 5). For instance, Mexico's largest media corporation, Televisa, produces up to 78 percent of its programming domestically and is one of the largest exporters of programming to Latin America and Spain. Its production facilities churn out "more programming than the four US networks and the major producers combined" (Sinclair 1996, 49). Its *telenovelas* (a Latin American variant of the soap opera) are popular not only with Spanish-speaking audiences but also in Germany, Poland, the Philippines, and even the Middle East. Televisa has also overtaken Britain as the primary exporter of programming to the U.S. market. As a regional power, then, Televisa has a greater impact on television flows within certain culturo-linguistic markets than even the largest U.S.-based multinational media corporations.

The original UNESCO report also paid no attention to issues of scheduling and popularity within the television systems-importing programs. Later studies compared the number of imported programs scheduled with the hours of TV actually viewed by domestic audiences and found that viewing hours tended to be lower for imports than for domestic programming. In Brazil, for example, 39 percent of the broadcast hours were devoted to imported programming in 1982, but that programming accounted for only 22 percent of the viewing hours, with only

19 percent of viewing hours going to U.S. programs. This finding indicates that viewing audiences prefer domestic programming when it is available and of adequate quality. More recent research indicates that imported programming most often occupies the lower-rated time slots, whereas prime-time hours are reserved for domestic programs. The influence of U.S. programming on foreign audiences is, thus, mitigated by issues of scheduling and audience preference. Some theorists have even argued that program importation is a temporary condition that will eventually be eclipsed by the increase in domestic production enabled by new financing and new technologies. This argument may be overstating the case, however, because foreign programming is likely to remain a staple for smaller nations incapable of generating sufficient support for native production.

In general, research on global television traffic has discovered a system of "flows within flows" that complicates the "simplistic model of the total domination of international television by the United States" identified in the original UNESCO report (Tracey 1993, 167). The picture that emerges instead is of an "arterial structure" of television flows that "is not a one-way street—rather, a number of main thoroughfares, with a series of not unimportant smaller roads leading off of these" (Tracey 1993, 167). Add to this a capillary system for the informal circulation of recorded media (videotapes, DVDs, and Internet downloads of TV programs), and we find a much more complex structure of ownership, control, and influence than the cultural imperialism thesis allows for.

Global Homogenization or Local Hybridization?

Because the original UNESCO study was limited to counting the number and direction of television exports, the authors also failed to consider how program content and reception might affect the impact of foreign programming on audiences. Qualitative media scholars have dedicated themselves to filling in these gaps. Their analyses have complicated the presumption of an automatic media effect from foreign programming whereby structural imbalances in media flows necessarily translate into cultural influence or dominance.

Much of this research was ignited by the global popularity of the prime-time U.S. soap opera *Dallas* in the 1980s. At the time cultural theorists and political leaders alike interpreted the *Dallas* phenomenon as a sign of the degradation and homogenization of global culture. Widespread anecdotal evidence held that social activity either stopped or was rescheduled to accommodate viewing of the program and that such popularity represented the colonization of cultural life by U.S. imperatives. Critics of

the phenomenon also assumed that people watched the program because they embraced the values of selfishness and materialism embodied by its central characters. A series of audience reception studies sought to test these assumptions; the studies indicated that the program's popularity was greatly exaggerated and that its reception was far more complex. First, its popularity varied from nation to nation and was often related to factors other than content. Researchers pointed out, for example, that the program never caught on in Japan because of linguistic barriers and failed in Peru because of the scheduling of the program opposite a popular, locally produced comedy program. Not only was the popularity of *Dallas* far from unanimous, but also the interpretation of its contents was negotiated by individuals based on their local value systems. Both Arabs and Russians, for example, tended to view the program as morally degenerate, but Arabs related this degeneracy to personal and familial failings, whereas Russians attributed it to "rotten capitalism" (Liebes and Katz 1990, 209). Neither group pas-

sively accepted the program's celebration of materialism. Instead, the groups used the raw material of the program as an occasion to discuss local personal and political concerns. They were influenced, in other words, by a "sedimentation of other social practices" responsible for shaping their cultural identities (Silj 1988, 40). Such research challenges the assumption that TV is an all-powerful medium capable of overriding the cultural training of individuals and implanting foreign notions in their heads.

Drawing on this insight, other qualitative studies of television exports have contested the notion that homogenization is likely to result from the structural imbalance of media flows. They argue that program exports are embraced by native populations and effectively indigenized, or turned into local cultural materials. For instance, Danish audiences have incorporated *Disney's Christmas Show* into their sense of national identity, transforming the annual viewing of the program into a rite of national renewal. Trinidadian audiences have adopted the U.S. soap opera *The Young and the Restless* as an expression of a local cultural attitude known as "bacchanal." Watching the program teaches Trinidadians important lessons about the impermanence and instability of the material life when compared with the constancy of family relations and personal character. Thus, the origin of the cultural text "does not dictate the process of local consumption" (Miller 2000, 514). Individuals may "think with American cultural products, but they do not [necessarily] think American" (Naficy 1993, 2). Other theorists have focused on the importation and indigenization of program formats, like the game show, soap opera, and news program, to argue that global traffic in TV programming may actually encourage cultural differentiation rather than homogenization. These formats, once adopted by local producers and filled with local talent, become something altogether new: hybrids reflecting the tastes and desires of local communities as much as the needs of corporations.

Finally, the growing importance of TV exports to the financing of media corporations within the United States means that program content and style are increasingly tailored for a global market in advance. In some cases this means just adding more action and investing more in the production values, including set design, costuming, and star power, all of which translate across linguistic barriers more easily. In other cases, however, this may mean entering co-production arrangements with local media producers who use local writers, directors, actors, and stories and so produce programs that speak more directly to local concerns than do U.S. programs. Media corporations have increasingly adopted strategies of co-production to enhance their globalization through localization, thereby relinquishing a measure of control (however small) over the content of their cultural productions. This feedback effect, whereby global audiences impact local production even in

A lifeguard stand on a beach, like the one on the television show *Baywatch*, a show which was an important source of images of U.S. popular and youth culture around the world. Source: istock.

the most developed media capitals, complicates the argument for cultural imperialism by showing that the process is not necessarily unidirectional.

Beyond Cultural Imperialism

The cultural imperialism thesis rests on the assumption that ownership and control of the television infrastructure necessarily translate into political and cultural influence. This assumption not only fails to account for the impact of local reception practices and contexts on global media messages, but also implies that the global media system is singular and unidirectional. It ignores important regional and local webs of production and completely discounts those informal networks of exchange (from pirating to file-sharing) that cut across the official national and international broadcasting regime. U.S.-based producers *are* likely to continue dominating the formal systems of global exchange because they enjoy a significant "domestic opportunity advantage (DOA)" related to the size and wealth of the U.S. audience (Wildman and Siwek 1993, 14). They also enjoy a linguistic advantage because English is the most widely spoken language in the world and because audiences prefer programs recorded in their native tongue. This structural dominance does not mean, however, that the United States will dominate global politics or culture. For one thing, media corporations have become relatively independent of the nations that once controlled them. Although these corporations clearly intervene in national politics to accomplish their economic goals, they do not necessarily reflect or transmit nationalist ideologies.

The cultural imperialism thesis may thus hamper efforts to understand and challenge the concentration of media ownership in transnational corporate hands because it still assumes that media systems are national in scope. Also, the official media infrastructure is shot through with alternate flows and informal webs of exchange that threaten the power of established interests, which is why media corporations have attacked piracy and file-sharing with such vehemence. Local reception practices also make it difficult to conclude that technological preeminence will necessarily translate into ideological dominance. Because the cultural imperialism thesis neglects this systemic complexity, it may have exhausted its utility.

Stacy Takacs

Further Reading
Ang, I. (1985). *Watching Dallas: Soap opera and the melodramatic imagination.* New York: Methuen.

Biltereyst, D. (1991). Resisting American hegemony: A comparative analysis of the reception of domestic and US fiction. *European Journal of Communication, 7,* 469–497.

Cooper-Chen, A. (1994). *Games in the global village: A 50-nation study of entertainment television.* Bowling Green, OH: Bowling Green University Popular Press.

Dunn, H. (1995). *Globalization, communications and Caribbean identity.* New York: St. Martin's Press.

Golding, P., & Harris, P. (1997). *Beyond cultural imperialism: Globalization, communication and the new international order.* Thousand Oaks, CA: Sage Publications.

Lee, C. (1980). *Media imperialism reconsidered: The homogenizing of television culture.* London: Sage Publications.

Liebes, T., & Katz, E. (1990). *The export of meaning: Cross-cultural readings of "Dallas."* New York: Oxford University Press.

MacBride, S., Abel, E., et al. (1984). *Many voices, one world: Communication and society, today and tomorrow: Towards a new more just and more efficient world information and communication order.* Paris: UNESCO.

Miller, D. (2000). The young and the restless in Trinidad: A case of the local and the global in mass consumption. In P. Marris & S. Thornham (Eds.), *Media studies: A reader* (pp. 503–515). New York: New York University Press.

Naficy, H. (1993). *The making of exile cultures: Iranian television in Los Angeles.* Minneapolis: University of Minnesota Press.

Noam, E., & Millonzi, J. (Eds.). (1993). *The international market in film and television programs.* Norwood, NJ: Ablex Publishing.

Nordenstreng, K., & Schiller, H. (Eds.). (1993). *Beyond national sovereignty: International communication in the 1990s.* Norwood, NJ: Ablex Publishing.

Nordenstreng, K., & Varis, T. (1974). *Television traffic—A one-way street?* Paris: UNESCO.

Rogers, E., & Antola, L. (1985). Telenovelas: A Latin American success story. *Journal of Communication, 35*(4), 24–35.

Schiller, H. (1969). *Mass communications and American empire.* New York: Kelley.

Schiller, H. (1991). Not yet the post-imperialist era. *Critical Studies in Mass Communication, 8,* 13–28.

Silj, A. (1988). *East of Dallas: The European challenge to American television.* London: British Film Institute.

Sinclair, J. (1996). Mexico, Brazil, and the Latin world. In J. Sinclair, E. Jacka, & S. Cunningham (Eds.), *New patterns in global television: Peripheral vision* (pp. 33–56). New York: Oxford University Press.

Sinclair, J., Jacka, E., & Cunningham, S. (Eds.). (1996). *New patterns in global television: Peripheral vision.* New York: Oxford University Press.

Sreberny-Mohammadi, A., Winseck, D., McKenna, J., & Boyd-Barret, O. (1997). *Media in global context: A reader.* New York: Edward Arnold Publishing.

Straubhaar, J. (1991). Beyond media imperialism: Asymmetrical interdependence and cultural proximity. *Critical Studies in Mass Communications, 8,* 39–59.

Tomlinson, J. (1991). *Cultural imperialism.* Baltimore: Johns Hopkins University Press.

Tracey, M. (1993). A taste of money: Popular culture and the economics of global television. In E. Noam & J. Millonzi (Eds.), *The international market in film and television programs* (pp. 163–198). Norwood, NJ: Ablex Publishing.

Tunstall, J. (1977). *The media are American: Anglo-American media in the world*. London: Constable.

Varis, T. (1993). Trends in the global traffic of television programs. In E. Noam & J. Millonzi (Eds.), *The international market in film and television programs.* (pp. 1–12). Norwood, NJ: Ablex Publishing.

Wasko, J., Phillips, M., & Meehan, E. (Eds.). (2001). *Dazzled by Disney? The global Disney audiences project.* New York: Leicester University Press.

Wells, A. (1972). *Picture-tube imperialism: The impact of US television on Latin America*. Maryknoll, NY: Orbis.

Wildman, S., & Siwek, S. (1988). *International trade in films and television programs.* Cambridge, MA: American Enterprise Institute/Ballinger Publications.

Wildman, S., & Siwek, S. (1993). The economics of trade in recorded media products in a multilingual world: Implications for national media policies. In E. Noam & J. Millonzi (Eds.), *The international market in film and television programs* (pp. 13–40). Norwood, NJ: Ablex Publishing.

Radicalism and Populism, U.S.

Radical and populist movements in the United States have had a mixed reception, sometimes using violence to attain ends such as unionization, other times using the political process to effect change as with the New Deal.

Whereas the concept of radicalism is generally applied to the advocacy of political or social reform and thus implies a basis in liberal or left-wing ideological values, certain U.S. movements that are typically regarded as radical in the U.S. context, such as agrarian radicalism, were at least in part movements of resistance. The dynamic of U.S. society, seen in the sometimes ruthless behavior of industrial and extractive capitalism and in the exploitation of agrarian classes, produced radical movements that sought to resist the changes engendered by this dynamic.

Agrarian Radicalism

Tensions between the urban and the rural were always present in U.S. history. The more recognized agrarian radical movements of U.S. history postdated the Civil War, first with the conventionally named Greenback Party. This party was active especially in midwestern states from around 1874 to about 1884, pushing a policy for government control of the currency to benefit agrarian interests. In 1878 the party became the Greenback Labor Party after amalgamation with trade union groups. Its presidential candidate, James Baird Weaver (1833–1912), won 3.3 percent of the national vote in 1880. However, the more famous agrarian movement was the later People's Party, the Populists, active nationally from the 1880s into the 1890s. Running again for president as its candidate, Weaver won 8.5 percent of the national vote in 1892. In 1896 the party supported the Democratic candidacy of William Jennings Bryan (1860–1925), although it nominated its own candidate for vice president, Georgia's Thomas Edward Watson (1856–1922). Historiography once used to recognize the Populists as a quintessentially radical party, opposing eastern moneyed interests with a policy of bimetallism (the use of both gold and silver as the monetary standard, with fixed values in relation to each other) and opposing exploitation by railroad interests in such matters as freight rates. However, the revisionist view of the Populists espoused by historians such as Richard Hofstadter (1916–1970) in his 1955 *The Age of Reform* saw in them characteristics of narrow-mindedness, intolerance and often anti-Semitism in the nature of their resistance to financial interests; in that sense they qualify as a movement of resistance rather than one of radicalism.

Although surviving to a degree in the South, Populism by the late 1890s was largely a spent force nationally. However, agrarian radicalism had a number of well-established state-based manifestations during the twentieth century. One was the Non-Partisan League in North Dakota, founded in 1915 as an alliance of farmers and labor by Arthur Charles Townley (1880–1959), who had been a leader of the Socialist Party of America (SPA) in the state. Another was the Minnesota Farmer-Labor Party, founded in 1918 and supporting the interests of farmers and workers, including state ownership of certain industries and a form of welfare state. In the 1920s and 1930s it elected both state governors and U.S. senators. There was also the Wisconsin Progressives, originally a faction established in 1900 within the state Republican Party by Robert Marion La Follette Sr. (1855–1925), founder of the La Follette political dynasty in Wisconsin. La Follette was a U.S. senator for Wisconsin from 1905 to 1925 and in 1924 ran for president on a Progressive Party ticket, winning 16.6 percent of the national vote and being endorsed by many labor groups for his demands for nationalization of, among other institutions, the railroads.

Labor Radicalism

Although it has long been a maxim that the United States has had no "socialism" or at least no social-democratic party on the model seen in Europe, some people have claimed that the United States did ultimately have a social-democratic party of sorts in terms of how the Democratic Party from 1936 emerged, especially in the East, as a party with a strong blue-collar social base not dissimilar in program to European social-democratic parties. In addition, the social-democratic SPA was founded in 1898. Indeed, besides the SPA, there were smaller and more sectarian worker parties, based in part on political tendencies brought from Europe by immigrants, such as the Socialist Labor Party (SLP) and the Industrial Workers of the World (IWW). The SLP, founded before the SPA and later coexisting with it, was then dominated by Daniel DeLeon (1852–1914); it never achieved mass status but was important as the base for DeLeon, undoubtedly one of the most influential Marxist

EXTRACT FROM THE CRISIS BY THOMAS PAINE

Thomas Paine's stirring prose helped spread wide support for the colonies' cessation from the British Empire in the late 1700s, and is considered by many to be one of America's first popular radical thinkers. The excerpt below, from The Crisis: 23 December 1776, became so popular that its readership at that time can be compared—by percentage of the population—to the amount of people who today watch the Super Bowl. This pamphlet remains well-known for its quotable opening line.

These are the times that try men's souls. The summer soldier and the sunshine patriot will, in this crisis, shrink from the service of their country; but he that stands it now, deserves the love and thanks of man and woman. Tyranny, like hell, is not easily conquered; yet we have this consolation with us, that the harder the conflict, the more glorious the triumph. What we obtain too cheap, we esteem too lightly: it is dearness only that gives every thing its value. Heaven knows how to put a proper price upon its goods; and it would be strange indeed if so celestial an article as FREEDOM should not be highly rated. Britain, with an army to enforce her tyranny, has declared that she has a right (not only to TAX) but "to BIND us in ALL CASES WHATSOEVER," and if being bound in that manner, is not slavery, then is there not such a thing as slavery upon earth. Even the expression is impious; for so unlimited a power can belong only to God.

Whether the independence of the continent was declared too soon, or delayed too long, I will not now enter into as an argument; my own simple opinion is, that had it been eight months earlier, it would have been much better. We did not make a proper use of last winter, neither could we, while we were in a dependent state. However, the fault, if it were one, was all our own we have none to blame but ourselves. But no great deal is lost yet. All that Howe has been doing for this month past, is rather a ravage than a conquest, which the spirit of the Jerseys, a year ago, would have quickly repulsed, and which time and a little resolution will soon recover.

I have as little superstition in me as any man living, but my secret opinion has ever been, and still is, that God Almighty will not give up a people to military destruction, or leave them unsupportedly to perish, who have so earnestly and so repeatedly sought to avoid the calamities of war, by every decent method which wisdom could invent. Neither have I so much of the infidel in me, as to suppose that He has relinquished the government of the world, and given us up to the care of devils; and as I do not, I cannot see on what grounds the king of Britain can look up to heaven for help against us: a common murderer, a highwayman, or a house-breaker, has as good a pretence as he.

Source: Paine, T. (1776, December 23). The crisis. Retrieved April 5, 2007, from http://www.ushistory.org/paine/crisis/c-01.htm

thinkers produced in the United States. The failure of an indigenous social-democratic party has been attributed to a number of factors, such as the material rewards of U.S. capitalism, U.S. society's general success in economically integrating immigrant groups, and particularly tensions and mutual suspicions between immigrant ethnic groups who would collectively have been the natural constituency of such a party.

There were other difficulties, especially after World War I, when all forms of militancy in the United States faced repression during the "Red Scare" period. As it was, Eugene Victor Debs's (1855–1926) SPA candidacy for the presidency in 1912 was his most successful, winning 6 percent of the vote nationwide; even in 1920, after the attacks on labor radicalism during the Red Scare, Debs managed 3.4 percent of the presidential vote. Socialists had later modest successes; for example, the muckraking writer Upton Sinclair (1878–1968) ran for governor of California on a socialist ticket and later, in 1934, was almost elected on the Democratic ticket, running on the campaign theme of "End Poverty in California." Still, even the event that otherwise might have shaken political complacency and produced a radical and autonomous social-democratic politics, the Great Depression of the 1930s, failed to do so in any significant way, although it did convert the

Democratic Party to the New Deal and alter its character from 1936 into a more obviously blue-collar-based party.

Labor Violence and Unionization

If labor radicalism in the form of organized politics had a checkered history in the United States and was ultimately unsuccessful, it remains true that U.S. labor history is marked by major instances of industrial violence in attempts to secure unionization. The IWW's attempts to mobilize support in mining and logging communities, for example, were often harshly suppressed, and indeed the U.S. labor movement was split on the issue of tactics.

The alternative approach was the narrow and nonideological one of the American Federation of Labor (AFL), craft-based and exemplified by its president, Samuel Gompers (1850–1924), who had founded the AFL in 1886. That is in contrast to the focus on the establishment of a wider industrial base, in which the IWW was prominent in the early years of the twentieth century. This difference was later seen in the breakaway from the AFL of the Congress of Industrial Organizations (CIO) at the inspiration of

John Llewellyn Lewis (1880–1969). Lewis favored the strategy of unionizing workers in such mass-production industries as automobile manufacturing. Lewis himself was first president of the CIO from 1936 to 1940 and president of the United Mine Workers of America (UMWA) from 1920 to 1960.

Progressivism as a Type of U.S. Radicalism

The ultimate failure of labor-based politics came about because much of its natural constituency was captured instead by so-called machine politics in major cities such as Chicago, Detroit, New York, and Philadelphia. The machine was corrupt in many ways but ensured much of its ascendancy and popularity by providing a crude and particularistic form of social welfare, outside any formal public-sector provision, as well as by bringing municipal facilities into local neighborhoods. By such measures—as well as by vice and corruption in the granting of contracts and licenses to private interests—did, for example, John "Bathhouse" Coughlin (1860–1938) and Michael "Hinky Dink" Kenna (1857–1946) control, as aldermen or ward committeeman, Chicago's First Ward through most of the first forty years of the twentieth century. Even more famous was New York's George Washington Plunkitt (1842–1924) of Tammany Hall, known for his commitment to "honest graft."

Civil Rights Radicalism

Almost autonomous from labor and agrarian radicalism has been the activism associated with the issue of race. From the pre-Civil War abolition movement through the civil rights mobilization of the 1950s and onward, civil rights radicalism had remarkably little concerted interface with other forms of U.S. radicalism. The Populist period does afford certain examples of interracial cooperation, but it equally gives examples of where that cooperation did not happen. Of course, the civil rights movement attracted sympathy and support from many in the mainstream political parties, but the movement itself was autonomous and often opposed to mainstream politics. The confrontation between Martin Luther King Jr. (1929–1968) and Chicago Mayor Richard Joseph Daley (1902–1976) over racial segregation in that city was one of the more notorious examples. African-American activism, even its more moderate wings represented by, for example, the National Association for the Advancement of Colored People (NAACP), had an ambiguous relationship with mainstream white politics. The NAACP was founded in 1909 by, among others, William Edward Burghardt (W. E. B.) Du Bois (1868–1963); although not revolutionary, its leaders were nonetheless critical of the accommodationist approach favored by Booker Taliaferro Washington (1856–1915).

Right-wing Radicalism

The ambiguity inherent in U.S. radicalism is further exemplified by the fact that the United States had fostered a form of right-wing radicalism. The concept of "radical right" was introduced into U.S. political analysis in the early 1950s by the political sociologist Seymour Martin Lipset (1922–2006). The label was seen as justified because the movements concerned, despite formal claims to be right-wing and conservative, were instead ones of resistance against the prevailing political orthodoxy, opposed to and wanting to change many aspects of the existing political system. In short, the movements represented a revolt against liberalism. At the time, Lipset particularly had in mind the McCarthyism of Senator Joseph Raymond McCarthy (1908–1957), but Lipset later extended the idea, also using the "extremism" label, to encompass right-wing movements of the past and subsequently including the right-wing movements appealing to the dispossessed in the 1930s (e.g., the Share Our Wealth movement of Louisiana Senator Huey Pierce Long [1893–1935]) and later the American Independent Party of George Corley Wallace (1919–1998).

A review of radical phenomena in U.S. history shows not so much the "obsolescence of left and right" (Lasch 1991, 21-39) as the ambiguity of these terms. Movements such as Populism with radical demands for reform of financial institutions nonetheless contained strong, and perhaps justified, elements of resistance to particular forms of change. Even movements that might, in a contemporary perspective, be seen as in little sense radical, such as the prohibition and temperance movements, nonetheless contained elements of a radical agenda.

Christopher T. Husbands

See also Alternative U.S. History

Further Reading

Argersinger, P. H. (1995). *The limits of agrarian radicalism: Western populism and American politics.* Lawrence: University Press of Kansas.

Bell, D. (Ed.). (1964). *The radical right: The new American right expanded and updated.* Garden City, NY: Anchor Books.

Goodwyn, L. (1976). *Democratic promise: The populist moment in America.* New York: Oxford University Press.

Gutfeld, A. (2002). American exceptionalism: *The effects of plenty on the American experience.* Brighton, UK: Sussex Academic Press.

Hofstadter, R. (1955). *The age of reform: From Bryan to F.D.R.* New York: Vintage.

Lasch, C. (1991). *The true and only heaven: Progress and its critics.* New York: W. W. Norton.

Laslett, J. H. M., & Lipset S. M. (Eds.). (1974). *Failure of a dream?: Essays in the history of American socialism.* Garden City, NY: Doubleday.

Lipset, S. M. (1996). *American exceptionalism: A double-edged sword.* New York: W. W. Norton.

Lipset, S. M., & Raab, E. (1977). *The politics of unreason: Right-wing extremism in America, 1790–1970* (2nd ed.). Chicago: University of Chicago Press.

Pope, D. (Ed.). (2000). *American radicalism.* Malden, MA: Blackwell.

Rosenblum, G. (1973). *Immigrant workers: Their impact on American labor radicalism.* New York: Basic Books.

Weinstein, J. (1967). *The decline of socialism in America 1912–1925.* New York: Monthly Review Press.

Relations with Africa, U.S.

The United States and African nations share the goal of promoting peace and security across Africa. Nevertheless, U.S. relations with African organizations, such as the AU, are the most underappreciated in U.S. foreign policy.

The African Union (AU) is a regional intergovernmental organization whose priorities are development, security, and good governance in Africa. Those priorities may seem to differ from the United States' international priorities of controlling weapons of mass destruction, nuclear proliferation, and terrorism. Nevertheless, all of these priorities rely on the assurance of peace and security in Africa. Thus, the American Assembly (a U.S. nonpartisan public affairs forum) concluded in 1997 that the United States should preserve and enhance Africa's security as a means of consolidating U.S. economic and political gains and protecting its own interests.

In this endeavor the key partner of the United States should be the African Union, which shares these objectives. Peace and security are at the top of the AU agenda because the resolution of conflicts and the creation of a peaceful environment are considered to be the foundation for development and integration of the continent. However, in general the AU and the United States have had a poor record in collaborating to promote peace, security, and stability in Africa. U.S. policymakers have more often pursued policies that appear to undercut African regional organizations, particularly the AU and its predecessor, the Organization of African Unity (OAU).

Background

The African Union was founded in 2002 to replace the OAU, which was established in 1963 in Addis Ababa, Ethiopia, by heads of state of thirty-two African nations. OAU goals included promoting the unity and solidarity of African states; coordinating their cooperation to achieve a better life for the peoples of Africa; defending their sovereignty, territorial integrity, and independence; eradicating colonialism from Africa; and promoting international cooperation. The AU has fifty-three members and has the goals of unifying Africa; defending the sovereignty, territorial integrity, and independence of its members; integrating the continent; encouraging international cooperation; and promoting peace, security, stability, human rights, sustainable development, democracy, and good governance on the continent.

History of U.S.-OAU Relations

U.S. foreign policy has generally marginalized or neglected African international organizations. Despite U.S. active engagement with international organizations such as the United Nations (U.N.), European Union (EU), Organization of American States (OAS), North Atlantic Treaty Organization (NATO), and Southeast Asia Treaty Organization (SEATO), the United States has never shown much interest in African international organizations, particularly the OAU and the AU.

The U.S. reluctance to forge strong ties with international organizations and to participate in multilateral activities such as humanitarian intervention, dispute resolution, and peacekeeping operations has been influenced by a fear that such involvement would come at the cost of U.S. national sovereignty. Understandably, the United States has preferred to deal bilaterally or unilaterally with Africa countries and issues affecting the continent rather than deal with African international organizations. However, this approach is "directly at odds with Africa's efforts to build multilateral approaches to the continent's greatest challenges" (Colgan 2003).

The United States has applied its policy in Africa in a selective way and in most cases contrary to OAU positions and policies. One of the issues on which the United States and OAU took opposite sides was the liberation struggles in Africa. On one hand, the OAU, by virtue of its objectives of liberating the continent from colonial domination, became an active supporter of freedom fighters in Rhodesia (now Zimbabwe), Angola, Mozambique, Cape Verde, South West Africa (now Namibia), and South Africa. On the other hand, the United States either gave lukewarm support to these movements or actively supported the Portuguese colonialists and white-minority regimes that the freedom fighters were fighting against. The United States supported Portugal in its fight against African liberation movements mainly because of U.S. NATO obligations, whereas the United States supported the white-minority regimes because of the fear that if African liberation movements took over power they would fall under the influence of the Soviet Union, then the major rival of the United States. Whereas the OAU made consistent declarations of sup-

port for liberation movements on the continent, the United States enacted policies that many people saw as totally undercutting those movements.

The United States has not actively worked with the OAU to resolve African conflicts or build peace on the continent. In general, the United States has been unwilling to make real commitments to OAU priorities in these efforts and has provided, at most, minimal support unilaterally to peace initiatives in the Sudan, Democratic Republic of the Congo (DRC, formerly Zaire), and Burundi. The United States in the past did make commitments to support the OAU in its peacekeeping efforts. For instance, when the OAU established a conflict prevention, management, and resolution mechanism in 1993, the United States offered to assist it by providing the necessary infrastructure and sharing with it U.S. standards and principles for the establishment of peacekeeping operations. In 1994 President Bill Clinton signed into law the African Conflict Resolution Act, which provided U.S. financial and technical support of the conflict resolution mechanism and authorized funding to support OAU efforts at conflict resolution.

However, this support was cut short because of the OAU's dalliance with Muammar al-Qaddafi of Libya. The fundamental reason for U.S. government hostility to Libya was Qaddafi's use of terrorism and subversion and his foreign military adventurism. Two incidents show how the rivalry between the United States and Libya worked to the detriment of the OAU. In 1981 the United States provided funding for the OAU peacekeeping force in Chad after the Libyan forces who had been supporting President Goukouni Oueddei pulled out of the country. However, the Reagan administration was later accused of undermining the OAU effort in Chad by providing arms to Hissen Habre's forces, who were fighting to oust Oueddei from power. With U.S. support Habre marched through the country and, by maneuvering around the OAU peacekeepers who wanted to avoid combat, took over the government.

The second incident was the bombing of PanAm flight 103 over Lockerbie, Scotland, in December 1988. The United States implicated Libya in the terrorist act and singled it out for punishment. As part of this punishment, Libya was isolated internationally in a campaign led by the United States. As Libya became an international pariah state, Qaddafi looked south in Africa for friendship from radical states and liberation movements such as South Africa's African National Congress (ANC). He also increased his participation in the OAU and spearheaded efforts to transform it into a more viable pan-African organization. As Qaddafi developed closer ties with the OAU, the United States reacted by scaling back and eventually almost freezing all its ties to the continental organization. The OAU was the first regional organization to defy sanctions against Qaddafi, and through the diplomatic initiatives

of former South African President Nelson Mandela the Lockerbie issue was resolved and sanctions against Libya were lifted. The OAU had a choice of strengthening its relations with the United States or Gadhafi, and it chose the latter.

A number of facts explain low U.S. interest in African international organizations and Africa in general. First, African international organizations, particularly the OAU, have not endeared themselves to the United States and the world in general through their poor performance record. In general, the record of the OAU in settling African conflicts was poor. Unlike the OAS, where the presence of the United States was a restraint on performance, the main restraint in the OAU was its lack of capacity and political will. The OAU distinguished itself as a "club of African big men" known for their brutal dictatorships. OAU effectiveness in addressing African problems was also hampered by its decision-making process, which was vested in the Assembly of African Heads of State and Government, who were reluctant to speak out against flagrant violations of human rights and misrule that were rampant on the continent because almost all of them were culpable. Hiding behind the cover of "sovereignty" and "noninterference" in each other's internal affairs, African leaders overlooked all forms of bad rule and mismanagement of public affairs on the continent. Although dictators of some OAU nations were friendly to the United States, the United States apparently preferred to deal with them individually rather than in a club. Furthermore, the OAU did not offer the United States the opportunities that it needed to wage the Cold War with the Soviet Union, nor did the OAU have the attractions for superpower contention and control.

Second, the end of the Cold War left the United States unsure of what role to play and how to play it in Africa. A desire to curtail defense spending and to limit military involvement overseas existed when U.S. leadership was most needed in resolving African problems. A paradox exists in the United States in that many Americans feel a moral compulsion to help countries in need and to defend the weak but a reluctance to be drawn into unpredictable and open-ended conflicts. One such moment came in the early 1990s when the Somali state collapsed after the ouster of dictator Siade Barre left a humanitarian catastrophe that attracted international attention.

Lost Opportunities

Although the AU is significantly different from the OAU, the United States has yet to develop relationships with the AU. The United States instead has shown a preference for the New Partnership for Africa's Development (NEPAD), a development plan that aims to attract international development finance and investment

to African countries that subscribe to good governance practices. However, when NEPAD became a part of the AU, the United States cooled off considerably toward NEPAD. An opportunity to support NEPAD is being lost because the United States has pegged its support on how its standards are being applied to Zimbabwe. African leaders also commit themselves to check on each other's behavior through the African Peer Review Mechanism (APRM). As proof of its commitment to NEPAD, the United States has challenged the AU and African leaders in general to apply the APRM to Zimbabwe's Robert Mugabe for violating the human rights of his people. This challenge has not gone down well with most African countries, which see it as a form of blackmail and arm-twisting because the United States has remained silent when similar violations take place in countries, such as Morocco and Ethiopia, that are regarded as strategically important to the United States.

The low level of U.S. commitment to the OAU and, later, the AU was glaringly displayed in the support of these organizations' peace support operations. In 2003 the Bush administration asked Congress to allocate $108 million for the Peacekeeping Operations Account, which funds U.S. voluntary contributions to multinational peacekeeping operations (outside of U.N.-run operations). Of this total, $30 million was for African regional peacekeeping operations ($41 million had been allocated the previous year). This money was to assist (1) the peacekeeping initiatives of the Economic Community of West African States (ECOWAS); (2) the Joint Military Commission (JMC) to build peace in the DRC, particularly in the disarmament, demobilization, and reintegration of combatants; and (3) the OAU Liaison Office in Ethiopia and Eritrea. In contrast, peacekeeping activities in the Balkans and diplomacy missions of the Organization for Security and Cooperation in Europe (OSCE) received $47 million. Moreover, of the $1.33 billion in U.S. foreign military financing appropriated for Africa in 2001, the OAU had received only $100,000, the bulk ($1.3 billion) going to Egypt.

The United States has supported the development of regional mechanisms such as ECOWAS to promote peace in West Africa. Nevertheless, the United States has received criticism for engaging in peace operations outside the framework of African international organizations. The African Crisis Response Initiative (ACRI) trained small units of African armies for peacekeeping duties. In 2004 ACRI was transformed into the African Contingency Operations Training and Assistance (ACOTA), which will train military trainers and equip African national militaries to conduct peace support operations and humanitarian relief. No agreement exists between the United States and the AU on how to deploy ACRI-trained troops as part of the AU's standby force. The United States prefers that ACRI partners (Benin, Ghana, Malawi, Mali,

Senegal, and Uganda) make their own decisions on how to contribute to multinational peace support operations. However, critics of ACRI and ACOTA have pointed out that such initiatives undercut Africa's peace agenda and multilateral efforts to promote it. People also have criticized these initiatives' emphasis on training Africans for peacekeeping in view of the fact that AIO's (African international organizations) peacekeeping operations are mainly challenged by a lack of logistics and sustainability.

Because this ACOTA initiative, like external ones such as France's Reinforcement of African Peace-Keeping Capacities (RE-CAMP), has not complemented the conflict-management framework and structures established by the OAU and AU, the United States can reorient ACOTA to focus on the AU's standby force. The standby force has aims similar to ACRI/ACOTA's, which are to create rapidly deployable regional peacekeeping brigades that can be deployed in a humanitarian crisis or in a traditional peacekeeping operation.

Successful U.S. Policy toward the AU

In analyzing U.S.-AU relations, three questions serve as a backdrop:

- ❏ What are the primary problems that the United States needs to be aware of in constructing its foreign policy toward the AU and other African international organizations?
- ❏ What does the United States need from its relationship with the AU? That is, what priorities should guide the formulation of U.S. policy toward the AU and African regional organizations?
- ❏ What type of "architecture" should be set up to deal with African problems? Should the United States act unilaterally, bilaterally, with selected African countries, with African regional groupings, or with the AU?

These questions are difficult to answer. Although problems are easy to catalog, the challenge is to determine their sources and agree on common strategies for addressing them. Prioritizing goals is more difficult because it forces policymakers to critically examine what is to be achieved by the policy and the cost to be paid.

Constructing an "architecture" is even more difficult because, first, many choices are available; second, the chosen architecture might not work as planned; and third, the architecture must be compatible with existing architectures.

Despite these problems the United States stands to gain considerably from improved cooperation with the AU on peace and security issues. The United States might find an entry point into the

AU through the AU's support of a continental policy on antiterrorism. Just as the U.S. war on terrorism is a priority in U.S. global security policy, it is also a priority in the AU peace and security agenda. In particular the United States and the AU could work closely to help African governments reduce the capacity of terrorists to act on the continent by focusing on certain critical aspects, including coastal and border security; immigration and customs; airport and seaport security; law enforcement training; terrorist tracking databases; disruption of terrorist financing; regional information sharing and cooperation; and community outreach through education, assistance, and public information. The AU's peace and security agenda also contains transnational security issues that are of interest to the United States: curbing arms proliferation, drug trafficking, international criminal activities, terrorism, the spread of infectious diseases, and environmental degradation. The United States can work closely with the AU in combating these threats to mutual security interests. The need for collaboration to address such threats presents a significant opportunity for the United States and the AU to strengthen their relations.

Most significantly, U.S. policy objectives toward Africa are a mirror image of the AU's agenda for the continent:

❑ Promoting peace by preventing, managing, or resolving conflicts
❑ Providing humanitarian assistance to alleviate suffering and hunger
❑ Fostering democracy, good governance, rule of law, and respect for human rights
❑ Combating the spread of HIV/AIDS and other infectious diseases that threaten Africa's economic growth
❑ Supporting economic growth and sustainable development

The Future

U.S. relations with African international organizations are the most underappreciated in U.S. foreign policy. U.S. relations with the AU suffer from neglect because the United States has not formulated a clear policy on these relations. Indeed, the United States can build a relationship with the AU based on a partnership and friendship rather than on aid. The United States, through the AU, can help Africa find peace, stability, and prosperity.

Despite past problems with African international organizations, the United States cannot overlook the developing trend toward multilateralism on the continent and has an opportunity to promote its African policy by cooperating with the AU in a mutually beneficial partnership. Problems should not arise as to whether the United States should pursue policies with individual African countries or with African regional and continental organizations because both relations are complementary.

This fact means that the U.S. approach of dealing with Africa unilaterally will have to change. For the United States to maximize its African foreign policy objectives, it must pursue direct relations with African international organizations, particularly the AU.

Wafula Okumu

See also IMF, World Bank, and IDB, U.S. Role in; Slavery and Abolitionism

Further Reading

Clough, M. (1997). *Free at last? United States policy toward Africa and the end of the Cold War.* New York: New York University Press.

Cohen, H. J. (2000). Intervening in Africa: Superpower peacemaking in a troubled continent. New York: St. Martin's Press.

Colgan, A.-L. (2003). *The state of U.S. Africa policy.* Paper presented at the meeting of Africa Action's First Annual Baraza. Retrieved January 29, 2007, from http://www.africaaction.org/events/baraza/2003/policy.php

Gordon, D. F., Miller, D. G., & Wolpe, H. (1998). *The United States and Africa: A post–Cold War perspective.* New York: W. W. Norton.

Huband, M. (2001). *Skull beneath the skin: Africa after the Cold War.* Boulder, CO: Westview Press.

Kansteiner, W. H., & Morrison, J. S. (2004). *Rising stakes in Africa: Seven proposals to strengthen U.S.-Africa policy.* Washington, DC: Center for Strategic & International Studies.

Morrison, J. S., & Cooke, J. G. (2001). Africa policy in the Clinton years: Critical choices for the Bush administration. Washington, DC: CISI Press.

Relations with APEC, U.S.

The United States has been a supporter of APEC because it provides secure economic access to the region, helps spread value systems preferred by Americans, and prevents domination of the region by other powers like China.

APEC (Asia-Pacific Economic Cooperation) is the major forum for facilitating economic growth, cooperation, trade, and investment in the Asia-Pacific region on both sides of the ocean. It has been an important forum for emerging and developed economies to discuss share interests.

As of 2007 APEC had twenty-one members: Australia; Brunei; Canada; Chile; People's Republic of China; Hong Kong, China; Indonesia; Japan; South Korea; Malaysia; Mexico; New Zealand; Papua New Guinea; Peru; Philippines; Russian Federation; Singapore; Chinese Taipei; Thailand; United States; and Vietnam. APEC is headquartered in Singapore. Its members account for more than one-third of the world's population, for about $19.3 trillion in output (60 percent of the global gross domestic product or GDP), and for about 47 percent of world trade.

The United States did not play an active role in the decision to found a new institution for Asia-Pacific economic dialogue rather than work through existing institutions. Because APEC is the creation of sovereign states (excluding Taiwan and Hong Kong), each economy has its own set of interests determined through its domestic decision-making processes. The U.S. government's perspective on APEC is a reflection of U.S. national interests, such as human rights and access to Asian markets.

History of APEC and the United States

APEC was founded in 1989 as an informal ministerial meeting of twelve Pacific Rim economies: six Association of Southeast Asian Nations (ASEAN) nations (Brunei, Indonesia, Malaysia, Philippines, Singapore, and Thailand), five developed nations (Australia, Canada, Japan, New Zealand, and the United States), and South Korea. Australian Prime Minister Robert Hawke issued the call to create the framework of APEC.

The framework of APEC uses three basic models: a minimalist model, the Organisation for Economic Cooperation and Development (OECD) model, and the North American Free Trade Agreement (NAFTA) model. The minimalist model draws from the early history of ASEAN (composed of Brunei, Cambodia, Laos, Indonesia, Malaysia, Myanmar, Philippines, Singapore, Thailand, and Vietnam). Under this model APEC should essentially be a forum for consultations and constructive discussions on economic issues. Under the OECD model APEC should provide a venue for identifying and discussing international economic issues. OECD is not a rules-based institution; its flexibility, combined with access to rules makers through its networks, have been used to considerable effect. However, many of the most important Asian economies, such as China and Taiwan, were not OECD members. Lastly, the NAFTA model makes trade liberalization the overriding goal, to be achieved through a formalized process similar to that of other regional trade schemes.

Two developments have completely changed APEC since its founding. The first was diplomatic. It occurred when U.S. President Bill Clinton invited all APEC members to a summit in Seattle, Washington, in 1993 to discuss world economic issues, such as the reduction of trade and investment barriers, economic cooperation and interdependence, expansion of the world economy, and support for an open international trading system. According to the APEC leaders' declaration, "Our meeting reflects the emergence of a new voice for the Asia Pacific in world affairs. As we prepare to enter the twenty-first century, we believe our dynamic region, representing forty percent of the world's population and fifty percent of its GNP, will play an important role in the global economy, leading the way in economic growth and trade expansion" (APEC Secretariat 1993).

Prior to the 1993 summit, APEC was merely a ministerial meeting with high-level officials from the member countries, but not the heads of the governments, and was based on the notion of "getting to know you." After Clinton's invitation, Indonesian President Suharto followed with an invitation to APEC leaders in 1994. Since then annual APEC summits have been considered prominent international events.

The second development that changed APEC was economic. At the 1994 meeting in Bogor, Indonesia, APEC set the ambitious goal of achieving free and open trade and investment among APEC members by 2010 for members with developed economies and by 2020 for all members. The APEC leaders' declaration concludes, "We also ask the Eminent Persons Group and the Pacific

Business Forum to review the interrelationships between APEC and the existing sub-regional arrangements [ASEAN Free Trade Area (AFTA), Australia-New Zealand Closer Economic Relations Trade Agreement (ANZCERTA), and NAFTA] and to examine possible options to prevent obstacles to each other and to promote consistency in their relations" (APEC Secretariat 1994). In other words, the 1994 APEC meeting indicated a need for a free trade agreement for the Asia-Pacific region.

U.S. Perspectives of APEC

Even though APEC is often cast in economic terms, politics certainly play a major role in its founding. Many world political leaders (Australians Malcolm Fraser and Robert Hawke, Japanese Takeo Miki and Masayoshi Ohira, Korean Roh Tae Woo, and Thai Thanat Khoman) pushed the idea of APEC. A number of members of the U.S. Congress also supported the idea of APEC. Since the 1970s many people in U.S. leadership circles recognized the changed circumstances in the Asia-Pacific region and the

potential for responding to those circumstances by establishing a new institution. Senators John Glenn and William V. Roth Jr. and Congressman Lester Wolff endorsed the idea of APEC in the 1970s. In the late 1980s Senators Alan Cranston and Bill Bradley made proposals for Asia-Pacific intergovernmental cooperation prior to the Hawke initiative.

The United States supported the creation of APEC in large part because Americans and Canadians who advocated Asia-Pacific economic institutions in the 1980s wanted to open Japan and other Asian markets using multilateral, rather than bilateral, external pressures. This would boost the North American economies through their increased association with the dynamic east Asian economies and providing an international economic alternative to what some people perceived as a less and less open Europe. Several of the prominent Americans associated with such organizations as Pacific Trade and Development Forum (PAFTAD), the Pan-Pacific Community Association, and the successor U.S. Committee for Pacific Economic Cooperation had a deep interest in Japan and saw positive benefits of the U.S.-Japanese relationship in establishing a broader Asia-Pacific context.

APEC DECLARATION 2001

At the conclusion of the October 2001 meeting of the member countries of the Asia-Pacific Economic Cooperation, the APEC leaders outlined their vision for the next century in light of September 11, 2001, terrorist attacks and the rise of the Asia-Pacific region.

Meeting New Challenges in the New Century

1. We, the Economic Leaders of APEC, gathered today in Shanghai for the first time in the twenty-first century. We are here to explore ways to meet the new challenges confronting us. Convinced of the great potential of the Asia-Pacific region, we have resolved to achieve common prosperity through broader participation and closer cooperation.

2. Our meeting has taken place at a crucial juncture. The major world economies are experiencing a slowdown more severe than anticipated. Most economies in the Asia-Pacific region have experienced an economic downturn, with some emerging economies particularly affected by unfavorable external market conditions. In addition, the terrorist attack on the United States risks undermining some industries as well as consumer and investor confidence. In the long run, a major challenge for the Asia-Pacific community is to manage the profound changes brought forth by globalization and the New Economy and to benefit from the opportunities that abound.

3. As the premier forum for regional economic cooperation in the Asia Pacific, APEC is well suited to play a leading role in helping its

member economies embrace these opportunities and challenges. We wish to send a clear and strong message on the collective resolve of the Asia-Pacific community to counter terrorism. We are determined to reverse the current economic downturn and maintain public confidence at a time of uncertainty by fighting protectionism and committing to the launch of the new WTO round at the upcoming WTO Ministerial Conference. These efforts are consonant with and contribute to the pursuit of the APEC vision of peace, harmony and common prosperity.

4. Inspired by such a vision, we are determined to work together for a more dynamic and prosperous Asia Pacific in the new century by promoting sustainable economic growth, sharing the benefits of globalization and the New Economy, and advancing Trade and Investment Liberalization and Facilitation (TILF). To this end, we reaffirm our commitment to achieving the Bogor Goals of free and open trade and investment in the Asia Pacific by 2010 for developed economies and 2020 for developing economies. We have also charted the course for the development of APEC in its second decade and beyond by adopting the Shanghai Accord.

Source: APEC economic leaders' declaration: Meeting new challenges in the new century. (2001, October 21). Retrieved June 8, 2007, from www.ustr.gov/assets/Trade_Agreements/Regional/APEC/asset_upload_file986_3564.pdf

After APEC was founded the United States became one of the most active members, participating intensively in developing APEC's program of work, hosting the 1993 meeting at Blake Island. However, the U.S. government has not played an active role when APEC economies have been in crisis, including a currency crisis that plagued Thailand, Philippines, South Korea, Hong Kong, and Indonesia in 1997–1998. During the 1998 APEC meeting in Kuala Lumpur, Malaysia, the U.S. government merely worked through existing institutions, such as the World Bank, International Monetary Fund (IMF), and Asian Development Bank. Unlike Asian countries, such as China (which vowed not to devalue its yuan currency) and Japan (which proposed $30 billion to support economic recovery in Asia), the United States simply stood by and watched the crisis. However, when issues threatened U.S. national interests, the United States voiced its objections and fought back. For instance, when Prime Minister Mohamad Mahathir of Malaysia proposed that the East Asia Economic Caucus (EAEC), made up only of east Asian nations, meet in the 1990s, the United States strongly objected because it feared exclusion from regional councils and the loss of access to the resources offered by Asia's dynamic growth. At the 1996 APEC meeting in the Philippines, the United States placed highest priority on a goal that was of direct interest to U.S. business interests—to obtain APEC endorsement of elimination of tariffs on computers and telecommunications equipment at an upcoming meeting of the World Trade Organization (WTO). In the APEC leaders' declaration, economies of APEC "endorse initiatives for freer and nondiscriminatory trade in goods and services" (APEC Secretariat 1996). Once again, with President Clinton in attendance at the Philippines meeting, the U.S. goal was achieved.

During the post–Cold War era the United States, as the only remaining superpower, still needs the influence of an international institution such as APEC. President George W. Bush attended the 2001 APEC summit in Shanghai a month after the September 11, 2001, terrorist attacks on New York City and Washington, D.C., indicating the importance of the APEC summit for the United States. Although the APEC summit usually addresses only economic issues, the 2001 summit also addressed a global political agenda, including antiterrorist measures. The APEC leaders' declaration on counterterrorism reflected U.S. national interests. At APEC summits in 2004 and 2006 leaders, apparently pressured by President Bush's either-you-are-with-us-or-against-us foreign policy attitude, again addressed the issue of antiterrorism in their declaration.

Fundamental U.S. objectives in the Asia-Pacific region have been remarkably consistent over time. These objectives have included securing economic access to the region (e.g., opening Asian markets to U.S. goods), spreading value systems preferred by Americans (e.g., human rights and democracy), and preventing domination of the region by other powers (e.g., preventing Japan and China from being competitors of the United States). U.S. presidents have used APEC summits to gain international influence and affect world politics.

U.S. Unilateral Behavior and the Fate of APEC

Since the September 11, 2001, terrorist attacks the United States has been isolated on many fronts in international relations. The Bush administration's seeming disregard and distaste for international law and institutions, such as the United Nations, has illustrated the significant differences between U.S. unilateralism and European multilateralism, in particular in tensions between the United States and France and Germany. U.S. unilateralism has also created dissatisfaction among members of APEC. For example, during the 2004 APEC summit in Santiago, Chile, some members of APEC worried that APEC's focus—economics—had been eclipsed by President Bush's concern about security and the war on terrorism. Malaysian Prime Minister Abdullah Ahmad Badawi called for a deeper understanding of the causes of terrorism and stated, "Punitive action (alone) cannot really provide a permanent solution but will create more hardened criminals and for every one we kill, five more will emerge to continue their struggle" (David Williams 2004, 2).

Moreover, in 2004 President Bush wanted to add condemnation of nuclear proliferation by North Korea and Iran to the APEC leaders' declaration at the summit in Santiago, Chile. After meeting with leaders from China and South Korea, as well as Russian President Vladimir Putin, President Bush shouted at TV reporters, "The will is strong, the effort is united, and the message is clear to Mr. Kim Jong-il [North Korea's leader]: get rid of your nuclear weapons programs" (Harding and Taylor, 2004, 6). President Bush repeatedly mentioned the nuclear threats of North Korea and Iran to Asia-Pacific leaders; however, most APEC leaders were skeptical in light of Bush's erroneous claims about weapons of mass destruction (WMDs) in Iraq before the Iraq War (2003). When President Bush discovered that the final draft of the leaders' declaration did not condemn the nuclear threats of North Korea and Iran, he demanded that all people attending the banquet on the final day of the summit pass through U.S.-operated metal detectors (in fact, U.S. security services had a near-violent confrontation with Chilean police at the summit dinner of the previous night; Bush himself intervened to get his own secret service agents into the hall). In the end the banquet was attended only by APEC leaders, not even their spouses were allowed to attend. The U.S.

news media, including Cable News Network (CNN), generally covered the behavior of President Bush in a cautiously admiring tone, but other members of APEC laughed at Bush's demands. He seemed not to understand why APEC leaders refused to add his nuclear condemnation to their declaration. He did not realize that he had lost a lot of credibility among other world leaders because of his unilateral foreign policy, including his stance on the Iraq War.

Asian economies of APEC are able to choose alternative economic partners. That is, European countries have considered their interests unrepresented by APEC. Competition between North America and western Europe over Asia has escalated. In 1996 Europe and east Asia inaugurated the ASEM (Asia-Europe Meeting) in Bangkok, Thailand. APEC and the ASEM represent attempts by state policymaking elites of east Asia to consolidate the channels of economic and political communication with the other two developed regions of the world. By 2006, ASEM members including France and Germany, had a 50 percent global GDP, 60 percent world trade and 40 percent world population, comparable with 48 percent global GDP, 48 percent world trade and 40 percent world population in APEC, including the United States.

However, without more U.S. support for the economic and trade agenda of APEC, reaching the 1994 APEC goal of free trade among the developed member economies by 2010 and among all member economies by 2020 will be difficult. Because the U.S. security agenda dominated the 2004 and 2006 APEC summits, free trade was not the key issue despite being one of the hottest topics among other members of APEC.

A week after the 2004 APEC summit ASEAN+3—ASEAN and China, Japan, and South Korea—shocked the United States at a summit in Laos. ASEAN+3 heads agreed to a name change, as indicated by the chairman's statement, "We agreed to transform the ASEAN+3 summit into East Asia Summit (EAS) and to hold the first EAS in Malaysia in 2005" (A revealing melee . . . 2004, 14). The EAS originally had been proposed by former Prime Minister Mohamad Mahathir of Malaysia under the name "East Asia Economic Caucus" (EAEC) in the 1990s, but the United States had prevented its establishment. Subsequently, Chinese Premier Wen Jiaboa offered to host the second EAS; though it was actually held in the Philippines. With the world gross domestic product at $32.3 trillion and the world population at 6.2 billion, EAS has only $7 trillion GDP, compared with $19.7 trillion for APEC and $15 trillion for ASEM, and 2 billion people, compared with 2.6 billion for APEC and 2.3 billion for ASEM. Interestingly, India, Australia, and New Zealand were also invited to EAS, as a means to counterbalance the influence of the uninvited U.S. and to undermine the fundamental structure of APEC. Unilateralist policies pursued by President George Bush resulted in creation of

the EAS at the Laos summit. It is possible that the creation of the EAS will one day be seen as a turning point, marking the decline of U.S. influence on the world stage.

Unryu Suganuma

See also IMF, World Bank, and IDB, U.S. Role in

Further Reading

Allen, Mike. (2004). At Summit, Bush Sets Sights on Alliances. (2004, November 22). *Washington Post*, p. A16

APEC Secretariat. (1993). *Leaders' declaration—Blake Island*. Singapore: Author.

APEC Secretariat. (1994). *APEC economic leaders' declaration of common resolve*. Singapore: Author.

APEC Secretariat. (1995). *APEC economic leaders' declaration for action*. Singapore: Author.

APEC Secretariat. (1996). *APEC economic leaders' declaration: From vision to action*. Singapore: Author.

APEC Secretariat. (1997). *APEC economic leaders' declaration: Connecting the APEC community*. Singapore: Author.

APEC Secretariat. (1998). *APEC economic leaders' declaration: Strengthening the foundations for growth*. Singapore: Author.

APEC Secretariat. (1999). *The Auckland challenge: APEC economic leaders' declaration*. Singapore: Author.

APEC Secretariat. (2000). *APEC economic leaders' declaration: Delivering to the community*. Singapore: Author.

APEC Secretariat. (2000). *APEC getting result for business*. Singapore: Author.

APEC Secretariat. (2001). *APEC economic leaders' declaration: Meeting new challenges in the new century*. Singapore: Author.

APEC Secretariat. (2002). *APEC economic leaders' declaration*. Singapore: Author.

APEC Secretariat. (2003). *Bangkok declaration on partnership for the future*. Singapore: Author.

APEC Secretariat. (2004). *Trade facilitation and trade liberalisation: From Shanghai to Bogor*. Singapore: Author.

APEC Secretariat. (2004). *12th APEC economic leaders' meeting: Santiago declaration, "one community, our future."* Singapore: Author.

ASEAN finalizes plans for pan-Asian bloc. (2004, November 30.). *Japan Times*. p. 1

A revealing melee in Chile. (2004, November 27). *Japan Times*. p. 14

Baker, R. (1998). The United States and APEC regime building. In V. K. Aggarwal & C. E. Morrison (Eds.), *Asia-Pacific crossroads: Regime creation and the future of APEC*. pp. 165–189. New York: St. Martin's Press.

Bergsten, C. F., & Noland, M. (1993). Introduction and overview. In C. F. Bergsten & M. Noland (Eds.), *Pacific dynamism and international economic system*. pp. 3–13. Washington, DC: Institute for International Economics.

Cumings, B. (1993). Rimspeak; or, the discourse of the "Pacific Rim." In A. Dirlik (Ed.), *What is in a rim? Critical perspectives on the Pacific region idea*. pp. 29–47. Boulder, CO: Westview Press.

Dua, A., & Esty, D. C. (1997). *Sustaining the Asia Pacific miracle.* Washington, DC: Institute for International Economics.

Harding, J. and Taylor, P. (2004, November 21) Hand-on Bush practices Pacific Rim diplomacy. In *Financial Times.* p. 6

Morrison, C. E. (1998). APEC: The evolution of an institution. In V. K. Aggarwal & C. E. Morrison (Eds.), *Asia-Pacific crossroads: Regime creation and the future of APEC.* pp. 1–22. New York: St. Martin's Press.

Ruland, J. (Ed.). (2002). *Asia-Pacific Economic Cooperation (APEC): The final decade.* Richmond, UK: Curzon.

Suganuma, U. (2002). Asia-Pacific Economic Cooperation forum. In D. Levinson & K. Christensen (Eds.), *Encyclopedia of modern Asia* (Vol. 1, pp. 169–170). New York: Charles Scribner's Sons.

Williams, David. (2004). APEC talk tough but ducks free trade. (2004, November 23). *Courier Mail,* p. 2.

World Bank. (1993). *The east Asian miracle: World Bank policy research report.* Washington, DC: Author.

Yamamoto, Y., & Kikuchi, T. (1998). Japan's approach to APEC and regime creation in the Asia-Pacific. In V. K. Aggarwal & C. E. Morrison (Eds.), *Asia-Pacific crossroads: Regime creation and the future of APEC.* pp. 191–211. New York: St. Martin's Press.

Relations with Latin America, U.S.

In the twenty-first century Latin American nations are increasingly asserting their sociopolitical and economic independence from the heavy-handed hegemony the United States has exercised over the entire region since 1823.

In February 2001 U.S. president George W. Bush met with newly elected Mexican president Vicente Fox to discuss a range of issues, including free trade, drug trafficking, and a U.S. immigration policy agreeable to both domestic constituencies. In March 2007 President Bush visited five Latin American countries to shore up relations with the region, negotiate trade agreements, and counter the growing influence of Venezuela's populist president Hugo Chavez.

During the intervening years U.S. attention had been turned toward responding to the terrorist attacks of September 11, 2001. As a result Latin America and the Caribbean have received very little attention from their northern neighbor. This pattern of significant attention and benign neglect is by no means a new characteristic of hemispheric relations. The relationship between the United States and its southern neighbors vacillated during the nineteenth century, the early twentieth century, the Cold War, the post–Cold War era, and since September 11, 2001.

In 1823 President James Monroe gave a speech in which he congratulated the newly independent nations of South America and warned that the hemisphere was no longer open to European colonial endeavors. His Monroe Doctrine became the basis for U.S. foreign policy for the next two centuries. For the remainder of the nineteenth century the United States was largely concerned with internal expansion through purchase or conquest. One of the most notable expansions came as a result of the defeat of Mexico in 1848. Under the Treaty of Guadalupe Hidalgo, the United States paid Mexico $15 million in return for much of the West and the Southwest.

For the remainder of the nineteenth century most of Latin America was mired in internal struggles over the postcolonial direction. Divisions over whether to adopt a market or a mercantilist economic system, a monarchy or a republic, and the role of the Catholic Church separated much of the region.

Waves of European immigration, the issue of slavery, and the Industrial Revolution directed U.S. attention inward until the end of the century. Most scholars characterize this period of U.S. history as one of isolationism. Isolationism suggests a level of intent in the direction of policy that is not supported by the historical record. Instead, the leadership and popular opinion focused on a series of domestic issues. In addition, the country was militarily and economically unable to support aggressive action abroad.

New Military Might

With the Spanish-American War of 1898 the United States emerged as a military power capable of defeating a declining European power and established a longstanding presence in the Caribbean in Cuba and Puerto Rico. The United States justified the war on the grounds of liberal concerns about human rights abuses in Cuba, but the war also provided the United States with a naval base that would be relevant in the aftermath of September 11, 2001.

For the Cuban nationals who had been fighting a guerrilla war against Spain for decades, the U.S. victory offered the hope of legitimate independence. This hope was quickly dashed as the United States established a protectorate and semipermanent control over Cuban commercial and military relations through the Platt Amendment in 1904. The resentment of explicit U.S. control over Cuba would be exploited with great success during and after the 1959 revolution in Cuba.

President Franklin D. Roosevelt's "Good Neighbor Policy" represented a shift away from the previous policy of military, political and economic intervention in the region. His goal was to create more harmonious relations between the United States and other nations in the hemisphere. In the early 1950s President Dwight D. Eisenhower sought to differentiate his foreign policy from that of his predecessors with a greater emphasis on covert action and nuclear force buildup. This policy was first tested with the CIA intervention in Guatemala in 1953. The United States was concerned about the election of leftist Jacobo Arbenz and his economic policies. In June 1954 the CIA supported a Guatemalan colonel who, through a combination of psychological operations, was able to force Arbenz from power. This power play was viewed as a success by the U.S. intelligence community because it achieved its goal with a low financial and human cost.

U.S. concern about the spread of leftist ideology centered on

Cuba after the 1959 revolution. The failed Bay of Pigs invasion (April 1961) and the Cuban Missile Crisis (October 1962) increased Cold War tensions between the two countries.

Throughout most of the 1970s the United States continued to support right-wing dictatorships in Central and South America against the threat of Soviet influence. In 1979 the U.S.-supported Nicaraguan strongman Anastasio Somoza was overthrown by the Sandanista National Liberation Front (FSLN), a broad coalition led by the Sandinistas. The Sandinistas would control Nicaragua for most of the decade and undertake a broad program of socio-economic reform supported in part by Cuba. The Nicaraguan and Cuban governments provided military and economic aid to guerrillas in neighboring El Salvador and Guatemala. During the 1980s Central America became the new battleground in the Cold War. The administration of President Ronald Reagan came to office explicitly disavowing President Jimmy Carter's foreign policy emphasis on human rights. Under the new president every attempt would be made to root out the sources of left-wing insurgency in the region. The Reagan administration used covert operations and direct military aid to prop up governments in the region and to undermine the Sandinista government.

In South America a dramatic political change began to take place. In Argentina, Brazil, Chile, and Peru authoritarian military regimes were gradually replaced by democratically elected governments. Political parties and civil society emerged or were strengthened. This trend would spread throughout South America and ultimately Latin America by the end of the decade. Most nations in the hemisphere had adopted periodic, free, and fair elections, universal suffrage, and a minimum level of civil rights.

However, as nations were shifting to procedural democracy, the economies of the region were collapsing in what would be the worst depression in memory. The cause of the depression was twofold: High levels of external debt, coupled with a recession in the United States and elsewhere in the West, made demand for Latin American exports less attractive. Nations were expected to pay more money to service their debt but were generating less revenue from exports to do so. In 1982 Mexico issued a temporary moratorium on debt payment. In 1986 the Peruvian president limited debt service to 10 percent of foreign earnings. On top of the external crisis, inflation at home had reached triple and quadruple digits in some countries. In response to the crisis international financial institutions and the United States implemented a neoliberal economic reform model that would allow nations to restructure foreign debt in exchange for significant macroeconomic changes. These changes included making significant cuts in public spending, laying off public-sector workers, privatizing state-owned resources, eliminating barriers to trade, and promoting significant foreign investment. The import-substitution industrialization model of eco-

nomic development, which had dominated the region since the end of World War II, was rapidly abandoned. The results were mixed. In some countries foreign investment increased significantly, as did economic growth, but the new policies seemed to have little immediate impact on the dire poverty that kept tens of millions searching for clean water to drink and enough food to eat.

Improving Economy

Gradually the economic situation improved against the backdrop of increasingly transparent and accountable political institutions. As the century drew to a close Latin America approached the new millennium in a position to take advantage of its new position. U.S. foreign policy under the Bill Clinton and George W. Bush administrations took a two-pronged approach, emphasizing political reforms toward democracy and neoliberal market reforms. Frequently these policies and the aid that accompanied them contradicted the antiguerrilla policies promoted in Colombia and Peru and throughout Central America. The traditional goal of political stability continued to outweigh larger concerns about human rights violations. This policy disconnect separated the average citizen from the broader U.S. goals of political and economic reform.

After the Cold War, people of Latin America grew increasingly discontent with the political and economic model recommended by the United States and the International Monetary Fund/World Bank. Patterns of income distribution had not improved dramatically, and poverty rates remained largely stagnant. This discontent was reflected in the election of left-wing populist leaders: Hugo Chavez in Venezuela, Evo Morales in Bolivia, Luiz Inácio Lula da Silva in Brazil, and Alan Garcia in Peru. In Nicaragua one-time Sandinista leader Daniel Ortega was elected president. These elections elicited popular support for the new leaders as the new leaders gave voice to the discontent with the economic model and the political institutions that had failed to improve the quality of life for the average citizen in Latin America. However, with the notable exception of Chavez in Venezuela and Morales in Bolivia, most of the leaders have maintained the economic policies of their predecessors, publicly criticizing the International Monetary Fund and U.S. policy but making little movement away from the largely neoliberal policy model.

The early twenty-first century represents a great opportunity for the region. Greater social, political, and economic independence from the United States exists, as do new relationships with Europe and China. Nonetheless, Latin America must rely on preferential trade deals to get its exports to U.S. markets. More important, the issue of immigration remains unresolved, although a new Mexican

president and a lame-duck U.S. president with opposition control of the legislature suggest a rare opportunity. Strong leadership will be needed from all quarters.

David M. Goldberg

See also Drug Trade and the War on Drugs; Immigration to the United States; Special Relationship (U.S.-Mexico)

Further Reading

Gilderhus, M. (2000). *The second century: U.S.-Latin American relations since 1889*. Wilmington, DE: Scholarly Resources Books.

Goldberg, D. (2007). Caricom and the Haitian crisis of 2004. In T. Legler, S. Lean, & D. Boniface (Eds.), *Promoting democracy in the Americas*. Baltimore, MD: Johns Hopkins University Press.

Skidmore, T., & Smith, P. (2007). *Modern Latin America* (6th ed.). New York: Oxford University Press.

Smith, P. (2005). *Democracy in Latin America: Political change in comparative perspective*. New York: Oxford University Press.

Valenzuela, A. (2005). Beyond benign neglect: Washington's diplomatic myopia. *Current History 104*(679), 58–63.

Relations with the European Union, U.S.

During the Cold War there was basic agreement about the threat of Communism and some of the methods to face it, but since September 11th U.S. and European security perspectives and concerns have diverged and may well remain so.

Recently the United States has demonstrated an adversarial attitude toward a more assertive and integrated Europe, especially as expressed by the European Union (EU), an international economic and political union. In particular, the political and economic establishment that has controlled the decision-making mechanisms in the United States since the terrorist attacks of September 11, 2001, considers the move toward a deeper EU foreign policy to be costly to U.S. interests.

This situation seems to be a mild case of déjà vu. An influential sector of the U.S. leadership, confirmed after the 2004 reelection of President George W. Bush, has been experiencing the same feeling experienced at the beginning of the deepening process of the EU that led to implementation of the Maastricht Treaty in 1992 (which created the EU) and the adoption of the euro as the common currency of twelve countries.

At the beginning of the 1990s Washington did not take these EU trends and movements too seriously. Experts believed that transforming the European Community (also known as the "Common Market") into the EU and adopting the euro would fail. The most that the U.S. establishment was ready to accept was that the European experiment would be at least as slow as the painful evolution of the Common Market from the late 1950s to the mid-1980s. Experts predicted that the Europeans would be incapable of getting their act together.

After the cohesiveness of the still-imperfect three EU "pillars" (economic and social policies; military and foreign policies, and police and judicial matters) and the efficacy of the euro became evident, this leading sector in the United States proceeded to catch up with evolving events. The analysts who had warned in the 1990s about the seriousness of the European process were vindicated.

The terrorist attacks of September 11 caught Washington flat-footed in many dimensions, particularly military and intelligence dimensions. However, it did not surprise the White House and the Pentagon in their ideological perspectives. In spite of what could be expected, the new design of foreign policy, as expressed in successive declarations of President Bush and his advisers, was solidly grounded on a cohesive, fundamental U.S. doctrine that can be traced back to the Kennan memorandum of 1947 by which

the U.S. policy towards the Soviet Union was set. By a combination of factors and beliefs, the rise of the European process and its deepening, simultaneously with its unstoppable widening, began to be the target first of uneasiness and then of preoccupation and animosity and finally of fear.

The euro ceased to be the subject of badly intentioned op-ed articles and think-tank analyses as a potential source for the resurgence of European confrontations and even wars. It became a well-identified enemy, labeled as the cause of the fall of the value of the dollar.

Paradoxically, the U.S. pressure of past decades on the Europeans to share the burden in defense spending has given way to a call for what appears to be a serious theoretical design of a real common foreign and security policy. The EU first responded with the creation of the position of high representative of the common foreign and security policy, a post entrusted to Javier Solana, who was drafted out of his job as secretary-general of the North Atlantic Treaty Organization (NATO). Now the EU seems to be poised for serious development of a foreign policy.

Deepening into a more historical perspective, the U.S. attitude today and the U.S. attitude of satisfaction at being present at the creation of the European Community are starkly different. The initial encouragement of U.S. leaders (such as Presidents Dwight D. Eisenhower and John F. Kennedy) in the 1950s and 1960s for the process of European integration as a mechanism complementary to NATO has been transformed today into an erratic, contradictory, and aggressive policy of what was sarcastically called "disaggregation" (separation into component parts).

Washington has turned upside-down the opportunity to end the artificial European division caused by the reapportionment of War World II by executing an act of political justice with the ambitious and costly enlargement of the EU. The opportunity has been manipulated by the U.S. leadership, most significantly since September 11 and especially since the split of European attitudes toward the Iraqi War (2003). The "new Europe" invented by then-Secretary of Defense Donald Rumsfeld has been labeled as a sort of dissidence movement opposed to Brussels (seat of the EU executive body), following the cues of the White House.

Dollars and euros shown balanced on a scale. Source: istock/José Luis Gutiérrez.

The sensitive issue of the future membership of Turkey in the EU was erratically and undiplomatically converted into a weapon of pressure brandished by the U.S. Department of Defense and Department of State at the worst time. The issue was raised not only at the height of the Iraq War controversy, but also during the final months of the evaluations of the credentials of Turkey for EU membership. Brussels and some key European capitals replied sternly to the bad timing and lack of diplomacy.

The lack of any reference to the EU in any fundamental declarations or speeches by President Bush since September 11 has been a confirmation of the fundamental distrust not only of multilateral schemes of integration and cooperation, but also of treaties and organizations to which the United States does not belong. This fact does not mean, however, that President Bush has demonstrated ease in settings such as the United Nations or even the World Trade Organization.

This situation contrasts to the energetic admonition of the Bush administration against an autonomous foreign and defense policy for the EU, reacting to the suggestion made by then-German chancellor Gerhard Schroder in looking for additional forums to deal with European security. Bush insisted that NATO is the only valid setting.

The insertion of the NATO issue into discussions of the development of an autonomous EU foreign and defense policy contributes a concrete anchoring for the negative assessment of the European design. Far from making vague declarations covering domestic interests of dominance, when the United States op-

poses an assertive Europe, a victim is seen by the United States as unnecessary collateral damage: NATO. All the history and accomplishments of the organization, in addition to its current capabilities, are used in rationalizing against the development of an independent defense and security mechanism for Europe. This strategy sanitizes the rather pragmatic principles of the alliance and misses several historical points that not only respond to innate patterns of U.S. foreign policy, but also reflect important chapters of foreign policy practices.

In essence, the United States seems to consider too many dimensions of the new EU to be detrimental to U.S. national interests. The U.S. attitude sometimes looks like a zero-sum (relating to a situation in which a gain for one side entails a corresponding loss for the other side) calculation: If the EU wins something and makes some progress, these advances must be at the cost of a U.S. vital interest.

Means to Oppose

In what ways do the U.S. leadership and its allies elect to oppose the process of a deeper EU integration and especially its project of an autonomous foreign and security policy? Many ways exist. Some are blunt and open; others are covert and discreet.

The usual way is the perennial Roman method of divide and conquer. This method was used heavily during the months leading to the 2003 Iraq War, and it was helped by a cadre of European

governments and individuals that expressed publicly its support for Bush, making any cohesive European front difficult if not impossible. This cadre coincides with the governments of countries that showed a deeper reluctance to accept the reformed voting system in the council of ministers, from a weighted vote in the Treaty of Nice to the double majority (55 percent of countries and 65 percent of the population) combination in the Constitution. Even today some members of the pro-Bush camp during the months before the Iraq War who subsequently lost power are still executing a campaign that has as a limited result the endemic division of the European front.

Assessment

The U.S. perception of an autonomous foreign, security, and defense policy for the EU is almost at the end of a downward move in a roller-coaster cycle. After encouraging European integration and backing that integration with military guarantees at the beginning, the United States descended into a deep sense of disinterest, disdain, and then economic concern for what appeared to be the building of "Fortress Europe" in the early 1990s. Washington met this challenge in a competitive fashion and contributed to the establishment of other free-trade mechanisms designed to protect some spheres of influence in Latin America and the Pacific. The cloudy atmosphere inaugurating the new century has given way to a more aggressive attitude to the EU integration process and especially to the design of a European autonomous foreign, security, and defense policy. September 11 and its consequences have propelled the U.S. mission of dominating the world after the Cold War.

However, the U.S. leadership seems to be poised to execute a mild correction to this trend, forced by the limitations of military and economic power, as well as by the worldwide erosion (if not absolute disappearance) of persuasion and influence as "soft power" techniques. With U.S. recognition of the useful alliance with a stronger EU, the gap across the Atlantic may shrink considerably. Nonetheless, that shrinkage will depend on the depth and substance of the recognition of an autonomous EU foreign policy by the U.S. leadership and the nature of the coordinated missions to be implemented in substitution for the existing unilateral strategy of its variance conformed as a coalition of the willing. The recent past and the idiosyncrasies of the U.S. political culture do not seem to predict a too ambitious outcome.

EXTRACT FROM TRANSATLANTIC DECLARATION ON EC-U.S. RELATIONS, 1990

Perhaps one of the strongest diplomatic relationships the United States has is the one it shares with the European Union, and the European Commission (EC) as its executive body.

Common Goals
The United States of America and the European Community and its Member States solemnly reaffirm their determination further to strengthen their partnership in order to:

❑ Support democracy, the rule of law and respect for human rights and individual liberty, and promote prosperity and social progress world-wide;

❑ Safeguard peace and promote international security, by cooperating with other nations against aggression and coercion, by contributing to the settlement of conflicts in the world and by reinforcing the role of the United Nations and other international organizations;

❑ Pursue policies aimed at achieving a sound world economy marked by sustained economic growth with low inflation, a high level of employment, equitable social conditions, in a framework of international stability;

❑ Promote market principles, reject protectionism and expand, strengthen and further open the multilateral trading system;

❑ Carry out their resolve to help developing countries by all appropriate means in their efforts towards political and economic reforms;

❑ Provide adequate support, in cooperation with other states and organizations, to the nations of Eastern and Central Europe undertaking economic and political reforms and encourage their participation in the multilateral institutions of international trade and finance.

Principles of U.S.–EC Partnership
To achieve their common goals, the European Community and its Member States and the United States of America will inform and consult each other on important matters of common interest, both political and economic, with a view to bringing their positions as close as possible, without prejudice to their respective independence. In appropriate international bodies, in particular, they will seek close cooperation.

The EC-US partnership will, moreover, greatly benefit from the mutual knowledge and understanding acquired through regular consultations as described in this Declaration.

Source: Transatlantic declaration on EC-U.S. relations. (1990). Retrieved March 22, 2007 from ec.europa.eu/comm/external_relations/us/ intro/index.htm

Nonetheless, the pressure for an understanding comes from the overwhelming amount of EU-U.S. trade, which flows at all times and with a normal pace without problems in spite of disputes and threats of sanctions. At the end of the day, an agreement is found, among other reasons because a notable two-way investment helps a lot and ends up imposing its own logic. The two regions are each other's most important partner in trade and investment, making the economic interests the most significant dimension of the transatlantic relationship.

Other issues, especially foreign and security policy, are not so simple. Both sides simply have to accept that they have to "agree to disagree." Both have to come to terms with the evidence that this trend will not be temporary—it will be permanent. During the Cold War a basic agreement existed regarding the common threat and some of the methods to face it. Now the situation is different. And this situation causes an uncomfortable feeling. However, that feeling should not mean that it is catastrophic.

Still, if a pragmatic meeting of the minds occurs between the U.S. and European leaderships, observers may be tempted to believe that the concept of West is still a reality. However, if the U.S. electorate continues to exert pressure to favor an even, unilateralist U.S. policy, distrustful of European initiatives, while Europeans back a hardening of defense and security policies, following a more autonomous path, one may conclude that the West is not as cohesive as it once was believed to be. The gap between the two regions might be as wide as the split of a civilization into two branches, making cooperation a dubious enterprise. The outcome depends not only on the evolution of popular attitudes, but also on effective political and intellectual leadership.

Joaquín Roy

See also IMF, World Bank, IDB, U.S. role in; NATO, U.S. role in; Relations with the United Nations, U.S.; Special Relationship (U.S.-U.K.); World War II

Further Reading

Asmus, R. D., Blinken, A. J., & Gordon, P. H. (2005, January/February). Nothing to fear. *Foreign Affairs,* 174–177.

Balis, C., & Collett, E. (2003, April 16). Europe's constitutional contentions. *Euro-Focus, 9*(4).

Balis, C. V., & Serfaty, S. (Eds.). (2004). *Visions of America and Europe: September 11, Iraq, and transatlantic relations.* Washington, DC: Center for Strategic and International Studies Press.

Burghardt, G. (2000). A transatlantic agenda for 2010. *Transatlantic Internationale Politik, 2,* 31–34.

Chalmers, M. (2001). The Atlantic burden-sharing debate—Widening or fragmenting? *International Affairs, 77*(3), 569–585.

Cimbalo, J. (2004, November/December). Saving NATO from Europe. *Foreign Affairs, 83*(6), 111–120.

Daalder, I. (2001). Are the United States and Europe heading for divorce? *International Affairs, 77*(3), 553–567.

Drozdiak, W. (2005, January/February). The North Atlantic drift. *Foreign Affairs,* 88–98.

Hunter, R. E. (2004, September/October). A forward-looking partnership: NATO and the future of alliances. *Foreign Affairs,* 13–18.

Kennedy, C., & Bouton, M. M. (2002, November/December). The real trans-Atlantic gap. *Foreign Policy,* 66–74.

Kupchan, C. A. (2004–2005, Winter). The travails of union: The American experience and its implications for Europe. *Survival, 46*(4), 103–120.

Lambert, R. (2001, March/April). Misunderstanding each other. *Foreign Affairs, 82*(2), 62–74.

Markovits, A. (1985). *On antiamericanism in West Germany.* Cambridge, MA: Harvard University Press.

Moisi, D. (2001, July/August). The real crisis over the Atlantic. *Foreign Affairs, 80*(4), 149–153.

Moravsik, A. (2003, July/August). Striking a new transatlantic bargain. *Foreign Affairs, 82*(4), 74–89.

Niblett, R., & Mix, D. (2005, January 31). Europe in 2005: A distracted partner. *Euro-Focus, 11*(1).

Peel, Q. (2004, December 2). Euroscepticism spreads west. *Financial Times.*

Roy, J. (2005, March). Spain's return to "old Europe": Background and consequences of the March 11 and 14, 2004 terrorist attacks and elections. Miami European Union Center. Retrieved April 12, 2007, from http://www.miami.edu/eucenter/royaznarfinal.pdf

Serfaty, S. (2004, June 1). Purpose and commitment. *Euro-Focus, 10*(2).

Tucker, R. W., & Hendrickson, D. C. (2004, November/December). The sources of American legitimacy. *Foreign Affairs, 83*(6), 17–32.

Relations with the United Nations, U.S.

Many nations see the United States as having little or no interest in the U.N. and believe that the U.S. uses the U.N. for its own ends. But both the U.S. and the U.N. need each other to retain global credibility.

Global institutions such as the United Nations (U.N.), when properly structured and cartelized, ensure good relations among member nations. However, the identity of each member is paramount to that nation, which sometimes minimizes that nation's commitment to other members of the institution. The challenge of cooperation is increased because such an institution is supposed to comprise all actions that one member can take against another via a unified communication procedure to be accepted by all members. Such an arrangement also introduces a power struggle among members as each legitimately protects its interests. The relationship between the United States and the U.N. is a dexterous combination of compliment and challenge.

Two schools of thought exist regarding U.S-U.N. relations. The basic argument of the first school, the Americentric ideology, holds that any attempt by the United States to adhere to the rules of the U.N. translates to the United States surrendering sovereignty to this weak, inconsistent, and socialist global institution. This ideology further describes the U.N. as an international malignancy, undermining free societies, providing a platform for racism, and transferring wealth from the industrialized North to the less-developed South.

The second school of thought, which speaks mostly for the developing world, argues that the United States has little or no interest in the U.N. and that the former uses the latter to achieve its political and military goals only when a U.N. resolution advances U.S. interests.

Brief History

Established in 1945 with only fifty-one member nations, the U.N. after World War II was the closest thing to a global government the world had ever seen. However, the U.N. must not be mistaken for a world government, although the U.N.'s charter does make it unique. The charter is based on the principles that all countries are equal and sovereign under international law regardless of size, form of government, political ideology, and population.

The U.N. has played a prominent role in international security

over the years. The U.N., as a symbol of international peace and order, provides a forum where nations resolve their differences to reach agreement on bilateral and/or multilateral issues. Additionally, the universality of its membership, which has increased to nearly two hundred nations, has helped to normalize relationships among nations. It provides a platform for international negotiations to seek economic growth, promotes better relationships, makes peace through its peacekeeping mission, and provides security as nations, especially in the Third World, make the transition from military to democratic governance.

U.S. Self-interests and U.N. Universalism

The United States, like other member nations, has one vote in the General Assembly. However, the United States (along with France, Britain, Russia, and China) is also a permanent member of the Security Council, which has veto power over U.N. resolutions. The U.S.-U.N. relationship is like roller coaster: It undulates depending on the issues at stake at any given time. The United States uses its financial muscle not only to dictate to the U.N. but also to influence financially disadvantaged countries to support U.S. interests despite the democratic principles of the General Assembly. For example, over the years many Third World countries have complained that the United States has too much power at the U.N. because the U.N. is effective only when the interests of the United States are at stake, especially in international security affairs. However, when Third World countries use the U.N. platform as a forum to criticize the United States, the United States shows its displeasure by withholding its U.N. dues, which sometimes surpass $1 billion. (The United States is the largest financial contributor to the U.N.) Therefore, it was not surprising when the United States withdrew its participation from the United Nations Educational, Scientific, and Cultural Organization (UNESCO) in 1980 because of a disagreement. Indeed, for years afterward the United States failed to pay dues to the U.N. despite criticisms from U.S. allies who accused the United States of not honoring its international

commitments. (The United States resolved to honor its financial commitments with renegotiated terms for the future.)

Kofi Annan, U.N., and U.S. Relations

The U.S. Congress also voiced discontentment over Boutros Boutros-Ghali of Egypt, who was U.N. secretary-general from 1992 to 1996. This discontentment led to his being replaced by a favorite of the United States, Kofi Annan of Ghana. Annan was secretary-general from 1997 to 2006. Despite the initial support of Annan by the United States, he, too, experienced his share of demands and attempts at control by the United States. Although

Annan conformed to the course of the United States by reforming the U.N. through budget cuts and internal restructuring, the United States was not pleased with the $64 billion U.N.-Iraq oil-for-food program. Critics of the U.N. and Annan, including the U.S. Congress and persons such as Pat Buchanan (former Republican Party presidential aspirant and ultraconservative political pundit) and Senator Norm Coleman, faulted the U.S.-educated Annan for lax management of the program. Annan's secretaryship was tainted by $1.5 billion in kickbacks to the regime of Saddam Hussein.

In his 2006 farewell address, Annan criticized the United States for its love-hate relationship with the U.N. He insisted that the most powerful nation on Earth must obey the principles of the U.N. Charter, arguing that "if America remains true to

EXCERPT FROM U.S. DEPARTMENT OF STATE VISION STATEMENT ON WORKING WITHIN THE UNITED NATIONS

Like many nations, the United States participates in organizations to advance national security, foreign policy interests, and to promote U.S. values. Below are the three guiding principles, as outlined by the U.S. State Department under President George W. Bush's administration, to participation in the United Nations.

Principle #1: We want the United Nations to live up to the vision of its founders.

America's leadership can mobilize like-minded nations and multilateral institutions to stand up for common principles. We have seen this outcome, for example, in the war against terrorism, efforts to protect refugees and provide humanitarian aid, and the consensus that world leaders reached in Monterrey, Mexico, on the most effective ways to finance development.

Americans want us to make sure the U.N. and its many agencies hold fast to founding principles. This is true whether the objective is to disarm Iraq, promote peace in the region, or ensure that the elected members of the Commission on Human Rights (CHR) respect, protect, and promote human rights. The credibility of the CHR rightfully came under attack after Libya was elected chair in 2003. We had opposed that nomination; we are now working within the Commission to make sure its actions reflect its mandate and uphold the principles elaborated in the Universal Declaration of Human Rights and other international agreements. A revitalized CHR will find that it has the support of Americans and others around the world.

Principle #2: We seek multilateralism that is effective.

Americans want us to make sure the U.N. is doing a good job of preserving international peace; advancing freedom, human rights, democratic institutions, good governance, and sustainable development; and improving health, nutrition, and education for those in desperate need. When it does a good job, we will continue to be supportive. When it falls short, we will say so. The U.S. government will continue to defend our country and promote its values independently as need be, of course; but we will not hesitate to work with the Security Council when collective action is useful or justified to meet threats to international peace and security and the promotion of democracy.

One way to make the U.N. more effective is for countries that share its founding principles to become increasingly engaged in its work. We will encourage these countries to play stronger roles in the CHR to ensure that its members are firmly and actively committed to human rights. We are also encouraging the hiring of more American citizens at every level of the United Nations. By vigorously engaging more Americans in the work of the U.N., we can be more confident that our values and interests are represented fairly and the work is results oriented and rooted in founding purposes—particularly when it comes to peace and security.

Principle #3: We want good stewardship of U.N. resources.

As we strive to make the work of the U.N. more effective, we must not neglect scrutiny of its management and finances. We must meet our pledge to American taxpayers to ensure their dollars are spent wisely. We will continue to promote meaningful reforms that will make the U.N. more efficient and effective in the future.

Source: Vision statement: U.S. multilateral diplomacy and the U.N.: Our principles and priorities. (2007). Retrieved June 8, 2007, from http://www.state.gov/p/io/c9703.htm

its principles, including in the struggle against terrorism," then it must respect the rule of law. He insisted that anytime "military force is used, the world at large will consider it legitimate only when convinced that it is being used for the right purpose...in accordance with broadly accepted norms." Annan, who opposed the invasion of Iraq (2003) by the administration of President George W. Bush, argued that the U.S. war on Iraq has created more terrorists than the United States claims to be killing. However, the Americentric school of thought maintains that the war is in the U.S. interests, which are superior to the interests of the rest of the world.

To Annan's critics, his legacy will be a "failed leadership." Buchanan, for example, insisted that the United States must not listen to "a UN bureaucrat from a failed state, Ghana [who] is telling us that US soldiers must be subjected to prosecution by a UN war-crimes tribunal with jurisdictions we have never accepted" (Buchanan 2004, para. 3). U.S. soldiers do not serve under the command of any other country when the United States is part of a U.N. peacekeeping mission.

Ignoring the U.N.

Some people in the United States regard the U.N. as an anti-democratic institution formed to block the good intentions of the United States toward the rest of the world. To such people the U.N. is irrelevant to the development of the United States; therefore, the United States must ignore the U.N. because the so-called communist activities of the U.N. do not serve the interests of the world's only superpower. In fact, during the Cold War both political blocs—east and west—saw the U.N. as irrelevant when it came to the interests of either the Soviet Union or the United States. "The UN appeared somewhat irrelevant in a world order structured by two opposing alliance blocs" (Goldstein and Pevehouse 2006, 260).

This school of thought argues that, apart from the United States, the other four permanent members of the Security Council are "socialist or communist nations" and that the U.N. as a body does not provide much security to the world. Although the U.N. Charter says the body exists to "practice tolerance" and to help nations live together in peace as good neighbors, those people who think the U.N. is irrelevant to the United States argue that the noble ideals of the U.N. over the decades have proven useless and that, in fact, the U.N. poses a threat to democracy and freedom. The unflinching support of Israel by the United States has on many occasions marred the relations between the U.N. and United States as the latter always rejects any U.N. resolution that directly or indirectly condemns Israel. For example, the United

The United Nations headquarters in New York City. Source: istock/ Jeremy Edwards.

States saw the Durban (South Africa) Conference against racism in 2001 as a "horror of racism aimed against Israel" and therefore withdrew its delegates, a withdrawal that threatened the viability of the conference.

International politics does not revolve around truth and morality but rather around interest, power, and cooperation. These three variables tend to work against the U.N. because a country does not surrender its sovereignty when it joins the U.N. For example, anytime U.S. interests are at stake, Americans are quick to view the U.N. as an impediment to its growth and therefore declare the U.N. irrelevant. Just before the United States invaded Iraq for allegedly possessing weapons of mass destruction (WMDs), the U.N. failed to coerce the Bush administration into respecting the provisions of the U.N. Charter. And while the United States has

criticized the U.N. for failing to impose sanctions on nations that are that are trying to acquire biological, chemical, and nuclear weapons, the United States possesses these weapons and continues to improve their potency.

U.N. and U.S. Influence and Unity

The United States cannot totally ignore the diplomatic weight of the U.N. Each needs the other to retain its credibility. For example, the U.N. swiftly condemned the September 11, 2001, terrorist attacks on the United States and regarded the attacks as a "threat to international peace and security." Members of the U.N. not only offered their support to the United States but also formed a counterterrorism committee to fight international terrorism despite the debate about the definition of "terrorism." The unified U.N. action was appreciated by the United States. "We [United States] have a right to act on our own . . . but we really need a united front against this," an official of the U.S. State Department stated (Jordan 2001). The duel between the U.N. and Washington has led some U.N. member nations to accuse the United States of being isolationist or unilateralist, in part because of the Bush administration stance on many global issues, including global warming, biological warfare, and the powers of the international criminal court (ICC) in world affairs. For example, a former U.S. ambassador to the U.N., John Bolton, has said that either the U.N. should not exist or the United States should not be part of it. He described the ICC under the auspices of the U.N. as "a product of fuzzy-minded romanticism (that) is not just, but dangerous" to world peace and democracy (Williams 2005).

Some Americans, including members of fringe groups, see the U.N. as an instrument of a foreign policy conspiracy to overpower the United States. One such group, Move America Forward, describes itself as "the organization leading the effort to evict the United Nations from American soil and halt American funding of the UN" (Williams 2005).

Power Play

Perhaps U.S. relations with the United Nations can best be understood in the context of hypocrisy. For example, if the United States accepts an international law, then it obeys that law. Otherwise, the

United States breaks international law to impose international law on others. Unfortunately, the hypocrisy and absurdity of U.S.-U.N. relations seem to escape most ultraconservative commentators who are, arguably, under the chimera that America *is* the world. The reality remains, however, that despite U.S. military and economic power and its status as the lone global superpower, the United States is just another part of the world.

Kwame Badu Antwi-Boasiako

Further Reading

Annan, K. (2006, December 11). Address at the Truman Presidential Library and Museum. Retrieved April 11, 2007, from http://www.foxnews.com/projects/pdf/121106_annan_speech.pdf

Buchanan, P. (2004, June 28). Another step toward world government. Retrieved April 11, 2007, from http://www.ghanaweb.com/Ghana HomePage/NewsArchive/artikel.php?ID=60546

Durch, W. J. (1996). *UN peacekeeping, American politics, and the uncivil wars of the 1990s.* New York: Palgrave Macmillan.

Franck, T. M. (1985). *Nation against nation: What happened to the UN dream and what the US can do about it.* New York: Oxford University Press.

Goldstein, J. S., & Pevehouse, J. C. (2006). *International relations* (7th ed.). New York: Pearson, Longman.

Jordan, M. J. (2001, October 5). Ties that bind: Changing relations between US and UN. *Christian Science Monitor.* Retrieved April 11, 2007, from http://www.csmonitor.com/2001/1114/p7s1-wogi.html

Katz, A. Z. (2000). *Mixed messages: American politics and international organization 1919–1999.* Washington, DC: Brookings Institution Press.

Malone, D. M., & Khong, Y. F. (2003). *Unilateralism and US foreign policy: International perspective.* London: Lynne Rienner Publishers.

Nau, H. R. (2007). *Perspective on international relations: Power, institutions, and ideas.* Washington, DC: CQ Press.

Nye, J. S. (2003). *Understanding international conflicts: An introduction to theory and history* (4th ed.). Boston: Longman.

Perkins, J. (2004). *Confessions of an economic hit man.* New York. Plume.

Williams, I. (2005, March 18). Bolton vs. United Nations. *In These Times.* Retrieved April 11, 2007, from http://www.inthesetimes.com/article/2031/

Religion

See Religious Fundamentalism, U.S.; Christian Nation, United States as; Religious Pluralism, United States and

Religious Fundamentalism, U.S.

One of America's most important founding principles is the separation of church and state. Yet President George W. Bush's religious rhetoric appears to some as transforming America's democratic mission into a Christian crusade.

A striking paradox of U.S. society at the beginning of the twenty-first century is that much of its culture is secular and materialist, while its politics has a strong religious element, not just in political rhetoric but also in the way issues are framed and debated. The most salient aspect of this paradox is the conservative nature of the activists involved in bringing their religious views into the political arena. The members of the "religious right," as they are most often called in the media, are descendants of early twentieth-century fundamentalists. The term *fundamentalism,* often used pejoratively with the intent of dismissively maligning its adherents, requires careful definition to understand its historical development and notoriety.

Defining Fundamentalism

In *Fundamentalism Project,* editors Martin Marty and Scott Appleby propose a generic definition of *fundamentalism* useful for historical and cross-cultural comparisons. They suggest that fundamentalism movements are growing out of mainstream religions that represent both a reactive and an adaptive response to modernization. That is, people attracted to fundamentalist movements are responding religiously, usually in a negative and resistive way, to the economic, political, social, intellectual, and cultural changes produced by the transition to an industrial society. At the same time, fundamentalist ideology provides them with a framework for interpreting the meaning of, and eventually adjusting to, those changes. The degree of accommodation, though, is limited by fundamentalists' understanding of which of their beliefs and practices are nonnegotiable and which can be adjusted to modern society. Some might retreat into insular communities trying to ignore developments in the outside world. Others might cheerfully accept the conveniences of modern life while maintaining within their homes and religious organizations their core values and traditions.

Although a variety of fundamentalism movements find a home in U.S. religion, the ones with the deepest roots and greatest notoriety are the Protestant variety. Members of this variety are part of the broader evangelical tradition within U.S. Protestantism. Evangelicalism is a variation of Protestantism that places reli-

gious authority in the Bible, emphasizes conversion as the central religious experience, pursues an aggressive but individualistic approach to missions and social action, and stresses the Crucifixion as the key event in the Bible. Evangelicalism's historic roots were in the revivals of the eighteenth century, particularly the Great Awakening in the United States and the development of Methodism in the British Isles. Thus, fundamentalists are evangelicals, but not all evangelicals are fundamentalists. In broad outline a good deal of overlap exists in terms of theology, but the key differences are that fundamentalists take a more rigid line in interpreting that theology, seeing the most minor of variations tending toward the slippery slope of apostasy (renunciation of a religious faith), and that fundamentalists more aggressively pursue efforts to reverse what they see as the decline of U.S. culture and society.

Fundamentalism's Origins

In a seminal article, Arthur Schlesinger Sr. described the years 1875–1900 as a critical period in U.S. religious history. Those years might easily be extended through the beginning of World War I. He suggested that Protestantism faced two broad challenges: one to its "program" and the other to its "system of thought." In the former Schlesinger noted that the massive immigration of the era brought waves of Catholics and Jews who threatened Protestant hegemony (influence), particularly in the cities where the immigrants were concentrated. Furthermore, Protestant churches were not reaching the working class, leaving large numbers of people outside the social control of the dominant institution of moral authority. Also, the materialism born out of the Gilded Age's laissez-faire capitalism distracted many from the spiritual concerns that Protestants believed should be a priority.

Although Protestants recognized that renewed efforts at evangelism—such as Dwight Moody's urban crusades and the development of social programs to meet the needs of immigrants and the working class, enticing them to visit Protestant congregations—might overcome this crisis, the more serious challenge, and the one most directly related to the origins of fundamentalism, was intellectual. These years brought at least two developments that shook Protestantism's thinking by calling

A young preacher speaking from the pulpit in a very traditional Protestant/ Evangelical church. Source: istock/ Glenn Frank.

into question assumptions about the uniqueness, accuracy, and reliability of the Bible. Biblical scholars used higher criticism to analyze the Bible as they would any ancient other text. They observed a variety of contradictions and inaccuracies and speculated that various parts, such as the Pentateuch (the first five books of Jewish and Christian Scriptures) and the Book of Isaiah, were a compilation of many sources. For some Protestants these conclusions seemed to undermine the Bible's inspiration as well as Jesus's divinity because if Moses did not write the Pentateuch, then Jesus was mistaken in attributing authorship of the first five books of the Old Testament to him.

Fundamentalism, 1920–1945

The general cultural crisis of the 1920s had a religious dimension that drew in the fundamentalists. As fundamentalists battled liberals within the denominations, they realized that their fight was only one campaign in the war for U.S. society. In trying to defend their interpretation of Christian orthodoxy, they saw themselves contending for what they believed was the foundation of the United

States. However, as their defeats in denominational politics denied them the institutional base to fight this wider conflict, they joined William Jennings Bryan's crusade against evolution. For Bryan and the fundamentalists, evolution became the symbol of the modern world and all that was wrong with 1920s United States. They argued that evolution was the philosophical foundation for German aggression that led to war and that allowing the dissemination of the theory of evolution in public schools would eventually undermine the United States. That an event such as the Scopes Monkey Trial took place in the South is somewhat serendipitous, but it does suggest where fundamentalists would find a haven after the savaging they endured in the press and public opinion as a consequence of the trial.

Defeated in denominational politics and spurned by the public who did not believe their cries of an impending apocalypse should evolution and liberal theology be accepted, fundamentalists beat a strategic retreat and began creating a network of religious institutions that would give an organized structure to their movement. Some abandoned their denominations and created new ones that would faithfully teach fundamentalist doctrine. They built colleges and seminaries that became hubs of a network of churches.

They proved adept at using modern media such as newspapers, magazines, and the radio and filling them with fundamentalist content. They established agencies to send missionaries around the world and youth groups to keep their children within the fold. The result was that fundamentalism developed a rather comprehensive subculture, not unlike the one immigrants create in their new countries. Such is the suggestion of George Marsden, who offered it as one interpretation of the fundamentalist experience. However, unlike most immigrants who move geographically and willingly, fundamentalists, according to Marsden, were immigrants in time forced to endure the transition from a nineteenth century in which their faith was dominant to a modern, secular twentieth century where their faith was marginalized by society.

In those years when fundamentalism was building its own institutions, its geographic base was also shifting to the South. Fundamentalists had been active in the South since the start of the twentieth century, building networks of conferences and some Bible colleges. The itinerant fundamentalist preachers who toured the South found a region where cultural values still supported a conservative interpretation of Christian doctrine.

Fundamentalism, 1945–1975

Although it appeared to be a spent force in U.S. religion after 1925, fundamentalism reemerged in the last quarter of the twentieth century to play a critical role in shaping political debate as the new millennium began. This development has not been the subject of careful historical studies, and only the outline of the story may be sketched. The first generation of fundamentalists after 1925 abandoned organized political engagement, expending most of its energy on building its own institutions. Furthermore, a debilitating schism occurred in the early 1940s, with the larger faction abandoning fundamentalist militancy and adopting the label "evangelical" to signal a more cooperative spirit and theological position. Billy Graham, who gained international recognition with his massive evangelistic rallies, was the most visible symbol of these new evangelicals. Despite being a regular guest in the White House and fiercely patriotic, Graham was largely apolitical and did not use his position to try to influence political debate. Although he commented on problems in U.S. culture, the solution he offered was spiritual, converting the individual rather transforming society through political means. That stance seemed to be acceptable to most evangelicals, despite growing concerns during the 1960s and 1970s over sexual morality, crime, drugs, a coarsening of culture, and generational conflict. However, Supreme Court rulings on prayer in public schools (in 1962) and abortion (in 1973), in evangelical

eyes, indicated that the United States was straying too far from its religious heritage and values.

Fundamentalism, 1976–2004

The 1976 presidential election signaled the reentry of evangelicals into politics, or, perhaps more precisely, they were noticed as a large and thus potentially decisive voting bloc. Democratic candidate Jimmy Carter's open admission of being "born again" and his frank confession in a *Playboy* interview to having "lusted in his heart" for women other than his wife prodded news organizations to investigate his faith, and they discovered that 30 to 40 million Americans claimed to be born again. For their part evangelicals

BORN AGAIN

This extract from one of the many writings of American evangelist Dwight L. Moody sets forth his interpretation of one the basic tenets of Christian fundamentalism: new birth.

Now if the words of this text are true they embody one of the most solemn questions that can come before us. We can afford to be deceived about many things rather than about this one thing. Christ makes it very plain. He says, "Except a man be born again, he cannot see the kingdom of God"—much less inherit it. This doctrine of the new birth is therefore the foundation of all our hopes for the world to come. It is really the A B C of the Christian religion. My experience has been this—that if a man is unsound on this doctrine he will be unsound on almost every other fundamental doctrine in the Bible. A true understanding of this subject will help a man to solve a thousand difficulties that he may meet with in the Word of God. Things that before seemed very dark and mysterious will become very plain.

The doctrine of the new birth upsets all false religion—all false views about the Bible and about God. A friend of mine once told me that in one of his after-meetings, a man came to him with a long list of questions written out for him to answer. He said: "If you can answer these questions satisfactorily, I have made up my mind to become a Christian." "Do you not think," said my friend, "that you had better come to Christ first? Then you can look into these questions." The man thought that perhaps he had better do so. After he had received Christ, he looked again at his list of questions; but then it seemed to him as if they had all been answered. Nicodemus came with his trouble mind, and Christ said to him, "Ye must be born again." He was treated altogether differently from what he expected, but I venture to say that was the most blessed night in all his life. To be "born again" is the greatest blessing that will ever come to us in this world.

Source: Moody, D. L. (1884). The way to God and how to find it (pp. 23–24). Chicago: The Bible Institute Colportage Association.

heard a politician using their language in a genuine and authentic way, but soon they discovered that, although President Carter may have believed as they did, it did not mean that he would pursue policies that reflected evangelical values. In 1980 Ronald Reagan began tying the evangelical vote to the Republican Party by promising action on their policies, despite his inability to aptly describe his faith and his being divorced, which seems counterintuitive to the fundamentalist ideal.

The agenda of this new religious right, though, was not set by evangelicals but rather by fundamentalists. In 1979 Jerry Falwell, pastor of a fundamentalist Baptist church in Lynchburg, Virginia, founded the Moral Majority. The Moral Majority was essentially a political action committee that claimed conservative Jews, Catholics, and Mormons as members. Falwell and the fundamentalist Protestants who dominated the organization supported candidates who promised to restrict abortions, opposed the Equal Rights Amendment and gay rights, would reintroduce prayer in schools, and supported the teaching of creationism in public schools. Disbanded in 1989, the Moral Majority was succeeded by the Christian Coalition under the leadership of Pat Robertson, a televangelist based in Virginia Beach, Virginia, who failed in a bid to win the 1988 Republican nomination for president. With much the same program, the coalition was much more effective in mobilizing evangelicals for the polls through activities such as distributing in churches "nonpartisan" voter guides that compared the positions of candidates in a particular race on a laundry list of religious issues. The guides rarely left any doubt as to which candidate should be the choice of the Christian voter. Usually the candidate would be the Republican, and during the 1990s this evangelical/fundamentalist bloc became a reliable part of the Republican base that helped the GOP gain control of Congress and that supplied a crucial measure of votes in George W. Bush's narrow victories in 2000 and 2004.

Fundamentalism and the U.S. Image in the World

The world meets this religious United States in several ways. One way is through the thousands of Americans serving as Christian missionaries around the world. Some work for the mainstream Protestant denominations as doctors, educators, or church planters, whereas many others are affiliated with the hundreds of independent mission organizations that seek to convert non-Christians. The latter, more typically, come from the evangelical/fundamentalist branch of U.S. Protestantism. The overwhelming majority are motivated by a sense of religious duty to evangelism, but non-

Christians may have difficulty distinguishing between the religious message and culture of the messengers.

This traditional missionary impulse, though, is connected to a broader way in which conservative Christians influence the U.S. image in the world through U.S. foreign policy. The reports from these missionaries to local churches, amplified by Christian media, alert the fundamentalists and evangelicals to a variety of international issues and circumstances. Of particular interest is the treatment of the missionaries' converts by their governments. In the last two decades of the twentieth century evangelicals increasingly pressured administrations to document and protest the treatment of Christian minorities as a part of U.S. support for human rights.

Strong U.S. support for Israel also reflects some fundamentalist/evangelical influence, although it grows more out of fundamentalist doctrine than missionary experience. Most fundamentalists and many evangelicals are premillennialists, believing that the prophetic passages in the Bible teach that world conditions will worsen until Jesus returns to establish and rule a millennial kingdom on Earth. An important sign heralding these events is the establishment of Israel as an independent nation. Thus, these conservative Christians add their voices to those calling for U.S. foreign policy to be pro-Israel.

A final way is more subtle and has deep roots in U.S. nationalism. One of the central themes in U.S. history is the nation's sense of mission. The Puritan settlers believed they were making their colony "a city set on a hill," an example to the rest of the world of the virtue of organizing society on the basis of their religious values. The American Revolution secularized that sense of mission with the purpose of the new republic being to show how a state could be organized on Enlightenment (a philosophic movement of the eighteenth century marked by a rejection of traditional social, religious, and political ideas and an emphasis on rationalism) democratic principles. Over the course of the nineteenth and twentieth centuries, this secular mission merged with U.S. industrial, economic and military growth, so that by the end of the nineteenth century the nation was not just an example for others to emulate, it had the power and obligation to spread democracy and freedom.

First, the policy of manifest destiny of the 1840s justified the acquisition of land to the Pacific; then the imperialism of the late nineteenth and early twentieth centuries supported the annexation of Hawaii and the Philippines; and President Woodrow Wilson claimed that the mission of the United States in World War I was to "make the world safe for democracy." In World War II the United States stood as the "arsenal of democracy" against fascism, and then the democratic United States waged the Cold

War against Communism. In each era, and with each redefinition of the U.S. mission, religious rhetoric of a rather generic sort was a part. At times it was quite explicit, as in President McKinley's justifying annexing the Philippines in order to Christianize the natives or in Congress in the 1950s affirming that the United States is not only democratic but also religious by adding "under God" to the Pledge of Allegiance and making the national motto "In God We Trust."

However, in the early twenty-first century the United States twice elected as president George W. Bush, a man whose religious experience and political policies mirrored those of his fundamentalist/evangelical supporters. As David Domke and Kevin Coe point out, no president since Franklin Roosevelt had mentioned God as much in his inaugural addresses or State of the Union speeches. However, Bush's invocations of the Almighty come in the context of a United States feeling threatened by an enemy with a religious, not political, ideology in the form of fundamentalist Islam. Thus, his religious rhetoric may appear to some as transforming the democratic mission of the United States into a Christian crusade.

William R. Glass

See also Christian Nation, United States as

Further Reading

Abrams, D. C. (2001). *Selling the old time religion: American fundamentalists and mass culture.* Athens: University of Georgia Press.

Balmer, R. (2000). *Mine eyes have seen the glory: A journey into the evangelical subculture of America* (3rd ed.). New York: Oxford University Press.

Carpenter, J. (1999). *Revive us again: The reawakening of American fundamentalism.* New York: Oxford University Press.

Dalhouse, M. T. (1996). *An island in a lake of fire: Bob Jones University, fundamentalism, and the separatist movement.* Athens: University of Georgia Press.

Domke, D., & Coe, K. (2005). Bush, God, and the state of the union. Retrieved March 8, 2007, from http://www.commondreams.org/views05/0129_26.htm

Glass, W. R. (2000). *Strangers in Zion: Fundamentalists in the South, 1900–1950.* Macon, GA: Mercer University Press.

Hangen, T. (2002). *Redeeming the dial: Radio, religion, and popular culture in America.* Chapel Hill: University of North Carolina Press.

Hankins, B. (2004). *Uneasy in Babylon: Southern Baptist conservatives and American culture.* Tuscaloosa: University of Alabama Press.

Harding, S. F. (2000). *The book of Jerry Falwell: Fundamentalist language and politics.* Princeton, NJ: Princeton University Press.

Larson, E. J. (1997). *Summer for the gods: The Scopes trial and America's continuing debate over science and religion.* Cambridge, MA: Harvard University Press.

Marsden, G. M. (1980). *Fundamentalism and American culture: The shaping of twentieth-century evangelicalism, 1879–1925.* New York: Oxford University Press.

Martin, W. (1996). *With God on our side: The rise of the religious right in America.* New York: Broadway Books.

Marty, M., & Appleby, R. S. (1991). *Fundamentalisms observed.* Chicago: University of Chicago Press.

Morgan, D. T. (1996). *The new crusades, the new Holy Land: Conflict in the Southern Baptist Convention, 1969–1991.* Tuscaloosa: University of Alabama Press.

Noll, M. A., Bebbington, D. W., & Rawlyk, G. A. (Eds.). (1994). *Evangelicalism: Comparative studies of popular Protestantism in North America, the British Isles, and beyond, 1700–1990.* New York: Oxford University Press.

Rozell, M., & Wilcox, C. (1996). *Second coming: The new Christian right in Virginia politics.* Baltimore: Johns Hopkins University Press.

Sandeen, E. R. (1970). *The roots of fundamentalism: British and American millenarianism, 1800–1930.* Chicago: University of Chicago Press.

Schlesinger Sr., A. M. (1932). A critical period in American religion, 1875–1900. *Massachusetts Historical Society Proceedings, 64,* 523–547.

Szasz, F. M. (1982). *The divided mind of Protestant America, 1880–1930.* Tuscaloosa: University of Alabama Press.

Watson, J. (1999). *The Christian coalition: Dreams of restoration, demands for recognition.* New York: St. Martin's Press.

Wilcox, C. (2000). *Onward Christian soldiers?: The religious right in American politics* (2nd ed.). Boulder, CO: Westview Press.

Religious Pluralism, United States and

The political, social, and economic realities of the world may well make the United States a model for other nations as the acceptance of religious pluralism becomes an essential condition of global peace.

When John Adams, Benjamin Franklin, and Thomas Jefferson accepted the phrase "E Pluribus Unum" for the national motto in August 1776, they set a unique course for the future of the new nation that was still to win its independence in war: "Out of Many, One." Quite unintentionally, as the Founding Fathers refused to make any one denomination the official state religion of their fledgling nation, they turned the United States into a social science lab and set up a multicentury experiment to test the effectiveness of religious pluralism to help maintain the many united in the one. Now, with the advent of the Internet, satellite communication, rapid transportation, and ever-increasing global population shifts, the U.S. experiment can, if successful, become a sign of hope for the world.

Religious Pluralism Defined

Religious pluralism is the belief that no single religion should be privileged and that people of all faith communities should be respected and allowed to live by the principles of their tradition without interference. In practice the implementation of religious pluralism as a guiding principle protected by law is closely related to the separation of church and state. However, for ordinary people hoping to live peacefully in a community, at least as important as the officially guaranteed liberty of religion and conscience are the attitudes and actions of their neighbors who identify with a different religion or denomination. In the latter sense, especially, religious pluralism is diametrically opposed to the kind of fundamentalism that assumes that the teachings of a particular religious tradition, interpreted a certain, unchanging way, represent an absolute truth and that consequently all other interpretations, religions, and ideologies are in error and in need of being corrected.

U.S. Paradox

One of the ironies of the U.S. enigma, as a flexible, loosely tied, mammoth bundle of contradictions, is that in addition to a centuries-old, pervasive tradition of religious pluralism, the United States has inherited from its Puritan ancestors a persistent strand of precisely the kind of fanatical religious fundamentalism that is most offended by pluralism. It is this strand of inherited religious fundamentalism that is responsible for the 16 November 1688 execution of Ann ("Goody") Glover for daring to remain Catholic in Cotton Mather's Boston and that today blows up abortion clinics and posts "God hates fags" signs.

In fact, pluralism in the United States manifests itself by permitting diverse and even diametrically opposed tendencies to coexist, but in an uneasy and potentially prolific and creative tension. Consider George Whitefield's emotional revivals of the Great Awakening yoked to the cerebral deism of Thomas Jefferson and John Adams. Both religious forms, evangelical enthusiasm and rational restraint, are equally characteristic of the U.S. paradox.

Compared with Europe, the United States is astoundingly religious but also extraordinarily secular. According to George Marsden, "Vast majorities of Americans profess belief in God, and more than two-thirds affirm such traditional Christian doctrines as the deity of Jesus Christ and the authority of the Bible. Probably only about half of those Christians are active in churches, but if you add practicing Jews, Muslims, and devotees of other religions, the proportion of seriously religious Americans is far higher than in other large highly industrialized nations" (Marsden 2004).

Challenges of Globalization

In an article published in 2004, Stephen J. Stein argues that in the wake of globalization, privatization, localization, and polarization religion in the United States is undergoing a major shift, away from formerly significant theological issues, concern with denominational identities, conventional moral standards, and traditional patterns of worship, leading to "an emerging American religious bricolage that defies easy description" (Stein 2004). Stein elaborates:

> Globalization is one force reshaping American religious pluralism. The nation once described as Christian, and then as

Judeo-Christian, now defies easy characterization. Post-1965 immigrants brought the traditions of Asia into the diverse religious mix at the same time that several truly indigenous communities, including the Mormons and the Jehovah's Witnesses, have grown exponentially. The Latino presence in the Roman Catholic Church is reorienting that huge community, too. The challenge now facing scholars is to construct a new descriptive model for this decentered religious world in America. (Stein 2004)

Combining Religious Chaos and Cooperation

However, even before the arrival of post-1965 immigrants and the effects of globalization on U.S. religious pluralism was more than "Christian" or "Judeo-Christian" and could be accurately characterized as "decentered" for centuries. From the beginning, as Greeley noted in 1972, U.S. religion has been loosely structured and multidenominational. Variations in local conditions and the absence of official guardians of orthodoxy produced major variants of even a single denomination in different regions of the country.

In the United States the multiplicity of churches did not result from the splintering of a single established national church. For Americans the variety of churches was simply a given to be accepted as an aspect of life in the New World. As Will Herberg put it in his classic *Protestant, Catholic, Jew:*

> In America religious pluralism is thus not merely a historical and political fact; it is, in the mind of the American, the primordial condition of things, an essential aspect of the American Way of Life, and therefore in itself an aspect of religious belief. Americans, in other words, believe that the plurality of religious groups is a proper and legitimate condition. However much he may be attached to his own church, however dimly he may regard the beliefs and practices of other churches, the American tends to feel rather strongly that total religious uniformity, even with his own church benefiting thereby, would be something undesirable and wrong, indeed scarcely conceivable. Pluralism of religions and churches is something quite axiomatic to the American. (Herberg 1955, 85)

"Despite all this pluralism, which at times may seem to the outsider to become dangerously close to religious chaos, particularly with its constant proliferation of new sects and new branches of denominations," Greeley observed, "there has also been a strong strain toward cooperation among American religious groups, and more recently, a quite powerful ecumenical movement" (Greeley 1972, 104). Religious conflict and competition are moderated "first

of all, by the consciousness that certain rules must be kept lest the larger social structure be destroyed and, secondly, by the belief that at least some of the heretics and schismatics with which we are surrounded are also men of good will with whom we can cooperate. It does not seem too much to say that the social basis for ecumenism may well be stronger in American society than it is in many European countries where the heavy hand of history is more obvious than it is in the United States" (Greeley 1972, 104). It seems no accident that William James, the early advocate of religious pluralism as a sign of healthy mindedness, was an American or that in 1893 the First Parliament of the World's Religions took place not in Paris or London or Vienna but in Chicago. Today Margarete Payer in her comprehensive German web site dealing with religion in the United States points to the Graduate Theological Union in Berkeley as an example of interreligious cooperation unthinkable in Germany—shared theological studies for Catholics (Dominicans, Franciscans, and Jesuits), Orthodox, Lutherans, Anglicans, Presbyterians, Baptists, Unitarians, Jews, and Buddhists.

Freedom as Fountainhead of Religious Diversity

The Founding Fathers of the United States had no way of envisioning the bewildering scope of religious diversity their descendants would encounter at the beginning of the third millennium. As Diana Eck notes in *A New Religious America:*

> When they wrote the sixteen words of the First Amendment, "Congress shall make no law respecting an establishment of religion or prohibiting the free exercise thereof," they unquestionably did not have Buddhism or the Santeria tradition in mind. But the principles they articulated—the "nonestablishment" of religion and the "free exercise" of religion—have provided a sturdy rudder through the past two centuries as our religious diversity has expanded. (Eck 2001, 7)

Source of Stability, Strength, and Unity

Even before the arrival of the Europeans, Native Americans had lived by diverse religions. And this practice has been perpetuated ever since. In the colonial days the United States was a multidenominational society. The religious pluralism of the original colonies rendered any attempt to impose a state church impractical. From that perspective the separation of church and state was simply the only way to ensure that multiple state patches could be

successfully stitched together to form a single national quilt—a pragmatic way of adjusting the law of the land to the realities of the situation. Political pluralism followed as the natural consequence of an already religiously pluralistic society.

As more people came to settle in the United States from other parts of the world, practicing their faith traditions came to provide a counterweight to alienation, a way of creating an accepting community, a place to belong, a home away from home, essential for emotional health, especially in times past when emigration generally meant a loss of all connections, except for occasional letters that might take months in transit, with those left behind.

Evolution of Religious Pluralism

Stephen J. Stein is, of course, correct to direct attention to the changes precipitated by new waves of immigrants as well as global-

An Amish horse and buggy on a country road in the Midwest. The Amish have been involved in several precedent-setting lawsuits involving religious freedom. Source: istock/Juan Monino.

ization. In the present radically new opportunities exist for swift and relatively inexpensive travel as well as Internet and satellite communication. As Eck also notes, emigration no longer means leaving one's country of origin behind, and new immigrants may become true world citizens, equally at home in their place of origin and the United States. Hence, Greeley's "belonging vacuum" may no longer be as important as it had been in the past. However, the changing conditions also provide new and important challenges and opportunities.

Eck points out that today "the United States has become the most religiously diverse nation on earth" (Eck 2001, 4), adding that,

> In the past thirty years massive movements of people both as migrants and refugees have reshaped the demography of our world. Immigrants around the world number over 130 million, with about 30 million in the United States, a million arriving each year. The dynamic global image of our times is not the so-called clash of civilizations but the marbling of civilizations and peoples. Just as the end of the Cold War brought about a new geopolitical situation, the global movements of people have brought about a new georeligious reality. Hindus, Sikhs, and Muslims are now part of the religious landscape of Britain, mosques appear in Paris and Lyons, Buddhist temples in Toronto, and Sikh gurdwaras in Vancouver. But nowhere, even in today's world of mass migrations, is the sheer range of religious faith as wide as it is today in the United States. (Eck 2001, 4–5)

Beyond Tolerance and Inclusivity

In his landmark study *Religious Pluralism in America*, William Hutchison insists that at the present juncture in U.S. history "pluralism as tolerance and pluralism as inclusivity have by now, after long struggles, become intrinsic to the social covenant; there can be no turning back" (Hutchinson 2001, 234–235). He argues that an even more evolved form of contemporary pluralism goes beyond inclusivity and becomes "mutually respectful and nonpatronizing" (Hutchinson 2001, 235). This fully respectful pluralism rests in the realization that "if I do concede your right to hold firmly to your beliefs, it makes no sense at all for me to deny or compromise that same right in relation to myself. Pluralism in its leading contemporary meaning—support for group identity and the integrity of competing beliefs—emphatically does not imply 'lack of all conviction,' either for historically dominant American faiths and their adherents or for the society at large" (Hutchinson 2001, 235).

Ultimately, and ironically, despite fearful foes who are convinced that religious pluralism is somehow part of a demonic plot to destroy this nation or Christianity, "the pluralist is on firm ground in pointing out that in the Judaic, Christian, and other traditions 'only God is God'; all apart from God is penultimate—less than absolute. Given that theological stance, neither 'we' nor 'others' can claim that our institutions embody final truth" (Hutchinson 2001, 236). In other words, religious pluralism is fully compatible with all religious traditions and none.

Global Perceptions of U.S. Religious Pluralism

World assessment of religious pluralism in the United States is a function of the ideological "lenses" worn by the interpreter and varies widely from country to country and within countries. The above-mentioned Margarete Payer, for example, in an academic German site, commends the United States for providing a healthy environment for the flourishing of religion by its combination of religious liberty and the separation of church and state. She favorably compares the U.S. model with the German situation, where the various state-supported churches are busy competing in an attempt to maintain their official privileges. The late Susan Sontag is cited in another German article observing that probably the most important source of U.S. radicalism is what used to be considered the source of conservative values—religion. Many observers have pointed out that the greatest difference between the United States and Europe consists in the fact that religion still plays a central role in public discourse in the United States, as Brian Anderson notes in "Secular Europe, Religious America."

On the other hand, Patricia M. Y. Chang describes her experience as academic director of a couple of U.S. State Department–sponsored study programs that bring Islamic scholars from around the world to the United States in order to show off the U.S. way "of separating church and state, and demonstrating how American society is able to both nurture faith traditions and support religious diversity. The implied intent is to promote an American-style separation of mosque and state in Muslim countries" (Chang 2003). Chang discovered that "rather than appreciating the benefits that religious pluralism offer, to the larger society, some of our guests were clearly puzzled. On the second day of the program, Munib Ur Rehmman, a Pakistani cleric, asked me 'If you believe your religion to be true and you believe it is your duty to share this truth with others, then why would you think that religious pluralism is good thing?' I realized that the religious tolerance that we celebrate in the U.S. could be perceived by someone from a religiously homogeneous country as a lack of religious conviction or, worse, a shameful hypocrisy" (Chang 2003).

Chang adds, "After the program ended, many of the Muslim scholars wrote to say that their visit had convinced them of the basic kindness of the American people. They were also surprised in some cases to find that Americans were not as irreligious as they had thought. Still, the differences in perspective remained large" (Chang 2003). Yet, pious Muslims may have more in common with pious Christians than either would expect. At the conclusion of a long sociological analysis of religious pluralism in the United States, David Machacek identifies an issue that almost led to schism at the 2001 meeting of the General Assembly of Presbyterian Church, USA: "[H]ow do religious believers rectify the respect for the legitimacy of other religions even while sustaining a faith in their own"? (Machacek 2003). Chang's Pakistani cleric would agree. He might also applaud Cardinal Joseph Ratzinger, arguably the second-most powerful Roman Catholic voice at the end of the twentieth century (and now, as Pope Benedict XVI, the most powerful), who called the theology of religious pluralism "the gravest threat facing the church" in 1996 (Allen 2000). At the same time, religious pluralism, even bearing a U.S. face, is naturally more attuned to the Far East where, in the worlds of the Malay theologian Edmund Chia, "any discussion of Christianity's presence and contribution . . . has to be done in acknowledgement of the presence and contributions of the other religions of Asia. Put another way, one cannot look at Christianity in Asia without at the same time looking at the other great Asian religions" (Chia n.d.).

No matter what one's position on religious pluralism, the political, social, and economic realities of the world may well make its acceptance an essential condition of global peace. In the words of the Baptist theologian Alan Neely, "Given the fact that this country—as most countries in the West—is becoming increasingly multicultural and multi-religious, how we Christians relate to non-Christians will determine whether we are able to live together in a truly pluralistic society or whether we will become a tangle of competing, mutually suspicious, antagonistic neighbors" (Neely 2001).

Revisiting the Multicentury Experiment

The time has come to examine the results of the multicentury experiment mentioned at the beginning of this essay. Does the exponential increase in religious diversity lead to a breakdown of pluralistic principle? Have the tendencies toward ecumenical dialogue and cooperation Greeley mentioned in the early 1970s

matured to help diffuse potentially explosive situations in the wake of the September 11, 2001, terrorist attacks? Is Hutchinson's optimism justified, and is religious pluralism indeed a "work in progress" (Hutchinson 2003, 238) that can expose the imperialism inherent in Christianity? Is there hope for the future not only in United States but also throughout the world?

Diana Eck provides evidence that the last question can be answered at least tentatively in the affirmative. Yes, the terrorist attacks spawned retaliatory hate crimes and even killings. However, we would have to say that these incidents of backlash unleashed by the terrorist attacks ultimately revealed something more complex and more heartening about U.S. society. The response evoked by each ugly incident made clear that the multireligious and multicultural fabric of the United States was already too strong to rend by random violence. Despite new fears of "sleeper cells" of Islamic terrorists and "assimilated terrorists" lounging by the condominium pool, Americans would not condone indiscriminate violence against neighbors of any faith or culture. The Palestinian bookstore owner in Alexandria, Virginia, stunned by the shattered glass and its message of hatred soon discovered hundreds of supportive neighbors he did not know who sent him bouquets of flowers and cards expressing their sorrow at what had happened. In Toledo, Cherrefe Kadri, the woman president of the Islamic community, reflected on the September 11 rifle fire: "That small hole in the dome created such a huge outpouring of support for our Islamic community" (Eck 2001). She said, "A Christian radio station contacted me wanting to do something. They called out on the airwaves for people to come together at our center to hold hands, to ring our mosque, to pray for our protection. We expected three hundred people and thought that would be enough to circle the mosque, but two thousand people showed up to hold hands around the mosque. I was amazed!" (Eck 2001).

Eck's examples illustrate the kind of mutual, interreligious, interideological bridge-building suggested in Leonard Swidler's "Dialogue Decalogue" and David Tracy's call to "a communal conversation on behalf of the *kairos* of this our day—the communal and historical struggle for the emergence of a humanity both finally global and ultimately humane" (Tracy 1981, 453).

Ingrid H. Shafer

Further Reading

Allen, J. L. (2000, September 15). The perils of pluralism. *National Catholic Reporter*. Retrieved November 29, 2004, from http://www.natcath.com/NCR_Online/archives/091500/091500e.htm

Anderson, B. C. (2004, Spring). Secular Europe, religious America. *Public Interest*. Retrieved October 23, 2004, from http://www.findarticles.com/p/articles/mi_m0377/is_155/ai_n6143340

Barrows, J. H. (Ed.). (1893). *The world's parliament of religions*. Chicago: Parliament.

Butler, J. (1990). *Awash in a sea of faith; Christianizing the American people*. Cambridge, MA: Harvard University Press.

Carpenter, J. A. (1997). *Revive us again; The reawakening of American fundamentalism*. New York: Oxford University Press.

Chang, P. M. Y. (2003, September 6). Puzzled by pluralism: Muslim visitors question the American way. *Christian Century*. Retrieved December 29, 2005, from http://www.findarticles.com/p/articles/mi_m1058/is_18_120/ai_107760337

Chia, E. (n.d.). Dialogue with religions of Asia: Challenges from without. Retrieved November 25, 2004, from http://www.sedos.org/english/without_chia.html

Cox, H. (1995). *Fire from heaven: The rise of Pentecostal spirituality and the reshaping of religion in the twenty-first century*. Reading, MA: Addison-Wesley.

Douglas, M., & Tipton, S. M. (Eds.). (1982). *Religion and America: Spiritual life in a secular age*. Boston: Beacon.

Eck, D. L. (2001). *A new religious America; How a "Christian country" has now become the world's most religiously diverse nation*. San Francisco: Harper.

Glazer, N. (1997). *We are all multiculturalists now*. Cambridge, MA: Harvard University Press.

Glazer, N., & Moynihan, D. P. (1963). *Beyond the melting pot*. Cambridge, MA: MIT Press and Harvard University Press.

Greeley, A. M. (1972). *The denominational society: A sociological approach to religion in America*. Glenview, IL: Scott, Foresman and Company.

Herberg, W. (1955). *Protestant, Catholic, Jew: An essay in American religious sociology*. Garden City, NY: Doubleday.

Hollinger, D. A. (1995). *Postethnic America: Beyond multiculturalism*. New York: Basic.

Hudson, W. S. (1953). *The great tradition of the American churches*. New York: Harper and Brothers.

Hutchinson, W. H. (2003). *Religious pluralism in America: The contemporary history of a founding ideal*. New Haven, CT: Yale University Press.

James, W. (1902). *The varieties of religious experience*. Retrieved October 29, 2004, from http://etext.lib.virginia.edu/toc/modeng/public/JamVari.html

Lambert, F. (2003). *The founding fathers and the place of religion in America*. Princeton, NJ: Princeton University Press.

Machacek, D. W. (2003, Summer). The problem of pluralism—"New religious pluralism" in the United States. *Sociology of Religion*. Retrieved October 29, 2004, from http://www.findarticles.com/p/articles/mi_m0SOR/is_2_64/ai_104733006

Marsden, G. M. (1980). *Fundamentalism and American culture: The shaping of twentieth century evangelicalism, 1870–1925*. New York: Oxford University Press.

Marsden, G. M. (2004, October 25). The paradox of American religion. *The Chronicle Review*. Retrieved October 29, 2004, from http://chronicle.com/prm/weekly/v51/i09/09b00701.htm

Marty, M. E. (1997). *The one and the many: America's struggle for the common good.* Cambridge, MA: Harvard University Press.

McDermott, G. R. (2000). *Jonathan Edwards confronts the gods: Christian theology, enlightenment religion, and non-Christian faiths.* New York: Oxford University Press.

McGraw, B. A. (2003). *Rediscovering America's sacred ground: Public religion and pursuit of the good in a pluralistic America.* Albany: State University of New York Press.

Neely, A. (2001, Winter/Spring). Religious pluralism in the United States and other lands: A challenge for Baptists and other Christians in the 21st century. *Baptist History and Heritage.* Retrieved January 1, 2005, from http://www.findarticles.com/p/articles/mi_moNXG/is_2001_Wintr-Spring/ai_94160922

Noll, M. A. (1992). *A history of Christianity in the United States and Canada.* Grand Rapids, MI: Eerdmans.

Stein, S. J. (2004). A decentered religious world. *The Chronicle Review.* Retrieved October 29, 2004, from http://chronicle.com/prm/weekly/v51/i09/09b00701.htm

Swidler, L. (1990). *After the absolute: The dialogical future of religious reflection.* Minneapolis, MN: Augsburg-Fortress.

Swidler, L. (2004, October 25). The dialogue decalogue. Retrieved October 29, 2004, from http://astro.temple.edu/~dialogue/Antho/decalog.htm

Tocqueville, A. de. (n.d.). *Democracy in America: Vol. 1.* New Rochelle, NY: Arlington House.

Tracy, D. (1981). *The analogical imagination: Christian theology and the culture of pluralism.* New York: Crossroad.

Wills, G. (1990). *Under God: Religion and American politics.* New York: Simon & Schuster.

September 11, 2001

In the immediate aftermath of 9/11, most nations and people around the world expressed solidarity and support for the United States—and for a short time the world was bound together in singular horror.

People have said that the world was forever changed on September 11, 2001, by the terrorist attacks on the World Trade Center in New York City and on the Pentagon in Washington, D.C. Jean-Marie Colombanii of France's *Le Monde* newspaper echoed the sentiment of millions around the world when he said, "We are all Americans." The rest of the world seemed to feel the shock and pain that Americans felt. For a moment in history the terrorist attacks bound the world together in horror as the enormity of the events overwhelmed the public consciousness.

In the immediate aftermath of September 11, the world expressed solidarity and support for the United States. Messages of condolence poured in to U.S. embassies and consulates. From Europe to Africa to Southeast Asia sympathy for the United States as a victim of terrorism manifested itself in tacit support for apprehension of those responsible for the attacks.

Suspicion immediately fell on the terrorist network al-Qaeda and its Taliban supporters in Afghanistan. In countries around the world people favored extradition and trial of the suspects rather than military action. The notable exception was the staunchest ally of the United States: Israel.

Public Opposition to U.S. Militarism

International public opinion was slow to recognize that the United States had decided al-Qaeda and the Taliban were legitimate targets for military retribution. Despite the growing political consensus for the invasion of Afghanistan, public sympathy for the United States did not manifest itself in support of the invasion. In cities as diverse as London, Paris, Berlin, Moscow, Damascus, Islamabad, Tokyo, and Jakarta thousands of antiwar protesters filled the streets in opposition to the invasion of Afghanistan.

A majority of the world saw the military campaign to oust the Taliban as collective punishment of innocent civilians. Each image of an Afghan child killed by high-altitude bombing reinforced the notion that the United States was punishing innocent Muslims. Resentment spread throughout the world, especially in the Arab world, as increasing numbers of people questioned the persistent use of aerial bombing in a country with no capacity to resist.

The invasion mobilized antiwar sentiment throughout western Europe. In Germany, France, Spain, and Italy majorities of the public were against the war in Afghanistan. Public good will toward the United States quickly dissipated. Anti-U.S. protests grew larger. In France public opinion of U.S. foreign policy grew more negative as the war progressed. In Germany polls showed that people considered President George Bush to be a greater danger than Iraq's Saddam Hussein. In eastern Europe countries such as Romania, Hungary, Bulgaria, the Czech Republic, and Poland felt caught between the United States and the European Union, which they would soon join.

Despite the acquiescence of Muslim countries to the attack on Afghanistan, leaders in Muslim countries increasingly faced domestic resistance by allying themselves with the United States. Throughout the Islamic world—from Indonesia to Turkey, from Pakistan to Saudi Arabia—Muslims across the political spectrum—from traditionalist Islamists to secular nationalists—expressed their displeasure with the U.S. military campaign in Afghanistan because they perceived the attack on Afghanistan as an attack on the *umma* (believers).

War in Afghanistan

In short order the U.S.-dominated alliance attacked al-Qaeda training camps in Afghanistan and quickly toppled the Taliban regime. Whatever its military justification, the bombing of Afghanistan with the inevitable collateral damage began to diminish the moral authority that the United States had enjoyed as a consequence of the terrorist attacks. International public support of the United States fell precipitously after the bombing began. By the time Kabul fell on 13 November 2001, clear majorities were against the bombing.

U.S. unilateralism in Afghanistan led to fissures within the North Atlantic Treaty Organization (NATO). Under intense pressure from the United States, NATO invoked Article V of its charter for the first time. Article V stipulated that an armed attack against one of its members was an attack against all its members. Consequently, member states could exercise the right of individual or collective security. France, Germany, and the Netherlands opted not to contribute troops to the NATO contingent in Afghanistan, whereas other NATO countries sent token troop contingents.

Despite the international public outcry against the bombing of Afghanistan, the U.S. war on terrorism reinvigorated U.S. relations with China, Russia, and India, each of which faced its own separatist-terrorist threat in Xianjiang, Chechnya, and Kashmir, respectively. The United States emphasized cooperation and mutual assistance in fighting terrorism. Thus, the U.S. response to the attacks of September 11 gave legitimacy to a crackdown on domestic "subversives" around the world. From Xianjiang to Chechnya and from Tashkent in Uzbekistan to Manila in the Philippines, governments have used extraordinary powers to suppress dissident Islamist movements.

Transformed Relations in Asia

The attacks of September 11 also transformed major power relations in Asia. The attacks temporarily stabilized the Chinese-U.S. relationship that had developed after the May 1999 accidental bombing of the Chinese embassy in Belgrade, Serbia, and the collision of a U.S. EP-3 reconnaissance aircraft with a Chinese jet fighter over the South China Sea. The attacks of September 11 presented Japan, as a reliable ally of the United States, with an opportunity to review its relationship with the United States while expanding its overseas security role.

Much of the transformation in Asia after September 11 has been in Southeast Asia. Pakistan, a long-time strategic partner of China, has given the United States an opening. India has taken advantage of the war on terrorism to strengthen its cooperation with the United States. The attacks of September 11 also had an impact on the Association of Southeast Asian Nations (ASEAN) countries. Singapore authorities uncovered a plot by al-Qaeda-linked terrorists of Jamaah Islamiyah to bomb U.S. and other Western targets in Singapore. As a consequence, countries with sizable Muslim populations—Singapore, Indonesia, and Malaysia—have carefully balanced their support of the U.S.-led war against al-Qaeda with domestic considerations.

Decision to Invade Iraq

After the ouster of the Taliban regime, the United States turned its attention to Saddam Hussein and began linking al-Qaeda leader Osama bin Laden and his network with Iraq. Despite the repeated denials of Hussein's regime, U.S. justification quickly built for the invasion of Iraq. The Bush administration believed that it could invade Iraq, with or without the consent of the United Nations, because the administration expected a replay of Afghanistan: Military resistance would dissipate in the face of superior firepower. Iraqis would welcome the Americans and their allies, and the

OSAMA BIN LADEN ON FIGHTING THE UNITED STATES

A month after the September 11, 2001, terrorist attacks on the United States, Osama bin Laden taped a message that appeared to justify the destruction wreaked on the United States. An extract from that message follows.

God Almighty hit the United States at its most vulnerable spot. He destroyed its greatest buildings.

Praise be to God.

Here is the United States. It was filled with terror from its north to its south and from its east to its west.

Praise be to God.

What the United States tastes today is a very small thing compared to what we have tasted for tens of years.

Our nation has been tasting this humiliation and contempt for more than eighty years.

Its sons are being killed, its blood is being shed, its holy places are being attacked, and it is not being ruled according to what God has decreed.

Despite this, nobody cares.

When Almighty God rendered successful a convoy of Muslims, the vanguards of Islam, He allowed them to destroy the United States.

I ask God Almighty to elevate their status and grant them Paradise. He is the one who is capable to do so.

When these defended their oppressed sons, brothers, and sisters in Palestine and in many Islamic countries, the world at large shouted. The infidels shouted, followed by the hypocrites.

One million Iraqi children have thus far died in Iraq although they did not do anything wrong.

Despite this, we heard no denunciation by anyone in the world or a fatwa by the rulers' ulema [body of Muslim scholars].

Israeli tanks and tracked vehicles also enter to wreak havoc in Palestine, in Jenin, Ramallah, Rafah, Beit Jala, and other Islamic areas and we hear no voices raised or moves made.

But if the sword falls on the United States after 80 years, hypocrisy raises its head lamenting the deaths of these killers who tampered with the blood, honour, and holy places of the Muslims.

The least that one can describe these people is that they are morally depraved.

They champion falsehood, support the butcher against the victim, the oppressor against the innocent child.

May God mete them the punishment they deserve.

I say that the matter is clear and explicit.

In the aftermath of this event and now that senior US officials have spoken, beginning with Bush, the head of the world's infidels, and whoever supports him, every Muslim should rush to defend his religion.

Source: Bin Laden's warning: full text. (2001, October 7). Retrieved June 8, 2007, from http://news.bbc.co.uk/1/hi/world/south_asia/1585636.stm

Ground Zero in New York City.
Source: istock.

U.S.-led coalition would install a regime capable of controlling and rebuilding Iraq quickly.

The U.S. decision to invade Iraq, with or without the consent of the United Nations, provoked international complaints and led to the collapse of international political and public support as countries made strategic policy choices calculating domestic and international self-interests. Fractures in the U.S.-led alliance began to appear as countries such as France, Russia, and China expressed grave concern about the invasion of Iraq in the U.N. Security Council. China and Russia went so far as to call for indefinite continuation of weapons inspections in Iraq. From receiving nearly universal sympathy in the first weeks after September 11, the United States had become an international pariah.

Changed Perceptions of the United States

The unilaterally inclined U.S. leadership dismissed most of the civilities and practices—international rules, treaties, security procedures—that many other nations identified with common civilization. Institutions such as NATO and the United Nations operate by consensus; diplomacy is the common language. The decision to ignore multilateral institutions discouraged international cooperation. U.S. unilateralism endangered coalition-building efforts of the United Nations in postwar Afghanistan and Iraq.

Nations such as France and Germany that opposed the U.S. decision to invade Iraq have been reluctant to contribute to the effort of nation-building.

In the aftermath of September 11 the subsequent U.S.-led military campaigns in Afghanistan and Iraq altered international relations and redefined global priorities. The United States declared it would make no distinction between suspected terrorists and the country that harbors them. It also declared that the United States was henceforth engaged in a "war against global terrorism" that would last indefinitely. In short, the United States disregarded international laws and norms. The United States would define who "global terrorists" are and pursue them wherever they might be in whatever manner was deemed necessary. In essence, the United States would use its global reach and military superiority to launch unilateral asymmetrical warfare against its enemies, real or imagined. What began as a "coalition of the willing" had become, in effect, a unilateral military expedition against any perceived enemy. Any challenge to Washington's freedom to act was treated as a hostile act. Much of the world began to view the United States as a greater long-term threat than terrorists.

In the final analysis the cause of the deepening anti-Americanism around the world was the U.S. unilateral approach in imposing a political vision on the Muslim world that would be acceptable to Washington regardless of the wishes of the international community. What started out as a military response to terrorist attacks had become a crusade to remake the entire political culture of the

Middle East. Whether democracy can be "planted" in the Middle East through military occupation remains to be seen.

Further damaging the international image of the United States was the perceived double standard concerning the rule of law and human rights. The United States has long been the defender of human rights around the world, but places such as Guantànamo in Cuba, Abu Ghraib in Iraq, and Bagram in Afghanistan became synonymous with the abuse of Muslim prisoners, tarnishing the reputation of the United States as well as undermining U.S. standards of judicial fairness.

Keith A. Leitich

See also Foreign Policy after September 11, 2001, U.S.; Iraq Wars; Islamic Worldview; Middle East Peace Process

Further Reading

Bernstein, R. (2003, September 11). Foreign views of U.S. darken since September 11. *New York Times*, A-1.

Brunn, S. D. (2004). *11 September and its aftermath: The geopolitics of terror.* Portland, OR: Frank Cass Publishers.

Coker, C. (2002). *September 11th and its implications for EU and NATO.* Oslo, Norway: Norske Atlanterhavskomité.

Colombani, J.-M. (2001, September 12). We are all Americans. *Le Monde*, 1.

Freidman, T. L. (2002). *Longitudes and attitudes: Exploring the world after September 11.* New York: Farrar, Straus, & Giroux.

Godzimirski, J. M. (2002). *11 September 2001 and the shift in Russia's policy towards NATO.* Oslo, Norway: Norske Atlanterhavskomité.

Han, S.-J. (2003). *Coping with 9-11: Asian perspectives on global and regional order.* Tokyo: Japan Center for International Exchange.

Hershberg, E., & Moore, K. W. (2002). *Critical views of September 11.* New York: W. W. Norton.

National Commission on Terrorist Attacks upon the United States. (2004). *The 9/11 commission report: Final report of the National Commission on Terrorist Attacks upon the United States.* Washington, DC: Government Printing Office.

Pond, E. (2004). *Friendly fire: The near-death of the transatlantic alliance.* Washington, DC: Brookings Institution Press.

Smith, M. (2001). *Russia & the West since 11 September 2001.* Camberley, UK: Conflict Studies Research Centre, Royal Military Academy, Sandhurst.

Talbott, S., & Chanda, N. (2001). *The age of terror: America and the world after September 11.* New York: Basic Books.

Wright, M. W. (2002). *Geographies of power: Placing scale.* Malden, MA: Blackwell Publishers.

Slavery and Abolitionism

The institution of slavery prevented the U.S. from reaching its full potential in many ways. Political energy was spent attacking it or defending it while England and France stood in judgment and played one side against the other.

Slavery is considered one of the greatest sins of the United States, costing millions of lives and economic and career opportunities and preventing the United States from reaching its full potential. The inhumanity shown toward slaves outraged some Europeans, whereas others, especially in England, tended to largely identify with the aristocratic South, even after the end of the institution of slavery in England.

Britain's first black slaves arrived in America in 1619. Settling in Virginia, they developed friendships with white indentured servants who, in some respects, had even fewer rights. Sharing the same quarters and living conditions as well as contempt toward landowners, servants and slaves communicated with each other, developing friendships that disturbed Virginia's wealthy power structure.

By the mid-1650s increased competition in the tobacco trade had cut profits, and newly freed servants were not getting the land or wealth they thought they would receive. Fearing a coalition of angry and frustrated poor whites and blacks, the Virginia and Maryland colonies took the lead in passing laws that mandated discrimination. Laws regarding marriage, punishment, personal property, and status of children born to slave mothers were all designed to give whites a common cause. Henceforth, nonwhites, particularly African-Americans, were treated as the new enemy, and the "peculiar institution" of slavery enhanced the ideas that blacks were inferior beings and that slavery was their natural and deserved status.

Sentiment for Slavery

It was natural for settlers to consider servitude and slavery as viable because many had been themselves threatened with enslavement while in England. During the seventeenth century the British floated the idea of enslaving all citizens who were not contributors to society. The idea of making the poor work for little or nothing was seen as a way to relieve chronic problems of poverty and vagrancy. Debtor prisons, for example, were founded, and prisoners were put to work without pay, which, in effect, made them slaves. Although full-scale slavery did not come about in England, those who came to the United States were aware of the sentiment for

slavery back home and acted upon that sentiment upon arrival in Virginia and elsewhere.

Slavery's increasing importance in the United States did not mean that all Southern blacks were subject to the master's whip. Thousands of blacks were free, and several owned slaves. However, no matter their status as free men, they were constantly reminded that slavery was but a step away. Any anger or suspicion toward free blacks may be understood within the context of the understanding that they were all symbols of what could be to current slaves. That they were free gave them a certain status.

Whites were well aware of this fact, but they understood that free blacks represented more than a status symbol. Many slave rebellions were allegedly plotted by free blacks. Thus, they were viewed as potential leaders of uprisings, and those who could read and write, be they slave or free, were viewed as dangerous rebellion leaders. An educated African-American challenged the very notion of slavery and black inferiority as slavery's defenders during the first half of the nineteenth century frantically came up with theories that justified the institution. Abolitionists, white and black, including a few runaway slaves, traveled to England, where they refuted the notion of black inferiority as a reason for slavery. Frederick Douglass is the most notable example.

Douglass in 1845 traveled to England, where he lived for two years. Speaking on a celebrated lecture campaign, Douglass attacked slavery and the system that forced him to run away from his home and country. By the time Douglass' campaign was done, he had aroused the sympathies of the British working class against slavery. Other speakers gave credence and support to Douglass' lectures, which effectively hardened the working class's opinion against the slave system.

Meanwhile, in the United States the abolitionist movement and guilty feelings of slaveholders compelled proponents of slavery during the eighteenth century to defend a system that was the dominant factor in the Southern way of life. Central to this defense was the portrayal of African-Americans as inferior and subhuman. Slavery's defenders based their portrayal on two essential fallacies. The first was the claim that blacks came from a primitive culture that had always been inferior to European culture. The essence of this argument was that Africans were better off as slaves in the United States than as free people in Africa.

The second fallacy claimed that Africans could be civilized but needed a great deal of time learning at the feet of the white race in order to be civilized.

Culture and Civilization

These two fallacies tied together in several ways. The obvious tie-in concerns culture and civilization. First, the primitive lifestyle meant that African Americans had a longer learning curve to become civilized—if they could be civilized at all. Second, the fallacies reinforced the notion that African-Americans did not have the ability to receive a liberal education. The ability of a slave to read and write meant more than the potential to read books about freedom and pass the knowledge on to other slaves. It challenged the claim that blacks were decades and even centuries from being civilized. Moreover, it challenged the idea that African-Americans did not have the ability to read, write, add, subtract, or multiply. To disprove these notions would challenge the institution and rationale behind slavery, and would lead to other questions about alleged black inferiority. To institutionalize this, governments made it illegal to teach a slave to read and write.

Obviously not all of white United States or white Europe agreed with the proslavery faction. England's Parliament had passed the Slavery Abolition Bill three decades into the early nineteenth century. From August 1834, with a few exceptions, slavery was officially abolished in the British Empire and the British became the world's foremost abolitionists.

Where the British were mixed in their opinion of slavery, the French were more united in their sympathies for the South. Heavily dependent upon Southern cotton and commerce, the French public favored mediation between the two sides that would ensure Confederate independence when the U.S. Civil War broke out in the 1860s, as opposed to war.

Man of the Moment

During the Civil War (1861–1865) the country needed a strong leader, and although many did not think so at the time, Abraham Lincoln turned out to be just the man. The 1860 presidential campaign became a referendum on the Southern way of life, and Lincoln won despite receiving less than 40 percent of the vote and not appearing on the ballot in ten slave states.

When the Civil War began, Lincoln refused to admit that slavery was a factor. He merely stated his desire to "keep the Union together." Undoubtedly this was Lincoln's goal. A closer look, however, reveals deeper reasons for why this was his only publicly stated objective until September 1862.

A plantation manor in South Carolina. Source: istock/Dirk G. Hilbert.

EMANCIPATION PROCLAMATION

The Emancipation Proclamation *as declared by President Abraham Lincoln on 1 January 1863 set out to free the slaves in the Confederacy.*

Whereas, on the twenty-second day of September, in the year of our Lord one thousand eight hundred and sixty-two, a proclamation was issued by the President of the United States, containing, among other things, the following, to wit:

"That on the first day of January, in the year of our Lord one thousand eight hundred and sixty-three, all persons held as slaves within any State or designated part of a State, the people whereof shall then be in rebellion against the United States, shall be then, thenceforward, and forever free; and the Executive Government of the United States, including the military and naval authority thereof, will recognize and maintain the freedom of such persons, and will do no act or acts to repress such persons, or any of them, in any efforts they may make for their actual freedom.

"That the Executive will, on the first day of January aforesaid, by proclamation, designate the States and parts of States, if any, in which the people thereof, respectively, shall then be in rebellion against the United States; and the fact that any State, or the people thereof, shall on that day be, in good faith, represented in the Congress of the United States by members chosen thereto at elections wherein a majority of the qualified voters of such State shall have participated, shall, in the absence of strong countervailing testimony, be deemed conclusive evidence that such State, and the people thereof, are not then in rebellion against the United States."

Now, therefore I, Abraham Lincoln, President of the United States, by virtue of the power in me vested as Commander-in-Chief, of the Army and Navy of the United States in time of actual armed rebellion against the authority and government of the United States, and as a fit and necessary war measure for suppressing said rebellion, do, on this first day of January, in the year of our Lord one thousand eight hundred and sixty-three, and in accordance with my purpose so to do publicly proclaimed for the full period of one hundred days, from

the day first above mentioned, order and designate as the States and parts of States wherein the people thereof respectively, are this day in rebellion against the United States, the following, to wit:

Arkansas, Texas, Louisiana, (except the Parishes of St. Bernard, Plaquemines, Jefferson, St. John, St. Charles, St. James Ascension, Assumption, Terrebonne, Lafourche, St. Mary, St. Martin, and Orleans, including the City of New Orleans) Mississippi, Alabama, Florida, Georgia, South Carolina, North Carolina, and Virginia, (except the forty-eight counties designated as West Virginia, and also the counties of Berkley, Accomac, Northampton, Elizabeth City, York, Princess Ann, and Norfolk, including the cities of Norfolk and Portsmouth[]], and which excepted parts, are for the present, left precisely as if this proclamation were not issued.

And by virtue of the power, and for the purpose aforesaid, I do order and declare that all persons held as slaves within said designated States, and parts of States, are, and henceforward shall be free; and that the Executive government of the United States, including the military and naval authorities thereof, will recognize and maintain the freedom of said persons.

And I hereby enjoin upon the people so declared to be free to abstain from all violence, unless in necessary self-defence; and I recommend to them that, in all cases when allowed, they labor faithfully for reasonable wages.

And I further declare and make known, that such persons of suitable condition, will be received into the armed service of the United States to garrison forts, positions, stations, and other places, and to man vessels of all sorts in said service.

And upon this act, sincerely believed to be an act of justice, warranted by the Constitution, upon military necessity, I invoke the considerate judgment of mankind, and the gracious favor of Almighty God. . . .

Source: National Archives & Records Administration. (2007). Retrieved June 8, 2007, from http://www.archives.gov/exhibits/featured_documents/emancipation_proclamation/transcript.html

The border states of Delaware, Maryland, Missouri, and Kentucky did not secede from the Union even though they were slave states. Having clapped their pro-secessionist leaders in irons and sent them to prison, President Lincoln replaced them with pro-Union men. His hold on these states, however, remained tenuous. An initial declaration that the war was being fought to end slavery would have most likely resulted in these states joining the Confederacy.

Lincoln also realized that most Northerners were opposed to slavery but were not willing to fight to end it. Keeping the Union together was worth fighting for as far as Northern and, to a lesser

extent, border states were concerned. This was a key component in their willingness to fight even after Lincoln issued the Emancipation Proclamation. Such subtleties and hard political realities, though, eluded the British, who waited for Lincoln to declare that the war was being fought to end slavery. When the president continually insisted on "keeping the Union together," the British government took him at his word. The result was that views of the United States and its slave system were split depending upon one's social and economic position.

In northern England laborers were pro-Union. Abolitionists' speeches affected them as they began to realize that they had

commonalities with slaves. They hoped for a Union victory even if it affected the cotton supply upon which their jobs depended. A Confederate victory would be a blow to their morale.

Factory owners and government officials supported a Confederate victory. The owners needed Southern cotton to keep their businesses running, although they eventually received cotton from India and Egypt. Government officials were from the British upper crust, and they felt a kinship with the Southern aristocracy. A Union victory would make the economic lower classes more difficult to deal with. England's cultural wars were being fought on U.S. battlefields.

The Emancipation Proclamation was a prime example of Lincoln's genius. When he had campaigned for the presidency Lincoln had not campaigned to end slavery but rather to prevent its extension. As president, Lincoln moved cautiously on the slavery issue despite pressure from abolitionists. After the narrow Union victory in the Battle of Antietam, Lincoln issued the Emancipation Proclamation. A brilliant domestic and foreign policy stroke, the proclamation subtly and effectively added slavery to the war's official agenda.

The Emancipation Proclamation freed few slaves. Implying that states in rebellion could keep their slaves if the states stopped fighting against the Union, Lincoln made sure that the proclamation did not include the loyal border states, ensuring their continued loyalty. Most importantly, Lincoln made the Civil War a war to end slavery.

As important as it was domestically, the Emancipation Proclamation was just as important to Lincoln's foreign policy. The British government had come to the conclusion that a breakup of the Union would be in its best interest. The proclamation ended any thought of recognizing the Confederacy, leaving only the possibility that bitter feelings after the war would prevent a reunification of North and South.

Such a reunification did come about, however, and its manner and speed impressed the British. The Reconstruction era was a frightening and exhilarating time for former slaves. The Thirteenth, Fourteenth, and Fifteenth Amendments began the long push for equal rights for African Americans. Taking advantage of the Homestead Act, a few freedmen moved west, where they received parcels of land. Those who could ride a horse or were willing to learn how worked for cattle barons and took part in cattle drives. The United States was still in the process of "taming" the West, and former slaves took advantage by joining the military. Some of these freedmen, at least for a time, were able to quickly adjust to freedom. Most freedmen, however, faced problems. And the problems were many.

Trusting white men was one such problem. Freedmen had just been released from slavery; memories were still fresh. Those who had been physically abused by Union troops had even fewer reasons to trust whites. Now that freedmen were legally able to learn to read and write, educational facilities for freedmen were in demand. Freedmen also needed health services, and thousands of Southern blacks and whites were homeless with little money and fewer prospects.

Freedmen's Bureau

Congress recognized these problems and in March 1865 created the Bureau of Refugees, Freedmen, and Abandoned Lands. The Freedmen's Bureau, as it was commonly known, was an organization designed to "provide food, clothing, and medical care for both white refugees and Black freedmen; to settle them on abandoned or confiscated lands; and in general to help the freedmen in the period of transition from slavery to freedom" (Stampp 1962, 131).

However, conflicts over administering and continuing Reconstruction marred President Andrew Johnson's relationship with Congress, resulting in his impeachment. Johnson survived removal from office by one vote in the Senate. However, President Johnson's relationship with Congress did not improve. When his term ended, Johnson went home to Tennessee and was elected to the Senate in 1874.

With Ulysses S. Grant's election to the presidency in 1868, Reconstruction apparently would continue to help African-Americans. They were elected to political offices, and by all accounts most were "men of ability and integrity" (Stampp 1962, 167). None ever became a governor, but two were elected to the Senate (Mississippi), two were lieutenant governors (Louisiana and Mississippi), and others were elected to state positions, including secretary of state, superintendent of education, and treasurer. On the surface all seemed well.

However, a loud undercurrent of trouble flowed. For example, the Ku Klux Klan, which was founded in 1866, used terrorism against freedmen and their supporters. In 1871 Congress was compelled to pass an anti-Klan bill, which effectively banned the Ku Klux Klan. Things were not this easy, however. Organizations sympathized with the Klan, and violence was the essential mode of operation in its crusade to redeem the South against reformers and their sympathizers. That there was a military occupation of the South certainly helped the redeemers' cause.

After an initial rush to help African-Americans during Reconstruction, Congress appeared to lose interest. Despite laws against their running for office, former Confederate leaders were elected to Congress and served. The Republican Party's Radical Reconstruction leaders were retired or had moved on to other

interests while President Grant presided over one of the most corrupt administrations in U.S. history.

After a fraudulent presidential election in 1876 a bipartisan congressional committee awarded the presidency to Rutherford B. Hayes over his Democratic rival, Samuel Tilden. In exchange for internal improvements in the South and the removal of federal troops, Southern Democrats agreed to a Hayes presidency. Reconstruction ended in March 1877. This meant the end of hopes for civil rights for African-Americans as the issue of African-American rights was abandoned in favor of reunification of the white North and the white South.

Perspectives on Reunification

Few people in England or France were optimistic about the United States becoming one nation again. Yet, after the war the British were impressed by how well the South was treated. Fights over Reconstruction and the treatment of African-Americans aside, allowing the former Confederate states back into the Union with little punishment and relatively little fanfare encouraged many British citizens to move to the United States. By the 1870s the English press became fascinated with the growth of the U.S. West. Many ranchers out west were Irish and British. Moreover, the physical recovery from the war was rapid, and the British were almost as impressed by this recovery as they were by reunification. Napoleon III had used the Civil War to control the government in Mexico. He believed that an independent U.S. South would support his government in Mexico. The Union victory dashed all of his hopes and, with them, his dreams of at least starting a new French empire in North America.

The Aftermath of Slavery in the United States

While the United States regained some political traction globally after abolishing slavery, it took many decades for the image of a free nation to emerge. Through the end of the nineteenth century, and the first half of the twentieth, the United States was still overcoming its slave nation past with segregation, Jim Crow laws, and the civil rights movement highlighting this tumultuous relationship. In the eyes of the world, the United States took a long time to change its image as a slave nation.

Julian Madison

See also Human Rights; U.S. Civil Rights; U.S. Civil War

Further Reading

Bailey, T. (1980). *A diplomatic history of the American people.* Englewood Cliffs, NJ: Prentice-Hall.

Blassingame, J. (1972). *The slave community: Plantation life in the antebellum South.* Oxford, UK: Oxford University Press.

Fredrickson, G. M. (1971). *The black image in the white mind: The debate on Afro-American character and destiny, 1817–1914.* New York: Harper Torchbooks.

Hankinson, A. (1982). *Man of wars: William Howard Russell of* The Times. London: Heinemann.

Morgan, E. (1975). *American slavery, American freedom.* New York: W. W. Norton.

Pease, W. H., & Pease, J. H. (1969). Antislavery ambivalence: Immediatism, expediency, race. In A. Meier & E. Rudwick (Eds.), *The making of black America: Essays in Negro life and history.* New York: Atheneum.

Rogers, J. A. (1984). *Sex and race: Vol. 2* (pp. 153). St. Petersburg, FL: Helga Rogers.

Stampp, K. (1956). *The peculiar institution: Slavery in the ante-bellum South.* New York: Vintage Books.

Stampp, K. (1962). *The era of Reconstruction, 1865–1877.* New York: Vintage Books.

Tocqueville, A. de. (2000). *Democracy in America* (H. Mansfield & D. Winthrop, Trans. & Eds.). Chicago: University of Chicago Press.

Soviet Empire, Collapse of

The Soviet communist utopia once inspired millions in search of a better world. But in practice the system caused enormous suffering, ultimately leading to the dissolution of the USSR and the deterioration of global communism.

The year 1989 has been seen as a watershed time in history—when the Cold War and the looming danger of a third world war came to an end. Since 1945 the United States bore the brunt of responsibility for preserving peace and for defending itself and its allies in case of an attack from the Soviet Union. The United States government felt it could not afford to fall behind in any aspect of the race with the other superpower, be it the arms race, space exploration, or winning the sympathy of ordinary people around the globe. The Cold War was rightly called a political "Ice Age": The front lines were immovable, and the balance of the two sides had to be carefully guarded—not allowing any change or any defection, lest one of the parties consider itself strong enough to try overcome the other. The sudden collapse of the Soviet Empire and the death of its ideology, the communist utopia, was totally unexpected. The United States found itself the sole superpower; a position that no country in history had ever held.

Background

Entering 1989 the Soviet Union and its informal but very real empire were already facing serious economic difficulties and a lack of confidence about attaining the ambitious aims of its philosophy of Marxism-Leninism. However, no politician or analyst foresaw that by the end of the year all the Communist one-party states of central and southeastern Europe would renounce dictatorship and switch to political pluralism. In 1990 they all held free elections won by parties opposed to the Communists, discarded even the vestiges of Soviet-type socialism, and started restoring capitalism, that is, the market economy, while proclaiming their aim to return to the basic values of the West and the institutions built upon those values.

On 1 July 1991 the Warsaw Pact, the political-military organization of the Soviet empire, was dissolved by common consent, a consent approved by Mikhail Gorbachev, president of the Soviet Union. On 25 December the Soviet Union itself was officially dissolved, and its member states became internationally recognized sovereign, independent countries, all professing a commitment to political pluralism and the market economy. Never before had

an empire disappeared so suddenly and without bloodshed; never before had such profound political, economic, and social changes taken place in such a short time and over such a large territory.

Inherent Faults

The Soviet experiment of turning the German political philosopher Karl Marx's (1818–1883) vision into reality was doomed from the outset. U.S. historian and diplomat George F. Kennan argued in 1947 "that Soviet power, like the capitalist world of its conception, bears within it the seeds of its own decay, and that the sprouting of these seeds is well advanced" (Kennan 1947, 580). "Of all the reasons for the collapse of communism, the most basic is that it was an intrinsically nonviable, indeed impossible, project from the beginning.... And the perverse genius of Marxism is to present an unattainable utopia as an infallibly scientific enterprise" (Malia quoted in Edwards 2000, 71). In pursuit of the attractive aims of utopian Communism, "the Communists violated everything we know from anthropology that human beings, even in the most primitive circumstances, desire and practice. They virtually outlawed religion, property, and free speech, which are common to all societies" (Pipes quoted in Edwards 2000, 46).

From the beginning the Communist system was built on intimidation, repression, and terror inflicted on the whole society—methods that can work only temporarily because people never genuinely acquiesce to them. The strongest appeal of Communism to members of the poorer section of society was its promise of radical improvements in their standard of living, first by expropriating the well-to-do and eventually by creating abundance in all material goods. However, an economic system that banned all private property and stifled individual initiatives was unable to improve living conditions. For more backward national communities—primarily for the Russians, but to a lesser extent for all people living in the eastern half of Europe—Communism held out the hope of catching up with the advanced West and even overtaking it. However, with growing prosperity in the West this hope evaporated, and by the 1980s hardly anyone in the Communist world believed in a bright economic future.

Fundamental Shortcomings

Vladimir Ilyich Lenin (1870–1924) and his Bolshevik Party, having attained power in a coup on 7 November (25 October, old calendar) 1917, sincerely believed that Communism would quickly spread to the rest of the world but were realistic enough to give a push to history with weapons. The Bolsheviks owed much of their victory to the non-Russian population of the czarist empire, for whom they promised self-determination and the right to secede. By 1922, however, the Bolsheviks brought most territories of the former Russian empire under their control and established the Soviet Union. Nominally it was a federation, but in fact it was a strongly centralized state run by Russians or people assimilated by the Russians, such as the Georgian Djugashvili, who assumed the name "Joseph Stalin." After Stalin (1879–1953) eliminated all his potential rivals in the "Great Terror" and defeated German Nazi leader Adolf Hitler, Stalin directed his Red Army, relying on a few local Communists, to impose the Communist system on all the countries in the eastern half of Europe, which came under Soviet control by the end of World War II. However, "Marxism-Leninism was an alien doctrine imposed on the region by an imperial power whose rule was culturally repugnant to the dominated peoples" (Brzezinski quoted in Edwards 2000, 21).

The captive nations attempted to escape from the oppressive system (Hungary with the uprising in 1956, Czechoslovakia with the "Prague Spring" in 1968, and Poland on several occasions), but the armed interventions of the Soviet Union and the Brezhnev Doctrine (any "threat" to socialism, perceived as such by the Soviet leadership, should be answered by common intervention) assured continued Soviet domination—for the time being. These interventions shattered many illusions about Soviet Communism in the West and in the Third World, discrediting the slogans, which were propagated by paid agents and credulous intellectuals.

After the death of Stalin, successor Nikita Khrushchev (1894–1971) revealed many of Stalin's crimes, and cautious economic reforms started. Detente apparently signaled the end of plans to launch an invasion of western Europe, but in Latin America, Africa, and Asia Soviet policies continued to spread revolution and the doctrines of Communism. Those policies, however, put a great strain on the flagging Soviet economy. With the easing of terror intellectual opposition grew, helped by the publicity given to it by the Western media, especially radio broadcasts, notwithstanding the jamming of them.

Incidental Causes

Marxism declared the victory of Communism as historically inevitable, but a system based on coercion, economic irrationality, and incompetent leadership was bound to fail on the long run. Also, quite a few providential incidents, mainly related to individuals, helped undermine the system and brought closer its demise.

The Conference on Security and Cooperation in Europe (CSCE) was meant by the Soviets to consolidate and legalize the

A Russian submarine, an important component of the Soviet arsenal during the Cold War. Source: istock/James Steidl.

division of Europe, but it backfired. The signing of the Helsinki Final Act and the follow-up conferences gave a boost to dissent all over the Communist bloc by "firmly entrenching human rights on the diplomatic agenda" (Kovrig 1991, 167).

Most political leaders in western Europe (except British Prime Minister Margaret Thatcher) acquiesced to the division of Europe and did not even dream of "winning" the Cold War. In the 1970s the United States negotiated treaties (SALT I and the ABM Treaty) with the Soviet Union in order to reduce the level of armaments and ventured beyond merely containing the Soviet threat when two foreign-born national security advisers, Henry Kissinger and Zbigniew Brzezinski, initiated differentiation within the Soviet bloc, rewarding any country that diverted a bit from the Soviet line. "Most favored nation" status and, as a concomitant, increasing exports to the United States were a real carrot for the command economies always in dire need of convertible currency. Polish-born Brzezinski advised President Jimmy Carter to show at least as much interest in eastern Europe as the Soviets were showing in Latin America. The insincerity of Soviet slogans about detente was exposed by conducting activity in the Third World, building up the Soviet fleet, commissioning a large number of nuclear submarines, and deploying medium-range SS-20 missiles in the western region of the Soviet Union and (unannounced) in the central European satellites. The response of the North Atlantic Treaty Organization (NATO) was the decision to deploy ground-launched Cruise missiles and Pershing II rockets on the territory of the west European allies, disregarding the protests of a large number of well-meaning but gullible people. The election of Ronald Reagan (1911–2004) in 1979 as president placed at the helm of the United States a man who had strong convictions about Communism. He undiplomatically called the Soviet Union "the Evil Empire," which it really was in the eyes of the peoples whose misfortune brought them under its control. Reagan did not like the prospect of "mutually assured destruction," the prospect that in case of a nuclear war between the two superpowers, each side had the capability to destroy the other, even after suffering a first strike. Being aware of the great strides the United States had made in high-tech weapons as well as in computer and space technology, he ordered work on SDI (Strategic Defense Initiative) to build a protective shield over the United States so that incoming enemy missiles and their nuclear warheads could be destroyed in space, never reaching their targets in the United States. That was a project that the Soviet Union was unable to answer.

The man who was expected to reform the Soviet system without changing its basic nature was Mikhail Gorbachev, a man raised in the Communist Party apparatus and the KGB (the Soviet security, secret police, and intelligence agency). He was elected secretary-general (de facto leader) in 1985 at the relatively young age of fifty-four. By that time socialism was in an obvious crisis all over the Soviet empire: Production figures were falling (or at best stagnating), corruption and crime were rising, alcoholism was rampant, and heavy pollution led to deteriorating health conditions and decreasing life expectancy. Gorbachev hoped to save the system by controlled change, to make it more effective, to advance its obsolete technology, and to maintain the Soviet Union's status as a superpower. His much-acclaimed "openness" policy (glasnost) exposed the depth of the crisis before the Soviet public and before the whole world. His other policy, "restructuring" (perestroika), tried to reduce the influence of the incompetent, corrupt, and increasingly senile party leadership and to increase the role of elected central and local bodies.

People in western Europe were elated to see such an enlightened Soviet leader, especially when he started a "peace offensive" by unilaterally reducing his armed forces in central Europe and recognizing the right of every country (by implication also those in the Soviet bloc) to choose its own political course.

Immediate Cause: Poland and Hungary

Undoubtedly the most effective weapon of the West in the later phase of the Cold War was prosperity; Western consumer goods, especially the car, became the most important status symbol. That prosperity won over the citizens of all the Communist countries; even their leaders became keen on Western contacts, scholarships, and visits to the department stores. Obviously the Soviet Union would never catch up with the West, let alone bury it, as had been promised by Khrushchev in the early 1960s.

Against that background Poland and Hungary, two nations that had already defied Communism and Soviet domination in 1956 and were ahead of all other members of the bloc in tolerating diversions from Communist orthodoxy, bent to popular pressure and introduced measures that went much further than any previous attempts at change.

In Poland after 1956 the strong Catholic church was no longer persecuted, the peasants were allowed to keep their private farms, and limited cultural freedom was tolerated. Repeated local riots against food price increases took place, culminating in July 1980 in a massive strike in Gdansk. Its outcome was a genuine working-class movement (the dream of Marx), the Solidarity Free Trade Union. Authorities were compelled to recognize the union when its membership rose to ten million in a country of thirty-six million inhabitants. This development was rightly termed a "self-limiting revolution" because its avowed aim was not to overthrow the hated regime but rather to improve the living conditions and to guarantee

the right of the workers to strike. Lech Walesa proved not only a charismatic but also a sensible leader of Solidarity, balancing between radicalism and compromise. This "dual power" lasted for one and a half years. The Soviet Union did consider military intervention, but with the war in Afghanistan and the need for European technological and humanitarian aid, that intervention was not feasible. The alternative was martial law, introduced on 13 December 1981, planned and carried out by General (by then Prime Minister and party leader) Wojciech Jaruzelski. This was indeed "war on Polish society," with Solidarity banned and ten thousand people held in detention, but it was far from being a repetition of the brutal repression of the Hungarians in 1956 and of the Czechs in 1968. Western sanctions (prompted by the United States) hit the economy and especially the party cadres. Finally a compromise was reached between the Communist leadership and the still-banned Solidarity leaders at roundtable discussions in 1989, leading to the "semi-free elections" in June, which were won by Solidarity. Jaruzelski felt compelled to appoint Tadeusz Mazowiecki, a non-Communist Solidarity adviser, as prime minister. Poland immediately started a return to the market economy.

After the mid-1960s the repression in Hungary was eased, and feeble economic reforms were introduced. Elements of the market and some private initiatives, especially in agriculture, were permitted. Gorbachev, whose earlier responsibility had been agriculture, found those reforms promising. With the economy stagnating and with prices starting to reflect real costs, Hungarian leaders had recourse to massive borrowing to prevent a decline in the standard of living. By the end of the 1980s the foreign debt of Hungary was $21 billion for a population of ten million. Growing business ties with the West made the Hungarian Communist leaders interested in survival through change. The example of Spain—where a peaceful transition from dictatorship to democracy took place—came to inspire the leaders of the modernizing central and east European countries. The CSCE follow-up conferences in Madrid, Geneva, and Budapest were utilized by the Hungarian "dissidents," too, who openly criticized the regime, and a kind of alliance was formed between them, the conservative patriots, religious groups, and discontented workers. Janos Kádár (1912–1989), the party leader who betrayed the revolution in 1956 and was responsible for the subsequent repression but who later became a cautious reformer, was replaced in May 1988. The leader of the 1956 revolution, Imre Nagy (1896–1958), and his fellow martyrs were given a moving reburial on 16 June 1989—attended by the world media and inspiring neighboring countries. Round-table talks started between the Communist leadership and the by-then legally recognized opposition parties. President George H. W. Bush gave strong encouragement to the

movement for change by visiting Poland and Hungary in July 1989. By September the political talks resulted in an agreement changing the constitution, restoring a multiparty democracy, and scheduling free elections for spring 1990. The elections were won by the center-right Hungarian Democratic Forum, led by József Antall (1932–1993).

In August 1989 a social event known as the "Pan-European Picnic" was organized on the border between Austria and Hungary by opposition parties in Hungary. It was used by close to a thousand East German citizens to escape through that temporary hole in the Iron Curtain. Tens of thousands of their compatriots followed, coming to Hungary in hopes that they too could leave for the West. Pressed by that crowd, and also by the political opposition and by the Federal Republic, the Hungarian government announced on 10 September 1990 that the citizens of the "German Democratic Republic" would be permitted to cross the border and leave for the West. By then the East German umbrella organization Neues Forum started to demand changes, including the right to visit fellow Germans in the Federal Republic. The successful escape through Hungary made it pointless to keep the Branderburger Gate in the Berlin Wall closed. When a new, reformist East German leadership decided to open it, the people tore the Wall into pieces on 9 November 1989. With the demise of that iconic physical barrier, a new democratic coalition was formed in East Berlin, preparing the way for the reunification of Germany.

All that was too much for the Czechs to watch passively, and a series of mass demonstrations in Prague in late November led to the "velvet revolution" directed by the Civic Forum and Slovak Openness against Violence. On 29 November the Communists started negotiations with the opposition and agreed to form a new government of national unity, headed by a reformist Communist, while the parliament elected the dissident playwright Vaclav Havel provisional president on 29 December 1989.

In mid-December bloody reprisals followed protests against the removal of a popular and outspoken Hungarian Calvinist pastor in the southwestern town of Timisoara. A mass rally called by the dreaded Romanian dictator Nicolae Ceausescu in Bucharest turned against him and ended in his having to escape by helicopter from his palace. After widespread fighting between his security forces and the insurgents Ceausescu and his wife were captured and summarily executed. The Council of National Liberation, headed by a former close associate of the dictator, Ion Iliescu, was formed.

Under far less dramatic circumstances Bulgaria, too, changed. Todor Zivkov, the long-time party boss, was replaced on 10 November 1989 by a reformist Communist. The most closed and self-isolated Communist country, Albania, also discarded Communism in two steps by the end of 1991.

DISSOLVING THE SOVIET UNION

On 25 December 1991, Mikhael S. Gorbachev delivered the following speech as he resigned as president of the Union of Soviet Socialist Republics (USSR). This was the final act in the dissolution of USSR.

Dear compatriots, fellow citizens, as a result of the newly formed situation, creation of the Commonwealth of Independent States, I cease my activities in the post of the U.S.S.R. president. I am taking this decision out of considerations based on principle. I have firmly stood for independence, self-rule of nations, for the sovereignty of the republics, but at the same time for preservation of the union state, the unity of the country.

Events went a different way. The policy prevailed of dismembering this country and disuniting the state, with which I cannot agree. And after the Alma-Ata meeting and the decisions taken there, my position on this matter has not changed. Besides, I am convinced that decisions of such scale should have been taken on the basis of a popular expression of will.

Yet, I will continue to do everything in my power so that agreements signed there should lead to real accord in the society, (and) facilitate the escape from the crisis and the reform process. Addressing you for the last time in the capacity of president of the U.S.S.R., I consider it necessary to express my evaluation of the road we have traveled since 1985, especially as there are a lot of contradictory, superficial and subjective judgments on that matter.

Fate had it that when I found myself at the head of the state it was already clear that all was not well in the country. There is plenty of everything: land, oil and gas, other natural riches, and God gave us lots of intelligence and talent, yet we lived much worse than developed countries and keep falling behind them more and more.

The reason could already be seen: The society was suffocating in the vise of the command-bureaucratic system, doomed to serve ideology and bear the terrible burden of the arms race. It had reached the limit of its possibilities. All attempts at partial reform, and there had been many, had suffered defeat, one after another. The country was losing perspective. We could not go on living like that. Everything had to be changed radically.

The process of renovating the country and radical changes in the world turned out to be far more complicated than could be expected. However, what has been done ought to be given its due. This society acquired freedom, liberated itself politically and spiritually, and this is the foremost achievement which we have not yet understood completely, because we have not learned to use freedom.

However, work of historic significance has been accomplished. The totalitarian system which deprived the country of an opportunity to become successful and prosperous long ago has been eliminated. A breakthrough has been achieved on the way to democratic changes. Free elections, freedom of the press, religious freedoms, representative organs of power, a multiparty (system) became a reality; human rights are recognized as the supreme principle.

The movement to a diverse economy has started, equality of all forms of property is becoming established, people who work on the land are coming to life again in the framework of land reform, farmers have appeared, millions of acres of land are being given over to people who live in the countryside and in towns.

Economic freedom of the producer has been legalized, and entrepreneurship, shareholding, privatization are gaining momentum. In turning the economy toward a market, it is important to remember that all this is done for the sake of the individual. At this difficult time, all should be done for his social protection, especially for senior citizens and children.

We live in a new world. The Cold War has ended, the arms race has stopped, as has the insane militarization which mutilated our economy, public psyche and morals. The threat of a world war has been removed. Once again I want to stress that on my part everything was done during the transition period to preserve reliable control of the nuclear weapons.

We opened ourselves to the world, gave up interference into other people's affairs, the use of troops beyond the borders of the country, and trust, solidarity and respect came in response.

The nations and peoples of this country gained real freedom to choose the way of their self-determination. The search for a democratic reformation of the multinational state brought us to the threshold of concluding a new Union Treaty. All these changes demanded immense strain. They were carried out with sharp struggle, with growing resistance from the old, the obsolete forces.

The old system collapsed before the new one had time to begin working, and the crisis in the society became even more acute.

The August coup brought the general crisis to its ultimate limit. The most damaging thing about this crisis is the breakup of the statehood. And today I am worried by our people's loss of the citizenship of a great country. The consequences may turn out to be very hard for everyone.

I am leaving my post with apprehension, but also with hope, with faith in you, your wisdom and force of spirit. We are the heirs of a great civilization, and its rebirth into a new, modern and dignified life now depends on one and all.

Some mistakes could surely have been avoided, many things could have been done better, but I am convinced that sooner or later our common efforts will bear fruit, our nations will live in a prosperous and democratic society.

I wish all the best to all of you.

Source: Gorbachev speech dissolving the Soviet Union (USSR). (1999). Retrieved March 15, 2007, from http://www.publicpurpose.com/lib-gorb911225.htm

Aftermath

Half-hearted economic and legal changes brought the Soviet economy almost to a standstill in 1990. Its former satellites were moving toward the West as fast as they could and called for the dissolution of the Warsaw Pact. All of the fifteen Soviet republics pressed for decentralization, and the Baltic republics demanded full independence. In June 1991 the Russian Republic elected its own president, the popular radical reformist Boris Yeltsin, with a claim for sovereignty. The hard-liners, probably with the connivance of Gorbachev, answered with a coup attempt on 19 August 1991, trying to restore central authority, but the people of Moscow, led by Yeltsin, took to the streets, and the coup attempt collapsed. The Communist Party was banned, the Baltic states declared their independence, and the other republics soon followed suit. Gorbachev was sent into retirement, and on 25 December the red flag, the symbol of Communism, was lowered from the Kremlin.

The Communist utopia, once firing the imagination of millions in search of a better world but causing enormous suffering and the deaths of tens of millions of innocent victims, ended fully discredited. The only good thing that can be said about it is that its downfall did not claim more lives. Contrary to Marx's predictions, it was not the state but rather Marxist Communism that withered away.

Implications for the United States

The disappearance of the Communist bloc was first welcomed as "not just the end of the Cold War, or a passing of a particular period of postwar history, but the end of history as such: that is, the end point of mankind's ideological evolution and the universalization of Western liberal democracy as the final form of human government" (Fukuyama 1989, 2). President George H. W. Bush confidently announced the coming of a "New World Order," in which the noble principles embodied in the Charter of the United Nations would finally prevail, guaranteed by the authority of the United States. But the "peace dividend," a massive reduction in military expenditure, proved illusory, as new threats ("rogue" states, weapons of mass destruction, nationalism leading to local wars, an upsurge of violence in the Middle East, and, finally, terrorism) needed new, even more sophisticated and more expensive weapons as well as soldiers trained for new types of war.

With the terrorist attack on the World Trade Center in New York and its repercussions from Afghanistan to Iraq, the pre-1990 bipolar world may appear more stable. It should not be forgotten, however, that the Cold War could have at any time turned into a hot war, ending human life on Earth. Also with the common danger presented by the Soviet Union gone, not a few people thought that Europe should disentangle itself from what they called the American "hyperpower" and emerge as an independent superpower. But those who remember Nazism and Communism, or suffered under those two evil systems, tend to remain "Atlanticists," committed to the maintenance and strength of NATO and its leading power, the United States. They are convinced that all the new threats to peace and democratic values can be answered only jointly by Europe and America, while fearing that "the only real alternative to American leadership is international anarchy" (Brzezinski 1997). Most friends and allies of the United States believe that the post–Cold War role of the Republic can be fulfilled only if its "hard power"—military, economic and political strength—is matched by the "soft power" of diplomacy, genuine partnership, and intellectual excellence.

Géza Jeszenszky

See also Cold War; Cold War, Post Era; Special Relationship (U.S.-Russia)

Further Reading

Ash, T. G. (1993). *The magic lantern: The revolution of '89 witnessed in Warsaw, Budapest, Berlin, and Prague.* New York: Vintage Books.

Brown, A. (1996). *The Gorbachev factor.* New York: Oxford University Press.

Brown, A., & Shevtsova, L. (Eds.). (2001). *Gorbachev, Yeltsin, and Putin: Political leadership in Russia's transition.* Washington, DC: Carnegie Endowment for International Peace.

Brzezinski, Z. (1989). *The grand failure: The birth and death of Communism in the twentieth century.* New York: Scribner.

Büky, B. (2001). *Visszapillantás a hidegháborúra* [Looking back at the Cold War]. Budapest, Hungary: Balassi.

Cipkowski, P. (1991). *Revolution in eastern Europe: Understanding the collapse of Communism in Poland, Hungary, East Germany, Czechoslovakia, Romania and the Soviet Union.* New York: Wiley.

Conquest, R. (1990). *The great terror: A reassessment.* London: Hutchinson.

Dallin, A., & Lapidus, G. W. (Eds.). (1995). *The Soviet system: From crisis to collapse.* Boulder, CO: Westview Press.

Edwards, L. (2000). *The collapse of Communism.* Stanford, CA: Hoover Institution Press.

English, R. D. (2000). *Russia and the idea of the West: Gorbachev, intellectuals and the end of the Cold War.* New York: Columbia University Press.

Fukuyama, F. (Summer 1989). The end of history? *The National Interest, 16*, 2.

Gati, C. (1990). *The bloc that failed: Soviet–East European relations in transition.* Bloomington: Indiana University Press.

Grachev, A. (1995). *Final days: The inside story of the collapse of the Soviet Union.* Boulder, CO: Westview Press.

Hough, J. F. (1997). *Democratization and revolution in the USSR 1985–1991.* Washington, DC: Brookings Institution.

Hutchings, R. L. (1997). *American diplomacy and the end of the Cold War: An insider's account of U.S. policy in Europe, 1989–1992.* Baltimore: Johns Hopkins University Press.

Kennan, G. F. (1947, July). The sources of Soviet conduct. *Foreign Affairs, 26,*. 580.

Kissinger, H. (1994). *Diplomacy.* New York: Simon & Schuster.

Kotkin, S. (2001). *Armageddon averted: The Soviet collapse 1970–2000.* Oxford, UK: Oxford University Press.

Kovrig, B. (1991). *Of walls and bridges: The United States and eastern Europe.* New York: New York University Press.

Matlock, J. F. Jr. (1995). *Autopsy on an empire: The American ambassador's account of the collapse of the Soviet Union.* New York: Random House.

McFaul, M. (1995). *Russia's unfinished revolution: Political change from Gorbachev to Putin.* Ithaca, NY: Cornell University Press.

Menges, C. C. (1990). *The twilight struggle: The Soviet Union v. the United States today.* Washington, DC: AEI Press.

Remnick, D. (1993). *Lenin's tomb: The last days of the Soviet empire.* New York: Random House.

Stokes, G. (1993). *The walls came tumbling down.* Oxford, UK: Oxford University Press.

Special Relationship (U.S.-Canada)

Since the Vietnam War many Canadians feel that their society is more peace-loving and socially conscious than the United States. Yet despite societal differences, Canadians also value their deep bonds with the United States.

Former Canadian prime minister Pierre Trudeau once likened living next to the United States to "sleeping with an elephant," and it would be hard to better describe the asymmetrical nature of the Canada-U.S. relationship. Since the early twentieth century the two nations have forged ever-deepening bonds of friendship. They share a vast undefended border, work together as allies in international affairs, and reap the benefits of the greatest bilateral trading relationship in the world. Yet, when one sleeps with an elephant—in this case an elephant ten times larger by population and with an even greater edge in military and economic might—one always faces the risk of being crushed. Canadians have therefore tended to have mixed feelings about the United States. They consider Americans to be their best friends but worry that immense U.S. power and influence pose a danger to Canada's political, economic, and cultural independence.

Early Relationship, 1775–1914

History has taught Canadians to be suspicious of the United States. Revolutionaries invaded Quebec in 1775, and a more serious U.S. effort to conquer Canada sparked the War of 1812. That bloody conflict ended in a draw and earned "Yankees" a withering reputation north of the border as a crass and warlike people. Tensions eased and trade flourished in ensuing decades, but in the 1860s Anglo-U.S. hostilities flared. The United States abrogated an 1854 reciprocity pact with Canada, and rumors spread that an invasion would follow. Fenian—Irish nationalists who were seeking retribution against Britain—border raids in 1866 further pressed four of the British North American colonies—what is now Quebec, Ontario, New Brunswick and Nova Scotia—to finalize confederation, the scheme that united them in the new Dominion of Canada on 1 July 1867.

The threat of war soon faded, and trade replaced it as the premier bilateral issue. In the late nineteenth century both nations erected tariff walls to protect domestic industries. Prime Minister Sir John A. Macdonald (1815–1891) labeled this high-tariff approach the "National Policy" and argued that Canada had to promote interprovincial trade to reduce its dependence on the colossal U.S. market. His opponent and later successor, Wilfrid Laurier (1841–1919), countered with "unrestricted reciprocity" in 1891 and 1911, but these free trade proposals were defeated by the charge that Laurier was trying to sell out Canada to the United States. The success of that unjust charge, coupled with bitter feelings that oozed from the Alaskan Boundary Dispute of 1903, revealed continuing anti-U.S. sentiments in Canadian society in the early twentieth century.

Special Relationship, 1914–2007

World War I (1914–1918) spurred Canada and the United States to overcome old animosities and establish a genuine friendship. Canadians fought from the outset as a British colony. Many people were disdainful of U.S. neutrality but rejoiced on 6 April 1917 when President Woodrow Wilson (1856–1924) brought the United States into the war against Germany and its allies. This war was the first time that Canadian and U.S. soldiers had fought against a common enemy, and their shared sacrifices on the Western front helped to improve the Canada-U.S. relationship.

In the interwar years the two peoples found that they had much in common. Both felt detached from Europe and uninterested in becoming embroiled once more in its affairs. Canada and the United States finally exchanged diplomatic legations in 1926, the same year that the Americans permanently surpassed the British as Canada's leading trading partners. The Great Depression blackened the 1930s, but one bright spot was the warm friendship that developed between Prime Minister William Lyon Mackenzie King (1874–1950) and President Franklin D. Roosevelt (1882–1945). When Germany began World War II on 1 September 1939, concerns for North American security propelled the two leaders toward unprecedented arrangements for bilateral cooperation.

Once again Canada sided with Britain from the beginning, and U.S. neutrality made early collaboration awkward. In 1940 and 1941 King and Roosevelt signed the historic Ogdensburg and

Hyde Park agreements, linking the military and economic futures of the two countries and creating the Permanent Joint Board on Defense. When Japan attacked Pearl Harbor on 7 December 1941, Canada and the United States were formal allies again. They fought together in various theaters of war, including the Normandy invasion of 6 June 1944, and Canada played a modest role in the top-secret Manhattan Project that produced the U.S. atomic bombs dropped on Japan.

In the aftermath of the war, Canadian leaders followed the U.S. lead as the threat of communism loomed and the Cold War began between the United States and the Soviet Union. When Louis St. Laurent (1882–1973) took over from King in November 1948, he committed Canada to even further cooperation with the United States. His government helped found the North Atlantic Treaty Organization (NATO) in April 1949 and lent troops to the U.S.-led coalition that fought the Korean War from 1950 to 1953. He even approved a series of radar outposts in the Canadian north, including the Distant Early Warning Line, which was controversial in Canada because it was staffed with U.S. military personnel. In 1957 the North American Air Defense agreement (NORAD) entailed intimate military cooperation and shared responsibility for meeting the potential threat of a Soviet attack on North America.

Some Canadian leaders privately questioned what they perceived to be a reckless and overly militaristic slant to U.S. foreign policies. This questioning was apparent between 1957 and 1963, when Prime Minister John Diefenbaker (1895–1979) refused to accept U.S. nuclear weapons on Canadian soil and engaged in an ugly public feud with President John F. Kennedy (1917–1963). The gradual escalation of the Vietnam War exposed further differences of opinion between Canadian and U.S. leaders. As the United States suffered through that draining conflict from 1961 to 1975, Prime Ministers Lester Pearson (1897–1972) and Pierre Trudeau (1919–2000) declined to send troops and allowed thousands of U.S. draft dodgers to cross the Canadian border.

The Vietnam War also reinforced in Canadians a sense that they lived in a more peace-loving and socially conscious society than that of the United States. They took pride in the Canadian role in various United Nations peacekeeping missions and, after 1968, in their universal health-care program. These feelings did not prevent the remarkable expansion of Canadian-U.S. trade. The 1965 Auto Pact, integrating the two automotive industries, was symbolic of the close linkage. Efforts by the Trudeau government in the 1970s and early 1980s to seek new markets and reduce U.S. ownership in certain critical industries garnered many headlines but had a negligible impact on the immense flow of daily traffic over the border.

In 1987 the Canada-U.S. economic partnership became more inextricably linked when the governments of Prime Minister Brian Mulroney (b. 1939) and President Ronald Reagan (1911–2004) negotiated the Canada-U.S. Free Trade Agreement. Canadian nationalists branded it the "Sale of Canada Act" and claimed

A bridge between Canada and the United States with the seagull in flight as symbol of free trade. Source: istock/Frances Twitty.

that its passage would doom Canadians to eventual absorption by the Americans. The 1988 Canadian federal election was fought over the issue of free trade. Mulroney won and implemented the deal. Five years later the North American Free Trade Agreement (NAFTA) brought Mexico into the fold, and the Canadian and U.S. governments have since pursued even broader free trade pacts extending throughout the Western Hemisphere.

The 1990s were a decade of generally positive Canadian-U.S. relations. When President George H. W. Bush (b. 1924) launched Operation Desert Storm to expel Iraq from Kuwait in 1991, Prime Minister Jean Chretien (b. 1934) provided modest military support. From 1993 to 2001, a period of sustained economic growth, President Bill Clinton (b. 1946) got along well with Chretien and was fairly well regarded in Canada. Relations chilled when President George W. Bush (b. 1946) assumed office in January 2001 because Bush appeared to take more interest in Mexico than Canada and pursued an international agenda that few Canadians supported. A great outpouring of Canadian sympathy followed the September 11, 2001, terrorist attacks on the United States, but these feelings soon dissipated as Bush aggressively pursued his "war on terrorism." Chretien supported the invasion and then occupation of Afghanistan late in 2001 but refused to commit Canadian forces to the invasion of Iraq in March 2003 unless the United Nations endorsed military action.

The Future

The decision to sit out the Iraq War (2003) has proven popular in Canada, largely because it represented a welcome assertion of Canadian sovereignty. Such foreign policy disagreements have emerged periodically between the two governments, but these ought not to overshadow the friendly character of the day-to-day Canada-U.S. relationship. Canadians grumble about the aggressive streak in U.S. foreign policy, but they have normally supported its guiding principles. They are quick to defend their separate identity but also value their deep bonds with the United States. Sleeping with the U.S. "elephant" has at times been nerve-wracking for Canadians, but the vast imbalance of power between the two nations has not kept Canada and the United States from developing a special relationship that seems likely to continue long into the future.

Christopher John Pennington

Further Reading

Bothwell, R. (1992). *Canada and the United States: The politics of partnership.* New York: Twayne Publishers.

Bothwell, R. (1998). *The big chill: Canada and the Cold War.* Toronto, Canada: Irwin Publishers.

Carment, D., Hampson, F. O., & Hillmer, N. (Eds.). (2003). *Canada among nations 2003: Coping with the American colossus.* Toronto, Canada: Oxford University Press.

Edmonds, J. D. (1989). *Friends so different: Essays on Canada and the United States in the 1980s.* Ottawa, Canada: University of Ottawa Press.

Granatstein, J. L. (1996). *Yankee go home? Canadians and anti-Americanism.* Toronto, Canada: HarperCollins.

Hillmer, N., & Granatstein, J. L. (1994). *Empire to umpire.* Toronto, Canada: Addison-Wesley.

Lipset, S. M. (1990). *Continental divide: The values and institutions of the United States and Canada.* New York: Routledge.

Martin, L. (1983). *The presidents and the prime ministers: Washington and Ottawa face to face: The myth of bilateral bliss, 1867–1982.* Markham, Canada: Paper Jacks.

Ross, D. A. (1984). *In the interests of peace: Canada and Vietnam 1954–1973.* Toronto, Canada: University of Toronto Press.

Stacey, C. P. (1981, 1984). *Canada and the age of conflict* (Vols. 1, 2). Toronto, Canada: University of Toronto Press.

Thompson, J. H. (2002). *Canada and the United States: Ambivalent allies.* Athens: University of Georgia Press.

Special Relationship (U.S.-Mexico)

U.S.-Mexico relations have always been challenged by issues of interdependence. The old saying, "Poor Mexico, so far away from God and so close to the U.S." captures the historically ambivalent nature of this relationship.

Geography is not destiny, but when neighboring countries of such deep, long-term cultural, political, and economic asymmetries as Mexico and the United States share a 2,500-kilometer-long land border, geography can cause those two countries to have complex and sometimes contradictory perspectives of one another. This fact applies in particular to Mexico, the weak party in the relationship, whose leaders and population have generally had an ambiguous perspective of and relationship with the United States. They have felt both admiration and rejection, a wish to emulate but also a fundamental distrust, the economic-political need to be close but also a wish that geography had put something in between. These contradictions can be explained best by looking at the key historical periods through which the U.S.-Mexico special relationship has evolved.

These periods can be divided into five major historical themes in the U.S.-Mexico relationship. First, the theme of foreign wars/ occupations dominated the relationship in the half-century after Mexico's independence from Spain in 1821. Second, between 1867 and 1910 the relationship was dominated by Mexico's dependence on U.S. technology and investment, while at the same time Mexico kept U.S. influence at bay through links with Europe. Third, the Mexican Revolution and its long aftermath (1910–1940) opened a new chapter in the relationship, characterized by mutual uncertainty, which was punctuated by political confrontation but eventual accommodation. Fourth, during World War II (1939–1945) and the Cold War (1948–1989/1991) Mexican leaders forged a good working relationship with the United States despite the fact that Mexico was not a liberal democracy. Fifth and last, economic crisis (1982), the end of the Cold War (1989/1991), and technological developments in transport and communications (since the early 1990s) gave way to a process of globalization, which has affected the U.S.-Mexico special relationship decisively and permanently

HOW MY MOM GOT TO THE UNITED STATES

The passage below presents a slightly different view on Mexico-U.S. migration. It was written by a sixth-grader from Virginia based on his memories and an interview with his mother about her migration experience.

My little brother could not stop crying. It was the day my mom left us in Mexico. She began her journey to the U.S. for a better life and job.

My mom is kind, honest, and has a positive mind. She wanted to leave Mexico because she needed money to support our family. One afternoon my brother, sister, and I were at home. My mom was there too—somewhere. My brother, sister, and I were in a little store which my grandma has. Finally, my mom came up to the store and at first she said nothing. A few seconds later she called me and said, "I just called a taxi. I am going to the U.S."

I could see that she had tears in her eyes "But why?" I said. She didn't say anything, and instead she me gave a big hug. Before I knew it, the taxi was there parked on the street waiting for my mom to get into it. She gave each of us another hug and got into the taxi and left. My little brother could not stop crying because our mom was leaving

us alone. My sister started crying too; but even though I wasn't crying, I felt my heart was broken.

Weeks passed, and we had no news from our mom. One day, in the afternoon I was playing outside when my grandma got a call from my mom. My grandma was relieved because my mom had made it to the States okay. A few days later she called again. I was so excited to hear her voice again. She didn't have a lot of time to talk, so she just talked to me. I asked her if she was okay, and how she got there. She told me that she was fine, but her feet were still hurting from the long walk. First she told me how she got to the U.S. First, she went to Hermosillo, Sonora by car. She went to Arizona crossing the desert and finally got to Virginia. It actually took her one week and a day. Of course she wasn't the only one who was coming to the U.S. There were about eleven people. After she hung up, I was so relieved knowing she was okay.

Two years later my mom was able to bring us here to Virginia.

Source: Interviews with today's immigrants. (2003). Retrieved March 21, 2007, from http://memory.loc.gov/learn/features/immig/interv/ toc.php

EXTRACT FROM THE TREATY OF GUADALUPE HIDALGO

The signing of the Treaty of Guadalupe Hidalgo on 2 February 1848 marked the official end of the two-year-long Mexican-American War. The treaty resulted in Mexico's ceding a large percent of its territory, and establishing the modern-day U.S.-Mexico border.

ARTICLE V

The boundary line between the two Republics shall commence in the Gulf of Mexico, three leagues from land, opposite the mouth of the Rio Grande, otherwise called Rio Bravo del Norte, or Opposite the mouth of its deepest branch, if it should have more than one branch emptying directly into the sea; from thence up the middle of that river, following the deepest channel, where it has more than one, to the point where it strikes the southern boundary of New Mexico; thence, westwardly, along the whole southern boundary of New Mexico (which runs north of the town called Paso) to its western termination; thence, northward, along the western line of New Mexico, until it intersects the first branch of the river Gila; (or if it should not intersect any branch of that river, then to the point on the said line nearest to such branch, and thence in a direct line to the same); thence down the middle of the said branch and of the said river, until it empties into the Rio Colorado; thence across the Rio Colorado, following the division line between Upper and Lower California, to the Pacific Ocean.

The southern and western limits of New Mexico, mentioned in the article, are those laid down in the map entitled "Map of the United Mexican States, as organized and defined by various acts of the Congress of said republic, and constructed according to the best authorities. Revised edition. Published at New York, in 1847, by J. Disturnell," of which map a copy is added to this treaty, bearing the signatures and seals of the undersigned Plenipotentiaries. And, in order to preclude all difficulty in tracing upon the ground the limit separating Upper from Lower California, it is agreed that the said limit shall consist of a straight line drawn from the middle of the Rio Gila, where it unites with the Colorado, to a point on the coast of the Pacific Ocean, distant one marine league due south of the southernmost point of the port of San Diego, according to the plan of said port made in the year 1782 by Don Juan Pantoja, second sailing-master of the Spanish fleet, and published at Madrid in the year 1802, in the atlas to the voyage of the schooners Sutil and Mexicana; of which plan a copy is hereunto added, signed and sealed by the respective Plenipotentiaries.

The boundary line established by this article shall be religiously respected by each of the two republics, and no change shall ever be made therein, except by the express and free consent of both nations, lawfully given by the General Government of each, in conformity with its own constitution.

Source: The Avalon Project at Yale Law School. (1996). Retrieved March 21, 2007, from http://www.yale.edu/lawweb/avalon/diplomacy/mexico/guadhida.htm

in the areas of economic integration, mass immigration, cultural and social cross-fertilization, and shared political challenges.

Foreign Wars and Occupations (1821–1867)

Opinion about the United States divided Mexican leaders since their country's independence from Spain in 1821. The liberals took the United States as their model. They highlighted the virtue of the republican form of government as opposed to the conservatives, who supported the creation of a monarchy based on a European model. This foundational split between liberal and conservative elites led to a half-century of civil wars, which were accompanied on several occasions by foreign wars and occupations. The most difficult for Mexico were the secession of Texas (1835–1836) and the Mexican-American War (1846–1848), followed by the French invasion and occupation (1863–1867). As a consequence of the first two, Mexico lost more than half of its original 1821 territory to the United States. This loss remains the deepest historical trauma

in Mexican history since independence. Thus, for Mexicans since the nineteenth century the United States represented a model of good political organization/government but also an aggressive and expansionist nation whose military strength led to Mexico's partition.

Restored Republic and Porfiriato (1867–1910)

The increased political and economic strength and influence of the United States after its Civil War (1861–1865) confirmed Mexican leaders' admiration and wish to emulate the United States as a successful nation (the U.S. government supported the Mexican government-in-exile against the French occupation of Mexico under Habsburg emperor Maximilian in 1863–1867). However, at the same time, growing U.S. power increased Mexican leaders' distrust and fear of their northern neighbor. During the long dictatorship of General Porfirio Díaz (1876–1910), Mexico's cultural and economic links were steered closer to European countries to

countervail U.S. influence. Mexicans still repeat Don Porfirio's dictum, "Poor Mexico, so far away from God and so close to the United States," to justify their ambivalent feelings toward the economic, political, and cultural power of the United States since the late nineteenth century.

Mexican Revolution: Mutual Uncertainty (1910–1940)

A civilian-led movement under Francisco I. Madero overthrew Díaz's regime in 1910–1911. This overthrow began a long revolution in Mexico. During the most violent phase of this revolution (1913–1920) the United States intervened diplomatically and militarily in Mexico. U.S. marines occupied the port of Veracruz in 1914, and in 1916 the U.S. Army sent an expedition into northern Mexico in a vain attempt to capture revolutionary leader Pancho Villa. During the 1920s successive Mexican and U.S. governments engaged in disputes over U.S. investors' rights in Mexican oil and land, as well as mutual recriminations over the Mexican government's suppression of the Catholic church (1926–1929) and the U.S. occupation of Central American (Nicaragua) and Caribbean (Dominican Republic, Haiti) nations. Further clashes

were averted in 1938 when Mexican president Lázaro Cárdenas (1934–1940) nationalized the oil industry, partly because Mexico offered compensation to foreign investors, but primarily because U.S. president Franklin D. Roosevelt (1933–1945) did not press the issue, wanting Latin American nations to come out strongly in support of the United States in the event of major war in Europe.

World War II and the Cold War (1939–1989/1991)

Mexico supported and fought with the Allies in World War II. After victory Mexican leaders recognized the United States as the triumphant and leading power in the West whose interests were partly in congruence with Mexico's. However, Mexican leaders also insisted that Mexico should pursue its political and economic autonomy through nationalism and neutrality in the U.S.-USSR Cold War confrontation. Mexican nationalism was anchored in the country's political system. This system was dominated by a hegemonic (relating to influence) party, the PRI (Partido Revolucionario Institucional), which stayed in power for seven decades (1920–2000). The regime pursued nationalist policies such as an independent foreign policy, nationalization of resources and industries, land

Flags on a garage in a Mexican-American neighborhood in Chicago, Illinois. Source: istock/John Rodriguez.

reform, and redistributive social legislation, which were not the U.S. government's preferred policies. Nonetheless, by and large the U.S. political and economic elites accepted and worked with their southern neighbor because the PRI regime delivered social peace and security, as well as political order and economic growth until 1982.

Globalization and North American Integration (since 1982)

Financial and economic collapse because of Mexico's external debt crisis in 1982 killed nationalist policies and forced successive Mexican governments to stabilize, adjust, and open markets. These actions culminated with the economic integration of the United States, Canada, and Mexico through NAFTA (North American Free Trade Agreement), which started operating in 1994. As a result, since the mid-1990s up to 80–90 percent of Mexico's annual imports/exports come from and go to the United States. In 2001 Mexico became the second-largest trading partner of the United States (after Canada). Economic integration has been the key force shaping the U.S.-Mexico special relationship since the mid-1990s, but other less-institutionalized forces such as mass migration and cultural and social cross-fertilization will become even more influential in the future.

Of these forces, mass migration is probably the most influential. Hispanics were declared the largest nonwhite minority in the United States after the country's census of 2000. By the year 2050, the official projections estimate, 25 percent of Americans will be Hispanic (in contrast to 15 percent African-American, 8 percent Asian-American, and 5 percent Native-American and Pacific Islander). Of these Hispanics, 67 percent will be Mexicans and Mexican-Americans. Los Angeles will remain the second-largest city in the world that is inhabited by Mexicans after Mexico City well into the twenty-first century. The annual remittances of Mexican workers in the United States have overtaken foreign investment plus foreign aid as a proportion of Mexico's gross domestic product since 2001—with the amount of remittances growing yearly (more than $25 billion in 2005 and some $30 billion in 2006). As a consequence of Mexicans settling in the United States, Mexican culture, cuisine, art, and traditions have been integrated into and enriched the U.S. Southwest. The worst aspect of this mostly positive phenomenon concerns illegal workers. In 2006, there were almost 12 million illegal workers in the United States, 80 percent of whom were Latino (two-thirds of which were Mexi-

can). Despite their contribution to the economic growth of both Mexico and the United States, the vast majority of these workers suffer anxiety, rejection, and on many occasions abuse from both countries' authorities. Despite repeated attempts of the Mexican and U.S. governments to find a solution to this complex problem, it remains the most pressing concern for Mexican leaders and the public at large when they assess the special relationship with the United States.

To these driving forces must be added the more recent challenge of peace and security. This challenge became a priority for U.S. leaders, policymakers, and the U.S. public after the terrorist attacks in New York City and Washington, D.C., on September 11, 2001. Since then, the 2,500-kilometer-long land border between Mexico and the United States has become a strategic area in the war against terrorism. Thus, new common political challenges have also become preeminent in the U.S.-Mexico shared agenda.

These driving forces of the U.S.-Mexico special relationship are mainly issues of interdependence. As such, they have made common geography an even more important influence on leaders and populations on both sides of the border. These forces will dominate Mexicans' perspectives of the special relationship with the United States in the first half of the twenty-first century. However, from the perspective of Mexicans the special relationship with the United States first has to create a basic framework of understanding between two countries that are as close but as unequal as the United States and Mexico.

Francisco E. Gonzalez

See also Immigration to the United States; Relations with Latin America, U.S.

Further Reading

Aguayo Quezada, S. (1998). *El Panteon de los Mitos: Estados Unidos y el nacionalismo mexicano.* Mexico City: Grijalbo.

Camp, R. A. (1999). *Politics in Mexico: The decline of authoritarianism* (3rd ed.). Oxford, UK: Oxford University Press.

Coatsworth, J. (1981). *Growth against development: The economic impact of railroads in Porfirian Mexico.* DeKalb: Northern Illinois University Press.

Gutiérrez, D. G. (1995). *Walls and mirrors: Mexican Americans, Mexican immigrants and the politics of ethnicity,* Berkeley and Los Angeles: University of California Press.

History of Texas. (n.d.). Retrieved February 9, 2007, from http://www.republic-of-texas.net/history.shtml

Holden, R. H., & Zolov, E. (Eds.). (2000). *Latin America and the United States: A documentary history.* Oxford, UK: Oxford University Press.

Katz, F. (1981). *The secret war in Mexico: Europe, the United States, and the Mexican Revolution.* Chicago: University of Chicago Press.

Knight, A. (1987). US-Mexican relations, 1910–1940: An interpretation. San Diego: University of California Press.

The Mexican War. (n.d.). Retrieved February 9, 2007, from http://www.latinamericanstudies.org/mexican.htm

NAFTA Resources. (n.d.). Retrieved February 9, 2007, from http://lanic.utexas.edu/la/Mexico/nafta/

Ruiz, R. E. (2000). *On the rim of Mexico: Encounters of the rich and poor.* Boulder, CO: Westview Press.

Stevens, D. F. (1991). *Origins of instability in early republican Mexico.* Durham, NC: Duke University Press.

U.S. Census Bureau. (2004). Facts for features. Retrieved February 9, 2007, from http://www.census.gov/Press-Release/www/releases/archives/facts_for_features_special_editions/002270.html

U. S. Census Bureau. (2004). Projected population of the United States by race and Hispanic origin. Retrieved February 9, 2007, from http://www.census.gov/ipc/www/usinterimproj/natprojtab01a.pdf

Special Relationship (U.S.-Russia)

The especially friendly relationship between the United States and Russia that arose after the September 11 attacks has reverted back to one reminiscent of the twentieth century, marked by criticism, mistrust, and competition.

A special relationship between the United States and Russia existed during the period 2001–2002, after the September 11, 2001, terrorist attacks on the United States. However, this relationship of cooperation quickly became adversarial and competitive because of diverging strategic interests. As the only country with the capacity to destroy the United States with its nuclear stockpile, Russia plays an important role in international politics, particularly in such areas as terrorism, energy resources, proliferation of weapons of mass destruction (WMDs), and relations with countries such as Iran, North Korea, and China. To better analyze the U.S.-Russia special relationship and its deterioration, we must understand the historical relationship between these two countries from World War II to the Cold War and beyond.

World War II

Prior to the twentieth century the United States and Russia did not have significant relations except for isolated events, such as the U.S. purchase of Alaska from Russia in 1867. With its growing presence on the world stage, the United States cooperated with Russia when the strategic interests of both countries coincided, as in the 1900 Boxer Rebellion and World War I (1914–1918). Strategic interests continued to direct U.S.-Soviet relations, with President Franklin Roosevelt formally recognizing the Soviet Union in 1933 because he feared the rise of German and Japanese power. After the United States was attacked by Japan in 1941, the United States and Soviet Union forged part of an alliance during World War II (1939–1945) that defeated the fascist powers.

Cold War

As the world's only superpowers after World War II, the United States and the Soviet Union started an ideological rivalry between democracy and communism across the globe that became known as the "Cold War" (1947–1991). The Cold War's most dramatic moment was the Cuban Missile Crisis (1962), when the Soviet Union tried to establish nuclear weapons in Cuba. After this humiliation over Cuba, the Soviet Union embarked on a military buildup that achieved parity in nuclear forces with the United States. With the United States seeking to withdraw from the Vietnam War (1955–1975) and both nations wanting to prevent a nuclear war, President Richard Nixon and Soviet general secretary Leonid Brezhnev pursued a policy of détente: Both countries would compete with each other within their prescribed spheres of influence. The crowning achievement of détente was the Strategic Arms Limitation Talks (SALT I and II in 1972 and 1979, respectively), which produced the Antiballistic Missile Treaty (ABM) that regulated the use of nuclear weapons.

However, détente was cast aside when the Soviet Union invaded Afghanistan in 1979, and Ronald Reagan was elected U.S. president in 1980. The United States embarked on a dramatic military buildup, which included the controversial Strategic Defense Initiative (SDI), which would intercept Soviet missiles aimed at the United States. Confronted with a stagnating economy, the Soviet Union was unable to match the U.S. military buildup. Led by General Secretary Mikhail Gorbachev, the Soviet Union entered the Strategic Arms Reduction Talks (START I and II in 1991 and 1993, respectively) to reduce nuclear and conventional weapons. Intermediate-range nuclear weapons also were abolished in Europe by the Intermediate-Range Nuclear Force Treaty (INF) in 1987. Gorbachev withdrew the Soviet military from Afghanistan in 1989 and stopped financial assistance to the eastern European communist states, which effectively destroyed the Communist Party rule over these countries. Weakened, Gorbachev did not object to German reunification (1990) and supported the U.S. coalition against Iraq in the Gulf War (1990–1991). When the Soviet Union collapsed on 31 December 1991, the Cold War was over.

Post–Cold War Relations

The Soviet Union was succeeded by the Russia federation, ruled by President Boris Yeltsin, who sought a partnership with the United States because Russia was in dire need of economic assistance to

restructure its economy. In order to obtain Western economic aid, Yeltsin had to demonstrate his credibility as a ruler who supported democracy and a free-market economy—objectives that coincided with Yeltsin's desire to destroy the still-influential Russian Communist Party. With the election of Bill Clinton as U.S. president in 1992, Yeltsin had a genuine partner to reform Russia's political and economic system.

During this era both countries also cooperated to prevent further nuclear proliferation. However, in spite of this shared objective, domestic and international factors played a significant role in preventing a complete partnership between the United States and Russia. Yeltsin was confronted with anti-Western and nationalist parliaments elected in 1993 and 1995 and had to collaborate with Russian criminal organizations to be reelected as president in 1996. Furthermore, Yeltsin's economic reforms of "shock therapy" created economic hardship for millions of his citizens, who saw Western financial assistance as a way to keep Russia weak. Finally, the fear of a further breakup of the Russian federation led to the Russian invasion of Chechnya to suppress its independence movement from 1994 to 1996 and from 1999 to today. These domestic factors made Yeltsin adopt a more nationalist approach to foreign affairs, which sometimes conflicted with U.S. strategic interests.

This shift to a nationalist foreign policy was manifested in Bosnia (1993–1996) and Kosovo (1999), where Russian public support of the Serbians prompted Yeltsin to criticize the campaign of the North Atlantic Treaty Organization (NATO) in the former Yugoslavia. Yeltsin also objected to the expansion of NATO to the former communist states of eastern Europe and to U.S. expansion into the oil- and gas-rich region of the Caspian Sea. Continuing U.S. trade restrictions on Russian exports and U.S. complaints about Russia's weapons agreements with anti-U.S. regimes also cooled U.S.-Russian relations.

Special Relationship

With the election of Vladimir Putin and George W. Bush as the respective Russian and U.S. presidents in 2000, relations between the two countries changed drastically. During the 2000 U.S. presidential election, one of the issues raised was "Who lost Russia?" as events that hinted at the recurrence of former troubles occurred, including the suppression by Putin of dissent movements and the press in Russia. However, Bush changed his attitude after he met Putin in June 2001, when Bush declared that he had "stared into Putin's soul" and found him to be "an honest, straightforward man." In spite of this personal relationship between the two leaders, the U.S. declaration of its intention to withdraw from the ABM Treaty and implement the second round of NATO enlargement, and Russia's second war in Chechnya created some strain in the relations between the two countries. It would take the September 11, 2001, terrorist attacks to change the relationship between the United States and Russia into a "special" one.

The Kremlin Wall and the Kremlin in Moscow. Source: istock/Denis Babenko.

Putin was the first foreign leader to call Bush to offer his condolences after the September 11 attacks. As the United States planned to invade Afghanistan in October 2001, Putin promised logistical and intelligence support and had no objections to temporary U.S. military bases being installed in central Asia. In exchange for this support, Putin asked Bush to consider Russia's war against Chechnya as part of the global war on terrorism, to keep the United States in the ABM Treaty, and to ask for Russian consultation on political but not military matters in NATO as the alliance expands to the borders of Russia. Soon after this agreement, U.S. businesses invested in Russia, particularly in the oil, gas, and mineral industries, while Putin expanded Russian oil output to undercut quotas of the Organization of Petroleum

Exporting Countries (OPEC). For the first time since 1945, the two countries faced a common threat and managed to align their strategic interests.

Diverging Strategic Interests

However, as the strategic interests of the United States and Russia started to diverge, their special relationship reverted to an adversarial and competitive one. After its expulsion of the Taliban government from Afghanistan in 2002, the United States attempted to establish a permanent military base in central Asia, which not only is rich in natural resources but also is a place from where the

SEPTEMBER 11, 2001: ATTACK ON AMERICA

The following is a joint statement on counterterrorism, following the September 11, 2001, attacks on the U.S., as issued by the U.S. president George W. Bush, and Russian president Vladimir Putin from the APEC conference on 21 October 2001.

The President of the United States and the President of Russia categorically reject and resolutely condemn terrorism in all its forms and manifestations, regardless of motive. The Presidents stress that the barbaric act of terrorism committed in the United States on 11 September 2001, represents a crime against all humanity.

The Presidents note that terrorism threatens not only the security of the United States and Russia, but also that of the entire international community, as well as international peace and security. They believe that terrorism poses a direct threat to the rule of law and to human rights and democratic values. It has no foundation in any religion, national or cultural traditions, and it only uses them as a cover for its criminal goals.

The Presidents agree that every effort must be undertaken to bring the perpetrators to justice, while protecting the rights and welfare of civilians. They stress that the fight against terrorism requires the unity of the entire international community to counter new challenges and threats on the basis of international law and the full use of the United Nations and other international organizations.

The Presidents call for all states to join a sustained global coalition to defeat international terrorism. Nations must make use of diplomatic, political, law enforcement, financial, intelligence, and military means to root out terrorists and their sponsors and bring them to justice.

The Presidents emphasize that the current situation in Afghanistan is a direct consequence of the policies pursued by the Taliban, which turned that country into an international center of terrorism and extremism. They reaffirm that the United States and Russia are ready to cooperate closely with the United Nations to promote a post-conflict settlement in Afghanistan that would provide for the formation of a

representative, broad-based government capable of ensuring the restoration of a peaceful Afghanistan that maintains good relations with countries of the region and beyond it.

The leaders of the two countries view U.S.-Russian cooperation as a critical element in the global effort against terrorism. They reaffirm their personal commitment and that of their two countries to fight this deadly challenge through active cooperation and coordination, both bilaterally and within the framework of international institutions.

The Presidents note with satisfaction the fruitful cooperation between the United States and Russia in the United Nations and the U.N. Security Council, in the NATO-Russia Permanent Joint Council, and in the G-8. They also instruct their governments to reinforce bilateral cooperation throughout the U.S.-Russia Working Group on countering terrorist and other threats emanating from Afghanistan.

The Presidents agree that the financial, communications, and logistics networks of terrorist organizations must be destroyed. They call upon all nations without exception to take measures to block access of terrorist organizations to financial resources, to enhance law enforcement tools to combat terrorism, and to strengthen procedures to stop the transit of terrorists and their material within and between countries. They stress the importance of speedy ratification and implementation of existing international counterterrorism conventions.

The two Presidents are resolved to advance cooperation in combating new terrorist threats: nuclear, chemical and biological, as well as those in cyberspace. They agreed to enhance bilateral and multilateral action to stem the export and proliferation of nuclear, chemical and biological materials, related technologies, and delivery systems as a critical component of the battle to defeat international terrorism.

Source: Joint statement by President Bush and President Putin. (2001, October 21). Retrieved June 8, 2007, from http://www.whitehouse. gov/news/releases/2001/10/20011022-11.html

United States could closely monitor Russia and China. Both Russia and China have called for the United States to set a date for the withdrawal of its military from central Asia and, to underscore this point, conducted their first joint military exercise in 2005. The United States has ignored both Russia's and China's demands, and, after the Uzbek government quelled riots by a mass killing of its citizens, the United States did not withdraw its military bases but instead tried to establish new ones in Kazakhstan.

U.S.-Russian relations also became strained when President Bush announced that the United States would withdraw from the ABM Treaty in order to test antimissile defense systems and that such technology would be placed in Poland and the Czech Republic. When the United States aided the democratic revolutions in the former Soviet republics of Ukraine, Georgia, and Moldova in 2004–2006, Russia objected to Western meddling in regions that Russia historically had controlled and influenced. Russia's support of North Korea and Russia's $300 million arms trade agreement with Iran, along with promises to help Iran develop nuclear technology for civilian use, increased tensions between the United States and Russia.

Iraq War (2003)

All these diverging strategic interests came to the forefront at a meeting of the United Nations (U.N.) when the United States sought authorization to invade Iraq. In February 2003 Russian Foreign Minister Igor Ivanov proclaimed that Russia would use its veto in the U.N. Security Council on any resolution that sought to resolve the Iraqi problem by the use of direct or indirect force. Besides the cited differences between the United States and Russia, Iraq's leader, Saddam Hussein, had long-standing military ties with Russia and had made secret oil agreements with Putin. The upcoming December 2003 parliamentary elections and 2004 presidential elections also played a crucial role in the calculation of Putin's opposition to the U.S. invasion of Iraq.

Options for the Future

Although Bush and Putin have close personal ties, these ties were unable to shape an effective foreign policy between the two countries. After September 11, 2001, Bush's foreign policy priorities do not include Russia with his focus on Iraq, Iran, North Korea, Islamic terrorism, and the growing power of China. The U.S. support of democratic values in Russia's neighboring states, its military bases in central Asia, and its unwillingness to remove U.S. trade restrictions on Russian exports have increased tensions between the United States and Russia. In return Putin has embraced an anti-Western, nationalist foreign policy empowered by a strong, oil-exporting economy. Confronted with domestic terrorism, the war with Chechnya, and the suppression of human rights and the domestic media, Russian leaders have resorted to a Cold War rhetoric that denounces Western values while seeking an alliance with China as a counterweight to U.S. hegemony (influence).

As Russia continues its slide into autocracy and expands its imperial ambitions, the United States is confronted with several options to repair its relationship with Russia. One option is an aggressive containment of Russian power and influence; a second option is to isolate and ignore Russia because of its lost status as an international power; a third option is to offer cooperation with Russia on strategic matters while criticizing Russia's abuse of democratic principles. Although its power is diminished, Russia, with its ties to Iran, North Korea, and China and its stockpile of nuclear weapons, still can thwart U.S. strategic objectives. In spite of their recent disagreements, the United States and Russia share several threats, from terrorism to the proliferation of WMDs to illegal narcotic trafficking and possibly even China. Whether the United States and Russia will cooperate against these common threats remains to be seen.

Lee Trepanier

See also Cold War, Post Era; Soviet Empire, Collapse of

Further Reading

Dmitri, T. (2006). Russia leaves the West. *Foreign Affairs, 85,* 87–96.

Gorodetsky, G. (2003). *Russia between East and West: Russian foreign policy on the threshold of the twenty-first century.* London: Frank Kass.

LaFeber, W. (2006). *America, Russia, and the Cold War, 1945–2006.* New York: McGraw-Hill.

MacLean, G. A. (2006). *Clinton's foreign policy in Russia: From deterrence and isolation to democratization and engagement.* Burlington, VA: Ashgate.

McFaul, M., & Goldgeier, J. M. (2005, October–November). What to do about Russia. *Policy Review, 135,* 45–62.

Special Relationship (U.S.-U.K.)

Though their history is rife with revolution, suspicion, and acrimony, the United States and Britain share a special relationship based on common political values including the rule of law, democracy, and civil rights.

The notion of a special relationship existing between the United States and the United Kingdom has been a common reference point for politicians on both sides of the Atlantic for more than a half-century. Originating in the close collaboration of the two nations as allies in World War II, the relationship was sustained thereafter by successive leaders in Washington, D.C., and London, regardless of their party affiliations. The terrorist attacks of September 11, 2001, and the Iraq War (2003) again confirmed the apparently unique affinity between the two nations.

Yet, the history of U.S.-U.K. relations is one rich with contradictions and mutual hostility. Assisted by the French, the United States was born in a revolution against British rule in the eighteenth century. The most serious foreign assault on mainland United States, prior to the terrorist attacks of September 11, 2001, was perpetrated by the British in the War of 1812. Relations between the two nations remained marked by mutual suspicion, trade disagreements, and occasional acrimony well into the twentieth century. Even during World War II Prime Minister Winston Churchill and President Franklin Roosevelt clashed repeatedly over military strategy and politics. Churchill championed a British Empire that the United States detested.

As early as the 1950s the asymmetrical nature of the relationship had become clear to both parties. Dean Acheson was quoted as say the United Kingdom had "lost an empire and not yet found a role," (Dobson 1995, 126) a predicament that arguably still exists today. U.S. military, economic, and cultural influence had powerfully eclipsed that of the declining Britain. Moreover, whereas London regularly adapted policies to suit Washington, rarely did Washington accommodate London in comparable fashion. Lend-lease (whereby the U.S. lent the U.K. destroyers in return for the lease of bases on British islands in the Caribbean and Newfoundland) was abruptly terminated by the administration of President Harry Truman after World War II, with minimal warning. Cooperation on nuclear affairs was, similarly, subject to an abrupt halt by the U.S. Pressure was heightened to dissolve the British Empire, and humiliation was visited on British prime minister Anthony Eden, who resigned his office in 1956 because of the joint British, French, and Israeli attack on Egypt. After Argentina invaded the British Falkland Islands in 1982, the U.S. State Department recom-

mended against supporting the British. President Ronald Reagan ordered the U.S. invasion of the British dependency of Grenada in 1983 without advance consultation with Prime Minister Margaret Thatcher. U.S. policy toward Northern Ireland, especially under President Bill Clinton, was distinctly equivocal toward successive British governments' preferences. And the Tony Blair government support for the Iraq War was granted against the opposition of most British citizens.

In spite of this checkered history and the existence of multiple "special relationships" for the United States, the one with the United Kingdom has been far deeper, longer lasting, and more resilient than that of most alliances. In what, then, does the "special" element of this relationship consist? Three aspects seem especially important.

"Anglosphere"

First, for all the differences between the political and economic systems and societies of the two nations, a basic agreement on fundamental political values has prompted some writers to discuss the existence of an "Anglosphere": an ideological construct comprising commitment to the rule of law, democracy, liberty, property rights, civil rights, and liberties that together provide a common lens by which the world is viewed in both nations. This commonality is hardly complete (attitudes in the United Kingdom and United States differ substantially on issues such as gun control, abortion rights, capital punishment, religion in public life, and government-provided health insurance). Furthermore, even where the U.S.-U.K. relationship is closest and most reliable—defense and intelligence cooperation—it remains anything but equal. The United Kingdom is heavily dependent on the United States for intelligence, far weaker in resources, and only marginally more capable of operating with the U.S. military in terms of technological and logistical capacities than other European nations. However, many in the U.K. political class believe that Britain's global influence is greater as a consequence of its closeness to the United States. At the same time, many in Washington value the greater political legitimacy of U.S. actions that British support—in the U.N. Secu-

rity Council, North Atlantic Treaty Organization (NATO), and the G8 economic forum—can sometimes lend and the constraints on the development of a rival European/European Union (EU) power that the United Kingdom invariably offers.

Second, this rudimentary shared political outlook helps to frame broadly similar views of the two countries' respective national interests—and threats to them—that are mutually reinforcing. Certainly, profound differences in priorities and preferences continue to exist on matters as varied as genetically modified food, climate change, "rogue states," and the Israeli-Palestinian conflict. Trade, too, remains as much a source of conflict and competition as of cooperation. However, the United States has represented one of the largest and most lucrative markets for British companies since 1945. The Confederation of British Industry estimated that U.K. firms invested $220 billion in the United States in 2003, 40 percent of all British overseas investment. Americans in turn have invested $156 billion in the United Kingdom, 35 percent of all U.S. investment in Europe. The U.S.-U.K. trade relationship is worth $74 billion, equally balanced between the two nations, and many U.S. business practices have been embraced in the United Kingdom (from executive remuneration structures to supplier handling and productivity measures). One million Britons are currently employed by U.S. companies in the United Kingdom, one million Americans by U.K. firms in the United States.

Third, mutual cultural influences and a shared language have reinforced the sense that the Americans and British are more at ease with one another than the peoples of many other nations. Exposure to the United States clearly assists this sense. For example, in 1998, 93 percent of Britons named Bill Clinton accurately from a picture of his face, and 97 percent correctly identified him as president of the United States. By comparison, only 22 percent recognized Jacques Chirac, although 49 percent correctly identified him as leader of France (only 12 percent recognized Bertie Ahern, and only 24 percent identified him as the Irish prime minister). Most British citizens also instinctively appreciate the strength and durability of the U.S.-U.K. bond. Their cultural choices—in music, clothes, bookstores, the cinema—underline the closeness. In no other EU member state is a mass sense of being "European" so still-born and U.S. cultural presence so pervasive as in the United Kingdom.

None of this is to suggest a perfect or consistent harmony of interests, values, or outlooks. British attitudes—elite and popular—toward the United States frequently exhibit a mixture of cultural snobbery, envy, prejudice, and stereotyping that U.S. global power compounds, a group feeling about a United States that seems not only "indispensable" but also inescapable. Some of these beliefs—for example, that the United States comprises

unrestrained individualism and homogenized sameness—are inherent contradictions. Most have a long lineage. According to Robin Harris, in 1944 the British Foreign Office described its U.S. policy as being to "steer this great unwieldy barge, the US, into the right harbor"(*Policy Review* 2002, 113). In the early 1960s British prime minister Harold Macmillan famously saw the British as the sophisticated, worldly "Greeks" and the Americans as the belligerent, bluff "Romans" (happily overlooking the fact that most Greeks were slaves in the days of imperial Rome).

Base of Cooperation

Despite the differences, the relationship has endured not only over the decades but also in the face of profound political changes in both Washington and London. With the exception of Conservative Prime Minister Edward Heath (1970–1974), every British postwar prime minister, whether Tory or Labor, has actively sought close relations with the White House, whether Democratic or Republican. The degree of closeness has varied markedly (from the distance of Richard Nixon and Heath to the closeness of Reagan and Thatcher, Tony Blair and Clinton). However, the mixed personal relationships of the leaders have rested on a strong and enduring base of institutionalized diplomatic and military cooperation that is unlike that of most nations. Historical ties, invented myths, shared language, and common values have reflected and reinforced shared perceptions of affinity and interest.

Whether this affinity continues to endure may perhaps be questioned. In the United States geopolitics (the EU's economic challenge, the rise of China, the war on terrorism), combined with domestic influences such as demographic changes (the disappearance of the World War II generation, the increased influence of Latinos and Asian Americans), may encourage a more "Pacific" or hemispheric focus by U.S. decision makers. In the United Kingdom the effects of immigration and multiculturalism, devolution, and above all the EU may prompt a more "European" focus by London. For both parties the Atlantic relationship may become less central than it was in the second half of the twentieth century. However, the factors making for continuity are, arguably, at least as strong as those suggesting change. The British remain—geographically, politically, and culturally—between Europe and the United States. A stronger Europe may not challenge the United States as a global equal, but a stronger Europe can certainly cause the United States problems even as a second-order power. The United Kingdom and the United States each retain an interest in sustaining this alliance of unequals that has, for the most part, been mutually beneficial over the years. Unless a choice is made by either party to abandon

the other, the Atlantic relationship promises to remain a shared and valuable reference point for countries.

Robert Singh

See also Colonial and Early Nationhood;
Perspectives on the United States, Visitors'

Further Reading

Dobson, A. (1995). *Anglo-American Relations in the Twentieth Century.* London: Routledge.

Dumbrell, J. (2006). *A special relationship: Anglo-American relations in the Cold War and after* (2nd ed.). New York: St. Martin's Press.

Gamble, A. (2003). *Between Europe and America: The future of British politics.* Basingstoke, UK: Palgrave Macmillan.

Garton Ash, T. (2004). *Free world: Why a crisis of the West reveals the opportunity of our time.* London: Allen Lane.

Harris, R. (2002). The state of the special relationship. *Policy Review,* 113. Retrieved April 5, 2007, from http://www.policyreview.org/JUN02/harris_print.html

Peterson, J., & Pollack, M. (2003). *Europe, America, Bush: Transatlantic relations in the twenty-first century.* London: Routledge.

Riddell, P. (2003). *Hug them close: Blair, Clinton, Bush and the "special relationship."* London: Politicos Publishing.

Sports

American sports culture differs in many ways from the international sports scene with greater focus on commercialization, individual rather than team potential, and rivalries between regions or cities, rather than other nations.

In the late 1990s a U.S. television executive claimed that football was too complicated for women and children to understand; he may also have been thinking of non-Americans. Despite the offensive tone of such a comment, it reflects the parochial following of the sport often referred to as the U.S. "national sport." The comment also accurately reflects the fact that football is the sport of the U.S. male, particularly the U.S. male spectator. By contrast, soccer, the "world game," is the sport of women and children in the United States, as demonstrated by the popularity of junior soccer leagues and the World Cup successes of the U.S. women's team.

Interestingly, the world's most dominant military and economic power favors a sport—U.S. football—that has limited international appeal despite the marketing and communications clout of the United States, while its men's national soccer team could be considered an also-ran (a contestant who loses the contest) in soccer. These facts could easily lead one to hold up soccer and U.S. football as examples of U.S. exceptionalism. However, taking the example of Australia, the same pattern could be seen to exist. Soccer is popular among children but struggles to get coverage on television, whereas the sport of choice of Australian male spectators is Australia's own Australian Rules Football. As Ian Tryell has argued, the allure of U.S. exceptionalism as an explanation can often lead us to exaggerate the differences between the United States and elsewhere while ignoring the commonalities.

What seems more significant is the United States's lack of noted international sporting rivalries, particularly in team sports. Apart from rare moments when the Cold War was played out on the basketball court, such as at the Olympics in 1972 or on the chessboard between Bobby Fischer and Boris Spassky, also in 1972, the United States's most important sporting competitions have been domestic contests such as those between the New York Yankees and the Boston Red Sox. At the college level basketball games between North Carolina State and Duke and football games between the University of Michigan and Ohio State are also strikingly intense, and many visitors to the United States are astounded by the record crowds and national coverage of these college contests. At the same time, the United States has a marked lack of success or involvement in many of the major international team sporting events. In male sports the United States is underwhelming in the world cup competitions for the three major sports of soccer, cricket, and rugby union. Such national sporting differences, particularly in nations such as England and France, give us an insight into the inward-oriented nature of U.S. culture and U.S. nationalism. This argument nonetheless holds more credence in team sports than in individual sports. Further, the dominance that the United States enjoys in the medal tally at the Olympics every four years mirrors U.S. global power. U.S. success at the Olympics is largely the result of individual triumphs on the track or in the gymnasium. The obvious exception to this record is the sport of basketball.

Basketball, the Global Game?

One cannot deny the global reach and cultural impact of basketball, a U.S. invention that grew out of YMCA culture to become a global sport and fashion phenomenon. Although some lament the decline of teamwork in basketball, it is undoubtedly still the most significant U.S. contribution to international team sports. The stars of the U.S. National Basketball Association (NBA) are global icons, recognized as much for the clothes and shoes they wear and promote as for their abilities on the court.

In his recent study of globalization the historian Walter LaFeber centers his inquiry on former basketball star Michael Jordan, possibly the most widely recognized person on the planet in the 1990s, to provide insight into this historical epoch. LaFeber's analysis of Jordan's endorsement of Nike products and the advertising of these products around the world—what LaFeber calls "the swooshifying of the world" (LaFeber 2000)—raises many questions about the values of professional sportspersons and U.S. business. For many people Jordan and Nike represent U.S. cultural and economic imperialism, with the spread of basketball more generally seen as another element of insidious Americanization. With its growing popularity in China, basketball is often cited as the world's second-most popular sport. For those people who worry about Americanization, the resilience of soccer as the world's most popular sport offers some solace.

Two boys playing basketball on a court in Hong Kong. Source: istock/ Christine Gonsalves.

Not Americanization but Commercialization

One of the theories for why soccer has never become popular in the United States is that the game's forty-five-minute continuous halves (plus injury time) are ruinous for commercial television because not enough opportunities exist to place advertising between the play. By contrast the opportunities for advertising on television in the big three U.S. sports—U.S. football, baseball, and basketball—are far greater.

The commercial element of U.S. sports is also part of those sports' global reach—more insidious than the popularity of the sports themselves is the spread of ideas and strategies on how sports, particularly in the commercial arena, can be played, usually with the aim of maximum commercial advantage. For critics of U.S. sports, the market ethos (distinguishing character, sentiment, moral nature, or guiding beliefs) reigns supreme, with the fans, the teams, and youth development too often secondary to the goal of making money.

A much-cited example is the franchise team that is moved from city to city. The Los Angeles Lakers basketball team was originally from Minneapolis, Minnesota, just as the Los Angeles Dodgers baseball team was originally from Brooklyn, New York. The owners had relocated the teams to new markets in search of a bigger fan base and more money. Demographics and the expansion of leagues to new cities are important in other countries, too,

but the commercial calculation is chilling to many sports fans. In Australia old inner-urban Melbourne Australian Rules teams were relocated to the cities of Sydney and Brisbane to create a national league. Such moves are more than occasionally lamented as an unfortunate Americanization of sporting culture.

Another example of commercialization in U.S. sports is the high number of games played per season in the sport of baseball. Whereas baseball has never caught on with any real gusto beyond the places where the United States could be described as a former colonial or neocolonial presence, the competing summer sport of cricket has always had broader global appeal and reach. Whereas baseball is at times argued to be a game derived from cricket, recently cricket has drawn many business lessons from Major League Baseball in order to make it more profitable and more popular. In the late 1970s cricket underwent the "Packer revolution" when businessman Kerry Packer used his Australian television network to promote a shorter one-day version of cricket. The new format even took its name from the yearly baseball World Series. In the new World Series Cricket, the players wore colored shirts, belted the ball for a day only, sometimes under lights at night, and played many more international games per season. Previously international cricket had been played in all-white uniforms, had been limited to daytime play, and had only the one format of a five-day test match, with long breaks between matches. The revolution offended many traditionalists, with concerns regularly voiced about the volume of international cricket reducing its quality and

significance (a common lament about professional sports across the board). However, the changes to cricket brought many new fans to the game and provided many more players with a decent income from their sport.

The belief that the United States is the home of the capitalistic approach to sports was recently challenged in an article on the web site Slate.com that argued that U.S. sports are often surprisingly socialist when compared with the ultracapitalist world of international club soccer. Undoubtedly, sports that are largely played in one nation or with the elite club competition centered in one country definitely have more ability to split income and star players more equitably across clubs than do global sports in which competition across borders often occurs. However, although this approach has been successful in U.S. football, in baseball the ultrawealthy and star-studded New York Yankees seem to play for the pennant with great frequency.

Triumphant Individual

Apart from the "Dream Team"—the U.S. national basketball team—U.S. sports are known internationally for the dominance of certain individuals rather than for teams that have captured either the U.S. or international imagination. Further, the Dream Team's dominance of international basketball (until very recently) and the relative strength of the NBA compared with international competition meant that the Dream Team's games were more a novelty than anything else. U.S. involvement in international sports would seem not to carry the passion that national teams such as the Indian cricket team, the Brazilian soccer team, or the New Zealand rugby union team carry. The hopes of their respective nations rest on their performance, a phenomenon far less familiar to Americans.

Americans do deserve special mention in international competition as individuals on the tennis court, in the boxing ring, on the golf course, on the athletic track, and in the bicycle seat. In these sports the United States has produced more than its share of champions. Among the most impressive sportspersons of recent decades are Carl Lewis, the multitalented track athlete and winner of nine Olympic gold medals; swimmer Mark Spitz, winner of seven gold medals at the 1972 Olympics; Martina Navratilova, winner of more professional tennis titles than any other player; and Lance Armstrong, winner of six consecutive Tour de France bicycle races. These athletes became sporting personalities, and although the celebrity sportsperson is certainly not just a U.S. tradition, few sporting icons have captured international attention more than U.S. boxers, from Joe Louis to Mike Tyson. The United States is the home of international boxing, with many of

the world title fights held in U.S. locations such as Madison Square Garden in New York City.

The transformation of athletes such as Michael Jordan into international sporting celebrities is often seen as the triumph of commercialism over sports. However, this view often ignores the skill, charisma, and narrative associated with particular athletes. A classic example is boxer Muhammad Ali, an athlete of tremendous fame across the globe whom few would associate with any particular commercial product or company (aside from the one-man marketing machine Don King). The story of Ali, not surprisingly the subject of a recent Hollywood film, makes sports broadly appealing with their ups and down, unpredictable twists and turns, and moments of great triumph. The United States is certainly not alone in producing such heroes—it is just more noted for presenting (and exposing) their stories to the rest of the world. In part this phenomenon occurs because of the reach of U.S. television and the U.S. commercial media. The historical remembrance of U.S. sporting icons is also the product of the strong U.S. culture of sports writing—a culture that could rightly be called "literary sports journalism." Great U.S. writers have often turned their pen to portraying boxers and boxing bouts: Norman Mailer on the "rumble in the jungle," David Remnick on Mike Tyson, and Joyce Carol Oates on boxing come to mind. Many of the great essays about the stars and wannabes of the full panoply of U.S. sports have been collected every year since 1991 in Glenn Stout's series *The Best of American Sports Writing*. These essays offer insight into U.S. culture and set a standard of popular sports writing that is rarely met in other English-language nations, which is only a little ironic, given the impact that U.S.-styled commercialism has at times had on the integrity and wonder of modern sports.

Brendon O'Connor

┌ **Further Reading**

Foer, F. (2004). *How soccer explains the world.* New York: Harper Collins.

LaFeber, W. (2002). *Michael Jordan and the new global capitalism.* London: W. W. Norton.

Mandelbaum, M. (2004). *The meaning of sport.* New York: Public Affairs.

Markovits, A. S., & Hellerman, S. L. (2001). *Offside: Soccer and American exceptionalism.* Princeton, NJ: Princeton University Press.

Stout, G. (1991–2004). *The best of American sports writing.* New York: Houghton-Mifflin.

Terrorism

See Foreign Policy after September 11, 2001, U.S.

Tourism

A leading global industry, tourism has its controversies, with debates on whether it helps or hurts local economies, promotes or hinders cross-cultural understanding, and preserves or destroys major historical sites.

The dramatic growth in tourism has made it the world's number one industry, accounting for more than 12 percent of the world's economy. With the changing demography and significant aging of the populations of Europe, Japan, and the United States, this growth is expected to accelerate dramatically.

Tourism is like an invisible export in terms of its economic impact in generating foreign exchange earnings for the country of destination, and it is particularly important for the U.S. given its growing trade deficit. Tourists coming to the U.S. from abroad help to improve the balance of payments (an economic measure of imports minus exports), and provide other economic benefits. Every year for the past eleven years, the U.S. had a positive tourist trade balance, meaning that international tourists in the U.S. spend more than U.S. citizens traveling abroad. Preliminary estimates for 2006 indicate that the U.S. will earn $1.074 billion from tourism.

In the wake of the attacks on September 11, 2001, U.S. earnings from tourism diminished significantly. In 2001, U.S. tourist earnings declined 13 percent and in 2002, they declined 7 percent. Through tighter visa requirements, the U.S. government has made it more difficult for international visitors to enter the country. In-country tourism, however, seems to have stayed steady and even increased in some instances. Tourism is mostly promoted at the state and local level. Within the U.S., the natural wonders of the West are particularly attractive for tourists, but there are many destinations including historic landmarks, gambling sites, and major cities.

Travel to distant lands is not new. Despite the lack of modern technologies in earlier times, people have been traveling long distances for millennia. Particularly notable are the movements of groups from Asia to the Americas, which are well-documented, for example, in the National Museum of Anthropology in Mexico City. The Pacific was populated as people moved from what is now Southeast Asia to as far away as the Polynesian triangle: New Zealand, Hawaii, and Easter Island. People also moved from what is now Southeast Asia to the island of Madagascar off the coast of southeast Africa. Mobility was a prominent feature of ancient Greek culture and of Christian, Judaic, and Islamic cultures in the Middle Ages. Arab and Indian people also traveled vast distances to spread Islam and Buddhism far beyond the Middle East and India/Nepal.

In recent decades travel has become a popular leisure industry, and organized tourism has considerable impact on the economies and cultures of many countries. Tourism provides limitless opportunities for increasing understanding of the world and of one's own country because, as Mark Twain wrote, "travel is fatal to prejudice, bigotry, and narrow mindedness" (Twain 1902, 650).

We define "international tourists" as people who travel outside the borders of their own country for a relatively short time for leisure purposes, frequently as part of an organized group. Tourism is part of the larger industry of leisure services that provide opportunities to travel to other countries, including transportation, tour businesses, advertising, guides, and lodging. Many people also travel to other countries for purposes other than leisure, for example, migration, formal education, or employment. For instance, many colleges offer research and learning opportunities that allow students and faculty members to travel to other countries. Such people are not tourists per se, although they normally do touring in addition to their formal studies and teaching. Tourism is generally a kind of organized travel, but in reports and studies it is often hard to distinguish from other forms of travel. Not discussed here is the huge industry of domestic tourism, in which people travel within their own nation's borders. For example, in Japan 22,297 hot springs attract 138 million overnight visitors each year.

Size of the Tourist Sector and the Economics of Tourism

In terms of economics, tourism actually functions in the same way as exports. Tourists to a nation generate hard currency for that nation in the same way that selling its exports does. For the year 2002 the World Tourism Organization reports that international tourism receipts totaled $474.2 billion or $1.3 billion per day, with the total number of international tourists exceeding 700 million for the first time. In terms of receipts the top-ranked country, the United States, had $66.5 billion. The next four countries in order were Spain ($33.5 billion), France ($28.2 billion), Italy ($26.9 billion), and China, excluding Hong Kong ($20.4 billion). In terms of actual numbers of tourists, France ranked first, Spain second, the United States third, Italy fourth, and China fifth. Such flows of tourists are affected by many factors. One important factor is the relative value of different currencies. The rise of the Euro and decline of the dollar in 2003–2004 have made the United States more attractive and Europe less attractive to potential tourists. With respect to visiting the United States, Canada ranks first (14.6 million tourists), Mexico second (10.3 million), Japan third (5.1 million), United Kingdom fourth (4.7 million), and Germany fifth (1.8 million). Of course, a nation's geographical size and location influence travel immensely; one can travel thousands of miles before leaving Russia, Brazil, or the United States, but only perhaps a hundred miles within Switzerland. Not surprisingly, many Americans have not traveled outside their own country. The magazine *Travel Agent* in 2004 reported that only 21 percent of Americans had passports.

With respect to Americans traveling abroad, 43 percent travel to Europe, 33 percent to Latin America and the Caribbean, and 23 percent to Asia/Oceania; 48 percent travel for business and conventions and 43 percent for leisure and visits to relatives or friends. The average age of male travelers is 45.5 years and that of females is 42.7 years. Currently 59 percent of travelers are male and 41 percent are female. This ratio may change because in the United States as many as 40 percent of all women older than forty are either single, divorced, or widowed. Currently 9 percent of U.S. travelers are retired. That percentage also will increase dramatically with the aging of the population.

In the aftermath of the 9/11 terrorist attacks and recognition of the growing importance of cultural understanding and knowledge, a surge has occurred in the number of students going abroad for study. The 2002–2003 academic year had an 8.5 percent increase, reaching a record total of 174,629 students, more than double (an increase of 145 percent) since the 1991–1992 academic year.

Kinds of International Tourism

The kinds of international tourism are related to people's motives—what they want to gain from the tourist experience. Lepp and Gibson classify tourists by the degree of novelty and familiarity they seek and the degree of risk they perceive, such as exposure to strange food, health hazards, crime, and terrorism. We stress the difference between shallow and deep tourism, which reflects the degree of serious interest in learning about other countries and their cultures. Many people travel simply for relaxation and pleasure.

Tourism for Recreation: Broadly viewed, one kind of international tourism could be called simply *recreative tourism*. A common image of recreative tourists, one that is promoted by television advertising, is of people eating or dancing on cruise ships or lying on beaches with palm trees in the background. Their aims are fundamentally relaxation and enjoyment. Sometimes the recreation is available to tourists at home, but they prefer going abroad. For instance, Japanese tourists travel to Thailand to play golf inexpensively. Some tourists seek *adventurous entertainment*, such as bungee jumping in New Zealand and hiking in the Andes or Himalayas. Among the motives for travel, romance and *sex tourism* must also be mentioned. Although usually labeled as such, sex tours, largely in less-developed countries, are offered for men often from the richer countries of the West or Asia. Sex tourists often leave highly negative images of their native cultures in the countries they visit

Tourism for Exploration and Learning: There are several kinds of tourism beyond simple recreative tourism, such as intentional exploratory tourism and adjunctive tourism. In both, people seek to learn about another country and are likely to have more depth of motive than are recreative tourists. *Intentional exploratory tourism* is exemplified by *ecotourism*, in which tourists explore the natural ecology of another country. Costa Rica and the Galapagos Islands

A large cruise ship docked in Barbados. Source: istock/David Partington.

(Ecuador) are quite popular for ecotourism. Uganda has encouraged tourism to its gorilla reserves. Usually this kind of tourism involves hiking, camping, or swimming in relatively less-inhabited areas such as mountains, upland rivers, or coral reefs. *Cultural and historical tourism* concentrates on the great monuments of the past and on performances revealing the traditions of a country, such as its dances and stories. Examples of this kind of tourism are visits to the Pyramids (Egypt), Machu Picchu (Peru), Easter Island (Chile), the Plain of Jars (Laos), and the new Guggenheim museum in Bilbao (Spain). And the Stanford Alumni Association travel program emphasizes visits to world heritage sites such as Angkor Wat (the world's largest religious monument) in Cambodia or Ha Long Bay in Vietnam. In *nostalgia tourism*, sometimes called "heritage tourism," people from the United States, for example, travel to Europe to seek out the towns from which they emigrated or to locate scenes from pictures their parents have shown them. Another example of heritage tourism would be Korean adoptees returning to Korea to learn about their heritage. A new kind of tourism is *adoption tourism*, in which people travel to another country to adopt a child. China and Cambodia have been particularly popular sites for such tourism. This kind of tourism became better known when the U.S. movie star Angelina Jolie adopted a boy from Cambodia.

Adjunctive tourism is associated with work or research in a foreign country. For instance, in *research tourism* people with grants or other financial sponsorship tour as a sideline. For example, during a Fulbright-supported study of south Indian dance a graduate student might explore the Himalayas, using her experience to broaden her understanding of India. Closely related to this kind of tourism is *business* or *work tourism;* for instance, a World Bank employee on business in east India might tour Rajasthan to explore both personal interests and future work possibilities. In *civil engagement tourism* people tour other countries with the intent of helping or informing other people; examples are Mobility International, Mercy Corps, Global Volunteers, and some missionary groups. Another kind of tourism *raises political consciousness,* as illustrated by the Argentinean revolutionary leader Ché Guevara's youthful travels around Latin America by motorcycle, which made him aware of poverty and social injustices.

A negative kind of tourism is *illicit traffic in cultural property.* People travel to other countries to purchase precious cultural art and artifacts, which are then taken illegally from the countries. In a rather notorious case many decades ago, André Malraux, the French adventurer and author who eventually became minister of culture, was caught smuggling valuable art from Angkor Wat out of Cambodia.

Seldom mentioned and not covered in this discussion is *in-country contrast tourism,* in which domestic tours are conducted as

if to another country. For instance, tourists from Nebraska might visit Chinatown in San Francisco, or tourists from São Paulo, Brazil, might travel to learn about diverse ethnic communities in the upper Amazon.

In vicarious travel—*armchair tourism*—people who stay at home watch television shows (on the Discovery Channel, for example) about travel. Reading books and magazines such as *National Geographic* also gives opportunities to know about other places vicariously. *The Travel Book* provides twelve hundred images of all 230 countries of the globe. Some children and adults have hobbies, such as stamp collecting, that involve learning about other countries. The Internet also has many opportunities for exploration of distant places. Preparation for actual travel ideally would involve prior armchair exploration of the destination.

Sharing the Tourist Experience

Tourists often preserve their memories and share their travel experiences through photos and souvenirs. The artist R. Padre Johnson published a volume of more than five hundred portraits of people encountered in traveling to 139 countries during a thirteen-year period. Other tourists write about their travels. A lot of this writing is informal, but the work of many professional writers is inspired by their travels. One of the best known contemporary writers of this type is Paul Theroux, the author of many books describing his adventures traveling by train around Asia and Latin America and paddling around the Pacific. *Tales of the South Pacific,* which launched James Michener's career as a popular novelist, derived from his travels in that part of the world. The Englishwoman Isabella Bird wrote forty-eight hundred pages in twelve volumes about her travels to such areas as Tibet, Japan, China, Persia, and Kurdistan.

Resources for Tourism

In addition to the wide range of guidebooks to specific countries and regions, other resources exist. Heinike-Motsch and Sygall provide a valuable guide to resources to facilitate the international travel of people with disabilities in *Building an Inclusive Development Community: A Manual on Including People with Disabilities in International Development Programs.* Evelyn Hannon (http://www.journeywoman.com) and Marybeth Bond (http://www.womentraveltips.com) give valuable information for women travelers. For people seeking wellness and spirituality to change their lives, Karen Baji Holms provides *101 Vacations to Change Your Life: A Guide to Wellness Centers, Spiritual Retreats, and Spas.* For those

THE DEVELOPMENT OF TOURISM ON THE ISLAND OF ANAFI, CYCLADES, GREECE

The growing global tourism industry has had a considerable impact on the economies and cultures of many tourist destinations. The passage below illustrates the changes that can occur in small economies when tourism starts to increase.

Islanders were initially at a loss when, from the mid-1970s onwards, increasingly large numbers of people, Greeks and foreigners, with no previous connection to the island, began to come to Anafi as holidaymakers, deliberately seeking an "unspoiled" island by choosing a destination unmentioned in guidebooks or described in them as off the beaten tourist track, or simply by letting chance decide where they would get off the steamer. They found the island almost too "unspoiled" for a holiday, with hardly any facilities for travelers or tourists. There was no bakery, water came from rain-fed cisterns, cafés opened at times to suit working men and were closed at lunchtime and in the weekday afternoons, the harbor and beaches had no cafés, restaurants, or rooms to rent, and the lack of electricity meant no refrigeration, hence problems with food storage. Inevitably, those who stayed on the island were equipped to be self-sufficient; those who were not left on the next boat, but a few were put up by local residents (such as café owners) or taken to the village guesthouse, mainly used by visiting meat-merchants. Over the years word-of-mouth recommendation, further guidebook attention, electrification (1974), and speedier and more frequent steamer

services resulting from government improvement programs brought more and more holidaymakers to the island each summer.

By the 1980s, hundreds of passengers were disembarking from the steamers that called at the island from Piraeus and Rafina three times a week during the summer months. Travelers now found eight restaurants and café-bars, two bar-discos, and eleven people with rooms to let—about eighty beds in all. In the high season there were now far too many arrivals to be serviced by existing facilities. Some evidence of the volume of tourist traffic to the island comes from passenger figures supplied by one of the domestic ferry lines running steamers to the island and from records of vehicles transported kept by the Statistical Service of the Greek Merchant Navy. Although these figures do not represent all arrivals on the island, they suggest that at least 4,000 people came to the island between April and September 1987, bringing with them 45 cars, 25 lorries and 150 motor-bikes, scooters, and other small-wheeled vehicles—despite the lack of any properly-surfaced motor-road. The only stretch of road on Anafi was begun in 1988 and finished in 1991, linking the harbor with the main beach and then continuing up to the village.

Source: Kenna, M.E. (1993). Return migrants and tourist development: an example from the Cyclades. Journal of Modern Greek Studies 11, (1), 80-81.

interested in becoming global citizens through international experiences, Elizabeth Kruempelmann has written *The Global Citizen: A Guide to Creating an International Life and Career.* Norman D. Sundberg has listed tips for increasing tourists' understanding of places and peoples visited in "Tips for Tourists" in *International Psychology Reporter,* and K. Cushner has written *Beyond Tourism: A Practical Guide to Meaningful Educational Travel.*

Looking Down the Road

Travel, through its promotion of interconnectedness, is an integral factor in globalization. The reduced cost of travel over time in terms of constant dollars and the increased influence of the Internet and media have resulted in what Cairncross has termed the "death of distance" (Cairncross 2001). Another factor is the increase in the number of older people, even in developing countries, calling attention to important influences, such as demography and gerontology, in contributing to the accelerated growth in international tourism. In the United States and elsewhere in the West retired people make up a large percentage of people on

formal tours. Another factor for the future is the unpredictability of world events, which can affect tourism dramatically, such as the 9/11 terrorist attacks, the nightclub bombing in Bali, the war in Iraq, and weather, such as Caribbean hurricanes and Hong Kong typhoons. Tourism is sometimes promoted to recover from disasters, such as the violence in Uganda.

Clearly international tourism, with its rapid growth, can be a contentious issue. For many countries it is an industry of growing importance, providing crucially needed foreign exchange. For the United States, with its huge and growing trade deficit, incoming tourism is important to reduce its balance of payments deficit and strengthen the dollar. Critics of international tourism point to its many adverse dimensions, such as the growing commercial sex industry and tourism's contribution to the destruction of the world's precious cultural and physical landscapes. Numerous cultural sites, such as the Charles Bridge in Prague, Angkor Wat in Cambodia, and La Casa de la Música in Havana, Cuba, are dominated by the presence of tourists, not by people from the culture itself.

Promoters of international tourism, on the other hand, see such tourism as a healthy industry that is likely to encourage local handicrafts, display of local customs, and learning about others.

Learning about others is likely to promote peace and cultural understanding and to reduce prejudice. People through travel may develop an international identity and discover organizations and friends with whom they communicate in different lands. Although tourists often have limited contact with locals, remain in enclaves, and have stereotyped interpretations, many may still broaden their horizons. Cultural and historical tourism may promote cultural preservation and identity. For instance, people in southern Mexico, Guatemala, and Belize have learned a great deal about the ancient Maya because of the interest generated by tourism. Overall, a positive relationship has existed between the development of cultural world heritage sites and international tourism. However, the planning of places for tourism, including marketing, must consider the influences on the existing cultural geography. To maintain their world heritage site status, sites must follow strict rules and regulations related to both cultural and environmental preservation.

Finally, inevitably international tourism will also improve understanding of one's own country. The British poet T. S. Eliot wrote:

> We shall not cease from exploration,
> And the end of all our exploring,
> Will be to arrive where we started,
> And to know the place for the first time.

The ideal is that increasing numbers of tourists will become knowledgeable and intelligent travelers, especially as the number of tourists continues to rise. According to Francoise Frangialli, president of the UN World Tourism Organization, global tourism is expected to grow 4 percent each year in the years to come (statement in Berlin, March 15, 2007). In 2006, global tourism spending rose 4.5 percent. If tourism continues to grow at 4 percent per year as expected, despite war and natural disasters, the global tourist industry will double in size every 18 years. The key challenge facing the United States is how to increasingly benefit from the world's largest industry. Will its tourist market share increase or decline? With its remarkable diversity of sites and its prominence in popular global culture, the U.S. still has tremendous unrealized tourism potential. A commitment to reducing barriers for tourists to come to the U.S., while encouraging U.S. citizens to explore the world will provide both its citizens and foreign visitors greater opportunity to develop and understand diverse global perspectives.

Gerald W. Fry and Norman D. Sundberg

See also Globalization, Economic; Overseas Americans (Expatriates); Perspectives on the United States, Visitors'

Further Reading

Bird, I. (1998). *Collected travel writings of Isabella Bird.* Bristol, UK: Ganesha Publishing.

Bonington, C. (1982). *Quest for adventure.* New York: C. N. Potter.

Brooke, J. (2004, December 12). Watering down the healing waters of Japan. *New York Times,* pp. 5, 6.

Cairncross, F. (2001). *The death of distance: How the communications revolution is changing our lives.* Boston: Harvard Business School Press.

Capodiferro, A. (2004). *Wonders of the world: Masterpieces of architecture from 4000 B.C. to the present.* New York: Barnes & Noble Books.

Clift, S., & Carter, S. (Eds.). (2000). *Tourism and sex: Culture, commerce and coercion.* London and New York: Pinter.

Cushner, K. (2004). *Beyond tourism: A practical guide to meaningful educational travel.* Lanham, MD: Scarecrow Education.

Engle, J. (2004, November 28). Female travelers are growing market. *Los Angeles Times.*

Fahn, J. D. (2003). *A land on fire: The environmental consequences of the Southeast Asia boom.* Boulder, CO: Westview Press.

Guevara, E. (2004). *Motorcycle diaries of Che Guevara.* London: Fourth Estate.

Heinicke-Motsed, K., & Sygall, S. (2004). *Building an inclusive development community: A manual on including people with disabilities in international development programs.* Eugene, OR: Mobility International USA.

Holmes, K. R. (1999). *101 vacations to change your life: A guide to wellness centers, spiritual retreats, and spas.* Secaucus, NJ: Carol Publishing Group.

Johnson, R. P. (1992). *Journeys with the global family: Insights through portraits & prose.* Cody, WY: World View Art & Publishing.

Kruempelmann, E. (2002). *The global citizen: A guide to creating an international life and career.* Berkeley, CA: Ten Speed Press.

Lepp, A., & Gibson, H. (2003). Tourist roles, perceived risk and international tourism. *Annals of Tourism Research, 30*(3), 606–624.

Leung, P. (2003). Sex tourism: The case of Cambodia. In T. G. Bauer & B. McKercher (Eds.), *Sex tourism: Journeys of romance, love and lust* (pp. 181–195). New York: Haworth Press.

Lonely Planet Publications. (2004). *The travel book: A journey through every country of the world.* Melbourne, Australia: Author.

Lutz, C. A., & Collins, J. L. (1993). *Reading National Geographic.* Chicago: University of Chicago Press.

McGregor, E., Boorman, C., & Uhlig, R. (2004). *Long way round: Chasing shadows across the world.* New York: Atria Books.

Medina, L. K. (2003). Commoditizing culture: Tourism and Maya identity. *Annals of Tourism Research, 30*(2), 353–368.

Møgelhøj, H. (1999, December 1). Tourism the world's largest industry—Is it given the credibility it deserves? Retrieved December 5, 2004, from http://www.pkf.co.uk/web/PKFWeb.nsf/pagesbyID/ID1B27E8E1F1B0FC4580256B4B0055ACDE?OpenDocument

Morris, J. (2004). *The world: Travels 1950–2000.* New York: W. W. Norton.

Peart, N. (1996). *The masked rider: Cycling in west Africa.* Lawrencetown Beach, Canada: Pottersfield Press.

Pelton, R. Y. (2003). *Robert Young Pelton's the world's most dangerous places.* New York: HarperCollins.

Poria, Y., Butler, R., & Airey, D. (2003). The core of heritage tourism. *Annals of Tourism Research, 30*(1), 238–254.

Prott, L. V. (2004, November). The fight against illicit traffic in cultural property: The importance of case studies. *IIAS Newsletter, 35,* 24.

Ringer, G. (2002). Gorilla tourism: Uganda uses tourism to recover from decades of violent conflict. *Alternative Journal, 28,* 16–19.

Ringer, G. (2004). Geographies of tourism and place in Micronesia: The "sleeping lady" awakes. *Journal of Pacific Studies, 26,* 131–150.

Ryan, C. (2001). *Sex tourism: Marginal people and liminalities.* London: Routledge.

Scheiser, R., & Zellman, U. (2005). *Mobility and travel in the Mediterranean from antiquity to the Middle Ages.* Munster, Germany: Lit Verlag.

Schultz, P. (2003). *1,000 places to see before you die.* New York: Workman.

Sundberg, N. D. (2001, Summer). Tips for tourists. *International Psychology Reporter, 5*(2), 17, 20.

Theroux, P. (2000). *Fresh air fiend: Travel writings, 1985–2000.* Boston: Houghton Mifflin.

Twain, M. (1902). *The innocents abroad.* Hartford, CT: American Publishing Company.

Van Den Abbeele, G. (1992). *Travel as metaphor: From Montaigne to Rousseau.* Minneapolis: University of Minnesota Press.

World Tourism Organization. (2003). *Tourism highlights edition 2003.* Madrid, Spain: Author.

Trade Agreements

U.S. economic conditions have become ever more dependent on foreign markets, and trends in the global economy now demand more elaborate trade arrangements—like NAFTA and the WTO—than were previously necessary.

U.S. foreign policy hinges heavily on U.S. economic foreign policy as expressed chiefly through international trade. International trade involves the exchange of goods and services through barter or sale between states, multinational corporations (MNCs), and international institutions. In an era of accelerating globalization and interdependence, no country, including the United States, is so economically self-sufficient that it can afford to ignore the rest of the world. Hence, international trade helps to satisfy U.S. needs in at least three principal dimensions, all of which are secured legally through agreements. First, U.S. commercial exchanges involve bilateral agreements with other states; second, financial transactions involve agreements between the United States and other states, private agents, and multilateral institutions; and third, private U.S. corporate enterprises pursue agreements with foreign governments to invest in their states.

International Commerce

The main facet of U.S. trade involves commercial agreements with agents of other states. This trade occurs on three levels: (1) bilateral commerce directly between the United States and other state governments or their corporate agents; (2) select U.S. agreements that set commercial transactions with governments in a regional organization, the members of which are usually protected by custom or tariff benefits; and (3) U.S. participation in multilateral institutions, created by international agreements, that aim to regulate and facilitate interstate commercial relations.

Background

The Great Depression and the destruction wrought by World War II deeply upset patterns of world trade. In the postwar era the United States seized the initiative to design multilateral institutions created by international agreements that could reinvigorate international commerce. In 1944 the United States convened the Bretton Woods Conference in New Hampshire. This conference created the International Monetary Fund (IMF) to promote mon-

etary cooperation among states and the International Bank for Reconstruction and Development (World Bank) to furnish development aid to needy states. In 1947 the United States sought to facilitate international trade through tariff reductions in a conference with twenty-two other governments in Geneva, Switzerland. This conference resulted in the General Agreement on Tariffs and Trade (GATT), which lowered trade barriers and eliminated discriminatory treatment in commerce for the participants. Taken together, the IMF, World Bank, and GATT became pillars of the Bretton Woods system, which functioned for nearly three decades until its collapse in the early 1970s. GATT was an international agreement; it was not, as often perceived, an international organization. Although developing countries subsequently called for a new international economic order to correct worldwide economic inequalities, this call proved fruitless. Even so, the creation on 1 January 1995 of the World Trade Organization (WTO) after seven years of negotiations heralded the rise of near-universal legal rules governing contemporary trade relations. The WTO is now the preeminent institution for regulating global commercial relations. Its 150 member states account for more than 97 percent of world trade, and the organization's decisions affect nearly all the goods and services moving in international commerce. In 2005 more than $12.5 trillion worth of commercial goods and services was exchanged.

World Trade Organization

The WTO provides a code of rules (called "agreements") and a forum for governments to discuss and resolve trade disputes and to continue negotiations toward expanding world trade opportunities. The thirty thousand pages of WTO agreements cover goods, services, and intellectual property; they articulate principles of liberalization and permissible exceptions; they prescribe special treatment for developing countries; and they require governments to make their trade policies transparent.

The WTO performs other roles that benefit U.S. interests. The General Agreement on Trade in Services furnishes a set of enforceable multilateral legal rules covering international trade in services. Consequently, all internationally operating U.S. banks,

insurance firms, telecommunication companies, hotel chains, and transport companies enjoy the same principles of free and fair trade under the WTO that originally applied to trade in goods. The Agreement on Trade-Related Aspects of Intellectual Property Rights (TRIPS) incorporates for the first time intellectual property rules into the multilateral trading system. These rules are aimed at protecting original products created by industries, such as films, music recordings, books, computer software, and online services. U.S. corporations clearly gain from these legal protections.

Multinational Corporations

While international commerce engages the U.S. government, U.S. multinational corporations are the main agents that carry out that commerce, and they do so through bilateral agreements. Today nearly 70,000 international MNCs and their 820,000 foreign affiliates engage in transnational sales that produce 25 percent of the world's gross product. Moreover, MNCs cover not only the movement of investment capital, but also the offering of private loans through services such as banking, insurance, and transportation. Although only 3,400 MNCs are headquartered in the United States, they negotiate bilateral commercial agreements to formalize trade exchange with foreign governments and other MNCs.

Regional Organizations

Patterns of international commerce are strongly influenced by multilateral associations and agreements that promote duty-free transactions among their membership. For the United States one of these trade associations—the European Union (EU)—and one agreement—the North American Free Trade Agreement (NAFTA)—make especially important contributions. NAFTA and the EU were created through multilateral agreements.

The implementation of NAFTA in 1994 established the North American Free Trade Zone between Canada, Mexico, and the United States. NAFTA contains rules on nine thousand categories of goods exchanged among the three states and on legal particulars for the free-trade zone. NAFTA is a trade agreement, not an organization. It aims to increase trade and investment among its partners by tariff elimination and reduction of nontariff barriers, as well as by comprehensive provisions concerning the conduct of business in the free-trade area. These activities include the regulation of investment opportunities, services, and intellectual property competition. The 440 million people in NAFTA states produce $12.5 trillion in goods and services annually, and dismantling trade barriers and opening North American markets since

1993 have contributed to impressive economic growth in all three countries as each of the partners have registered more than 30 percent economic growth during that period. By lowering trade barriers and developing clear rules for commerce, NAFTA expanded trade investment opportunities among the United States, Canada, and Mexico. From 1993 to 2005 the total volume of annual trade

PREAMBLE TO THE NORTH AMERICA FREE TRADE AGREEMENT

The Government of Canada, the Government of the United Mexican States and the Government of the United States of America, resolved to:

STRENGTHEN the special bonds of friendship and cooperation among their nations;

CONTRIBUTE to the harmonious development and expansion of world trade and provide a catalyst to broader international cooperation;

CREATE an expanded and secure market for the goods and services produced in their territories;

REDUCE distortions to trade;

ESTABLISH clear and mutually advantageous rules governing their trade;

ENSURE a predictable commercial framework for business planning and investment;

BUILD on their respective rights and obligations under the General Agreement on Tariffs and Trade and other multilateral and bilateral instruments of cooperation;

ENHANCE the competitiveness of their firms in global markets;

FOSTER creativity and innovation, and promote trade in goods and services that are the subject of intellectual property rights;

CREATE new employment opportunities and improve working conditions and living standards in their respective territories;

UNDERTAKE each of the preceding in a manner consistent with environmental protection and conservation;

PRESERVE their flexibility to safeguard the public welfare;

PROMOTE sustainable development;

STRENGTHEN the development and enforcement of environmental laws and regulations; and

PROTECT, enhance and enforce basic workers' rights

Source: North American Free Trade Agreement. (2007). Retrieved June 6, 2007, from http://www-tech.mit.edu/Bulletins/nafta.html

between the three NAFTA parties increased from $297 billion to $810 billion (up 173 percent), and U.S. exports in 2006 alone to Canada and Mexico grew from $134 billion to $368.6 billion. As the three economies grew, North America became a magnet for worldwide foreign direct investment (FDI). In 2005, Mexico attracted an additional $209.6 billion, Canada attracted $356.9 billion, and the United States attracted $1.626 trillion, bringing the combined FDI in the NAFTA states to more than $15 trillion, or one-third of the world's total.

International Finance

The globalization of international trade for the United States is revealed in its international financial transactions. Currency flows worldwide exceed $1.5 trillion each day, or $550 trillion every year, two-thirds of which moves through four states—the United States, Germany, Japan, and the United Kingdom. In the United States central banks and the Treasury Department use monetary reserves (foreign exchange and gold) to control exchange rates and reduce fluctuations. Although no international banking and finance system truly exists—because banks operate under the laws of the state in which they conduct their banking and financial business—international financial institutions assist in coordinating and facilitating this massive flow of money between states. The United States assumes a leading role in these processes.

U.S. banks play a central role in international commercial transactions. Payments made through U.S. banks are the means by which a person in the United States transfers value for goods purchased to a person in another country. U.S. banks thus supply channels through which international commerce is conducted and consummated by U.S. corporations. U.S. banks also manage international commerce by providing customers with credit, settlement, and venture capital through loans and financial investment services.

International banking and financing are conducted through agreements negotiated by private banks and multilateral financial institutions. The latter are not privately owned because their funds are contributed by member states. Their main function is to facilitate and support the economic development of member states. Paramount among these international financial institutions is the International Monetary Fund, the main purpose of which is to provide loans to countries experiencing balance-of-payments difficulties in order to restore conditions for sustainable economic growth. Significantly, the U.S. role is preeminent in decision making because its contributions give it 17 percent of the IMF vote.

Foreign Investment

U.S. investment abroad has proliferated dramatically as the U.S. economy has become more heavily affected by foreign investment. The Bureau of Economic Analysis of the Department of Commerce calculates that U.S.-owned investment assets abroad totaled nearly $8 trillion in 2003. Most of these foreign investments are private assets committed by U.S. firms in developed (mainly European) countries. Yet, at the same time, foreign agents invest in the United States even more heavily. The Department of Commerce

Migrant workers picking strawberries in a field. Source: istock/Glenn Frank.

estimates that by 2005, direct foreign investment in the United States amounted to $12.7 trillion, much of which came in securities and other liabilities to finance U.S. corporate spending and government deficits that ballooned since the 1980s.

The Future

Intensified globalization means that greater international commerce, more financial arrangements, and expanding monetary exchange will foster greater intermeshing of U.S. domestic economics with international trade, as revealed in new trade agreements. Consequently economic conditions in the United States, especially employment, inflation, and overall growth, will depend more on the stability of foreign markets, imports of goods and services, currency exchange rates, capital flows, and other international economic factors. This complex situation will engender increased global economic interdependence for both the U.S. government and U.S. corporations.

For the United States and its corporate agents, the complex interdependent process of internationally trading goods and services through international agreements will expand. Although worldwide interdependence and financial globalization will persist in drawing U.S. traders into close commercial ties with firms in other countries, these same forces make it essential that rules guide those processes. Thus, the United States should assist in establishing through international institutions new rules, anchored in new trade agreements, as they become needed in the conduct of international economic transactions.

Christopher C. Joyner

See also Drug Trade and the War on Drugs; Globalization, Economic; IMF, World Bank, and IDB, U.S. Role in; International Agreements and Summits; International Law

Further Reading

Articles of agreement of the International Bank for Reconstruction and Development. (1945). *Treaties and Other International Acts Series No. 1502, United Nations Treaty Series, 2,* 134.

Articles of agreement of the International Monetary Fund. (1945). *Treaties and Other International Acts Series No. 1501, United Nations Treaty Series, 2,* 9.

Bureau of Economic Analysis, Department of Commerce. (2007). U.S. net international investment at year end 2005. Retrieved February 12, 2007, from www.bea.gov/bea/di/intinv05_t3.xls

European Union. (2007) . Europa—Gateway to the European Union. Retrieved February 12, 2007, from http://europa.eu.int/index_en.htm

Friedman, T. L. (1999). *The Lexus and the olive tree: Understanding globalization.* New York: Farrar, Straus, Giroux.

General Agreement on Tariffs and Trade. (1947). *Treaties and Other International Acts Series No. 1700, United Nations Treaty Series, 55,* 194.

Gilpin, R. (2000). *The challenge of the global capitalism: The world economy in the 21st century.* Princeton, NJ: Princeton University Press.

International Monetary Fund. (2007). IMF members' quotas and voting power, and IMF board of governors. Retrieved February 12, 2007, from www.imf.org/external/np/sec/memdir/members.htm#t

Jackson, J. H., Davey, W. J., & Sykes, A. O. (1995). *Legal problems of international economic relations: Cases, materials and text on the national and international regulation of transnational economic relations* (4th ed.). St. Paul, MN: West Group.

North American Free Trade Agreement. (1994). Department of Foreign Affairs and International Trade (Canada). Retrieved February 12, 2007, from http://www.dfait-maeci.gc.ca/nafta-alena/agree-en.asp

Office of the United States Trade Representative. (2004). NAFTA: A decade of success. Retrieved February 12, 2007, from http://www.ustr.gov/Document_Library/Fact_Sheets/2004/NAFTA_A_Decade_of_Success.html

Office of the United States Trade Representative. (2007) . Snapshot of the WTO cases involving the U.S. Retrieved February 22, 2007, from http://www.ustr.gov/Trade_Agreements/Monitoring_Enforcement/Dispute_Settlement/WTO/Section_Index.html?ht=

Rothgeb, J. M. Jr. (2001). *US trade policy: Balancing economic dreams and political realities.* Washington, DC: CQ Press.

Spero, J. E., & Hart, J. (2002). *The politics of international economic relations.* Belmont: CA: Wadsworth.

World Bank. (2007). The World Bank: IBRB and IDA: Working for a World Free of Poverty. Retrieved February 22, 2007, from www.worldbank.org/

World Trade Organization. (1994). Marrakesh agreement establishing the World Trade Organization. *World Trade Organization, the Legal Texts: The Results of the Uruguay Round, 1999,* 4.

World Trade Organization. (2007). What is the WTO? Retrieved February 22, 2007, from http://www.wto.org/english/thewto_e/whatis_e/whatis_e.htm

Yergin, D., & Stanislaw, J. (1999). *The commanding heights: The battle between government and the marketplace that is remaking the modern world.* New York: Simon & Schuster.

Transnational Corporations

See Multinational Corporations

U.S. Agency for International Development

The U.S. is perceived by some to be operating USAID more to exert control and exploit resources than to provide humanitarian development assistance. Others see it as essential for creating economies capable of generating wealth.

The U.S. Agency for International Development (USAID) was established in 1961 by President John F. Kennedy to assist in long-range economic and social development in poor and developing countries. Providing economic and humanitarian assistance in more than one hundred countries, USAID has provided many opportunities for people around the world to form perspectives on the United States. The USAID mission contains two interrelated premises. The first is that foreign assistance remains a valuable foreign policy tool in terms of promoting U.S. security and economic interests. The second is that the interdependence of nations means that the United States will continually be affected—for better or worse—by economic and political events in other parts of the world.

USAID developed with the dual aims of furthering U.S. foreign policy interests while attempting to improve the lives of citizens in the developing world. The first aim is constant, whereas the second is ephemeral. The first aim creates a perception abroad of deceptiveness in development assistance and gives the United States an unscrupulous reputation around the world; U.S. policies are not consistent, and they change as conditions around the world change. One day a country is considered a friend and given millions of dollars in aid; the next day this same country is considered a foe, and aid is withdrawn. Furthermore, policy interests are not just political; they include the economic interests of national and U.S.-based transnational corporations. This situation means that U.S. policies are designed first and foremost to support U.S. economic interests abroad. The second aim, to improve the lives of people in the Third World, is not a deception, and indeed many lives have been improved. However, after fifty years and billions of dollars spent in development aid, most receiving countries remain poor and underdeveloped. As USAID struggles to balance its dual responsibility mandated by the U.S. government, its development programs are considered by many people in aid-receiving nations and elsewhere to be a cause for continued poverty and underdevelopment. This situation is the contradiction of development.

Two Perceptions of U.S. Development Assistance

Perception, perspective, and underlying interests are key considerations when analyzing the United States and development aid. USAID, as an independent agency that gets its foreign policy direction from the U.S. State Department, combines funding and monitoring of police training and counterinsurgency efforts with agricultural research, local health initiatives, as well as women in development projects (including education, farming, small-scale animal husbandry and other micro-enterprise projects). In reviewing what has been written about U.S. development efforts, one finds two clear perspectives. The first perspective maintains that the United States is a capitalist giant that uses aid assistance to further its own interests; that poor and underdeveloped nations are marginalized in the international arena by aid programs; and that aid programs configure the conditions for exploitation of developing nations' resources by foreigners, create market forces beyond the control of indigenous populations, encourage privatization and economic dependence on the United States, and have driven poor nations deeper into poverty. This perspective positions development aid as an instrument of dependency and neocolonial policies of the United States. Supporters of this perspective claim that development aid turns the developing world into nothing more than a source of raw materials used to underpin the U.S. economy. Development aid is simply a new way to ensure economic superiority by ensuring either the expansion of traditional primary-product exports or creation of labor-intensive, low value-added manufacturing exports, leaving many of the poorest in the developing world even poorer.

A competing perspective on USAID development assistance maintains that aid is responsible for development throughout many developing countries. In this perspective the most prosperous developing and least-developed nations are those that adhere to U.S. programs and policies because the United States sets up productive economies capable of generating wealth. This perspective contends,

for example, that the cash crop-producing areas and trading ports of west Africa and the mineral-producing areas of sub-Saharan Africa are proof that development aid is successful. Indeed, according to this perspective, without development assistance, nations would not be able to export cocoa, cotton, tobacco, groundnuts, or palm oil. Copper, zinc, rubber, and other natural resource industries would not be developed and would not earn much-needed foreign currency. This perspective claims that modern education and health care, hospitals and the control of disease, as well as fundamentals such as public security and law and order; mechanical transport, airports, roads, railways, and ports; the application of science and technology to economic activity, and the development of towns with substantial buildings, clean water, and sewage facilities are all the result of development assistance.

Perspectives on the United States

The perception of many people is that the United States dominates, drives, perpetuates, and disproportionately prospers from the spread of global capitalism. USAID is partially responsible, as the answer to the question "Why, despite billions of dollars in aid to the developing world, have many nations failed to develop?" demonstrates: Development assistance is more about establishing U.S. hegemony (influence) than it is about encouraging development of free sovereign nations, helping to establish national agricultural programs to feed people, or educating people. In seeking access to global markets and cheap exports, the U.S. government is seen as using development aid or withholding promised aid to block local development priorities and state-regulated markets in favor of limited state involvement and lower policy-induced trade barriers. In Asia, Africa, and Latin America, since the inception of USAID, the push for free trade, open markets, and unregulated growth as a development policy has resulted in impoverished people and destabilized governments in many countries.

Under the guise of development and democratization, the United States is seen as protecting corrupt client regimes to protect its own continued access to strategically important resources. A U.S. State Department report from 1955 declared:

> Our foreign policy is aimed at achieving the kind of world community in which trade and investment can move with a minimum of restrictions and a maximum of security and confidence. Thus, almost every aspect of our foreign policy has some ultimate effect, directly or indirectly, upon the flow of private investment abroad. (Curtis 1998, 68)

In other words the ideology behind U.S. development assistance, and the creation of USAID, envisioned that economic aid offers political leverage to persuade recipient states to follow foreign policies consistent with those of the United States. In discussing U.S. aid to Egypt, William J. Burns says:

> Aid could be offered as an incentive to reinforce certain desirable behavior patterns on the part of the recipient country; or aid could be denied as a political sanction for behavior considered contrary to U.S. interests. A whole hierarchy of inducements exists based upon the quantity, quality, and duration of the aid promised or provided. (Burns 1985, xi)

The one-third to one-half of humanity living in poverty as a result of this strategy is an unfortunate corollary to the positive results garnered to the United States.

The contradiction of development then appears to entail the political and economic actions of USAID through the provision of financial aid to foreign governments. Every year the testimony to Congress in favor of the foreign aid bill stresses the multiplier

USAID IN LEBANON

The text below is an extract from the USAID/Lebanon objectives document on building tourism.

Lebanon's tourism sector is making steady gains, with tourist arrivals, mainly from Arab countries, 13 percent higher this past year, notably for cultural and historical tourism, ecotourism and business travel. Hotels and other tourist establishments are continually coming on-stream, with $2 billion of investment over the past decade. Growth in tourism will spur substantial employment opportunities for women and disadvantaged groups, as well as foreign exchange receipts. There are also excellent new prospects to extend tourism activities to areas outside Beirut. Tourism activities include an agro-tourism integrated park in Marjaoun, a World War II interactive museum at Khiam, tourist attraction sites at Derdra, Tel Debbine, recreation centers at Chebaa Lake, Hebbariyye, Kfar Hamam, Rachaiya, sports-oriented tourism such as hiking trails at Mount Hermon and river adventures at Wazzani. On a national level, activities will include a national marketing venture to update a Lebanon tourism attractions database and a national website, a hospitality worker training for hotels and other tourism institutions to participate in. A rural tourism development forum is also planned to involve the stakeholders of the tourism industry in holding meetings and discussions as well as implement priority initiatives.

Source: USAID Lebanon. (2003–2005). Retrieved March 14, 2007, from http://lebanon.usaid.gov/

effect of this aid to the United States. Thus, working through friendly politicians, bureaucrats, and nongovernmental organizations abroad and funneling substantial sums of money to groups and individuals overseas, USAID has systematically furthered the strategic aims of the United States. Furthermore, the U.S. government deemed that vital interests were threatened by any experiment that didn't mimic the U.S. economic model—the free market and unlimited private accumulation of productive assets. Any nation seeking to alter these economic ground rules—Nicaragua, for example—was immediately perceived as having "gone over to the other camp" and thus was an enemy. Punishment was swift, usually including the suspension of aid and the arming of opponents of the offending government.

Aid Benefits the Donor

The United States is perceived by many people as selfish and aggressive. One key criticism of USAID development assistance and the United States is that although the United States almost always touts development as a local phenomenon, where control is supposedly relinquished to the local government, authority, or agency, in truth the opposite is the case. In keeping with U.S. foreign policy objectives the money provided under development aid goes back to the United States. The recipient country is tied to the donor and must make purchases of goods and supplies from the donor country. Even projects that are designed with local growth and governance in mind tend to benefit the United States more than the developing country. More than 70 percent of bilateral aid commitments from the United States are tied to purchase of goods and services from the United States. This money ends up supporting Americans and U.S. businesses, not local aid-receiving communities. A 1997 USAID newsletter declared that "The principal beneficiary of America's foreign assistance has always been the United States.... Foreign assistance programs have helped the United States by creating major markets for agricultural goods, new markets for industrial exports and hundreds of thousands of jobs for Americans" (Shah 2004). The same newsletter urged that the amount of money spent on aid be upped significantly in order to maintain U.S. leadership in the global arena.

The USAID 2004 Performance and Accountability Report supports the contention that aid is primarily designed to benefit the donor country. The report opens with the statement that USAID and "development" are playing a critical role, along with diplomacy and defense, in addressing the United States' most pressing national security demands. In 2007, USAID Director Randall Tobias noted in testimony before U.S. congress that providing foreign assistance was not just a moral obligation to alleviate suffering, but it provides

a foundation for U.S. national security strategy. USAID-funded projects provide the United States insight into, and some control of, the receiving country's economy and government. Leagues of foreign experts, known as "development consultants," are relied on to make important economic decisions. These decisions tend to be centered on the donor country's search for market goods and services or its need to develop exports. These decisions are not based on cultural sensitivity to local conditions or on what is good for local markets and sustainability of the country receiving aid. The primary function of development funded by USAID is to create an indispensable precondition for the recipient county to attract foreign private investment. The end result is an unequal exchange: developing nations suffer from low prices paid for their exports and higher prices paid for imports. Development aid has not led to "take-off" development, to use Rostow's metaphor. This arrangement is at best a misconception and at worst a deception of development.

The Future

Globalization in the twenty-first century means that the world is politically and economically interconnected. The United States is perceived as having three motivations for operating USAID: humanitarian development, commercial development, and political control of foreign governments. The United States is perceived as being concerned more with commercial development and political control than with providing humanitarian development assistance that will help the receiving country. Some USAID projects have provided real improvement in living standards for a large segment of the world's poorer countries. However, the United States is not seen as altruistic. The free-market model of development aid advocated by USAID is understood to benefit the needs of international firms rather than to promote development. Effective aid programs are those that promote access to developed country markets, including creating links between producers in developing country markets and those people who control the markets in the United States. USAID must help build institutions that facilitate broad-based sharing of the fruits of development rather than support development for elites. Expanding markets without improving people's lives is simply exploitation and not development.

Lorna Lueker Zukas

Further Reading

Bauer, P. T. (1992). *Colonialism is not responsible for Africa's problems.* In C. Wekesser (Ed.), *Africa: Opposing viewpoints.* San Diego, CA: Greenhaven Press.

Burns, W. J. (1985). *Economic aid and American policy toward Egypt, 1955–1981.* Albany: State University of New York Press.

Chua, A. (2004). *World on fire: How exporting free market democracy breeds ethnic hatred and global instability.* New York: Anchor Books.

Curtis, M. (1998). *The great deception: Anglo-American power and world order.* London: Pluto Press.

Escobar, A. (1995). *Encountering development: The making and unmaking of the Third World.* Princeton, NJ: Princeton University Press.

Lappé, F. M., Collins, J., Rosset, P., & Esparza, L. (1998). Myths: More US aid will help the hungry. Retrieved March 8, 2007, from http://www.globalissues.org/TradeRelated/Poverty/FoodDumping/USAid.asp

Reinert, E. S. (2004). *Globalization, economic development and inequality: An alternative perspective.* Northampton, MA: Edward Elgar Publishing.

Shah, A. (2004). The U.S. and foreign aid assistance. Retrieved March 8, 2007, from http://www.globalissues.org/TradeRelated/Debt/USAid.asp

USAID. (2004). Performance and accountability report fiscal year 2004. Retrieved March 8, 2007, from http://www.usaid.gov/policy/par04

USAID. (2007). Testimony of Ambassador Randall L. Tobias Director of U.S. Foreign Assistance & USAID Administrator: Hearing on Foreign Assistance Reform and FY 2008 Budget. Retrieved March 20, 2007, from http://www.usaid.gov/press/speeches/2007/sp070308_1.html

Wiegersma, N., & Medley, J. E. (2000). *US economic development policies towards the Pacific Rim: Successes and failures of US aid.* New York: St. Martin's Press.

U.S. Civil Rights

The U.S. advancement of civil rights over the past two centuries has in many ways laid the foundation for equality across the world. Even so, the fight for U.S. civil rights and equality continues to be waged on many fronts.

The quest for freedom and equality in the United States has inspired Americans for more than four centuries. Americans pride themselves on their compassion and fairness. In their pursuit of life, liberty, and happiness, Americans have positioned themselves as global caretakers and civil rights champions. The U.S. advancement of civil rights has endowed the United States with a unique ability to advance civil rights globally.

However, not everyone views Americans as stalwart champions of the civil rights of others. The practices and philosophies leading to the U.S. Civil War and the civil rights movement in the United States have aroused skepticism and cynicism among other nations. Continued racial, social, and political conflict in the United States leads many people in other nations to question the effectiveness of civil rights policies and laws in the United States. Some people find it hypocritical that the United States would champion civil rights in other nations while allowing civil injustice to continue in the United States. Such skepticism diminishes the effectiveness of U.S. global civil rights intervention. Nevertheless, the United States continues to address civil rights issues at home and elsewhere.

As the rest of the world views past and present U.S. struggles to advance civil rights at home, people have mixed feelings about U.S. global presence. Other countries have acknowledged the noble U.S. fight for civil rights. Willing to fight for the unity of their country and for individual liberties, Americans confront their own problems and the problems of others. The U.S. Civil War and the civil rights movement of the 1960s provide insight into how the United States addresses internal conflict.

History of the Civil Rights Movement in the United States

The term *civil rights* has no clear definition in the United States. Generally civil rights are those privileges given to citizens of a country. Civil rights are not the same as civil liberties, although the terms are often used interchangeably. Thomas Jefferson (1743–1826) warned that rights must be given to the individual and protected from government intrusion. John Locke (1632–1704) suggested that the rights to life, liberty, and property are part of a social contract between the government and its citizens. The belief that all should have access to equal rights to life, freedom, and happiness caused the Puritans to view the British colonies in North America as the land of promise. Throughout history people immigrating to the United States have expected to find a land of freedom and equality. This expectation remains an important part of the civil rights movement.

Early settlers in the United States found a vast untamed frontier rich in resources. Unlike European countries that were close and crowded, the United States had an expanse that seemed a God-given gift for new beginnings. Using the resources of this new frontier, the new settlers set out to establish a place for religious, political, and social equality. The vision for the United States was one of limited government and individual rights. Although no set definition was established, the individual's right to enjoy life in freedom constituted U.S. civil rights.

The European explorers who came to North America were looking for riches to take back to their home countries. These explorers eventually saw an opportunity to establish a country independent of Europe. As settlers adjusted to their new land, their dependence on Europe was diminished. Despite hardships, the attraction of a vast new frontier motivated settlers to build communities. The excitement of starting a new country overshadowed the ideal of equality for all. Land ownership, voting, and other political privileges were reserved for white Anglo-Saxon men. After the Revolutionary War (1775–1783), Americans began to build a nation on principles of justice and fairness. Their intentions were noble, but the recipients were primarily white Anglo-Saxon men.

Skin color and race relations played an enormous role in Americans' quest for civil rights. When Europeans had migrated to the United States, they had found a land geographically and culturally different from Europe. Predominantly white, these settlers viewed the Native American people occupying the land as backward and savage. Seeing themselves as potential saviors and believing themselves entitled to the new land, whites established policies giving special privileges to those of Anglo-Saxon descent, particularly men. When the United States brought in

U.S. CIVIL RIGHTS

people from other lands, those people who were deemed inferior were used as slaves.

The practice of slavery in the southern United States contradicted the U.S. promise of freedom. Legislation and cultural practices did not recognize all people as free. Slavery identified a particular segment of society, Africans, as property and as less than human. Between 1820 and 1822 the Missouri Compromise, regulating slavery in the western territories, offered a solution to the slavery conflict. An 1857 Supreme Court decision fueled the civil rights debate: The Dred Scott decision denied citizenship to anyone of African descent. Based on this decision and similar laws, Americans increasingly found themselves at odds over how freedom and justice were achieved. The Civil War (1861–1865) tore the young nation apart on ideological, political, and cultural principles.

Along with race, gender played an integral role in formulating U.S. civil rights policy. President Abraham Lincoln's Emancipation Proclamation (1863) offered freedom to black men but not to black women. White women also were excluded from many privileges given to men. After the Civil War the momentum for civil rights shifted from race to gender.

How the U.S. Civil Rights Movement Influenced the World

During the Reconstruction era the opportunity for people to achieve freedom regardless of race and economic status was threatened by the southern states' reluctance to abolish slavery. The Black Codes (1865) prevented blacks from participating in the political process. The Ku Klux Klan (1866) and other hate groups used intimidation to spread fear. Such an atmosphere caused some people in the rest of the world to view the United States with suspicion.

The rest of the world had viewed slavery in the United States apprehensively. During the 1800s most of the world began to make the change from oppressive policies to policies of universal freedom. Europe led the way as many countries abandoned the practice of slavery. Unfortunately, the economic benefits of slavery had caused the United States, particularly the South, to continue slavery as other nations abandoned it. Thus, other countries, such as Japan, Mexico, and Caribbean nations, watched with great interest during Reconstruction to see how the United States would heal its national wounds caused by slavery and the war. In China the

---

THE GREAT SOCIETY

The passage below is an excerpt from U.S. president Lyndon Johnson's "Great Society" speech delivered at the University of Michigan commencement in 1964 in which he set forth a platform for social change including the reduction of poverty and racial injustice. It was during his presidency that the Civil Rights Act of 1964 and the Voting Rights Act of 1965 were passed.

I have come today from the turmoil of your Capital to the tranquility of your campus to speak about the future of your country.

The purpose of protecting the life of our nation and preserving the liberty of our citizens is to pursue the happiness of our people. Our success in that pursuit is the test of our success as a nation.

For a century we labored to settle and to subdue a continent. For half a century we called upon unbounded invention and untiring industry to create an order of plenty for all of our people.

The challenge of the next half century is whether we have the wisdom to use that wealth to enrich and elevate our national life, and to advance the quality of our American civilization.

Your imagination, your initiative, and your indignation will determine whether we build a society where progress is the servant of our needs, or a society where old values and new visions are buried under unbridled growth. For in your time we have the opportunity to move not only toward the rich society and the powerful society, but upward to the "Great Society."

The "Great Society" rests on abundance and liberty for all. It demands an end to poverty and racial injustice, to which we are totally committed in out time. But that is just the beginning.

The "Great Society" is a place where every child can find knowledge to enrich his mind and to enlarge his talents. It is a place where leisure is a welcome chance to build and reflect, not a feared cause of boredom and restlessness. It is a place where the city of man serves not only the needs of the body and the demands of commerce but the desire for beauty and the hunger for community.

It is a place where man can renew contact with nature. It is a place which honors creation for its own sake and for what is adds to the understanding of the race. It is a place where men are more concerned with the quality of their goals than the quantity of their goods.

But most of all, the "Great Society" is not a safe harbor, a resting place, a final objective, a finished work. It is a challenge constantly renewed, beckoning us toward a destiny where the meaning of our lives matches the marvelous products of our labor.

Source: Lyndon Baines Johnson: The great society. (1964). Retrieved April 20, 2007, from http://americanrhetoric.com/speeches/lbjthe greatsociety.htm

period from 1850 to 1870 was plagued by rebellion and poverty. The Taiping Rebellion (1850–1864) resulted in about 20 million deaths in the quest for equality and social justice. In Russia the Crimean War showed the antiquated and oppressive policies of the Russian autocracy. Excessive taxation and unequal land distribution caused peasants and other poor people to demand better treatment.

Reconstruction allowed Americans an opportunity to show that universal liberty and justice are possible. The U.S. ideal of equality could have laid the foundation for equality across the world. However, U.S. ideals as a compassionate and fair neighbor wavered during Reconstruction. Legislation that might have ended inequalities could not counter the pull toward racial and even gender discrimination. Women were excluded from voting and many other rights enjoyed by men. Several constitutional amendments attempted to correct inequalities based on race and gender. The Thirteenth Amendment (1865) abolished slavery. The Fourteenth Amendment (1868) guaranteed citizenship to all persons born in the United States. The Fifteenth Amendment (1870) gave all citizens the right to vote regardless of race, creed, or gender.

During the 1900s legislation attempted to advance racial civil rights. The Supreme Court case *Brown v. Board of Education* (1954) noted the inequality of segregated schools. In 1955 the refusal of Rosa Parks (1913–2005) to stand on a bus sparked the civil rights movement of the 1960s. Dr. Martin Luther King Jr. (1929–1968) and the march on Washington in 1963 attempted to unite Americans along racial, economic, and religious lines. The Civil Rights Act of 1964 prohibited discrimination in public places.

However, in 1964 Americans faced a conflict that marred the impressive civil rights legislation. The Vietnam War (1959–1975) caused many Americans to question the U.S. presence overseas. The war began a military effort based on civil discord outside the United States. During World War I (1914–1918) the United States had remained largely uninvolved until 1917. During World War II (1939–1945), unable to remain uninvolved, Americans fought to maintain freedom in the United States and elsewhere. By the Vietnam War, Americans were weary of fighting to ensure freedom in other countries. Not officially declared a war, the Vietnam conflict caused Americans to question their interference in the affairs of other countries.

Future of U.S. and Global Civil Rights

The twenty-first century presents a new challenge for the United States and for civil rights. As globalization introduces new cultures

and methods, Americans continue to view themselves as compassionate and fair champions of freedom. President George W. Bush (b. 1946) used the term *compassionate conservatism* to explain the U.S. plan for civil rights. Since the 1960s civil rights movement, other groups have pushed for a greater voice in the United States. Any group claiming marginalization from mainstream United States uses the ambiguous term *civil rights movement.* The women's liberation movement used many strategies of the 1960s civil rights movement. However, the Equal Rights Amendment (1972–1982), guaranteeing women pay and status equal to those of men, was soundly defeated at the polls. Gay rights activists often equate their plight with that of African-Americans.

The new and diversified civil rights movement has not changed the global perspective of the United States. As Americans continue to view themselves as the world champions of freedom and equality, other countries remain skeptical. In 2003 the U.S. war against Iraq caused a bitter debate at home and abroad as the United States declared its right to apply a policy of containment against other countries. This policy included economic sanctions, no-fly zones, and cultural interference. U.S. cultural interference led to military-backed regime changes. The United States justified this action as preventative: Containing enemies prevents those enemies from destroying the United States and helps the nation to build on democratic principles. However, globally people viewed U.S. interventions as self-serving and destructive.

Interference in the affairs of other countries and the failure to provide equality for all people in the United States have done much to discredit the U.S. claim to fairness. The vision of a land where everyone has the right to a good life and liberty is clouded by racial, gender, and economic disparity. The promise of inalienable rights is contradicted by the lack of civil rights for all people in the United States. Thus, other countries doubt the sincerity of the U.S. quest for freedom and equality. This doubt casts a shadow over future global efforts by the United States for civil rights.

Janice E. Fowler

See also Human Rights; Slavery and Abolitionism; U.S. Civil War and Reconstruction

Further Reading

Bender, T. (2006). *A nation among nations: America's place in world history.* New York: Hilland and Wang.

Golinger, E. (2006). *The Chavez code: Cracking US intervention in Venezuela.* Northampton, MA: Olive Branch Press.

Snow, N. (2007). *The arrogance of American power: What U.S. leaders are doing wrong and why it's our duty to dissent.* Lanham, MD: Rowman & Littlefield.

U.S. Civil War and Reconstruction

Faced with concerns about the westward expansion of the U.S., the French and English considered political and economic issues, as well as the morality of slavery, before aligning themselves with the North in the U.S. Civil War.

The U.S. Civil War, one of the defining moments in U.S. history, was a largely internal conflict that played a major role in shaping international perspectives of the United States. History has framed the Civil War as a war over two issues: union and slavery.

These two issues were critical for both President Abraham Lincoln of the Union and President Jefferson Davis of the Confederacy in garnering international support. Politics, economics, and a degree of morality weighed on the European powers that were being lobbied for support. In the end, though, Lincoln and Davis were forced to consider domestic politics. These considerations might have extended the war because foreign powers were unwilling to back the Union as long as it did not state that it was fighting the war to end slavery and were unwilling to back the Confederacy as long as it opposed abolition.

Two Global Powers

France and England—the two major global powers during the 1860s—were monarchies with established aristocracies. Their class system made it easy for the French and English to identify with the South and to forgo support of the North. Additionally, France and England saw an advantage to a weakened or divided United States, especially because the prewar United States had started to expand westward.

However, neither England nor France was willing to support the Confederate states as long as they fought to preserve slavery. Slavery had been abolished in most of Europe. Similarly, neither country would support the Union as long as its stated reason for fighting was to preserve the United States as a country and not to abolish slavery.

Lincoln's Emancipation Proclamation, published 23 September 1862, countered this reticence and cemented international support for the Union's cause. However, the proclamation's application was more symbolic than practical because it freed only slaves in the states that had rebelled and that didn't recognize the Union as their government. The proclamation did not abolish slavery in

states, including Maryland, that supported the Union and had refused to secede but also had not abolished slavery.

When the Emancipation Proclamation was published, the tide of international isolationism started to ebb. Although he had drafted the document months earlier, Lincoln waited for more decisive Union victories in the war before making the document public so it would not appear to be a tactical maneuver. Between the time Lincoln wrote the proclamation and the time it was published, he publicly stated that Union troops were fighting to preserve the Union and not to abolish slavery—a reflection of the precarious situation of the Union.

Economics

The industries of England and France were still reliant on the United States for the crops of the South, particularly cotton, and for the industry of the North. Thus, France and England were not in a position to align themselves with either side of the war, although both Union and Confederate actions nearly forced the hand of both England and France.

On 19 April 1861, Lincoln ordered a blockade of all Southern ports, cutting off any imports they were receiving and cutting off the ability of the South to raise revenue through cotton and other agricultural exports. This blockade put the Civil War in a new context because a blockade was considered by many in Europe to be a de facto recognition of the Confederate states as a sovereign country and not merely a group of rebellious states. The distinction made was that a country blockades another country's ports, whereas a country merely closes its own ports.

Economically the blockade started off slowly. Without enough ships at the outset of the war to effectively close Southern ports, the blockade was more a sieve than the "anaconda" that Union general Winfield Scott had envisioned. However, by the end of the war the industry of the North had supplied the Union navy with enough ships to tighten the blockade and to cause great financial hardship to the Confederacy.

The Confederacy tried to use the blockade to its own advantage

by employing it as a leverage point with those European countries that relied on cotton for their textile industries. Toward that end the Confederacy made no concerted effort to run the blockade and to maintain exports to Europe. The Confederacy reasoned that by withholding its cotton from Europe, with the excuse of the blockade, the economic hardship would cause one or more European powers to intervene militarily to open the Southern ports and thus to side with the Confederacy.

Economically the blockade and its restrictions on the cotton trade came close to dragging international powers, including France, Britain, and Russia, into the war. However, this complication was avoided "by the exploitation of new sources of cotton, notably Egypt, and Lincoln seizing the moral high ground by the emancipation of the slaves which, especially with regards the British public, put the Southern cause beyond the pale" (Hunt 2007).

Additionally, as the war persisted Northern forces were able to wrap the blockade along the eastern and southern coasts and up the

Mississippi River. Union victories in Mississippi in July 1863 closed off the western portions of the Confederacy and eliminated supply routes. "The fall of Fort Fisher and the city of Wilmington, North Carolina, early in 1865 closed the last major port for blockade runners, and in quick succession Richmond was evacuated, the Army of Northern Virginia disintegrated, and General Lee surrendered. Thus, most economists give the Union blockade a prominent role in the outcome of the war" (Elekund et al. 2004).

Trent Affair

The war nearly reached the international theater in the autumn of 1861 when the Union ship USS *San Jacinto* shot at and boarded the British mail steamer RMS *Trent*. Two Confederate diplomats, James Mason and John Slidell, had taken a blockade runner from Charleston, South Carolina, to Havana, Cuba. The two men were

A closeup of the carving of Confederate leaders at Stone Mountain Park, near Atlanta, Georgia.
Source: istock/Gabriel Eckert.

LINCOLN'S SECOND INAUGURAL ADDRESS

The following is an extract from President Abraham Lincoln's second inaugural speech on 4 March 1865. He delivered this speech after a landslide election and just weeks before both the official end of the U.S. Civil War and his own death.

On the occasion corresponding to this four years ago all thoughts were anxiously directed to an impending civil war. All dreaded it, all sought to avert it. While the inaugural address was being delivered from this place, devoted altogether to saving the Union without war, insurgent agents were in the city seeking to destroy it without war—seeking to dissolve the Union and divide effects by negotiation. Both parties deprecated war, but one of them would make war rather than let the nation survive, and the other would accept war rather than let it perish, and the war came.

One-eighth of the whole population were colored slaves, not distributed generally over the Union, but localized in the southern part of it. These slaves constituted a peculiar and powerful interest. All knew that this interest was somehow the cause of the war. To strengthen, perpetuate, and extend this interest was the object for which the insurgents would rend the Union even by war, while the Government claimed no right to do more than to restrict the territorial enlargement of it. Neither party expected for the war the magnitude or the duration which it has already attained. Neither anticipated that the cause of the conflict might cease with or even before the conflict itself should cease. Each looked for an easier triumph, and a result less fundamental and astounding. Both read the same Bible and pray to the same God, and each invokes His aid against the other. It may seem strange that any men should dare to ask a just God's assistance in wringing their bread from the sweat of other men's faces, but let us judge not, that we be not judged. The prayers of both could not be answered. That of neither has been answered fully. The Almighty has His own purposes. "Woe unto the world because of offenses; for it must needs be that offenses come, but woe to that man by whom the offense cometh." If we shall suppose that American slavery is one of those offenses which, in the providence of God, must needs come, but which, having continued through His appointed time, He now wills to remove, and that He gives to both North and South this terrible war as the woe due to those by whom the offense came, shall we discern therein any departure from those divine attributes which the believers in a living God always ascribe to Him? Fondly do we hope, fervently do we pray, that this mighty scourge of war may speedily pass away. Yet, if God wills that it continue until all the wealth piled by the bondsman's two hundred and fifty years of unrequited toil shall be sunk, and until every drop of blood drawn with the lash shall be paid by another drawn with the sword, as was said three thousand years ago, so still it must be said "the judgments of the Lord are true and righteous altogether."

With malice toward none, with charity for all, with firmness in the right as God gives us to see the right, let us strive on to finish the work we are in, to bind up the nation's wounds, to care for him who shall have borne the battle and for his widow and his orphan, to do all which may achieve and cherish a just and lasting peace among ourselves and with all nations.

Source: The Avalon Project at Yale Law School. (1996). Retrieved June 6, 2007, from http://www.yale.edu/lawweb/avalon/presiden/inaug/lincoln2.htm

---

bound for France and England to lobby the governments. After the *Trent* left Cuba the crew of the *San Jacinto* boarded the ship and detained Mason and Slidell and their staffs. Captain Charles Wilkes of the *San Jacinto* interpreted international law to justify his detainment of Slidell and Mason.

The incident, labeled the "*Trent* Affair," sparked an immediate backlash from Britain, which readied fifty thousand troops in Britain, increased militias in Canada by the tens of thousands, put its navy on standby, and warned Washington not to interfere with British ships carrying legal passengers.

Further international conflict and a war with Britain—and with France, which had pledged its support to Britain—were averted when Lincoln issued an apology to Britain and released the two diplomats and their staffs.

Thus, what could have become an international incident that almost surely would have brought the Union army into a war on two fronts ended peacefully, although not without some political damage to Lincoln's administration. Had the incident ended differently, with the Union drawn into war with Britain, better equipped and better financed than the Confederacy, the outcome of the Civil War would have been decidedly different.

Reconstruction

The postwar effort to rebuild the Confederacy and to reunite the two sides (called alternately "restoration" by President Andrew Johnson and "reconstruction" by Congress) was as important to the global image of the United States as the war had been. Generally the era of Reconstruction is considered to have occurred from two years before the end of the war in 1863 through 1877. The rebuilding effort under Lincoln and the reintegration of the Confederacy's citizenry garnered particular praise in Europe, where the U.S. government's efforts were seen as generous and forgiving. When the Confederate forces, under General Robert E. Lee, surrendered to the Union forces, led by Ulysses S. Grant,

at Appomattox Courthouse, Virginia, on 9 April 1865, the terms were considered to be generous because the Union insisted on the surrender of only weapons and equipment, allowing Southern officers and soldiers to retain their sidearms and horses and to return to their homes.

Initially states that had seceded were required to reform, first under provisional governors and then under new state constitutions, and to pledge loyalty to the Union. Soldiers were allowed to live freely as long as they took loyalty oaths and said that they had fought under orders from their superiors. Lincoln described his position in his second inaugural address:

> With malice toward none; with charity for all; with firmness in the right, as God gives us to see the right, let us strive on to finish the work we are in; to bind up the nation's wounds; to care for him who shall have borne the battle, and for his widow, and his orphan—to do all which may achieve and cherish a just, and a lasting peace, among ourselves, and with all nations. (Avalon Project 1996)

Confederate government officials, including President Jefferson Davis, were not hanged for treason, as was allowable under law. Davis was indicted for treason, but the charges were dropped after he spent two years in jail. Lee, the general who had led the Army of Northern Virginia and ultimately had commanded the entire Confederate army, was allowed to return to his home.

The tide of open reconciliation subsided after Lincoln was assassinated on 14 April 1865. The assassination left the White House to Vice President Andrew Johnson. Johnson, and Lincoln before him, administered reconstruction under the auspices of "war powers." Among the initiatives was Lincoln's "ten percent plan," which allowed a state to rejoin the Union if 10 percent of the state's citizens who had voted in the 1860 presidential election took a loyalty oath.

With the war over, Congress reasserted its authority in dictating the terms of reconstruction. With Congress controlled by Union states, the terms of readmittance to the Union were decidedly harder. In 1866, with electoral victories by the Radical Republican Party, Congress and Johnson clashed more and more, eventually leading to his impeachment (he was narrowly acquitted). Congress used its power to veto Johnson's initiatives and to enforce its policies in the South. Congress sent the army to Southern states to enforce voting rights and took suffrage away from ten to fifteen thousand former Confederate soldiers and officers.

Reconstruction in the South was not met favorably by poor white residents, who saw Northern interests and Southern interests aligned with factions of the Republican Party as meddling and exploitative. This resentment led to the growth of Southern resistance movements, most notably the Ku Klux Klan, born out of

resistance to Reconstruction and "carpetbaggers" from the North trying to rebuild the South. The Klan, as it became known, was started by Confederate veterans but persisted in various forms for more than a century, with pockets of activity through the twentieth century.

Going Forward

The harder it became to be a former Confederate state as federal forces were sent in and Northern ideals were legislated upon the South, the longer it took for the South to heal from the war. Directly reacting to the hardline Radical Republicans in the North, the growth of the Democratic Party in the South, and the creation of "separate but equal" Jim Crow laws, the Ku Klux Klan, segregation, racial violence, and more than one hundred years of racial strife in the United States can be traced to Reconstruction. The Civil War, which abolished slavery, also set in motion a century of racial struggles that came to define the United States to the rest of the world—for better and worse.

Scott Eldridge II

See also Slavery and Abolitionism; U.S. Civil Rights

Further Reading

Avalon Project. (1996). Second inaugural address of Abraham Lincoln. Retrieved June 12, 2007, from http://www.yale.edu/lawweb/avalon/presiden/inaug/lincoln2.htm

Davis, L. & Engerman, S. L. (2006) *Naval blockades in peace and war: An economic history since 1750.* Cambridge, UK: Cambridge University Press.

Elekund, R. B., Jackson, J. D., & Thornton, M. (2004, Spring). The "unintended consequences" of Confederate trade legislation. *Eastern Economic Journal.*

Harrison, M. & Gilbert, S. Eds. (1996) *Abraham Lincoln: In his own words,* New York: Barnes & Noble.

Hunt, P. (2007). Naval warfare in the American Civil War. Retrieved June 12, 2007, from http://www.hksw.org/american%20civil%20war_naval%20part%20II.htm

Jones, H. (1992) *Union in peril: The crisis over British intervention in the civil war,* Chapel Hill, NC: University of North Carolina Press.

Lincoln, A. (1863). Annual message to Congress. Retrieved June 12, 2007, from http://teachingamericanhistory.org/library/index.asp?document=426

Report of the Joint Committee on Reconstruction. (n.d.). Retrieved June 12, 2007, from http://odur.let.rug.nl/~usa/D/1851-1875/reconstruction/repojc.htm

U.S. Congress. (2007). Biographical directory of the U.S. Congress, Davis, Jefferson—Biographical information. Retrieved June 12, 2007, from http://bioguide.congress.gov/scripts/biodisplay.pl?index=D000113

United States Information Agency

Originally conceived in response to anti-American propaganda at the start of the Cold War, the USIA was the most extensive information organization ever mounted to influence attitudes and actions around the world.

The United States Information Agency (USIA) was founded on 1 August 1953 to distribute information beneficial to the United States overseas during the Cold War. As the propaganda arm of the U.S. government, the USIA did not have legal permission to operate within U.S. borders. Instead, at the height of its operations, it had the most extensive overseas presence of any U.S. government agency. Although the USIA aimed to promote the long-range interests of Americans, it was officially separate from the U.S. government. It did not officially speak for the U.S. government, accepted no special treatment or assistance from U.S. officials or government organizations, and strove for balanced and accurate news reporting. The USIA became the biggest information and cultural effort ever mounted by one society to influence the attitudes and actions of people beyond its borders.

In the years before World War II the United States was the only major global power that did not have a strategy for carrying out ideological operations beyond its borders. In the 1930s every major world power, especially Germany, capitalized on radio's ability to influence public opinion. The United States, uninterested in playing a role in world affairs, did not see the value in developing a system of international radio propaganda. However, the fall of France to Nazi Germany, prompted in part by Nazi Germany's use of propaganda to destroy the French will to fight, changed U.S. opinion. President Franklin D. Roosevelt realized that ideas could be as useful as tanks in a military effort, and he began to mobilize for propaganda warfare. In 1941 Roosevelt established the U.S. Foreign Information Service (FIS), and the first U.S. government-sponsored radio broadcast was delivered on 24 February 1942 from New York City to Europe. The Japanese attack on Pearl Harbor that prompted U.S. entrance into the war led to widespread support for a propaganda agency. Propaganda operations subsequently became part of a massive mobilization of resources, with the United States establishing the Office of War Information (OWI) in 1942. Voice of America (VOA), authorized in December 1942, became the best-known part of the OWI. When the war ended, OWI's operations were cut back drastically. In August 1945 the office's functions were transferred to the De-

partment of State, and the office was redesignated as the "Interim International Information Service."

U.S. propaganda at first seemed to be unnecessary after World War II ended, but the start of the Cold War changed that feeling. The Soviet Union engaged in international broadcasting hostile to the United States. In response the U.S. Congress created a tool for democratic propaganda. On 1 August 1953 the USIA began operations. Linked by its organizational charter to the Department of State, the agency followed State Department policy guidelines both in Washington, DC, and at overseas embassies. However, the two agencies had different bureaucratic cultures. USIA's staff consisted largely of media professionals trained to produce information for public use. They described the details of U.S. foreign policy on an around-the-clock basis to foreigners, often to the discomfort of State Department officials accustomed to carefully worded and committee-approved messages.

Getting the Word Out

Most of the more than one hundred nations created out of former European colonies in the years after World War II had little or no previous contact with Americans or their cultural products before the war. The USIA addressed this deficiency. Its information and cultural posts—the U.S. Information Service (USIS)—eventually operated in almost three hundred cities. A USIS center was typically located in the center of town on a main street. Its most prominent feature was a library available to everyone. These libraries had open shelves where patrons could browse in the stacks and borrow books to take home, something without precedent in most cities where the USIS operated. The libraries proved so popular in some places that patrons had to be assigned a time slot in which to visit.

The United States used most of the conventional propaganda techniques of its allies and enemies. However, it also had unique resources that distinguished its ideological offensive: massive networks of mass media that no other society could match. VOA broadcast worldwide and was heard by 100 million people weekly

during the Cold War. In 1959 VOA inaugurated *Special English,* a slow-paced broadcast of simplified English for non-native speakers that was designed to facilitate comprehension. In 1994 VOA entered the television market with a Chinese-language program beamed by satellite. In 1996 VOA television studios were completed, and the agency simulcast some portions of its programming on both radio and television in twelve languages: Albanian, Arabic, Bosnian, English, Indonesian, Mandarin Chinese, Persian, Russian, Serbian, Spanish, and Ukrainian. It also provided programming to twelve hundred radio stations around the world. Other USIA activities included publishing magazines, books, pamphlets, leaflets, and news bulletins in more than one hundred languages and distributing them in tens of billions of copies as well as producing documentary films, newsreels, and television programs that presented U.S. culture around the world. It also administered educational fellowships, such as those of the Fulbright program, that sent scholars to and from the United States.

Foreign Fulbright participants have included former United Nations Secretary-General Boutros Boutros-Ghali, British politician Shirley Williams, Italian author Umberto Eco, and Bangladeshi women's activist Salma Shan. U.S. participants have included writers John Updike and Eudora Welty, poet Maya Angelou, and composer Aaron Copland.

Befitting an agency developed to address the Cold War, the USIA focused its activities at first on the Soviet Union. The confrontational tone that had marked much of VOA's programs in the early postwar years ended in 1955 with a thaw in U.S.-Soviet relations. This change of tone was a critical step in establishing VOA as a more credible source of news and information among its audiences. VOA's audience rose steadily over the next decades, particularly in the Soviet Union and eastern Europe, because of this new moderation. The number of broadcasts delivered by VOA rose dramatically as the agency responded to the information needs of people behind the Iron Curtain and in politically unstable countries.

Cold War Thaw

As another result of the thaw in U.S.-Soviet relations during the Eisenhower administration, cultural and information exchanges between the United States and the Soviet Union began in 1959. The USIA sponsored and organized these exchanges. Large exhibits showed aspects of U.S. life. Each exhibit featured a specific theme, ranging from architecture to farming. The exhibits traveled across the Soviet Union, attracting long lines of visitors at each stop. Smaller versions of the exhibits also toured most of the Communist-dominated countries of eastern Europe.

The Soviet Union in the late 1950s offered support to Communist and left-wing groups in newly independent countries, particularly in Africa and Asia. In response the USIA shifted its program focus to Third World concerns. The agency's operations in Europe and Japan were steadily scaled back in favor of programs in developing nations. In 1959 the USIA had twenty-four posts in thirteen African countries. By 1963 the USIA had fifty-five posts in thirty-three African countries, largely in response to movement of decolonization within the continent. Colonial governments had resisted USIS operations during the years leading up to independence, with Belgian authorities in the Congo once warning the USIA that the local population would not be capable of using a library for fifty years. In South Africa officials rejected plans for a library in the capital of Johannesburg after learning that it would be available to both black and white users. The library eventually opened, creating a small but symbolic breach in apartheid laws.

The USIA had mixed success in Asia. After the French withdrawal from France's Southeast Asian colonies in the late 1950s, the United States became more involved with the South Vietnamese government's attempt to turn back Communist-led guerrilla advances. The USIS produced and distributed propaganda materials for the South Vietnamese government. Increasingly the USIA was drawn deeper into the Vietnam quagmire as U.S. policy and operations shifted away from a reliance on ideological and economic programs to plans for a military solution. The USIA had better luck in other Asian nations. It was particularly active in Thailand, the Philippines, and Laos in combating insurgencies in these countries.

Some events presented a challenge to the USIA's mission to present a fair and balanced view of the United States. The agency found it particularly difficult to explain the domestic fight over civil rights. The State Department had been generally unresponsive to warnings about the overseas impact of civil rights events. In 1957 a USIA public opinion survey revealed the negative impact on the overseas images of the United States caused by the strife over the attempt to integrate Little Rock High School in Arkansas. The USIA made continual reports to the White House about overseas reactions to the civil rights movement. It also produced a documentary film, *Nine from Little Rock,* which won an Oscar. Gradual race relations improvements, including the Civil Rights Act of 1964, gave the USIA a positive story to tell abroad.

The USIA faced its biggest challenge with the 1972 Watergate scandal. Originally dismissed by the Nixon administration as a minor burglary, the thwarted attempt by Republican Party operatives to steal documents from the Democratic National Committee offices in the Watergate building soon took on the trappings of a serious political event. At first there was little interest abroad in Watergate. This lack of interest changed when it became clear that

the head of the world's oldest constitutional democracy could be driven from office as the result of a botched attempt to play dirty politics. Despite efforts by the White House to manipulate the story, the USIA accurately reported developments in the scandal. A watch group of agency officials was formed to check all VOA scripts and agency newsfile stories for balance and accuracy. Overall, the agency received acclaim for reporting a story that dramatized the U.S. democratic process.

The end of the Cold War made the USIA seem irrelevant to many people within the U.S. government. In 1999 the USIA closed. Its information and cultural operations were moved as a single unit to a new State Department bureau, headed by an undersecretary for public diplomacy.

Caryn E. Neumann

See also Government Controlled Media, U.S.

Further Reading

Dizard, W. P. Jr. (2004). *Inventing public diplomacy: The story of the U.S. Information Agency.* Boulder, CO: Lynne Rienner.

Fitzgerald, M. I. (1987). *The Voice of America.* New York: Dodd, Mead.

Hansen, A. C. (1989). *USIA: Public diplomacy in the computer age.* New York: Praeger.

Henderson, J. W. (1969). *The United States Information Agency.* New York: Praeger.

Piresein, R. W. (1979). *The Voice of America: A history of the international broadcasting activities of the United States government 1940–1962.* New York: Arno Press.

Snow, N. (1998). *Propaganda, Inc.: Selling America's culture to the world.* New York: Seven Stories Press.

Use of Force Internationally, Views on U.S.

The U.S. has lost much of its international prestige in the twenty-first century, mainly caused by the 2003 invasion of Iraq, the actions of the Bush administration, and the U.S. status as the last remaining military superpower.

Even the most powerful nation cannot base their foreign policy solely on the old maxim *oderint dum metuant*—let them hate us, as long as they fear us. Public support in other countries is indispensable for a nation's foreign policy to succeed. "To win the hearts and minds of other people" has therefore become a recognized goal of foreign policy and public diplomacy around the world. The United States, as a major world superpower, needs international cooperation to pursue its interests effectively and to address common issues. Studies of public opinion have shown, however, that the United States has suffered in recent years a loss of much of its international support and trust it enjoyed among other nations, allies in particular.

Sympathy for and trust of the United States were high at the time of the terrorist attacks of September 11, 2001, in the immediate aftermath, even still as the U.S. went to war against the Taliban regime in Afghanistan soon after. But since then U.S. foreign policy—particularly its decisions leading up to and throughout the Iraq War—have met with increasing criticism, both in Europe among its allies and in the world at large. Since that time, the United States has taken on an approach of unilateralism based on a fundamental distinction between "good and evil" on which to base its actions. In contrast, many countries around the world and particularly in Europe, support a multilateral approach to international affairs taking into account the complexity of global relations. The majority of Europeans agree that the United Nations, a multilateralist institution, has suffered as a result of the Iraq crisis. The U.S. use of military force in Iraq has raised the question in the minds of many of whether the United States is still qualified to be a global leader.

Iraq War (2003)

At the level of mass public opinion the war created deep divisions both within the United States and within the countries that were part of the U.S.-led international coalition. Outside of this coalition opposition to the war was the norm. In countries, such as Spain and Poland, who provided troops to fight with the Ameri-

cans, there were no clear majorities in support of the decision for war, with the exception of the United Kingdom and Australia. Public support for the war in the U.K. and Australia came only after the invasion of Iraq; however, this support soon started to wane, just as it did in the United States between 2003 and 2007. During this time the number of Americans still in favor of the war dropped by half.

The war has had deep and lasting consequences. According to one poll held in forty-four countries after the end of the initial fighting, majorities in only seven of these countries thought that the war against Iraq had been justified, even though it specifically stipulated "now that Saddam Hussein is removed from power." This feeling was echoed in many international polls that were held around the same time. Several reasons probably contribute to this sentiment. One was a perceived lack of overall progress in Iraq. Then there was the discovery about the absence of weapons of mass destruction (WMDs), the presence of which was the initial justification for the invasion. And the questionable treatment and detention of Iraqi prisoners and suspected terrorists around the world continued to devastate U.S. international standing. In the context of the fight against terrorism, many around the world have taken the view that the war in Iraq has hurt, not helped this fight. And in general a variety of trend poll data suggest an overall decline in desire for U.S. world leadership.

By 2004 support for the United States had more or less evaporated in Europe, above all in western Europe and as of 2007 there are no signs of recovery. Also, in 2004 a plurality of 47 percent (in twenty-two countries worldwide) said they saw U.S. influence in the world as "mainly negative," while only 38 percent saw it as "mainly positive." In 2005, some recovery seemed on its way, but by the end of 2006 American prestige had further deteriorated (to 50 percent "mainly negative" versus 31 percent "mainly positive"). At that time, among the twenty-four countries included in the poll that year U.S. influence was seen as "mainly positive" only by majorities in Kenya, Nigeria, and the Philippines.

A severe decline of support for the United States occurred even in those countries that had supported President Bush's policy in the Iraq crisis or had been traditional allies. The most remarkable

change was in Germany, where 81 percent of citizens (as opposed to 55 percent in 2002) stated in 2003 that Europe was more important to their vital interests than the United States. Only 9 percent (as compared with 20 percent a year earlier) gave their preference to the United States in this respect. In 2006 only 13 percent of all Germans approved of Bush's international policies and 39 percent saw U.S. world leadership as desirable.

Structural or Personal Factors?

What has caused the decline of U.S. standing in international opinion? Some argue that it is the result of personal factors, that is, President George W. Bush, his personality, and the policies pursued by his administration. The coincidence in time as well as the results of some opinion polls suggest that the decline in U.S. standing in the world had less to do with a growing antipathy to the United States per se and more to do with the current administration. One opinion poll (2004) showed that among those people who said that their views of the United States had become less positive, many people in many countries replied specifically that this feeling was not because of the United States as such, but rather because of President Bush.

The degree to which President Bush shaped views of the United States was evident in another international poll taken in July and August of 2004 in thirty-five countries. The poll showed that in thirty countries a majority or plurality (by an average 2–1 majority margin) preferred to see Senator John Kerry win the U.S. presidential election of 2004. Kerry was more popular in every region of the world and was especially popular among traditional U.S. allies. The poll also showed that in thirty countries, when people were asked how the foreign policy of President Bush had affected their feelings toward the United States, a majority or plurality (on average 53 percent) said that it made them feel "worse," whereas only in three countries more people said that it had made them feel "better." In twelve out of twenty-two countries pluralities or majorities said at the end of 2004 that the reelection of Bush had made them feel worse about "the Americans." For others Bush was less prominent in determining their opinions on the U.S.

Some people argue, however, that the decrease in the United States' approval ratings and the increase in criticism of its military role are not caused by the President Bush, but are the result of more general, structural factors like the fact that the United States is the only remaining military superpower, which creates fear and perhaps even hatred, as well as awe and envy, regardless of the party or leader in power. Other structural factors that could play a role include traditional U.S. foreign policies, economic power, and the global impact of the U.S. economic system.

Still others believe it is a combination of personal and structural factors. This is because views of the United States abroad were often better during Democratic presidencies (such as Kennedy, Carter, or Clinton) than during Republican presidencies (such as Nixon, Reagan, or George W. Bush). Moreover, dissension on certain issues—for instance, on the use of force—often occurs not between the U.S. and Europe, but within the United States itself, as Democrats and Europeans often share similar views of the world. The origin of the critical views of the United States would therefore be ideological rather than geopolitical.

Cycles of International Opinion

People have often argued that a deep and troublesome gap across the Atlantic has been developing since the end of the Cold War. In the past, whatever differences of view existed—and they were frequent and often intense—Europeans and Americans remained always convinced that they shared many values and interests, particularly an aversion to Soviet Communism. Since the end of the Cold War, however, Europeans and Americans no longer appear to share the same view of the world, particularly as far as fundamental ideas about the nature of international relations, the meaning of power, and the use of military force are concerned.

Some observers argue, however, that the decline in U.S. standing in the world, particularly in Europe, is only the most recent manifestation of earlier waves of criticism and part of a recurrent pattern of the ebb and flow in transatlantic relations, implying that the end of the Cold War was not a watershed and that U.S. standing will improve again after some time, as it has in the past.

Relations with Europe and views of the United States in mass public opinion were generally good in the 1950s and 1960s during the height of the Cold War. They turned sour during the Vietnam War, which not only divided U.S. society, but also was generally deeply unpopular in countries outside the United States. Mass public opinion was also negative during the late 1970s and 1980s, particularly during the Reagan administration, which was characterized by deep controversies over nuclear weapons and the policies toward the Soviet Union. However, even then relations recovered again, and it can be argued that the controversies were less serious than sometimes alleged. Analyses of the situation during the 1980s stressed an important continuity of past relations: stable and general support for the Atlantic alliance and the Western principles of defense.

The ebb and flow in the feelings toward the United States are shown in Figure 1, which displays the evolution of attitudes toward the United States in terms of "favorable" versus "unfavorable" for four European countries during a long period of time. The troughs

Figure 1. Favorability Ratings of the United States in percent of "Favorable Opinion"

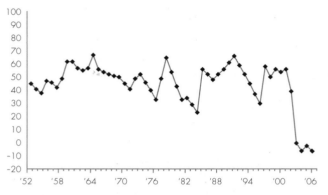

Note: Combined net scores ("favorable" minus "unfavorable") are given for France, Germany, Italy, and United Kingdom. Averages have been calculated for years in which numerous poll results were available. Data for missing years have been interpolated. Polls were not always held in all countries, and the average figure presented in the graph may not always reflect important differences among the four countries.

Source: Collected by P. Isernia, University of Siena, using data from numerous sources including Eurobarometer, Pew Global Attitudes Project, and U.S. Information Agency.

in the graph coincide with periods of (hot and cold) war that divided people of the United States and Europe: Vietnam, the Cold War (a term which originated as a result of the confrontational stance taken by the Reagan administration), Bosnia, and Iraq. The figure also suggests that even though the United States' favorability ratings are at their lowest point in fifty years as of 2006, ratings are likely to go up again in the future.

A New and Different Situation?

Statistical evidence, like that shown in Figure 1, leads some observers to conclude that in spite of historical precedents the present U.S. standing in international opinion is different from earlier ones because the recognition of common values and interests between Europe and the United States, which has constituted "a reservoir of goodwill" in the past, now may not be sufficient to overcome fundamental disagreements that cover a range of international issues, particularly the international use of force.

Still, others argue that the "reservoir of goodwill" cannot be dismissed so easily because critical opinions of U.S. foreign and military policies continue to coexist with strong feelings of friendship, a recognition of shared values, and considerable sympathies with many other aspects of U.S. society. Thus, despite reports of

rising anti-U.S. sentiment in Europe, annual polls in *Transatlantic Trends* of the German Marshall Fund of the United States (2002–2006) indicated that Europeans continued to like Americans as much as—if not even more than—they like each other when asked to rate their feelings in general toward various countries on a "thermometer" scale from 0 to 100. Public opinion in the six European countries and in the United States shows remarkable similarity and warmth. Americans, on their side, largely reciprocate these warm feelings for the European countries.

Anti-U.S. Sentiment

This diversity also makes it hard to accept the concept of "anti-Americanism" as a deep-seated, prejudice-like set of attitudes, which is sometimes presented as an explanation of the present wave of negative feelings. It is used often to describe a set of attitudes characterized by a general and often emotional, visceral, and wholesale rejection of anything having to do with the United States. This concept continues to enjoy popularity as an analytical term in spite of its inherent ambiguity, compounded by frequent use as a polemical tool. Anti-Americanism can be found on the left, where opposition focuses on the alleged destructive nature of U.S. capitalism and the imperialist nature of its traditional foreign policies, as well as on the right, where it centers on the alleged lack of culture and the negative sides of U.S. mass culture. Proponents argue that the phenomenon has longstanding historical roots and is related to traditional global perceptions of the United States as either a bad and corrupt society or a state bent on conquest of the world. As such the phenomenon can be traced back to the eighteenth century. In considering the roots of anti-Americanist sentiment, a dislike of U.S. policies has often been set off against a disdain for U.S. values. Some would consider President George W. Bush to be the realization of a two-century-long nightmare of anti-Americanism because he fits both elements of the longstanding anti-American stereotype—a simpleminded cowboy, religious, conservative, and unintellectual who also has set forth many controversial U.S. policies.

However, problems exist with this kind of explanation too. What is sometimes passionately rejected or criticized about the United States is sometimes a result of distorted or selective images and stereotypes. For example, many developed countries over the last century have participated in a process of modernization, but since the United States is commonly considered a major symbol of modernity, it is also gets singled out in criticisms of modernity. Whatever people do not like about the way the world is heading—urbanization, secularism, mass culture, and so on—is then portrayed as a specifically U.S. characteristic.

The line is often hard to draw, moreover, between strong criticism of particular policies and the attribution of evil motives or even outright hatred. In foreign policy the question is whether actions are viewed as ill-conceived and mistakes or as crimes proving the evil nature of the United States as imperialistic and aggressive.

Although we generally account for the roots of "anti-American" feelings, they offer no explanation for the ebb and flow of these feelings. In particular the anti-Americanism-as-a-prejudice theory does not seem able to account for the past periods of rapid recovery of pro-American feelings. Moreover, it overlooks the specific conditions of the present period of post–Cold War adaptation, new international threats and continuous and legitimate differences of opinion on how to handle these threats.

Future Trends and Perspectives

There is little room for doubt that the worsening image of the United States has been enhanced by the personality and policies of the Bush administration (2001–present). However, focusing exclusively on this presidency tends to make one forget that this is not the first period of a "transatlantic gap," and that there is more to consider than the idiosyncrasies of an individual president of the United States. Therefore, a second perspective which stresses the ebb and flow of international relations, which are strongly related to controversies that come and go, may be a better lens for examining world opinion of the United States. Without this second perspective, it is hard to explain the periods of often sudden decline or increase in anti-U.S. attitudes. One may question, however, whether the development of the international relations will continue to follow the traditional pattern of peaks and troughs and particularly, whether the alleged "reservoir of goodwill and common values" among U.S. allies will be large enough to sustain relations through the uncertainties of these first decades of the twenty-first century, which have so far been characterized by greatly diverging perspectives in terms of international policies, particularly the international use of force.

Philip Everts

See also Foreign Policy after September 11, 2001, U.S.; Iraq Wars; Perspectives on the United States, Theory of

Further Reading

Asmus, R., Everts, P., & Isernia, P. (2004, February–March). Power, War and Public Opinion. Looking behind the Transatlantic Divide. *Policy Review*, 123, 73–88.

Asmus, R., Everts, P., & Isernia, P. (2004). Across the Atlantic and the political aisle: The double divide in U.S.-European relations. Retrieved June 18, 2007, from http://www.gmfus.org/publications/article.cfm?id=46

Crockatt, R. (2003). *America embattled: September 11, anti-Americanism, and the global order*. London: Routledge.

Deutsch, K. (1967). *Arms control and the Atlantic alliance: Europe faces coming policy decisions*. New York: John Wiley & Sons.

Deutsch, K., Burrell, S. A., & Kann, R. A. (1957). *Political community and the North Atlantic area: International organization in the light of historical experience*. Princeton, NJ: Princeton University Press.

Eichenberg, C. R. (1989). *Public opinion and national security in western Europe*. London: Macmillan.

Everts, P. (2002). *Democracy and military force*. London: Palgrave.

Everts, P., & Isernia, P. (Eds.). (2001). *Public opinion and the international use of force*. London: Routledge.

Flynn, H. G., & Rattinger, H. (Eds.). (1985). *The public and Atlantic defense*. Totowa, NJ: Rowman and Allanheld.

Hollander, P. (1992). *Anti-Americanism: Critiques at home and abroad, 1965–1990*. New York: Oxford University Press.

Isernia, P. (2005). Anti-Americanism and European public opinion. In S. Fabbrini & M. Gilbert (Eds.), *America contested: The limits and future of American unilateralism*. London: Routledge.

Kagan, R. (2003). *Paradise & power. America and Europe in the new world order*. London: Atlantic Books.

Mandelbaum, M., & Schneider, W. (1979). The new internationalisms: Public opinion and American foreign policy. In K. A. Oye, D. Rothchild, & R. J. Lieber (Eds.), *Eagle entangled: U.S. foreign policy in a complex world* (pp. 34–88). New York: Longman.

Nacos, B. L., Shapiro, R. Y., & Isernia, P. (Eds.). (2000). *Decisionmaking in a glass house: Mass media, public opinion, and American and European foreign policy in the 21st century*. Lanham, MD: Rowman & Littlefield.

Noelle-Neumann, E., & Köcher, R. (Eds.) (2002). *Allensbacher Jahrbuch der Demoskopie 1998–2002*. Munich, Germany: Saur.

Rubin, B., & Rubin, J. C. (2004). *Hating America: A history*. Oxford, UK: Oxford University Press.

Vietnam War

The Vietnam War stirred up anti-American sentiment around the world and displaced the WWII image of America as a liberator. What remained was an image of American military power wielded without mercy or reason.

The United States' military involvement in the Vietnam conflict, beginning in the mid-1950s and lasting until 1973 (South Vietnam did not surrender until 1975; the country was reunited in 1976), provoked a range of responses from its allies, from large-scale military support to overt diplomatic and political opposition.

U.S. Entrance into the Vietnam Conflict

The partition of Vietnam into a northern, Communist-controlled section and a southern, U.S.-supported zone was accomplished by an international agreement concluded at the Geneva Conference on Indochina in 1954. This Conference was convened after the disastrous French defeat by Communist-led troops at Dien Bien Phu in northern Vietnam, and was attended by Britain, the Soviet Union, France, the People's Republic of China, and the United States, as well as by representatives from the contending local governments and Communist movements from the French possessions in Indochina—Vietnam, Laos, and Cambodia. Although the petition agreement was designed as a temporary arrangement, with national reunification elections slated for 1956, the United States disassociated itself from the agreement.

Initially U.S. resistance was intended as a protest against the turnover of Vietnamese territory north of the seventeenth parallel to a Communist administration based at Hanoi and led by Ho Chi Minh (1890–1969). By 1956, however, the focus of U.S. policy had shifted. The government of South Vietnam, led by the U.S.-supported bureaucrat Ngo Dinh Diem (1901–1963), was deeply unpopular, and it was widely believed that any elections would produce a victory for Ho's Communists. In Washington, President Dwight D. Eisenhower's administration determined that elections must not be held and that U.S. aid was necessary to shore up Diem's regime in the South. Vietnam's Communists responded by reactivating their networks in the South, and beginning in 1959, Hanoi developed lines of communication to deliver military and eventually manpower assistance to the Communists of South Vietnam.

As John F. Kennedy assumed the U.S. presidency in 1961, pressures to escalate U.S. military involvement were growing. In South Vietnam itself, Diem was employing increasingly brutal methods to preserve the country's internal security. By the time Kennedy's successor, Lyndon B. Johnson, secured Congressional approval for the direct use of U.S. military power against the Communists in August 1964, the United States was pushing its allies to support its stand against Communist insurgents in South Vietnam and their sponsors in the North.

French Reactions to the U.S. Involvement

Franco-American relations were deeply damaged in 1954 when Eisenhower refused to reinforce the besieged French forces at Dien Bien Phu. Indeed, some diplomats placed the blame for France's complete collapse in Indochina on Washington, believing that if the United States had credibly threatened to intervene in Vietnam, as they had in Korea in 1950, French political authority could have been preserved. Paris also objected to the U.S. selection of Ngo Dinh Diem to head the Saigon government, in part because Diem had opposed French rule in the 1930s. French officials began agitating to reunify Vietnam in the late 1950s by opening contacts with Hanoi. Washington continued to reject the notion of reunification. In August 1963 President Charles de Gaulle of France offered to help Kennedy by negotiating an end to the Communist insurgency in the South. When Kennedy rejected the offer, Franco-American relations—already suffering from disagreements over nuclear weapons and European security issues—deteriorated even further.

The French public, weary of its own wars in Vietnam and Algeria, overwhelmingly backed de Gaulle. In a 1966 speech delivered in Phnom Penh, Cambodia, de Gaulle challenged the United States to recognize the futility of fighting for South Vietnam and to withdraw from Indochina altogether. In 1967 de Gaulle again spoke out, charging that the United States was responsible for the war in Vietnam. When the U.S. vice president, Hubert H. Humphrey, visited Paris that year, he was met by Vietnam War

protestors at every stop. Street demonstrations in Paris grew, and in May 1968 clashes between protesters and police disrupted the city for weeks.

French opinion began to change when Richard M. Nixon assumed the U.S. presidency in 1969. France accepted his promises to extract U.S. forces from Vietnam. The new French president, Georges Pompidou, was largely free of anti-American resentment, and he improved communications between Paris and Washington. France agreed to host U.S. negotiations with the Vietnamese Communists, which produced the 1973 Paris Accords on U.S. military withdrawal from Vietnam.

Other European Reactions

President Johnson's decisions in 1964–1965 to escalate U.S. military involvement in Vietnam were generally viewed with grave concern in the rest of Western Europe. West Germany, for example, relied upon the continued presence of U.S. troops to dissuade the Soviet Union from invading the West across its borders. As U.S.

troop deployments to Vietnam rose quickly during the late 1960s, German diplomats feared that the United States' post–World War II commitment to European security was unraveling. Criticism of U.S. policy in Scandinavia became commonplace. Stockholm (Sweden), Copenhagen (Denmark), and Oslo (Norway) were the sites of major anti-American demonstrations, and all three cities hosted meetings of the International Commission of Enquiry into U.S. Crimes in Indochina, a private initiative organized to highlight the destruction in Southeast Asia.

The British reaction was more complex. Britain supported the partition of Vietnam, and when the United States decided in 1954 to create a collective security organization in Southeast Asia, Britain signed on. At this stage, however, Britain's regional interests focused upon its own colonial possessions, including Malaya (now part of present-day Malaysia), which became independent in 1957 after a Communist-led insurgency was quelled by Commonwealth forces. As security conditions in South Vietnam deteriorated in 1960–1961, Britain supported U.S. policy by sending military advisers, but it did not follow the U.S. lead in providing massive military aid. When U.S. ground forces entered South Vietnam

EXCERPT FROM THE PARIS ACCORDS, JANUARY 27, 1973

Article 11

Immediately after the cease-fire, the two South Vietnamese parties will: achieve national reconciliation and concord, end hatred and enmity, prohibit all acts of reprisal and discrimination against individuals or organizations that have collaborated with one side or the other; -ensure the democratic liberties of the people: personal freedom, freedom of speech, freedom of the press, freedom of meeting, freedom of organization, freedom of political activities, freedom of belief, freedom of movement, freedom of residence, freedom of work, right to property ownership, and right to free enterprise. . . .

Chapter V. The Reunification of Viet-Nam and The Relationship Between North and South Viet-Nam

Article 15

The reunification of Viet-Nam shall be carried out step by step through peaceful means on the basis of discussions and agreements between North and South Viet-Nam, without coercion or annexation by either party, and without foreign interference. The time for reunification will be agreed upon by North and South Viet-Nam. Pending reunification:

(a) The military demarcation line between the two zones at the 17th parallel is only provisional and not a political or territorial boundary, as provided for in paragraph 6 of the Final Declaration of the 1954 Geneva Conference.

(b) North and South Viet-Nam shall respect the Demilitarized Zone on either side of the Provisional Military Demarcation Line.

(c) North and South Viet-Nam shall promptly start negotiations with a view to reestablishing normal relations in various fields. Among the questions to be negotiated are the modalities of civilian movement across the Provisional Military Demarcation Line.

(d) North and South Viet-Nam shall not join any military alliance or military bloc and shall not allow foreign powers to maintain military bases, troops, military advisers, and military personnel on their respective territories, as stipulated in the 1954 Geneva Agreements on Viet-Nam. . . .

Article 21

The United States anticipates that this Agreement will usher in an era of reconciliation with the Democratic Republic of Viet-Nam as with all the peoples of Indochina. In pursuance of its traditional policy, the United States will contribute to healing the wounds of war and to postwar reconstruction of the Democratic Republic of Viet-Nam and throughout Indochina.

Source: Documents relating to American foreign policy: Vietnam. (2007). Retrieved June 7, 2007, from http://www.mtholyoke.edu/acad/intrel/vietnam.htm

The Ho Chi Minh Museum in Vietnam.
Source: istock/Kris Vandereycken.

in 1965, British forces were tied down protecting Borneo from Indonesia. Furthermore, Britain's Labour government, elected in 1964, prioritized domestic issues and generally disapproved of U.S. policy in Vietnam.

British youth, workers, and students harshly criticized the war. One left-wing group, the Vietnam Solidarity Campaign (VSC), arranged street demonstrations beginning in 1966. By 1968 VSC-run marches in London were attracting 100,000 participants. Other smaller groups held public protests at the U.S. embassy in London.

The Commonwealth Countries

Several Commonwealth countries became engaged in the Vietnam conflict while still maintaining a distance from U.S. policies. Both India and Canada served (with Poland) on the tripartite International Control Commission (ICC) created in 1954 to monitor the cease-fire arrangements in Indochina. India was generally neutral toward U.S. policies until the late 1950s, when it began to back South Vietnamese and U.S. claims that the Communists were violating the cease-fire. India and the United States cooperated to contain Chinese influence in the Himalayas, and in the early 1960s the United States increased its aid programs to India. By that time, with the Vietnam conflict intensifying, the ICC slipped into obscurity. India's extension of diplomatic recognition to Hanoi in 1972 signaled the end of ICC activity.

During the late 1950s, Canadian officials on the ICC generally supported the U.S. view that the Communists regularly violated the 1954 cease-fire. Hoping to preserve close U.S.-Canadian relations, officials in Ottawa gave public support to U.S. goals in Vietnam but privately urged Washington to exercise caution in committing military forces. However in 1965 Prime Minister Lester Pearson, speaking in Philadelphia, openly advised President Johnson to downgrade the U.S. bombing of North Vietnam. The Canadian public was generally suspicious of the U.S. military involvement and was more sharply critical of U.S. economic policies, which damaged Canada's export businesses. In 1972 the Canadian government was dismayed by Nixon's renewed bombing of North Vietnam. It was relieved when a peace agreement was finalized in 1973.

Both Australia and New Zealand, as treaty partners of the United States, were inclined to support U.S. policies in Vietnam in the late 1950s. As the United States began committing military advisers in the early 1960s, Australia too provided a small cohort of advisers, but New Zealand was more reluctant, eventually agreeing only to send small medical teams. Under heavy pressure from the United States, and hoping to preserve its broader relationship with Washington, New Zealand agreed in mid-1964 to send a team of military engineers, and in 1965 it deployed an artillery battery. Following repeated demands from the United States for a greater show of force, Wellington finally sent two infantry companies in 1967, but other personnel rotated home, allowing New Zealand to maintain a maximum presence in South Vietnam of only five hundred troops in 1969. A limited antiwar movement

developed in Auckland and Wellington in the late 1960s, but it quickly merged with New Zealand's new antinuclear and environmental movements.

The Australian government responded forcefully to U.S. appeals for military assistance in Vietnam, providing combat troops as early as June 1965. As U.S. troop deployments grew, so did those of Australia, albeit on a much smaller scale. The Australian government faced bitter domestic criticism from 1968 on, including street protests in many cities, some of which inspired comparisons to Australia's conscription resistance movement in World War I. Nonetheless the government maintained a military presence in South Vietnam until mid-1972, sending fifty thousand Australians to South Vietnam over a ten-year period. Australian forces also participated in the evacuation of civilian refugees from the Saigon area in March 1975.

The United States' Asian Allies

Japan, like France, had a history in Southeast Asia that complicated its reactions to U.S. involvement in Vietnam. After Japan's defeat in World War II, it paid reparations to France's colonies and their successor states, which Japan had occupied during the war. Those payments continued until 1960. By that time, South Vietnam had emerged as an important buyer of Japan's exports. However, Tokyo also maintained economic ties with North Vietnam, which supplied coal for Japan's electricity industry. Under pressure from the United States, Japan stopped selling key products such as copper wire and steel sheets to Hanoi in 1965. Japan's new prime minister, Sato Eisaku, had determined that Japan's strategic interests, including hopes for the recovery of Okinawa from the United States, required that Japan support U.S. policy in Vietnam, despite the wide unpopularity of that stance. Sato authorized the use of U.S. military bases in Japan for support of operations in the Vietnam theater. Japan also hosted U.S. servicemen on leave and realized millions of dollars by filling U.S. supply contracts for construction materials, electronics, uniforms, and chemicals.

Nonetheless, the Japanese public opposed the war. As early as 1964, minority political parties and labor unions organized protests against U.S. policy, including marches against port calls by U.S. nuclear submarines, which were seen as part of the Vietnam-related American force build-up in East Asia. Petitions circulated calling for the denial of base privileges to the United States, and student protesters organized a grassroots anti–Vietnam War movement known as Beheiren. This movement reflected the pacifism of Japan's post–World War II generation, and it adopted the street demonstration tactics popular in Europe and the United States. Under the pressure of an October 1966

nationwide antiwar strike and growing protests at U.S. bases, the United States began shifting its B-52 bombing operations from Japan to bases in Thailand. Even so, street protests continued, and in Tokyo Beheiren adherents held regular demonstrations against U.S. policies in Vietnam every month between September 1965 and October 1973.

By contrast, South Korea supported U.S. policies, undertaking a major military commitment in South Vietnam. U.S. pressures for a South Korean contribution to the defense of South Vietnam met with positive responses in Seoul, where maintaining the United States' large deployment of troops along the demarcation line with North Korea was a strategic priority. In 1963 U.S.-trained South Korean military advisers began arriving in South Vietnam, and eventually some 320,000 Korean servicemen were deployed to South Vietnam. Although open protests were not tolerated in South Korea, government officials recognized by the late 1960s that dissent was building. At soon as peace agreements were signed in Paris in January 1973, South Korea announced the immediate withdrawal of Korean forces from South Vietnam.

The Rise of Global Anti-Americanism

The United States suffered a long-term loss of political prestige among some allies, particularly New Zealand and Japan, because of its military policies in Vietnam. However, the same policies were interpreted elsewhere, including in South Korea, as demonstrating U.S. resolve to support non-Communist governments under threat. Beyond intergovernmental relations, however, the conflict had a broad impact in stirring anti-Americanism in Europe, Asia, and beyond. The post–World War II image of U.S. soldiers as liberators was largely displaced by a less favorable image as the U.S. involvement in Vietnam produced civilian casualties, incidents of military misconduct, and scores of media images unfavorable to Americans. Together, these developments contributed to emerging popular notions of U.S. military power wielded without mercy or reason. Critics of U.S. foreign policies have subsequently referred to the Vietnam engagement as a prototype of superpower hubris, and the episode has proven to be a turning point in the development of international anti-American sentiments.

Laura M. Calkins

Further Reading

Busch, P. (2003). *All the way with JFK? Britain, the U.S. and the Vietnam War.* Oxford, UK: Oxford University Press.

Debre, M. (1971). France's global strategy. *Foreign Affairs, 49*(3), 395–406.

Devillers, P. (1962). French policy and the Second Vietnam War. *World Today 23*(6), 249–261.

Freedman, L. (2000). *Kennedy's wars: Berlin, Cuba, Laos and Vietnam.* Oxford, UK: Oxford University Press.

Havens, T. R. H. (1987). *Fire across the sea: The Vietnam War and Japan, 1965–1975.* Princeton, NJ: Princeton University Press.

Hsiao, G. T. (Ed.). (1973). *The role of external powers in the Indochina crisis.* Edwardsville: Southern Illinois University Press.

Kesavan, K. V. (1977). The Vietnam War as an issue in Japan's relations with the United States. *International Studies, 16*(4), 501–519.

Kolodiej, E. (1974). *French international policy under de Gaulle and Pompidou: The politics of grandeur.* Ithaca, NY: Cornell University Press.

Mayer, F. (1996). *Adenauer and Kennedy: A study in German–American relations, 1961–1963.* London: Macmillan.

McNeill, I. (1993). *To Long Tan: The Australian Army and the Vietnam War, 1950–1966.* St. Leonards, Australia: Allen & Unwin.

Ninkovic, F. (1994). *Modernity and power: A history of the domino theory in the twentieth century.* Chicago: University of Chicago Press.

Pemberton, G. (1987). *All the way: Australia's road to Vietnam.* Sydney, Australia: Allen & Unwin.

Pickering, J. (1998). *Britain's withdrawal from East of Suez: The politics of retrenchment.* Basingstoke, UK: Macmillan.

Ross, D. A. (1984). *In the interests of peace: Canada and Vietnam, 1954–1973.* Toronto, Canada: University of Toronto Press.

Sullivan, M. P. (1978). *France's Vietnam policy: A study in French–American relations.* Westport, CT: Greenwood Press.

Voice of America

See Government Controlled Media, U.S.

War

See Civil War and Reconstruction; Iraq Wars; Use of Force Internationally, Views of U.S., Vietnam War; World War I; World War II

Western Europe, Cultural Relations with

Western European attitudes toward the U.S. may be derisive on the part of the intellectual elite, but the average cultural consumer continues to embrace the "dream of America," adopting its music, cuisine, and Hollywood lifestyle.

There has been a saying in western Europe for many years: "The United States is the country we love to hate and the country we hate to love." Few topics are more debated in western Europe than its relationship with the United States. U.S. foreign affairs and pop culture, Hollywood movies, and Americans in general are among the most disputed topics in western European media, literature, and public debates at the beginning of the twenty-first century. The strong positive and negative reactions toward the United States can more easily be understood by considering the historical relationship across the Atlantic Ocean for the last five hundred years.

Six "social levels" explain the long-term ambivalence of western Europe toward the United States:

1. European views versus non-European views of the United States: Non-Europeans generally do not have the long colonial European tradition of regarding U.S. culture as something of less value than their own.
2. Views of the United States in western Europe versus in eastern Europe: Eastern Europe generally lacks the western European tradition of deep political skepticism toward U.S. foreign policy. This difference can be explained by the Cold War (1945–1989), when eastern Europeans were under the domination of the Soviet Union and not members of the North Atlantic Treaty Organization (NATO).
3. Views of U.S. culture by "the elite" versus "the people": Parts of the European intellectual elite (authors, academics, politicians) have had a long tradition of criticizing U.S. culture from jazz to Hollywood, thereby being at odds with the average European cultural consumer.
4. Cultural (what people are) versus political (what people do) views of the United States: The negative western European views of U.S. culture were created a long time before the United States even had an active foreign policy.
5. Premodern versus modern views of the United States among European elites: From the times of Columbus, Thomas More, and Shakespeare, leading Europeans looked upon the continent on the other side of the ocean with great enthusiasm—as

the new utopia. After Americans declared their independence from Great Britain in 1776, the enthusiasm for the country and the U.S. way of life was more a part of the average European immigrant, farmer, or consumer.
6. Conservative versus radical traditions in western European views of the United States: The western European critique of the United States since the eighteenth century has often been based on so-called conservative and elitist cultural arguments. The political European critique of U.S. foreign affairs is a newer tradition, originally stemming from the radical left-wing protests in the 1960s but in later years also including parts of the conservative cultural arguments.

In short, the historical western European animosity toward the United States can be explained as cultural conservative or elitist arguments among western European intellectuals after U.S. independence from England in 1776. The term *anti-Americanism* is often used to describe such negative feelings toward Americans, but that term will not be used here. The Norwegian author Jens Bjørneboe in 1952 called these deep-felt and long-lasting skeptical attitudes in western Europe the "fear of America," a term that might be more appropriate.

In order to understand this western European "fear of America," one must understand the European "dream of America." These two antitheses are intertwined in European history.

"Dream of America": From Plato to More and Shakespeare

The Greek philosopher Plato (c. 428–348 BCE) was the first European to create a myth of a great utopian country on the other side of the ocean. In the dialogue *Timaeus*, Plato refers to Solon, who in Egypt learns about the mythical island Atlantis. The utopian Atlantis "was larger than Libya and Asia put together, and was the way to other islands, and from these you might pass to the whole of the opposite continent which surrounded the true ocean" (Plato 360 BCE).

When Atlantis sank into the ocean, it disappeared to the west of the Mediterranean Sea where the sun sets, Plato explains. This legend of Atlantis was revived after Columbus (1451–1506) crossed the Atlantic eighteen hundred years later in 1492. In the 1500s the new continent was looked upon as a "resurrected" Atlantis among educated Europeans. Several maps were drawn with the name "Atlantis" on the continent we call "North America." The ocean between Europe and North America was named the "Atlantic" Ocean in honor of the Atlantis legend. The Dutch geographer Mercator (1512–1594) coined the term *atlas* to refer to a general collection of maps, a term that refers to the giant Atlas, who lived on the middle of Atlantis island.

Columbus wrote in his diary that he had arrived at the world's "terrestrial paradise" (Columbus 1989, 383). The word *utopia* in English can also be related to the European "dream of America." In 1505 the English author Thomas More (1478–1535) wrote his fictional *Utopia*, describing his utopian dream of the island Utopia on the coast of the "New World": "there is in no place of the world either a more excellent people or a more flourishing commonwealth" (quoted in Gunn 1989, 41).

During the sixteenth, seventeenth, and eighteenth centuries America was described as "the New Canaan," "the New World," "Arkadia," "Eden," "Atlantis," and "Utopia." William Shakespeare (1564–1616) was one of many who followed suit. In his drama *The Tempest* (1611), also called his "American Fable," Miranda—the main character's daughter—describes her newfound island like this: "O, wonder! How many goodly creatures are there here! How beauteous mankind is! O brave new world, That has such people in 't!"

The notion of a "brave new world" also became the title of English novelist Aldous Huxley's best-known novel in 1932. However, something had changed in the European intellectual attitude during those three hundred years. Whereas More and Shakespeare had looked upon "America" as a utopia, Huxley described the modern United States rather as a "dystopia" (an imaginary place where people lead dehumanized and often fearful lives).

Ambivalence after 1776: Elites versus the People

The main change of spirit among the intellectual elite came during the colonies' break from the mother country in 1776. The British author and aristocrat Samuel Johnson (1709–1784) set the tone with the pamphlet *Taxation No Tyranny* in 1775, where he wrote that he was willing to love all mankind except Americans. In the pamphlet he describes Americans as greedy, concerned only with money and business.

Throughout the nineteenth century leading writers and scholars in Europe commonly described the U.S. way of life as a contrast to the classic and more worthy European way of life, filled with romantic spirit, tradition, and history. More than two hundred travelogues about the United States were published in England between 1815 and 1860. One of the best known and most influential was *Domestic Manners of the Americans* (1832) by Fanny Trollope (1779–1863). She wrote of Americans: "I do not like their principles, I do not like their manners, I do not like their opinions" (Trollope 1997, 314).

The same attitude toward the United States was found throughout Europe. Nikolaus Lenau (1802–1850), called the "German Lord Byron," had a similar impact on Germany that Trollope had on England: "The American knows nothing, seeks nothing but money, he has no ideas; consequently, the state is not an intellectual and moral institution (fatherland), but merely a material convention" (quoted in Diner 1996, 34–35). Even writers who were genuinely interested in learning from the new society came home with the conception that Americans were not as free thinking as Europeans or at least were very different. The French aristocrat Alexis de Tocqueville (1805–1859) wrote in *Democracy in America* (published in 1835) that there is "no country in which there is so little independence of mind and real freedom of discussion as in America" (Tocqueville 2003, 297–298).

Not all western European intellectuals bought into the widespread fear of the United States. After a trip to the United States in 1881, the Norwegian Nobel Prize winner in literature, Bjørnstjerne Bjørnson (1832–1910), wrote a critique of European stereotyping of the United States under the title "An Endless Slandering of a Whole Nation." At the same time millions of poor Europeans voted with their feet and moved to the "land of opportunity" rather than remain in their native country.

Whereas the fear of the United States during the nineteenth century was about democracy and the will of the masses, the fear of the United States at the beginning of the twentieth century was more about modern life, popular culture, and materialism. The debate in Europe was not about what Americans ought to do in their own country but rather about what Germany, France, Great Britain, and other European countries should choose for themselves in the future. The fear of the United States became a fear of the future. The French author Georges Duhamel (1884–1966) compared the U.S. cinema with a brothel in *America the Menace* in 1930, a book that helps one understand the French view of the United States during the 1930s.

This trend only increased after World War II. Europe was devastated, whereas the United States was stronger than ever, both as a symbol and as an economic, cultural, political, and military superpower. The United States originally had been viewed as

"Europe's daughter"—as French President Charles de Gaulle put it—but after 1945 the daughter had to take care of the injured "parents." For many people in Europe that role reversal was not easy to accept. As the French political analyst Maurice Duverger wrote in the French newspaper *Le Monde* in 1964: "It must be said, it must be written. There is only one immediate danger for Europe, and that is American civilization" (quoted in Kuisel 1996, 191).

On the other hand, the average European consumer for the last sixty years more than ever has embraced U.S. culture and the U.S. way of life. Hollywood, Disney, Las Vegas, New York, California, Route 66, pop, rock, jazz, blues, country, and rap music: These parts of U.S. culture keep the "dream of America" alive among ordinary Europeans, not unlike More's utopian dream of five hundred years ago. For several authorities and leading intellectuals the success of U.S. culture is viewed as a threat to classic European culture. At the end of the twentieth century most western European countries imposed limits on U.S. and other foreign films for television and cinemas in order to preserve European cultural traditions.

New Political Criticism and the New Century

During the Vietnam War in the 1960s, a new political criticism of the United States was gaining ground in western Europe. This criticism was originally from the radical left wing. However, at the beginning of the twenty-first century, global polls showed that western Europeans are among the most critical in the world toward U.S. foreign affairs, and toward the United States as such. A poll by the Program on International Policy Attitudes (PIPA) of thirty-four thousand people in thirty-five countries in 2004 found that Africans and Asians—excluding people in Middle Eastern nations—in general were far more positive to the U.S. foreign policy or the U.S. as such than were Western Europeans (PIPA 2004).

A BBC World Service poll taken in late 2006 confirms earlier PIPA-findings. Even with worsening worldviews of the United States, more people than not in the billion-populated democratic India answered that they view U.S. influence as "mainly positive." And while 70 percent of people in Nigeria—Africa's most populous country—regard the United States positively, and only 20 percent negatively, the figures are opposite in Western European countries: Some 74 percent of Germans view U.S. influence in the world as "mainly negative," while 20 percent regard it as positive (BBC 2007).

These trends cannot be attributed just to world opinions of recent U.S. policies. The Pew Research Center's Global Attitude Survey of 2002, just after 9/11, found that seven out of ten Germans and French disliked "American ideas and traditions" (Pew Research Center 2002). In England, Italy, Germany, and France, as many people were negative as positive about U.S. ideas on democracy. Eastern Europeans, Africans, Asians, and Latin Americans answered far more positively than did western Europeans.

These polls indicate that there still is a special animosity towards the United States among western Europeans, and especially when it comes to the "cultural view" upon the country. This can be explained by the long-term European disregard for the lack of intellectual potential in the newfound land "over there." But at same time, Europeans continue to adopt American popular culture, cuisine, and traditions into their lives as never before. The dual European fears and dreams about America continue—some five hundred years after Thomas More's utopian writings.

Stian Bromark and Dag Herbjørnsrud

See also NATO, U.S. role in; Perspectives on the United States, Visitors'; Relations with the European Union, U.S.; Special Relationship (U.S.-U.K.); World War I; World War II

Further Reading

BBC World Service Poll. (2007). Israel and Iran share most negative ratings in global poll. Retrieved April 15, 2007, from http://www.worldpublicopinion.org/pipa/articles/home_page/325.php?nid=&id=&pnt=325&lb=hmpg1#US

Columbus, C. (1989). *The diario of Christopher Columbus's first voyage to America, 1492–1493.* Norman: University of Oklahoma Press.

Diner, D. (1996). *America in the eyes of the Germans: An essay on Antiamericanism.* Princeton, NJ: Markus Wiener Publishers.

Duhamel, G. (1974). *America the menace: Scenes from the life of the future.* New York: Arno Press.

Gunn, G. (1994). *Early American writings.* New York: Penguin Books.

Kuisel, R. (1996). *Seducing the French: The dilemma of Americanization.* Berkeley and Los Angeles: University of California Press.

Pew Research Center. (2002, December 4). What the world thinks in 2002. Retrieved January 10, 2005, from http://people-press.org/reports/display.php3?ReportID=165

Program on International Policy Attitudes (PIPA). (2002, September 8): Global public opinion on the US presidential election and US foreign policy. Retrieved April 15, 2007, from http://www.pipa.org/OnlineReports/Views_US/USElection_Sep04/USElection_Sep04_rpt.pdf

Plato. (360 BCE) *Timaeus.* Retrieved April 15, 2007, from http://www.gutenberg.org/dirs/etext98/tmeus11.txt

Revel, J. F. (2003). *Anti-Americanism.* San Francisco: Encounter Books.

Tocqueville, A. de. (2003). *Democracy in America.* New York: Penguin Classics. (Original work published 1835)

Trollope, F. (1997). *Domestic manners of the Americans.* London: Penguin Classics. (Original work published 1832)

World War I

Benefiting from a period of neutrality in the early years of World War I, the United States emerged from the conflict with a powerful military and a dynamic economy, promoting them to a leadership role in global affairs.

World War I, fought from July 1914 to November 1918, was one of the most cataclysmic events in modern history. It badly weakened the great powers of Europe, introduced the world to the horrors of trench warfare, and resulted in roughly twenty million deaths. It also had the unanticipated effect of vaulting the United States into a leadership role in global affairs. As a neutral power in the first three years of the war, the United States enriched itself by trading with the warring European nations. As a combatant from April 1917 to November 1918 it had a decisive impact on the outcome of the war, turning the tide against Germany and in favor of Britain and France. The United States emerged from World War I as a leading creditor nation, an economic colossus, and a proven military power. This shift caused a major rethinking of global perspectives toward the United States, which had previously been dismissed by European leaders as little more than a distant regional power.

Outbreak of War, 1914

The origins of the war were complex, rooted in the imperialist competition of all the great European powers, an accelerating naval arms race between Britain and Germany, and rigid alliance systems. The immediate spark was the June 1914 assassination of the heir to the throne of Austria-Hungary, Archduke Franz Ferdinand, as he visited Serbia. This assassination set in motion a full-scale confrontation between the Triple Entente (Britain, France, Russia) and the Central Powers (Germany, Austria-Hungary, Ottoman Empire). Vast armies were mobilized across the continent, with leaders making the mistaken assumption that the war would be short and glorious.

At first the war had little to do with the United States. President Woodrow Wilson (1856–1924) disdained it as a product of greedy European imperialism. His democratic instincts favored an Entente victory over the autocratic Central Powers, but in 1914 the United States had no pressing reason to get involved. Wilson thus settled on a policy of "strict neutrality," keeping Americans out of the war but allowing them to trade with the belligerent European powers. Not until the casualties in Europe began to mount, and the immense economic and human sacrifices needed to wage modern war became painfully clear did the particulars of U.S. neutrality became crucially important.

Period of Neutrality, 1914–1917

The basic problem with "strict neutrality" was that in practice it heavily favored the Entente powers of Britain and France. The United States had always exported more to them than to Germany, but this disparity was made more pronounced during the war. In 1914 exports totaled $754 million to Britain and France and $345 million to Germany, but in 1916 the United States exported a stunning $2.75 billion in goods to Britain and France and just $2 million to Germany. U.S. banks also lent $2.3 billion to the British and French governments in the first three years of the war, whereas Germany received a paltry $27 million.

Wilson argued that the imbalance was simply the product of economic blockades. The British used their superior surface fleet to patrol the North Sea and stop ships bound for Germany. This tactic was more effective and less deadly than German submarines, which were effective only when they struck without warning. Wilson was displeased with the British approach, but the submarines were intolerable. He made unrealistic demands of German submarines, insisting that they give fair warning before taking any action and implying that war would be declared if the rights of U.S. citizens were not respected. For the most part, the Germans sullenly restricted their submarine warfare to avoid antagonizing the United States into entering the war against them.

Wilson often spoke with a moralistic tone that irritated the warring European nations. When the British liner *Lusitania* was sunk in April 1915, with a more than one thousand people dying and 128 of them Americans, Wilson was ridiculed for his refusal to declare war on the grounds that the United States was "too proud to fight." He also tried to play the role of impartial mediator, urging both sides to state their war aims and attempting to bring them to the negotiating table. This was a noble effort, but it was not appreciated by European leaders. They resented his pious

attitude and doubted that the United States acted only for selfless reasons. At home, former President Theodore Roosevelt argued that Wilson could not win the trust of European leaders simply by sitting around and getting rich off of their urgent requirements for war material.

Eventually the Germans decided that they had little to lose by declaring unrestricted submarine warfare, which was almost certain to bring the United States into the war. On 1 February 1917 German submarines were let loose on all Atlantic shipping. In March 1917 the U.S. government was informed by the British about the "Zimmerman telegram," a foolish attempt by Germany to recruit Mexico as an ally. In the same month the czar of Russia, Nicholas II (1870–1918) was deposed by a democratic uprising. This event was important because it further convinced Wilson that the Entente occupied the moral high ground. Now able to justify U.S. entry as part of a historic campaign to "make the world safe for democracy," on 6 April 1917 Wilson declared war on Germany with the overwhelming support of Congress.

Associate Power, 1917–1918

The question in the spring of 1917 was whether the Americans could get their forces into the field fast enough to make a difference before Britain and France were starved into submission by unrestricted submarine warfare. The German cause was bolstered when Russia was seized by the Bolsheviks under Vladimir Lenin (1860–1924), who in January 1918 pulled Russia out of the war. This move freed German forces to participate in a final assault on the Western front. Although the U.S. doughboys were initially slow to arrive, by May 1918 one million were on the Western front to help block the last German offensive. Two million U.S. troops had reached Europe when, on 11 November 1918, an armistice brought hostilities to an end.

The United States had played a critical role for the Entente, but the British and French were not entirely thrilled with their ally. For one thing, Wilson had refused to accept that the United States was an "ally" of these imperialist powers at all. He preferred the term *associate power* and tried to keep U.S. troops apart from other Entente forces. In January 1918 he unilaterally introduced his "Fourteen Points of Light," a plan for the postwar peace that embraced political and economic liberalism, the League of Nations to enforce collective security, and "self-determination" as a basic right of nationalities around the world. Wilson also promised "peace without victory," implying that a peace settlement should treat all sides fairly. The Germans expediently adopted this philosophy as their military forces collapsed in the summer of 1918, and they signed the armistice of 11 November assuming that the peace settlement would be premised on the Fourteen Points and "peace without victory." This development frustrated the British and French, neither of whom had agreed to Wilson's forgiving approach beforehand.

The World War I memorial in Kansas City, Missouri. Source: istock/Jennifer Trenchard.

Wilsonian Dream, 1919

The Fourteen Points were of central importance at the Paris Peace Conference of 1919, which set out the peace terms to be presented to the vanquished Central Powers. Along with Wilson, French Prime Minister Georges Clemenceau (1841–1929) and British Prime Minister David Lloyd George (1863–1945) made most of the important decisions. Clemenceau and Lloyd George found Wilson difficult; Clemenceau remarked that talking to Wilson was like talking to Jesus Christ. The "self-determination" idea in-

EXTRACT FROM THE FOURTEEN POINTS

Speaking to a joint session of Congress on 8 January 1918, President Woodrow Wilson outlined his plan of fourteen points that would lead to lasting peace in Europe. While the armistice with Germany ending World War I would not come for another ten months, Wilson's Fourteen Points were used as terms of surrender with the German government.

The program of the world's peace, therefore, is our program; and that program, the only possible program, as we see it, is this:

I. Open covenants of peace, openly arrived at, after which there shall be no private international understandings of any kind but diplomacy shall proceed always frankly and in the public view.

II. Absolute freedom of navigation upon the seas, outside territorial waters, alike in peace and in war, except as the seas may be closed in whole or in part by international action for the enforcement of international covenants.

III. The removal, so far as possible, of all economic barriers and the establishment of an equality of trade conditions among all the nations consenting to the peace and associating themselves for its maintenance.

IV. Adequate guarantees given and taken that national armaments will be reduced to the lowest point consistent with domestic safety.

V. A free, open-minded, and absolutely impartial adjustment of all colonial claims, based upon a strict observance of the principle that in determining all such questions of sovereignty the interests of the populations concerned must have equal weight with the equitable claims of the government whose title is to be determined.

VI. The evacuation of all Russian territory and such a settlement of all questions affecting Russia as will secure the best and freest cooperation of the other nations of the world in obtaining for her an unhampered and unembarrassed opportunity for the independent determination of her own political development and national policy and assure her of a sincere welcome into the society of free nations under institutions of her own choosing; and, more than a welcome, assistance also of every kind that she may need and may herself desire. The treatment accorded Russia by her sister nations in the months to come will be the acid test of their good will, of their comprehension of her needs as distinguished from their own interests, and of their intelligent and unselfish sympathy.

VII. Belgium, the whole world will agree, must be evacuated and restored, without any attempt to limit the sovereignty which she enjoys in common with all other free nations. No other single act will serve as this will serve to restore confidence among the nations in the laws which they have themselves set and determined for the government of their relations with one another. Without this healing act the whole structure and validity of international law is forever impaired.

VIII. All French territory should be freed and the invaded portions restored, and the wrong done to France by Prussia in 1871 in the matter of Alsace-Lorraine, which has unsettled the peace of the world for nearly fifty years, should be righted, in order that peace may once more be made secure in the interest of all.

IX. A readjustment of the frontiers of Italy should be effected along clearly recognizable lines of nationality.

X. The peoples of Austria-Hungary, whose place among the nations we wish to see safeguarded and assured, should be accorded the freest opportunity to autonomous development.

XI. Rumania, Serbia, and Montenegro should be evacuated; occupied territories restored; Serbia accorded free and secure access to the sea; and the relations of the several Balkan states to one another determined by friendly counsel along historically established lines of allegiance and nationality; and international guarantees of the political and economic independence and territorial integrity of the several Balkan states should be entered into.

XII. The Turkish portion of the present Ottoman Empire should be assured a secure sovereignty, but the other nationalities which are now under Turkish rule should be assured an undoubted security of life and an absolutely unmolested opportunity of autonomous development, and the Dardanelles should be permanently opened as a free passage to the ships and commerce of all nations under international guarantees.

XIII. An independent Polish state should be erected which should include the territories inhabited by indisputably Polish populations, which should be assured a free and secure access to the sea, and whose political and economic independence and territorial integrity should be guaranteed by international covenant.

XIV. A general association of nations must be formed under specific covenants for the purpose of affording mutual guarantees of political independence and territorial integrity to great and small states alike.

Source: President Woodrow Wilson's Fourteen Points. (2006). Retrieved March 19, 2007, from http://net.lib.byu.edu/~rdh7/wwi/1918/14points.html

spired national groups, but its application was hugely problematic. The terms finally delivered to Germany shocked its population, which had expected a lenient settlement that neither Clemenceau nor Lloyd George was willing to concede. Wilson did get his League of Nations, but this body failed to prevent Germany from resurrecting itself and seeking retribution in World War II two decades later.

Shift in Global Perspectives

Whatever the outcome, the undeniable new reality at the Paris Peace Conference was the dramatic increase in the power and prestige of the United States. Wilson was the central figure at the conference. His nation had benefited greatly from its period of neutrality, becoming a leading creditor and expanding the most dynamic and productive economy in the world. The United States had also proven itself capable of mobilizing vast armies, even if it did not maintain them in peacetime. Nor had Wilson been afraid to press his vision of a liberal and democratic world order (one that, not coincidentally, closely reflected U.S. interests) upon everyone else. In practice his ambitious ideas were difficult to apply, but they did lay much of the groundwork for the international structure of the later twentieth century.

Americans generally enjoyed good relations with most nations after the war, especially with wartime allies. Canada and the United States, for example, drew closer together because of their shared sacrifices. Britain and France became more intimate friends of the United States because of the war, largely because of their shared democratic values and desire to build a safer world order. The Anglo-American "special relationship," a pillar of each nation's foreign policy ever since, was cemented during World War I. The British and French did harbor some ill will toward the United States, however. Neither nation agreed wholly with the Fourteen Points, which seemed tailored to serve U.S. interests. The issue of war debts poisoned relations for years, as the U.S. government insisted on repayment, and the British and French replied that they had already paid a high enough cost in human lives for the Entente victory.

Predictably, the Germans adopted a negative view of the United States after the war. They were bitter about the one-sided character of U.S. neutrality and, of course, about the eventual entry of the United States into the war against them. The harsh terms at Paris angered many Germans, who felt so betrayed by Wilson that when he died in 1924, the German government refused to lower its flags to half staff. Oddly, however, German leaders continued to think little of Americans as major players in world affairs. Nazi leader Adolf Hitler (1895–1945) dismissed the United States in the 1930s

as a "mongrel nation." He would regret that assessment during World War II.

Perhaps the most lasting damage to the U.S. image was done in Russia. There Lenin and the Bolsheviks saw U.S. foreign policy at its most hypocritical; U.S. troops backed anticommunist White Russians from 1918 to 1920 at the same time that the president was preaching the right of "self-determination." That intervention was a total disaster, earning the United States nothing but the lasting hatred of the Soviet Union. This hatred was unfortunate because of the critical importance of Russian-U.S. relations for the rest of the twentieth century. Hostile feelings persisted between the two during the interwar period, eased briefly during World War II, and finally dominated global affairs throughout the Cold War.

Overall, the rest of the world keenly felt the sudden increase in U.S. power that resulted from World War I. U.S. culture also spread abroad in the 1920s as Ford cars and Hollywood movies proliferated across Europe, and "Americanism" came to stand for progress, technological innovation, and mass culture. Wilson's self-appointed mission of spreading U.S. liberalism around the world had its limitations, as the Paris Peace Conference revealed, but his dream of a peaceful, democratic world order remained a widely held inspiration. The irony was that Americans themselves were slow to embrace their new role on the world stage. Wilson failed to persuade the U.S. Senate to join his beloved League of Nations, and the United States pursued aloof foreign policies in the interwar years. Not until the early years of the Cold War would the United States finally complete the transition to superpower status that had been unexpectedly accelerated by World War I.

Christopher Pennington

See also Cold War

Further Reading

Ambrosius, L. (2002). *Wilsonianism: Woodrow Wilson and his legacy in American foreign relations.* New York: Palgrave Macmillan.

Bailey, T., & Ryan, P. B. (1975). *The* Lusitania *disaster: An episode in modern warfare and diplomacy.* New York: Free Press.

Burk, K. (1985). *Britain, America and the sinews of war, 1914–1918.* London and Boston: G. Allen & Unwin.

Burton, D. H. (1999). *British–American diplomacy 1895–1917: Early years of the special relationship.* Malabar, FL: Krieger Publishing.

Coogan, J. W. (1981). *The end of neutrality.* Ithaca, NY: Cornell University Press.

Devlin, P. (1975). *Too proud to fight: Woodrow Wilson's neutrality.* New York: Oxford University Press.

Ferguson, N. (1999). *The pity of war.* New York: Basic Books.

Foglesong, D. S. (1995). *America's secret war against Bolshevism: U.S. intervention in the Russian Civil War, 1917–1920.* Chapel Hill: University of North Carolina Press.

Gilbert, M. (1994). *The First World War: A complete history.* New York: H. Holt.

Keene, J. D. (2000). *The United States and the First World War.* Harlow, NY: Longman.

Knock, T. (1995). *To end all wars: Woodrow Wilson and the quest for a new world order.* Princeton, NJ: Princeton University Press.

Levin, N. G. (1968). *Woodrow Wilson and world politics.* New York: Oxford University Press.

Link, A. S. (1979). *Woodrow Wilson: Revolution, war and peace.* Arlington Heights, IL: AHM Publishing.

MacMillan, M. (2003). *Paris 1919.* New York: Random House.

Paterson, T., Larry, J., Hagan, C., & Hagan, K. (1999–2000). *American foreign relations: Vol. 2* (5th ed.). Boston: Houghton-Mifflin.

World War II

When fighting broke out in Europe in 1939 the United States declared its neutrality, but by 1942 the United States had been thrust into a war that would fundamentally alter the course of U.S. and world history, for better or worse.

When World War II (1939–1945) erupted in September 1939 the United States declared its neutrality. Just as it had during the first three years of World War I (1914–1918), the United States watched as much of Europe, Asia, North Africa, and the Middle East were consumed by the largest and deadliest war in history. Only after the Japanese attack on Pearl Harbor, Hawaii, in December 1941, did the United States join the conflict, fundamentally changing the war and emerging as the most powerful nation on Earth. In many respects World War II was one of the biggest turning points in history in ushering in a new global era dominated by U.S. military, economic, and political influence that still exists today.

World War I and the Interwar Period

The interwar period (1919–1939) preceding World War II was marked by extremes. On the one hand, there was until 1929 an economic boom premised primarily on recovery after World War I. Untouched by the physical devastation of the war and with an economy flush from wealth garnished as a neutral country trading with belligerents, the United States became the world's bank. U.S. investment helped to rebuild Europe's shattered economies, and in the process industry and commerce in the United States dramatically expanded. A new "consumer society" quickly emerged, complete with radios, refrigerators, washing machines, telephones, and the automobile. During the so-called Roaring Twenties U.S. society also underwent great change. The war empowered women, who gained not only the right to vote (August 1920) but also economic and political power in running farms and factories while men were overseas. Even before the war women had championed movements and reforms designed to promote the social welfare of Americans in what historians call the "Progressive Era." Both men and women were deeply affected by the war and its unprecedented savagery. Many began to challenge social norms and class structures by adopting "radical" lifestyles that included various degrees of sexual liberation, smoking, drinking, and experimentation—in effect rebelling against the Victorian mentality prevalent before 1914. U.S. culture spread throughout the world with the export of Hollywood movies, jazz music, and writers such as F. Scott Fitzgerald, Ernest Hemingway, and Henry Miller. In some ways the United States became the focal point of the world and the cultural model upon which many Europeans based their own rebellions against the old order.

On the other hand, in many respects the interwar period was anything but "roaring" or "progressive." The war had been so destructive that many people around the world were left with nothing. Often scarred mentally and physically, soldiers returned from the war to face hardship reintegrating with societies so different than the ones they had left. Many brought with them radical ideas that had taken root in Europe during the war such as communism, which posed a fundamental challenge to the capitalist system that dominated the United States and Europe. It advocated violent revolution against those who controlled business and industry and predicted that by winning global struggles the working-class peoples of the world would ultimately build more egalitarian societies. With millions suffering from the war, communism seriously threatened already shaky governments throughout Europe. Russia endured a brutal revolution and civil war (1917–1921) that produced the world's first communist state in the Soviet Union, utterly transforming international relations in the process.

World War I also gave life to extreme nationalisms that took root in the devastation that followed. In Italy, Germany, and Japan resentment over the war and the peace that followed spawned radical movements that were built upon the anger and frustration of millions. By fanning the flames of ethnic, religious, and racial prejudices ultranationalist movements also emerged in other countries, including the United States. Many of these radicals blamed both the war and its aftermath on particular groups: Jews, Catholics, immigrants, and others. Fascist movements in Italy and Germany depended on nationalist sentiments to exclude such people, ultimately dehumanizing them. In the United States organizations such as the Ku Klux Klan (KKK) enjoyed a huge surge in membership, in part a reaction to the changes that war had brought. Extremists gained even more strength after the collapse of the global economy, beginning in the United States with the stock market crash of October 1929. With the apparent failure of both capitalism and democracy many people turned to radical solutions. It was in this context that Adolf Hitler (1889–1945) came to power

in Germany in 1933 and that militarists took over the government of Japan come 1940—two developments that ultimately paved the way for World War II.

Isolationism

During the 1920s and 1930s the United States remained detached from events in Europe and Asia. It never joined the League of Nations—the brainchild of U.S. president Woodrow Wilson (1856–1924, served 1913–1921)—and shunned binding alliances with other countries. Responding to strong isolationist sentiments in many parts of the United States, successive presidential administrations avoided foreign conflicts and thus did little to prevent the rise of radical regimes in Europe and Japan. In fact, in some respects the United States even facilitated them. The government of Franklin Roosevelt (1882–1945, served 1933–1945) refused to place economic sanctions on Japan when it invaded the Chinese province of Manchuria in 1933 or on Italy when it invaded Ethiopia in 1935. Roosevelt also prevented Americans from joining antifascists fighting the civil war in Spain between 1936 and 1939. U.S. loans and investment contributed substantially to German economic reconstruction and rearmament under Hitler. Japan was critically dependent on U.S. trade and used much of it to build its military. The United States even continued to trade with Japan after its brutal invasion of China beginning in 1937. Americans were by no means alone in failing to meet these challenges to peace and stability. Great Britain and France actively appeased the Italians, Germans, and Japanese throughout the 1930s in the hopes of avoiding conflict. However, the notion that the United States was simply an innocent bystander on the way to war is as naïve and misleading as the belief that the United States single-handedly won the conflict after it entered.

War Breaks Out in Europe

When another war in Europe erupted, most Americans sympathized with the Allies, which primarily consisted of Britain and its Commonwealth and France and its colonies. However, few were willing to fight foreign wars. After a valiant defense, Poland was divided between Nazi Germany and the Soviet Union and surrendered in early October 1939. Just more than a week before war broke out Soviet leader Joseph Stalin (1878–1953, ruled 1922–1953) signed a formal treaty with Germany promising mutual nonaggression and secretly agreeing to divide Poland. Anxious to avoid alienating the Soviets, Roosevelt did nothing to help the Poles or, initially, the Allies who went to war over the invasion. Moreover,

when the Soviet Union invaded neighboring Finland that November the United States offered little more than token support for the beleaguered Finns.

In the spring of 1940 German armies swept through Belgium, Netherlands, Luxembourg, Denmark, and Norway en route to France, which surrendered after just four weeks of fighting that June. The fall of France put most of Europe under Hitler's control. Only Britain and its Commonwealth stood in the way of his total victory. The German air force (Luftwaffe) began systematic bombing of the United Kingdom in preparation for an invasion. Confronted with the likely defeat of Britain should this happen, Roosevelt finally responded. In June he appointed two prominent interventionist Republicans to his cabinet as the secretary of war (Henry Stimson) and the secretary of the navy (Frank Knox). In July the president signed an act authorizing a two-ocean navy as part of a $10 billion appropriation for refurbishing the U.S. military. In September he implemented the first peacetime conscription in U.S. history. Most important, also in September 1940 he transferred fifty destroyers to the British Navy in exchange for rights in British possessions, including Newfoundland, Jamaica, Bahamas, and Trinidad. The Bases for Destroyers Agreement was designed to protect the vulnerable Atlantic convoys on which Britain was critically dependent for supplies from North America. Technically a violation of the Neutrality Acts passed in the 1930s designed to keep the United States out of another European war, the Bases for Destroyers Agreement illustrated Roosevelt's resolve to help the Allies even in the face of congressional and public reluctance.

Lend-Lease Act

Roosevelt extended U.S. support in March 1941 with the controversial Lend-Lease Act. Through it Roosevelt was authorized to lend, lease, sell, exchange, or transfer title on anything related to military defense. Critics, particularly those isolationists who feared that Roosevelt was drawing closer to war, accused the president of being a dictator and warned that Congress was being undermined. Originally aimed at providing Britain and China with aid, the program was eventually extended to include the Soviet Union when it was attacked by Germany in June 1941. Between 1941 and 1945 more than $50 billion worth of military goods was sent to the Allies—the majority of this to Britain and the Commonwealth ($31.5 billion) and the Soviet Union ($11.3 billion). In exchange the United States received only about $8 billion worth of primarily services, such as rent costs on air bases and other facilities. Despite some difficulties in the administration and transfer of goods, Lend-Lease proved critical to the success of Allied military efforts. From the German perspective, the program in effect brought the United States into the war. Spinning Roosevelt's metaphor that the United States was simply lending a garden hose to help a neighbor

put out a fire, the German ambassador in Washington commented that "if your neighbor's house is on fire, you don't just lend him a hose, you help him put out the fire."

Roosevelt followed this up with the Atlantic Charter, devised in August 1941 during a meeting off the coast of Newfoundland with British prime minister Winston Churchill (1874–1965, prime minister 1940–1945 and 1951–1955). Amid much secrecy, the two leaders agreed to like-minded principles that would govern the postwar order, including the right of self-determination, disarmament, and increased international trade and cooperation. Most important, the Atlantic Charter called for the defeat of Nazi Germany and other Axis powers, notwithstanding the fact that the United States was still a neutral. That November Congress authorized changes to neutrality laws to allow merchant ships to be armed and to allow the U.S. Navy to escort Atlantic convoys. Several incidents at sea, including attacks on two U.S. ships by German submarines, made it clear that the United States was no longer really neutral. Still, neither Roosevelt nor Hitler was prepared to declare war. The president still faced strong isolationism, while Hitler was preoccupied with the German invasion of the Soviet Union.

The Coming of War in Asia-Pacific

Relations with Japan were in many respects even worse. The United States did little to prevent the Japanese conquest of China begun in 1937, but by the summer of 1940 it was clear to Roosevelt that U.S. interests in the Pacific were seriously threatened. The surrender of France and the Netherlands to the Germans left colonies in Southeast Asia virtually abandoned. For Japan resource-rich French Indochina and the Dutch East Indies were alternative sources of the oil and metals it got from the United States. The question was how far Japan could extend its empire without drawing Britain and, more important, the United States into a conflict. For the United States the problem was how to prevent Japanese expansion without risking war. After much deliberation in July 1940 Roosevelt made the decision to limit trade in scrap metals and oil with Japan. He followed that up with a formal embargo on iron and steel in September. In response Japan immediately signed the Tripartite Pact—a formal alliance with both Germany and Italy—and then applied pressure to the Dutch East Indies to gain further oil shipments. Critically short of resources needed to fuel their conquest of China, in September 1940 Japanese leaders decided to occupy Tonkin—the northern part of Vietnam—and then, in July 1941, to invade the rest of French Indochina. In retaliation Roosevelt placed a full embargo on Japan and froze all its assets in the United States—in effect the last step toward war.

Historians debate whether Roosevelt was intent on war with Japan even at this stage. Some note that he intended to reverse the embargo and ship oil in exchange for an end to Japanese expansion. Others point out that despite its increasingly strong stance on China the Roosevelt administration was not prepared to go to war over it. However, events in Japan made a peaceful settlement almost impossible. In October 1941 the ostensibly civilian government in Tokyo fell, and the military under General Hideki Tojo (1884–1948, prime minister 1941–1944) came to power. Although negotiations designed to avert a conflict with the Americans continued, plans for war accelerated. The Japanese military was not prepared to abandon its occupation of China or plans for empire in the South Pacific, even if it meant war with the United States. Resigning themselves to the inevitability of a conflict with the United States, Japanese leaders prepared to attack.

Pearl Harbor

At 6 A.M. on Sunday, 7 December 1941 (8 December, Tokyo time), the Japanese launched a massive aerial assault against the U.S. Pacific naval base at Pearl Harbor, Hawaii, as part of a plan developed by Admiral Isoroku Yamamoto (1884–1943). Nearly simultaneously the Japanese attacked U.S. bases at Guam, Wake Island, and Philippines, invaded Thailand, and assaulted British positions in Hong Kong and Malaya. In just over three hours at Pearl Harbor the Americans lost six battleships, three destroyers, three light cruisers, and four other vessels. Many more were damaged. The raids destroyed 164 airplanes and damaged another 128. By the time it was over 2,403 U.S. servicemen and civilians were killed and more than 1,100 wounded. In the short term the Japanese had succeeded in taking out the U.S. battle fleet and thus won a strategic victory. However, in the long term the attack was a catastrophic failure. Repair facilities and fuel installations at Pearl Harbor were left intact, and the principal target of the attacks, the three aircraft carriers and their heavy cruiser escorts, were not even there. Two were out to sea, and the third was in San Diego, California. With the core of the fleet still afloat and facilities at Pearl Harbor still operable, the United States could fight back in the Pacific. Moreover, the attack galvanized U.S. public opinion like never before. Rallying the nation in response to what he called "a day of infamy," on 8 December President Roosevelt asked Congress for a declaration of war, which passed with only one dissension. A vigorous debate still rages over whether the Roosevelt administration had intelligence about the attack in advance. Some argue that the Pearl Harbor attack was in fact a set-up designed by the president to draw the United States into World War II whereas others contend that although intelligence

information about Japanese plans was available it was not properly interpreted and analyzed. Despite a congressional inquiry and decades of exhaustive research by historians and conspiracy theorists alike, no incontrovertible evidence has been found to prove that Roosevelt was in any way involved with the attack.

The United States Goes to War

What is clear is that Japan had shaken an economic and military giant. Still, the United States took time to fully wake up. The Great Depression had ravaged the U.S. economy, leaving nearly 15 percent of the population unemployed. Investment was low, and industrial infrastructure was lacking. To make matters worse, there was considerable tension between businesspeople and labor unions as well as within the unions themselves. Providing the necessities of war was a monumental challenge after a decade of depression. Similarly, building the military to fight the war was no small task. The armed forces were kept to a bare minimum for most of the 1930s. In 1940 the army counted only 269,023 personnel, while the navy had 160,997 and the marines 28,345. Come war on two fronts in 1941 military planners aimed at rallying some twelve million men for service, not to mention all the material, resources, food, and money to equip them. On top of that was the need to provide for U.S. allies under Lend-Lease.

In what some experts consider one of the worst mistakes of the war, on 11 December Adolf Hitler responded to the attack on Pearl Harbor by declaring war on the United States. Although the Tripartite Pact did not oblige Germany to do so, Hitler hoped that the declaration would encourage Japan to attack the Soviet Union and ideally open a front in Mongolia or Siberia. Moreover, Hitler knew that in his struggle to control the Atlantic, war with the United States was very likely. However, there is little evidence that Roosevelt was immediately prepared to fight in Europe after Pearl Harbor. He did not command sufficient military force and had no public resolve for a war with Germany, too. Plus, the focus was on fighting across the Pacific Ocean, not on battling on multiple fronts. Thus, the German declaration brought the United States fully into the European theater of war as well, much to the relief of the Allies. By mid-1942 U.S. soldiers began moving into Britain, where they were trained for the eventual invasion of Europe. The U.S. Army Air Force (USAAF) saw action much sooner in the systematic Allied bombing campaigns against Germany beginning in the summer of 1942 and became critically important to the war effort. It also underwent nearly unimaginable expansion: from 2,320 planes and 20,000 personnel in 1939 to 80,000 aircraft and nearly 2.5 million men by 1945.

In fact, the U.S. war machine as a whole was unquestionably one of the most important factors securing the Allied victory in World War II. By late 1942 the unemployment rate in the United States had dropped to almost nothing. There was a massive migration of workers from rural to urban areas to meet the demand of factories producing materiel for the war. Women, African-Americans, the elderly, and youth joined the workforce in unprecedented numbers, raising their standard of living and gaining recognition for their service. The pressures of war also changed the dynamics of family, marriage, gender, and class distinctions. Many Americans were strongly patriotic and contributed to the war effort through hard work, consumer rations, and the purchase of war bonds to help fund the fight. With enhanced efficiency and key industries running factories around the clock, productivity soared. By 1943 the United States produced nearly two-thirds of the world's oil supply. By 1944 it turned out one-half of the world's steel. By 1945 U.S. factories made $181 billion worth of munitions, which included 300,000 aircraft, 147 aircraft carriers, 952 other warships, and an almost endless supply of ammunition, guns, and tanks as well as food, clothing, and medicine. There were, of course, still substantial problems with the economy and U.S. society itself. Racism and sexism were still widespread, and neither minorities nor women were considered the equals of white men. Americans of German, Italian, and Japanese descent had their loyalties questioned and were often harassed during the war, none worse than the thousands of Japanese-Americans who were forced from their homes along the West Coast and interned in camps. Still, in many respects the war represented renewal and prosperity for Americans at home, while on a global scale the United States emerged from World War II as an economic and military superpower. But that superpowerdom came with suffering and sacrifice. The United States lost 291,557 dead and 671,846 wounded in nearly four years of war. In comparative terms this was nothing compared with the approximately 30 million who perished in the Soviet Union, 20 million Chinese, or the 7.5 million Germans who died. It was sacrifice nonetheless. U.S. forces fought in almost every major theater and were of critical importance in each.

The War in Asia-Pacific

Indeed, in Asia-Pacific Americans bore the brunt of the war against Japan. Just a few days after their attack on Pearl Harbor Japanese soldiers landed in the Philippines, then a commonwealth under the protectorate of the United States. U.S. defenses there were severely damaged during the 7 December raids, and, outnumbered and ill-equipped, U.S. forces withdrew from the capital of Manila to the Bataan Peninsula, expecting reinforcements. When none was forthcoming, their commander, General Douglas

A cemetery for American soldiers at Normandy, France, the site of the D-day invasion in 1944. Source: istock/ Joe Brandt.

MacArthur (1880–1964) evacuated the Philippines for Australia along with most of the Filipino government, vowing famously that he would return. His army surrendered to the Japanese in early April 1942 after a three-month siege. Almost twelve thousand Americans, together with sixty-six thousand Filipino soldiers and twenty thousand civilians—the majority suffering from disease and malnutrition—were then force-marched in ferocious heat over 104 kilometers to Japanese camps, many beaten and tortured along the way. In what became known as the "Bataan Death March" as many as ten thousand soldiers and civilians died. Although they were humiliated in defeat, Americans steeled their resolve to fight after the loss of the Philippines and the Japanese atrocities that followed.

The fight was long and hard across the Pacific Ocean in what some refer to as a campaign of "island hopping." That required control of the sea, and in the first few months after Pearl Harbor the U.S. Navy was at a distinct disadvantage against the larger and better-prepared Japanese fleet. Still, in May 1942 the U.S. and Australian navies won a strategic victory over the Japanese during the Battle of the Coral Sea. Then, in early June the Americans faced the bulk of the Japanese fleet at Midway in what many historians consider the most important naval engagement of the war. Hoping to draw the remaining operational U.S. aircraft carriers into a trap, the Japanese planned on seizing tiny Midway atoll at the northeastern end of the Hawaiian Island chain about 2,129 kilometers east of Honolulu. From there they could attack Fiji,

Samoa, and Hawaii and gain mastery of the Pacific. Admiral Yamamoto anticipated that after the Battle of the Coral Sea, where one U.S. aircraft carrier was sunk and another badly damaged, the U.S. Navy had only two left. He also believed that after several months of defeats, the Americans had low morale and no will to fight. What Yamamoto did not realize was that the damaged carrier, the USS *Yorktown*, was repaired enough to head back to sea in just seventy-two hours, giving the Americans considerably more punch. He also did not know that after months of exhaustive work, U.S. and British cryptanalysts had broken the Japanese code on which orders for the Battle of Midway were scrambled. Through this the Americans could anticipate the movements of the Japanese fleet and focus their attacks. The battle raged on and under the sea, in the skies, and on land for over three days. In the end four of the six Japanese aircraft carriers were sunk and with them went hopes of controlling the Pacific.

After Midway the Americans went on the offensive with two major thrusts: one in the southwest Pacific through New Guinea to the Philippines and the other through the north Pacific. In August 1942 U.S. forces launched their first major assault at Guadalcanal, a mosquito-infested island in the southern Solomon Islands chain, forcing the Japanese to withdraw after months of heavy fighting. Then, in November 1943, the Americans won another important victory at Tarawa in the Gilbert Islands after fierce resistance by Japanese defenders. Together with Australian and New Zealand contingents the Americans also gained control of the Papuan

peninsula of New Guinea. Meanwhile, in the north Pacific, U.S. forces secured the Marshall Islands before striking at the Caroline and Marianas Islands chains. Held by Japan since World War I, both were strongly fortified and resolutely defended. By July 1944 the Americans took Saipan in the Caroline Islands but only after incurring more than fourteen thousand casualties. Nearly thirty thousand Japanese soldiers—virtually the whole contingent on Saipan—died, along with twenty-two thousand civilians. Convinced by propaganda that the Americans were demons and cannibals, many civilians committed suicide rather than surrender. That same month U.S. forces also took Tinian and Guam after similarly heavy fighting.

Tightening the Noose

From these bases the Americans could launch long-range bombing missions against Japan and strangle its shipping. From the south Pacific they tightened the noose even further. Considered the largest naval engagement of the war, the Battle of Leyte Gulf in October 1944 paved the way for the U.S. liberation of Philippines and MacArthur's triumphant return. Fierce fighting throughout the islands dragged out for months, with pockets of Japanese troops holding out until the end of the war. Several even hid out for years.

The approach to Japan in early 1945 was marked by key U.S. victories at Iwo Jima and Okinawa. Just 8 kilometers long and 4 kilometers wide, Iwo Jima (Iwoto) lies just 1,046 kilometers southeast of Tokyo and thus became a primary objective for the Americans as a base for bombers. A sulfurous island dominated by Mount Suribachi, an extinct volcano, Iwo Jima is covered in ravines, crevices, ridges, and caves: ideal terrain for digging in and defending. After seventy-two days of near-constant aerial assaults and naval bombardment, sixty thousand U.S. marines went ashore, only to be met by fierce fire from some twenty-two thousand Japanese defenders who had dug underground bunkers and tunnels to withstand the shelling. It took thirty-six days for the Americans to prevail but not before 5,931 marines had been killed and 17,372 wounded: fully one-third of the entire force committed to the operation, making it the bloodiest single battle in marine history. In testament to the savagery of the fight, five of the twenty-four Medals of Honor awarded to marines in the course of World War II were given for service at Iwo Jima. The island was also the scene of one of the most famous photographs in U.S. history: five marines and a U.S. Navy corpsman raising the U.S. flag atop desolate Mount Suribachi. On the Japanese side more than 20,000 Japanese were killed, with only 216 eventually surrendering.

At Okinawa, just 869 kilometers from Japan, the Americans faced a similarly tenacious defense. With 1,213 warships and nearly 500,000 men committed to the operation, Okinawa was for the Americans the largest and costliest battle in the Pacific during the war. The Japanese had seventy-seven thousand soldiers and twenty thousand local militia dedicated to the island's defense in cave networks similar to those of Iwo Jima. They also used about nineteen hundred *kikusui* (floating chrysanthemum) suicide plane attacks—*kamikaze* to the Americans—against U.S. Navy ships. After nearly three months of fighting only 7,400 Japanese soldiers were left to surrender. Worse yet, as many as 150,000 Okinawan civilians died in what some called the *tetsu no ame* (rain of steel): relentless bombing and shelling of the island by U.S. forces. U.S. losses were also high. Thirty-six warships were destroyed and 368 damaged. Navy personnel killed in action numbered 4,900, with an additional 4,300 wounded. The marines and army suffered 7,613 dead and more than 31,000 wounded, along with 763 destroyed aircraft. Okinawa saw the highest casualty rate in the war for U.S. forces, and in both size and cost the invasion was second only to D-Day. However, for the Japanese, the loss of Iwo Jima and Okinawa was even more important. They were a severe blow to Japanese confidence and the defense of the home islands and put U.S. forces within a few hundred miles of Tokyo.

Elsewhere in Asia U.S. servicemen were vital in British, Commonwealth, and Chinese efforts to dislodge the Japanese. After the British retreat from Burma (Myanmar) in early 1942, Allied efforts focused on the protection of India and the relief of besieged Chinese Nationalist (Kuomintang) armies. Under the controversial command of General Joseph Stilwell (1883–1946) U.S. forces supplied both British and Chinese armies despite receiving far less materiel than their counterparts operating in Europe or the Pacific. Nicknamed "Vinegar Joe" for his brutal honesty and difficult personality, Stilwell was charged with training Chinese soldiers in India. He also had the unenviable task of convincing their leader, Generalissimo Chiang Kai-shek (Jiang Jieshi, 1887–1975), to use Lend-Lease aid against the Japanese rather than his communist adversaries in China's simultaneous civil war. Under Stilwell's command the famous Ledo Road, stretching more than 1,609 kilometers from India to China, was built through mountains and jungle to aid the beleaguered Chiang. U.S. forces were also instrumental in Allied efforts to push the Japanese out of Southeast Asia and China in 1944–1945.

Operation Torch in Africa

In Africa U.S. forces saw their first concerted action beginning in November 1942 with Operation Torch—a joint Allied offensive aimed at securing Morocco, Tunisia, and Libya. British and Com-

monwealth armies had been fighting in North Africa since July 1940 and by October 1942 had succeeded in forcing German and Italian retreats from Egypt and the strategically vital Suez Canal. The British occupation of French territories in Lebanon and Syria and consolidation of the British hold on Iraq and Iran furthered the Allied position. But the Germans did not easily yield. Under the command of Field Marshal Erwin Rommel (1891–1944) the *Afrika Korps* continued to push the Allies back, winning, in fact, a tactical victory against inexperienced U.S. forces at the Battle of Kesserine Pass (Tunisia) in February 1943 during the first serious engagement of the war between German and U.S. troops. But British forces, together with the U.S. Army's II Corps under Lt. General George Patton (1885–1945), soon squeezed Rommel's forces. With a lack of supplies and the weight of U.S. entry into the war the Germans were ultimately doomed, and by May 1943 their forces in North Africa either withdrew to Europe or were captured.

The War in Italy

Victory in Africa exposed a rift between the Allies over long-term strategy. By the beginning of 1943 the Soviets had reversed their fortunes and began pushing the Germans back. Incurring unbelievable losses in the process, they demanded that a second front be opened in western Europe. The British wanted that to be in Italy, which Churchill referred to as the "soft under-belly" of the Axis powers. The Americans preferred to wait, preserve their armies, and prepare for a massive assault on France. In the end the British prevailed, and in July 1943 Allied forces invaded Sicily. In less than one month defenders on the island surrendered, and in Rome the fascist government of Benito Mussolini (1883–1945, ruled Italy 1922–1943, Italian Social Republic 1943–1945) collapsed. A new government began secret peace talks with the British and Americans. Encouraged by this the Allies pressed on and launched invasions on both the Mediterranean and Adriatic coasts of Italy in September 1943, forcing its surrender just five days later. However, in the ensuing chaos German forces moved in to halt the Allied advance. The Germans also protected Mussolini, who was installed at the head of a puppet fascist government in the northern part of the country. By the winter of 1943–1944 the Allies were stalled south of Rome against an array of German defenses nicknamed the "Gustav Line." Despite repeated assaults the line held, inflicting on the Allies some of the heaviest losses of the war. In response to Churchill's estimation, the commander of Allied forces in Italy, General Mark Clark (1896–1984), referred to the campaign as "a tough old gut."

Between January and May 1944 the Allies repeatedly attempted to break through the line head-on at Cassino, a small town 128 kilometers south of Rome at the heart of German defenses in the Liri and Garigliano Valleys and capped at 335 meters by a sixth-century Benedictine monastery. Four major thrusts claimed the lives of fifty-four thousand Allies and twenty thousand Germans before Free Polish forces finally broke through. Critics accused Clark of poor planning in the headlong assaults and his decision not to pursue withdrawing German units. Instead he drove for Rome, which was liberated amid much fanfare by U.S. forces on 4 June after Clark issued stern warnings to British and Canadian armies not to enter first. His vanity bought the Germans time to refortify a second line of defenses south of Bologna and nullified British plans to break northeast into Austria, Hungary, and Yugoslavia to prevent Soviet domination of eastern Europe. Not until April 1945 did Allied forces manage to breach German defenses in the north, by which point the war was almost over.

D-Day

Events in Italy were quickly overshadowed. Just two days after Clark rolled into Rome, the Allies launched their biggest operation of World War II on the shores of Normandy, France. Operation Overlord, better known as "D-Day," involved 120 Allied divisions or nearly two million men, more than half of whom were Americans, under the leadership of future U.S. president General Dwight Eisenhower (1890–1969), the supreme commander of all Allied forces in Europe. The invasion required years of careful planning, including elaborate intelligence operations designed to convince Hitler that the invasion would come at Calais, some 321 kilometers to the north. Despite their array of defenses from France to Denmark, the so-called Atlantic Wall, the Germans were ill-prepared. Nearly 90 percent of their forces were defending against the Soviet advance in the east; thus, only fifty thousand soldiers defended Normandy when the Allies came ashore. Along five major beach sites U.S., British, and Canadian forces led the assaults. Mostly because of poor weather many of the men and their equipment landed off their marks. In addition, naval and aerial bombardment did not destroy German defenses. As a result, the Americans in particular endured high casualties at Omaha Beach. However, the bluff worked, and by the time Hitler realized that Normandy was no decoy it was too late to dislodge the Allies. On 26 June the Americans took the key port of Cherbourg, and on 9 July British and Canadian forces liberated Caen. By mid-August Allied forces had broken through the last lines of German defense

en route to Paris. On 25 August the French capital was liberated by the Free French forces.

The Road to Berlin

The Germans were, however, not finished. The bulk of their remaining soldiers in the west retreated into Belgium and Holland, where they amassed to protect against an invasion of Germany. Allied attempts to broach their defenses in Operation Market Garden that September failed before winter set in. In December Hitler ordered the last major German offensive: a drive aimed to break through primarily U.S. lines in the Ardennes region of southern Belgium. In what came to be known as the "Battle of the Bulge," German units surrounded U.S. forces centered on the town of Bastogne. However, without reinforcements or provisions, the 101st Airborne Division spearheaded a fierce defense and repulsed numerous German attacks. By the time it was finally relieved the 101st had successfully stalled the German offensive. Indeed, many German troops were quickly cut off by Allied reinforcements. In January 1945 the Allies punched through remaining German defenses in various sectors and pushed into Germany. By early March they successfully crossed the Rhine River and fanned out to sweep east through the country. In mid-April U.S. forces met Soviet troops pushing west at the Elbe River in central Germany. On 30 April Adolf Hitler committed suicide in his bunker in Berlin, and on 7 May the last German forces offered their unconditional surrender.

Truman and the Atomic Bomb

As the Allies celebrated victory in Europe, the war against Japan continued. New factors had significant bearing on that front in addition to the defeat of Germany and Italy. Roosevelt died of a cerebral hemorrhage on 12 April 1945. His successor, Harry S. Truman (1884–1972, served 1945–1953), had been vice president for just eighty-two days before Roosevelt's death and knew little about management of the war or foreign affairs. He had not been privy to any major decisions and knew almost nothing of Roosevelt's grand strategy, particularly with respect to the postwar. As he took office, Soviet forces continued to push into eastern Europe, and it was unclear if or how agreements devised at wartime Allied conferences such as Tehran (November–December 1943) and Yalta (February 1945) would be implemented. With such heavy issues on his mind, shortly after being sworn into office Truman told reporters that he "felt like the moon, the stars, and all the planets had fallen on me."

In one of his first debriefings the new president learned of the top-secret Manhattan Project to develop the world's first atomic bomb. It was originally designed with Germany in mind, but the collapse of the Nazi regime in May 1945 changed that. Truman headed to his first meeting with Soviet leader Stalin at the Potsdam Conference outside Berlin in July 1945 just as the project went into final testing. In fact, it was during the Potsdam proceedings that Truman learned of the first successful detonation of an atomic bomb in the New Mexico desert. Although the focus at Potsdam was on the fate of Germany, Allied leaders also wrangled over the war against Japan. Truman was wary of promising the Soviets anything in exchange for their entry into the Pacific war but feared that going it alone would result in a substantially longer conflict with many more U.S. deaths. With the atomic bomb in mind, Truman warned Japanese leaders that unless the Allies received their unconditional and immediate surrender, they would face "prompt and utter destruction."

When the Japanese ignored the Potsdam Declaration, Truman followed through on his threat. On 6 August 1945, the city of Hiroshima was destroyed by a single atomic bomb. Approximately ninety thousand were killed instantly, and up to fifty thousand more died of radiation poisoning and other injuries in the first few months afterward. In the confusion that followed Japanese leaders in Tokyo were initially unsure of what had happened. It was not until their own aerial surveillance of the city and an official announcement from Washington that they learned the true nature of the attack. Still, they did not surrender. Instead Japanese leaders planned on continued attempts via the Soviet Union to negotiate terms, particularly with respect to the emperor being allowed to remain in power. Then, on 9 August, the Soviet Union announced its intention to unilaterally break the treaty with Japan and declare war. In response Tokyo declared martial law, and senior militarists censored any attempts to make peace. That same day Truman ordered the second atomic bombing of Japan at Nagasaki. As many as seventy thousand died instantly. After continued debate within the Japanese government, Emperor Hirohito (1901–1989, reigned 1926–1989) announced the decision to surrender on 14 August. Japan formally surrendered to the Allies on 2 September, ending World War II.

The decision to use the atomic bomb against Japan remains highly controversial today. Some argue that it was an entirely political, not military, decision aimed at the Soviets—in effect a demonstration of U.S. power calculated for the postwar balance of power. Others object to the timing of the bombs, in particular the one dropped on Nagasaki, pointing out that insufficient time was given the Japanese to respond. Still others consider the decision on more philosophical and moral grounds, accusing the Americans of not only war crimes but also crimes against humanity in

unleashing such weapons under any circumstances. Those who defend the decision argue that the Japanese resolutely refused to surrender and that based on fighting across the Pacific an invasion of the home islands by conventional means would have resulted in dramatically higher deaths on both sides. Defenders also note that the Japanese started the war, were guilty of horrendous war crimes, and threatened to kill more than 100,000 Allied prisoners if an invasion was launched.

The Coming Cold War

Despite the debate, it is clear that Truman's decision ultimately ushered in a new atomic age. It is also clear that as World War II came to a close a new world order had emerged, dominated by two "superpowers" in the Soviet Union and the United States, but the two were hardly allies. Mistrust and animosity had dominated U.S.-Soviet relations since 1917, and with the exception of their mutual crusade against Hitler between 1941 and 1945 the two nations were rivals. Even before Germany surrendered some observers, like General Patton, predicted and even welcomed a war between the United States and Soviet Union. Fortunately, cooler heads prevailed. Still, the potential for conflict in 1945 was great. The newsreels showing Americans and Russians celebrating the end of the war together in Germany masked serious geopolitical divisions and ideological differences, and the war-time alliance against Nazi Germany quickly gave way to mutual suspicion and conflict and ultimately led to the "Cold War" between them that would last nearly fifty years.

The Myth of the "Good War"

Despite its enormous power in 1945 the United States was not simply a military juggernaut. Amid the ashes of World War II the country took the leading role in rebuilding many countries around the world, including Germany and Japan. American values and ideas helped shape postwar institutions like the United Nations, World Bank, International Monetary Fund, and others that are still prominent international organizations today. And for many people, even with its inherent flaws and problems, the United States emerged as a symbol of hope, freedom, and progress in a world ravaged by war. In this light World War II was for the United States and its allies a "good war." Americans had fought against tyrannical regimes and saved millions of people through their sacrifices. But that is not the only interpretation.

Critics argue that the "good war" is nothing more than a myth created by the victors. They point out that the United States en-

tered and fought the war for its own global interests, and indeed prospered immensely as a result. They also contend that ultimately Americans were no different than the Germans, Japanese, or Italians they fought. They all fought for their countries and all believed that they were righteous in doing so. Moreover, some critics note that although the Allies did not carry out atrocities at the same level as the Nazis or Japanese, they were also guilty of war crimes including not only the atomic bombings of Hiroshima and Nagasaki, but also instances such as the British and American firebombing of Dresden in February 1945 and other episodes involving the execution of prisoners or murder of civilians. Whereas the United States and its allies established international war crimes tribunals after the war to deal with both German and Japanese offences, no similar hearing addressed their own. Some point to the tremendous hypocrisy this illustrates, particularly in light of Soviet atrocities in Eastern Europe.

These interpretations of World War II have been shaped to a degree by events since 1945. Over the course of the past sixty years Americans have fought and died in numerous other conflicts, often with less tangible objectives. Some, like the Vietnam War and the war in Iraq (2003), have sharply divided public opinion in the United States and abroad about the motives and means of U.S. foreign policy. Today many observers view the United States and its power with skepticism, concern, and even hatred. However, it is important to note that the United States that went to war in 1941 was a very different nation than exists today. So too has the international context changed. It is also important to consider that for the veterans who fought for Allied nations in World War II the "good war" is no myth, but rather the most important event in their lives. While some might acknowledge that all armies are capable—and possibly even guilty—of excesses in war, few would agree that American or British actions were anything like those of their Nazi or Japanese counterparts. Nor was the United States in any way like the ruthless dictatorships it fought. Aside from any mistakes the United States might have made in the years since, most Americans continue to consider the Allied cause in World War II a noble crusade against tyranny, and it is safe to say that most people in the world agree. What is beyond contention is that in entering World War II the United States changed fundamentally as a nation, and fundamentally changed the world as well.

Arne Kislenko

See also Cold War; World War I

Further Reading

Adams, M. C. C. (1994). *The best war ever: America and World War II.* Baltimore: Johns Hopkins University Press.

Dallek, R. (1995). *Franklin Roosevelt and American foreign policy 1932–1945* (Rev. ed.). New York: Oxford University Press.

Dear, I. C. B. (Ed.). (1995). *The Oxford companion to World War II*. Oxford, UK: Oxford University Press.

Doenecke, J. D. (2005). *Debating Franklin D. Roosevelt's foreign policies, 1933–1945*. Lanham, MD: Rowman & Littlefield.

Folly, M. H. (2002). *The United States and World War II: The awakening giant*. Edinburgh, UK: Edinburgh University Press.

Keegan, J. (1990). *The Second World War*. New York: Penguin Books.

Kennedy, D. M. (1999). *Freedom from fear: The American people in depression and war, 1929–1945*. Oxford, UK: Oxford University Press.

Kimball, W. F. (2004, March). Franklin Roosevelt and World War II. *Presidential Studies Quarterly, 34*(1), 83–99.

Lyons, M. J. (2004). *World War II: A short history* (4th ed.). Upper Saddle River, NJ: Prentice Hall.

Reynolds, D. (2001). *From Munich to Pearl Harbor: Roosevelt's America and the origins of the Second World War*. Chicago: Ivan R. Dee.

Reynolds, D. (2006). *From World War to Cold War: Churchill, Roosevelt, and the international history of the 1940s*. Oxford, UK: Oxford University Press.

Roehrs, M. D. (2004). *World War II in the Pacific*. London: M. E. Sharpe.

Stoler, M. A. (2005). *Allies in War: Britain and America against the Axis Powers, 1940–1945*. London: Hodder Arnold.

Sulzberger, C. L. (1987). *World War II*. Boston: Houghton Mifflin.

Zeiler, T. W. (2004). *Unconditional defeat: Japan, America, and the end of World War II*. Wilmington, DE: Scholarly Resources.

U.S. Agencies and Organizations

Today most U.S. government and nongovernment agencies and organizations have Internet websites. A good starting place for obtaining information on U.S. agencies and organizations is Web World at http://www.fedworld.gov (U.S. Department of Commerce Technology Administration, National Technical Information Service, Springfield, VA 22161). At that website one can find the following:

INTEREST AREA	ACTIVITY
Top government websites	Access to key agencies and topical sites
Search the website USA.gov	30 million government webpages
Government jobs	Daily-updated listing of government jobs
Government science, engineering, and technology websites	Access to U.S. government resources (www.scitechresources.gov)
Government research and development publications	Scientific and technical publications from all government agencies (www.ntis.gov)
Supreme Court	1937–1975 Supreme Court decisions
Internal Revenue Service	IRS archived forms and publications through Fedworld (http://www.fedworld.gov/taxsear.html)

The Library of Congress (http://www.loc.gov), with its searchable online collection, is another source of a vast amount of information. First Government (http://www.firstgov.gov or http://firstgov.com) is another portal to a vast amount of U.S. government information. It has sections for citizens, businesses and nonprofit organizations, federal employees, and government-to-government relations. It also has many links to government agencies.

The FedStats home page (http://www.fedstats.gov) is the entryway to statistics from more than one hundred U.S. federal agencies. It also has search capabilities to locate information.

U.S. Agriculture

The Department of Agriculture (USDA) home page at http://www.usda.gov/wps/portal/usdahome has search capabilities and contains current news, forms, weather, commodities, recall announcements, events, and links to other agricultural and government information websites. The site is also available in Spanish.

The National Agricultural Library (http://www.nalusda.gov) has some excellent search engines and many agricultural publications. The *Agricultural Fact Book* (http://www.un.org/english) contains a wealth of USDA information on U.S. agriculture. The Animal and Plant Health Inspection Service (APHIS) website is located at http://www.aphis.usda.gov. APHIS's responsibility is safeguarding U.S. agriculture.

The Food Safety and Inspection Service (FSIS) of the USDA (http://www.fsis.usda.gov) protects public health through food safety. For example, the Grade A Pasteurized Milk Ordinance (http://vm.cfsan.fda.gov/~acrobat/pmo99-1.pdf) regulates the production, handling, pasteurization, and distribution of milk. USDA food composition data can be found at http://www.nal.usda.gov/fnic/foodcomp/Data/index.html, which is a standard reference for the chemical composition of 6,839 foods.

The U.S. Food and Drug Administration (FDA) is located at http://vm.cfsan.fda.gov/list.html. The FDA ensures that food, cosmetics, medicines, and medical devices are safe and effective and that radiation-emitting products will not harm people. Feed and drugs for pets and farm animals also come under FDA scrutiny. The FDA also ensures that these products are labeled truthfully. The First Government website, previously mentioned, also contains agricultural information.

The Foreign Agriculture Service (FAS) website at http://www.fas.usda.gov/country.html provides exporter assistance, country pages, import and export data, market reports, trade policy, embassies, satellite imagery, and weather maps.

The Agricultural Research Service (ARS) at http://www.ars.usda.gov has a search system and links to research, products and services, people and places, partnering, careers, and employee resources. It also has sections on science of interest to children, nutrition, an arboretum, and a library. This website is also available in Spanish. It also has a link to First Government.

The General Accounting Office (GAO) report at http://www.gao.gov/new.items/d01866.pdf documents the impact of the U.S dairy industry and contains seventy-four tables.

Environment

The U.S. Environmental Protection Agency website at http://www.epa.gov/compliance contains information on planning and results, compliance assistance, compliance incentives and auditing, compliance monitoring, civil enforcement, cleanup enforcement, criminal enforcement, environmental justice, and the National Environmental Policy Act (NEPA). This site also has a search system geared to each state. The websites of the Office of International Affairs (OIA) at http://www.epa.gov/oia and the Environmental Protection Agency (EPA) at http://www.epa.gov cover international affairs, air and climate, countries and regions, environment and trade, grants and cooperative agreements, technical assistance, toxins, and water. The National Aeronautics and Space Administration (NASA) Visible Earth website at http://visibleearth.nasa.gov has links to agriculture, atmosphere, biosphere, cryosphere, human dimensions, hydrosphere, land surface, oceans, radiance or imagery, solid Earth, and satellites/sensors. It also has photographs from space and a search engine. The Space Science and Engineering Center (SSEC, 1225 W. Dayton Street, Madison, WI 53706), located on the web at http://www.ssec.wisc.edu/data/composites.html, also has satellite images of the Earth in several formats.

Energy

The International Energy Agency (IEA) website is http://www.iea.org. This agency is an intergovernmental body committed to advancing security of the energy supply, economic growth, and environmental sustainability through energy policy cooperation. The IEA's focus is the impact of high oil prices on the economy, oil stocks and emergency response potential, and the world energy outlook.

International Development

The United States Agency for International Development (USAID) at http://www.usaid.gov provides links or information on USAID, employee news, presidential initiatives, First Government, USA Freedom Corps, the White House, Volunteers for Prosperity, foreign aid in the national interest, federal forms, regulations, Freedom of Information Act (FOIA) requests, the No Fear Act, and the Office of Inspector General (OIG) investigations hotline.

State Department

The State Department home page (http://www.state.gov) has information about U.S. embassies and consulates, press and public affairs (publications), traveling and living abroad (travel warnings, emergencies abroad, passports for U.S. citizens, visas for foreign citizens), countries and regions, international topics (environment and conservation, human rights, land mines), history, education and culture, a business center (regarding business in international markets and contracting opportunities), children's services, em-

ployee services, and employment (civil service, foreign service, student programs, international organizations). The International Information Programs (USINFO) webpage at http://usinfo.state.gov covers news, regions, resource tools, and products in several languages. Travel Government at http://travel.state.gov provides information on international travel for U.S. citizens, passports for U.S citizens, and visas for foreign citizens. Travel warnings are posted at http://travel.state.gov/travel/warnings.html under the subheading of "Travel Warnings," and more information can be found under the links "Public Announcements," "Consumer Information Sheets," and "Country Notes Background." Passport Authority at http://travel.state.gov/passport/index.html has information on applications, renewals, types of passports, processing time, lost or stolen passports, publications, policies, and application locations.

Defense

The *World Fact Book* of the Central Intelligence Agency (CIA; http://www.cia.gov and http://www.cia.gov/cia/sitemap.html) supplies up-to-date background information on all countries: geography, location, area, land boundaries, coastline, maritime claims, climate, terrain, natural resources, land use, natural hazards, environment, geography, people, population, migration rates, sex ratio, health, nationality, ethnic groups, religions, languages, literacy, government, capital, national holidays, constitution, legal system, suffrage, elections, executive branch, legislative branch, judicial branch, political parties and leaders, international organization participation, diplomatic representation in the United States, contact information, flag description, economy, income, labor, unemployment, budget, electricity, oil, natural gas, agriculture, exports, imports, currency, radio, television, transportation, ports and harbors, airports, and military. In addition, each of these major headings is usually subdivided for additional information.

The U.S. Department of Defense website (http://www.defenselink.mil) contains a global posture update and news on the latest overseas trouble spots.

Commerce

The U.S. Census Bureau at http://www.census.gov has information on the 2000 census: people, economics, geography. In addition, the Census Bureau (http://www.census.gov/ipc/www/idbsum.html) publishes summary demographic data and population pyramids for each country. It also publishes an AIDS database (http://www.census.gov/ipc/www/hivaidsd.html), including summary tables, maps, and links to other international AIDS sites.

Trade

The office of the United States Trade Representative (USTR) at http://www.ustr.gov contains information on trade agreements, world regions, trade and development, trade sectors, and the World Trade Organization. The U.S. Trade Development Agency (USTDA) at http://www.tda.gov advances economic development and U.S. commercial interests in developing and middle-income countries. The U.S. Government Export Portal at http://www.tradenet.gov provides assistance and market information on all export-related information offered by the federal government, including trade leads, free export counseling, and help with the export process.

Banking

The Export-Import Bank of the United States (ExIm) at http://www.exim.gov supports the financing of U.S. goods and services, turning export opportunities into real transactions and creating and maintaining U.S. jobs. Under some conditions the ExIm can assume credit and country risks that the private sector is unable or unwilling to accept. The Bank Information Center (BIC) at http://www.bicusa.org/bicusa/index.php is the principal source of information on and strategic support to nongovernment organizations (NGOs), affected communities, indigenous peoples, and grassroots movements in developing countries. The BIC addresses the negative effects of economic globalization so that field personnel can achieve more sustainable development outcomes. The BIC stresses citizen participation, transparency, full adherence to environmental and social policies, and public accountability.

The Federal Reserve Bank of San Francisco (http://www.frbsf.org/publications/fedinprint/index.html) is one of twelve regional Federal Reserve banks across the United States and offers search capabilities for banking publications. The Federal Reserve banks have three functions: managing the nation's supply of money and credit, regulating banking institutions to ensure safety and soundness, and serving as depository banks.

The World Bank's (http://www.worldbank.org) mission is to fight poverty and improve the living standards of people in the developing world. It is a development bank that provides loans, policy advice, technical assistance, and knowledge-sharing services to low- and middle-income countries to reduce poverty. The bank

promotes growth to create jobs and to empower poor people to take advantage of these opportunities.

Travel

The U.S. State Department (http://www.travel.state.gov./travel/warnings.html) issues travel warnings and consular information sheets when the State Department recommends that Americans should avoid travel to a certain country. The Centers for Disease Control (CDC) at http://www.cdc.gov or http://www.cdc.gov/travel gives health and safety tips, including vaccination and immunization advice, for various areas of the world.

Embassies

The U.S. State Department (http://usembassy.state.gov) provides links to U.S. embassies around the world. Embassy World (http://www.embassyworld.com/embassy/inside_usa_a.htm) lists contact information for foreign embassies located in the United States.

Assistance and Exchange

The mission of the Peace Corps (http://peacecorps.gov) is to help the people of other countries meet their need for trained men and women, to help people of other countries better understand Americans, and to help Americans better understand people of other countries. The Fulbright Council for International Exchange of Scholars (CIES) at http://www.cies.org is a program for international educational exchange that promotes "mutual understanding between the people of the United States and the people of other countries of the world." Fulbright grants are made to U.S. citizens and nationals of other countries for a variety of educational activities, primarily university lecturing, advanced research, graduate study, and teaching in elementary and secondary schools.

Famine

The Famine Early Warning Systems (FEWS) network, funded by USAID, is located at http://www.fews.net and has links to current events, geographic centers, livelihoods, hazards, risk analysis, and a learning center. The mission of FEWS is to collaborate with international, national, and regional partners to provide timely early warning and vulnerability information on emerging food security issues.

Justice

The National Institute of Justice (NIJ) International (http://www.ojp.usdoj.gov/nij/international) addresses the issues of crime, law, and justice across national borders.

Refugees

The Office of Refugee Resettlement (ORR) at http://www.acf.dhhs.gov/programs/orr/geninfo/index.htm is part of the Department of Health and Human Services. Its mission is to assist refugees and other special populations in obtaining economic and social self-sufficiency in their new homes in the United States. ORR funds and facilitates programs that offer, among other benefits, cash and medical assistance, employment preparation and job placement, skills training, English language training, social adjustment, and aid for victims of torture.

Nongovernment

The United Nations Statistics Division (http://unstats.un.org/unsd) compiles statistics from many international sources and produces global updates, including the Statistical Yearbook, World Statistics Pocketbook, and statistical yearbooks in specialized fields. It also provides to countries specifications for the best methods of compiling information so that data from different sources can be readily compared.

Organizations

Political Resources on the Net (http://www.politicalresources.net) lists political sites on the Internet, sorted by country. It has links to parties, organizations, governments, and media from all around the world. It also has a search capacity for finding information on individual countries. The Culturelink Network (http://www.culturelink.org/dbase/links.html) has links to intergovernmental organizations, national institutions, research institutions, arts organizations, publications, and resources. It also has information on networking, activities, and a databank. Yahoo! Government Countries (http://dir.yahoo.com/government/countries) supplies information on individual countries and has subcategories on embassies, consulates, the Executive Branch, government officials, law, military, national symbols and songs, politics, and web directories. The Organization of American States (OAS) at http://www.oas.org/main/english brings together the countries of the Western Hemisphere to strengthen cooperation and advance common interests. The core of the OAS mission is a commitment

to democracy. The OAS promotes good governance, strengthens human rights, fosters peace and security, expands trade, and addresses the problems caused by poverty. The European Union (EU), at http://europa.eu.int/index_en.htm, is a family of democratic European countries committed to working together for peace and prosperity. The member countries have set up common institutions to which they delegate some of their sovereignty so that decisions on matters of joint interest can be made democratically.

The United Nations (U.N.) website at http://www.un.org has links to daily briefings, radio, TV, photos, documentation, maps, databases, publications, stamps, peace and security, economic and social development, human rights, humanitarian affairs, and international law. The goals of the U.N. are to eradicate extreme poverty and hunger, achieve universal primary education, promote gender equality and empower women, reduce child mortality, improve maternal health, and combat HIV/AIDS, malaria, and other diseases.

International Foundations and Volunteer Organizations

Many international foundations and volunteer organizations have websites. For example, Rotary International is a global network of community volunteers at http://www.rotary.org. The motto of the Kellogg Foundation (http://www.wkkf.org) is "To Help People Help Themselves." The mission of the Ford Foundation (http://www.vault.com/companies/company_main.jsp?product_id=791&ch_id=256&co_page=2&tabnum=2&v=1) is to strengthen democratic values, reduce poverty and injustice, promote international cooperation, and advance human achievement. Winrock International's (http://www.winrock.org) mission is to help the poor and disadvantaged around the world. The mission of Agricultural Cooperative Development International and Volunteers in Overseas Cooperative Assistance (ACDI/VOCA; (http://www.acdivoca.org/acdivoca/acdiweb2.nsf/acdivoca?OpenPage) is to empower people to succeed in a global economy.

U.S. Universities

A gateway to the home pages of many U.S. universities is at the University of Texas website at http://www.utexas.edu/world/univ/state.

Want More?

Most of these websites of U.S. agencies and organizations branch in many directions and contain more information than can be listed in a brief appendix. Although web addresses sometimes change, often one can enter the name of the agency or organization into a web search engine and find the new address. Additional sites can often be located by including the name of the organization in a search engine. However, this search procedure is often more difficult and takes additional time.

Herbert W. Ockerman and Lopa Basu

INDEX

Note: **Bold** entries and page numbers
denote encyclopedia entries.

Note: **Bold** entries and page numbers
denote encyclopedia entries.

Note: **Bold** entries and page numbers denote encyclopedia entries.

435